The

WRITER'S HARBRACE HANDBOOK

THIRD EDITION

The Writer's HARBRACE HANDBOOK

CHERYL GLENN

The Pennsylvania State University

LORETTA GRAY

Central Washington University

THOMSON

WADSWORTH

Australia • Brazil • Canada • Mexico • Singapore • Spain
United Kingdom • United States

THOMSON

WADSWORTH

The Writer's Harbrace Handbook, **Third Edition**
Cheryl Glenn, Loretta Gray

Publisher: *Michael Rosenberg*
Senior Acquisitions Editor: *Dickson Musslewhite*
Senior Development Editor: *Michell Phifer*
Editorial Assistant: *Jonelle Lonergan*
Technology Project Manager: *Tim Smith*
Managing Marketing Manager: *Mandee Eckersley*
Marketing Assistant: *Dawn Giovanniello*
Associate Marketing Communications Manager:
    Patrick Rooney
Senior Project Manager, Editorial Production:
    Lianne Ames

Senior Print Buyer: *Mary Beth Hennebury*
Senior Permissions Editor: *Isabel Alves*
Permissions Editor: *Nora Piehl*
Production Service: *Lifland et al., Bookmakers*
Text Designer: *Linda Beaupre*
Photo Manager: *Sheri Blaney*
Photo Researchers: *Billie Porter/Cheri Throop*
Cover Designer: *Linda Beaupre*
Cover Printer: *Phoenix Color*
Compositor: *Pre-Press Company, Inc.*
Text Printer: *QuebecorWorld*

Library of Congress Control Number: 2005937962

ISBN 1-4130-1032-6

Thomson Higher Education
25 Thomson Place
Boston, MA 02210-1202
USA

For more information about our products, contact us at:
Thomson Learning Academic Resource Center
1-800-423-0563

For permission to use material from this text or product, submit a request online at
http://www.thomsonrights.com
Any additional questions about permissions can be submitted by e-mail to
thomsonrights@thomson.com

Credits appear on pages 805–808, which constitute a continuation of the copyright page.

CONTENTS

D   PART III WRITING IN THE DISCIPLINES

G   **PART IV** GRAMMAR

S **PART V** EFFECTIVE SENTENCES

P	

PART VII PUNCTUATION

M   PART VIII MECHANICS

Chapter 40   Spelling, the Spell Checker, and Hyphenation   733   sp

Chapter 41   Capitals   744   cap

Chapter 42   Italics   755   ital

PREFACE

What are the origins of first-year writing handbooks?

The first writing handbook of rules and conventions was Edwin A. Abbott's 1874 *How to Write Clearly.* Abbott's aim was to help his classics students at the City of London School produce more fluent English translations of their Greek and Latin lessons, and his handbook was the first college-level text to equate clear writing with the mastery of specific rules, fifty-six of them, to be precise. In the United States, *How to Write Clearly* became wildly popular—not in classics, but in English composition courses, because it provided easy-to-use, error-based rules for writers.

With the 1862 Morrill Act, the U.S. Government provided funding for the establishment of Mechanical and Agricultural Colleges (which later became the major state universities), and the country's university population exploded. Higher education was no longer reserved for the sons and daughters of the upper classes. College writing classes suddenly expanded from thirty to one hundred students—a flood of students who needed to learn how to write—and teachers desperately sought ways to handle the workload of grading weekly themes. *How to Write Clearly,* along with a number of other popular rule-governed and exercise-based handbooks, tried to meet this need. The handbook had established itself as the *sine qua non* of writing instruction.

How did the *Harbrace Handbook* get started?

The book you have in your hands is not the first handbook, but, since 1941, it has served as the paradigm for all successful handbooks. In the 1930s, John C. Hodges obtained federal funding to support his study of the frequency of errors in college students' essays. Hodges, an English professor at the University of Tennessee, collected some twenty thousand student papers that had been marked by sixteen different professors of rhetoric from all over the United States. Then, working with a cadre of graduate students, he counted and analyzed the errors in those papers, creating a taxonomy that he used to organize the 1941 *Harbrace Handbook of English* into thirty-five sections.

In the preface to that first edition, Hodges wrote:

> The *Harbrace Handbook of English* is a guide to the correction of student themes and also a text for use in class. It presents well-known subject matter in an easily usable form, and thus lightens the instructor's task of grading papers. The book contains only thirty-five major sections.

Thus, his handbook became a masterpiece of organized minimalism, easily accessible to teachers and students alike. The *Harbrace Handbook of English* captured the attention of both groups, as it responded to their needs in a material (and easy-to-use) way.

What makes *The Writer's Harbrace Handbook* so good?

Firmly established as the granddaddy of all handbooks, the *Harbrace Handbook of English* evolved into *The Writer's Harbrace Handbook,* Third Edition, which continues the Hodges' tradition of up-to-date reliability and practicality. Like all of its predecessors, this edition of *The Writer's Harbrace Handbook* responds to the material needs of teachers and students. Still providing teachers with a simplified method for marking student papers, this handbook also gives both teachers and students the ease of reference and attention to detail that have made the Harbrace handbooks the standard of reliability. Without diminishing its longstanding commitment to helping students make the best decisions in terms of grammar, style, punctuation, and mechanics, this "writing first" handbook also guides them as they develop their abilities as writers. Therefore, *The Writer's Harbrace Handbook* provides priorities for any writing course, on any topic of composition.

What's new about this edition?

This edition enhances the important changes made in the previous edition in two readily apparent ways: rhetorical principles now underpin the entire book, and the purposeful use of visuals is emphasized throughout. These changes reinforce our commitment to helping students understand the rhetorical situation as the starting point for their reading and writing and to guiding them in the interpretation and production of visuals, which are ubiquitous in contemporary culture.

- **Opening with the Rhetorical Situation** Perhaps the most significant substantive change is in the opening chapter, which now emphasizes even more strongly the constituent parts of the rhetorical situation: writer, audience, message, purpose, context, and exigence (the specific reason for writing). Decisions about the most effective information to include, the best arrangement of that information, and the most appropriate language to use all grow out of an understanding of the rhetorical situation.

  Chapter 1, "The Rhetorical Situation," lays the rhetorical foundation for the entire book, from the writing chapters through the research and grammar chapters that follow. When students are guided by the rhetorical situation, they can read and write more effectively and efficiently, whether in an English or science course or in the workplace.

  Chapter 2, "Reading Rhetorically," applies the rhetorical situation to the interpretation (rather than the production) of words by helping students focus on the relationships among the writer, the reader, the writer's purpose, and the context within which the writing takes place. In this chapter, students are guided through an analysis of a Pulitzer Prize–winning book, beginning with the front cover and the table of contents and including a sample page, an explanatory figure, and the review blurbs on the back cover. They learn to read both words and images. Students who can read rhetorically better comprehend content and can separate their understanding of what is on the page (or screen) from their personal response to that content.

- **Chapter 5, "Planning for Academic Success,"** demonstrates specific methods students can use to ease the pressures of academic reading and writing through understanding course requirements, seeking out academic support opportunities, managing deadlines, and preparing for in-class essay examinations.

- **Chapter 7, "Visual Documents,"** introduces students to visual rhetoric, the specific ways in which any visual image communicates meaning to viewers, by way of the image as a whole, the elements of the image, the arrangement of those visual elements, and the relationship between an image and the surrounding text. Students will also learn about the conventions of document design in terms of the relationships between design and function and graphics and purpose.

- **Thinking Rhetorically About . . . Boxes** New to this edition, these boxes prompt students to consider the impact of the choices they make in grammar, style, and punctuation. Many of the boxes present situations in which a writer has multiple options or in which a conventional rule may be broken. These possibilities move students away from thinking that "one rule fits all" to gauging the rhetorical effect of the sentence-level decisions they make.

■ **Revised Chapters** Attention to the rhetorical situation has invigorated all of the writing and research chapters and many of the grammar ones, whether those chapters are thoroughly revamped or completely new. The following chapters have been extensively revised in light of contemporary composition pedagogy, while maintaining those aspects of traditional rhetorical theory that are still widely respected.

Chapter 6, "Online Documents," helps students assess the rhetorical situation in the online environment, whether they are participating in electronic messaging or a discussion forum or composing documents for online presentation. The chapter covers netiquette and the use of hyperlinks to enhance online documents.

Chapter 9, "Finding Sources in Print, Online, and in the Field," guides students through the process of formulating a research question, conducting research, and choosing appropriate sources—all in terms of the elements of the rhetorical situation. The methods of conducting research presented in this chapter include traditional library research, online research, and field research (through interviews, discussion forums, and questionnaires).

Chapter 11, "Using Sources Effectively and Responsibly," reminds students of the importance of establishing an ethos as a writer, one firmly grounded in integrity. This chapter, then, helps students understand the importance of taking notes, organizing those notes, and responding to sources in terms of a specific rhetorical situation. Students are introduced to the basic methods necessary for creating a bibliography, writing an annotated bibliography, and integrating sources into a text of their own. Perhaps the most important feature of this chapter is its focus on helping students learn ways to use sources responsibly and thereby avoid plagiarism.

Chapters 16 through 19, "Writing to Interpret Literature," "Writing in the Social Sciences," "Writing in the Natural Sciences," and "Writing in Business," now emphasize how writers respond to differing rhetorical situations in various academic areas. These chapters contain information on discipline-specific ways of reasoning, uses of sources and evidence, and conventions for style and formatting.

■ **Updated Style Guides for Researched Writing** In this edition, we continue our thorough and updated coverage of the style guidelines from the Modern Language Association (MLA), the American Psychological Association (APA), *The Chicago Manual of Style* (CMS), and *The CBE Manual for Authors, Editors, and Publishers* (CSE/CBE). (*The Writer's Harbrace Handbook* itself is edited according to *The Chicago Manual of Style,* which is the style guide used by most publishers.) We have added over forty-five new citation examples to the MLA chapter, giving special attention to the citing of sources accessed through databases. All of the documentation chapters have easy-to-follow, color-coded visual examples of each type of citation (for a book, an article, and an online source), showing the major components and their exact arrangement. In addition, tip boxes remind students of all the steps they need to follow as they compose their bibliographies.

■ **More Visuals** Additional images now reinforce or demonstrate the written components of this handbook. Most chapters now feature instructive visuals. For instance, in Chapter 8, "Writing Arguments," cartoons illustrate many of the rhetorical fallacies. In the research and documentation chapters, annotated visuals, such as screen shots of databases and Web sites, help students learn how to locate in these kinds of sources the information they need for their bibliographies. In Chapter 16, "Writing to Interpret Literature," a new student paper analyzing "Everyday Use," a short story by Alice Walker, incorporates stills from the film version of the story. Most of the student-generated papers in this handbook now include some kind of visual—photograph, table, or figure. In the process of referring to the visuals in this book, students will come to understand the specific ways these features communicate meaning to an audience, meaning that supplements and enhances what words convey.

Supplements

Instructor Supplements

Instructor's Flex-Files

Flex-Files, written by Professors Wendy Sharer (East Carolina University) and Eve Weiderhold (University of North Carolina, Greensboro), are designed to give you maximum flexibility in planning and customizing your course. Providing an abundance of materials, the Flex-Files are organized in two main sections. "Part One: Questions for Teachers" raises a variety of pedagogical questions (and gives possible solutions) for you to consider when teaching your course with this handbook. "Part Two: Sample Syllabi and Activities" offers sample syllabi with possible assignments for a semester-long course and for a quarter-long course. Additionally, this section contains sample in-class collaborative learning activities, technology-oriented activities, and critical thinking and writing activities. The Flex-Files also include the following supplementary materials: (1) an ESL insert aimed at helping mainstream instructors teach writing effectively to their ESL students, (2) an insert on disability issues as they relate to teaching first-year composition, (3) the Answer Key for the exercises in the handbook, and (4) the Answer Key for the *College Workbook.*

ThomsonNOW™

Help your students boost their writing skills by empowering them with this Web-based, multimedia, writing assessment and learning program— ThomsonNOW. This study system helps students understand what they know, as well as what they don't know, and build study strategies to "fill in the gaps" and master the crucial rudimentary concepts of writing. Using a variety of technologies to accommodate many learning styles, ThomsonNOW covers all aspects of writing, arming students with interactive learning tools, such as *Diagnostic Quizzes, Personalized Study Plans,* a direct link to vMentor™ tutoring, and *Multimedia Tutorials.* These tools will help students master the fundamentals of writing and build their confidence as they become more effective writers.

Instructor's Correction Chart

To make marking your students' papers easier, you can prop up on your desk this oversized, laminated chart, which lists all of the sections of the handbook and shows the editing symbols correlated to them.

Student Supplements

The Writer's Harbrace Animated Handbook

A fully interactive version of the handbook, this online resource includes over 200 animated examples of the most important choices and conventions for writers, as well as explanations of the Beyond the Rule topics and a library of model student papers.

The Writer's Harbrace Handbook Web Site

The free companion Web site provides links, sample syllabi, quizzes and tests, sample student papers, and other student and instructor resources.

Thomson InSite™ for Writing and Research

 This all-in-one online writing and research tool includes electronic peer review, an originality checker, an assignment library, help with common errors, and access to InfoTrac® College Edition. InSite makes course management practically automatic. Visit **http://insite.thomson. com**.

Turnitin®

 This online plagiarism-prevention program promotes fairness in the classroom by helping students learn to cite sources correctly and allowing instructors to check for originality before reading and grading papers. Turnitin checks student papers against billions of pages of Internet content, millions of published works, and millions of other student papers and generates a comprehensive originality report within seconds.

InfoTrac® College Edition

 Do in-depth research for class right from your desktop or catch up on the latest news online—using your four months of access to InfoTrac College Edition. You can search this virtual university library's more than 18 million reliable, full-length articles from 5,000 academic and popular periodicals (including the *New York Times, Newsweek, Science, Forbes,* and *USA Today*) and retrieve results almost instantly. You can also use InfoMarks—stable URLs that you can link to articles, journals, and searches to save you time when doing research—and the InfoWrite online resource center, where you can access guides to writing research papers, grammar help, critical thinking guidelines, and much more.

College Workbook

With cross-references to sections of this handbook, the *College Workbook* covers grammar, punctuation, usage, style, and writing. This printed workbook combines exercises with clear examples and explanations that supplement the information and exercises found in the handbook.

Think About Editing: An ESL Guide

A self-editing manual for ESL writers, *Think About Editing* is designed to help intermediate to advanced students edit their writing to correct grammar, structure, and usage. The manual is prefaced with a correlation guide that links its units to corresponding sections in *The Writer's Harbrace Handbook.*

Dictionaries

The following dictionaries are available for a nominal price when bundled with the handbook: *The Merriam-Webster Dictionary,* Second Edition; *Merriam-Webster's Collegiate® Dictionary,* Eleventh Edition; *Merriam-Webster Pocket Thesaurus;* and *Heinle's Newbury House Dictionary of American English with Integrated Thesaurus.* The latter was created especially for ESL students.

Acknowledgments

Who wrote this handbook?

John C. Hodges carried forward his vision of a useful handbook for many editions of the *Harbrace Handbook*—and his influence continues with every edition. With the fifth edition, he was assisted by Mary E. Whitten (North Texas State University—now University of North Texas), who guided the book from the sixth through the tenth editions. Suzanne S. Webb (Texas Woman's University) joined the handbook on the tenth edition to enhance its rhetorical elements and add a section on logical thinking. In the eleventh edition, Winifred Bryan Horner (Texas Christian University) and Robert K. Miller (University of St. Thomas) joined the team, so that Win could add her rhetorical expertise and Bob could rework the research paper chapter.

The twelfth, thirteenth, and fourteenth editions profited from the three-person team of Sue, Win, and Bob, with remarkable results. Three new chapters, "Writing Arguments," "Reading and Thinking Critically," and "Writing under Pressure," were included in the handbook. By the fourteenth edition, the *Harbrace Handbook* appeared in three different versions to meet the growing diversity of handbook users: *Hodges' Harbrace Handbook* continued to emphasize grammar first, while *The Writer's Harbrace Handbook* and *The Writer's Harbrace Handbook,* Brief Edition, as their titles suggest, gave primary emphasis to writing, thereby rounding out the family of Harbrace handbooks.

With Win's retirement, rhetoric and composition specialist Cheryl Glenn (The Pennsylvania State University) and linguist Loretta (Lori) Gray (Central Washington University) joined Sue and Bob to produce the fifteenth edition of *Hodges' Harbrace Handbook* and the second edition of both *The Writer's Harbrace Handbook* and its briefer version.

This edition is the result of a spectacularly successful collaboration between Cheryl and Lori. They had the advantage of building on the terrific work of past Harbrace authors as they wrote what they hope is the best edition so far, one responsive to the rhetorical demands of the twenty-first century.

Who helped?

The third edition of this handbook and the other two versions took shape through extensive phone conversations and e-mail correspondence between the authors as well as with a number of members of the Thomson Wadsworth Higher Education editorial staff. For their collective ideas, enthusiasm, support, and wise counsel, we remain grateful. In particular, we thank Michael Rosenberg, Publisher, whose pride in the Harbrace family of handbooks has never wavered as he supported the two-person author team and their new ideas through many months of work. We're especially grateful to Dickson Musslewhite, Senior Acquisitions Editor, who brought Cheryl and Lori into partnership with his bolder vision for the Harbrace handbooks. On a number of occasions, he plied a tired author duo with more ideas and, therefore, more work, but he always tempered his direction with the goodwill and good sense that characterize the best of rhetors. Lianne Ames, Senior Production Project Manager, helped to bring this huge project to completion, and Jane Hoover carried out the copyediting with style and care. Linda Beaupre gave the book its clear and aesthetically pleasing interior design and cover. Without the help and support of these imaginative people, we simply could not have produced *The Writer's Harbrace Handbook.*

But it is Michell Phifer, Senior Development Editor Extraordinaire as well as friend—to whom we owe a special thanks. A scrupulously careful editor—and our constant intellectual companion—Michell successfully helped us balance our writing deadlines with our other professional commitments (teaching, for instance!). She regularly prodded us to think critically about each chapter, about our choice of images or textual examples, and especially about the project as an intellectual whole. She massaged our sometimes convoluted writing and thinking into accessible prose and challenged us to locate more effective examples of professional and student writing. Michell was always on our team, guiding our collaboration until the very last minute, until the presses rolled.

The successful completion of our work would not have been possible without the research assistance of Stacey Sherrif and Rosalyn Collings Eve, both at The Pennsylvania State University. In addition, this project benefited from the support and encouragement of those overseeing our university schedules and workloads: Patsy Callaghan, Chair of the

Department of English, and Liahna Armstrong, Dean of Arts and Humanities, both at Central Washington University; and Melanie Ekdahl, Staff Assistant in the Office of the Provost at The Pennsylvania State University. Angelique Bacon-Woodard and Rachel Smith, Administrative Fellows in Central Administration at The Pennsylvania State University, offered support, suggestions, and good company.

We would also like to thank the students whose indefatigable efforts went into the model student papers in this edition: Melissa Schraeder, Nicole Hester, and Kaitlyn Andrews-Rice, The Pennsylvania State University; Laura Klocke, Andy Pieper, Nikki Krzmarzick, and Geoffrey Rutledge, University of St. Thomas; Mike Demmon, University of Nevada, Reno; and Heather Jensen and Roxanne Kirkwood, Texas Woman's University. For writing and revising—and revising some more—we remain indebted to you. After all, good student writing, the kind that you have produced, is what this book is all about.

And we cannot forget our valued and imaginative colleagues, Stacey Sherrif (The Pennsylvania State University) and Brent Henze (East Carolina University), who served as our technology consultants for this project. Consummate professionals, they helped us envision and frame Chapter 6, "Online Documents," and Chapter 7, "Visual Documents," providing more good information than we could possibly use.

We want to thank those colleagues who reviewed *The Writer's Harbrace Handbook* throughout the course of its development. Their astute comments, frank responses, and thoughtful suggestions helped shape what is the final version—until the next edition. We thank them for taking the time out of their already busy schedules to help us.

Handbook Reviewers

James Barcus, Baylor University; Patrick Christle, University of Tennessee-Knoxville; Elaine Coney, Southwest Mississippi Community College; Laurie Cubbison, Radford University; Twyla Davis, Bladen Community College; Tiffany Griffith, University of Evansville; Terriann Gaston, University of Texas at Arlington; Richard Hay, University of Wisconsin-Milwaukee; Keith Hunter, North Idaho College; Khristian Kay, Lakeland College; Thomas Long, Thomas Nelson Community College; Margaret Loweth, Loyola University-Chicago; Kelly Martin and Peggy Vera, Collin County Community

College; Sandee McGlaun, North Georgia College and State University; Michelle Sidler, Auburn University; Allison Smith, Middle Tennessee State University; Phillip Wedgeworth and Cheryl Windham, Jones County Junior College.

Focus Group Participants

John Buckuold, Scott Downing, Laura Durnell, Janet Flood, Brenda Kilianski, Carolyn Leeb, Scott Markwell, Michael Meyer, Eileen Seifert, Salli Berg Seeley, and Christine Sneed, De Paul University; Dale Adams, Lee College; Diane Whitley Bogard, Austin Community College; Linda Brender, Macomb Community College; Hugh Burns, Texas Woman's University; Amy Childers, North Georgia College and State University; Maria Clayton, Middle Tennessee State University; Daniel Ferguson and Patricia Knight, Amarillo College; Bea Hugetz, Alvin Community College; Glen Hutchinson, University of North Carolina-Charlotte; Craig Jacobsen, Mesa Community College; Patricia Jenkins, University of Alaska-Anchorage; Martina Kusi-Mensah, Montgomery College; Marjorie Lynn, University Michigan-Dearborn; Beth Maxfield, Blinn College; Donald Pardlow, Floyd College; Carolyn Poor, Wharton County Junior College; Beverly Reed, Stephen F. Austin State University; Marti Singer, Georgia State University; Sarah Spring, Texas A&M University; Stephanie Woods, Hinds Community College.

Finally, we are grateful to our friends and families. Although our faces toward the screen meant our backs toward you, you were never far from our thoughts. After all, without you, our work would be neither possible nor worthwhile.

To all of you reading this preface and using or considering using this handbook for the first time, know that we are grateful to you too. In fact, if you have advice for how we might improve the next edition or if we can help you in any way, write us c/o Thomson Wadsworth, English Editorial Department, 25 Thomson Place, Boston, MA 02210.

Cheryl Glenn
Loretta Gray
January 2006

The

WRITER'S HARBRACE HANDBOOK

WRITING AND THE RHETORICAL SITUATION

Elements of the rhetorical situation.

1   THE RHETORICAL SITUATION

Rhetoric, the purposeful use of language, pervades your daily activities. You cannot read your mail, fill out an employment application, or answer an exam question without using rhetoric to analyze what you are reading or to produce language that others will understand. Every day, you use rhetoric as you read and write—whether you are reading class assignments, directions for your stereo system, course syllabi, or e-mails or submitting written assignments, answering questions in class, instant messaging with your friends, or writing a memo to your professor. Every day, you are surrounded by rhetoric and rhetorical opportunities, and you have been reading, writing, and speaking rhetorically for most of your life.

This chapter explains reading and writing rhetorically as processes, each a series of sometimes overlapping steps that help you understand these four elements of the rhetorical situation (**1a**):

- exigence (**1b**),
- purpose (**1c**),
- audience (**1d**), and
- context (**1e**).

Writing rhetorically helps you to fulfill a variety of class assignments, some of which are discussed in this handbook:

- an essay from personal experience (**4h**),
- an argument from personal experience and research (**8j**),
- an argument based on research (chapters **9–15**),
- an interpretation of a literary text (**16g**),
- a field report and a lab report (**17d**, **18d**),
- a Web page for an organization (**6e–f**),
- a business letter and a résumé (**19b**, **19d**), and
- a business plan (**19f**).

Whatever form an assignment takes, writing rhetorically (just like reading rhetorically) involves a process of active engagement, an ability to interact with a text, step by step, until it fulfills its purpose, transferring its meaning to its audience.

1a Understanding the rhetorical situation

As a communicator, you use visual and verbal language purposefully, every day, in terms of a **rhetorical situation,** the context in which you are interpreting a reading or composing a piece of writing or a visual (see fig. 1.1). When you read and write rhetorically—whether in or out of school, as the sender or the receiver—you have a clear sense of the rhetorical situation and the specific elements that constitute it.

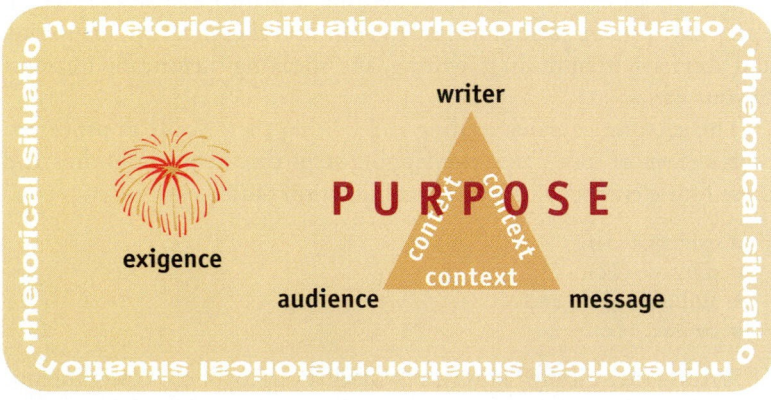

Fig. 1.1. The rhetorical situation.

The **writer** in a rhetorical situation is the person who identifies the **exigence,** the reason or problem that impels that person to write in the first place. When purposeful language can resolve the exigence, the situation is rhetorical. The writer then prepares a **message** (information delivered through visual or verbal means) with the **purpose** of resolving that exigence. But to fulfill that purpose, the writer must gauge the message in terms of the intended **audience,** the reader or readers who have the capability of resolving the exigence or problem. Whether or not that audience works to resolve the exigence, it reads, hears, or sees the message within a specific **context,** the constraints (obstacles) and resources (positive influences) in the environment surrounding the rhetorical situation. Those constraints and resources include whatever else has already been said on the subject; when, where, and through what medium the transaction between writer and audience takes place; and the writer's relationship with the audience, the writer's credibility (or believability), and the appropriateness of the message in terms of both content and delivery.

Reading and writing rhetorically offer you the opportunity to consider each of these elements separately as well as in combination. You can actively engage a text by establishing the writer's credibility, purpose, intended audience, context, and overall message and establishing the necessary interdependence of these elements. For instance, a writer's purpose must be appropriate for the intended audience and the context; the writer's choice of audience might change according to the purpose or context; the context affects the audience and the writer's purpose (see **1e**).

By reading and writing rhetorically, you can also evaluate the thesis statement, the key points, and the amount of support each point merits, as well as what needs to be said and what is purposefully left unsaid. Therefore, when you *read* rhetorically, you read more efficiently and effectively—and you can talk knowledgeably about what you have read (see chapter **2**). When you *write* rhetorically, you generate new ideas and communicate them clearly and concisely to your audience (see chapters **3** and **4**)—and you improve your understanding of what you have read.

1b Writing to an exigence

The exigence is the particular problem or situation that calls for words. A parking violation, a birth, a college application, and an engagement—these are all events that compel people to write. Words—either spoken or written—can resolve the problem of fining a parking violator, announcing a birth, awarding college admission, or inviting wedding guests. Once you determine the exigence for your writing—the reason that impels you to write—you will be better able to gauge all the elements of your writing (from word choice to organizational pattern) in terms of your overall purpose.

Natural disasters provide exigencies for writing and speaking, often with the purpose of stimulating fundraising and relief efforts.

BEYOND THE RULE

EXIGENCE

Historical events of varying significance often serve as the exigencies for writing. When, over the past few years, the football teams of the University of Oregon, the University of Southern California, and Auburn University were excluded from the national championship, journalists and fans alike complained to Bowl Championship Series officials. The December 2004 earthquake and tsunami disaster in southeast Asia provided many people— from journalists to schoolchildren—with a reason to write and speak. For more information, see **www.harbrace.com**.

1c   Writing with a specific purpose

As soon as you know that words can resolve an exigence or address a particular need or situation, you can concentrate on the general purpose of those words. Writers must clarify their purpose, and readers should be influenced according to that purpose—whether the writer wants to express feelings about something, amuse or entertain, report information, explain or evaluate the significance of information, analyze a situation, clarify a point, invite the audience to consider alternative points of view, or argue for or against a course of action.

Depending on the writer's overall purpose, then, the message (whether composed or read) can be classified as expressive, expository, or argumentative. Any of these types of writing can be used to help fulfill a writer's overall purpose.

(1) Expressive writing emphasizes the writer's feelings and reactions to people, objects, events, or ideas.

Personal letters and journals are often expressive, as are many essays and short stories. The following example (paragraph 1) comes from an essay designed to convey how the author feels about the relationship he had with his father. (For ease of reference, each of the sample paragraphs in this chapter is numbered.)

1   At just about the hour when my father died, soon after dawn one February morning when ice coated the windows like cataracts, I banged my thumb with a hammer. Naturally I swore at the hammer, the reckless thing, and in the moment of swearing I thought of what my father would say: "If you'd try hitting the nail it would go in a whole lot faster. Don't you know your thumb's not as hard as that hammer?" We were both doing carpentry that day, but far apart. He was building cupboards at my brother's place in Oklahoma; I was at home in Indiana putting up a wall in the basement to make a bedroom for my daughter. By the time my mother called with the news of his death—the long distance wires whittling her voice until it seemed too thin to bear the weight of what she had to say—my thumb was swollen. A week or two later a white scar in the shape of a crescent moon began to show above the cuticle, and month by month it rose across the pink sky of my thumbnail. It took the better part of a year for the scar to disappear, and every time I noticed it I thought of my father.

—**SCOTT RUSSELL SANDERS,** "The Inheritance of Tools"

(2) Expository writing focuses more on objects, events, or ideas than on the writer's feelings about them.

Textbooks, news accounts, scientific reports, and encyclopedia articles are usually expository, as are many of the essays students are expected to write in college. When you report, explain, clarify, or assess, you are

practicing exposition. Paragraph 2 is excerpted from a book that explains how paleoanthropologists—in this case, a paleoanthropologist named Mac—discover their prizes.

2   Searching only in the most promising areas isn't the key to [Mac's] success; perseverance is. He walks the same territory over and over again, changing courses around obstacles, and he tells his people to do the same. If you walked to the left around this bush yesterday, then walk to the right today. If you walked into the sun yesterday, then walk with the sun at your back today. And most of all, walk, walk, walk, and *look* while you are doing it. Don't daydream; don't scan the horizon for shade; ignore the burning sun even when the temperature reaches 135°F. Keep your eyes on the ground searching for that elusive sliver of bone or gleaming tooth that is not just any old animal, fossilized and turning to rubble, but a hominid. Those are the prizes we seek; those are the messengers from the past.

                              —ALAN WALKER AND PAT SHIPMAN, *The Wisdom of the Bones*

(3) Argumentative writing is intended to influence the reader's attitudes and actions.

Most writing is to some extent an argument. Through the choice and arrangement of material, even something as apparently straightforward as a résumé can be an argument for an interview. However, writing is usually called argumentative if it clearly supports a specific position (see chapter **8**). In paragraph 3, note how the writer calls for students to claim their own educations.

3   The first thing I want to say to you who are students, is that you cannot afford to think of being here to *receive* an education; you will do much better to think of yourselves as being here to *claim* one. One of the dictionary definitions of the verb "to claim" is: *to take as the rightful owner; to assert in the face of possible contradiction.* "To receive" is *to come into possession of; to act as receptacle or container for; to accept as authoritarian or true.* The difference is that between acting and being acted-upon, and . . . it can literally mean the difference between life and death.   —ADRIENNE RICH, "Claiming an Education"

Writers need to identify their overall purpose for each piece of writing, knowing that they can tap various methods of development (such as narration, description, and cause-and-effect analysis; see **3g**) to work toward that goal. Whether you are the reader or the writer, however, you must assess the rhetorical purpose. For instance, when you are the reader, you want to assess the overall purpose of the writing in order to know how best to respond. If you can identify specific words or passages that convey the writer's purpose, you can discern whether the writer wants you to be entertained, informed, or persuaded. When you are the writer, you want to compose a message that responds to an exigence and fulfills a purpose while also alerting your intended audience to that purpose. If you are writing in response to a specific assignment, talk with your instructor or examine your assignment sheet to review which elements of the rhetorical situation (purpose, context, and audience) have already been set for you (see **5a(2)**).

CHECKLIST for Assessing Purpose

- Has your instructor provided a purpose for your writing, or are you defining a purpose on your own? Are you trying primarily to express how you feel?

- Are you writing to improve your self-understanding or trying to help others understand you better?

- Are you trying to be entertaining or inspiring? How easily does your topic lend itself to your purpose? What examples or choice of words will help you fulfill that purpose?

- Are you writing primarily to convey information? Are you trying to teach others something they do not know or to demonstrate that you have knowledge in common?

- Are you writing primarily to argue for or against a course of action? Do you want your readers to stop a certain behavior, to undertake a specific action, or to consider alternative points of view?

- Do you have more than one purpose in writing? Which one is primary? How can the other purposes help you achieve your primary one? Or are some of your purposes in conflict?

Exercise 1

Select one of the following subjects, and write two paragraphs that begin to develop an expressive, expository, or argumentative essay on that subject.

1. your finances
2. your generation
3. your career goals
4. your computer expertise
5. your favorite musical group
6. volunteer work
7. a memorable lesson
8. music or dance performances
9. student housing
10. your closest relative

1d   Considering audience

A clear understanding of the audience—its values, concerns, and knowledge—helps writers tailor their writing in terms of length, quality and quantity of details, the kind of language used, and the examples that will be most effective. Of course, the audience is anyone who reads the text, but that broader audience includes the writer's intended audience, those people whom the writer considers capable of being influenced by the words or who are capable of bringing about change. Some writers like to plan and draft essays with their purpose and their audience clearly in mind; others like to focus first on purpose and attend to their audience when they are revising. (See chapters **2** and **3**.) As a writer, you will need to think clearly, at some point, about who exactly will be reading what you write and ask yourself whether your choices are appropriate for that audience.

(1) A specialized audience is predisposed to the message.

A **specialized audience** has a demonstrated interest in the subject. If a relative died as the result of drunk driving, you might become a member of a specialized audience: people whose lives have been affected by alcohol abuse. You would probably be interested in alcohol-abuse information that is specifically geared to people who have had experiences like yours. And if you decided to write about the harm done through alcohol abuse, you would probably direct your text to members of an organization such as Alcoholics Anonymous or Mothers Against Drunk Driving, who constitute a specialized audience.

Any group (such as nutritionists, police officers, or social workers) that has an area of expertise, an agenda, or a specific interest can be a specialized audience, one that you will want to address accordingly. Depending on the topic, then, you can usually assume that every member of a specialized audience has an interest in your subject and some knowledge of it.

You will want to consider your specialized audience—what they know that you do not, how much and what sorts of information you might provide them, and how best to develop your information—in terms of your overall purpose. You will be writing to readers with some degree of expertise, so you will want to establish common ground with them by mentioning areas of agreement, acknowledging their expertise, and adjusting your tone and language choices to their knowledge and attitudes. (See **4a(3)** and chapter **32**.) You will also want to provide your audience with new information—or a new way of understanding information with which they are already familiar.

A general reader might be surprised by the emotional content of the following excerpt, which was created for a specialized audience, one already familiar with the dire consequences of drunk driving.

When writing to a specialized audience, take into account the needs, interests, and values of its members.

4   Early on Sunday morning, September 18, 1999, Jacqueline Saburido, 20, and four friends were on their way home from a birthday party. Reggie Stephey, an 18-year-old star football player, was on his way home from drinking beer with some buddies. On a dark road on the outskirts of Austin, Texas, Reggie's SUV veered into the Oldsmobile carrying Jacqui and the others. Two passengers in the car were killed at the scene and two were

rescued. Within minutes, the car caught fire. Jacqui was pinned in the front seat on the passenger side. She was burned over 60% of her body; no one thought she could survive. But Jacqui lived. Her hands were so badly burned that her fingers had to be amputated. She lost her hair, her ears, her nose, her left eyelid and much of her vision. She has had more than 50 operations since the crash and has many more to go.

In June 2001 Reggie Stephey was convicted of two counts of intoxication manslaughter for the deaths of Jacqui's two friends. He was sentenced to seven years in prison and fined $20,000.

—**TEXAS DEPARTMENT OF TRANSPORTATION,** "Jacqui's Story"

Even knowing the meaning of every word in the preceding paragraphs does not guarantee that you will be interested in what the author is arguing or that you will make any changes in your drinking habits. Nevertheless, the passage is aimed at a specialized audience of people, who are committed to ending drunk driving.

Many of the essays you will be assigned to write in college—in English, history, economics, psychology, and the sciences, for example—are for a specialized audience, and often that audience is your instructor, who is already familiar with the subject matter. For example, if you are writing an essay about molecular mapping for your biology instructor, it is not necessary to define *chromosomes*. Instead, use your essay to communicate your understanding of the molecular process or of its connections with various physical characteristics. (See chapter **18**.)

Writing for a specialized audience does not mean that you have to know more than the members of that audience, nor does it mean that you have to impress them with your interpretation. Since no one knows everything about a subject, members of a specialized audience will usually appreciate thinking about their subject in a new way, even if they are not learning new information.

(2) A diverse audience represents a range of expertise and interest.

A **diverse audience** consists of readers with differing levels of expertise and varying interest in your subject. For example, if you are writing about upgrading computer software in a report that will be read by all the department heads of a company, you should be aware that some of your readers probably know more about software than others, including you. But you can also assume that all of your readers share a willingness to learn about new material if it is presented clearly and respectfully by someone who is establishing common ground with them.

Paragraph 5 helps a diverse audience of readers understand an unusual illness that put a young man in the hospital.

5   I first met Greg in April 1977, when he arrived at Williamsbridge Hospital. Lacking facial hair, and childlike in manner, he seemed younger than his twenty-five years. He was fat, Buddha-like, with a vacant, bland face, his blind eyes roving at random in their orbits, while he sat motionless in his wheelchair. If he lacked spontaneity and initiated no exchanges, he responded promptly and appropriately when I spoke to him, though odd words would sometimes catch his fancy and give rise to associate tangents or snatches of song and rhyme. Between questions, if the time was not filled, there tended to be a deepening silence; though if this lasted for more than a minute, he might fall into Hare Krishna chants or a soft muttering of mantras. He was still, he said, "a total believer," devoted to the group's doctrines and aims.

—**OLIVER SACKS,** "The Last Hippie," *An Anthropologist on Mars*

Oliver Sacks writes to a diverse audience. Although its members share an interest in science writing, and medical stories in particular, they come to Sacks's essay with varying levels of expertise. Therefore, Sacks describes a medical condition in words easily understood by a wide audience. When you are writing to a diverse audience, you too need to establish what the members are likely to have in common in order to make appropriate word choices (see chapters **32–34**) and include appropriate details (see **3f(1)**).

There will be times, however, when you simply will not know much about your audience, even though your purpose for writing might be to evaluate a product or argue for a course of action. When this is the case, it may help you to imagine a thoughtful audience of educated adults, with whom you may even share common ground. Such an audience is likely to include people with different backgrounds and cultural values (see **8e(2)**), so be careful not to assume that you are writing for readers who are exactly like you (see **32d**). To a considerable extent, the language you use will determine whether diverse readers feel included in or excluded from your work. Be careful to avoid jargon or technical terms that would be understood only by a specialized audience. If you must use a specialized term, explain what you mean by it. (See **32c** and **32e**.)

(3) Multiple audiences read for different reasons.

Writers often need to consider multiple audiences, a task related to—yet different from—addressing a diverse audience. When you address a diverse audience, you try to reach everyone. When you consider multiple audiences, you gauge your choice of words and tone according to your primary audience, knowing that a secondary audience might have access to your text. At work, for instance, you address your research report, employee evaluation, or proposal to your boss. But if you know that she will circulate the text among your colleagues, you adjust your words and tone accordingly. You might not be as frank in writing as you would be in person; you might omit potentially hurtful information or temper your words. If you are asked to evaluate the performance of an employee under your supervision, you might be asked to send the evaluation to your boss, who is looking to see whether you are a competent supervisor, and a copy of it to the employee, who is looking for praise. When you know that your rhetorical situation includes multiple audiences, you can better select your words.

 The use of e-mail for communication (see **6b**) has increased the likelihood of writing for multiple audiences because messages can be forwarded easily—and not always with the writer's permission. Other electronic texts, such as those generated by listserv dialogues or online conversations through a Web site, also reach multiple audiences. When writing for electronic submission, consider whether anyone outside your primary audience might read your work.

When writing essays in college, you may also find yourself writing for multiple audiences. For example, you may use an English essay as the foundation for developing another essay for your psychology or history class. You may take a linked or team-taught course in which you submit written work for evaluation by two instructors (your two primary audiences). Or you may write an essay for a general audience (which constitutes your secondary audience) and submit it to an instructor who is a specialist in your subject (and your primary audience).

In each of these cases, you are writing for multiple audiences. This kind of writing requires that you consider a variety of attitudes and positions (see **8d–e**). Considering different points of view is helpful when planning an essay and also when reading what you have drafted as you prepare to revise it (see chapter **4**). The following checklist may also help you assess your audience.

CHECKLIST for Assessing the Audience

- Who is going to be reading what you write?
- What do you know about the members of your audience? What characteristics can you safely assume they have? What do they have in common? How are they different?
- What values do you share with them? How do you differ from them?
- How much do they already know about your topic?
- What kind of language is appropriate or inappropriate for this audience?
- How open are the members of this audience to views that may be different from their own?
- What level of expertise will they expect from you?
- What do you *not* know about this audience? What assumptions would be risky?
- Are you writing with a primary audience in mind but expecting a secondary audience to also read what you have written? If so, have you clearly identified the primary audience so that you can address that audience specifically, while recognizing the expectations of the secondary audience?

Exercise 2

Examine an introductory and an advanced textbook in a discipline of your choice, and locate a passage in each devoted to the same issue or concept. Photocopy these passages, and prepare a class presentation in which you explain how they reveal differences in audience.

1e Sending and receiving a message within a context

Context includes time and place, writer and audience, and the medium of delivery—the circumstances under which writer and reader communicate. Social, political, religious, and other cultural factors influence context, as do the constraints and resources of the rhetorical situation. Therefore, what you are able to produce in writing is always influenced (positively or negatively) by the context.

Your background and beliefs often shape the stance (or attitude) you take when writing. An essay written shortly before your school's winter break, for example, could be influenced by both your anticipation of a combined religious holiday and family reunion and your uncertainty as to whether your audience shares that anticipation. Or an international crisis, such as the war in Iraq or the tsunami in southeast Asia, might prompt you to reconsider the purpose of an essay you are drafting for your international economics course. Writers who consider the time, place, and other factors of the context in which they are writing, as well as their audience, are more likely to communicate their ideas effectively.

The medium in which you are writing is also part of the context. Writing material for a Web page or another online medium requires you to think differently about organization, design, and style than does writing a traditional academic essay or business letter. Depending on your familiarity with and aptitude in using the technology, writing electronically may demand a good deal more time from you, too. Considering the method of delivery for a Web page, for example, requires making different kinds of rhetorical decisions than you would make for a text in a wholly static print medium. (See chapter **6**.)

When you read the work of other writers, you will sometimes find that the context is specifically stated, as in the following passage. You can tell the time, place, and event that Churchill refers to in this one sentence.

6   In the twenty-second month of the war against Nazism we meet here in this old Palace of St. James, itself not unscarred by the fire of the enemy, in order to proclaim the high purposes and resolves of the lawful constitutional Governments of Europe whose countries have been overrun; and we meet here also to cheer the hopes of free men and free peoples throughout the world.   —**WINSTON CHURCHILL**, "Until Victory Is Won"

Often, however, the context must be inferred. Whether the context is announced or not, it is important that writers and readers identify and consider it.

CHECKLIST for Assessing the Context

- Under what circumstances of time and place are you writing?
- Under what circumstances will your writing probably be read? Will it be one among many texts or documents being received, or is your particular message eagerly awaited? In either case, how can you help your reader quickly see the purpose and thrust of your work under these circumstances?
- How has your response to the task been influenced by other events in your life, your country, or the world?
- Have you been asked to write a text of a specific length? If length has not been specified, what seems appropriate for your purpose and audience?
- What document design (see chapter 7) is appropriate given the context for your writing?

READING RHETORICALLY

2

Reading is more pleasurable and profitable when undertaken as a series of steps. Every time you pick up a newspaper, glance over the headlines, turn to the sports section, skim over the first page, and then go back to read the story that most intrigues you, you are reading rhetorically. Sometimes, as with an article about baseball players who claim that they and many of their teammates use steroids, you find yourself rereading the text to make sure that you understand the differences between what the sportswriter is reporting and what the baseball players (whom the writer quotes) are alleging.

Whether you are reading the sports pages, a church bulletin, or your biology assignment, you are reading rhetorically every time you find yourself previewing a text, reading for content, responding, and rereading. When you follow these steps, you can more easily determine how difficult the text will be to understand, what you are likely to learn from it, and how useful it will be to you—assessments that will improve your reading comprehension. In addition, you can use these steps to consider the features of the rhetorical situation (writer, audience, exigence, purpose, and context).

This chapter explains the process of reading rhetorically and describes ways for you to monitor your personal and intellectual responses to a text. Whether **chronological** (in order of occurrence) or **recursive** (alternating between moving forward and looping back), reading rhetorically is a process of

- previewing (**2a**),
- reading for content (**2b**), and
- rereading (**2c**).

This chapter will not only help you move through the process but will also

- help you distinguish between actual content and your personal response to that content (**2d**) and
- encourage you to write daily about your reading (**2e**).

🖨 Click to Print

Caminiti comes clean

Ex-MVP says he won award while using steroids

Posted: Tuesday May 28, 2002 4:16 PM

ATLANTA (CNNSI.com) -- Former major leaguer Ken Caminiti says he was on steroids when he won the National League Most Valuable Player Award in 1996, according to an exclusive report in this week's issue of *Sports Illustrated*.

But even though it left him with health problems that continue to this day, Caminiti defended his use of steroids and told SI's Tom Verducci the practice is now so rampant in baseball that he would not discourage others from doing the same. Caminiti told Verducci that he continued to use steroids for the rest of his career, which ended last season when he hit .228 with 15 home runs and 41 RBIs for the Texas Rangers and the Atlanta Braves.

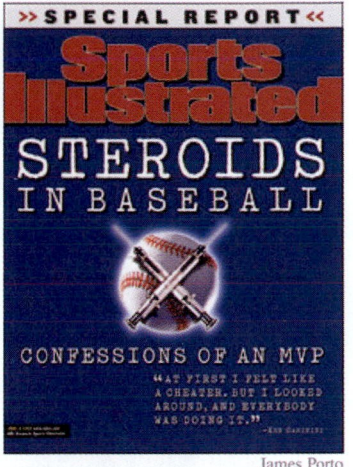

James Porto

•SI Report: Caminiti comes clean

An article about a controversial situation or issue may require careful rereading.

| 2a | Previewing for an initial impression |

You often preview reading material—when you thumb through a newspaper or a magazine looking for articles that stir your interest. A systematic preview, though, gives you more reliable results and makes your reading more efficient. When reading rhetorically, you systematically preview a text by reading the author's name and the title, then skimming the entire text to get a sense of how the information is organized and what you can expect from reading the text.

You will also want to assess what the reading demands of you in terms of time, effort, and previous knowledge. By previewing the length of a text, you can estimate how much time you need to set aside for reading. By reading the summary (often located in the preface or introductory chapter) or the abstract (usually preceding a scholarly article), you can decide whether the text will be useful. If the text is difficult, you can preview the major points, often found in headings (see **17c** and **18c**).

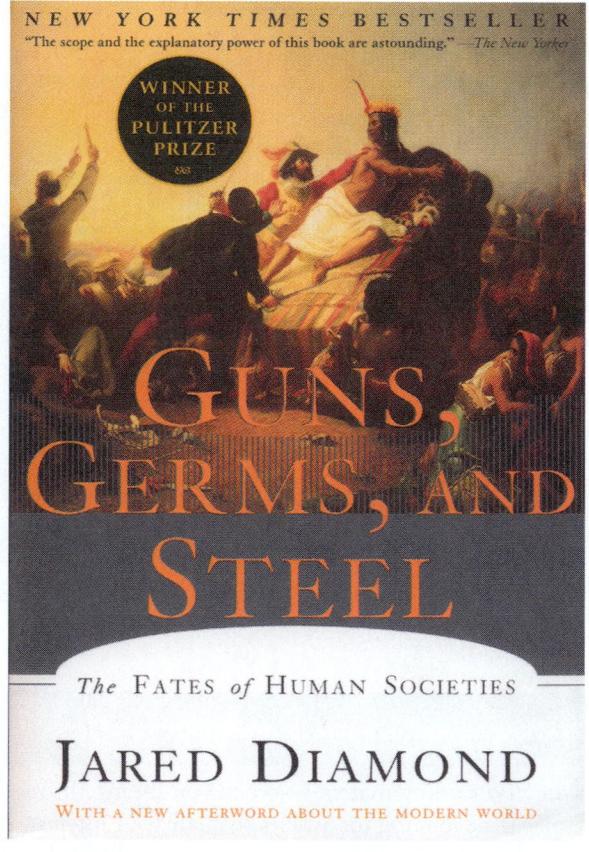

The title of Jared Diamond's book—*Guns, Germs, and Steel: The Fates of Human Societies*—accurately reflects the contents.

FEATURES OF A TEXT FOR PREVIEWING

Title

The title (and subtitle, if any) often reveals the focus of a text and sometimes even its thesis (see 3c). When a title does not provide much information, look at the chapter titles or section headings to get a clearer sense of the work as a whole as well as to gauge how much you may already know about the subject.

Author

If you know anything about the author, you may have an idea about the expertise or tone being brought to the topic. If Dave Barry is the author, you can expect the essay to be humorous, but if Anna Quindlen is the author, you can expect the essay to be timely and political. Jared Diamond's science writing is highly respected and widely read, for he has earned a Pulitzer Prize (for *Guns, Germs, and Steel*), membership in the MacArthur Foundation fellowship (otherwise known as a "genius award"), and a National Medal of Science.

Length

Considering a text's length allows you to estimate how much time you should set aside for reading. By checking length, you can also estimate whether a work is long enough to include useful content or so short that it might only skim the surface of the subject it addresses.

Directories

In addition to previewing title and author, you will also want to examine various directories. The **table of contents** identifies the chapters and main sections within a book, and the **index**, at the back, lists in alphabetical order the specific topics covered. A **bibliography**, or list of research sources and related works, indicates how much research was involved in writing the book and can also direct you to additional sources. Checking these directories can help you determine whether the book has the kind of information you are looking for, where you can find it, and how much or what sections of the book you want to read.

Visual Aids

The extent to which visual aids are useful varies, but a quick check for graphs and other illustrations can help you decide whether the work has the kind of information you need, depending on the topic you are researching.

(Continued on page 22)

(Continued from page 21)

Summaries

Both books and articles often contain summaries, and reading a summary can help you decide whether the work as a whole will be helpful. Reading a summary can also help you follow a difficult text because the summary tells you the major points. Summaries can often be found in the preface of a book, as well as in introductory and concluding chapters. Scholarly articles often begin with a summary identified as an abstract (see **9c** and **10b(2)**). Within other kinds of articles, the introductory and concluding paragraphs often include summaries (see **9c**). Sometimes, book summaries can be found on the inside or back cover.

CONTENTS

5

The table of contents shows how the material in Diamond's book is arranged and indicates how fully that material is developed.

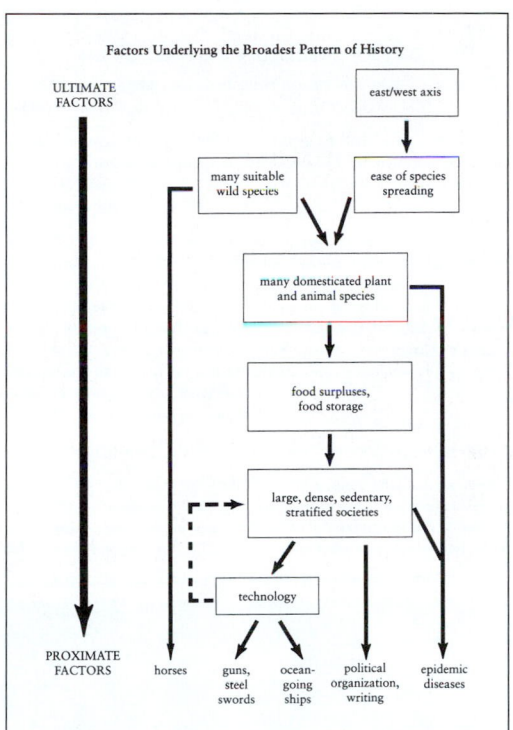

In chapter 4, Diamond uses a visual aid to map out the causal chain of factors that he believes underlies patterns of history—especially the development of steel and guns and the spread of germs.

In addition to assessing the title, author, length, directories, visual aids, and summary of a text you are previewing, assess how much you already know about the subject. If you are unfamiliar with the subject matter, you might want to start with a less demanding treatment of the topic, either in print or online. Finally, if you know that your values or opinions differ greatly from those of the author, you will want to pay close attention to passages in the text that you might be tempted to dismiss without reading carefully.

Previewing helps make your reading easier and helps you select appropriate research materials (see chapter **9**). But remember that previewing a text is not the same as reading it for understanding.

SCIENCE

OVER 1 MILLION COPIES SOLD

"Fascinating. . . . Lays a foundation for understanding human history."
—Bill Gates

"Artful, informative, and delightful. . . . There is nothing like a radically new angle of vision for bringing out unsuspected dimensions of a subject, and that is what Jared Diamond has done."   —William H. McNeill, *New York Review of Books*

"This is a brilliantly written, passionate, whirlwind tour through 13,000 years of history on all the continents—a short history of everything about everybody. The origins of empires, religion, writing, crops, and guns are all here. By at last providing a convincing explanation for the differing developments of human societies on different continents, the book demolishes the grounds for racist theories of history. Its account of how the modern world was formed is full of lessons for our own future. After reading the first two pages, you won't be able to put it down."   —Paul R. Ehrlich, Bing Professor of Population Studies, Stanford University

"An ambitious, highly important book." —James Shreeve, *New York Times Book Review*

"A book of remarkable scope, a history of the world in less than 500 pages which succeeds admirably, where so many others have failed, in analyzing some of the basic workings of culture process. . . . One of the most important and readable works on the human past published in recent years."   —Colin Renfrew, *Nature*

WINNER OF THE PHI BETA KAPPA AWARD IN SCIENCE

JARED DIAMOND is professor of geography at UCLA and author of the best-selling and award-winning *The Third Chimpanzee*. He is a recipient of a MacArthur Foundation fellowship and has been awarded a 1999 National Medal of Science.

With a new afterword extending the book's significance to today's economics and geopolitics

Cover design by Calvin Chu

Cover painting: Sir John Everett Millais, *Pizarro seizing the Inca of Peru*, 1845. Victoria & Albert Museum, London/Art Resource, NY

W. W. NORTON
NEW YORK • LONDON

ISBN 0-393-31755-2

$16.95 USA $24.99 CAN.

www.wwnorton.com

The reviewers have summarized Diamond's book as well as evaluated its importance.

CHECKLIST for Previewing a Reading Selection

- What do you already know about this subject that you can use to connect with the text?
- What do the title and subtitle reveal about the way the subject is being treated?

- How long is this work, and how is it organized? What do the major divisions indicate to you?
- What information do the table of contents and the index provide about the book?
- Does the article include an abstract, or does the book include a summary?
- What do you know about this author that contributes to his or her credibility? If the author is unfamiliar, what biographical information could help you assess that credibility? (See **8c** and **10a**.)
- If there are graphs, figures, or other visual aids, what do they illustrate?
- Is there a bibliography that indicates how extensive and current the research is?
- Is the text suited to your level of understanding, or should you start with a simpler treatment of the same subject?
- Do you have strong feelings about this subject that could interfere with your ability to understand how it is treated in this text? (See **2d**.)

2b Reading for content

Effective readers pay close attention to the words on the page and develop specific strategies for increasing their comprehension as well as for working through misunderstandings. After previewing a text, you should be able to determine what the author wants to communicate, to whom, and for what specific purpose. In other words, you can begin to read for content.

As you read, you will want to note the author's major points, perhaps by underlining or highlighting them. Particular words and key phrases often signal those important points: "There are *three* advantages to this proposal. . . . The *first* is . . . . The *second* is . . . ." The phrase *in other words* signals that the author is about to paraphrase a point—because it is important. And *in this article* (or *chapter*) introduces a statement of the author's focus or purpose, whereas *in summary*, *in conclusion*, and *the point I am making* place a significant emphasis on the information just presented. Thus, transitional words or phrases indicating sequencing (see **4d**) or movement within a text help you

HEMISPHERES COLLIDING • 3 5 7

Eurasia's diverse and protein-rich cereals; hand planting of individual seeds, instead of broadcast sowing; tilling by hand instead of plowing by animals, which enables one person to cultivate a much larger area, and which also permits cultivation of some fertile but tough soils and sods that are difficult to till by hand (such as those of the North American Great Plains); lack of animal manuring to increase soil fertility; and just human muscle power, instead of animal power, for agricultural tasks such as threshing, grinding, and irrigation. These differences suggest that Eurasian agriculture as of 1492 may have yielded on the average more calories and protein per person-hour of labor than Native American agriculture did.

[margin note: amazing— all by hand]

[margin note: interesting]

SUCH DIFFERENCES IN food production constituted a major ultimate cause of the disparities between Eurasian and Native American societies. Among the resulting proximate factors behind the conquest, the most important included differences in germs, technology, political organization, and writing. Of these, the one linked most directly to the differences in food production was germs. The infectious diseases that regularly visited crowded Eurasian societies, and to which many Eurasians consequently developed immune or genetic resistance, included all of history's most lethal killers: smallpox, measles, influenza, plague, tuberculosis, typhus, cholera, malaria, and others. Against that grim list, the sole crowd infectious diseases that can be attributed with certainty to pre-Columbian Native American societies were nonsyphilitic treponemas. (As I explained in Chapter 11, it remains uncertain whether syphilis arose in Eurasia or in the Americas, and the claim that human tuberculosis was present in the Americas before Columbus is in my opinion unproven.)

[margin note: oh! I want to hear more]

    This continental difference in harmful germs resulted paradoxically from the difference in useful livestock. Most of the microbes responsible for the infectious diseases of crowded human societies evolved from very similar ancestral microbes causing infectious diseases of the domestic animals with which food producers began coming into daily close contact around 10,000 years ago. Eurasia harbored many domestic animal species and hence developed many such microbes, while the Americas had very few of each. Other reasons why Native American societies evolved so few lethal microbes were that villages, which provide ideal breeding grounds for epidemic diseases, arose thousands of years later in the Americas than in Eurasia; and that the three regions of the New World supporting urban

[margin note: So contact w/ livestock/ animals was a major factor w/ disease]

When you annotate a printed text—that is, talk back to it—you read it actively and rhetorically.

grasp content. Transitional expressions—especially those indicating purpose, result, summary, repetition, exemplification, and intensification (see page 77)—alert you to important points. Such phrases identify opportunities for you to talk back to the text itself, as though you were carrying on a conversation with the author.

When reading from a book or periodical (a magazine or professional journal) that you own, you can underline, highlight, or add comments to passages that interest or confuse you, or that you question. Write in the margins and annotate key passages whenever you have something to say or a question to pose. If you have borrowed a book, you can use sticky notes to highlight and annotate the text. With an electronic text, you can print out a hard copy and annotate it or use your word-processing program to respond directly on the screen.

Reading for content means making sure you understand the words on the page. When you encounter a word that is new to you, the meaning may be defined in the text itself, or you may be able to infer the meaning from the way the word has been used. Whenever a new term appears in a critically important position such as a thesis statement (see **3c**) or a conclusion (**4b(2)**), look it up in a college-appropriate dictionary (**32e**). But even language that is well chosen can sometimes be misleading because words have different specific meanings (**denotations**) as well as strong associations (**connotations**) that vary from reader to reader (see **33a**) and culture to culture (see chapter **32**)—depending on the rhetorical situation.

Your challenge as a reader, then, is to try to understand what exactly the author wanted the words to mean within the particular rhetorical situation, to understand as much as you can but to keep that understanding flexible enough to accommodate what will come. If you are reading a twenty-page chapter, you probably need a preliminary understanding of the first ten pages if you are going to understand the next ten. But if you later reread the entire chapter, your understanding of all the material is likely to deepen. Accordingly, effective readers usually reread texts that are important to them in order to master the content.

2c Rereading for understanding

Rereading is the easiest way to check your understanding of the content. Effective readers use their second pass through the material to determine the author's specific purpose and to note how the information is

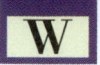

organized and how supporting ideas are developed (see chapter **3** and **6e**). In addition to noting these general features, you can also scan the first and last sentences in every paragraph. The central idea of a paragraph, which suggests a sense of content and overall organization, can occur anywhere in the paragraph (see **4c**), but it often appears in one of those two sentences.

2d   Recognizing a personal response

Critical readers consciously work to keep their personal responses from interfering with their ability to understand. So, in addition to reading for content, they also keep track of what they think about or how they are reacting to this content. That is not to say that they read passively. Reading rhetorically means reading actively, noting where you agree or disagree, become frustrated or intrigued, sympathetic or annoyed—and keeping track of what feature of the writing (or of yourself) triggered each response: was it the writer's tone (see **4a(3)**), an example that evoked a personal memory, a lapse in the organization (**3d**), the topic itself (**3b**), or a visual element such as a photo or illustration?

As you read, try to determine what the author thinks and why he or she holds that opinion. Then determine what *you* think and why *you* hold your opinion. In other words, what information do you agree or disagree with—and why? What passages brought to mind your own experience or expertise? What have you learned from your reading? What about this text confuses you? What would you like to know more about?

By noting personal responses and recognizing that they are independent of a work's content even if they are inspired by it, you can increase your understanding of the purposeful choices writers make when communicating with readers. Personal responses often serve as the basis for your own writing (see **2e**). Often, good readers and writers use techniques from the following list.

TIPS FOR RECORDING PERSONAL RESPONSES

- Note passages that capture your attention. Underline or highlight your own copy; highlight with color when reading on a computer screen.

- Put a question mark in the margin when you do not understand a passage—or if you question its accuracy.
- Put an exclamation point in the margin when a statement or an example surprises you.
- Write *yes* or *no* in the margin when you agree or disagree. When a passage reminds you of another passage (or something else you have read), note that association in the margin. Keep a reading journal (see **3a(1)**). Include at least one question or reservation about something you read each day.
- Correspond by e-mail with other people who are reading the same material (see chapter **6**).

2e Writing daily about your reading

Effective readers write daily about their reading. Whether you keep a personal journal, a writer's notebook, or a reading journal (or, in some classes, participate in an online discussion forum; see **6c**), you are taking the opportunity to write about your reading in terms of content and personal response. When you respond to a text in this way—listening to it, arguing with it, extending it, connecting it with your own experience—you will be more likely to engage the text, understand it, and remember it. Writing regularly about your reading, then, helps you increase your comprehension and identify responses that could be the seeds from which larger pieces of writing subsequently grow.

You can design your reading journal in such a way that you will benefit in terms of comprehension and creativity. One way to do this is to keep a **double-entry notebook,** a journal in which each entry has two distinct parts: summary and response. For example, if you keep your journal in a spiral notebook, you can use the left side of each page to summarize your understanding of what you have read (see **11b**) and the right side to record your responses to it. (Or you might prefer to format word-processing files into columns.)

A first-year student created a double-entry notebook for her world geography course. When she read the substantial prologue to Diamond's book, she summarized his views about the course of history on the left-hand side of a page and responded to his thinking on the right-hand side:

Summary	Response
Diamond gives an overview of the reasons why history has "proceeded very differently for peoples all over the globe." He mentions the rise of literacy in comparison to illiteracy, the development of metal tools in some societies and stone tools in others, and he uses these comparisons to explain why some societies have so easily been able to infiltrate and conquer other ones. Then he moves to his meeting with local New Guinean politician Yali, who had many questions, all of which can be summarized in the following: "Why is it that you white people developed so much cargo and brought it to New Guinea, but we black people had little cargo of our own?" Diamond uses the rest of the prologue to map out a response having to do with the inequalities of wealth and power in the modern world, which he plans to explain. He decides to work within the confines of genetics, climate, irrigation systems, and so on. Finally, he summarizes his book in this way: "History followed different courses for different peoples because of differences among peoples' environments, not because of biological differences among peoples themselves."	Diamond demonstrates a deep global and historical perspective about the course of history for different people, yet part of me still wonders if he's being "politically correct." He writes that he and Yali "both knew perfectly well that New Guineans are on the average at least as smart as Europeans" (114). Yet despite the equality of intelligence, by A.D. 1500 the die had been cast: "empires with steel weapons were able to conquer or exterminate tribes with weapons of stone and wood" (16). I see that he's not justifying the outcome; rather he's trying to understand it so that things don't always work out that way: the whites don't continue to dominant nonwhite people. In fact, he writes that he's going to explain how white people picked up the technologies that became the basis of "civilization." He's also going to talk about racism, about how people from all over the world (from the Japanese to the Australians) think about aboriginal people as uncivilized. What I find really interesting is his explanation of why the New Guineans he knows seem, on the whole, smarter than the European people he knows. He explains the differences as survival on the part of New Guineans and as genetic resistance on the part of Europeans. In other words, dumb New Guineans probably died off, whereas dumb Europeans have been protected by social and medical advances, so they grow up, reproduce, and continue to depend on their resistance. I'm pretty sure he's using the word "European" to mean "whites."

Like this student, you will want to keep the entries devoted to summarizing content separated from those devoted to your personal response. This separation will come in handy when you need to review what you have written. When you are preparing for a written examination (see **5f**), for example, you will be able to easily identify the entries that will help you remember content. And when you are involved in the brainstorming necessary for drafting an essay (see chapter **3**), you can turn to those entries in which you recorded your own ideas, interpretations, questions, or reflections.

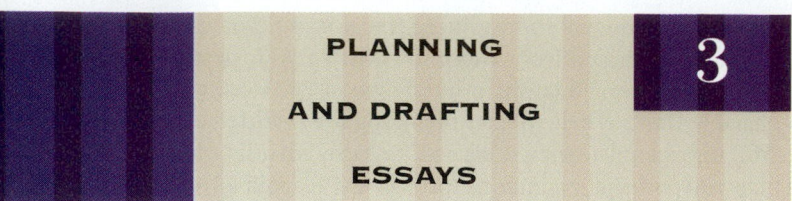

PLANNING AND DRAFTING ESSAYS

3

Experienced writers understand that writing is a process. Think of the writing you do out of school, and you will realize how experienced you already are at the process. When you compose an e-mail, for instance, you consider the audience, the message, and the tone you wish to convey. Even though you are writing quickly, you stop often to draft, cut and paste, and delete—just as you do when you are writing more slowly to fulfill an academic assignment. Whether you are writing in or out of school, you do so in terms of your purpose, audience, and context (see **1a**), revising and editing all along the way.

This chapter will help you understand writing as a process and

- find good topics (**3a**),
- focus your ideas (**3b**),
- write a clear thesis statement (**3c**),
- organize your ideas (**3d**),
- express your ideas in a first draft (**3e**), and
- use various strategies to develop effective paragraphs and essays (**3f** and **3g**).

Effective writers know they cannot do everything at once, so they generate, organize, develop, and clarify their ideas as well as polish their prose during a series of sometimes separate—but often overlapping—steps.

The writing process is **recursive,** which means that as you plan and draft an essay, you may need to return to a specific activity several times. For example, drafting may help you see that you need to go back and collect more ideas, modify your thesis, or even start over with a new one. Experienced writers expect the writing process to lead to new ideas as well as uncover passages in need of improvement.

Despite the infinite variations of the writing process, writing usually involves four basic, recursive stages, described below.

STAGES OF THE WRITING PROCESS

- **Prewriting** is the initial stage of the writing process. As soon as you begin thinking about a specific writing task, consider what is expected of you in terms of your intended audience, purpose, and context. Then start exploring your topic by talking with others working on the same assignment, keeping a journal, freewriting, or questioning. In short, do whatever it takes to energize your thinking and jump-start your writing.

- **Drafting** involves writing down your ideas quickly, writing as much as you can, without worrying about being perfect or staying on topic. The more ideas you get down on paper, the more options you will have as you begin to clarify your thesis and purpose for writing, organize, and revise. Progress is your goal at this stage, not perfection.

- **Revising** offers you the opportunity to focus your purpose for writing, establish a clear thesis statement (see **3c**), and organize your ideas toward those ends (**3d**). This is the time to start stabilizing the overall structure of your essay as well as the structure of the individual paragraphs (**3f** and **4c**) and to reconsider your introduction and conclusion (**4b**). Remember that revising means producing another draft for further revision and editing.

- **Editing** focuses on surface features: punctuation, spelling, word choice and Standardized English, grammar, and sentence structure (see **4f**). As you prepare your work for final submission, consider reading it aloud to discover which sentence structures and word choices could be improved.

3a Selecting worthwhile subjects for writing

Whether you are assigned a subject or are free to respond to an exigence of your own choosing, you must consider what you already know—or would like to learn about—and what is likely to interest your audience (see **1d**). The first step toward engaging an audience is to be interested in the subject yourself, so consider your interests and experience. Often the best subject is one drawn from your specific knowledge of hobbies, sports, jobs, or places. When subjects are important to you, they usually interest readers, especially when you write with a clear purpose and well-chosen details (see **1c** and **3f(1)**).

More often, however, you will be asked to write essays about subjects outside your personal experience but within your academic coursework.

If, for instance, you are assigned an essay for a course in ancient history, you may be responsible for choosing your topic—but it will have to be related to the course. In order to find material that interests you, look in your textbook, particularly in the sections listing suggestions for further reading. Go through your lecture notes, your reading journal, or any marginal annotations you have made for the course (see **2e**). Ask yourself whether any details of the subject have surprised, annoyed, or pleased you—if there is something you feel strongly about and would like to explore further. Writing about a subject is one of the best ways to learn about it, so use a writing assignment not only to impart information to your audience but also to satisfy yourself.

(1) Keeping a journal is one way to explore a subject.

Keeping a journal is a good way to generate subjects for essays. In a **personal journal,** you reflect on your experiences, using writing as a means to explore how you feel about what is happening in your life or in the world around you. You might focus on external events, such as what you think about a book or a film, or on your inner life, such as changes in your moods or attitudes. Writers who keep a personal journal usually write for their own benefit, but in the process of writing the journal—or reading it—they may discover subjects and exigencies they can use for essays.

Like a personal journal, a double-entry notebook (see **2e**) includes responses to experiences. In this case, however, the emphasis is on recording and exploring material for future projects. You might list quotations and observations that invite development; then, when time allows, you might also draft the opening pages of an essay, outline an idea for a story, or experiment with writing a poem.

Some writers prefer to keep a reading journal (see **2e**). You may find it convenient to keep your journal in a word-processing file on your computer, especially if you use a laptop. Whichever type of journal you keep or method you use to record your thoughts, feel free to write quickly, without worrying about spelling or grammar.

(2) Freewriting offers a risk-free way to explore a subject.

When **freewriting,** writers record whatever occurs to them, without stopping, for a limited period of time—often no more than ten minutes. They do not worry about whether they are repeating themselves or getting off track; they simply write to see what comes out. Freewriting is another good way to generate ideas for a writing assignment because no matter what you write, it will contain ideas and information you did not realize you had. Some writers use colored marking pens (or change the font in their word-processing program) to identify different topics generated by this activity.

In **directed freewriting,** you begin with a general subject and record whatever occurs to you about this subject during the time available. When Melissa Schraeder's English instructor asked her to write for five minutes, assessing some of the main challenges to being a happy and successful college student, she produced the freewriting shown below. (This freewriting represents the first step toward Melissa's essay, three different versions of which appear in chapter 4.)

Sometimes I feel like being successful in school and remaining sane are incompatible goals. Schoolwork's stressful, especially when working on those classes that I don't like, such as my math or science. This is why I have had to be creative in my study habits and patterns. One of the small compromises I make with myself is to invite a friend along to study with me. Studying seems less gloomy when done in pairs since it is comforting and motivating to know that you are not the only one who is working hard. The biggest challenge I face in maintaining my success and happiness as a college student though is balancing school and work. With tuition so high and all the extra expenses such as books and technology fees, most students have to work in order to stay afloat and I am certainly not exempt. I usually only work around 15 hours a week, but those 15 hours are crucial in the midst of exams and papers with strict deadlines. I always try to put my schoolwork first, so there are some weeks where I wish I didn't have to work at all!

As the color shading shows, Melissa's freewriting generated three possible strands of development for an essay about being a successful college student: managing stress, finding creative approaches to studying, and balancing work and school. Some of these strands overlap; all of them have to do with managing time and stress. But notice that she mentions the necessity of working while in school; she eventually decided to focus her essay on balancing the demands of her much-needed job with those of her schoolwork.

(3) Questioning pushes the boundaries of your subject.

You can also explore a subject by asking yourself some questions. The simplest questioning strategy for helping you explore a subject comes from journalism. **Journalists' questions**—*Who? What? When? Where? Why?* and *How?*—are easy to use and can help you discover ideas about any subject. Using journalists' questions to explore the subject of balancing schoolwork and a job could lead you to think about it in a number of ways: *Who* typically has to work part-time while in college? *What* should college students look for in a part-time job? *When* should students work? *Where* should students work? *Why* can part-time work be an important part of the college experience? And *how* can students balance part-time work with good schoolwork; *how* can a part-time job influence a student's attitude about schoolwork?

3b   Focusing a subject idea into a specific topic

By exploring your subject, you can discover productive strategies for development as well as a specific focus for your topic. As you prewrite, you will decide that some ideas seem worth pursuing but others seem inappropriate for your purpose, audience, or context. You will find yourself discarding ideas even as you develop new ones and determine your topic.

A simple analogy helps explain focus: when you take a picture of a landscape, you cannot photograph all that your eye can take in. You must focus on just part of it. As you aim the camera, you look through the viewfinder to make sure the subject is correctly framed and in focus. At this point, you may wish to move in closer and focus on one part of the scene, or you may decide to change the angle, using light and shadow to emphasize certain features of the landscape. You can think of your writing the same way—you focus and direct your ideas just as you focus and direct the lens of a camera, moving from a general subject to a more specific topic.

In addition to reviewing the ideas you have generated through strategies such as freewriting and questioning, you can also focus by thinking in terms of how the various rhetorical methods you might use for developing your ideas (see **3g**) might take you in different directions. Responding to the exigence of "balancing a part-time job with schoolwork," Melissa needed to focus her subject into a narrow topic. Thus, she considered the subject in terms of the following rhetorical methods of development:

Like photographers, writers need to focus their ideas, moving from a general subject to a more specific topic.

- *Narration.* What kind of story can I tell about part-time work for college students?
- *Description.* What kind of part-time job do I have? What is my place of work like? How do my employers treat me?
- *Process analysis.* How have I gone about balancing my own part-time job with my schoolwork?
- *Cause-and-consequence analysis.* What have been the causes of my success in balancing my job with my schoolwork? Concentration? Commitment? What were some of the consequences when I made mistakes in balancing these two in the past? Exhaustion? Frustration? What is the primary cause? What are contributory causes?
- *Comparison and contrast.* How do my study habits and academic skills compare with those of students who do not work and those of students who do? How does my work-and-school lifestyle compare to my previous school-only lifestyle?
- *Classification and division.* How can I classify the different types of jobs that college students take on? How can I divide up the desirable qualities of jobs and employers? How many college students feel they must take a job?
- *Definition.* How do I define "success" in college? Is career experience as important as good grades? What constitutes a "good attitude" toward your education?

The following sentence suggests a focus on comparison and contrast:

Before I came to college and took on a part-time job, I spent all of my free time either studying or hanging out with friends.

This sentence focuses on cause and consequence:

> Now that I'm working part-time and taking classes full-time, I have little free time to spend with my friends or relax.

Sometimes a combination of strategies leads to a focus:

> When I think of how much leisure time I had before I came to college, I almost get depressed. I used to spend Saturdays hanging out with my friends at the mall and Sunday afternoons reading a novel. Now that I'm in college, working part-time and carrying a full load of classes, I have little time to hang out with my friends, and no time for pleasure reading. So instead of getting depressed, I try to concentrate on the positive consequences of working while attending school.

Because writing is a form of thinking and discovering, your focus might not emerge until after you have written your first draft. When you compare the draft of Melissa's essay on working while attending school (see pages 83–87) with the final version of it (pages 96–99), you will see how drafting and revising can sharpen a writer's focus.

Whatever method you use to bring a topic into focus, your choice should be determined not only by your interests but also by your purpose, the needs of your audience, and the time and space available. The following checklist may help you assess your topic.

CHECKLIST for Assessing a Topic

- Are you interested in the topic?
- Is the topic appropriate for your audience?
- Can you interest the audience in your topic?
- What is your purpose in writing about this topic?
- Can you do justice to the topic in the time and space available to you? Or should you narrow it down or expand it?
- Do you know enough about the topic to write a paper of the length your instructor requires? If not, how will you get additional information?
- Are you willing to learn more about the topic?

Exercise 1

Use the journalists' questions to generate more ideas about a concept or subject that interests you. Then consider how you might focus that general subject into a specific topic appropriate for an essay.

3c Conveying a clearly stated thesis

Once you have focused your subject into a topic, you have come a long way toward developing the main idea you want to convey. By this point, you have probably also established your purpose for writing, whether to explain, teach, analyze, argue, or compare. Your subject, purpose, supporting information, and focus all come together in a controlling idea, or **thesis,** which is appropriate for your audience and context (see chapter 1). In the first draft or two, your thesis may be only tentative. By your final draft, however, you will have developed a clear thesis statement.

Most pieces of writing have a **thesis statement,** an explicit declaration (usually in one sentence) of the main idea. Your thesis statement, then, will convey a single idea, clearly focused and specifically stated. A thesis can be thought of as a central idea stated in the form of an assertion, or **claim** (see **8d**), which indicates what you believe to be true, interesting, or valuable about your topic.

An explicitly formulated thesis statement helps keep your writing on target. It identifies the topic, the purpose, and, in some cases, the plan of development. Notice how the following thesis statements fulfill their purpose. The first is from an expressive essay.

Dave Rahm was a stunt pilot, the air's own genius.   —ANNIE DILLARD

With this simple statement, the author establishes that the topic is Dave Rahm and indicates that she will discuss his genius as a stunt pilot. She conveys enthusiasm and awe about his expertise.

The following thesis statement (in two sentences) for an expository essay divides student excuses into five kinds, using humor to make a point.

With a show of energy and creativity that would be admirable if applied to the (missing) assignments in question, my students persist, week after week, semester after semester, year after year, in offering excuses about why their work is not ready. Those reasons fall into several broad categories: the family, the best friend, the evils of dorm life, the evils of technology, and the totally bizarre.

   —**CAROLYN FOSTER SEGAL**, "The Dog Ate My Disk, and Other Tales of Woe"

The main idea in an argumentative essay usually carries a strong point of view, as in the following, which unmistakably argues for a specific course of action.

Amnesty International opposes the death penalty in all cases without exception.

   —**AMNESTY INTERNATIONAL**, "The Death Penalty: Questions and Answers"

It is just as important to allow your thesis statement to remain tentative in the early stages of writing as it is to allow your essay to remain flexible through the first and second drafts. Rather than starting with a preconceived thesis, which you must struggle to support, you should let your final thesis statement grow out of your thinking and discovery process as you draft and revise. The following tips might help you develop a thesis statement that is neither too obvious nor too general.

TIPS FOR DEVELOPING A THESIS STATEMENT

- Decide which feature of the topic interests you most.
- Write down your point of view or assertion about that feature.
- Mark the passages in your freewriting, journal, or rough draft that support your position.
- Draft a thesis statement, and consider whether you can address the full scope of this tentative thesis in your essay or whether it is still too broad to be developed sufficiently.
- After your first or second draft, ask yourself whether your thesis is too broad for your essay (or vice versa). Revise your thesis to widen or narrow its scope in the direction your essay has taken.
- If you are unhappy with the results, start again with the first tip, and be even more specific.

A clear, precise thesis statement helps unify what you write; it directs your readers to the writing that follows. Therefore, as you write and revise, check your thesis statement frequently to see whether you have drifted away from it. It should guide your decisions about which details to keep and which to toss out as well as your search for appropriate additional information to strengthen your points or support your assertions. In addition, as you write and revise, test all of your supporting material against the thesis statement and scrupulously discard anything that does not pertain to it.

A thesis is usually stated in a declarative sentence with a single main clause—that is, in either a simple or a complex sentence (see **21d**). If your thesis statement presents two or more coordinate ideas, as a compound sentence does, be sure that you are not losing direction and focus. For example, the following thesis statement, composed of two sentences, coordinates and focuses two ideas, indicating a discussion that will contrast men's and women's use of language.

> Male students are more likely to be comfortable attacking the readings and might find the inclusion of personal anecdotes irrelevant and "soft." Women are more likely to resist discussion they perceive as hostile, and, indeed, it is women in my classes who are most likely to offer personal anecdotes.
>
> —**DEBORAH TANNEN**, "How Male and Female Students Use Language Differently"

If you wish to sharpen a thesis statement by adding information that qualifies or supports it, subordinate such material to the main idea:

> Many who today hear me somewhere in person, or on television, or those who read something I've said, will think I went to school far beyond the eighth grade. This impression is due entirely to my prison studies.
>
> —**MALCOLM X,** "Prison Studies"

As you clarify your thesis statement, resist using such vague qualifiers as *interesting, important,* and *unusual,* which can signal that the topic lacks interest or focus. For example, in the thesis statement "My education has been very unusual," the vague word *unusual* may indicate that the idea itself is weak and that the writer needs to find a sharper focus. However, this kind of vague thesis may disguise an idea of real interest that simply needs to be made specific: "Our family grew closer after my parents decided to teach me at home." The following examples show how vague thesis statements can be clarified and sharpened.

Vague   It is hard to balance work with school.

Better   Hardworking students who balance a part-time job with success in schoolwork can grow in maturity and self-confidence.

Vague	People wonder about the connection of thinking styles with intelligence.
Better	Thinking styles are largely distinct from intelligence or aptitude.
Vague	Harry Truman was an important president.
Better	President Truman's executive order in 1948 became an important step in the long-term struggle for civil rights.

The thesis statement most often appears in the first paragraph of an essay, although you can put yours anywhere that suits your purpose—occasionally even in the conclusion. The advantage of putting the thesis statement in the first paragraph is that readers know from the beginning what you are writing about and where the essay is going. Especially appropriate in academic writing, this technique helps readers who are searching for specific information to locate it easily. If the thesis statement begins the introductory paragraph, the rest of the sentences in the paragraph usually support or clarify it, as is the case in paragraph 1. (For ease of reference, each of the sample paragraphs in this chapter is numbered.)

1   *America is suffering from overwork.* Too many of us are too busy, trying to squeeze more into each day while having less to show for it. Although our growing time crunch is often portrayed as a personal dilemma, it is in fact a major social problem that has reached crisis proportions over the past 20 years.   —**BARBARA BRANDT,** "Less Is More"

If the thesis statement is the last sentence of the opening paragraph, the preceding sentences will build toward it, as is the case in paragraph 2.

2   The story of zero is an ancient one. Its roots stretch back to the dawn of mathematics, in the time thousands of years before the first civilization, long before humans could read and write. But as natural as zero seems to us today, for ancient peoples zero was a foreign—and frightening—idea. An Eastern concept, born in the Fertile Crescent a few centuries before the birth of Christ, zero not only evoked images of a primal void, it also had dangerous mathematical properties. *Within zero there is the power to shatter the framework of logic.*   —**CHARLES SEIFE,** *Zero: The Biography of a Dangerous Idea*

Most of the writing done for college courses contains an obvious thesis statement. The following checklist may help you assess the thesis of your essay.

CHECKLIST for Assessing a Thesis

- Does your thesis make a clear comment about your topic?
- Is your thesis an accurate reflection of what you believe to be true about your topic?
- Does your thesis match your essay in terms of focus and coverage?
- What two assertions can you make to support your thesis?
- What specific examples, illustrations, or experiences support your assertions?
- How does your thesis relate to the interests of your audience? To your purpose? To the context of your essay?
- Where is your thesis located in your essay? Would your readers benefit from having it stated earlier or later?

3d Arranging or outlining ideas

Many writers need a working plan to direct their ideas and keep their writing on course. Various plans of arrangement might be determined for them by their instructor, by the discipline in which they are writing, or by tradition.

Some writers quickly compose informal lists, which grow out of a collection of ideas. The ideas in these lists can overlap, be discarded, or lead to a tentative thesis statement, conclusions, and the beginning of an overall organizational plan. Other writers, however, rely on outlines. Either method (list or outline) can be especially helpful when you are writing lengthy papers (see chapters 8 and 9) and when you are writing under pressure (see chapter 5). Whatever method you choose for arranging your ideas, remember that you can always alter your arrangement to accommodate any changes your writing undergoes during the process.

You can simplify your thinking about arrangement if you accept Aristotle's claim that every speech needs "a beginning, a middle, and an end." Even the simplest outline offers an essay a structure, much like the basic framework of a house. And, like the framework of a house, a simple outline can quickly become more elaborate and detailed. As you work and think, you might introduce indentations, letters, and numbers into your rough outline to indicate various levels of subordination

and coordination in your material. Thus, an outline becomes a visual map of your thinking. The main points form the major headings, and the supporting ideas form the subheadings. An outline of Melissa's essay might look something like the following.

TENTATIVE THESIS STATEMENT: Balancing a part-time job with success in schoolwork is not only a manageable task, but also a valuable experience contributing to growth as a student and as an individual.

I. Balancing work with school is manageable

   A. Your own sacrifices will determine success

      1. Time with friends

      2. Use breaks at work wisely

      3. Get a good handle on your school schedule and determine how far ahead you need to start assignments

   B. Best if you have an understanding employer

      1. An employer who puts school first and values scholarship

      2. Take advantage of university-run work programs

   C. Flexibility in scheduling hours

      1. Plan ahead around exam and paper weeks

      2. Often need to sacrifice weekend time in order to get in hours

II. Balancing work with school is valuable experience for students

   A. Provides discipline

      1. In prioritizing schoolwork, those students who work part-time jobs often have a good handle on their academic schedules and stay on top of their studies

      2. Working students learn the importance of time management and set realistic goals and time lines for themselves

   B. Working to pay for education leads students to place more value on their education

      1. More serious about schoolwork

      2. Realize the importance of timely completion of degree

         a. Sleep becomes a priority

         b. Exercise seems less important

   C. Part-time work can offer career experience

      1. Internships

      2. Career-related work

D. Part-time work can motivate students to achieve excellence in school as a means of moving beyond the scope of part-time work

1. Face boredom or monotony in job

2. Face low wages

3. Constructive use of potential negativity

However streamlined or detailed your outline, you will need enough headings to develop your topic fully within the boundaries stated in your thesis.

3e Getting your ideas into a first draft

When writing a first draft, get your ideas down quickly. Spelling, punctuation, and correctness are not important in the first draft; ideas are. Experienced writers know that the most important thing about a first draft is to have done it, for it gives you something to work on—and against. If you are not sure how to begin, look over some of the journal writing, listing, or outlining you have already done, and try to state a tentative thesis. Then write out some main points you would like to develop, along with some of the supporting information for that development. Keep your overall plan in mind as you draft. If you find yourself losing track of where you want to go, stop writing and reread what you have already done. Talk with someone working on the same assignment, or write in your journal. You may find that you need to revise your plan—or you may need to rethink your topic. Experienced writers expect a change in plan as they write and revise.

If you feel stuck, move to another part of your essay and draft paragraphs that might appear later (see **5e**). Doing so may help you restart your engine, for when you are actually writing, you think more efficiently. You can then move on to another part that is easier to write, such as sentences that develop another supporting idea, an introduction, or a conclusion. But do not worry about writing a provocative introduction or a sensible conclusion at this point. Later, when you are revising, you can experiment with ways of polishing those sections of an essay (see **4b**). What is important at this stage is to begin writing, and then keep writing as quickly as you can. Save this early work so that you can refer to it as you revise (see chapter **4**).

Finally, remember that writing is a form of discovering, understanding, and thinking. As you draft, you are likely to discover that you have more to say than you ever thought you would. So, whenever drafting leads you in a direction you did not intend, allow yourself to explore if you sense that this side trip may hold a useful discovery. You can consider whether to integrate or suppress this new material when you prepare to revise.

3f Drafting well-developed paragraphs

You compose a draft by developing the information that will constitute the paragraphs of your essay. If you are working from an informal list (see **3d**), you will have a sense of where you want to take your ideas but may be uncertain about the number and nature of the paragraphs you will need. If you are working from an outline (see **3d**), you can anticipate the number of paragraphs you will probably write and what you hope to accomplish in each paragraph. In the first case, you enjoy the freedom to pursue new ideas that occur as you draft. In the second, you enjoy the security of a clear direction. In both cases, however, you need to develop each paragraph fully and then ask yourself whether any additional paragraphs (or additional supporting information within any paragraph) would help your audience understand the main idea of your essay.

Paragraphs have no set length. Typically, they range from 50 to 250 words, and paragraphs in books are usually longer than those in newspapers and magazines. There are certainly times when a long paragraph makes for rich reading, as well as times when a long paragraph exhausts a single minor point, combines too many points, or becomes repetitive. On the other hand, short, one-sentence paragraphs can be effectively used for emphasis (see chapter **30**) or to establish transition (see **4d**). Short paragraphs can also, however, indicate inadequate development. There will be times when you can combine two short paragraphs as you revise (see chapter **4**), but there will be many more occasions when you need to lengthen a short paragraph by developing it with specific details or examples.

Experienced writers do not worry much about paragraph length; rather, they concentrate on getting words on the paper or on the screen, knowing that all paragraphs can be shortened, lengthened, merged, or otherwise improved later in the writing process. So think of revising and developing your paragraphs as a luxury, an opportunity to articulate exactly what you want to say without anyone interrupting you—or changing the subject.

(1) You can develop a paragraph with details.

A good paragraph developed with details brings your idea to life. Consider the following well-developed paragraph by Alice Walker.

3   I stood in front of the mirror and looked at myself and laughed. *My hair was one of those odd, amazing, unbelievable, stop-you-in-your-tracks creations— not unlike a zebra's stripes, an armadillo's ears, or the feet of the electric-bluefooted boobie—that the Universe makes for no reason other than to express its own limitless imagination.* I realized I had never been given the opportunity to appreciate hair for its true self. That it did, in fact, have one. I remembered years of enduring hairdressers—from my mother onward— doing missionary work on my hair. They dominated, suppressed, controlled. Now, more or less free, it stood this way and that. I would call up my friends around the country to report on its antics. It never thought of lying down. Flatness, the missionary position, did not interest it. It grew. Being short, cropped off near the root, another missionary "solution," did not interest it either. It sought more and more space, more light, more of itself. It loved to be washed; but that was it.

—ALICE WALKER, "Oppressed Hair Puts a Ceiling on the Brain"

Notice how the series of details in paragraph 3 supports the main idea (italicized), the topic sentence (see 4c). Readers can easily see how one sentence leads into the next, creating a clear picture of the hair being described.

(2) You can develop a paragraph by providing examples.

Like details, examples contribute to paragraph development by making specific what otherwise might seem general and hard to grasp. **Details** describe a person, place, or thing; **examples** illustrate an idea with information that can come from different times and places. Both details and examples support your ideas in terms of the rhetorical situation.

The author of paragraph 4 uses several closely related examples (as well as details) to support the main idea with which he begins.

4   *Illiterates live, in more than literal ways, an uninsured existence.* They cannot understand the written details on a health insurance form. They cannot read the waivers that they sign preceding surgical procedures. Several women I have known in Boston have entered a slum hospital with the intention of obtaining a tubal ligation and have emerged a few days later after having been subjected to a hysterectomy. Unaware of their rights, incognizant of jargon, intimidated by the unfamiliar air of fear and atmosphere of ether that so many of us find oppressive in the confines even of the most attractive and expensive medical facilities, they have signed their names to documents they could not read and which nobody, in the hectic situation that prevails so often in those overcrowded hospitals that serve the urban poor, had even bothered to explain.

        —**JONATHAN KOZOL**, "The Human Cost of an Illiterate Society"

Exercise 2

Examine some of your own writing—such as an essay you have recently drafted, e-mail messages that are still on file, or entries in your journal—and select one paragraph that holds potential interest. Write out (by hand) the original paragraph, and then rewrite it, developing it with additional details or examples.

3g Employing rhetorical methods of development

When drafting essays, you can develop a variety of paragraphs using **rhetorical methods,** mental operations that help you think through various types of rhetorical problems—having to do with establishing boundaries (definition), making sense of a person, place, or event (description and narration), organizing concepts (classification and division), understanding or thinking critically about a process (process or cause-and-consequence analysis), or needing to convince someone (argumentation). The strategies used for generating ideas, focusing your topic (see **3b**), developing paragraphs and essays, and arranging ideas are already second nature to you. Every day, you use one or more of them to define a concept, narrate a significant incident, supply examples for an assertion, classify or divide information into specific parts, compare two or more things, analyze a process, or identify a cause or consequence.

When drafting an essay, you may discover that you need to define a term or explain a process before you can take your readers further into your topic. Writers have the option of tapping one, two, or several rhetorical methods to fulfill their overall purpose, which might be to explain, entertain, argue a point, or evaluate a situation.

(1) Narrating a series of events tells readers what happened.

A **narrative** discusses a sequence of events, normally in **chronological order** (the order in which they occur), to develop a particular point or set a mood. This rhetorical method, which often uses a setting, characters, dialogue, and description, usually uses transition words or phrases such as *then, later, that evening,* or *the following week* to guide readers from one incident to the next. Whatever its length, a narrative must remain focused on the main idea. Drawn from Charles Darwin's journal, written during his voyage on the *Beagle,* paragraph 5 uses narrative to convey a sense of wonder at the power of nature.

5   The day has been memorable in the annals of Valdivia, for the most severe earthquake experienced by the oldest inhabitant. I happened to be on shore, and was lying down in the wood to rest myself. It came on suddenly, and lasted two minutes, but the time appeared much longer. The rocking of the ground was very sensible. The undulations appeared to my companion and myself to come from due east, whilst others thought they proceeded from the southwest. This shows how difficult it sometimes is to perceive the direction of vibrations. There was no difficulty in standing upright, but the motion made me almost giddy; it was something like the movement of a vessel in a little cross-ripple, or still more like that felt by a person skating over thin ice, which bends under the weight of his body.

—**CHARLES DARWIN,** "Great Earthquake"

(2) Describing how something looks, sounds, smells, or feels adds useful detail.

By describing a person, place, object, or sensation, you can make your material come alive. Often descriptions are predominantly visual, but even visual descriptions can include the details of what you hear, smell, taste, touch; that is, descriptions appeal to the senses.

Description should suit your purpose and audience. In describing your car, for example, you would emphasize certain features to a

Combining appeals to several senses, through a photograph and descriptive words, brings information alive for the reader (and potential buyer).

potential buyer, others to a mechanic who was going to repair it, and still others to a friend whom you wished to impress. In paragraph 6, Judith Ortiz Cofer employs vivid descriptive details to convey her ideas about cultural influences on adolescent striving and embarrassment.

6   I came to remember Career Day in our high school, when teachers told us to come dressed as if for a job interview. It quickly became obvious that to the barrio girls, "dressing up" sometimes meant wearing ornate jewelry and clothing that would be more appropriate (by mainstream standards) for the company Christmas party than as daily office attire. That morning I had agonized in front of my closet, trying to figure out what a "career girl" would wear because, essentially, except for Marlo Thomas on TV, I had no models on which to base my decision. I knew how to dress for school: at the

Catholic school I attended we all wore uniforms; I knew how to dress for Sunday mass, and I knew what dresses to wear for parties at my relatives' homes. Though I do not recall the precise details of my Career Day outfit, it must have been a composite of the above choices. But I remember a comment my friend (an Italian-American) made in later years that coalesced my impressions of that day. She said that at the business school she was attending the Puerto Rican girls always stood out for wearing "everything at once." She meant, of course, too much jewelry, too many accessories. On that day at school, we were simply made the negative models by the nuns who were themselves not credible fashion experts to any of us. But it was painfully obvious to me that to the others, in their tailored skirts and silk blouses, we must have seemed "hopeless" and "vulgar." Though I now know that most adolescents feel out of step much of the time, I also know that for the Puerto Rican girls of my generation that sense was intensified. The way our teachers and classmates looked at us that day in school was just a taste of the culture clash that awaited us in the real world, where prospective employers and men on the street would often misinterpret our tight skirts and jingling bracelets as a come-on.

—JUDITH ORTIZ COFER, "The Myth of the Latin Woman:
I Just Met a Girl Named María"

(3) Explaining a process shows readers how something happens.

Process paragraphs, in explaining how something is done or made, often use both description and narration. You might describe the items used in a process and then narrate the steps of the process chronologically. Add an explanation of a process to a draft if doing so will illustrate a concept that might otherwise be hard for your audience to grasp. In

Descriptions of a process, such as boat building, often combine description and narration.

paragraph 7, Bernice Wuethrich explains the process by which a scientist studied the effects of alcohol on brain cells.

7   Mark Prendergast, a neuroscientist at the University of Kentucky, recently revealed one way these hyperactive receptors kill brain cells. First,

he exposed rat hippocampal slices to alcohol for 10 days, then removed the alcohol. Following withdrawal, he stained the tissue with a fluorescent dye that lit up dead and dying cells. When exposed to an alcohol concentration of about .08 percent, cell death increased some 25 percent above the baseline. When concentrations were two or three times higher, he wrote in a recent issue of *Alcoholism: Clinical and Experimental Research,* the number of dead cells shot up to 100 percent above the baseline.

—BERNICE WUETHRICH, "Getting Stupid"

(4) Analyzing cause or consequence establishes why something happens or predicts results.

Writers who analyze cause or consequence raise the question *Why?* and must answer it to the satisfaction of their audience, differentiating the **primary cause** (the most important one) from **contributory causes** (which add to but do not directly cause a situation) or the **primary consequence** (the most important one) from **secondary consequences** (which occur because of an event but are less important than the primary consequence). Writers who analyze cause or consequence usually link events along a time line, just as you would if you were describing a traffic accident to a police officer. Always keep in mind, though, that just because one event occurs before—or after—another event does not necessarily make it a cause—or a consequence—of that event. In paragraph 8, undergraduate student Robyn Sylves analyzes some causes of credit card debt among college students.

8   Experts point to several factors for excessive credit card debt among college students. High on the list is students' lack of financial literacy. The credit card representatives on campus, the preapproved applications that arrive in the mail several times a week, and the incessant

Although companies push credit cards on many campuses, some students do not realize that a possible consequence of card use is debt.

phone offers for credit cards tempt students into opening accounts before they really can understand what they are getting themselves into. The people marketing these cards depend on the fact that many students don't know what an annual percentage rate is. Credit card companies count on applicants' failing to read the fine print, which tells them how after an "introductory" period, the interest rate on a given card can increase two to three times. The companies also don't want students to know that every year people send money (in the form of interest charges) to these companies that there is no need to send. That annual fee that credit card companies love to charge can be waived. I think that many people, students and nonstudents alike, might be surprised how often and easily it can disappear if people call the company to say they don't want to pay it.

—**ROBYN SYLVES**, "Credit Card Debt among College Students: Just What Does It Cost?"

Writers can also demonstrate consequences, as in paragraph 9, which explores the effects automobiles have had on our society by asking us to imagine life without them.

9   Let us imagine what life would be like in a carless nation. People would have to live very close together so they could walk, or, for healthy people living in sunny climes, bicycle to mass transit stops. Living in close quarters would mean life as it is now lived in Manhattan. There would be few freestanding homes, many row houses, and lots of apartment buildings. There would be few private gardens except for flowerpots on balconies. The streets would be congested by pedestrians, trucks, and buses, as they were at the turn of the century before automobiles were common.

—**JAMES Q. WILSON**, "Cars and Their Enemies"

(5) Comparing or contrasting helps readers see similarities or differences.

A **comparison** points out similarities, and a **contrast** points out differences—to reveal information. When drafting, consider whether a comparison might help your readers see a relationship they might otherwise miss or whether a contrast might help them establish useful distinctions. In paragraph 10, Jane Tompkins uses descriptive details in her revealing comparison of her two kindergarten teachers.

10   The teachers, Miss Morget (pronounced *mor-zhay*) and Miss Hunt, were tall and thin but unalike in every other way. Miss Hunt was young and

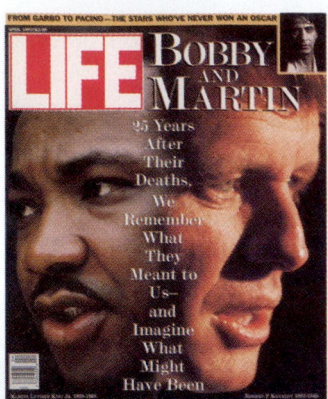

This magazine cover suggests a comparison of Martin Luther King, Jr., and Robert F. Kennedy as influential political leaders, while inviting a contrast of their individual backgrounds.

attractive. She had chestnut brown hair, stylishly rolled, hazel eyes, and a prominent chin. At first, her smart outfits and polished good looks fooled me into thinking she was the nice one. But there was a twist to her mouth sometimes and a troubled look in her eyes that frightened me, and when she spoke to the children, there was iron in her voice. Miss Morget was old and kind. Her frizzled white hair stuck out, softening her sharp nose; and her pale eyes, which held a twinkle, made me pretty sure she wasn't going to do or say anything mean. She spoke in a gentle, cracked voice that was never angry; but the children knew when she meant business, and they minded.

—JANE TOMPKINS, *A Life in School*

Two valuable kinds of comparisons are metaphors and analogies. A **metaphor** is a figure of speech that makes an indirect comparison of one thing to another, as in "He was a lion in uniform." (See **33a**.) An **analogy,** on the other hand, makes a direct comparison of the similarities between two things. Although analogies can invigorate your writing, you must remember that two things that are alike in some ways are rarely alike in all ways. (See **8i(7)** on false analogy.) In paragraph 11, Nelson Mandela uses a metaphor to compare leadership and gardening.

11   In some ways, I saw the garden as a metaphor for certain aspects of my life. A leader must also tend his garden; he, too, plants seed, and then watches, cultivates, and harvests the result. Like the gardener, a leader must take responsibility for what he cultivates; he must mind his work, try to repel enemies, preserve what can be preserved, and eliminate what cannot succeed.

—**NELSON MANDELA,** "Raising Tomatoes and Leading People"

(6) Classifying and dividing can give order to material.

To classify is to place things into groups based on shared characteristics. **Classification** is a way to understand or explain something by establishing how it fits within a category or group. For example, a book reviewer might classify a new novel as a mystery—leading readers to expect a plot based on suspense. **Division,** in contrast, separates an object or group into smaller parts and examines the relationships among them. A novel can also be discussed according to components such as plot, setting, and theme (see chapter **16**).

Classification and division represent two different perspectives: ideas can be put into groups (classification) or split into subclasses (division). As a strategy for organizing (or developing) an idea, classification and division often work together. In paragraph 12, for example, classification and division work together to clarify the differences between the two versions of the cowboy icon. Like most paragraphs, this one mixes rhetorical methods; the writer uses description, comparison and contrast, and classification to make her point.

12 First, and perhaps most fundamentally, the cowboy icon has two basic incarnations: the cowboy hero and the cowboy villain. Cowboy heroes often appear in roles such as sheriff, leader of a cattle drive, or what I'll call a "wandering hero," such as the Lone Ranger, who appears much like a frontier Superman wherever and whenever help is needed. Writers and producers most commonly place cowboy heroes in conflict either with "Indians" or with the cowboy villain. In contrast to the other classic bad guys of the Western genre, cowboy villains pose a special challenge because they are essentially the alter ego of the cowboy hero; the cowboy villain shares the hero's skill with a gun, his horse-riding maneuvers, and his knowledge of the land. What distinguishes the two, of course, is character: the cowboy hero is essentially good, while the cowboy villain is essentially evil.

—**JODY M. ROY,** "The Case of the Cowboy"

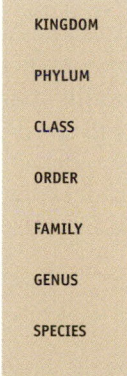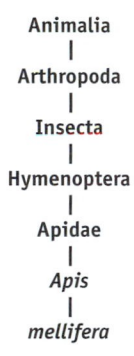

KINGDOM	Animalia
PHYLUM	Arthropoda
CLASS	Insecta
ORDER	Hymenoptera
FAMILY	Apidae
GENUS	*Apis*
SPECIES	*mellifera*

The scientific identification of the honeybee (*Apis mellifera*) requires a classification in the genus *Apis* and a division within that genus, into the species *mellifera*.

(7) Defining an important concept or term clarifies meaning.

By defining a concept or a term, writers efficiently clarify their meaning and develop their ideas. By defining a word for your readers, you can immediately connect with them; they know what you are and are not talking about. Definitions are usually constructed in a two-step process: the first step locates a term by placing it in a class; the second step differentiates this particular term from other terms in the same class. For instance, "A concerto [the term] is a symphonic piece [the class] consisting of three movements performed by one or more solo instruments accompanied at times by an orchestra [the difference]." A symphony belongs to the same basic class as a concerto; it too is a symphonic piece. However, a symphony is differentiated from a concerto in two specific ways: a symphony consists of four movements, and its performance involves the entire orchestra.

Paragraph 13 defines volcanos by putting them into a class ("landforms") and by distinguishing them ("built of molten material") from other members of that class. The definition is then clarified by examples.

13   Volcanos are landforms built of molten material that has spewed out onto the earth's surface. Such molten rock is called lava. Volcanos may be no larger than small hills, or thousands of feet high. All have a characteristic cone shape. Some well-known mountains are actually volcanos. Examples are Mt. Fuji (Japan), Mt. Lassen (California), Mt. Hood (Oregon), Mt. Etna and Mt. Vesuvius (Italy), and Paricutín (Mexico). The Hawaiian Islands are all immense volcanos whose summits rise above the ocean, and these volcanos are still quite active.   —JOEL AREM, "Rocks and Minerals"

Use the rhetorical methods just described to make your essay as a whole more understandable to your audience. Make sure, however, that you are using these methods to support your thesis and fulfill your overall purpose. If a paragraph or two developed with one of the methods is contributing to the main idea of your essay, then it is contributing to your purpose. If the development of a paragraph does not support the thesis, then you need to revise or delete it (see 4c and 4f).

4

REVISING AND

EDITING

ESSAYS

Revising, which literally means "seeing again," lies at the heart of all successful writing. When you see again, you see with a different set of eyes—those of the reader instead of the writer. **Revising** entails rethinking what you have already written in terms of your overall purpose: how successfully you have addressed your audience, how clearly you have stated your thesis, how effectively you have arranged your information, how thoroughly you have developed your assertions. **Editing,** on the other hand, focuses on issues that are smaller in scale. When you are editing, you are polishing your writing: you choose words more precisely (see chapter **33**), shape prose more distinctly (chapter **34**), and structure sentences more effectively (chapters **27–31**). While you are editing, you are also **proofreading,** focusing even more sharply to eliminate surface errors in grammar, punctuation, and mechanics. Revising and editing often overlap (just as drafting and revising do), but they are distinct activities that concentrate on large-scale and small-scale issues, respectively. Usually revising occurs before editing, but not always. Edited passages may be redrafted, rearranged, and even cut as writers revise further.

As you revise and edit your essays, this chapter will help you

- consider your work as a whole (**4a(1–2)**),
- evaluate your tone (**4a(3)**),
- compose an effective introduction and conclusion (**4b**),
- strengthen the unity and coherence of paragraphs (**4c**),
- improve transitions (**4d**),
- benefit from a reviewer's comments (**4e**),
- edit to improve style (**4f**),
- proofread to eliminate surface errors (**4g**), and
- submit a final draft (**4h**).

4a The essentials of revision

In truth, you are revising throughout the planning and drafting stages of the writing process, whether at the word, phrase, sentence, example, or paragraph level. But no matter how much you may have revised during those stages of the writing process, you will still do most of your revising after you have completed a draft. You may rewrite specific sentences and paragraphs as well as reconsider the draft as a whole. A few writers prefer to start revising immediately after drafting, while their minds are still fully engaged by their topic. But most writers like to let a draft "cool off," so that when they return to it, they can assess it more objectively, with fresh eyes. Even a twenty-four–hour cool-off period will provide you more objectivity as a reader and will reveal more options to you as a writer.

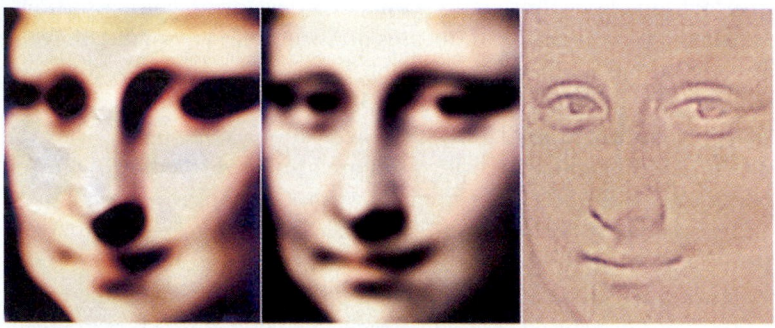

Just as changing the focus on the face in the portrait known as *Mona Lisa* alters viewers' perception of it, successful revision can alter your writing in effective ways.

 Most newer word-processing programs enable you to track your revisions easily, a feature that is especially useful if your instructor requires you to submit all drafts or if a peer group is reviewing your drafts. Go to your toolbar, and click on Tools in order to see the pulldown menu. Track Changes will be listed on that menu. If your word-processing program does not have this feature, you can save each new version of your work in a separate file and date each one. By opening two or more of those files on your computer screen, you can easily compare the different versions.

(1) Anything and everything on the page can be revised.

As you reread your essay as a whole, you will want to recall your purpose, restate your thesis, and reconsider your audience. Does your main point come through clearly in every paragraph, or do some paragraphs digress, repeat information, or contradict what has come before (see **3c**)?

In addition to sharpening your main idea, you will also want to revise in terms of audience expectations. Revising demands that you gauge what you have written to the audience you are addressing (see **1d**). How will your audience respond to your thesis statement? Which of your assertions will your audience immediately understand or accept? Which examples or details will interest your audience? Which of your language choices were aimed expressly at this audience? In other words, revising successfully requires that you examine your work both as a writer and as a reader. As a writer, you must ask yourself whether your words accurately reflect your intention and meaning. As a reader, you must ask yourself whether what is clear and logical to you will also be clear to others.

(2) What is not on the page can be more important than what is on the page.

Writers are always on the lookout for what they have put on the page—and what they may have left out. What information might the audience be expecting? What information might strengthen your thesis? Your best ideas will not always surface in your first draft; you will sometimes have an important new idea only after you have finished that draft and taken a good look at it. No matter how complete a draft seems, ask yourself whether something is missing. You might use questioning strategies to discover what is missing (see **3a(3)**). Or you might share your draft with a classmate or colleague who is working on the same assignment, asking that person to mark confusing or unclear passages (see **4e**).

(3) Your tone helps you fulfill your purpose.

Tone reflects a writer's attitude toward a subject, so you will want to make sure that your tone is appropriate to your purpose, audience, and context (see **1a**). Decide what you intend your tone to be (how you want to "sound"), and then read your piece aloud to see if it sounds the way you want it to. You want to present yourself as confident, well informed, and fair-minded, so you will want all of your words and sentences to convey that tone. If some passages sound defensive, self-centered, or apologetic, revise them. Such tones rarely sustain a reader's interest, let alone goodwill. Your challenge is to make sure that your tone contributes to eliciting from your readers the desired response—to you as well as to the information you are presenting.

Consider the tone in paragraph 1, written by a celebrated contemporary writer who grew up in Kentucky and is describing the consumer patterns of the typical U.S. family. (For ease of reference, each of the sample paragraphs in this chapter is numbered.)

1   I think a lot about those thirty citizens of India who, it's said, could live on the average American's stuff. I wonder if I could build a life of contentment on their material lot, and then I look around my house and wonder what they'd make of mine. My closet would clothe more than half of them, and my books—good Lord—could open a branch in New Delhi. Our family's musical instruments would outfit an entire (if very weird) village band, featuring electric guitars, violin, eclectic percussion section, and a really dusty clarinet. We have more stuff than we need; there is no question of our being perfect. I'm not even sure what "perfect" means in this discussion. I'm not trying to persuade my family to evaporate and live on air. We're here, we're alive, it's the only one we get, as far as I know, so I am keenly inclined to take hold of life by

its *huevos*. As a dinner guest I gratefully eat just about anything that's set before me, because graciousness among friends is dearer to me than any other agenda. I'm not up for a guilt trip, just an adventure in bearable lightness. I approach our efforts at simplicity as a novice approaches her order, aspiring to a lifetime of deepening understanding, discipline, serenity, and joy. Likening voluntary simplicity to a religion is neither hyperbole nor sacrilege. Some people look around and declare the root of all evil to be sex or blasphemy, and so they aspire to be pious and chaste. Where I look for evil I'm more likely to see degradations of human and natural life, an immoral gap between rich and poor, a ravaged earth. At the root of these I see greed and overconsumption by the powerful minority. I was born to that caste, but I can aspire to waste not and want less.

The expressive tone of Dorothea Lange's photograph of a poor mother and children added depth and richness to a photodocumentary of the Great Depression.

—**BARBARA KINGSOLVER,** "Lily's Chickens"

Exercise 1

Establishing your own tone, create a paragraph about the expectations for consuming or conserving in your family. Identify specific words and phrases from paragraph 1 that helped you with your version. Be prepared to read your paragraph aloud and share your findings with the rest of the class.

When Melissa Schraeder revised the first draft reprinted later in this chapter (see pages 83–87), she decided to change her tone in response to a comment from one of her readers that she sounded too breezy about her ability to balance work and school. Although she did not want to sound as though balancing work and school were impossible, Melissa surely did not mean to imply that doing so could be easy. A consistently easygoing tone was not appropriate for her rhetorical situation (see **1a**).

 The thesaurus and grammar checker in your word-processing program may give you advice that can affect the tone of your writing. Go to the toolbar, and click on Tools; the pulldown menu will reveal the spelling and grammar checkers and usually a dictionary and a thesaurus as well. These tools are easy to find and use; however, only you can make the choices that enhance the tone you wish to create. For example, a grammar checker may suggest that you change a word, one you have intentionally repeated in order to achieve a specific effect and create a certain tone. If you are using these features of your word-processing program as you revise your writing, give careful consideration to the suggestions they make.

4b Guiding readers with your introduction and conclusion

Your introduction and conclusion play a special role in helping readers understand your essay as a whole. In fact, readers look for these parts of an essay and read them carefully, expecting guidance and clarification from them.

(1) An effective introduction arouses your reader's interest and establishes your topic and tone.

Experienced writers know that the opening paragraph is important; it is their best chance to arouse the reader's interest with provocative information, establish the topic and writer as worthy of consideration, and set the tone. Effective introductions make readers want to read on. In paragraph 2, Nancy Mairs speaks directly to her readers—shocking them—in order to get their attention:

2   The other day I was thinking of writing an essay on being a cripple. I was thinking hard in one of the stalls of the women's room in my office building, as I was shoving my shirt into my jeans and tugging up my zipper. Preoccupied, I flushed, picked up my book bag, took my cane down from the hook, and unlatched the door. So many movements unbalanced me, and as I pulled the door open I fell over backward, landing fully clothed on the toilet seat with my legs splayed in front [of] me: the old beetle-on-its-back routine. Saturday afternoon, the building deserted, I was free to laugh aloud as I wriggled back to my feet, my voice bouncing off the yellowish tiles from all directions. Had anyone been there with me, I'd have been still and faint and hot with chagrin. I decided that it was high time to write the essay.   **—NANCY MAIRS,** "On Being a Cripple"

Mairs's unsettling introduction takes her readers off guard: they are in the bathroom with a cripple—and a witty one at that. Her especially strong introduction orients readers to the direction her essay will take: she will candidly reveal her daily humanity in order to remind her readers that "cripples" are people, too.

Introductions have no set length; they can be as brief as a couple of sentences or as long as two or more paragraphs. Although introductions always appear first, they are often drafted and revised much later in the writing process—for introductions as well as the thesis statements they so often contain (see **3c**) evolve naturally as writers revise their material, sharpening its focus and developing it to fulfill the overall purpose. You may wish to try several different introductions as you revise, to determine which is most effective.

You can arouse the interest of your audience by writing introductions in a number of ways.

(a) Opening with an unusual fact or statistic

3 In the course of a hundred days in 1994 the Hutu government of Rwanda and its extremist allies very nearly succeeded in exterminating the country's Tutsi minority. Using firearms, machetes, and a variety of garden implements, Hutu militiamen, soldiers, and ordinary citizens murdered some 800,000 Tutsi and politically moderate Hutu. It was the fastest, most efficient killing spree of the twentieth century.

—SAMANTHA POWER,
"Bystanders to Genocide"

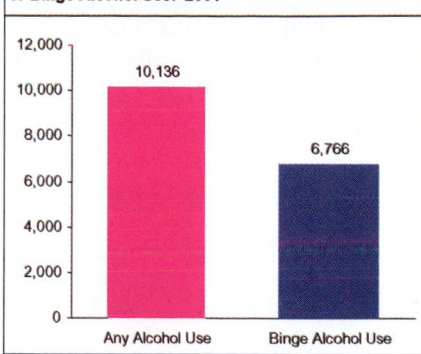

Figure 1. Estimated Numbers of Persons Aged 12 to 20 (in Thousands) Reporting Past Month Alcohol Use or Binge Alcohol Use: 2001

Opening with a thought-provoking statistic can be an effective introduction.

(b) Opening with an intriguing statement

4 In Afghanistan, nothing is ever what it seems. Including surrender.

—ALEX PERRY, "Inside the Battle at Qala-i-Jangi"

(c) Opening with an anecdote or example

5 Every morning, she wakes up earlier than everyone else in her family so she can pour a tiny bit of cereal and milk in her bowl, place the bowl and spoon in the sink, and slink upstairs to get ready for school. When she comes back down to catch the bus, she tells her mother that she's already eaten cereal and doesn't want anything else. She skips lunch at school, telling her friends that she doesn't like cafeteria food—and, besides, she eats lunch as soon as she gets home. But she doesn't. Instead, she goes home and drinks water as a way to fill up her stomach and give her a false sense of satisfaction before she sits down with her family to eat supper. She eats a little bit of food, but she spends most of her energy pushing the food around on her plate or cutting it up into small pieces so it looks like she ate some. She always leaves the table feeling hungry, but she's still angry at herself for eating anything at all. Her entire day is planned around what and when to eat, how to avoid eating, and mostly how to avoid confrontations with her mother. She is almost perfect—at deception. She has an eating disorder.

—LAUREN A. MAKUCH, "What Can We Do to Prevent Eating Disorders?"

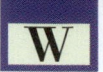

(d) Opening with a question your essay will answer

6   You ask me what is poverty? Listen to me. Here I am, dirty, smelly, and with no "proper" underwear on and with the stench of my rotting teeth near you. I will tell you. Listen to me. Listen without pity. I cannot use your pity. Listen with understanding. Put yourself in my dirty, worn out, ill-fitting shoes, and hear me.   **—JO GOODWIN PARKER,** "What Is Poverty?"

(e) Opening with an appropriate quotation

7   Wordsworth said we "half perceive and half create" the beauty we find in nature, and I guess that's what I'm saying, too. On the one hand I see the forest differently now because of the ideas and knowledge I bring to it. I accept it because I know more and am more confused about notions I used to take for granted. On the other hand my sense of this landscape, my pleasure in it, seems to come from outside, too, unbidden and uncontrolled, surprising. I didn't expect to feel the way I do and even resisted it. Satisfaction is the feeling actually produced in me when I walk here over time. Enjoyment is what I experience in the presence of these trees and these openings, just empirically, prior to thoughts and theories.

          —CHRIS ANDERSON, "Life on the Edge"

(f) Opening with general information or background about the topic

8   I fell in love with it—college basketball, that is—at a drafty old barn in Lincoln Square in Worcester, Massachusetts, not far from where one of my great-uncles once owned a saloon. This Worcester Memorial Auditorium was square and huge, and it had towering murals depicting men loading shells into the big guns of a dreadnought and firing artillery along the banks of the Somme. You had to walk up broad staircases to see the murals in their entirety, and I didn't have the courage for that until I was nearly ten. I continued to love it—the whole raucous, tumbling parade of it—through my undergraduate days at Marquette University, where Al McGuire put together a delightfully rambunctious program. I even loved it when I covered it for five years, more or less full-time, for the *Boston Herald.* I have missed one Final Four since 1982, and I can tell you exactly where and when I stopped loving college basketball: I stopped loving it in a hotel in Indianapolis in 1999, on a Saturday afternoon, before the national semifinals.

          —CHARLES P. PIERCE, "ConMen"

(g) Opening with a thesis, simply stated

9   Complaining was great when I was a kid. Well, maybe not great, just better than now. When you are a kid, your sense of entitlement is more intact. At least that's how it seems from this distance. Things are supposed to be a certain way—*yours*. Oh sure, things are supposed to go your way as an adult, but it's not always appropriate to mention this.

—**CARRIE FISHER**, "The Art of Complaining"

Whatever type of introduction you choose to write, use your opening paragraph to indicate your topic, engage your readers' attention, set your tone, and establish your credibility (see **8f(1)**).

(2) An effective conclusion helps readers understand the most important points of your essay and why they are significant.

Just as a good introduction tantalizes readers, a good conclusion satisfies them. It helps readers recognize the important points of your essay and the significance of those points while, at the same time, wrapping up the essay in a meaningful, often thought-provoking way. As you draft and revise, you may want to keep a list of ideas for your conclusion, especially ones that go beyond a simple restatement of the thesis (see **3c**). Some suggestions for writing effective conclusions follow, beginning with the technique of restating the thesis and main points.

(a) Rephrasing the thesis and summarizing the main points

10   The Endangered Species Act should not take into account economic considerations. Economics doesn't know how to value a species or a forest. Its logic drives people to exploit resources to the point of extinction. The Endangered Species Act tells us that extinction is morally unacceptable. It was enacted by a Congress and president in a wise mood, to express a higher value than a bottom line.

—**DONELLA MEADOWS**, "Not Seeing the Forest for the Dollar Bills"

(b) Calling attention to larger issues

11   Nonetheless, the greatest growth industry in this country is the one dedicated to the mirage of good grooming as the road to immortality. Immigrants past built bridges and schools, gilded the cherubim in the corners of churches. Today an entire immigrant class makes a living painting

toenails and opening pores. Advances in science and medicine have combined to offer this: the tattooing of permanent eyeliner, the bleaching of teeth, the lasering of sun spots. The waning days of a great nation can be charted only in hindsight. But surely it is a danger sign of some sort when a country is no longer able to care for its own cuticles.

—**ANNA QUINDLEN,** "Leg Waxing and Life Everlasting"

(c) Calling for a change in action or attitude

12   Our medical care system is in trouble and getting worse. While the experts try to figure out how to achieve utopian goals at affordable prices, let's do something practical about the suffering on our doorsteps. Primary care is the most affordable safety net we can offer our citizens. By all means, let's continue the debate about universal, comprehensive insurance to cover all medical costs, but, in the meantime, let's provide primary health care to all uninsured Americans—now!

—**GORDON T. MOORE,** "Caring for the Uninsured and Underinsured"

(d) Concluding with a vivid image

13   At just past 10 a.m., farm workers and scrap-yard laborers in Somerset County looked up to see a large commercial airliner dipping and lunging as it swooped low over the hill country of southern Pennsylvania, near the town of Shanksville. A man driving a coal truck on Route 30 said he saw the jet tilt violently from side to side, then suddenly plummet "straight down." It hit nose first on the grassy face of a reclaimed strip mine at approximately 10:05 Eastern Daylight Time and exploded into a fireball, shattering windowpanes a half-mile away. The seventy-two-year-old man who was closest to the point of impact saw what looked to him like the yellow mushroom cloud of an atomic blast. Twenty-eight-year-old Eric Peterson was one of the first on the scene. He arrived to discover a flaming crater fifty feet deep. Shredded clothing hung from the trees, and smoldering airplane parts littered the ground. It did not look much like the site of a great American victory, but it was.   —**RANDALL SULLIVAN,** "Flight 93"

(e) Connecting with the introduction

The introduction

14   Here's a memory. On an overcast morning in February, 1996, I received in the mail from my mother, in St. Louis, a Valentine's package containing

one pinkly romantic greeting card, two four-ounce Mr. Goodbars, one hollow red filigree heart on a loop of thread, and one copy of a neuropathologist's report on my father's brain autopsy.

In the essay that follows this introduction, Jonathan Franzen focuses on what Alzheimer's takes away from the human brain—from his father's brain, in particular. His conclusion loops back to his mom, his dad, and that autopsy report.

The conclusion

15   After we'd kissed him [Franzen's father] goodbye and signed the forms that authorized the brain autopsy, my mother sat down in our kitchen and uncharacteristically accepted my offer of undiluted Jack Daniel's. "I see now," she said, "that when you're dead you're really dead." This was true enough. But, in the slow-motion way of Alzheimer's, my father wasn't much deader now than he'd been two hours or two weeks or two months ago. We'd simply lost the last of the parts out of which we could fashion a living whole. There would be no new memories of him. The only stories we could tell now were the ones we already had.

—**JONATHAN FRANZEN,** "My Father's Brain"

Whatever technique you choose for your conclusion, provide readers with a sense of closure. Bear in mind that they may be wondering, "So what? Why have you told me all this?" Your conclusion gives you an opportunity to address that concern. If there is any chance that readers may not understand your purpose, use your conclusion to clarify why you have asked them to read what they have just read.

Exercise 2

Thumb through a magazine you enjoy, and skim the introductions of all the articles. Select two introductions that catch your attention. Copy them, word for word, and then consider the reasons *why* they interest you. What specific techniques for an introduction did the authors use? Next, look through the same or another magazine for two effective conclusions. Copy these, and analyze their effectiveness as well. Be prepared to share your findings with the rest of the class.

4c Revising for unified and coherent paragraphs

When revising the body of an essay, writers are likely to find opportunities for further development within each paragraph (see **3f** and **3g**) and to discover ways to make each paragraph more **unified** by relating every sentence within the paragraph to a single main idea (**4c(2)**), which might appear in a topic sentence. After weeding out unrelated sentences, writers concentrate on **coherence,** ordering the sentences so that ideas progress logically and smoothly from one sentence to the next. A successful paragraph is well developed, unified, and coherent.

(1) The topic sentence expresses the main idea.

Much like the thesis statement of an essay, a **topic sentence** states the main idea of a paragraph and comments on that main idea. Although the topic sentence is usually the first sentence in a paragraph, it can appear in any position within the paragraph. Sometimes, the topic sentence is implied by something in all of the sentences. If you need to work at improving the unity and coherence of your paragraphs, you might want to keep your topic sentences at the beginning. Not only will they serve to remind you of your focus, but they will also be obvious to your readers, who will grasp your main ideas immediately. More experienced writers may avoid repeating the same paragraph patterns by organizing their sentences differently within different paragraphs.

When you announce your general topic and then provide specific support for it, you are writing **deductively.** Your topic sentence appears first, like the one in italics in paragraph 16, which announces that the author will offer evidence as to why we are suspicious of rapid cognition.

16   *I think we are innately suspicious of . . . rapid cognition.* We live in a world that assumes that the quality of a decision is directly related to the time and effort that went into making it. When doctors are faced with a difficult diagnosis, they order more tests, and when we are uncertain about what we hear, we ask for a second opinion. And what do we tell our children? Haste makes waste. Look before you leap. Stop and *think.* Don't judge a book by its cover. We believe that we are always better off gathering as much information as possible and spending as much time as possible in deliberation. We really only trust conscious decision making. But there are moments, particularly in

times of stress, when haste does not make waste, when our snap judgments and first impressions can offer a much better means of making sense of the world. —MALCOLM GLADWELL, *Blink*

If you want to emphasize the main idea of a paragraph or give its organization some extra support, you can begin and conclude the paragraph with two versions of the same idea. This strategy is particularly useful for long paragraphs because it gives readers whose attention may have wandered a second chance to grasp the main idea. In paragraph 17, which is remarkably long, both the first sentence and the last convey the idea that the things the soldiers carried weighed heavily upon them.

17   *The things they carried were largely determined by necessity.* Among the necessities or near necessities were P-38 can openers, pocket knives, heat tabs, wrist watches, dog tags, mosquito repellant, chewing gum, candy, cigarettes, salt tablets, packets of Kool-Aid, lighters, matches, sewing kits, Military Payment Certificates, C rations, and two or three canteens of water. Together, these items weighed between fifteen and twenty pounds, depending upon a man's habits or rate of metabolism. Henry Dobbins, who was a big man, carried extra rations; he was especially fond of canned peaches in heavy syrup over pound cake. Dave Jensen, who practiced field hygiene, carried a toothbrush, dental floss, and several hotel-size bars of soap he'd stolen on R&R in Sydney, Australia. Ted Lavender, who was scared, carried tranquilizers until he was shot in the head outside the village of Than Khe in mid-April. By necessity, and because it was SOP [standard operating procedure], they all carried steel helmets that weighed five pounds including the liner and camouflage cover. They carried the standard fatigue jackets and trousers. Very few carried underwear. On their feet they carried jungle boots—2.1 pounds—and Dave Jensen carried three pairs of socks and a can of Dr. Scholl's foot powder as a precaution against trench foot. Until he was shot, Ted Lavender carried six or seven ounces of premium dope, which for him was a necessity. Mitchell Sanders, the RTO [radio telephone operator], carried condoms. Norman Bowker carried a diary. Rat Kiley carried comic books. Kiowa, a devout Baptist, carried an illustrated New Testament that had been presented to him by his father, who taught Sunday school in Oklahoma City, Oklahoma. As a hedge against bad times, however, Kiowa also carried his grandmother's distrust of the white man, his grandfather's old hunting hatchet. Necessity dictated. Because the land was mined and booby-trapped, it was SOP for each man to carry a steel-centered, nylon-covered flak jacket, Simonov carbines and black-market Uzis and .38 caliber Smith &

Wesson handguns and 66 mm LAWs and shotguns and silencers and blackjacks and bayonets and C-4 explosives. Lee Strunk carried a slingshot; a weapon of last resort, he called it. Mitchell Sanders carried brass knuckles. Kiowa carried his grandfather's feathered hatchet. Every third or fourth man carried a Claymore antipersonnel mine—3.5 pounds with its firing device. They all carried at least one M-18 colored smoke grenade—twenty-four ounces. Some carried CS or teargas grenades. Some carried white-phosphorus grenades. *They all carried all they could bear, and then some, including a silent awe for the terrible power of the things they carried.*

—TIM O'BRIEN, *The Things They Carried*

As you prepare to revise a draft, try underlining the topic sentences you can identify. If you cannot find a topic sentence, add a sentence stating the main idea of that paragraph. If you find that you open every paragraph with a topic sentence, you might try experimenting with another pattern, revising a paragraph so that the topic sentence appears at the end, as in paragraph 18.

18   I have been to big-money tribal casinos on both coasts and in Minnesota, and they tend to run together in the mind. They are of a sameness—the vast parking lots, the low, mall-like, usually windowless buildings, the arbitrary Indianish décor, the gleeful older gamblers rattling troves of quarters in their bulging pants pockets, the unromantic expressions in the employees' eyes. Also, going to a major Indian casino is so much like going to a non-Indian one, in Atlantic City or someplace, that you may have to remind yourself exactly why Indian casinos enjoy tax advantages non-Indian casinos don't. The idea of Indian tribal sovereignty, a bit elusive to begin with, can fade out entirely behind the deluge of generic gambling dollars. In the last few years, some state and federal legislators have begun to view tribal casinos in just this skeptical way. Their renewed attacks on tribal sovereignty usually include a lot of rhetoric about the supposed great gambling wealth of Indian tribes nowadays. Regrettably, the resentment against Indian casinos, whose largest benefits go to only a few tribes, may end up threatening the sovereignty of all tribes. Many Indians have worried more about loss of sovereignty since the casino boom began. Some say that entering into compacts with the states is itself a wrong idea, because it accepts state jurisdiction where none existed before. Concern for sovereignty has been a main reason why the Navajo have rejected casino gambling. *A Navajo leader said that tribes who accept outside oversight of their*

gambling operations have allowed a violation of tribal sovereignty; he added, "The sovereignty of the Navajo nation and the Navajo people is not and should never be for sale." —IAN FRAZIER, *On the Rez*

Placing the topic sentence toward or at the end of the paragraph works well when you are moving from specific supporting details to a generalization about those ideas—that is, when you are writing **inductively.** Effective writers try to meet the expectations of their readers, which often include the anticipation that the first sentence will be the topic sentence; however, writers and readers alike enjoy an occasional departure from the expected. And writers need to adjust their paragraph organization according to the rhetorical purpose of each paragraph.

(2) In a unified paragraph, every sentence relates to the main idea.

Paragraphs are **unified** when every sentence relates to the main idea; unity is violated when something unrelated to the rest of the material appears. Consider the obvious violation in paragraph 19.

19   The Marion, Ohio of my childhood offered activities to suit any child's taste. In the summer, I could walk to the library and spend the afternoon browsing or reading. On the way home, I could stop by Isaly's dairy and buy a skyscraper ice cream cone for twenty-five cents. I could swim every afternoon in our neighborhood swimming pool, where kids played freely and safely. If I wanted, I could meet up with my cousin Babs and walk downtown for a movie matinee or a grilled-cheese sandwich at Woolworth's lunch counter. *It's hard to find a good grilled-cheese sandwich these days.* If we didn't want to stay within walking distance, we could take a city bus out to the roller rink or, if something big was going on, out to the fairgrounds.

Easy to delete, the italicized sentence about today's grilled-cheese sandwiches violates the unity of a paragraph devoted to childhood activities in a small town. If the overall purpose of the essay includes a comparison of small-town life then and now, the writer could simply develop the idea of what is "hard to find" into a separate paragraph.

As you revise your paragraphs for unity, the following tips may help you.

TIPS FOR IMPROVING PARAGRAPH UNITY	
Identify	Identify the topic sentence for each paragraph. Where is each located?
Relate	Read each sentence in a paragraph, and decide if and how it relates to the topic sentence.
Eliminate	Any sentence that violates the unity of a paragraph should be cut (or saved for use elsewhere).
Clarify	Any sentence that "almost" relates to the topic sentence should be revised until it does relate. You may need to clarify details or add information or a transitional word or phrase to make the relationship clear.
Rewrite	If more than one idea is being conveyed in a single paragraph, either rewrite the topic sentence so that it includes both ideas and establishes a relationship between them or split the paragraph into two.

(3) Clearly arranged ideas contribute to coherence.

Some paragraphs are unified (see **4c(2)**) but not coherent. In a unified paragraph, every sentence relates to the main idea of the paragraph. In a **coherent** paragraph, the relationship among the ideas is clear and meaningful, and the progression from one sentence to the next is easy for readers to follow. Paragraph 20 has unity but lacks coherence.

Lacks coherence

20   The inside of the refrigerator was covered with black mold, and it smelled as if something had been rotting in there for years. I put new paper down on all the shelves, and my roommate took care of lining the drawers. The stove was as dirty as the refrigerator. *When we moved into our new apartment, we found that the kitchen was in horrible shape.* We had to scrub the walls with a brush and plenty of Lysol to get rid of the grease. The previous tenant had left behind lots of junk that we had to get rid of. All the drawers and cabinets had to be washed.

Although every sentence in this paragraph concerns cleaning the kitchen after moving into an apartment, the sentences are not arranged coherently. This paragraph can easily be revised so that the italicized topic sentence controls the meaningful flow of ideas—from what the roommates saw to what they did.

Revised for coherence

21 *When we moved into our new apartment, we found that the kitchen was in horrible shape.* The previous tenant had left behind lots of junk that we had to get rid of. The inside of the refrigerator was covered with black mold, and it smelled as if something had been rotting in there for years. The stove was as dirty as the refrigerator. [New sentence:] So we set to work. All the drawers and cabinets had to be washed. I put new paper down on all the shelves, and my roommate took care of lining the drawers. We had to scrub the walls with a brush and plenty of Lysol to get rid of the grease.

Paragraph 21 is coherent as well as unified.

To achieve coherence and unity in your paragraphs, study the following patterns of organization (chronological, spatial, emphatic, and logical), and consider which ones you might use in your own writing.

(a) Using chronological order, according to time

When you use **chronological order,** you arrange ideas according to the order in which things happened. This organizational pattern is particularly useful in narrations.

22 When everyone was finished, we were given the signal to put our silverware on our plates. Each piece of silverware had its place—the knife at the top of the plate, sharp edge toward us; then the fork, perfectly lined up next to the knife; then the spoon—and any student who didn't put the silverware in the right place couldn't leave the table. Lastly, our napkins were refolded and put in their original spot. When we stood, we pushed our chair under the table and waited for the signal to turn right. Then we marched outside, single file, while the kitchen staff started to clean the dining room.

—**ANNE E. BOLANDER AND ADAIR N. RENNING,** *I Was #87*

(b) Using spatial order, according to the movement of the eyes

When you arrange ideas according to **spatial order,** you orient the reader's focus from right to left, near to far, top to bottom, and so on. This organizational pattern is particularly effective in descriptions. Often the organization is so obvious that the writer can forgo a topic sentence, as in paragraph 23.

23 The stores on Tremont Avenue seemed to be extensions of my domestic space. Each one had sensory memories that I associate with my mother. On the corner was the delicatessen. From its counter, which was like a bar

complete with a brass footrest, came the deeply dark smell of cured meats, the tang of frankfurters, with the steaming background scent of hot knishes on the griddle. —**LENNARD J. DAVIS,** *My Sense of Silence*

(c) Using emphatic order, according to importance

When you use **emphatic order,** you arrange information in order of importance, usually from least to most important. Emphatic order is especially useful in expository and persuasive writing, both of which involve helping readers understand logical relationships (such as what caused something to happen or what kinds of priorities should be established). In paragraph 24, the writer emphasizes the future as the most important arena for change.

24   Among the first things Goldsmith had taught the executive was to look only to the future, because, whatever he had done to make people angry, he couldn't fix it now. "Don't ask for feedback about the past," he says. Goldsmith has turned against the notion of feedback lately. He has written an article on a more positive methodology, which he calls "feedforward." "How many of us have wasted much of our lives impressing our spouse, partner, or significant other with our near-photographic memory of their previous sins, which we document and share to help them improve?" he says. "Dysfunctional! Say, 'I can't change the past—all I can say is I'm sorry for what I did wrong.' Ask for suggestions for the future. Don't promise to do everything they suggest—leadership is not a popularity contest. But follow up on a regular basis, and you know what's going to happen? You will get better." —**LARISSA MACFARQUHAR,** "The Better Boss"

(d) Using logical order, moving from specific to general or from general to specific

Sometimes the movement within a paragraph follows a **logical order,** from specific to general or from general to specific. A paragraph may begin with a series of details and conclude with a summarizing statement, as paragraphs 18 and 25 do, or it may begin with a general statement or idea, which is then supported by particular details, as in paragraphs 21 and 26.

25   This winter, I took a vacation from our unfinished mess. Getting back to it was tough, and one morning, I found myself on my knees before the dishwasher, as if in prayer, though actually busting a water-pipe weld. To my

right were the unfinished cabinets, to my left the knobless backdoor, behind me a hole I'd torn in the wall. There in the kitchen, a realization hit me like a 2-by-4: for two years I'd been working on this house, and there was still no end in sight. It had become my Vietnam.

—**ROBERT SULLIVAN,** "Home Wrecked"

26　It was not the only disappointment my mother felt in me. In the years that followed, I failed her so many times, each time asserting my own will, my right to fall short of expectations. I didn't get straight As. I didn't become class president. I didn't get into Stanford. I dropped out of college.

—**AMY TAN,** "Two Kinds"

4d　Transitions within and between paragraphs

Even if the sentences are arranged in a seemingly clear sequence, a single paragraph may lack internal coherence and a series of paragraphs may lack overall coherence if transitions are abrupt or nonexistent. When revising your writing, you can improve the coherence by using pronouns, repetition, conjunctions, and transitional words or phrases (see also **23d**).

(1) Pronouns help establish links between sentences.

In paragraph 27, the writer enumerates the similarities of identical twins raised separately. She mentions their names only once, but uses the pronouns *both, their,* and *they* to keep the references to the twins always clear.

27　Jim Springer and Jim Lewis were adopted as infants into working-class Ohio families. **Both** liked math and did not like spelling in school. **Both** had law enforcement training and worked part-time as deputy sheriffs. **Both** vacationed in Florida, **both** drove Chevrolets. Much has been made of the fact that **their** lives are marked by a trail of similar names. **Both** married and divorced women named Linda and had second marriages with women named Betty. **They** named **their** sons James Allan and James Alan, respectively. **Both** like mechanical drawing and carpentry. **They** have almost identical drinking and smoking patterns. **Both** chew **their** fingernails down to the nubs. —**CONSTANCE HOLDEN,** "Identical Twins Reared Apart"

(2) Repetition of words, phrases, structures, or ideas can link a sentence to those that precede it.

In paragraph 28, the repetition of the key word *never* links sentences to preceding sentences and also provides emphasis. (See **30d**.)

28 **Never** is the most powerful word in the English language, or perhaps any language. It's magic. Every time I have made an emphatic pronouncement invoking the word **never,** whatever follows that I don't want to happen happens. **Never** has made a fool of me many times. The first time I remember noticing the powerful effect of this word I was a student at Indian school. My best friend, Belinda Gonzalez, and I were filling out our schedules for spring semester. She was Blackfeet, a voice major from Yakima, Washington. I was a painting major and checking out times for painting and drawing courses. She suggested I sign up for drama class with her. I said, no I will **never** go on stage. Despite my initial protest I did sign up for drama and dance troupes in the country, and now I make my living performing. **Never** is that powerful.

—**JOY HARJO,** "The Power of Never"

In this case, the author wished to stress the expectations many people hold when they declare "never." By repeating the word five times in one paragraph, Harjo emphasizes its power.

Parallelism, another kind of repetition, is a key principle in writing coherent sentences and paragraphs (see chapter **29**).

(3) Using conjunctions and other transitional words or phrases also contributes to coherence.

Conjunctions and other transitional words or phrases demonstrate the logical relationship between ideas. In the following sentences, in which two clauses are linked by different conjunctions, notice the subtle changes in the relationship between the two ideas.

The dog ran, **and** she threw the frisbee.

The dog ran **while** she threw the frisbee.

The dog ran **because** she threw the frisbee.

The dog ran, **so** she threw the frisbee.

The dog ran; **later** she threw the frisbee.

The following list of frequently used transitional connections, arranged according to the kinds of relationships they establish, can help you with your critical reading as well as your writing.

TYPES OF TRANSITIONAL CONNECTIONS

Addition	and, and then, further, furthermore, also, too, again, in addition, besides
Alternative	or, nor, either, neither, on the other hand, conversely, otherwise
Comparison	similarly, likewise, in like manner
Concession	although this may be true, even so, still, nevertheless, at the same time, notwithstanding, nonetheless, in any event, that said
Contrast	but, yet, or, and yet, however, on the contrary, in contrast
Exemplification	for example, for instance, in the case of
Intensification	in fact, indeed, to tell the truth, moreover, even more important, to be sure
Place	here, beyond, nearby, opposite to, adjacent to, on the opposite side
Purpose	to this end, for this purpose, with this objective, in order to, so that
Repetition	as I have said, in other words, that is, as has been noted, as previously stated
Result or cause	so, for, therefore, accordingly, consequently, thus, thereby, as a result, then, because, hence
Sequence	next, first, second, third, in the first place, in the second place, finally, last, then, afterward, later
Summary	to sum up, in brief, on the whole, in sum, in short
Time	meanwhile, soon, after a few days, in the meantime, now, in the past, while, during, since

The following checklist can guide you in revising your paragraphs.

CHECKLIST for Revising Paragraphs

- Does the paragraph have a clear (or clearly implied) topic sentence (4c(1))?
- Do all the ideas in the paragraph belong together? Do sentences link to previous and later ones? Are the sentences arranged in chronological, spatial, emphatic, or logical order, or are they arranged in some other pattern (4c(2))?
- How does the paragraph link to the preceding and following ones (4d)?
- Are sentences connected to each other with effective transitions (4d(2))?
- What evidence do you have that the paragraph is adequately developed (3f)? What idea or detail might be missing (4a(1))? What rhetorical methods have been used to develop each of the paragraphs (3g)?

When revising an essay, you must consider the effectiveness of the individual paragraphs at the same time as you consider how those paragraphs work (or do not work) together to achieve the overall purpose. Some writers like to revise at the paragraph level before addressing larger concerns; other writers cannot work on the individual paragraphs until they have grappled with larger issues related to the rhetorical situation (overall purpose, attention to audience, and context; see 1a) or have finalized their thesis (3c). All experienced writers use a process to write, but they do not all use exactly the same process. Since there is no universal, predetermined order to the writing process, you can follow whichever steps work best for you each time you are revising. Be guided by the principles and strategies discussed in this chapter, but trust also in your own good sense.

4e The benefits of peer review

Because writing is a form of communication, writers check to see whether they are communicating their ideas effectively to their readers. Instructors are one set of readers, but they are often the last people to see your writing. Before you submit your work to an instructor, take advantage of other opportunities for getting responses to it. Consult with readers—at the writing center, in your dorm, in your classes, or from online writing groups—asking them for honest responses to your concerns.

(1) Clearly defined evaluation standards help both writers and reviewers.

Although you will always write within a rhetorical situation (see **1a**), you will often address that situation in terms of an assigned task with specific evaluation standards. Instructors usually indicate their evaluation standards in class, on assignment sheets, or on separate handouts (see **5a(2)**). Whether you are working with a small writing group from class or a single reader, such as a classmate or a writing center tutor, you need to review the evaluation criteria at the beginning of a working session and use them to determine where you should focus your attention. For example, if your instructor has told you that your essay will be evaluated primarily in terms of whether you have a clear thesis (see **3c**) and adequate support for it (**3f** and **3g**), then those features should be your primary focus. Your secondary concerns may be sentence length and variety (see chapter **31**) and the effectiveness of your introduction (**4b(1)**).

Although evaluation standards or guidelines do not guarantee useful feedback every time, they help. They help you focus on the advice you want to ask for in a writer's memo (see **4e(2)**), and they help your reviewers focus on what kinds of advice to give. Reviewers can refer to the guidelines as they carefully and slowly read and reread your draft. They will then be able to respond with specifics and with respect. If a reviewer sees a problem that the writer did not identify, the reviewer should ask the writer if she or he wants to discuss it and should abide by the writer's decision. A reviewer's comments should point out what the writer has done well as well as suggest how to improve particular passages. For instance, the reviewer may frame recommendations in terms of personal engagement with the text (see page 85): "You say 'you should' a few times. How about changing this to 'I would recommend' or 'based on my experiences, the following methods have been helpful' in order to make your tone less presumptuous?" A reviewer can be honest and helpful simultaneously. Ultimately, however, the success of the essay is the responsibility of the writer, who will evaluate the reviewer's advice, rejecting any comments that would take the essay in a different direction and applying any suggestions that help fulfill the rhetorical purpose (see **1c**).

If you are developing your own criteria for evaluation, the following checklist can help you get started. Based on the elements of the rhetorical situation, this checklist can be easily adjusted so that it meets your specific needs for a particular assignment.

CHECKLIST for Evaluating a Draft of an Essay

- What is your purpose in the essay (**1c**)? Does the essay fulfill the assignment?
- Does the essay address a specific audience (**1d**)? Is that audience appropriate for the assignment?
- What is the tone of the essay (**4a(3)**)? How does the tone align with the overall purpose, the intended audience, and the context for the writing (**1c–e**)?
- Is your topic sufficiently focused (**3b**)? What is the thesis statement (**3c**)?
- What assertions do you make to support the thesis statement? What specific evidence do you provide to support these assertions?
- Are paragraphs arranged in an effective sequence (**3d** and **4c(3)**)? What pattern of organization are you using? Is each paragraph thoroughly developed (**3f** and **3g**)?
- Is the introduction effective (**4b(1)**)? How do you engage the reader's attention?
- Is the conclusion appropriate for the essay's purpose (**4b(2)**)? Does it draw the essay together, or does it seem disconnected and abrupt?

---

(2) You can help your reviewers by telling them about your purpose and your concerns.

When submitting a draft for review, you can increase your chances of getting the kind of help you want by introducing your work and indicating what your concerns are. You can provide such an orientation orally to a writing group, tutor, or peer reviewer in just a few minutes. Or, when doing so is not possible, perhaps because you are submitting a draft online, you can attach to your draft a cover letter consisting of a paragraph or two—sometimes called a **writer's memo.** In either case, adopting the following model can help ensure that reviewers will give you useful responses.

SUBMITTING A DRAFT FOR REVIEW

Topic and Purpose

State your topic and your exigence for writing (see **1b**). Indicate your thesis (**3c**) and purpose (**1c**). Providing this information gives reviewers useful direction.

Strengths

Mark the passages of the draft you are confident about. Doing so directs attention away from areas you do not want to discuss and saves time for all concerned.

Concerns

Put question marks by the passages you find troublesome, and ask for specific advice wherever possible. For example, if you are worried about your conclusion, say so. Or if you suspect that one of your paragraphs may not fit the overall purpose, direct attention to that particular paragraph. You are most likely to get the kind of help you want and need when you ask for it specifically.

Melissa's writer's memo follows.

Topic and purpose: I'm focusing on the good and bad consequences of working part time while attending school full time. Given that tuition is on the rise nationally, while employment opportunities are on the decline, I am imagining that more and more college students will have to hold a job while attending school. My purpose is to explain that doing this is hard, but it's doable, and, besides, when done well, it makes the college student a better, more responsible and grateful human being.

Concerns: My biggest concern is sounding like I think juggling the obligations of school and work is easy if you're organized. And I know from experience that that is not true. So I guess it's my tone that I'm worried about—tone plus examples.

Melissa Schraeder submitted the draft on pages 83–87 for peer review in a first-year writing course. She worked with a classmate, who was working on the same assignment, and a peer tutor from the university writing center, using a set of criteria that she had prepared. Because these students were learning how to conduct peer evaluations, their comments represent the range of responses you might receive in a similar situation. As members of writing groups gain experience and learn

to employ the strategies outlined in this section, their advice usually be-comes more helpful.

Some instructors may require students to do peer reviewing online, using e-mail or a computer network. You should always check with your instructor for specific peer-review guidelines and procedures, but here are some general suggestions for online reviewing.

- If you are responding to a classmate's draft via e-mail, reread your comments before sending them to be sure that your tone is appropriate and that you have avoided the kinds of misunderstandings that can occur with e-mail (see **6b** and **6d**).
- Always save a copy of your comments in case your e-mail message is lost or inadvertently deleted.
- If you are responding to a classmate's draft using an online course-management program, such as WebCT, Angel, or Blackboard, remember that your comments may be read by other classmates, too.
- Follow the advice in **4e(1)**, just as you would if you were commenting on a paper copy of your classmate's draft.

As you read the assignment and then Melissa's draft, remember that it is only a first draft—not a model of perfect writing—and also that this is the first time the peer reviewers, Bob Geiger and Michelle Clewell, responded to it. Melissa sent her draft electronically to Bob and Michelle, who used the Track Changes function of their word-processing program to add suggested changes and comments throughout the essay.

The assignment   Draft a three- to four-page, double-spaced essay in which you analyze the causes or consequences of a choice you have had to make in the last year or two. Whatever choice you analyze, make sure that it concerns a topic you can develop with confidence and without violating your own sense of privacy. Moreover, consider the expectations of your audience and whether the topic you have chosen will help you communicate something meaningful to readers. As you draft, then, establish an audience for your essay, a group that might benefit from or be interested in any recommendation that grows out of your analysis.

Draft—Working toward a Degree   Bob   *Michelle*

When I first decided to pursue my college education at Penn State University, a key factor in my decision was that as a state university, Penn State offered a relatively low tuition. *This first sentence doesn't seem to have much grounding. Maybe develop your own experience with choosing a school more, or use a different opening?* Adding this factor to the giving financial support of my parents and my fortune at receiving several grants and scholarships, I initially believed that my college education would be easily affordable. When I started classes however, I soon found that with all the additional expenses of school such as the cost of books, technology fees, and spending money, going to school meant finding a job. Though hesitant at first about how holding a job might affect my studies, I soon took on a part-time job ~~where I worked,~~ *working* about fifteen hours a week. *Up until this point your sentences seem sort of long. Maybe you can condense these introductory sentences into a central idea that will get us more quickly to your thesis statement. See my suggestion.* Based on my own experience, I feel confident in saying that balancing a part-time job with success in schoolwork is not only a manageable task, but also a valuable experience contributing to growth as a student and as an individual. ~~Since so many students of today need to work while going to school, I hope to show them that while holding a part-time job and doing well in school may seem difficult at first, in many ways these two undertakings are quite compatible.~~ *This sentence seems repetitive to me—I don't think it is needed.*

If you have the right attitude and some good advice about finding a part-time job, you will find that working while going to school *does not have to be a scary experience* ~~is not as scary as it may sound at first~~. As college students, the most important thing ~~that we need~~ to remember is that ~~our~~ schoolwork must always be ~~our~~ *your* first priority. *I think you should keep your pronouns consistent. Since you started with the second-person voice, why not stick with it?* Keeping this in mind, as with most things in life, your own individual sacrifices in this balancing act will determine your success. One of the sacrifices that you might have to make is the need to limit or carefully schedule the time that you spend

with your friends. *Since you are trying to show how work at school is both manageable and beneficial for a college student, maybe you shouldn't begin your evidence with such a negative example. Keep a consistent tone.* Not all sacrifices need to be so difficult though. A small sacrifice you can make is to bring your schoolbooks along with you to work and utilize your work breaks to get a ~~heads up~~ head start on your nightly schoolwork. In addition, ~~since part of your time is already committed to your employers, You~~ you will need to get a good handle on your school schedule and plan ahead ~~to determine the time you need to work on various assignments~~. *This section seems kind of vague. I think it would be better if you gave some of your own personal experiences with planning in order to show specific examples of this point.* This sacrifice however will have positive repercussions as it will encourage you to form early study and time management habits. *This is a good point, but I wonder if it might fit better on page 3 where you begin to discuss the positive repercussions of part-time work on the college experience.*

While it is important to make such sacrifices in balancing a part-time job with success in school, you need not put all of the pressure on yourself. In fact, a key factor in minimizing such pressure is to choose a job where you work for an understanding employer. *I don't like the way this is worded, it implies that you are putting pressure on the employer. Maybe rephrase "there are ways to limit the pressure that you might feel."* This is not always an easy task and is certainly easier said than done. You can, however, take advantage of the resources available to you such as older students, advisors, and internship coordinators in finding a student-friendly employer. You should look for an employer that understands the need to put schoolwork first and who values scholarship in employees. A good place to look for such an employer is in university-run businesses where supervisors are advised to view employees as students first and foremost. Planning ahead around exam or paper weeks, you should also look for a job that offers flexibility and variability in scheduling hours. Again, this is a feature that can be found in most university-related businesses or services since many of these follow the academic calendar in their hours of operation. For the understanding and flexibility that such jobs offer, you should take advantage of the many positions available within your own college or university. *This paragraph seems to repeat itself a little bit. I think you should condense this material and use a personal experience to drive home your point about university employment.* This paragraph is where you start to sound too "preachy." You say "you should" a few times. How about changing this to "I would recommend" or "based on my experiences, the following methods have been helpful" in order to make your tone less presumptuous?

Now that I have shown how college students can manage their schoolwork with a part-time job, I want to move on to demonstrating the ways in which the challenge of balancing work with school can be a valuable learning and growing experience for college students. First, this challenge provides students with a degree of self-discipline as working students need to prioritize their schoolwork carefully, thus learning the importance of realistic goal-setting and time management. *The tone of this is too definite. Remember that your previous paragraphs give good examples but are not the ultimate method for everyone.* Second, students who work to support their own education often develop a heightened sense of respect, value, and responsibility for that education. *Great point!* This means that working students often take their studies rather seriously and realize the importance of a timely completion of their degree. These two examples represent large-scale attitudes and outlooks on education, but part-time work can also have more immediate effects on the academic career of a college student.

Such immediate effects of part-time work can be categorized into two types of experiences ~~with part-time work~~, work which offers career experience and work which fuels academic and career motivation. The former category includes but need not be limited to arranged, paid internships or focused work programs implemented or overseen by your college or university. Career experience is also found in more unexpected ways, such as when a management student gets to observe her manager at work or when a communications student practices his skills in a sales job. While many students will be fortunate to have such experiences, others will find themselves working at jobs that have very little to do with their projected career goals. In such cases, there are still valuable lessons to be learned. Certain types of part-time work, such as factory, food service, or maintenance work, while less directly valuable to the education process, often have positive motivating effects on students' academic attitudes. A working student who faces boredom, monotony, or low wages in her or his part-time job, will often be motivated to achieve academic excellence as a means of moving beyond the scope of this part-time work. *I think you should add some personal experience here. Did you work at a job related to your major or that was monotonous yet motivating?*

With the right attitude and outlook, part-time work can have many positive effects on the experiences of a college student. Even the potential negativity of facing boredom or monotony at work can be used constructively to motivate students to do their best schoolwork. If your college years are the best and most important of your life, I assure you that combining work with academics will enrich that importance, as it will give you a greater appreciation for the education you worked doubly hard to receive. I like your conclusion. I think it is good that it ends on a very positive note and that it relates back to your title about "Working toward a Degree."

Melissa,

Generally, I think this is a very good essay. The overall progression of the paper going from "how to work and do well in school" to "why it is beneficial to work while in school" makes logical sense to me. I like that you emphasize the benefits of holding a job beyond just the obvious point of making money. I also think that you have strong credibility and show good will since you have personal experience with your topic. This credibility makes for a strong argument. Maybe it would behoove you to include specific examples of your working experiences in college. Although your credibility is strong, you might want to avoid being too "preachy" in your tone. I feel that this self-assured tone tends to weaken your argument. I do like, however, the way you note in your paper that not all work has to apply directly to your major in order for it to be valuable. And the way your working experiences reinforce this point. Finally, I like the point you make in the concluding paragraph about monotonous work motivating students to appreciate schooling and thus work harder at their education, as this is something that many college students don't think about. This is especially true for freshmen since many often take attending college for granted as they see it as the next logical step following high school.

—Bob Geiger

Melissa,

Your paper is well thought out and focused, yet combining several sentences and limiting the wordiness would intensify your point. The validity of the paper is strengthened because of your personal experience of holding a part-time job while attending college— tie some of these specific examples into your paper rather than using generic and general examples. This is a great draft—keep working, developing, and improving. Here are some specific suggestions for improvement.

- *First paragraph suggestion: "Because I decided to attend a state university, was fortunate to receive several grants and scholarships, and had the financial support of my parents, I initially believed my college education would be easily affordable. However, with all the additional expenses, such as the cost of books, technology fees, and spending money, going to school meant finding a part-time job."*
- *Paper has good structure and flow.*
- *Limit prepositional phrases and repeating yourself.*
- *Great points made about time management and valuing one's education.*
- *First half of the paper "you" is used talking directly to the student reading the paper, but the second half is written in a more generic third person. Try to be consistent with point of view.*
- *Add personal experiences and examples to strengthen points.*

—*Michelle Clewell*

Before revising, Melissa considered the comments she received from Bob and Michelle. Since she had asked both of them to respond to her introduction, conclusion, and organization, she had to weigh all the comments—relevant and irrelevant—and use the ones that seemed to be most useful for her next draft. For Melissa's own response to this draft, see pages 88–91. For Melissa's final draft, see pages 96–99.

Exercise 3

Reread "Working toward a Degree" and the comments it received. Identify the comments you think are the most useful, and explain why. Which comments seem to be less useful, even hurtful? Explain why. What additional comments would you make if Melissa asked you to review her draft?

After Melissa had time to reconsider her first draft and to think about the responses she received from readers (including the ones reprinted here), she made a number of large-scale changes concerning her attention to audience, improved her introduction and conclusion, and edited some of her paragraphs to make them more effective and clear. She also dealt with sentence-level issues of punctuation and word choice. The following pages show what her paper looked like midway through its revision. Melissa used the Track Changes function of her word-processing program as she revised so that she could see her changes.

Working toward a Degree

When I first decided to pursue my college education at Penn State University, a key factor in my decision was that as a state university, Penn State offered a relatively low tuition compared to other schools in the state, Temple, Pitt, Penn (of course), and many of the private schools. ~~That, together with my parents' support and the scholarships I'd won made me think that college would be easily affordable.~~ The relatively lower tuition, together with the generous financial support of my parents and my fortune to have received several grants and scholarships, led me to believe that my college education would be easily affordable. When I started classes, though ~~however,~~ I soon discovered that unexpected expenses meant I'd have to find a job. What with the cost of books, technology fees, and simple spending money, I realized that, for me, going to school meant going to work. ~~I was shocked by how many unexpected expenses I continued to have at Penn State. I knew I was going to have to find a job.~~ Though initially nervous about how a job would affect my schoolwork, ~~Soon,~~ I took on a part-time job at the Penn State Creamery where I worked about 15 hours a week—and I continue to do ~~still did~~ well in my coursework. ~~So I can now say that balancing a part-time job with success in schoolwork is not only manageable but valuable for students. Since so many students of today need to work while going to school, I hope to show them that while holding a part-time job and doing well in school may seem difficult at first, in many ways these two undertakings are quite compatible.~~ Based on my own experience, I feel confident in assuring you hardworking students that not only can you, too, balance a part-time job with success in schoolwork, but that the experience can be a valuable, life-long lesson for you.

If you think it through and try to keep a positive attitude, you~~'ll~~ will find that working while going to school is not as scary as it may sound at first. As college students, the most important thing we all need to remember is that our schoolwork must always be our first priority. ~~Keeping this in mind, as with~~ After all, like most things in life, ~~y~~our own individual sacrifices in this balancing act will determine ~~y~~our success. One of the first sacrifices you ~~must~~ might have to make is to ~~cut out time~~ limit, schedule, or reimagine the free time you spend with your friends~~—or schedule time with them (more about that below)~~. After you start working, you won't be able to spend long hours in the coffee shop with your friends, but you can spend study time with them. Not all sacrifices are difficult, though. Another small sacrifice might be to take ~~You can bring~~ your schoolbooks along with you to work and ~~utilize~~ consistently think of your work breaks ~~to get a heads up on~~ as pre-scheduled time to spend on your nightly schoolwork. Using work breaks for study time will also help you plan ahead in terms of your various assignment deadlines. ~~Besides, since you're already committed to work anyway, you'll need to get a handle on your school schedule and assignment deadlines. This sacrifice however will have positive repercussions early on because you'll immediately form better work and study habits.~~ Such small sacrifices can lead to big gains: you can learn quickly how to manage your time so you work and study efficiently.

While it is important to make such sacrifices in balancing a part-time job with success in school, you need not put all of the pressure on yourself. One key factor in reducing pressure will be your ability (or luck) in finding a job that includes ~~A key factor in reducing pressure is to find~~ an understanding employer.

Doing so is not easy, but is surely easier said than done, so you might want to take advantage of some of the on-campus or campus-sponsored job opportunities. Older students, academic advisors, and internship coordinators can help you locate student-friendly employers, an employer who expects you to be a reliable employee at the same time that she accepts the fact that your major responsibility is schoolwork. In fact, it was my academic advisor who told me about openings at the Creamery, a ~~This is not always easy. So take advantage of the resources available to you on campus. You should look for an employer that understands your need to put schoolwork first. A good place to look is in~~ university-run business where supervisors are advised to view employees as students first and foremost. The Creamery is one of a number of on-campus businesses that offer ~~You should also look for a job that offers~~ flexibility and variability in scheduling hours, ~~so take advantage of the many positions available within your own college or university,~~ especially during holiday breaks and finals' week. Again, this is a feature that can be found in most university-related businesses or services since they usually follow the academic calendar in their hours of operation. For these reasons, you should consider taking advantage of on-campus job opportunities.

Once you meet the challenge of balancing your schoolwork with the obligations of a part-time job, you'll find that the balancing act has its own rewards. First of all, this challenge provides you with self-discipline, the self-discipline that comes with prioritizing your schoolwork, setting realistic goals, managing your time, and becoming a reliable worker. ~~Now that I've shown how college students can manage their schoolwork with a part-time job, I want to move on to demonstrate the ways in which the challenge of balancing work with school can be a valuable learning experience for college students. First, this challenge provides students with self-discipline as they prioritize their schoolwork and learn to set realistic goals and time management.~~ Second, working students like us often value our education more because we've worked and paid (or helped pay) for it. Sometimes, we take more responsibility for our educations as well, which means that we study seriously enough to get out on time, even early. We understand the importance of a timely completion of our degree. ~~students who work value their education more. This means that working students take their studies seriously and realize the importance of a timely completion of their degree.~~ These two examples represent ~~large-scale~~ long-range attitudes and outlooks on education, but part-time work can also have more immediate effects on ~~the~~ your academic career as well. ~~of a college student.~~

Such immediate effects can be categorized into two types of experiences with part-time work~~,~~: work ~~which~~ that offers career experience and work ~~which~~ that fuels academic and career motivation. The former category includes but need not be limited to arranged, paid internships or focused work programs implemented or overseen by your college or university. Career experience is also found in more unexpected ways, such as when a management student gets to observe her manager at work or when a communications student practices his skills in a sales job. While many student~~s-workers~~ will be fortunate to have such experiences, others, like me, will find themselves working at jobs that have very little to do with their projected career goals. In such cases, there are still valuable lessons to be learned. While I'm grateful for my work environment, I don't plan to dip ice cream forever. Thus, c~~C~~ertain types of part-time work, such as factory, food service, or maintenance work, while less directly valuable to the education process, ~~often~~ can have positive motivating effects on your ~~students'~~ academic attitude. If you're a ~~A~~ working student who faces boredom, monotony, or low wages in ~~her or his~~ your part-time job, you might ~~will~~ be motivated to achieve academic excellence as a means of moving beyond the scope of this part-time work.

With the right attitude and outlook~~,~~ toward your part-time work, you might gain work experiences that are as positive as your academic ones. You can use the ~~can have many positive effects on the experiences of a college student. Even the potential negativity of facing~~ boredom at work as motivation ~~can be used constructively to motivate students~~ to do your ~~their~~ best schoolwork in order to move steadily through your requirements and graduate on time. You may also appreciate your career goals much more than someone who didn't work their way through school. Everyone tells us that our college years are the best years of our life—and I think they're right. By combining work with academics, we're earning a greater appreciation for our education, one we've worked doubly hard to receive.

After several more revisions, more peer review, and some careful editing and proofreading, Melissa was ready to submit her essay to her instructor. Her final draft is on pages 96–99.

4f Editing for clearer ideas, sentences, and paragraphs

If you are satisfied with the revised structure of your essay and the content of your paragraphs, you can begin editing individual sentences for clarity, effectiveness, and variety (see chapters 27–34). The following checklist for editing contains cross-references to chapters where you can find more specific information.

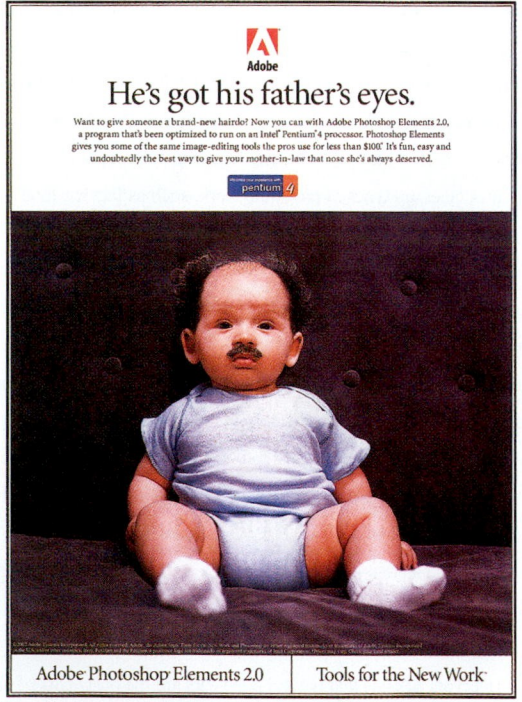

Just as photographic manipulation makes this image arresting, effective editing can make your writing more engaging.

CHECKLIST for Editing

1 Sentences

- What is the unifying idea of each sentence (**27**)?
- Are the sentences varied in length? How many words are in your longest sentence? Your shortest sentence?
- How many of your sentences use subordination? Coordination? If you overuse any one sentence structure, revise for variation (**31**).
- Which sentences have or should have parallel structure (**29**)?
- Do any sentences contain misplaced or dangling modifiers (**24**)?
- Do any of your sentences shift in verb tense or tone (**26c**)? Is the shift intentional?
- Does each verb agree with its subject (**26f**)? Does every pronoun agree with its antecedent (**25c**)?

2 Diction

- Have you repeated any words? Is your repetition intentional?
- Are your word choices exact, or are some words vague or too general (**33**)?
- Is the vocabulary you have chosen appropriate for your audience, purpose, and context (**1a** and **32**)?
- Have you defined any technical or unfamiliar words for your audience (**32c(4)**)?

4g | **Proofreading for an error-free essay**

Once you have revised and edited your essay, it is your responsibility to format it properly (see chapter **7**) and proofread it. Proofreading means making a special search to ensure that the final product you submit is free from error, or nearly so. An error-free essay allows your reader to read for meaning, without encountering incorrect spelling or punctuation that can interfere with meaning. As you proofread, you may discover problems that call for further revision or editing, but proofreading is usually the last step in the writing process.

With a computer, you can easily produce professional-looking documents. Showing that you care about presentation indicates respect for your audience. (See chapter **7**.) However, no matter how professional your paper looks when you print it, proofread it carefully. Mechanical mistakes can undermine your credibility.

Because the eye tends to see what it expects to see, many writers miss errors—especially minor ones, such as a missing comma or apostrophe—even when they think they have proofread carefully. To proofread well, then, you need to read your work more than once and read it aloud. Some people find it useful to read through the paper several times, checking for a different set of items on each pass. Other writers rely on peer editors to provide help with proofreading.

The proofreading checklist that follows refers to chapters and sections in this handbook where you will find detailed information to help you. Also, keep your dictionary (see **32e**) at hand to look up any words whose meaning or spelling you aren't sure of.

CHECKLIST for Proofreading

1 Spelling (40)

- Have you double-checked the words you frequently misspell and any the spell checker may have missed (for example, homophones or misspellings that still form words, such as *form* for *from*)?

- If you used a spell checker, did it overlook homophones (such as *there/their, who's/whose,* and *it's/its*) (**40c**)?

- Have you double-checked the spelling of all foreign words and all proper names?

2 Punctuation (35–39) and Capitalization (41)

- Does each sentence have appropriate closing punctuation, and have you used only one space after each end punctuation mark (**39**)?

- Is all punctuation within sentences—commas (**35**), semicolons (**36**), apostrophes (**37**), other internal marks of punctuation

(**35d–i**), and hyphens (**40f**)—used appropriately and placed correctly?

- Are direct quotations carefully and correctly punctuated (**38a**)? Where have you placed end punctuation with a quotation (**38d**)? Are quotations capitalized properly (**38a** and **41c(1)**)?
- Are all proper names, people's titles, and titles of published works correctly capitalized (**41a** and **41b**)?
- Are titles of works identified by either quotation marks (**38b**) or italics (**42a**)?

4h The final draft

After producing the intermediate draft reprinted on pages 88–91, Melissa continued to revise and edit her essay. Each subsequent draft became stronger. The essay that Melissa ultimately submitted to her teacher follows.

Melissa Schraeder successfully combined a part-time job with her college studies. Her hard work paid off—at graduation.

Melissa A. Schraeder

English 15

Professor Glenn

Working toward a Degree

With many private universities approaching $40,000 per year for tuition, it is all too obvious that getting a higher education is expensive. Fortunately, financial aid programs and state-funded schools, where tuition costs are normally less than half those of the average private school, have made higher education more affordable for Americans. When I decided to attend Penn State University, I was fortunate to receive several grants and scholarships as well as the promise of financial support from my parents. Little wonder that I initially believed that my college education would be easily affordable. When I started classes, however, I soon found that with all the additional expenses of school such as the cost of books, technology fees, and spending money, going to school meant finding a job—even for someone with financial support. Though hesitant about how holding a job might affect my studies, I soon took on a part-time job at the Penn State Creamery where I work about fifteen hours a week—and continue to do well in my coursework. Based on my experience, I feel confident in assuring hardworking students that not only can they balance a part-time job with success in schoolwork, but that the experience can be a valuable, life-long lesson, contributing to their growth as students and individuals.

If you have the right attitude and some good advice about finding a part-time job, you will find that working while going to school does not have to be an overwhelming experience. As a college student, the most important thing to remember is that schoolwork must always be your first priority. After all, like most things in life, your individual sacrifices in this balancing act will determine your success. One of the first sacrifices you might have to make is to limit, schedule, or reimagine the free time you have with your friends. After you start working, you won't be able to spend long hours in the coffee shop with your friends, but you can study with them. Not all sacrifices are difficult, though. Another small sacrifice might be to take your schoolbooks along with you to work and consistently think of your work breaks as pre-scheduled time to spend on your nightly coursework. Using work breaks for study time will also help you plan ahead in terms of your various assignment deadlines. I usually set up a calendar where I indicate the dates of all my major exams and due dates for papers and then tailor my work schedule around these dates. Such small sacrifices can lead to big gains: you quickly learn how to manage your time so you work and study efficiently.

While it is important to make such sacrifices in balancing a part-time job with success in school, you need not put all of the pressure on yourself. One key factor in reducing pressure will be your ability (or luck) in finding a job that includes an understanding employer. Doing so is not easy, so you might want to take advantage of some of the on-campus or campus-sponsored job opportunities. Older students, academic advisors, and internship coordinators can help you locate a student-friendly employer, one that expects you to be a reliable employee at the same time that the employer accepts the fact that your major responsibility is your studies. In fact, it was my academic advisor who told me about openings at the Creamery, a university-run business where supervisors are advised to view employees as students first and foremost. Supervisors at the Creamery release a monthly newsletter in which they highlight the academic achievements of student employees as a means of encouragement. The Creamery is also one of a number of on-campus businesses that offer flexibility and variability in scheduling hours, especially during holiday breaks and finals' week. This scheduling feature can be found in most university-related businesses or services since they usually follow the academic calendar in their hours of operation. For the understanding and flexibility that such jobs offer, I recommend that you try to take advantage of the many positions available within your own college or university.

Once you meet the challenge of balancing your college studies with the obligations of part-time work, you'll find that the balancing act has its own rewards: it can be a valuable learning and growing experience for you. First, this challenge can provide you with self-discipline, the self-discipline that comes with prioritizing your schoolwork, setting realistic goals, managing your time, and becoming a reliable employee. Second, students who work to support their own education often develop a heightened sense of respect, value, and responsibility for that education because we've worked and paid (or helped pay) for it. Because we take more responsibility for our educations, we usually study seriously enough to graduate on time, even early. We realize the importance of the timely completion of a degree. These two examples represent forward-looking attitudes and outlooks, but part-time work can also have more immediate effects on your academic career as well.

Such immediate effects of part-time work can be categorized into two types of experiences with part-time work: work that offers career experience and work that fuels academic and career motivation. The former category includes but need not be limited to arranged, paid internships or focused work programs implemented or overseen by your college or university. But career experience can also be found in more unexpected ways, such as when a management student gets to observe her manager at work or when a communications student practices his skills in a sales job. While many student-workers will be fortunate to have such experiences, others, like me, will find themselves working at jobs that have very little to do with their projected career goals. My experiences with work at college have fallen into the latter category, but there are still valuable lessons to be learned. Although the food service work I perform at the Creamery has little relevance to my English and history majors, I enjoy my time there as a release from my studies. Working at the

Schraeder 4

Creamery has also motivated me to do my best schoolwork, since I recognized that a food service job would not be fulfilling to me as a life-long career. If you find that the part-time work available to you is not directly related to your education, such work can still have positive motivating effects on your academic attitudes. A working student who faces boredom, monotony, or low wages in her or his part-time job will often be motivated to achieve academic excellence as a means of moving beyond the scope of this part-time work.

   With the right attitude, you might gain work experiences that are as positive as your academic ones. There are likely to be many jobs available within your university community that are student friendly and may even be directly related to your major area of studies. If that is not the case, you can use the less-than-fulfilling aspects of the work as motivation to do your best academic work in order to move steadily through your requirements and graduate on time. Any kind of employment may help you appreciate your career goals more than someone who isn't working their way through school. Everyone tells us that our college years are the best years of our life—and so far I think they're right. By combining part-time work with academics, we're not only earning a greater appreciation for our education, one we've worked doubly hard to receive, but we are also helping to pay for that education.

Exercise 4

Compare the three versions of "Working toward a Degree" reprinted in this chapter, and write a two-paragraph summary describing how Melissa revised her work. If she had shown her final draft to you, asking for your advice before submitting it for a grade, what would you have told her? Write a one-paragraph response to this draft.

PLANNING FOR ACADEMIC SUCCESS
5

You will not always have the luxury of planning, drafting, revising, getting feedback on, and editing a piece of writing over a stretch of days or weeks. Frequently, your college instructor or employer will ask you to produce an essay or a report during a class period or within a day or two. And the need for a timely response to current events or disasters often gives rise to an unscheduled writing assignment (a quickly prepared report, proposal, or analysis).

No matter what their time line, most writers feel some pressure. But when they are asked to write quickly or on demand, that pressure intensifies. The focus of this chapter is how to write well when faced with time constraints, especially when you feel as though you have only one shot at success. This chapter will help you

- ease the pressures of academic reading and writing (**5a**),
- take advantage of academic support services (**5b**),
- manage deadlines (**5c**),
- abbreviate the writing process (**5d**),
- manage writer's block (**5e**), and
- plan for essay examinations (**5f**).

The key to academic success is to use the available time as efficiently as possible.

5a Easing the pressures of academic reading and writing

Successful college students develop an understanding of the rhetorical situation of every class by reading carefully every course syllabus and assignment sheet—written texts that establish student rights and responsibilities.

(1) The syllabus states course requirements and the plan for meeting them.

On the first day of class, an instructor usually passes out a **syllabus,** a concise description of the course, which includes the readings, due dates, and sometimes the assignment sheets. You will want to become familiar with the syllabus, reading it carefully as you prepare for each class meeting and every assignment.

CHECKLIST for Reading a Syllabus

- Note your instructor's name, office number, and office hours. See whether your instructor has included an e-mail address and indicated any preferred method for getting in touch with her or him outside of class.
- Note the texts required for the course. Editions of textbooks change often, so be sure you purchase the correct one, new or used.
- Look closely at what the syllabus says about assignments. How much reading and writing does the course require? When are assignments due? Are there penalties for turning in papers late? Are there opportunities for revision?
- When are exams scheduled (see **5f**)? If there are quizzes, will they be announced in advance?
- Does the syllabus indicate that some assignments will be given more weight than others? If not, how will your final grade be determined?
- Does the syllabus indicate an attendance policy? Are there penalties for missing class or being late?
- Will there be a Web site or other online component for the course? If so, how will it be used, and how can you access it?

Many instructors post their syllabi on Web sites created for their courses. An electronic syllabus is easier for the instructor to modify once the course gains momentum. Be sure to review a course's electronic syllabus from time to time or, if your instructor uses a print syllabus, keep track of any changes. Every course Web site is different, but there are basic guidelines to follow.

Coding for Corporate Survival
IST 301 & ENGL 202C

Next Class Meeting: JanuaryEleven

CourseRoster - CodingSchedule - SyllaBus - DueDates - GroupFormations - WakkaFormatting -
DiscussionPapers - SemesterLongProject - ProjectTopics - TwoExams -
SoYouThinkYouCanWriteaFinalExam? - LogoContest -

Web sites, such as this one constructed by instructor Jeff Pruchnic, have become a
common source of course information—from reading and writing assignments to
recommendations for outside reading and study-group times.

CHECKLIST for Using a Course Web Site

- Access the course Web site immediately to find out which Web browser properly displays the site, including its specific links and other elements, and whether your Internet connection works quickly enough. See your instructor if you have any problems.

- Learn whether the course Web site contains information and resources that are not included on the syllabus. If an instructor briefly describes a writing assignment on the syllabus but includes extensive guidelines and deadlines only on the course Web site, it is vital that you have easy access to and the ability to navigate that site.

- Check the links on the course Web site. There may be a link to a Web-based newsgroup for the course or to a required reading. It is essential that such links work properly on your browser.

(2) Reading assignments rhetorically is essential to academic success.

Instructors write out assignments so that they receive the kind of writing they want to read; therefore, you will want to respond to each assignment exactly as directed in terms of length, focus, format, and purpose. Do not risk misunderstanding an assignment because you read it too quickly. Rather, read every assignment carefully, and concentrate on fulfilling what your instructor has asked you to do. Ask questions if you have any uncertainty about what is expected.

Discussion Papers

The discussion paper should both prepare students for solving problems in class and lead to better problem results. To quickly apply knowledge from the readings while working on the problems in class, students need to have synthesized the material for it to serve as an effective resource.

Instructions

1. Read the assigned question.

2. Read each article with the question in mind, and prepare a summary of each (for yourself, not to hand in).

3. Compare the summaries and identify how each article relates to the question.

4. Develop a thesis that is related to the question (this will often narrow the scope of the question).

5. Write a 600-700 word (about one single spaced page) response and post it to the wiki. This response should explain your thesis (in three sentences or less) and support this thesis primarily with evidence from the readings as well as, if appropriate, personal experiences or knowledge gained from other classes.

Grading

Clear thesis statement (two points)
Effective application of assigned reading(s) (two points)
Organization and arrangement (two points)

Assignment sheets, such as this one devised by Jeff Pruchnic, provide information that is crucial for successfully fulfilling instructors' assignments. Note that this sheet includes information on how the assignment will be evaluated.

Whether you are asked to submit an essay, an argument, a research paper, or another form of writing, you have a better chance of completing your project successfully if you read the assignment sheet with the following concerns in mind.

CHECKLIST for Reading an Assignment Sheet

- What does this assignment require you to do? Are there subject, formatting, or length restrictions? Are there guidelines for making choices?
- Have purpose, audience, context, and exigence been supplied for you, or will you choose these components of your assignment?
- What strengths can you bring to this assignment? What do you still need to learn if you are going to complete this assignment successfully?
- How much time should you devote to this assignment? When should you get started?
- How might a visit to the writing center help you? (See **5b(2)**.)
- Are you expected to submit all of your process writing along with your final copy?

5b Taking advantage of academic support opportunities

One of the biggest advantages of studying at a college or university is the availability of academic support services and trained personnel. All students inevitably need academic support at some point in their college careers. Too often, though, students do not get the help they need because they do not know what resources are available, where those resources are located, and—most important—how to use them for their own benefit. Successful students seek out the multiple means of support offered on their campus.

(1) Your instructor can clarify course assignments and requirements.

Your instructor should be able to help you with most of your course-related questions, whether they concern a reading assignment, the due date for an essay, or a concept essential to the subject matter. Although you can get answers or clarifications for most of your questions either in class or immediately afterward, you are likely to get more time and attention when you visit your instructor during office hours. The checklist that follows includes tips for making your office visit a productive one.

In addition to conferring with instructors in their offices, you may also be able to consult with them by e-mail or through a Web site created especially for a class. The course syllabus may include an e-mail (or other online) address as well as a policy about communicating online. If not, ask whether such communication is possible and under what circumstances it would be appropriate. Most instructors are happy to answer short questions online; however, questions needing longer answers probably merit an office visit.

CHECKLIST for Getting Help from Your Instructor

- Learn the instructor's office hours and the location of his or her office.
- Make an appointment during office hours, and then appear on time. Before the visit, write out your questions and concerns. What do you need to take away with you for the meeting to be productive?
- If you are planning to discuss a specific reading or writing assignment, bring a copy of it to the meeting.
- Tell your instructor what information or help you need.
- Once you have clearly stated your questions and concerns, pay close attention to the answers you receive, writing them down if necessary. Do not hesitate to return.

---

(2) Writing centers offer help from tutors.

Regardless of their major, many successful college writers benefit from visits to their school's writing center, where they can discuss their work-in-progress with fellow students who are trained to assist them with their writing. Because writing tutors usually represent many majors, they bring to their work a wide range of writing experiences from virtually all disciplines. Your school most likely has a writing center where this kind of student-to-student consultation takes place on a regular basis. The writing center probably maintains a Web site where you can get information about services, hours of operation, and additional resources for writing. Students who visit a writing center are demonstrating their commitment to writing well and to reaching their own writing goals. They do not expect tutors to write or correct an essay for them.

TIPS FOR VISITING A WRITING CENTER

- Learn when the center is open, whether you can drop in or need to make an appointment, and how long tutoring sessions last.

- If you are working on a specific assignment, bring the material with you: your assignment sheet and whatever you have already written, whether notes, an outline, or a draft.

- Be prepared to explain your understanding of the assignment to your tutor and to indicate the specific kind of help you need. If you bring along the instructor's comments or previously graded assignments, the tutor can use specific information from them to help you.

- Some students find that they benefit from a visit early in the writing process, after they have written a detailed outline or an initial draft. Others find that they benefit more toward the end of the process, during revision and before they are ready to edit and proofread.

- Recognize that tutors are ready to help you with your *writing;* rarely will they serve as proofreaders or editors. In fact, they may ask you to read aloud what you have written so that *you* can catch your own surface errors and organizational weaknesses. For this reason, you will want to visit the center at least a day or two before your assignment is actually due.

- If you have a good session with a tutor, learn his or her name so that you can develop a working relationship. Many writing centers encourage weekly meetings with the same tutor so that writer and tutor can develop a collaborative learning relationship.

- If you have a frustrating experience with a tutor, ask for someone else on your next visit, and do not judge the entire staff by a single bad experience.

5c Managing deadlines

You will almost always be working with deadlines—whether for essays, business plans, grant proposals, or other time-sensitive documents. Preparing ahead of time always helps. Even though an in-class essay exam may not be scheduled until midterm, start preparing on the first day of class. As you read your assignments and participate in class discussions, try to determine what is most important about the material you are learning. Pay attention to indications that your instructor considers certain material especially important. Whenever an instructor

gives you instructions or assignments, read them carefully, asking questions until you know exactly what is expected of you.

The best preparation for a writing assignment with a longer deadline, such as a research project, is to start early. If you are choosing your own topic, begin as soon as you can to narrow down your ideas (see **3b**). The sooner you identify a subject, the sooner you can discuss it with your instructor. You can make deadlines work for you by establishing your own time line. For an important project, you might even set yourself intermediate deadlines for writing an introduction with a thesis statement, composing a first draft, meeting with a classmate for review, revising your draft, and editing. If you carry a small notebook or hand-held computer with you, you will always have a place to jot down notes and ideas.

5d Abbreviating the writing process

Students and employees are often expected to write well with little notice. When faced with a short deadline, try to narrow the topic to a manageable scope or to relate the assignment to your academic or work experiences or personal knowledge. If you give your topic a sharp focus, you can write a thoughtful, in-depth analysis, rather than skimming the surface of a broader topic. Once you have a focused topic, organize your ideas. The following tips will help you abbreviate the writing process.

TIPS FOR ABBREVIATING THE WRITING PROCESS

- Generate ideas about the assignment or topic with a friend or colleague who is facing or has faced the same kind of deadline. That person can help you clarify your line of reasoning and develop counterarguments. Take notes.

(Continued on page 108)

(Continued from page 107)

- Draft an introductory paragraph that frames your position or approach and includes a clear thesis statement. E-mail your paragraph to your instructor or to a classmate to make sure that you are on the right track.

- If your thesis statement and basic approach are on track, write down your main points; then flesh them out with examples and supporting text until you have a first draft.

- Read your draft aloud, slowly. Make sure that your topic sentences are clear. Reading aloud will help you locate passages that need transitional words or phrases to help your reader along.

- Write a conclusion that reiterates your main points and suggests their implications, the directions in which they may point.

- Read over your text to make sure that it fulfills the assignment. Reread your introduction and conclusion to see whether they frame your piece. Examine your topic sentences and supporting paragraphs to make sure that they help you fulfill your purpose and are appropriate for your audience.

- Proofread one last time. Submit your work on time.

You can use your computer to help you manage writing tasks efficiently.

- If you do not have much time for revising and editing, you can use the grammar checker and spell checker of your word-processing program to help you proofread, even while you are drafting.

- A program such as Microsoft's Outlook can be used to schedule tasks and keep a calendar. You can set the Alarm function of this type of program to remind yourself to complete certain tasks for a writing assignment in time to meet the overall deadline.

- Many on-campus writing centers can receive drafts of student writing via e-mail or through a Web site, and writing tutors will often respond to a draft within twenty-four hours. If the writing center on your campus offers such a service, you can use it to get helpful advice on short notice when you have a tight deadline.

5e Managing writer's block

Writer's block can affect any writer at any time, no matter how experienced, no matter what the writing assignment. Many experienced and successful writers suffer from **writer's block,** which is nothing more than the inability to begin or continue writing for reasons other than lack of skill or commitment. Sometimes, it helps to stay put at the computer and keep typing away. Sometimes, it helps to focus on completing one small section of the writing assignment at a time. Other times, it helps to step away from the work.

A number of factors can contribute to writer's block: you may not think you are a very good writer; you may want the words to be "just right"; you cannot decide on a thesis statement, because there seem to be so many angles you could take; you find it difficult to organize information; or you may procrastinate.

One of the most common causes for writer's block is striving for perfection. Of course, you want your writing to be as good as it can be, in terms of grammar, spelling, structure, and development. But you will be better off turning in completed work that is less than perfect than submitting no work at all. In other words, do the very best you can, given your circumstances, and then move on. The deadline is a reality that must be honored by all writers.

> **CHECKLIST for Managing Writer's Block**
>
> - Allot your time with thought and care.
> - Prioritize your responsibilities, and allow time for each activity.
> - Establish regular writing habits, including when and where you write.
> - For an out-of-class assignment, draft without worrying about structure, content, or surface errors. You can revise later.
> - For an essay exam, read each question slowly and jot ideas in the margin as you read down the page.

5f Preparing for essay examinations

If your instructor has posed a clear question and provided explicit instructions, you are (almost) home free. Write out your answer, framing it with a thesis statement, main points, and supporting arguments or examples. If a question does not make clear what is called for, ask your instructor for clarification. The steps described in the following sections will help you improve your ability to take essay examinations.

(1) Set up a time schedule.

If the exam has more than one question, figure out how much time to allot to each one. If you are faced with two questions that are worth the same number of points, give half the time to one and half to the other. When certain questions are weighted more heavily than others, however, you need to divide your time accordingly. However you allocate your time, allow ten minutes for final revising and proofreading.

Stick to your time allotment for each question. If you do not finish, leave room to complete it later and move on to the next question. Partial answers to *all* questions usually gain you more points than complete answers to only *some* questions. Besides, you can use the ten minutes you saved to put the finishing touches on any incomplete answers, even if you have to draw arrows to the margins or to the back of the page, or if you have to supply rough notes (see **5f(3)**). Your instructor will probably appreciate the extra effort.

(2) Read instructions and questions carefully.

Students who take time to read instructions and questions carefully almost always do better than those who do not. Invest a few minutes in studying each question, putting that question in your own words, and then jotting down a few notes in the margin next to it. If you have been given a choice of questions to answer, choose those that best suit your knowledge yet do not overlap.

Most questions contain specific instructions about how, as well as what, to answer. Be alert for words such as *compare, define,* and *argue,* which identify the writing task and provide specific cues for organizing your response. Other words, such as *discuss* and *explain,* are less specific, so try to determine exactly what it is your instructor wants you to do. When these more general directions appear, be tuned in to such accompanying words as *similar* or *different* (which signal, respectively, a comparison or a contrast), *identify* (which signals a definition or description), and *why* (which signals the need to identify causes). You will also want to be clear as to whether you are being asked to call up course-related information from memory or to respond with your own ideas. Words such as *think, defend,* and *opinion* signal that you are to frame a thesis and support it.

Most essay exam questions begin with or contain one of the words in the following list and end with a reference to the information you are to discuss. Understanding these terms and framing your answer in response to them will help you focus on what is being asked.

TERMS USED IN ESSAY QUESTIONS

Compare	Examine the points of similarity (compare) or difference (contrast) between two ideas or things (**3g(5)**).
Define	State the class to which the item to be defined belongs, and clarify what distinguishes it from the others of that class (**3g(6)**).
Describe	Use details in a clearly defined order to give the reader a clear mental picture of the item you are being asked to describe (**3g(2)**).
Discuss	Examine, analyze, evaluate, or state pros and cons. This word gives you wide latitude in addressing the topic and is thus more difficult to work with than some of the others in this set, since you must choose your own focus. It is also the one that, unfortunately, appears most frequently on exam questions.
Evaluate	Appraise the advantages and disadvantages of the idea or thing specified (chapter **8**).
Explain	Clarify and interpret (**3g(3)**), reconcile differences, or state causes (**3g(4)**).
Illustrate	Offer concrete examples or, if possible, create figures, charts, or tables that provide information about the item.
Summarize	State the main points in a condensed form; omit details, and curtail examples.
Trace	Narrate a sequence of events that show progress toward a goal or comprise a process (**3g(1)** and **3g(4)**).

---

(3) Decide how to organize your response.

Even under time constraints, you should be able to draft a rough outline or jot down a few phrases for an informal list (see **3d**). Identify your thesis; then list the most important points you plan to cover. You might decide to rearrange ideas later, but the first step is to get some down on paper. Before you begin to write the answer, quickly review the list, deleting any irrelevant or unimportant points and adding any better ones that come to you (keeping in mind how much time you have allotted to the specific question). Number the points in a logical sequence determined by chronology (reporting events in the order in which they occurred), by causation (showing how one thing led to another), or by order of importance (going from the most important point to the least important). Although arranging points in order of increasing importance is often effective, it can be risky in an exam situation because you might run out of time and not get to your most important point.

Following is a thesis statement and a list of supporting points that was quickly composed and edited during the first few minutes of an essay exam. Biology major Trish Parsons was responding to the following question: "Discuss whether the term 'junk DNA' is an appropriate name for the nucleic DNA that does not code for proteins."

THESIS: The term "junk" applied to DNA with no apparent purpose is a misnomer; there are many possible purposes, both past and present, for the allegedly "junk" DNA.

1a.

1b. Though junk DNA sequences do not code for specific proteins, they may play an important role in DNA regulation. ⟶ go to point #5

2. Microbiology technology has had many amazing advances since the discovery of DNA. ~~Indeed,~~ DNA itself was not immediately recognized as the "plan for life." Further technological advances that are sure to come may find a definite purpose for "junk" DNA.

3. Junk DNA may have coded for proteins in our evolutionary past and a mechanism for disposing of it ~~never has~~ yet to evolve ~~evolved~~.

4. During DNA replication, the possibilities for mistakes are endless. The junk (filler) DNA decreases the chances of the more important, protein-coding DNA being mutated during this process.

5. Junk DNA may yet play an important role in the new field of eugenics, where it has been found that certain traits are heritable, but not directly coded for (possible relation to DNA regulation role in point #1)

← 1a Many terms have been applied in genetics that end up creating confusion because scientists came to conclusions too quickly — e.g., dominant and recessive alleles are too simplistic. b/c genetics is a relatively new field we have only recently begun to understand.
(BEGIN WITH THIS ONE)

Sometimes, the language of the question will tell you how you should organize your answer. Consider this example:

> Discuss how the two-party political system of the United States influenced the outcome of the Bush-Gore presidential election.

At first glance, this exam question might seem to state the topic without indicating how to organize a discussion of it. *To influence*, however, is to be responsible for certain consequences. In this case, the two-party political system is a cause, and you are being asked to identify its effects (see **3g(4)**). Once you have recognized this, you might decide to discuss different effects in different paragraphs.

Here is another example:

> Consider Picasso's treatment of the human body early and late in his career. How did his concept of bodily form persist throughout his career? How did it change?

The reference to two different points in the artist's career, along with the words *persist* and *change*, indicates that your task is to compare and contrast. You could organize your response to this question by discussing Picasso's concept of the bodily form when his paintings were realistic and when they were cubist—preferably covering the same points in the same order in each part of the response. Or you could begin by establishing similarities and then move on to discuss differences. There is almost always more than one way to organize a thoughtful response. Devoting at least a few minutes to organizing your answer can help you better demonstrate what you know.

(4) State your main points clearly.

If you state your main points clearly, your instructor will see how well you have understood. Make your main points stand out from the rest of the answer to an exam question by identifying them. For instance, you can make a main point be the first sentence of each paragraph. Or you can use transitional words such as *first, second,* and *third.* You might even create headings to separate your points. By the time you have outlined your essay exam answer, you should know which points you want to highlight, even if the points change slightly as you begin writing. Use your conclusion to summarize your main points. If you tend to make points that differ from those you had in mind when you started, try

leaving space for an introduction at the beginning of the answer and then writing it after you have written the rest. Or simply draw a line pointing into the margin (or to the other side of the paper), and write the introduction there.

(5) Stick to the question.

Always answer each essay exam question as precisely and directly as you can, perhaps using some of the instructor's language in your thesis statement. If your thesis statement implies an organizational plan, follow that plan as closely as possible. If you move away from your original thesis because better ideas occur to you as you write, simply go back and revise your thesis statement (see **3c**). If you find yourself drifting into irrelevant material, stop and draw a line through it.

If you find yourself facing a vague or truly confusing question, construct a clear(er) question and then answer it. Rewriting the instructor's question can seem like a risky thing to do, especially if you have never done it before. But figuring out a reasonable question that is related to what the instructor has written is actually a responsible move if you can answer the question you have posed.

(6) Revise and proofread each answer.

Save a few minutes to reread each answer. Make whatever deletions and corrections you think are necessary. If time allows, ask yourself if there is anything you have left out that you can still manage to include (even if you have to write in the margins or on the back of the page). Unless you are certain that your instructor values neatness more than knowledge, do not hesitate to make additions and corrections. Simply draw a caret (∧), marking the exact place in the text where you want an addition or correction to be placed. Making corrections will allow you to focus on improving what you have already written, whereas recopying your answer just to make it look neat is an inefficient use of time (and you may have recopied only half your essay when the time is up). Finally, check spelling, punctuation, and sentence structure.

6

ONLINE

DOCUMENTS

Word-processing software makes it easy to capture and arrange ideas for writing, plan a writing task, compose, revise, edit, proofread, and produce professional-looking documents. In addition to word-processing capabilities, computers offer you the opportunity to communicate with a wider, often global, audience when you compose for Web sites and other online forums and documents, such as chat rooms, listservs, and instant messages.

Online writing is often **interactive** (that is, a message is related to one or more previous or subsequent messages), and it can dramatically expand the audience, context, and style and presentation options for your work. Because composing in this medium differs somewhat from writing essays or research papers delivered in hard copy, it calls for different skills—many of which you already have. This chapter will help you

- assess the rhetorical situation for e-writing (**6a**),
- use electronic messaging effectively (**6b**),
- participate in online discussions (**6c**),
- understand conventions for electronic communication (**6d**),
- compose effective Web documents (**6e**), and
- manage visual elements of a Web site (**6f**).

6a Assessing the online rhetorical situation

Whenever you compose material for a Web page, engage in an online discussion forum, or instant-message a classmate, you are using rhetoric, or purposeful language, to influence the outcome of your interaction (see **1a**). In each case, you are responding to an online rhetorical situation that can be markedly different from that for a static, print medium.

Because the Web gives you access to so many different audiences, the unique nature of the online rhetorical situation becomes instantly evident when you begin composing for a Web site or a newsgroup posting. If you are constructing a Web page for a course assignment, your primary audience is probably your instructor and classmates. But as soon as you put your composition online, you open up your work to a variety of secondary audiences (see **1d(3)**), whose responses you will also want to consider as you compose.

Keep in mind that primary or secondary audiences for online documents may be specialized, diverse, or multiple (**1d**). When writing a message for a listserv (an e-mail–based discussion forum organized around a particular subject), you are addressing a specialized audience and can assume that its members share an interest in and some knowledge of your topic. When creating a Web page about an important historical event or place, such as the 1929 stock market crash that led to the Great Depression or Booker T. Washington's Tuskegee Institute, however, you should write for a diverse audience, whose members have varying levels of knowledge, understanding of specialized terms, and interest in your subject matter.

When responding to an online rhetorical situation, you also want to specify your purpose clearly. Your purpose for writing an online document is often much like that for writing a paper document: to express how you feel about something, create a mood, or amuse or motivate your audience. For example, for a Web site such as the one developed by The Green Belt Movement (shown in fig. 6.5), the purpose is to inform and then motivate the audience to become involved. Because readers may encounter your composition in a number of different ways—by having an e-mail message forwarded to them, by finding your Web page through a search engine, or by entering an online discussion forum—you need to take extra care to clarify your purpose and make it readily apparent.

Composing online also requires a greater responsiveness to context than you may have become used to for conventional academic writing projects (see **1e**). In the rhetorical situation for online composition, the boundary between writer and audience is often blurred, because participants are writing and responding simultaneously. In addition, the accessibility of electronic messaging and online discussion forums (see **6b–c**) encourages many people to add to or comment on a composition. This flow of new material contributes to an always evolving rhetorical situation, requiring you to be familiar with the preceding discussion and understand the conventions of the forum in order to compose effectively.

In addition, many Internet users have come to expect online compositions to be especially timely, given the relative ease of updating an electronic document compared to a print-based publication. For example, a Web site about tsunamis produced before the December 2004 disaster in Southeast Asia surely differed from one produced after that date. In the first place, chances are that many more people became familiar with the meaning of the word *tsunami* in December 2004. Second, the later Web site was more likely to take into account the international efforts to understand, avoid, and communicate the warning signs of an impending tsunami.

6b Using electronic messaging effectively

You probably write e-mails or instant messages on a daily basis, though you may never have thought of them as online documents. Both of these media are now widely used for sharing ideas and information with coworkers and classmates, for exchanging documents, and for discussing course-related, business-related, and personal issues. Ease and speed define electronic messaging and, at the same time, compromise the user's ability to establish a fitting tone—an essential feature of effective communication in any context. In deciding on the appropriate language and style for an electronic message, you need to consider elements of the rhetorical situation as you would for any document (see **1a**): who is your audience, and what do you hope to accomplish with your message? Conversational style may be acceptable for a message to a discussion group for your writing class, but a more formal style is required for a message to your instructor about the grade you received on an assignment. (See also **6c(2)**.)

(1) The basic rhetorical unit of e-mail is the screen (not the paragraph or the page).

Although computer screens come in a range of sizes, you can anticipate having only about twenty lines in which to present an e-mail message.

I hate to disagree with both Emily and Valerie, but I think the first real dictionary was published in 1604 (Kersey's didn't come out until 1702).

If you look on page 10 of the notes, under the first heading called "Dictionaries" you will find "Earliest English-to-English dictionary 1604." Then the notes explain it.

Also, the second-to-the-last paragraph on page 236 in the text talks about the 1604 dictionary.

Kersey's dictionary is discussed later on page 10 of the notes under the heading "Dictionaries between 1604 and Johnson's Dictionary." Kersey's was the "first English-English dictionary to contain everyday words." And yes, I agree with Valerie that Bailey's was the "best dictionary before Johnson's" because it was the "first to show stress placement."

BUT, the big clue for me that the 1604 dictionary is the first real dictionary of English is that both Kersey's and Bailey's are under the heading "Dictionaries between 1604 and Johnson's Dictionary." Therefore, 1604 was the first.

Does anyone agree with me or am I the only one who feels this way?

Meg Barry

I hate to disagree with both Emily and Valerie, but I think the first real dictionary was published in 1604 (Kersey's didn't come out until 1702). If you look on page 10 of the notes, under the first heading called "Dictionaries" you will find "Earliest English-to-English dictionary 1604." Then the notes explain it. Also, the second-to-the-last paragraph on page 236 in the text talks about the 1604 dictionary. Kersey's dictionary is discussed later on page 10 of the notes under the heading "Dictionaries between 1604 and Johnson's Dictionary." Kersey's was the "first English-English dictionary to contain everyday words." And yes, I agree with Valerie that Bailey's was the "best dictionary before Johnson's" because it was the "first to show stress placement." BUT, the big clue for me that the 1604 dictionary is the first real dictionary of English is that both Kersey's and Bailey's are under the heading "Dictionaries between 1604 and Johnson's Dictionary." Therefore, 1604 was the first. Does anyone agree with me or am I the only one who feels this way?

Meg Barry

Fig. 6.1. The top e-mail message uses white space advantageously in response to the rhetorical situation. The bottom one does not.

Keeping the length of your message to only one screen is especially important when your audience is work-related and your purpose is to inform or question. People tend to read only one screen of an e-mail message, so get to your point quickly: compose a message that fits on a single screen yet has the white space necessary for easy reading.

Because most people who use e-mail on a regular basis receive a large volume of messages, they have become used to scanning, quickly responding to, and deleting these communications. Clearly announcing your message in the subject line and then arranging and presenting it in concise, readable chunks help ensure that important information is not overlooked. In the e-mail shown in fig. 6.1, for example, Meg Barry's audience is her editing group from a course on the history of the English language; the exigence for her message is that the group is preparing for a midterm, and the context includes Meg's careful attention to tone ("I hate to disagree . . ."), her references to the textbook, and her purpose for sending the message—to make sure that the group has the right information. The content of the message responds to the features of the specific rhetorical situation and not only demonstrates Meg's logical and careful work but also enhances her credibility by showing her concern for her fellow students.

(2) Instant messaging reflects the speed and practical limits of real-time message entry.

Many users of instant messaging (IM), especially those using their cell phones, are able to read just a few lines of text at a time, so keep each message you send brief and to the point. Because instant messaging is **synchronous** (the text and multimedia elements are visible to the recipient at the moment the message is posted), messages sent between two users sometimes overlap, becoming disconnected from their original context (see **6c(2)**). To avoid confusion, especially when it is important that your message be clear (as when setting up a meeting or explaining the purpose of a project), allow a time delay when you respond. Consider pasting in "reminder" text from previous e-mails or messages in order to provide the context for a response. Remember, however, that because most IM users have come to expect immediate responses to their messages, you should notify the recipient if you are pausing in a given messaging exchange or leaving your computer.

BEYOND THE RULE

WHO OWNS YOUR ELECTRONIC MESSAGES?

Your e-mail is not necessarily private or secure. Employers have been vindicated in cases where they were charged with privacy violations for reading employees' e-mail, and university legal counsels and administrators have "confiscated" the e-mails of teachers and students when complaints were lodged about grades. Be sure to check your school's or employer's policy with regard to the use of electronic messaging. For additional information, visit **www.harbrace.com**.

TIPS FOR SENDING ATTACHMENTS WITH ELECTRONIC MESSAGES

E-mail

- Before you send an attachment, consider the size of the file—many inboxes have limited space and cannot accept or store the large files that contain streaming video, photographs, and sound clips.

- If you want to send a file larger than 500K or multiple files whose combined size is larger than that, call or e-mail your recipient first to ask permission. A large file could crash the recipient's e-mail program.

- If you do not know the type of operating system or software installed on your recipient's computer, send text-only documents in **rich text format (rtf),** which preserves most formatting and is recognized by many word-processing programs.

Instant Messaging

- Take the same care when attaching files to and including graphical elements in instant messages as with e-mails, so that you do not unintentionally send someone an inappropriate file or virus.

- Most instant-messaging programs use **file transfer protocol (ftp)** to transmit files. To protect your computer from viruses, make sure that the preferences on the program you are using are set so that you have to approve a file before it is downloaded. Then, open only files you are expecting or ones from users you know, and be sure to run a virus scan on all downloaded files before opening them. Or, in order to control what you receive, you might set your preferences to accept messages only from those on your buddy list.

Viruses

- Because attachments are notorious for transmitting computer viruses, never open an attachment sent by someone you do not know.

- Before opening attachments, make sure that you are working on a computer with antivirus software that will scan all incoming attachments for viruses.

- Check Web sites such as **www.symantec.com** for information and updates on viruses. You can also get virus-related updates and alerts on the Web site of the manufacturer of your computer or software (such as Apple or Microsoft).

6c The community of online discussion groups

Participating in online discussion groups is a good way to learn more about topics that interest you and to develop your writing skills. However, just as you evaluate information in print sources, you need to evaluate the information and advice you get from online forums (see chapter **10**). There are two main types of online discussion groups: asynchronous and synchronous forums.

(1) Asynchronous forums allow easy access, regardless of time and place.

Some examples of asynchronous forums are listservs, newsgroups, and blogs. A **listserv** is an e-mail–based discussion forum organized around a specific subject, such as short story writing, American history, or computer gaming, and distributed from a central e-mail address to everyone who has subscribed to the forum. Many listservs archive messages (as well as shared photographs, links, calendars, and membership lists), giving you the option of reading that information on a Web site rather than in your e-mail. A **newsgroup** (sometimes called a **bulletin board**) keeps messages on a server, organized by topic (or **thread**) so that users can search for, read, and respond to messages on particular features of the subject covered by the group (see fig. 6.2). A **blog** (from the phrase

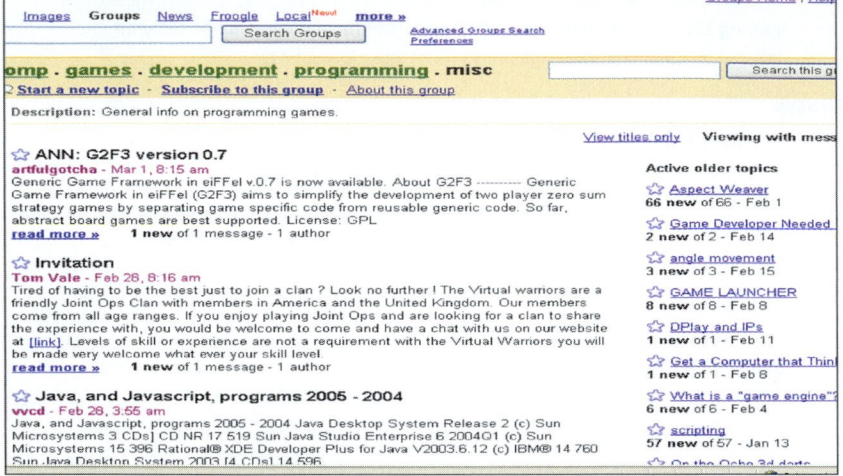

Fig. 6.2. A newsgroup allows participants to access and contribute to an online discussion at any time.

"Web log") is a Web site that is part online diary and part community forum; a blog allows users to post their responses to its creator's opinions and usually maintains archives of past postings. Some blogs also post "blogrolls" of other blogs that the original author recommends (see fig. 6.3).

The delay between posting and viewing contributions to an asynchronous forum often leads to thoughtful discussions because it emphasizes the importance of *responding* to the existing rhetorical situation. Before joining a listserv or newsgroup or responding to a blog, you might want to **lurk,** that is, remain anonymous while you read previous and current postings to understand the various topics of discussion and the histories of the different "conversations." When you have a good sense of the rhetorical situation, you can add your own comments to an existing thread or start a new one—always keeping in mind the information and overall tone in the messages posted by other users.

(2) Synchronous forums allow discussion in real time.

Synchronous forums, including chat rooms, electronic meeting software, and instant-messaging conferences, show the posted text (and any

Fig. 6.3. Some bloggers update their blogs on a daily basis, adding text and visuals.

multimedia elements) in real time. Such discussions resemble face-to-face interactions. They may or may not be archived, depending on their formality and the technology used to communicate.

Synchronous discussion groups offer a convenient way for people who are in different physical locations to interact. In business, for example, a project team in New York City can "meet" with members of another team in Los Angeles by using a program such as NetMeeting. Some academic courses use courseware (such as WebCT or Blackboard) to host synchronous discussion forums to supplement class meetings or to hold classes exclusively online. Offering not only a text-based environment but also voice and video capability, synchronous forums have the advantages of immediacy and a sense of physical presence.

Engaging in real-time online discussion can be disconcerting initially. Several different threads are usually being explored simultaneously, and it can take time to get used to having all the comments from current participants appear on your screen as though they were part of a single conversation (see fig. 6.4). Successful participation in a synchronous

```
ses963psu (8:32:24 PM): 😊
rhosarhetor (8:32:26 PM): ahem
rhosarhetor (8:32:38 PM): in any case, we have a list of several "issues" for
    sloop.
rhosarhetor (8:32:39 PM): mo?
raenalynn (8:32:40 PM): How does Signdefwegwqrhgwethwrty having problems with comptr
rhosarhetor (8:32:48 PM): i'd say
sallysarahfl (8:33:02 PM): these conversations move so quickly, quicker than i think!
rhosarhetor (8:33:06 PM): what an image i have in my mind: of both of you falling
    off your chairs!
ses963psu (8:33:09 PM): btw, i couldn't find the this american life show reference i heard! damn.
raenalynn (8:33:12 PM): yea for me too.
xkaren08 (8:33:20 PM): speaking of KB
rhosarhetor (8:33:29 PM): we can keep looking. in our spare time.
ses963psu (8:33:31 PM): they move fast and are fun...and fun and theory isn't bad
rhosarhetor (8:33:41 PM): fun isn't bad theory
xkaren08 (8:33:52 PM): what were you thinking we should focus on in RoM?
rhosarhetor (8:34:27 PM): the reason i thought of faigley earlier -- FRAGMENTS OF
    RATIONALITY -- is that he does a solid foucaudian and althusserian
    thing with this kind of mediated comm. it's vvvv early ... and kinda
    wrong. but it was powerful at the time
pplwhoh8snowcanstudyinfl (8:34:44 PM): The *speed* doesn't annoy me as much as the plurality of conversations--we can be
    discussing more than one thing at a time and I have to do investigative work to figure out which comments go with which
    conversations
```

Fig. 6.4. Participants in an instant-messaging discussion use different colors to distinguish their responses.

forum entails concentrating on who is participating and which thread each participant is pursuing, at the point you enter the discussion. Given the speed of these discussions, convention dictates that comments be short and to the point, much more so than in newsgroups or listservs. Successful users join the discussions judiciously, taking care not to overwhelm other participants with too many messages or unannounced changes of the subject under discussion.

Both asynchronous and synchronous forums are used by a variety of online communities—social groups, scholarly or special-interest groups, and business groups. Both kinds of forums can also be used for course-related online discussions, as extensions of the classroom discourse. But remember that when you work, volunteer, or take classes with the other people in an online group, your rhetorical situation is somewhat different from that for online interactions with groups of strangers. You may want to lurk for a while so that you can learn the conventions of an unfamiliar online forum; however, when you know the other participants in an online community, you can plunge right in, remembering to take along your netiquette (see **6d**).

Exercise 1

Join a listserv or online discussion forum devoted to a subject you are currently interested in or researching. Lurk for a few days to a week. Then, introduce yourself to the members of the group, and ask a question related to one of the topics they have been discussing. After reading the responses, write a paragraph describing the experience.

6d Netiquette and online documents

Netiquette (from the phrase "Internet etiquette") is a set of social practices that was developed by Internet users in order to regulate online language and manners. For the most part, you will find electronic communication pleasurable, especially if you try to convey respect.

TIPS FOR NETIQUETTE IN ELECTRONIC MESSAGES AND ONLINE DISCUSSION FORUMS

Audience

- Keep in mind the potential audience(s) for your message: those for whom it is intended and others who may read it.
- Make the subject line of your message as descriptive as possible so that your reader(s) will immediately realize the topic.
- Use a signature line for e-mail to identify yourself and your institution or company.
- Keep your message focused and brief. The recipient's time and bandwidth may be limited, so delete anything that is not essential (previous messages, for instance) when replying.
- Give people adequate time to respond.
- Consider the content of a message, especially anything that the sender might prefer to keep private, before forwarding it to others. When in doubt, seek the sender's permission before forwarding a message.

(Continued on page 126)

(Continued from page 125)

- Respect copyright. Never send something written by someone else or pass it off as your own.
- Do not send junk mail, such as chain letters, petitions, and jokes, unless you know the recipient likes that kind of material.

Style and Presentation

- Take care to establish a tone appropriate for your message and your audience.
- Be sure of your facts.
- Present ideas clearly and logically.
- Pay attention to spelling and grammar.
- Use emoticons (such as :>)) and abbreviations (such as IMHO for "in my humble opinion") only when you are sure your audience will understand them and find them appropriate.
- Do not use all capital letters. OTHERWISE, YOU WILL SEEM TO BE SHOUTING.
- Abusive or profane language is never appropriate.

Context

- Observe what others say and how they say it before you engage in an online discussion; note what kind of information participants find appropriate to exchange.
- If someone is abusive, ignore that person or change the subject. Do not participate in **flaming** (online personal attacks).
- Understand that sarcasm and irony may appear to be personal attacks.

Credibility

- Do not use your school's or employer's network for personal business.
- Be respectful of others even when you disagree, and be kind to new members of an online community.

6e Composing Web documents

The Web offers you the chance to communicate to many different audiences for a variety of purposes. More than an electronic library for information and research, the Web is also a kind of global marketplace, allowing people all over the world to exchange ideas. For example, the home page of The Green Belt Movement (fig. 6.5) presents to an international audience themes that are conveyed throughout the Web site,

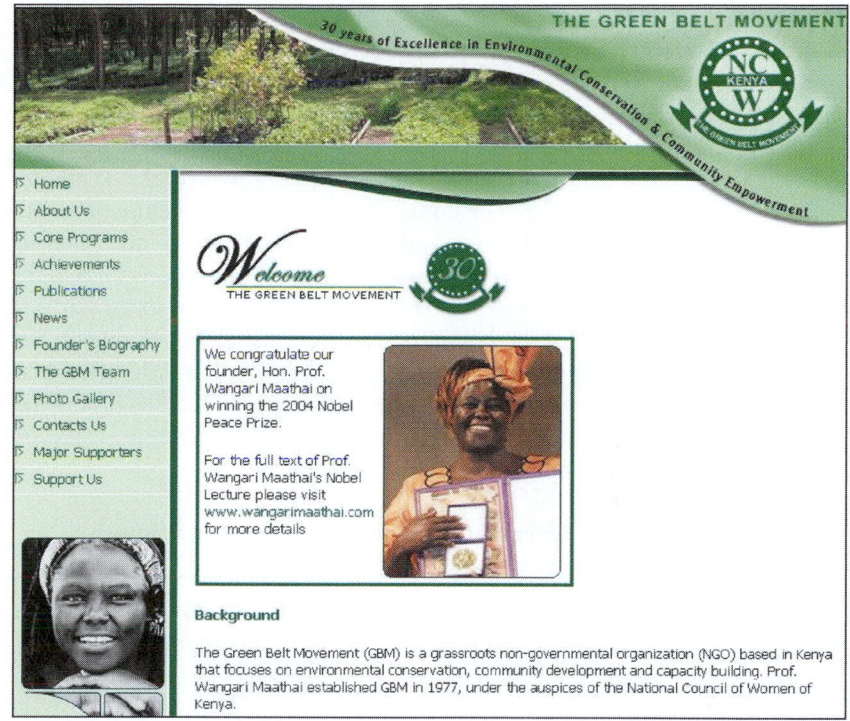

Fig. 6.5. The home page for The Green Belt Movement highlights the activities of the founder, Wangari Maathai, and emphasizes the group's values and focus: volunteerism, environmental conservation, accountability, and empowerment.

emphasizing the group's values and mission. The text on the page is designed to appeal to a diverse audience, from environmental activists to people interested in international development to conservationists planning to start their own grass-roots organizations. Even though the group is based in Kenya, its Web site strives for international appeal by highlighting the founder's Nobel Peace Prize, offering multiple ways of contacting the organization, and providing the option of making an online donation in various currencies.

Your intentions for Web composing may well be more modest than those of The Green Belt Movement. Nevertheless, you will want to remember that Web sites (and other online compositions) are available to diverse audiences, and so their composition should be given as much forethought as possible in terms of context, purpose, and message (see **1a**).

The home page of The Green Belt Movement introduces eleven main topics—from "About Us" to "Support Us"—each of which is the subject of a separate Web page. The **arrangement** (the pattern of organization of the ideas, text, and visual elements in a composition) of the site is clear. The site is thus easy to use: every page maintains the list of main topics in a navigation bar on the left. Arrangement also involves the balance of visual elements and text. The home page is unified by the use of several shades of green for the background, links, and headings, and the entire site is given coherence by the appearance of the organization's logo in the upper-right corner of every page. Finally, the trees shown in the bar that runs across the top of the home page create a visual link to one of The Green Belt Movement's key activities: planting trees as a means of fostering environmental consciousness and concern for the local environment. That visual link combines arrangement and **delivery** (the presentation and interaction of visual elements with content).

(1) Effective Web documents take advantage of the unique features of electronic composition.

Because of the flexible nature of electronic composition, you can have fun planning, drafting, and revising your Web documents.

(a) There are three basic kinds of Web documents.

You will find three types of documents on the Web:

- True electronic documents are constructed as Web pages or sites from the outset and are never intended to appear in print form.
- Print documents are frequently converted to Web pages or sites (for example, an article in the *New York Times* is placed on the newspaper's Web site).
- Electronically created documents (created with Adobe Acrobat or Illustrator, for instance) can be accessed on the Web but are often designed for printing out on paper.

A true electronic document contains **hypertext,** which includes links to other online text, graphics, and animations, as an integral part of its arrangement and content. That is, such a document is created and delivered with text, graphics, and animations integrated into the content. Although print documents converted for use on the Web can have hyperlinks as well as text and images (see 7f–j), these documents are not truly hypertextual compositions because they were not originally created with online capabilities in mind.

(b) Hypertext allows users to customize their approach to a Web document.

As you work to create an effective Web document, you need to consider the influences of hypertext on the use of that document. Basically, the inclusion of hyperlinks transfers control over the sequence of information from you (the writer) to your audience (the user). In other words, Web documents offer unlimited options for ordering the content, as users may click on links in any order they choose. Clearly, the individual interests and personalities of those who read your Web document will lead them to navigate it in different ways. Therefore, you will want to consider how users' differences may affect the intended purpose of your document and try to arrange your document accordingly.

You generally want to plan and compose a Web page or site with a more fluid arrangement of material than is typical of a print document. However, you can create some measure of consistency, as well as help orient users, by carefully placing design elements (such as a logo and color) and by including links to the home page on all other pages.

The visual elements included on a Web page or site create important associations among the concepts and ideas that underlie your online composition. For instance, the central image on The Green Belt Movement's home page (see fig. 6.5) is a photo of the organization's founder, which immediately creates an association for users who already know about Professor Maathai as well as connecting the organization to African women more generally.

Using HTML

To create a Web page, you do not have to understand the computer code (HTML) that allows a browser to display text. Programs such as FrontPage and Netscape Composer, referred to generally as WYSIWYG (What You See Is What You Get) HTML editors, will do such coding for you automatically. But some writers find that knowledge of the basic HTML commands can be useful for troubleshooting and editing a Web page. A number of tutorials on the use of HTML are available on the Web.

(c) Creating accessible Web documents requires attention to audience.

Because the Web gives you access to a wide variety of audiences, it is important to be sure to make your Web document accessible to users who do not have a fast Internet connection or who will access your online composition differently because of limitations in seeing, hearing, or keyboarding. To make your online document accessible, you may wish to simplify the design by using a limited number of graphic elements and to facilitate downloading by using low-resolution images (which have smaller file sizes). To accommodate users with physical disabilities or different means of accessing Web documents (for example, visually impaired users who employ talking computer programs that "read" Web pages), you may want to incorporate basic accessibility features such as **alt tags** (descriptive lines of text for each visual image that can be read by screen-reading software). Such accommodations will make your Web documents accessible to the greatest number of users.

BEYOND THE RULE

EVALUATING A WEB SITE FOR ACCESSIBILITY

Resources are available on the Web to help you evaluate whether your site is accessible to the users you want to reach. In the United States, the federal government's Access Board, in conjunction with the Departments of Education and Justice, has developed standards for electronic and online documents. Called Section 508 guidelines, these are available at **www.access-board.gov**. For more information, visit **www.harbrace.com**.

(2) Planning a Web site involves working out an arrangement for presenting ideas.

As you develop your Web document, you need to keep all the elements of the rhetorical situation in mind. Depending on your audience and purpose, you must decide which ideas or information to emphasize and then work out how best to arrange your Web document to achieve that emphasis. While you are generating the textual content, you need to consider the supplementary links that will help you achieve your overall purpose. But you do not have to do everything at once; fine-tuning the visual design can wait until the content is in place.

When you are planning a Web site, you may find it helpful to create a storyboard or other visual representation of the site's organization.

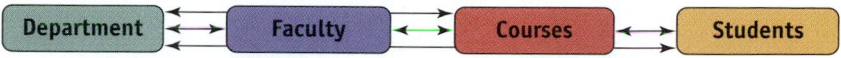

Fig. 6.6. Linear pattern for organizing a Web site.

You can sketch a plan on a sheet of paper or in a word-processing file if your site is fairly simple, or you can use index cards tacked to a bulletin board if it is more complex. If you have some time to devote to the planning process, you may want to learn how to use software such as Web Studio or FrontPage to help you map out your site (such Web site design programs are often available on computers in school labs).

Three basic arrangement patterns—linear, radial, and hierarchical—serve as starting points for planning your Web site. A linear site is easy to set up (see fig. 6.6). Hierarchical and radial arrangements are more complex to develop and may be better suited to group projects. The hierarchical arrangement branches out at each level (see fig. 6.7), and the radial arrangement, in which individual pages can be linked in a variety of sequences, allows the user to determine the sequence in which pages are viewed (see fig. 6.8).

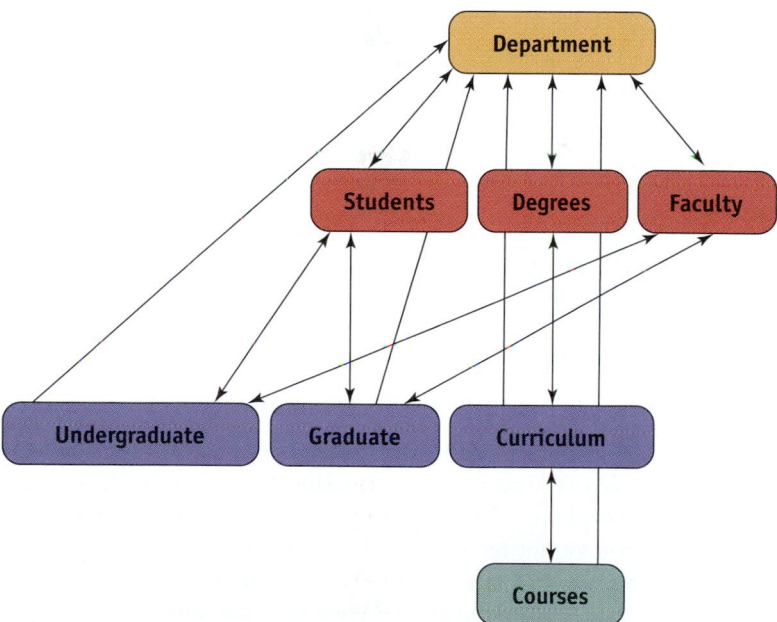

Fig. 6.7. Hierarchical pattern for organizing a Web site.

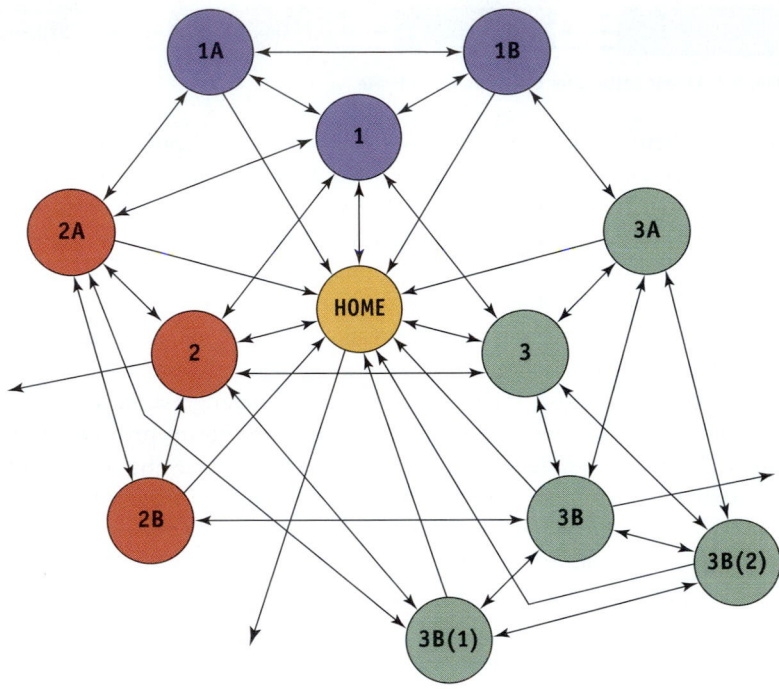

Fig. 6.8. Radial pattern for organizing a Web site.

The possibilities for organizing a Web site are endless. The most important consideration is how the arrangement of your site will affect a user's experience in navigating it. However you decide to organize your site, be sure to represent each main element in your plan. A good plan will be invaluable to you as you draft text, incorporate visual and multimedia elements, and refine your arrangement.

(3) Hyperlinks help fulfill the rhetorical purpose of a Web document.

You are probably accustomed to navigating Web sites by clicking on hyperlinks, one of the distinguishing features of online documents. However, you may not have thought about how valuable hyperlinks can be as tools for Web site development. Some basic principles can help you use hyperlinks effectively in your Web documents.

(a) Hyperlinks enhance the coherence of a Web document.

Hyperlinks should be a vital part of your organizational plan. Considering the ways in which users can exploit these links is an important part of your rhetorical strategy. You need to use hyperlinks purposefully to connect related ideas and to provide additional information. A site map is essential for a large site and helpful for a compact one. Refer again to the home page for The Green Belt Movement (fig. 6.5). Notice that the main sections of the site are featured as a list of links in a navigation bar running along the left side of the home page. A link to a relevant external site—Wangari Maathai's professional Web site—appears within the text. Hyperlinks to the individual pages of a site can provide transitions based on key words or ideas or logical divisions of the document. Because these links provide coherence and help users navigate your Web site, they are powerful rhetorical tools that aid you in creating an effective arrangement.

(b) Hyperlinks can be textual or graphical, linking to internal or external material.

You can use individual words, phrases, or even sentences as textual hyperlinks. Your hyperlinks can also be icons or other graphical elements, such as pictures or logos. If you do use graphical links, be sure that their appearance is appropriate for the transitions you are indicating. In addition, you must get permission for text, graphics, or multimedia elements you draw from other sources. Such material is often free online, but it still requires acknowledgment (see **10c**).

Internal hyperlinks are those that take the user between pages or sections of the Web site in which they appear. When choosing hyperlinks that take the user to content *external* to your Web site (such as a hyperlink in a Web page about tsunamis that links to a meteorologist's Web site), be sure to select sites containing relevant, accurate, and well-presented information. You should also use any contact information provided on a site to ask permission to link to it, and you should check your links periodically to be sure that they are still active.

(c) Hyperlinks have rhetorical impact.

Textual and graphical links establish persuasive rhetorical associations (see chapter **8**) for the user. Compare the rhetorical impact of linking an image of the Twin Towers in New York City to a page about public memorials with that of linking the same image to a page about global

terrorism. Because hyperlinks serve various rhetorical purposes, you will want to evaluate the impact of any you include on your Web document as you plan, compose, and revise it. You will also want to evaluate the rhetorical impact of the hyperlinks on Web documents you are reading or using.

(4) Drafting Web documents can transform your composing process.

As you plan, draft, arrange, and revise a Web document, you will undoubtedly discover better material to include as well as better ways to organize that material. You may draft text for a linear arrangement and then later break the text into separate sections for different pages, which you link in sequence. However, you may find that arrangement and delivery issues related to online documents force you to change your drafting process significantly. You may find that composing a Web site requires you to write the text in chunks. You might write the text for a single page, including hyperlinks, and then move on to the next page. Or you might wait until you revise to add hyperlinks or to replace some of your initial text links with graphical ones. When you replace text with graphics, the visual aspects of your site have become part of your composing process rather than merely decorative elements that are added later.

Once you have drafted and revised your site, get feedback from your classmates or colleagues, just as you would for an essay or report. Since a Web site can include many pages with multiple links and images, you may want to ask for feedback not only about the content of your site but also about layout, graphics, and navigation (see **6f**).

Professional Web developers often put a site that is still in a draft stage on the Web and solicit reactions from users, a process called **usability testing.** The developers then use those reactions to refine the site. Because Web sites are more interactive than printed texts, it is a good idea to seek input from users during site development. To solicit feedback, you may want to specify on your home page how users can contact you. Be careful, though, to consider your own security—you may want to use a free e-mail account through Yahoo! or Hotmail or allow users to post comments directly on your site.

The following checklist will help you plan a Web site and develop ideas for each page.

CHECKLIST for Planning and Developing a Web Site

- What information or ideas should a user take away from your site?
- How does the arrangement of your site reflect your purpose? How does it assist your intended users in understanding your purpose?
- How would you like a user to navigate your Web site? How might different users navigate within the arrangement of your site? To what purpose?
- Should you devote each page to a single main idea or combine several ideas on one page?
- How will you help users return to the home page and find key information quickly?
- What key connections between ideas or pieces of information might be emphasized through the use of hyperlinks?
- Will a user who follows external links be able to get back to your page?
- To ensure that your Web site has more impact than a paper document, have you used Web-specific resources—such as hyperlinks, sound and video clips, and animations—in creating it? How do those multimedia elements help you achieve your purpose?
- Do you need graphics—charts, photos, cartoons, clip art, logos, and so on—to enhance the site so that it will accomplish your purpose? Where should key visual elements be placed to be most effective?
- How often will you update your site?
- How will you solicit feedback for revisions to your site?

Exercise 2

Plan and compile information for a Web page that supports a paper you are writing for one of your classes. If you have access to a program that converts documents to Web pages, try starting with that. Then, critique your Web page.

6f Visual elements and rhetorical purpose

Visual design sends messages to users, inviting them to explore a Web site at the same time as it conveys the rhetorical purpose (see chapter 7). All the design elements of an online document, like the tone and style of a printed one, are rhetorical tools that help you achieve your purpose and reach your intended audience. For instance, if a user has a negative reaction to a photograph of dead seals on a Web site devoted to protecting wildlife, that reaction is likely to affect the user's view of the site in general. When you choose visual elements such as photographs, try to anticipate how your audience may react.

(1) Adhering to basic design principles makes an online document visually pleasing and easy to navigate.

A number of basic principles apply to the visual design of all documents, including those presented on the Web.

- **Balance** involves the way in which design elements used in a document are spatially related to one another. Web pages with a symmetrical arrangement of elements convey a formal, static impression, whereas asymmetrical arrangements are informal and dynamic.
- **Proportion** has to do with the relative sizes of design elements. Large elements attract more attention than small ones and will be perceived as more important.
- **Movement** concerns the way in which our eyes scan a page for information. Most of us look at the upper-left corner of a page first and the lower-right corner last. Therefore, the most important information on a Web page should appear in those locations. Vertical or horizontal arrangement of elements on a page implies stability; diagonal and zigzagging arrangements suggest movement.
- **Contrast** between elements can be achieved by varying their focus or size. For instance, a Web page about the Siberian Husky might show a photo of a dog of this breed in sharp focus against a blurred background; the image of the dog might also be large relative to other elements on the page. In text, you can emphasize an idea by presenting it in a contrasting font—for example, a playful display font such as **Marker Felt Thin** or an elegant script font such as *Edwardian Script*. (Remember, though, that older Web browsers may not display all fonts properly.) An easy-to-read font such as Arial, however, should be used for most of the text on a Web page.

- **Unity** refers to the way all the elements (and pages) of a site combine to give the impression that they are parts of a complete whole. For instance, choose a few colors and fonts to reflect the tone you want to convey, and use them consistently throughout your site. Creating a new design for each page of a Web site makes the site seem chaotic and thus is ineffective.

(2) Color and background play an important rhetorical role in online composition.

Like the other elements of a Web document, color and background are rhetorical tools that can be used to achieve various visual effects. Current Web standards allow the display of a wide array of colors for backgrounds, text, and frames. You can find thousands of background graphics on the Internet or create them with special software.

Designers recommend using no more than three main colors for a document, although you may use varying intensities, or shades, of a color (for example, light blue, dark blue, and medium blue) to connect related materials. Using more than three colors may create confusion on your Web pages. Besides helping to organize your site, color can have other specific effects. Bright colors, such as red and yellow, are more noticeable and can be used on a Web page to emphasize a point or idea. In addition, some colors have associations you may wish to take advantage of. For instance, reds can indicate danger or an emergency, whereas brown shades such as beige and tan suggest a formal atmosphere. Usually, textual hyperlinks appear in a color different from that of the surrounding text on a Web page. Also, links that have not yet been clicked usually appear in one color, and links that have been clicked change to a different color. Select the colors for textual hyperlinks to fit in with the overall color scheme of your document.

Background, too, contributes to a successful Web site. Although a dark background can create a dramatic appearance, it often makes text difficult to read and hyperlinks difficult to see. A dark background can also cause a printout of a Web page to be blank. If you do use a dark background, be sure that the color of the text is bright enough to be readable on screen and that you provide a version that will print clearly. Similarly, a background with a pattern can be dramatic but can obscure the content of a Web page or other online document. For example, the Web page in fig. 6.9 is difficult to read because of the background's busy appearance, which contributes nothing to the purpose or the content of

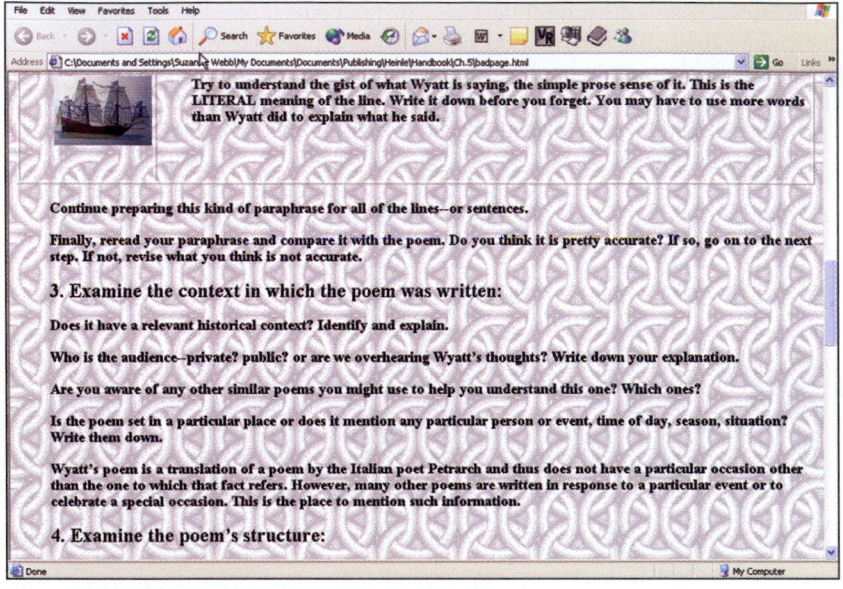

Fig. 6.9. Example of poor Web page design.

the page. Intended to teach close reading of a poem, this page inadvertently sends the message that poetry is as difficult to read as the page itself. If you want to use a pattern for your background, check the readability of the text. You may need to change the color of the text or adjust the pattern of the background to make the page easier to read.

Use different background colors or patterns for different pages of your online document only if you have a good rhetorical reason for doing so (as you might, for instance, if you were using a different color for each of several related categories of information). When you do this, follow the other design principles in **6f(1)** strictly so that your site appears coherent to your audience.

For examples and more information on Web site design and usability, you may want to check out the following:

Jakob Nielsen's *Alertbox* (**www.useit.com/alertbox/9605.html**),

Killersites.com (**www.killersites.com/gettingStarted.jsp**),

and design guru Jeff Glover's *Sucky to Savvy* (**jeffglover.com/ss.html**).

CHECKLIST for Designing an Online Document

- Have you chosen the background and text colors so that users can print copies of your pages if they wish?
- Have you used no more than three colors, but perhaps varied the intensity of one or more of them?
- Does a background pattern on your page make the text difficult or easy to read?
- Have you chosen a single, easy-to-read font such as Arial for most of your text? Are the type styles (bold, italic, and so on) used consistently throughout the document?
- Have you used visual elements sparingly? Are any image files larger than 500K, making it likely that they will take a long time to transfer? If so, can you shrink them by using a lower resolution or a smaller size?
- Have you indicated important points graphically by using bullets or numbers or visually by dividing the text into short blocks?
- Is any page or section crowded? Can users scan the information on a single screen quickly?
- Does each page include adequate white space for easy reading?
- Have you made sure that all links work?
- Have you identified yourself as the author and noted when the site was created or last revised?
- Have you run a spell checker and proofread the site yourself?

VISUAL DOCUMENTS

7

So far, your education has focused mostly on the production and interpretation of written or spoken words. For years, you have been taking writing and public speaking classes, and most of your other courses have required you to use words to communicate your ideas and knowledge. In your daily experiences, however, whether in school or out, you interpret images at least as often as you interpret words. After all, you experience the barrage of images that advertisers use to sell their products, the striking visual works that artists create to express their ideas, the often compelling pictures that various news sources employ to depict important events and people, and even the commonplace images of traffic signs that alert you to potential driving dangers, such as steep hills, winding roads, children at play, or railroad crossings.

All of us derive meanings from visual messages every day—even if we do not know exactly how we "read" images. Just as important as understanding how we make sense of visuals is understanding how we can use them to communicate meaning to others in the texts we compose. In this chapter, you will learn the basic principles of "reading" and using images. This chapter will help you

- express meaning through visual representations (**7a**),
- use principles of visual rhetoric to examine images (**7b**),
- consider the entire image (**7c**),
- analyze the visual elements of an image (**7d**),
- consider the presentation and arrangement of visual elements (**7e**),
- consider relationships between images and accompanying text (**7f**),
- adapt document design to purpose (**7g**),
- recognize conventions of document design (**7h**),
- use design to serve a function (**7i**), and
- use graphics to achieve a particular purpose (**7j**).

7a Visual representations of meaning

What constitutes an "image"? Are images limited to visual representations reproduced on a surface (such as a sheet of paper, a t-shirt, or a computer screen)? Is anything we see an image, or is an image nothing more than an idea—a mental representation that may or may not be associated with an actual object? After all, we frequently speak of things we imagine or "see" with our "mind's eye." For the purposes of this chapter, an **image** is any visual representation that expresses meaning, such as a photograph, painting, etching, sketch, illustration, or diagram. **Visual elements** refer to specific features of images, such as the people or things portrayed. Visual elements also refer to design and layout features of the larger documents in which images appear.

Just as we study a verbal text to understand a writer's messages, we can study a visual representation to understand the message communicated by the image's creator or designer. In many cases, visual and verbal elements appear together in a document, calling for analysis of how the two work together to convey a message. The growth of the Internet has made the purposeful integration of words and visuals more prevalent. Information that was traditionally text-heavy in its print form has become graphics-heavy on the Internet.

7b Examining images using principles of visual rhetoric

Some of the rhetorical principles for understanding the meanings of verbal texts also apply to visual representations. For instance, we can ask questions about the rhetorical situation—the exigence, audience, purpose, and context—of a specific image. We can analyze the image in order to determine its theme, organization, or style. We can even assess whether it makes an argument or seeks to persuade its viewers—and, if so, what rhetorical appeals it uses to argue or persuade.

Despite the extensive overlap of the methods and the terminology for analyzing words and images, we require some specific interpretive tools to examine images. We experience visual representations differently than we do verbal texts, often making different assumptions about how and why the two types of texts were created. When reading verbal texts, for instance, we are accustomed to making distinctions between the various rhetorical methods of development (such as description or argument), but in a visual text, we look for different kinds of clues. As the following sections show, the process of analyzing and interpreting an image requires looking at the image as a whole, the parts of the image, and the context in which it appears.

7c Considering the whole image

Like a verbal text, an image operates within a specific rhetorical situation. So, before analyzing the individual elements of any image, you want to consider the image as a whole, within its rhetorical situation: What exigence does it respond to? Who is the primary audience? What other audiences might have been anticipated? What purpose does the image carry? An illustration in a children's book, for instance, is clearly intended to be seen by children. But another important audience is parents who purchase the book and then read it to their children.

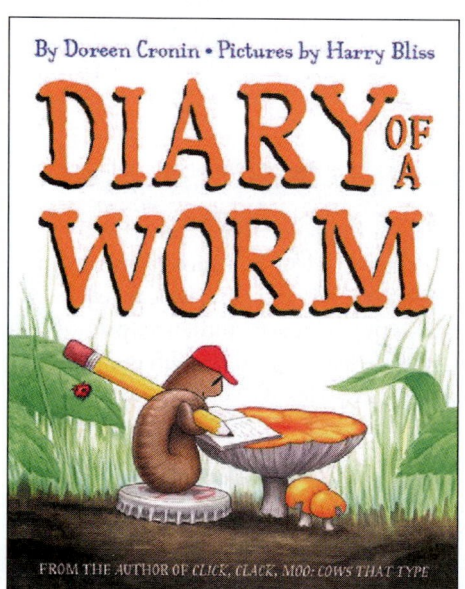

Fig. 7.1. A book's cover image can fulfill multiple purposes.

The purpose of any image may be obvious, unclear, or multiple. Consider the cover of a children's book in fig. 7.1. An obvious purpose of this image is to introduce the book's main character and theme, but it fulfills additional purposes as well: it attracts potential readers to pick up the book and entices parents to buy it for their children. Just as context shapes our interpretation of a verbal message, it informs our interpretation of a visual message. If the image on the cover appeared within the book, it would fulfill a different purpose within a different context. Hang the image in a museum gallery or include it in a scholarly book on the uses of illustration, and the purpose changes again—once more within a different context.

7d Analyzing the elements of an image

After considering the image as a whole, in context, you need to analyze its elements: the participants and the lines and spaces, which work together to convey the meaning of the image to the viewers. **Analysis** is the process of separating a whole into its constituent parts (see chapter 8), so you examine the individual parts of the image as well as their relationships to one another and how each contributes to the whole.

As you conduct an analysis of an image, you need to remember that images are composed by people who wish to communicate with others. Composing is basic to paintings and sketches, and it is also essential to naturalistic photography, which produces images that seem to spring directly from the real world. A photographer chooses where to point the camera, how to set the focus and lighting, when to snap the picture, and how to crop it. In some cases, the photographer may have no direct influence on the positions of objects within the frame; in others, the photographer selects the arrangement and camera angle, making numerous decisions to emphasize certain objects and deemphasize others.

(1) Participants include the image's characters and objects.

Participants, the people, animals, or things that an image depicts, are much like characters in a narrative. The image tells a story about the participants, about their relationships to one another and to the scene in which they are placed. The broader category of participants is divided into **characters** (people, animals, and things that have been personified) and **objects** (inanimate, unthinking things). The nonhuman characters in images often assume human characteristics, prompting viewers to identify with those characters in ways they do not generally identify with objects. Keep in mind that objects (elements that are neither people nor animals) can also function as characters in an image, often because they exhibit human features or are portrayed as having consciousness. In the SpeeDee advertisement in fig. 7.2, for example, an oil can is personified

Fig. 7.2. In many images, objects are personified to enhance their appeal.

as a cheery character, moving forward rapidly and wearing an oil-funnel cap on its "head."

(2) Lines can be used to unite or divide elements of an image.

Lines indicate relationships, connections, or boundaries in an image. A single line may appear as a distinct feature (a pen mark in a cartoon sketch or a brushstroke in a painting); a line or series of lines may constitute one or more of the participants (the straight line formed by the rail of a bridge in a travel magazine photo, a line of picketers photographed in front of a factory, or the curved line of a river in an aerial photograph). Thus, lines may be used to indicate boundaries (the aforementioned line of picketers), connections (two riverbanks joined by the bridge in the magazine photo), or some more abstract relationship among characters (between God and a human in Michelangelo's *The Creation of Adam*, as shown in fig. 7.3).

Just as lines express abstract as well as concrete relationships among objects and characters, **spaces** (unmarked or uninhabited areas of an image) indicate such relationships as well. A large area of space between two objects, for example, may emphasize their difference or isolation from one another. Conversely, two objects placed near one another,

Fig. 7.3. The relationship between God and Adam is expressed by the line of the characters' outstretched arms.

particularly within a larger and otherwise empty space, can be interpreted as belonging together, as being members of the same group.

(3) The viewer is also an element of any image.

Although not a part of the image itself, the **viewer** is another element of the image, since the elements of an image are always positioned in relation to the viewer's viewpoint. When we view an image, we often assume that the objects and characters within it are simply relating to one another, when, in fact, they are also relating to us. The relationship of the image to the viewer is perhaps most powerful in portraits, where the figure portrayed usually appears to be staring directly at the viewer (see fig. 7.4). Clearly, the position of the figure in a portrait—the orientation of body,

Fig. 7.4. Viewers of Escher's self-portrait look up at the figure—but the figure is also looking down at the viewers.

head, and eyes—is determined by assumptions the painter makes about the viewer's position.

7e The presentation and arrangement of visual elements

Once you have identified the most important elements of an image, you also consider characteristics of form, position, visual balance, and surface.

(1) Characteristics of form are shape and size.

Form concerns the shape and size of visual elements. What shapes are dominant in the image, and what impressions or cultural associations do these shapes communicate? Rounded, curving forms may suggest beauty, tranquility, or a natural state, whereas sharp angles and straight lines may suggest strength, industry, or aggressiveness. An image with contrasting forms might suggest a conflict between two different states—for example, the clash of nature with technology. Tall, skinny shapes can often seem less stable than short, stocky shapes. As viewers, we are apt to apply these interpretations whether the forms are humans, personifications, or abstractions.

The sizes of different forms may also provide clues about the image's message. Generally, larger objects are considered dominant, more important to the image's meaning. However, there are exceptions. In the image in fig. 7.11 (on page 152), for example, the focal point is the car. Although it is one of the smaller objects in the photo, the car's centrality is established by its position and its marked contrast to the elements surrounding it.

(2) Characteristics of position are relation, pointers, grouping, and order.

Visual elements can be interpreted according to where and how they are positioned in the image. **Relation** refers to the affiliation of different elements to one another and to space. Consider first the focal point of the image—which participant or space initially captures your attention? How is that element related to others in the image? If more than one element draws your attention, what pathway does your eye follow from one element to another?

Relation also involves the placement of participants with respect to the viewer of the image: which elements are in the foreground, closer to the viewer, and which are in the background, further away? Foreground participants are often, though not always, dominant, intended to be the focus of the viewer's attention. However, in images that use deep perspective (landscapes, for example), the background elements are often most prominent, while the foreground elements serve as a frame that draws the viewer's attention into the image. You will also want to think about the point of view the image creates for the viewer: are the image's elements positioned so that they are viewed from a point directly in front of them, from above or below, or from one side?

The elements in photos, paintings, and drawings do not actually move, but they may act as **pointers,** indicating movement or directing the viewer's gaze in a particular direction. For example, arrows, fingers, and other things that point imply movement between areas of the image that are related somehow. Similarly, the positioning of objects or characters often guides the viewer's attention in a particular direction. In fig. 7.5, notice how the woman's position on an overlook and her outstretched arms and upturned head direct attention toward the blue sky and the scenic valley beyond her.

Elements that slant toward one side of an image can also suggest instability, and this principle applies to real objects as well. For instance, viewers of the Leaning Tower of Pisa and Hanging Rock often feel anxious.

Other characteristics of position provide clues to an image's meaning as well. Similar items placed near each other are often assumed to belong together, as members of a group. Dissimilar items grouped together usually lead to a different assumption. In the composition in fig. 7.6, all of the boats stand out from the deep blue water. However, the eye quickly separates the white powerboat from the colored kayaks, not only because of the dissimilarity of color but also because of the positioning of the

Fig. 7.5. The woman's position and gesture point toward Virginia's natural beauty, thereby encouraging tourism in that state.

Fig. 7.6. A number of boats constitute the composition of this photograph.

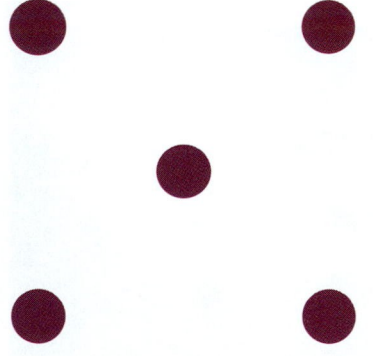

Fig. 7.7. Five dots can be arranged in the pattern of an X.

kayaks. Even though the kayaks have several colors and two sizes, their similar shapes and their clustering lead us to see them as a group.

As viewers, we also notice when elements of an image appear to be arranged in a significant order, in the pattern of a straight line, a circle, a square, a curve, or an X. We tend to interpret an ordered relationship among individual elements, such as the five dots in fig. 7.7, which we perceive as forming two intersecting lines and perhaps even as residing within a square border, as on one side of a die. As we try to make sense of visual elements, we often mentally match them to some familiar pattern rather than seeing them as randomly arranged.

(3) Visual balance can be achieved through symmetry or asymmetry.

In analyzing how elements of an image work together, you need to consider each element in the context of the others. Sometimes, a characteristic of one part of the image can be interpreted only in light of a characteristic of some other part of the image. In fig. 7.6, for example, the bright white powerboat is a prominent element partly because it stands out against the deep blue water, yet the water relates the boat to the other elements in the photo. The powerboat and the cluster of kayaks are two elements that balance each other by virtue of their positions (at opposite ends of the image) and their visual "weight" (both stand out from the blue background). The powerboat is larger, and its whiteness provides a stronger color contrast with the blue of the water. However, the repetitiveness of the kayaks sets off the singularity of the powerboat, and the bright but cool white of the powerboat differs from the generally warmer colors of the kayaks. Thus, overall, the image has balance.

(a) Symmetrical images tend to convey stability.

An image has **symmetry** when its elements are very similar in number, arrangement, form, or other characteristics on both sides of an **axis** (an imaginary horizontal or vertical line that splits an image into two separate parts). Images need not have identical halves to achieve symmetry; many natural forms, such as trees, flowers, and people, appear to be symmetrical, despite minor variations that add visual interest and variety (see fig. 7.8). Small differences between the two parts of an image create visual interest by asking the viewer to study the image more carefully than he or she might do if the image were perfectly symmetrical.

Fig. 7.8. This image of two girls is symmetrical, despite the small differences in the girls' appearance.

(b) Asymmetrical images achieve a more active kind of balance.

Balance in an image can also be achieved through asymmetry of position, color, brightness, size, or other characteristics. In fig. 7.9, for

Fig. 7.9. The right edge of the gravel road provides a diagonal axis.

instance, the right edge of the gravel road provides a strong diagonal axis that cuts the image into two roughly triangular areas, one containing the road itself (which is mostly in the foreground), and the other containing the small white building, which is the image's only other foreground object.

The dramatic tension in the image in fig. 7.9 is immediately apparent. The dominant object on the left is the road, which sweeps from the lower third of the frame nearly to the upper-left corner. But because the right edge of the road begins in the lower-right corner, the road also seems to encroach on the right side of the picture, nearly dominating the image with its detail and breadth. A road has thematic significance, as well; it acts as a pointer, suggesting transition, motion, or even progress. Because the road recedes into the distance, we imagine ourselves traveling through the scene, placing ourselves in the same position the photographer occupied. In balance to the road is the house, sitting peacefully near the center of the large triangular area in the upper right of the photograph. Although the road occupies most of the lower-left half of the photo, it is uniformly gray. The small house, on the other hand, stands in vivid contrast to the tall grass around it, and this high contrast compensates for its small size. Thus, the road and house achieve equal prominence, giving the image balance. The road suggests motion and progress; the house, sitting quietly alongside the deserted road, suggests repose and timelessness. In this case, asymmetry is used to achieve balance.

(c) Imbalance can also be used to express meaning.

Visual balance makes many images effective, but some images are effective precisely because they convey a sense of imbalance, which may communicate change, motion, instability, or unresolved tension. Of course, an image may lack balance simply because the creator has tried but failed to achieve it. As a viewer, you should consider whether a lack of balance is part of an image's message (perhaps because it is reinforced by other aspects of the image) or is instead a sign that the image simply fails to communicate its message.

(4) Characteristics of surface are color, brightness (or intensity), and texture.

Images also possess characteristics of surface that may affect our interpretations. Color, brightness (or intensity), and texture can communicate different messages. Brightly colored objects, for instance, may suggest happiness, youth, liveliness, or even chaos. Reds and oranges suggest heat, energy, or intensity, while blues and greens suggest coolness, stillness, or serenity. Some colors have cultural associations as well. Long-standing symbolic associations with color (such as the western European association of white with virtue and the Chinese association of white with death) may lead different viewers to read the same image differently.

Often, the color or brightness of an individual object is less important than how that characteristic relates to the same feature of surrounding objects. For instance, the brightly colored tree in fig. 7.10 takes center stage because it contrasts in both color and texture with the dim, foggy background; the same tree would be almost invisible if it were located in the midst of a forest of other trees with red leaves and black trunks. In addition, the crisp leaves and rough bark of the tree have much more surface texture than does the soft blurred background of sky, grass, and other trees. Even in the absence of distinct colors or textures, we notice the varying intensity among shaded elements in an image.

Fig. 7.10. A bright tree contrasts with its foggy background.

7f The relationships between image and accompanying text

Although it is worthwhile to know how to analyze images in isolation, most images are accompanied by text. Whether text is placed within an image or an image is inserted into text, combined text-and-image messages address various rhetorical situations and, therefore, can fulfill a variety of purposes. Combinations of text and image are delivered in a wide range of documents, from corporate reports, assembly manuals, and health brochures to comic strips, t-shirts, and billboards.

Your knowledge of the type and purpose of a document will help you interpret the relationship between image(s) and text and the ways in which specific techniques are used to convey meaning. Like any rhetorical analysis, then, analysis of a text-and-image document must begin by determining the basic facts about the rhetorical situation: To what exigence might the creator of the document be responding? Who is the creator? Who makes up the intended audience? What are the resources and constraints of the context? What is the document's purpose?

Whether you are examining a fiscal report, an article in a sports magazine, an advertisement, or a children's book, you want to account for any relationship between text and image in terms of the rhetorical situation of the document as a whole. You need to determine if the image illustrates, reinforces, contradicts, or reiterates the text. For instance, the images in a set of product-assembly instructions are meant to reinforce a process analysis and make assembly easier for the reader. Either words or images might suffice in this case, but, together, they offer more support to the reader. In other cases, however, words and images are a necessary bundle; neither can fulfill the document's purpose alone.

In fig. 7.11, the words and image of the advertisement work together to argue that the reader should consider buying a particular car. The image depicts three vehicles parked in a row in a clearing surrounded by stately trees. A large tree is stretched across the vehicles; the tree appears to have fallen, crushing the two large sport-utility vehicles at either end

Fig. 7.11. Both words and image are necessary to communicate this message.

of the row. The car in the middle, much shorter, is untouched. Considering the image alone, a viewer can see that the small vehicle is the focal point: prominently placed at the center of the frame, its unscathed body provides a strong contrast to the dramatically crushed vehicles on either side. The setting also contributes to the analysis, as the tall trees (one of which has fallen on the bigger, more rugged vehicles) convey an outdoorsy, back-to-nature mood. Ironically, the large vehicles are destroyed; the smaller vehicle remains intact. Along with the compelling image, the advertisement has three elements of verbal text. The first, printed on the license plate of the small car, is "ELECTRIC," a word that alerts the reader to the car's energy efficiency. Second, the sentence "HELLO, PARKING KARMA" appears below that car, the only ecologically sensitive vehicle in the image. Finally, the small type at the bottom of the image reads, "With the right car, everything's better. Introducing the electric ZAP Worldcar L.U.V.," followed by the company's contact information and logo.

Without the accompanying text, the image in fig. 7.11 might convey the message that the center car was lucky to have been parked between two bigger vehicles. But bundled with the three text elements, the message is clarified: the electric vehicle is environment-friendly, whereas the larger vehicles are gas hogs that burn fossil fuel and pollute the environment. The sentence about parking karma strongly suggests that the falling of the tree was not accidental but was, in fact, an ethical consequence; that is, nature is punishing the gas hogs and sparing the electric vehicle. The argument of this advertisement is clear: pick the "right car," one that is compact and environmentally sound, and you will be rewarded.

Any analysis of a document that combines image and text must take into account where the document appears and for whom it is intended. The ZAP Worldcar advertisement would probably work very well in magazines such as *National Geographic* and *Outside*, which cater to ecology-oriented readers for whom nature-friendly arguments are persuasive. If the same advertisement were printed on an urban billboard, on the other hand, its information about the car's compact size—particularly how easy it is to park—might be the most effective part of the message. On the other hand, either message might be completely lost on readers of *Off-Road* magazine, since they are unlikely to accept (or appreciate) the advertisement's criticism of large sportutility vehicles.

Exercise 1

Select a print image that has caught your attention. Write for five to ten minutes in response to that image. Then, analyze it in terms of its elements and its rhetorical situation. Be prepared to share your image and analysis with the rest of the class.

7g Document design and rhetorical purpose

As the volume of information in a particular document increases, so does the importance of its delivery. After all, document design provides readers with necessary cues for acquiring information, whether that information is presented in verbal or visual form. For print as well as Web-based documents, design shapes the reader's first impression and ongoing experience. Effective design addresses the organization of the content, its readability, and the relationship between text and images.

Document design is important from the moment a written communication is conceptualized. Like the arrangement of ideas for an essay (see **3d**), design helps you develop, organize, and present information in a document so as to meet the needs of your audience and fulfill your rhetorical purpose. At first glance, even before reading a word of a document, you see design features that immediately orient you to the document's content, style, quality, and purpose. These first impressions guide your interpretation and greatly influence whether the document achieves its purpose.

Effective document design involves attending to the rhetorical situation and understanding the design conventions for the particular type of document, that is, the physical, spatial, textual, and visual characteristics that reinforce the document's purpose.

7h The conventions of document design

Most academic papers share certain conventions of document design; for example, they have titles, paragraph indents, line spacing, and legible fonts (see the sample papers in **4h** and **8j**). The conventions that apply to academic writing work well in most classroom contexts: they are easy to learn and convenient to produce, and they make reading and commenting easier for instructors. However, when you are producing an academic paper that replicates a real-world communication task in the natural and social sciences or in business (see chapters **17–19**), you may be expected to use the design conventions for that type of professional document. Assignments such as business proposals, scientific research reports, newsletters, and résumés may require you to use specialized headings and even tables, charts, or illustrations. As a writer, you should become familiar with the document design conventions of the various academic disciplines you encounter. Knowing these conventions will help you to produce better documents for courses in these disciplines and in your professional life.

The scientific research report in section **18d** illustrates one set of specialized design conventions. The major sections are signaled by left-aligned, fully capitalized headings (such as "ABSTRACT," "INTRODUCTION," and "RESULTS"). In the results section, the writer includes italicized subheadings (for instance, "*INTERPHASE*" and "*PROPHASE*") to indicate divisions within the section. The use of specific section headings (Abstract, Introduction, Materials and Methods, Results, Discussion, and References) is a convention of scientific research reports; it is also customary in these papers to use subsections when the content within a section can be made clearer by further division. The specific formatting of the section and subsection headings may vary slightly from situation to situation (for instance, some instructors may ask for section titles to be underlined rather than printed in capital letters), but using the system of sections is a firm convention. The example paper demonstrates other conventions, too, such as the use of figures and tables to communicate data and results, and the positions of the figure and table titles (see pages 434–436).

You may be familiar with the conventions called for in some rhetorical situations, but not others. In terms of classroom assignments, for instance, you already possess basic knowledge about how to format and organize your papers. Without consciously learning them, you picked up certain conventions of academic writing—such as printing on white, unlined 8½-by-11-inch paper and using left-aligned paragraphs—from your experiences with such writing. Résumés call for different conventions regarding text placement, paper type, and paragraph structure than do academic papers, and the design conventions

for year-end business reports may vary from company to company. Beyond these context-related variations, you may find that different audiences and different purposes call for further adaptations. You know that novice computer users, for instance, need plenty of diagrams in order to set up their new computers, and general readers often find shorter, more reader-friendly paragraphs more attractive than do members of a specialized audience.

Like most conventions of writing, document design conventions vary somewhat according to the rhetorical situation. Therefore, you will want to evaluate the audience, purpose, and context for your document while you are making design choices. You will also want to consult examples of successful documents to see what design choices have worked for others.

7i Document design and function

Document design choices should support the document's message and purpose; they always arise from an understanding of the rhetorical situation. In fact, many of the principles of visual rhetoric discussed in **7a** through **7f** apply to document design, since readers perceive the pages of documents as visual objects. The following sections will help you make effective choices when designing documents.

(1) Simple, consistent document design reinforces organization, indicating differences and establishing unity.

One of the guiding principles of organization (see **3c–d** and **4c–d**) is to group the parts of a document that go together. In an essay, you use a thesis statement and transitions to show how ideas fit together. You can also use document design principles to reinforce the grouping of ideas, for example, using text formatting to highlight the connections between related sections or placing text sections to establish hierarchical relationships among different types of content.

Many professional documents use ordered relationships to draw together different types of information. Major sections contain subsections; subsections contain paragraphs or lower-level subsections; details may be presented in a bulleted list. Various levels of organization and types of content are signaled by such document design techniques.

Skillful use of these techniques not only reveals differences between types of content but also expresses their hierarchical relationships.

You want to use design elements that are distinctive enough to indicate differences among the document's parts but maintain enough consistency to indicate the overall unity of the document. For instance, headings should be more visually prominent than subheadings, whether that visual prominence results from a larger font, a different color, bolder type, more prominent positioning, or graphical accents (such as lines, boxes, or icons). But it is not necessary to vary every characteristic (font, color, placement on the page, and so on) for each type of content. Too much variety in typeface or other characteristics can actually make a document less effective. After all, if everything is varied, nothing will stand out.

You are already familiar with the ways simple document design choices express hierarchical relationships while emphasizing overall unity. The three-level system of headings used in this book provides a simple example: the numbered and lettered level-one headings, the numbered level-two subheadings, and the lettered level-three subheadings set up a clear hierarchy.

7a Level-one headings introduce major sections in a chapter.

(1) Level-two subheadings introduce topics within the chapter's major sections.

(a) Level-three subheadings are sometimes used to break topics into more specific subtopics.

Despite the ways in which these headings differ, however, they maintain strong connections. All use the same typeface (which is different from that used for the body text) and are boldfaced (so the headings stand out from the body text). All are left-aligned at the edge of the text, and all use **down-style capitalization** (which means that only the first word in a heading is capitalized, rather than capitalizing all the important words). In addition, the headings all use a labeling system involving numbers and letters. The ultimate effect is a coherent system of hierarchically related headings and subheadings, distinctive but clearly belonging to the same "family."

(2) Page design choices organize content into visual blocks.

Page design involves choices about the balance of elements on the page: the use of margins, columns, and grids to position major text elements; the use of lists and tables to organize certain types of information; and the use of white space, lines, shading, and boxes to organize space.

The conventional formats for academic papers will restrict your use of some page design elements (such as lines and boxes, multicolumn layouts, and centered text blocks). For many other writing projects, however, you can use a variety of these elements to improve a document's readability and visual interest. As in all areas of document design, you should base your page design decisions on how well your choices will support the document's purpose rather than how they serve as decoration.

(a) Page grids and columns structure usable areas of the page.

Compare a page from a standard college essay (such as the example in **4h**) with a typical newspaper front page (fig. 7.12). The first thing you might notice is that the newspaper uses images to illustrate the most important stories on the page. Next, you might notice that the text is laid out in multiple columns, not in the single-column format of academic papers. Both characteristics (the use of images and the arrangement of text into columns) work to organize the page into distinct areas. In fact, despite how tightly the text is packed on a newspaper page, you can very quickly separate one story from another by "reading" the visual and spatial clues available to you. Each article begins with a prominent title that spans the columns devoted to that story, and thin vertical lines highlight the boundaries between stories. Even more important, short segments of multiple columns are "chunked" together for each article. Although the page uses a six-column grid, articles extend across multiple columns rather than running from top to bottom along a single column, a technique that emphasizes the distinctiveness and unity of each story and supports readers' habit of reading newspaper articles individually rather than reading the entire page from top to bottom.

A newspaper's page design supports the specific ways in which readers typically use this kind of document. The chunking technique makes it easier to read an article while the paper is folded. The prominent images, the article titles, the text columns, and the compact, single-

Fig. 7.12. The front page of the *New York Times* is designed for ease in reading.

spaced lines all work together to organize the reader's view of the densely packed content. This page design helps readers move from story to story easily and in whatever order they wish, rather than directing them to read from left to right, top to bottom, and page to page (as readers of an academic essay would do).

(b) Lines, boxes, and white space establish borders.

Borders, formed from lines or boxes, help to distinguish one area of a page from another. Borders can also be formed from **white space** (blank areas around blocks of text) or with the use of background shading that highlights blocks of text. Prominent headings (such as those in fig. 7.12) imply borders, as do the folds of a brochure (particularly in combination with other techniques such as background shading or the placement of headings).

(3) Text elements are the basic building blocks of document design.

The most basic level of document design is the textual level. Text elements include typeface, type size, type color or highlighting, leading (the amount of space between lines), and kerning (the amount of space between letters in a word).

Some research has indicated that many readers prefer **serif** typefaces (those with little "feet" at the ends of letters) for large sections of text, either because newspapers and books have traditionally used such typefaces or because the shapes of serif letters are more readily recognized. Document designers often select a clear and readable serif typeface (such as Times New Roman, Palatino, or Garamond) for the body of the document and a **sans serif** (meaning "without feet") typeface (such as Arial, Century Gothic, or Tahoma) for headings, figure titles, and other visual accents.

Although word-processing software makes it easy to use a variety of fonts and type sizes on a single page, excessive font variation detracts from your content and distracts readers. It is better to use a single, highly legible font for the body text of a document, possibly complemented by a different font for headings and labels (if your document uses these elements). In addition, except for purely decorative purposes, avoid the more elaborate, hard-to-read display fonts, such as 𝕺𝕷𝕯 𝕰𝖓𝖌𝖑𝖎𝖘𝖍 and *Script*.

The color of type can also affect legibility. Although ink-jet printers offer the option of printing text in color, you should not do so in academic papers unless your instructor has specifically indicated that this formatting is acceptable. (Some documents such as flyers or announcements can be made more effective by the use of colored type.) Most instructors prefer that you use black ink (and a font such as Times Roman) for traditional academic assignments because it produces clear, dark text that is easy to read.

Word-processing software makes it easy to use italics for titles and foreign words and phrases, but you should resist the temptation to use italics or boldfacing for emphasizing words or phrases within lines of text. (See **42f**.) With respect to the use of italics, follow the recommendations of the style manual for the specific discipline in which you are writing.

Compare the two versions of a short document presented in fig. 7.13. The first version uses a hard-to-read typeface, no highlighting of any text or headings, uniform double-spaced lines, and uniformly indented paragraphs. With its undifferentiated lines of text, this document is harder to read than the other. A few modest design changes improve the layout and readability of the second version.

The typeface in the first version (Courier, once a typewriter standard) is replaced in the second version by Palatino, a more space-efficient typeface. The headings in the second version are set in Tahoma to distinguish them from the rest of the content; boldfacing reinforces this distinction. The body text is single-spaced, with an extra line space between paragraphs. This use of extra space makes the paragraphs stand apart from one another more clearly and also makes it unnecessary to indent the first line of each paragraph. Finally, a horizontal line between the memo header and the memo body reinforces the boundary between these two parts of the document. These subtle changes improve readability, while at the same time they make the text more space-efficient; space efficiency and legibility do not have to work at cross purposes.

7j Graphics and purpose

In addition to enhancing the visual characteristics of the text, document designers often incorporate visual displays, or **graphics,** into their documents. Graphics can be used to illustrate a concept, present data, provide visual relief, or simply attract readers' attention. Different types of graphics—tables, charts or graphs, and pictures—serve different purposes, and some may serve multiple purposes in a given document. Any of these types of graphics can enable readers to capture a message more quickly than they would by reading long sections of text. However, if there is any chance that readers might not receive the intended message, it is a good idea to supplement graphics with text discussion.

DATE: Friday, September 19, 2003
TO: Statewide Insurance Corporation
FROM: John Doe, Policy #H24-6802-46
SUBJECT: Hurricane Isabel Damage Report, Claim #: 12345-678-901234-56

The following damage to property insured by Policy #H24-6802-46 has resulted from Hurricane Isabel.

Rain has leaked through the roof to the vaulted ceiling in the living room. Three water marks have appeared on the ceiling, covering approx. 6' x 4' area. Damage is also apparent in the flashing at the chimney base.

Several shingles are missing or broken on both sides of the roof.

Water has entered the attic from the west end gable vent, soaking the wall sheathing and insulation on one end wall.

Date: Friday, September 19, 2003

To: Statewide Insurance Corporation

From: John Doe, Policy #H24-6802-46

Subject: Hurricane Isabel Damage Report, Claim #: 12345-678-901234-56

The following damage to property insured by Policy #H24-6802-46 has resulted from Hurricane Isabel.

Rain has leaked through the roof to the vaulted ceiling in the living room. Three water marks have appeared on the ceiling, covering approx. 6' x 4' area. Damage is also apparent in the flashing at the chimney base.

Several shingles are missing or broken on both sides of the roof.

Water has entered the attic from the west end gable vent, soaking the wall sheathing and insulation on one end wall.

Fig. 7.13. Two versions of an insurance agent's memo.

(1) Tables organize data so that they can be easily accessed and compared.

Tables use a row-and-column arrangement to organize data (numbers or words) spatially; they are especially useful for presenting great amounts of numerical information in a small space, enabling the reader to draw direct comparisons among data or even to locate specific pieces of data. When you design a table, be sure to label all of the columns and rows accurately and to provide both a title and a number for the table. Table number and title traditionally appear above the table, as table 7.1 demonstrates, and any notes or source information should be placed below it.

Most word-processing programs have settings that let you insert a table wherever you need one. You can determine how many rows and columns the table will have, and you can also size each row and each column appropriately for the information it will hold.

TABLE 7.1
Modified Monthly Tornado Statistics

Month	2002 Prelim.	2001 Final	2000 Final	1999 Final	3-Year Average
Jan	8	5	16	212	77
Feb	2	30	56	22	32
March	30	34	103	56	66
April	114	131	136	177	140
May	130	235	241	311	256
June	?	147	135	289	219
Jul	?	123	148	102	128
Aug	?	69	52	79	62
Sep	?	85	47	56	58
Oct	?	121	63	17	60
Nov	?	112	48	7	37
Dec	?	?	26	15	16
Total	290	1212	1071	1343	1151

Source: National Weather Service.

(2) Charts and graphs provide visual representations of data.

Like tables, charts and graphs display relationships among statistical data in visual form; unlike tables, they do so using lines, bars, or other visual elements rather than just letters and numbers. Data can be displayed in several different graphic forms: pie charts, line graphs, and bar charts are the most common examples.

Pie charts are especially useful for showing the relationship of parts to a whole (see fig. 7.14), but they can only be used to display data that add up to 100 percent (a whole).

Line graphs show the relationship between one variable (measured on the vertical y axis) and another variable (measured on the horizontal x axis) that changes in a regular way. The most common x-axis variable is time. Line graphs are very good at showing how a variable changes over time. A line graph might be used, for example, to illustrate progression of sleep stages during one night (see fig. 7.15), increases or decreases in student achievement from semester to semester, or trends in financial markets over a number of years.

Bar charts show correlations between two variables that do not involve smooth changes over time. For instance, a bar chart might illustrate gross national product for several nations, the relative speeds of various computer processors, or statistics about the composition of the U.S. military (see fig. 7.16).

In addition to charts, graphs, and tables, a variety of other graphics can be used to clarify complex ideas or to illustrate relationships among

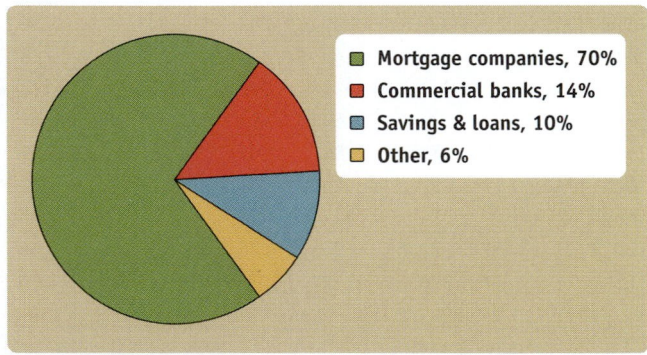

Fig. 7.14. Pie chart showing issuers of mortgage-based securities.

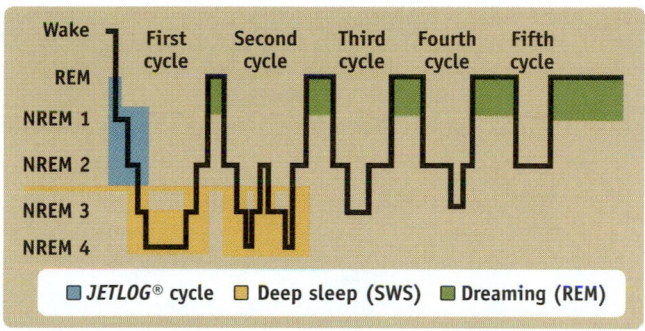

Fig. 7.15. Graph of nightly sleep stages.

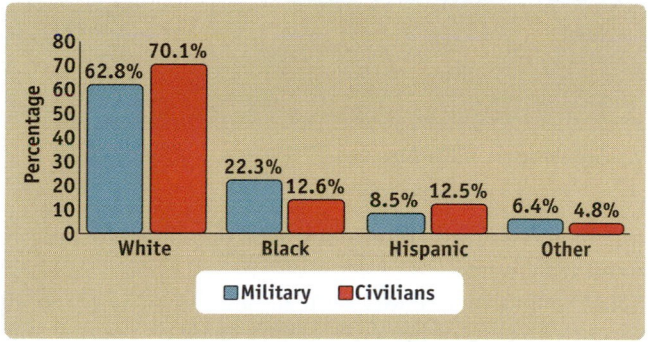

Fig. 7.16. Bar chart illustrating the composition of the U.S. military.

concepts. Figure 7.17 (a process diagram of the water cycle) uses a simple graphical convention (superimposing arrows and labels on a semirealistic drawing) to present information that, in textual form, would require a great deal of space. This process diagram shows the movement of water in different forms through the environment.

(3) Pictures illustrate how objects appear.

Pictures include photos, sketches, technical illustrations, paintings, icons, and other visual representations. Photographs are often used to reinforce textual descriptions or to show a reader exactly what something looks like. Readers of a used-car ad, for instance, will want to see exactly what the car looks like, not an artistic rendition of its appearance. Likewise, a Costa Rican travel brochure

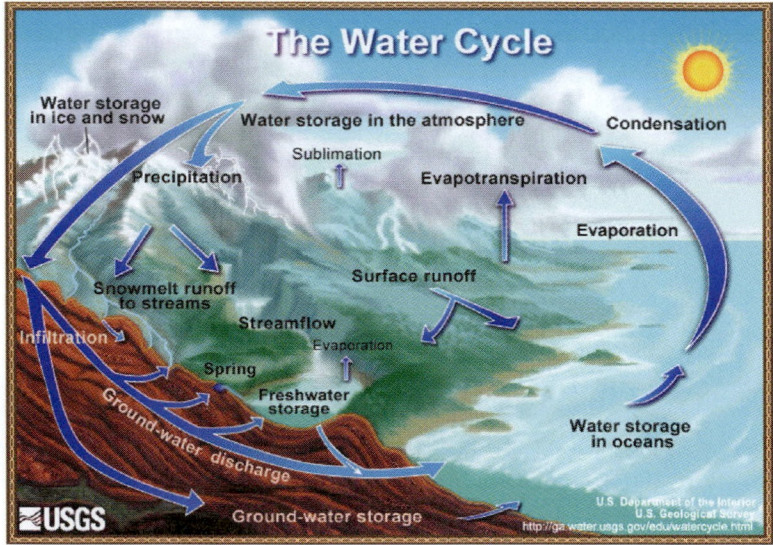

Fig. 7.17. Process diagram of the water cycle.

will contain lots of full-color photos of dazzling beaches, verdant forests, and azure water.

But photographs are not always the most informative type of picture. Compare the two parts of fig. 7.18: a photograph of a printer and a line drawing of the same printer. While the photograph is a more realistic image of the actual printer, the lines of the illustration reveal more clearly the printer's important features: buttons, panels, and so forth. With its simple lines and clear labels, the illustration is well suited to its purpose: to help the viewer set up and start to use the printer. Line drawings enable the designer of a document such as a user manual to highlight specific elements of an object while deemphasizing or eliminating unnecessary information. The addition of arrows, pointers, and labels adds useful detail to such an illustration.

Your ability to interpret images and use them in documents is greater than you might imagine. You have had years of practice at doing just those things—from responding to advertising to composing class papers, science projects, and 4-H exhibits. Consciously applying your knowledge to these tasks will help make your interactions with documents more productive.

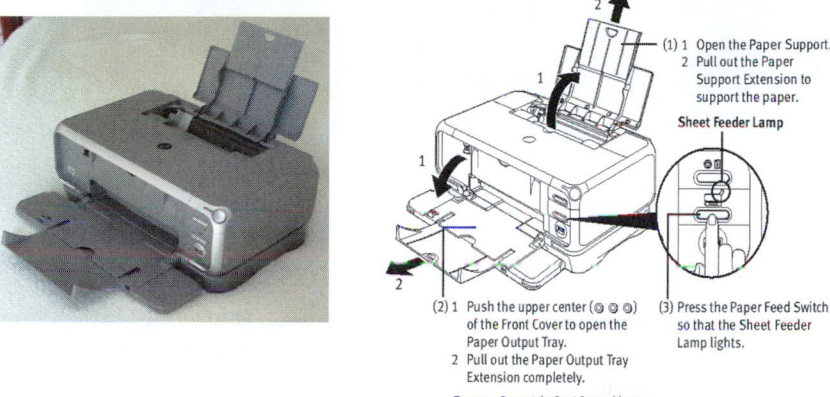

Fig. 7.18. A photo and a line drawing of the same printer.

Exercise 2

If you can locate a document that contains one or more images and that you composed for another class or an extracurricular activity, bring it to class or photograph it. Be prepared to explain how you created the document and chose the image(s). If you cannot locate a copy of such a document, write for ten to fifteen minutes, reconstructing the process by which you created the document, including what you knew how to do before you started and what you learned as you progressed.

WRITING

ARGUMENTS

8

You write arguments on a regular basis. When you send your business partner a memo to tell her that a client needs to sign a contract, when you e-mail your parents to ask them for a loan, when you petition your academic advisor for a late drop, or when you demand that a mail-order company refund your money, you are writing an argument. You are expressing a point of view and then using logical reasoning to invite a specific audience to accept that point of view or adopt a course of action. *Argument* and *persuasion* are often used interchangeably, but they differ in two basic ways. Traditionally, **persuasion** has referred to winning or conquering with the use of emotional reasoning, whereas **argument** has been reserved for the use of logical reasoning to convince listeners or readers. But because writing often involves some measure of "winning" (even if it is only gaining the ear of a particular audience) and uses both emotion and reason, this book uses *argument* to cover the meanings of both terms.

When writing arguments, you follow the same process as for all your writing: planning, drafting, and revising, as well as attending to

Argumentation is about problem solving.

audience and context (see **1d–e**). Argumentative writing is distinct from other kinds of writing in its emphasis on the inseparability of audience and purpose. Recognizing and respecting the beliefs, values, and expertise of a specific audience is the only way to achieve the rhetorical purpose of an argument, which goes beyond victory over an opponent. Argument can be an important way to invite exchange, understanding, cooperation, consideration, joint decision making, agreement, or negotiation of differences. Thus, argument serves three basic and sometimes overlapping purposes: to analyze a complicated issue or question an established belief, to express or defend a point of view, and to invite or convince an audience to change a position or adopt a course of action.

This chapter will help you

- determine the purpose of an argument (**8a**),
- consider different viewpoints (**8b**),
- distinguish fact from opinion (**8c**),
- take a position or make a claim (**8d**),
- provide evidence to support a claim (**8e**),
- use the rhetorical appeals to ground an argument (**8f**),
- arrange ideas (**8g**),
- use logical reasoning (**8h**),
- avoid rhetorical fallacies (**8i**), and
- analyze an argument (**8j**).

As you proceed, you will understand the importance of determining your purpose, identifying your audience, marshaling your arguments, arguing ethically, and treating your audience with respect.

8a Determining the purpose of your argument

To what exigence are you responding? What is your topic? Why are you arguing about it? What is at stake? What is likely to happen as a result of making this argument? How important are those consequences? Who is in a position to act or react in response to your argument?

When writing an argument, you need to establish the relationships among your topic, purpose, and audience. The relationship between audience and purpose is particularly significant because the audience often shapes the purpose.

- If there is little likelihood that you can convince members of your audience to change a strongly held opinion, you might achieve a great deal by inviting them to understand your position.
- If the members of your audience are not firmly committed to a position, you might be able to convince them to agree with the opinion you are expressing or defending.
- If the members of your audience agree with you in principle, you might invite them to undertake a specific action—such as voting for the candidate you are supporting.

No matter how you imagine those in your audience responding to your argument, you must establish **common ground** with them, stating a goal toward which you both want to work or identifying a belief, assumption, or value that you both share. In other words, common ground is a necessary starting point, regardless of your ultimate purpose.

8b　Considering differing viewpoints

If everyone agreed on everything, there would be no need for argument, for taking a position or questioning one held by anyone else. But everyone doesn't agree. Thus, a good deal of the writing you will do in school or at work will require you to take a position on a topic, an arguable position. The first step toward finding a topic for argumentation is to consider issues that inspire different opinions.

Behind any effective argument is a question that can generate more than one reasonable answer. If you ask "Is there racism in the United States?" almost anyone will agree that there is. But if you ask "Why is there still racism in the United States?" or "What can Americans do to eliminate racism?" you will hear different answers. Answers differ because people approach questions with various backgrounds, experiences, and assumptions. As a consequence, they are often tempted to use reasoning that supports what they already believe. As a writer, you, too, will be tempted to employ such reasoning, and doing so is a good place to start. But as you expand and shape your argument, you will want to demonstrate not only that you are knowledgeable about your topic but also that you are aware of and have given fair consideration to other views about it. To be knowledgeable and yet respectful of others' views constitutes a worthy goal.

When you write an argument, you are trying to solve a problem or answer a question—with or for an audience. When you choose a topic for argumentation, you will want to take a stance that allows you to question, that provides you an exigence (or reason) for writing. First, you focus on a topic, on the part of some general subject that you will address in your essay (see **3b**), and then you pose a question about it. As you craft your question, consider the following: (1) your own values and beliefs with respect to the question, (2) how your assumptions might differ from those of your intended audience, and (3) how you might establish common ground with members of your audience, while at the same time respecting any differences between your opinion and theirs. The question you raise will evolve into your **thesis,** an arguable statement.

The most important criterion for choosing an arguable statement for an essay is knowledge of the topic, so that you will be an informed writer, responsive to the expectations of your audience. When you are in a position to choose your own topic, you can draw on your knowledge of current events, politics, sports, fashion, or a specific academic subject. Topics may present themselves on television or the Web, as you find yourself agreeing or disagreeing with what you hear and read.

To determine whether a topic might be suitable, make a statement about the topic ("I believe strongly that . . . " or "My view is that . . . ") and then check to see if that statement can be argued.

TIPS FOR ASSESSING AN ARGUABLE STATEMENT ABOUT A TOPIC

- What reasons can you think of to support your belief about the topic? List those reasons.

- Who or what groups might disagree with your statement? Why? List those groups.

- Do you know enough about this topic to discuss other points of view? Can you find out what you need to know?

- What are other viewpoints on the topic and reasons supporting those viewpoints? List them.

- What is your purpose in writing about this topic?

- What do you want your audience to do in response to your argument? In other words, what do you expect from your audience? Write out your expectation.

If you can answer all these questions to your satisfaction, you should feel confident about your topic. As you move further into the writing process, researching and exploring your topic in the library or on the Web (see chapter **9**), you may be able to clarify your purpose and improve your thesis statement.

8c Distinguishing between fact and opinion

When you develop your thesis statement into an argument, you use both facts and opinions. It is important to distinguish between these two kinds of information so that you can use both to your advantage, especially in terms of establishing your credibility (see **8f(1)**), an essential feature of successful argumentation. **Facts** are reliable pieces of information that can be verified through independent sources or procedures. **Opinions,** on the other hand, are assertions or inferences that may or may not be based on facts. Opinions that are widely accepted, however, may seem to be factual when they are not.

Just because facts are reliable does not mean that they speak for themselves. Facts are significant only when they are used responsibly to support a claim; otherwise, a thoughtful and well-informed opinion might have more impact. To determine whether a statement you have read is fact or opinion, ask yourself questions like these: Can it be proved? Can it be challenged? How often is the same result achieved? If a statement can consistently be proved true, then it is a fact. If it can be disputed, then it is an opinion.

Fact	Milk contains calcium.
Opinion	Americans should drink more milk.

To say that milk contains calcium is to state a well-established fact: it can be verified by consulting published studies or by conducting laboratory tests. Whether or not this fact is significant depends on how a writer chooses to use it. As an isolated fact, it is unlikely to seem significant. But to say that Americans need to drink more milk is to express an opinion that may or may not be supported by facts. When considering the statement "Americans should drink more milk," a thoughtful reader might ask, "How much calcium does a human need? Why do humans need calcium? Is cow's milk good for humans? Might leafy green vegetables provide a richer source of calcium?" Anticipating questions such as these can help you develop an argument. These sorts of questions also help you recognize the evidence that will best support your argument, where you can obtain such evidence, and what to do if you discover conflicting evidence.

The line between fact and opinion is not always clear. Therefore, writers and readers of arguments should always be prepared to interpret and assess the reliability of the information before them, evaluating the beliefs supporting the argument's stance, the kinds of sources used, and the objections that could be made to the argument.

Exercise 1

Determine which of the following statements are fact and which are opinion. In each case, what kind of verification would you require in order to accept the statement as reliable?

1. Toni Morrison won the Nobel Prize in literature in 1993.
2. Women often earn less money than men who hold the same positions.
3. *The Lion King* was the best movie ever made about animals.
4. Writing well is a gift, like musical genius.
5. A college degree guarantees a good job.
6. Santa Fe is the oldest U.S. city that is a state capital.
7. Running is good for your health.
8. The United States won World War II.
9. In combination, ammonia and chlorine bleach result in a poisonous gas.
10. Researchers will find a cure for AIDS.

8d Taking a position or making a claim

When making an argument, a writer takes a position on a particular topic. Whether the argument analyzes, questions, expresses, defends, invites, or convinces, the writer needs to make clear his or her position. That position, which is called the **claim**, or **proposition**, clearly states what the writer wants the audience to do with the information being provided. The claim is the thesis of the argument and usually appears in the introduction and sometimes again in the conclusion.

(1) Effective writers claim no more than they can responsibly support.

Claims vary in extent; they can be absolute or moderate, large or limited. Absolute claims assert that something is always true or false, completely good or bad; moderate claims make less sweeping assertions.

Absolute claim	College athletes are never good students.
Moderate claim	Most colleges have low graduation rates for their athletes.
Absolute claim	Harry Truman was the best president we have ever had.
Moderate claim	Truman's domestic policies helped advance civil rights.

Moderate claims are not necessarily superior to absolute claims. After all, writers frequently need to take a strong position in favor of or against something. But the stronger the claim, the stronger the evidence needed to support it. Be sure to consider the quality and the significance of the evidence you use—not just its quantity.

(2) Types of claims vary in terms of how much they encompass.

(a) Substantiation claims assert that something exists.
Without making a value judgment, a **substantiation claim** makes a point that can be supported by evidence.

> The job market for those who just received a PhD in English is limited.
> The post office is raising rates again.

(b) Evaluation claims assert that something has a specific quality.
According to an **evaluation claim,** something is good or bad, effective or ineffective, attractive or unattractive, successful or unsuccessful.

> The graduation rate for athletes at Penn State is very high compared with that at the other Big Ten universities.
> The public transportation system in Washington, DC, is reliable and safe.

Sometimes, writers use evaluation claims as a way to invite their audience to consider an issue.

It is important for us to consider the graduation rate of college athletes.

(c) Policy claims call for a specific action.

When making **policy claims,** writers call for something to be done.

We must find the funds to hire better qualified high school teachers.

We need to build a light-rail system linking downtown with the airport and the western suburbs.

Policy claims, such as the one made by this famous Army recruiting poster, call for a specific action.

Much writing involves substantiation, evaluation, and policy claims. When writing about the job market for those with new PhDs in English, you might tap your ability to substantiate a claim; when writing about literature (see chapter **16**), you might need to evaluate a character. Policy claims are commonly found in arguments about social issues such as health care, social security, and affirmative action. These claims often grow out of substantiation or evaluation claims: first, you demonstrate that a problem exists; then, you establish the best solution for that problem.

TIPS FOR MAKING A CLAIM ARGUABLE

- Write down your opinion.
- Describe the situation that produced your opinion.
- Decide who constitutes the audience for your opinion and what you want that audience to do about your opinion.
- Write down the verifiable and reliable facts that support your opinion.
- Using those facts, transform your initial opinion into a thoughtful claim that considers at least two sides to the issue under discussion.
- Ask yourself, "So what?" If the answer to this question shows that your claim leads nowhere, start over, beginning with the first tip.

As an example of transforming an opinion into an arguable claim, consider the following scenario. Helen thinks that air pollution is a problem. She describes the situation that has inspired her opinion: she was jogging on a busy street and had difficulty breathing because of the excessive car exhaust. Describing this situation helps Helen focus her opinion. She decides to narrow her topic to reducing automobile emissions. Next, she imagines an audience for her topic, an audience who can do something about this issue. She decides to write to automobile manufacturers. Helen knows that she needs to do some research on this topic in order to write a convincing argument, so she researches the physics of automobile emissions and realizes that, with just a small amount of effort, car manufacturers could improve the efficiency of most automobile engines—and thereby reduce emissions. She also conducts a survey of fellow students and learns that most of them would prefer to buy cars with more efficient engines. Helen now has a specific audience, a specific claim for their consideration, and a specific reason for her audience to agree with her claim: despite a slight increase in automobile price, automobile manufacturers should work to produce more efficient engines; if they do so, young adults will be more likely to purchase their automobiles.

Exercise 2

The following excerpt is from an argument analyzing racial strife in the United States, written by Cornel West, a scholar specializing in race relations. Evaluate the claims it presents. Are they absolute or moderate? Can you identify a substantiation or evaluation claim? What policy claim is implicit in this passage?

[1]To engage in a serious discussion of race in America, we must begin not with the problems of black people but with the flaws of American society— flaws rooted in historic inequalities and longstanding cultural stereotypes. [2]How we set up the terms for discussing racial issues shapes our perception and response to these issues. [3]As long as black people are viewed as a "them," the burden falls on blacks to do all the "cultural" and "moral" work necessary for healthy race relations. [4]The implication is that only certain Americans can define what it means to be American—and the rest must simply "fit in." —**CORNEL WEST**, *Race Matters*

8e Providing evidence for an effective argument

Effective arguments are well developed and supported. You should explore your topic in enough depth to have the evidence to support your position intelligently and ethically, whether that evidence is based on personal experience or research (see chapters **3** and **9**). You will want to consider the reasons others might disagree with you and be prepared to respond to those reasons.

(1) An effective argument clearly establishes the thinking that leads to the claim.

If you want readers to take your ideas seriously, you must communicate the reasons that have led to your position, as well as the values and assumptions that underlie your thinking. When you are exploring your topic, make a list of the reasons that have led to your belief (see **3d** and **3f**). For example, when Laura Klocke was working on her argumentative essay (at the end of this chapter; see pages 198–204), she listed the following reasons for her belief that fair trade coffee should be used exclusively at her school:

1. The average price of coffee is $12.00/lb., while the average coffee grower is paid only 20–40 cents/lb.
2. The average latte costs $3.50, while the average coffee farmer makes $3.00/day.
3. The University of St. Thomas is committed to producing "morally responsible individuals who combine cultural awareness and intellectual curiosity." St. Thomas could easily support only fair trade coffee.

Although it is possible to base an argument on one good reason (such as "Buying fair trade coffee is the right thing to do"), doing so can be risky. If your audience does not find this reason convincing, you have no other support for your position. When you show that you have more than one reason for believing as you do, you increase the likelihood that your audience will find merit in your argument. Sometimes, however, one reason is stronger—and more appropriate for your audience—than several others you could advance. To develop an argument for which you have only one good reason, explore the bases underlying your reason: the values and assumptions that led you to take your stand. By demonstrating the thinking behind the single reason on which you are building your case, you can create a well-developed argument.

Whether you have one reason or several, be sure to provide sufficient evidence from credible sources to support your claim:

- facts,
- statistics,
- examples, and
- testimony, from personal experience or professional expertise.

This evidence must be accurate, representative, and sufficient. Accurate information should be verifiable by others (see **8c**). Recognize, however, that a writer may provide you with information that is accurate but neither representative nor sufficient, because it was drawn from an exceptional case, a biased sample, or a one-time occurrence. If, for example, you are writing an argument about the advantages of using Standardized English but draw all of your supporting evidence from a proponent of the English-Only movement, your evidence represents only the views of that movement. If you draw all of your evidence from just one person (Bill Cosby, for instance, has strong views on the use of Standardized English, especially as a means to stamp out the Ebonics movement), your evidence is neither representative of all the support for the use of Standardized English, nor is it sufficient to support a thoughtful argument. In order to represent a wider viewpoint, you should gather supporting evidence from sociolinguists, speakers of other dialects and languages, education specialists, professors, and other experts. In other words, consult more than a single source. (See chapter **9**.)

When gathering evidence, be sure to think critically about the information you find. If you are using the results of polls or other statistics or statements by authorities, determine how recent and representative the information is and how it was gathered. Consider, too, whether the authority you plan to quote is qualified to address the topic under consideration and is likely to be respected by your readers.

Whatever form of evidence you use—facts, statistics, examples, or testimony—you need to make clear to your audience exactly *why* and *how* the evidence supports your claim. As soon as the relationship between your claim and your evidence is clear to you, make that connection explicit to your readers, helping them understand your thinking.

(2) Effective arguments respond to diverse views.

Issues are controversial because good arguments can be made on all sides. Therefore, effective arguments consider and respond to other points of view, fairly and respectfully. In order for your argument to be effective and convincing, your audience must realize that you are knowledgeable about points of view other than your own. The most common strategy for addressing opposing points of view is referred to as **refutation:** you introduce diverse views and then respectfully demonstrate why you disagree with each of them. As you consider opposing points of view, you are likely to discover some you cannot refute, perhaps because they are based in a belief system markedly different from your own. You are also likely to discover that some of the other views have real merit. If you understand the reasons behind opposing viewpoints but remain unconvinced, you will need to demonstrate why.

When you find yourself agreeing with a point raised on another side of the issue, you can benefit from offering a **concession.** By openly admitting that you agree with opponents on one or more specific points, you demonstrate that you are fair-minded (see **8f(1)**) and at the same time increase your credibility. Concessions also increase the likelihood that opponents will be inclined to find merit in your argument.

Whether you agree or disagree with other positions, work to recognize and assess them. It is hard to persuade people to agree with you if you insist that they are entirely wrong. If you admit that they are partially right, they are more likely to admit that you could be partially right as well. In this sense, then, argument involves working with an audience as much as getting them to work with you.

Exercise 3

The following paragraph is taken from an argument by Martin Luther King, Jr., in which he defends the struggle for civil rights against public criticism from a group of prominent clergymen. Write a short analysis of this paragraph in which you note (a) an opposing viewpoint to which he is responding, (b) a refutation he offers to this viewpoint, (c) a concession he makes, and (d) any questions this excerpt raises for you.

[1]You express a great deal of anxiety over our willingness to break laws. [2]This is certainly a legitimate concern. [3]Since we so diligently urge people to obey the Supreme Court's decision of 1954 outlawing segregation in the public schools, at first glance it may seem rather paradoxical for us consciously to break laws.

[4]One may well ask: "How can you advocate breaking some laws and obeying others?" [5]The answer lies in the fact that there are two types of laws, just and unjust. [6]I would be the first to advocate obeying just laws. [7]One has not only a legal but a moral responsibility to obey just laws. [8]Conversely, one has a moral responsibility to disobey unjust laws. [9]I would agree with St. Augustine that "an unjust law is no law at all."

—**MARTIN LUTHER KING, JR.,** "Letter from Birmingham Jail"

8f   Using the rhetorical appeals to ground your argument

Effective arguments always incorporate several appeals to the audience simply because logical reasoning—providing good reasons—is rarely enough (see **8e** and **8h**). Human beings do not believe or act on the basis of facts or logic alone; if we did, we would all agree and act accordingly. In reality, we believe and act on the basis of our own concerns, experiences, and needs. When we do not listen to another point of view, we simply do not want to change our minds. An effective argument, then, is one that gets a fair hearing. If you want your views to be heard, understood, and maybe even acted on, you need to follow the necessary steps to gain a hearing.

(1) Three rhetorical appeals can shape any argument.

Aristotle, a Greek philosopher who lived over two thousand years ago, was the first to help speakers shape effective arguments through a combination of three persuasive strategies: the **rhetorical appeals** of ethos, logos, and pathos. **Ethos** (an ethical appeal) establishes the speaker's or writer's credibility and trustworthiness. An ethical appeal demonstrates goodwill toward the audience, good sense or knowledge of the subject at hand, and good character. Establishing common ground with the audience is another feature of ethos. But ethos alone rarely carries an argument; therefore, you also need to use **logos** (a logical appeal). Logos demonstrates an effective use of reason and judicious use of evidence, whether facts, statistics, comparisons, anecdotes, expert opinions, personal experiences, or observations. You employ logos in the process of supporting claims, drawing reasonable conclusions, and avoiding rhetorical fallacies (see **8i**). Aristotle also taught that persuasion comes about only when the audience feels emotionally stirred by the topic under discussion. Therefore, **pathos** (an emotional appeal) involves using language that will stir the feelings of the audience. If you misuse pathos in an attempt to manipulate your audience, it can backfire. But pathos can be used successfully when it establishes empathy and authentic understanding. Thus, the most effective arguments combine these three persuasive appeals responsibly and knowledgeably.

In the next three subsections, excerpts from Martin Luther King, Jr.'s "Letter from Birmingham Jail" illustrate how a writer can use all three of the classical rhetorical appeals.

(a) Ethical appeals establish a writer's credibility.

In his opening paragraph, King shows that his professional life is so demanding that he needs more than one secretary. He also indicates that he wishes to engage in "constructive work," thereby establishing common ground with his audience, whom he characterizes as being well-intentioned and sincere. He also establishes that he will argue in good faith.

1 My Dear Fellow Clergymen:
While confined here in the Birmingham city jail, I came across your recent statement calling my present activities "unwise and untimely." Seldom do I pause to answer criticism of my work and ideas. If I sought to answer all the criticisms that cross my desk, my secretaries would have little time for anything other than such correspondence in the course of the day, and I would have no time for constructive work. But since I feel that you are men of genuine good will and that your criticisms are sincerely set forth, I want to try to answer your statement in what I hope will be patient and reasonable terms.

(b) Logical appeals help an audience clearly understand the writer's ideas.

To help his audience understand why segregation is wrong, King defines key terms:

2 Let us consider a more concrete example of just and unjust laws. An unjust law is

As a writer and a speaker, Martin Luther King, Jr., successfully used the rhetorical appeals of ethos, logos, and pathos.

a code that a numerical or power majority group compels a minority group to obey but does not make binding on itself. This is difference made legal. By the same token, a just law is a code that a majority compels a minority to follow and that it is willing to follow itself. This is sameness made legal.

(c) Emotional appeals can move the audience to a new way of thinking or acting.

As he moves toward his conclusion, King evokes feelings of idealism as well as guilt:

3   I have travelled the length and breadth of Alabama, Mississippi, and all the other southern states. On sweltering summer days and crisp autumn mornings I have looked at the South's beautiful churches with their lofty spires pointing heavenward. I have beheld the impressive outlines of her massive religious-education buildings. Over and over I have found myself asking: "What kind of people worship here? Who is their God? . . . Where were their voices of support when bruised and weary Negro men and women decided to rise from the dark dungeons of complacency to the bright hills of creative protest?"

—**MARTIN LUTHER KING, JR.,** "Letter from Birmingham Jail"

The full text of King's argument includes other examples of ethos, logos, and pathos.

Although ethos is often developed in the introduction, logos in the body, and pathos in the conclusion, these classical rhetorical appeals often overlap and appear throughout an argument.

(2) Rogerian appeals show other people that you understand them.

Rogerian argument derives from the work of Carl R. Rogers, a psychologist who believed that many problems are the result of a breakdown in communication. Rogers claimed that people often fail to understand each other because of a natural tendency to judge and evaluate, agree or disagree, without really listening to, let alone understanding, what is being said. His model calls for suspending judgment until you are able to restate fairly and accurately what others believe. When each person in a conflict demonstrates this ability, the likelihood of misunderstanding is significantly reduced.

Skills such as paraphrasing and summarizing (see **11d(3)–(4)**) are essential to the Rogerian approach. Although this model can be used to achieve a number of goals, it is especially useful for building consensus. To demonstrate that you have given fair consideration to the views of others, you begin a Rogerian argument by paraphrasing these views and demonstrating that you understand the thinking behind them. Then, you introduce your own position and explain why you believe it has merit. Because the Rogerian model is designed to build consensus, you conclude your argument by showing how everyone concerned about the issue could benefit from adopting your proposal. This emphasis on being fair-minded and nonconfrontational gives ethos (see **8f(1)**) an essential place in a Rogerian argument.

The summary of benefits with which a Rogerian argument concludes gives you the opportunity to draw your threads together and appeal to your audience without simply restating what you have already said. In the following conclusion to an argument on public education, notice how the author cites benefits for students, teachers, and the public at large if her proposal is adopted.

4   Reducing the maximum class size in our secondary schools from thirty students to twenty-five will not solve all the problems in our system, but it will yield important benefits. Students will get more individualized instruction. Better able to give their full attention to the students who remain with them, teachers will gain greater job satisfaction. And in an era when events like the recent killings in Littleton, Colorado, raise legitimate concerns about the safety of public schools, an improved student-teacher ratio reduces the risk of a troubled student being overlooked—a comfort to parents as well as educators. Finally even those citizens who do not have children will benefit, because in the long run everyone benefits from living in a community where people are well educated.

—**LAURA BECHDEL**, "Space to Learn"

8g   Purposefully arranging an effective argument

No single arrangement is right for every written argument. Unless your instructor asks you to demonstrate a particular type of arrangement, the decisions you make about arrangement should be based on several factors: your topic, your audience, and your purpose. You can develop a good plan by simply listing the major points you want to make (see **3d**), deciding what order to put them in, and then determining where to include refutation or concession (see **8g(3)**). You must also decide whether to place your thesis statement or claim at the beginning or the end of your argument. Once you sort out the reasons supporting your claim, you need to develop each reason with a separate paragraph (unless, of course, you're summarizing your reasons in the conclusion).

No matter which arrangement you use, your conclusion should move beyond a mere summary of what has already been stated and instead emphasize your emotional connection with your audience, a connection that reinforces your rhetorical purpose: the course of action you want your audience to take, an invitation to further understanding, or the implications of your claim (see **8h**). The student paper by Laura Klocke at the end of this chapter (see pages 198–204) ends with a conclusion that not only reinforces her purpose but links her purpose with the stated mission of her university.

In addition, there are a few basic principles that may be useful.

(1) Classical arrangement works well if your audience has not yet taken a position on your issue.

One way to organize your argument is to follow the plan recommended by classical rhetoric, which assumes that an audience is prepared to follow a well-reasoned argument.

FEATURES OF THE CLASSICAL ARRANGEMENT

Introduction	Introduce your issue, and capture the attention of your audience. Try using a short narrative or a strong example. (See **3f(2)** and **3g**.) Begin establishing your credibility (using ethos) and common ground.
Background information	Provide your audience with a history of the situation, and state how things currently stand. Define any key terms. Even if you think the facts speak for themselves, draw the attention of your audience to those points that are especially important, and explain why they are meaningful.
Proposition	Introduce the position you are taking: present the argument itself, and provide the basic reasons for your belief. Frame your position as a thesis statement or claim. (See **3c** and **8d**.)

Proof or confirmation	Discuss the reasons that have led you to take your position. Each reason must be clear, relevant, and representative. Provide facts, expert testimony, and any other evidence that supports your claim.
Refutation	Recognize and disprove the arguments of people who hold a different position and with whom you continue to disagree.
Concession	Concede any point with which you agree or that has merit; show why this concession does not damage your own case.
Conclusion	Summarize your most important points, and appeal to your audience's feelings, making a personal connection. Describe the consequences of your argument in a final attempt to encourage your audience to consider (if not commit to) a particular course of action.

(2) Rogerian arrangement can help calm an audience strongly opposed to your position.

To write an argument informed by Rogerian appeals, use the following plan as your guide.

FEATURES OF THE ROGERIAN ARRANGEMENT

Introduction	Establish that you have paid attention to views different from your own. Build trust by stating these views clearly and fairly.
Concessions	Reassure the people you hope to persuade by showing that you agree with them to some extent and do not think that they are completely wrong.
Thesis	Having earned the confidence of your audience, state your claim, or proposition.
Support	Explain why you have taken this position and provide support for it.
Conclusion	Conclude by showing how your audience and other people could benefit from accepting your position. Indicate the extent to which this position will resolve the problem you are addressing. If you are offering a partial solution to a complex problem, concede that further work may be necessary.

For a sample student paper organized as a Rogerian argument, visit **www.harbrace.com**.

(3) Refutation and concession are most effective when placed where readers will accept them.

Classical arrangement places refutation after the proof or confirmation of the argument, an arrangement that works well for an audience familiar with this organizational model. Sometimes, however, that refutation can come too late. Readers unfamiliar with classical arrangement may have decided that you are too one-sided—and may even have stopped reading. Therefore, when you are taking a highly controversial stand on an emotionally loaded subject, strive to establish common ground, and then acknowledge opposing viewpoints and respond to them. This variation on classical arrangement assumes that readers will be unwilling to hear a new proposition unless they are first shown what is weak or incomplete about their current thinking.

In a Rogerian argument, a writer begins by reporting opposing views fairly and identifying what is valuable about them. The strategy here is not to refute the views in question but to concede that they have merit—thus putting the audience at ease before introducing a thesis or claim that might be rejected if stated prematurely.

However, sometimes readers may react negatively to a writer who responds to opposing views before offering any reasons to support his or her own view. These readers want to know from the start where an argument is headed. For this reason, writers often choose to state their position at the beginning of the argument and offer at least one strong reason to support it before turning to opposing views. They sometimes keep at least one other reason in reserve (often one responsibly laden with emotion, or pathos), so that they can present it after responding to opposing views, thereby ending with an emphasis on their confirmation.

Unless you are required to follow a specific arrangement, or organizational plan, you should respond to opposing views wherever your audience is most likely either to expect this discussion or to be willing to hear it. If your audience is receptive, you can place refutation and concession after your confirmation. If your audience adheres to a different position, you should respond to their views toward the beginning of your argument. You might also want to keep in mind that if you open a paragraph with an opposing view, you will want to move quickly to your response to that view so that your readers make only one shift between differing views. Your goal is to keep your readers focused on your line of thinking.

Exercise 4

Read the editorial pages of several consecutive issues of your community or college newspaper. Look for editorials that analyze or question an established belief, express or defend an opinion, invite consideration, or try to convince. Choose an editorial that strikes you as well argued, well developed, and well organized—even if it does not change your belief or action (it may only have changed your level of understanding). Bring several copies of the editorial to class, and be prepared to discuss its purpose, audience, use of appeals, and conclusion.

8h Using logic to argue effectively and ethically

Because writers cannot argue on the basis of ethos alone, they need to understand the ways in which **logic**—the reasoning behind an argument—enhances or detracts from the argument. Logic is a means through which you can develop your ideas, realize new ones, and determine whether your thinking is clear enough to persuade readers to agree with you. By arguing logically, you increase the likelihood that your arguments will be taken seriously.

(1) Inductive reasoning is the process of using a number of specific facts or observations to draw a logical conclusion.

You use inductive reasoning on a daily basis. If you get a stomachache within fifteen minutes of eating ice cream, you might conclude that there's a connection. Perhaps you are lactose-intolerant. This use of evidence to form a generalization is called an **inductive leap,** and the leap should be in proportion to the amount of evidence gathered.

Inductive reasoning involves moving (or leaping) from discovering evidence to interpreting it, and it can help you arrive at probable, believable conclusions (but not absolute, enduring truth). Making a small leap from evidence (a stomachache) to a probable conclusion (lactose intolerance) is more effective and ethical than using the same evidence to make a sweeping claim that could easily be challenged (ice cream is bad for everyone) (see **8d**). Generally, the greater the weight of the evidence, the more reliable the conclusion.

When used in argument, inductive reasoning often employs facts (see **8c**) and examples (see **3f(2)** and **3g**). When writers cannot cite all the information that supports their conclusions, they choose the evidence that is most reliable and most closely related to the point they are making.

(2) Deductive reasoning is the process of applying a generalization (or generalized belief) to a series of specific cases.

At the heart of a deductive argument is a **major premise** (a generalized belief that is assumed to be true), which the writer applies to a specific case (the **minor premise**), thereby yielding a conclusion, or claim. For example, if you know that all doctors must complete a residency and that Anna is in medical school, then you can conclude that Anna must complete a residency. This argument can be expressed in a three-part structure called a **syllogism.**

Major premise	All doctors must complete a residency. [generalized belief]
Minor premise	Anna is studying to become a doctor. [specific case]
Conclusion	Anna must complete a residency. [claim]

Sometimes premises are not stated, for the simple reason that the writer assumes a shared belief with the audience.

> Anna has graduated from medical school, so she must complete a residency.

In this sentence, the unstated premise is that all doctors must complete a residency. A syllogism with an unstated premise—or even an unstated conclusion—is called an **enthymeme.** Frequently found in written arguments, enthymemes can be very effective because they presume shared beliefs or knowledge. For example, the argument "We need to build a new dormitory because the present overcrowded dorms are unsafe" contains the unstated premise that we should approve proposals that reduce unsafe overcrowding.

(3) The Toulmin model of reasoning provides an alternative to inductive and deductive reasoning.

To create a working system of logic suitable for the needs of all writers, philosopher Stephen Toulmin defined *argument* as a logical progression, from the **data** (accepted evidence or reasons that support a claim), to the **claim** (a debatable or controversial statement), based on the **warrant** (the underlying assumption, like the major premise). If the warrant is controversial, it requires **backing** (independent support or justification). Writers who assume that they are drawing their evidence from reliable authorities should be able to cite the credentials of those authorities. And writers who base an argument on the law or another written code that has been widely agreed upon (a university's mission statement, for instance) should be able to cite the exact statute, precedent, or regulation in question or even include the law or code in the essay itself.

Like deductive reasoning, Toulmin's method establishes a reasonable relationship between the data and the claim. The following argument may help explain the progression:

Fair trade coffee should be served at the University of St. Thomas because doing so would foster social justice.

Data	Purchasing fair trade coffee promotes social justice.
Claim	The University of St. Thomas should purchase and serve only fair trade coffee.
Warrant	The University of St. Thomas believes in promoting social justice.

The warrant establishes a relationship with the data, providing a reasonable link with the claim that follows (see fig. 8.1).

Of course, few arguments are as simple as this example. For instance, the University of St. Thomas may wish to promote social justice but be unable to follow through on every opportunity to do so. In such cases, writers must make allowances for exceptions. Qualifiers such as *usually, probably, should,* and *possibly* show the degree of certainty of the conclusion, and rebuttal terms such as *unless* indicate exceptions.

Since the University of St. Thomas seeks to promote social justice, it **should** purchase and serve only fair trade coffee, **unless** doing so would cause other problems.

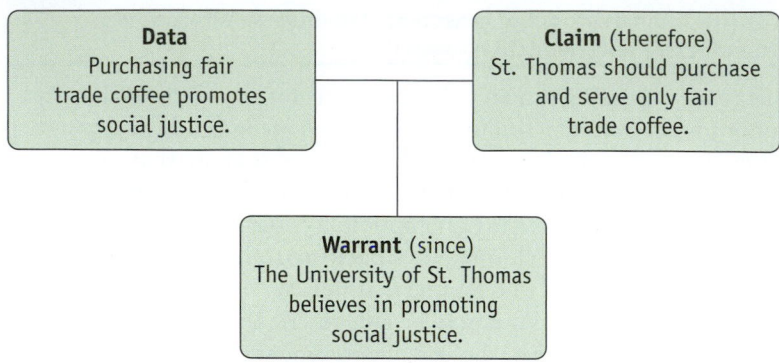

Fig. 8.1. A warrant linking data and a claim.

When using the Toulmin model to shape your arguments, you may be able to identify the claim, the data, and the qualifiers more easily than the warrant. Like the unstated premise in an enthymeme (see **8h(2)**), the warrant is often assumed and backed up by something left unsaid. In the example above, the backing is the university's mission statement, which calls for commitment to social justice. To determine the backing for a warrant in an argument you are writing, trace your thinking back to the assumptions with which you began. As you do so, remember that backing can take different forms. It may be a law or regulation (such as a university regulation about student housing), a belief that the data came from a reliable source or that what is true of a sample is true of a larger group, or a moral, political, or economic value that is widely accepted in your culture.

8i Avoiding rhetorical fallacies

Logical reasoning not only enhances the overall effectiveness of an argument, it also enhances the ethos of the speaker or writer. Almost as important as constructing an argument effectively is avoiding errors in argument, or **rhetorical fallacies.** Rhetorical fallacies signal to your audience that your thinking is not entirely trustworthy and that your argument is not well reasoned.

Therefore, you need to recognize and avoid several kinds of fallacies. As you read the arguments of others (see **10a**) and revise the arguments you draft (chapter **4**), try to keep the following common rhetorical fallacies in mind.

(1) *Non sequitur,* Latin for "it does not follow," means that just because the first part of a statement is true doesn't mean the second part will necessarily happen or become true.

Non sequitur is the basis for most of the other rhetorical fallacies.

Faulty   Eddie is smart; therefore, he will do well in college.
[This assertion is based on the faulty premise that *all* smart people do well in college. (See **8h(2)**.)]

(2) *Ad hominem* refers to a personal attack on an opponent that draws attention away from the issues under consideration.

Faulty   She is unfit to be a minister because she is divorced.
[The fact that a woman is divorced may reveal the condition of a previous marriage, but a divorce has little if anything to do with her spiritual beliefs and principles that could benefit a congregation.]

Ad hominem attacks focus their attention on an individual, rather than on the issue.

(3) *Appeal to tradition* **is an argument that says something should be done a certain way simply because it has been done that way in the past.**

Faulty   Because they are a memorable part of the pledge process, fraternity hazings should not be banned.
[Times change; what was considered good practice in the past is not necessarily considered acceptable now.]

"I don't know how it started, either. All I know is that it's part of our corporate culture."

These two employees have accepted an appeal to tradition: they don't question established corporate practices.

(4) *Bandwagon* **is an argument saying, in effect, "Everyone's doing or saying or thinking this, so you should, too."**

Faulty   Everyone drives over the speed limit, so why shouldn't we raise the limit?
[The majority is not always right.]

Not everyone wants to jump on the bandwagon.

(5) *Begging the question* **is an argument that assumes what in fact needs to be proved.**

Faulty   We need to fire corrupt officials in order to reduce the city's crime rate.
[If there are corrupt officials in city government, this point needs to be established.]

"Nothing important—nothing on fax, nothing on voice mail, nothing on the Internet. Just, you know, handwritten stuff."

Although the secretary says that the handwritten stuff is not important, that assertion has not been proved.

(6) *Equivocation* **is an assertion that falsely relies on the use of a term in two different senses.**

Faulty   We know this is a natural law because it feels natural.
[In the first use, *natural* means "derived from nature or reason"; when used again, it means "easy or simple because of being in accord with one's own nature."]

(7) *False analogy* **is the assumption that because two things are alike in some ways, they must be alike in others.**

Faulty   The United States lost credibility with other nations during the war in Viet Nam, so we should not get involved in the Middle East, or we will lose credibility again.
[The differences between the war in Southeast Asia in the 1960s and 1970s and the current conflict in the Middle East may well be greater than their similarities.]

(8) *False authority* is the assumption that an expert in one field can be credible in another.

Faulty We must stop sending military troops into Afghanistan, as Bruce Springsteen has argued.
[Springsteen's expertise in music does not automatically qualify him as an expert in foreign policy.]

(9) *False cause* is the assumption that because one event follows another, the first is the cause of the second—sometimes called *post hoc, ergo propter hoc* ("after this, so because of this").

Faulty When Coach Joe Paterno turned 75, Penn State's football team had a losing season.
[The assumption is that Paterno's age is solely responsible for the losing season, with no consideration given to the abilities and experience of the football players themselves.]

(10) *False dilemma* (sometimes called the *either/or fallacy*) is a statement that only two alternatives exist, when in fact there are more than two.

Faulty We must either build more nuclear power plants or be completely dependent on foreign oil.
[Other possibilities exist.]

(11) *Guilt by association* is an unfair attempt to make others responsible for a person's beliefs or actions.

Faulty Jon's father and grandfather were gamblers; therefore, Jon must be one, too.
[Several people can graduate from the same school, practice the same profession or religion, belong to the same family, or live in the same neighborhood without engaging in the same behavior.]

(12) *Hasty generalization* is a conclusion based on too little evidence or on exceptional or biased evidence.

Faulty Ellen is a poor student because she failed her first history test.
[Her performance may improve in the weeks ahead or be good in all her other subjects.]

In a clear case of guilt by association, Uncle Sam is stopped by
airport security guards who are profiling men with beards.

**(13) *Oversimplification* is a statement or argument that leaves out
relevant considerations in order to imply that there is a single
cause or solution for a complex problem.**

Faulty   We can eliminate unwanted pregnancies by teaching birth
control and abstinence.
[Teaching people about birth control and abstinence does not
guarantee the elimination of unwanted pregnancies.]

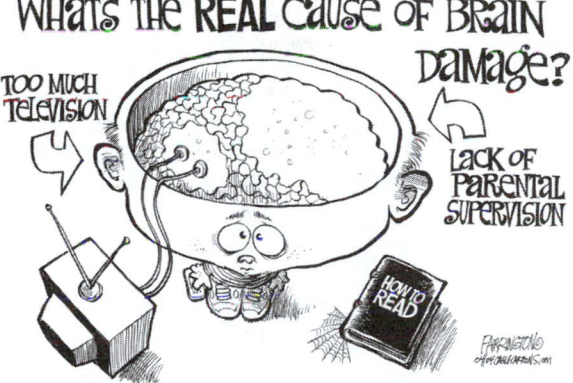

This cartoon begs the question "Are children brain-damaged?"
It also oversimplifies the potential causes of that damage.

(14) *Red herring* **(sometimes called** *ignoring the question***) means dodging the real issue by drawing attention to an irrelevant one.**

Faulty Why worry about violence in schools when we ought to be worrying about international terrorism?
[International terrorism has little if any direct relationship with school violence.]

(15) *Slippery slope* **is the assumption that if one thing is allowed, it will be the first step in a downward spiral.**

Faulty Handgun control will lead to a police state.
[Handgun control has not led to a police state in England.]

Be alert for rhetorical fallacies in your writing. When you find such a fallacy, be sure to moderate your claim, clarify your thinking, or, if necessary, eliminate the fallacious statement. Even if your argument as a whole is convincing, rhetorical fallacies can damage your credibility (see **8d** and **10a**).

Applying a slippery slope argument, this cartoon suggests that removing one potentially offensive word from the Pledge of Allegiance will result in removing almost all the words.

Exercise 5

For each of the following statements, write one or two sentences in which you identify and explain the faulty reasoning. Next, describe circumstances under which you might find these statements convincing. Finally, rewrite each statement so that it avoids rhetorical fallacies, regardless of the circumstances (if possible).

1. We must either build more dormitories or double up students in existing dormitories.
2. If we censor neo-Nazi demonstrations, we will ultimately lose freedom of speech.
3. If women dressed more conservatively, they would earn as much money as men.
4. We should cut social services because people on welfare are getting too many benefits.
5. Children would do a lot better at school if they didn't spend so much time watching television.

8j Studying a sample argument written by a student

The following paper was Laura Klocke's response to an assignment in argumentative writing. She was asked to write an essay that pointed to a specific problem in her living quarters, on her campus, in her town, or in the world at large and then recommended a solution for that problem.

As you read Laura's essay, consider whether—and how—she argued her case effectively. Note her use of classical rhetorical appeals (ethos, logos, and pathos) and arrangement and her inductive reasoning. Also, identify the kinds of evidence she uses (facts, examples, testimony, or authority).

Klocke 1

Just Coffee: A Proposal in the Classical Arrangement

Laura Klocke

Introduction

From the local café and the multinational chains to the gas station and the grocery store, you can buy lattes, cappucinos, fresh drip, and espresso. Everywhere and anywhere, it seems, coffee is "the best part of waking up."

Approximately 20 to 25 million people grow coffee for the world's drinkers and rely solely on coffee production for their income and survival. Coffee is a world beverage of choice, and this is perhaps most clearly evident in the United States, which consumes one-third of the world's coffee. Roughly $18 billion dollars is spent on coffee itself; almost just as much is invested in coffee equipment in the United States. It's not surprising, then, that coffee is the second-largest commodity traded on the market in the entire world, following oil (Dicum and Luttinger 3). With these large dollar figures and millions of cups of coffee in mind, you might wonder where all the money goes. Or, better yet, to whom?

Background
information

The answer has mostly to do with coffee plantations known as fincas, a modern-day version of pre-Civil War Southern plantations. The coffee grown and processed is taken from the fincas and enters into what is called the "coffee chain." This chain continues from the finca and its workers to a local speculator, or "coyote." The coyote draws up a contract with an exporter, and the chain proceeds to the roaster, distributor, retail outlet, and, finally, your cup. The goal of this chain, like the goal of most business transactions, is to maximize the final profit. Unfortunately for those at the beginning—the peasant farmers of the finca—their livelihood is not a consideration of their employer; the maximization of profit is the employer's sole concern. Grocery store gourmet coffee costs as much as

Klocke 2

$12.00 per pound, and yet some <u>finca</u> workers are paid only twenty to forty cents per pound. When considering that the average <u>finca</u> coffee farmer makes $3.00 a day, and the average latte is priced at $3.50 or more, it is clear that something doesn't add up in this coffee chain system (Rice and McLean 22). And, because the workers do not own the land, though they live and work on it in each stage of the coffee-growing production, they have relatively little say in their pay. Something akin to the sharecroppers of the past, the situation for those living on <u>fincas</u> is a present-day injustice. The emphasis for the world's production of coffee is on profit, and a speedy profit at that, which I will explain below.

When fair trade coffee organizations are part of the coffee-growing and coffee-selling equation, the emphasis is not only on speed and profit. Fair trade coffee organizations establish personal, gradually developing, and long-term buying relationships with coffee growers and encourage the farmers to organize into

Coffee is produced by many fair trade farms or organizations like this one. (Photo © AP Photo/Kent Gilbert/Wide World Photos)

cooperatives, where they are free to live, work, and grow coffee in a community supported by a guaranteed fair and livable wage. Fair trade coffee eliminates the middle people in the chain and thereby allocates the money that had gone to the coyotes to the growers themselves. Instead of the twenty to forty cents per pound they earned on the <u>fincas</u>, the workers can earn a minimum of $1.20 per pound. This pay raise is accomplished by

Klocke 3

eliminating the middle people and ensuring that the workers are paid fairly for their labor—not by raising the price of coffee noticeably. With the guarantee of a livable wage, many farmers would be able to put money into their community, building schools, recreation centers, churches, and businesses, improving the lives of everyone in the region.

Though I have never traveled to a <u>finca,</u> I am aware that my purchases are just one of the many ways that I can demonstrate my recognition of the inherent dignity of all people. Therefore, I do not want to support knowingly any flawed financial system with my purchases. My university is also working to make positive steps in its purchasing practices; however, with regard to fair trade food products, particularly coffee, the University of St. Thomas is not yet up to speed. In order to be fully engaged in ethical buying practices, St. Thomas must support a fully fair trade coffee supplier. Though the whole world may never be converted to the philosophy of fair trade, the sizable amount of money the university spends on coffee can still make a difference and set an example that other universities may want to follow.

Proposition

Since the university can choose between selling fair trade or unfairly traded coffee at every food service location on campus, I advocate that our university sell only that coffee that has been provided from fair trade organizations. Such a university-wide decision will reflect the ethics and politics of the university's buying power as well as align with the commitment of our University Mission Statement.

The switch from coffee drinker to conscientious coffee drinker is not difficult. The mission of the University of St. Thomas includes a commitment to "develop morally responsible individuals who combine . . . cultural awareness and intellectual curiosity." In addition, the tradition of

Proof

Klocke 4

the school seeks to foster "a value-oriented education needed for complete human development and for responsible citizenship in contemporary society"; an "international perspective"; and an "appreciation for cultural diversity." Finally, "the university embraces its role and our responsibilities in the world community," a statement that clearly connects the University of St. Thomas and the fair trade issue. The commitment to ethical activities in the university supports not only a continuation of international learning and experience, but also reflects an understanding of the inherent dignity of work and the workers that grow and process the coffee the university serves. Not only are the workers valuable as members of the human race, but their work, also, has value to them, and to the world.

Many other groups already support the fair trade coffee movement, including the Audubon Society and the MacArthur Foundation, so the University of St. Thomas would join a wide movement of people and organizations who recognize that drinking fair trade coffee is in good taste—financially, politically, and ethically (Rice and McLean 38).

Unfortunately, this proposal for a change to a completely fair trade coffee offering at the University of St. Thomas has been met with several concerns from the administration. St. Thomas does not desire to terminate its contract with Dunn Brothers Coffee, a local Twin Cities company that currently provides several varieties of certified fair trade coffee, including Guatemalan and Mexican. Though Dunn Brothers offers these choices, they are not a solely fair trade coffee company. Through a gradual approach of switching to an entirely fair trade coffee company, Dunn Brothers would be given a chance to improve their offerings as well as help St. Thomas to address some of its major concerns, in particular, those from a cost standpoint. As a student of this university, and given my

Refutation

Klocke 5

support of this mission statement, I prefer to approach this issue from an ethical stand. However, it is easy to show that the serving of fair trade coffee makes sense from a financial perspective as well.

First, however, to answer the concerns of the university is necessary. University administrators argue that, by supporting a small local company like Dunn Brothers, they are still using university money in an acceptable way. I argue that the university could use its money in an even better way. The fact that Dunn Brothers is not a solely fair trade company puts them at odds with the university mission. Besides, there are several local fair trade companies—Cloud Forest Initiatives and Peace Coffee, to name just two— that are small enough for the university to support at the same time that it does more with its buying power.

Next, the cost difference between fair trade and unfair trade coffee is an understandable concern for St. Thomas. While the movement continues to grow, fair trade coffee has the potential to cost slightly more (though hardly noticeably more) per pound than unfairly traded coffee. However, with an institution-sized order, many coffee cooperatives could be in a position to provide a contract that could work in the best way, financially, for both the growers and, in this case, the university. A worst-case scenario would be an increase of almost five cents more per cup. In answering this argument, however, the University of St. Thomas should recognize that the price difference for fair trade coffee is negligible when compared to the cost of unfairly traded coffee for communities, farmers, and families.

The last concern the administration of St. Thomas has expressed is the fear of losing the recognizable Dunn Brothers' name. The administration understandably wants to continue to sell coffee that is

Klocke 6

successfully marketed and doesn't yet know if students will support the move to fair trade coffee if there's no name recognition. To that objection, I would respond that relatively few students have taken an active interest in the coffee served at the University of St. Thomas (fair trade or otherwise). It is unlikely that once the switch to fair trade coffee is realized, my fellow students will notice—let alone protest against it. It seems that, at the heart, there is a discrepancy between the bottom lines in this issue. The University of St. Thomas would like to make the bottom line about cost, and yet the mission statement and foundation of the university clearly states otherwise. Also in response to this argument, it is worth mentioning that students are rarely consulted about the buying choices of the university. We live in a closed market system on campus, meaning, we have no choice about many of our food products (for example, the university is a "Pepsi" campus, and only Pepsi products are sold in beverage vending machines).

We at the University of St. Thomas have the chance not only to have our concerns answered but to affirm our mission statement and be a leader in the intra-campus community. We would convey a strong message with our purchase and sales of fair trade coffee, demonstrating that we are a community of concerned citizens. Our mission guides us in decisions that affect our local community as well as our global community. St. Thomas should be a leader in social justice as well as in academics.

Conclusion

We must support fair trade coffee growers and their communities, and, thereby, as a university, adhere to the mission that we profess. By helping to guarantee coffee growers a livable wage, the commitment to fair trade coffee at the University of St. Thomas is clearly the just choice.

Klocke 7

Works Cited

Dicum, Gregory, and Nina Luttinger. <u>The Coffee Book: Anatomy of an</u>
<u>Industry from Crop to the Last Drop</u>. New York: New Press, 1999.

Rice, Paul D., and Jennifer McLean. "Sustainable Coffee at the
Crossroads." <u>CCC Coffee Program</u>. 15 Oct. 1999. Consumer's
Choice Council. 23 Oct. 2001.
<http://www.consumerscouncil.org/coffee/coffeebook/coffee.pdf>.

University of St. Thomas. "Mission Statement."
<http://www.stthomas.edu>.

Exercise 6

Reread Laura Klocke's essay to establish her claim and proof. What values does Klocke reveal as she argues for the use of fair trade coffee? What personal experiences have shaped Klocke's values?

Primary sources, such as a report from an archeological dig, are useful for many research projects.

9 FINDING SOURCES IN PRINT, ONLINE, AND IN THE FIELD

When you hear the word *research*, you might think of laboratory experiments, archaeological digs, or hours spent in the library—forgetting about the ordinary research you yourself do every day as you decide what to buy, how to fix something, how to perform a function on your computer, which books to read, or where to spend your vacation. Research is common to everyone's experience. To conduct useful research efficiently, you must first develop skills in accessing information. This chapter will help you

- use the rhetorical situation to frame your research (**9a**),
- find books (**9b**),
- find articles (**9c**),
- find Web-based sources (**9d**), and
- conduct field research (**9e**).

9a Research and the rhetorical situation

To make the most of the time you spend doing research, determine your rhetorical situation early in the research process. By understanding your exigence, audience, and purpose, you can gather relevant sources efficiently.

(1) Identifying an exigence can help you form a research question.

The starting point for any writing project is your exigence—the issue or problem that has prompted you to write (see **1b**). For research assignments, the exigence also prompts you to find more information before you write. Once you are sure of the exigence, craft a question to guide your research. Your research will then become a quest to answer that question (in essence, to resolve your exigence).

Research questions often arise when you try to relate what you are studying for a course to your own experience. For instance, you may start wondering about voting regulations and procedures while reading about past elections for a history class and at the same time noticing the number of news stories about the role technology plays in elections or the unfair practices reported in some states. Such observations may prompt you to find more information. Each observation, however, may give rise to a different question. Focusing on the influence of technology may prompt you to ask, "What are the possible consequences of having electronic ballots only?" If, instead, you focus on unfair voting practices, you may ask, "How do voting procedures differ from state to state?" Because you can ask a variety of research questions about any topic, choose the one that interests you the most and that allows you to fulfill your assignment.

To generate research questions, you may find it helpful to ask yourself about causes, consequences, processes, definitions, or values, as in the following examples.

Questions about causes

Why did the United States invade Iraq?

What causes power outages in large areas of the country?

Questions about consequences

What are the consequences of taking antidepressants for a long period of time?

How would the climate in a school change if a dress code were established?

Questions about processes

How can music lovers prevent corporations from controlling the development of new music?

How are presidential campaigns funded?

Questions about definitions

How do you know if you are addicted to something?

What kind of test is "the test of time"?

Questions about values

Should the Makah tribe be allowed to hunt gray whales?

Would the construction of wind farms be detrimental to the environment?

If you have trouble coming up with a research question, you may need a jump start. The following tips can help you.

TIPS FOR FINDING A RESEARCH QUESTION

- Can you remember an experience that you did not understand fully or that made you feel uncertain? What was it that you did not understand? What were you unsure of?
- What have you observed recently (on television, in the newspaper, on campus) that piqued your curiosity? What were you curious about?
- What widely discussed local or national problem would you like to help solve?
- Is there anything (lifestyles, political views, fashion preferences) that you find unusual or intriguing and would like to explore?

Research and writing require a commitment of time and effort, so you will find these tasks more pleasant, and maybe easier, when you are sincerely interested in your question. By talking with other people, you may discover that they are interested in it too. On the other hand, they may help you see that you need to narrow your question or change it in some other way. After talking about your question with other people, you may even decide that it does not interest you very much. To get a conversation about your ideas started, have a friend or classmate ask you the following questions. You may also use these questions to initiate a focused freewriting exercise.

- Why is it important for you to answer this research question? Why is it important for your audience to know the answer to the question?
- Does the answer to your question require research? (There should not be a simple or obvious answer to the question.)
- What types of research might help you answer your question?
- Will you be able to carry out the necessary research in the amount of time allowed?

Exercise 1

Each of the following subjects would need to be narrowed down for a research paper. To experiment with framing a research question, compose two questions about each subject that could be answered in a ten-page paper (refer to the list on pages 208–209 for examples of questions).

1. terrorism
2. the job market
3. gender differences
4. globalization
5. civil rights
6. health care

(2) Research can help you address your audience and achieve a specific purpose.

Your audience and your purpose are interconnected. In general terms, your purpose is to have an impact on your audience; in more specific terms, your purpose may be to entertain your readers, to inform them, to explain something to them, or to persuade them to do something. Research can help you achieve any of these goals.

A research paper often has one of the following rhetorical purposes.

- *To inform an audience.* The researcher reports current thinking on a specific topic, including opposing views, without analyzing them or siding with a particular position.

  Example   To inform an audience about current nutritional guidelines for children

- *To analyze and synthesize information and then offer possible solutions.* The researcher analyzes a topic and synthesizes the available information about it, looking for points of agreement and disagreement and for gaps in coverage. Thus, part of the research consists of finding out what other researchers have written about the topic. After presenting the analysis and synthesis, the researcher sometimes offers possible ways to address any problems found.

  Example   To analyze and synthesize various national health care proposals

- *To convince or issue an invitation to an audience.* The researcher states a position and backs it up with data, statistics, testimony, corroborating texts or events, or supporting arguments. The researcher's purpose is to persuade or invite readers to take the same position.

Example To persuade people to support a political candidate

A researcher presenting results from an original experiment or study must often achieve all of these purposes. In the introduction of a lab report, for example, the researcher analyzes and synthesizes previous work done on the same topic and locates a research niche—an area needing further study. The researcher then attempts to convince the readers that his or her current study will help address the need for more research. The body of the report is informative, describing the materials used, explaining the procedures followed, and presenting the results. In the conclusion, the researcher may try, based on the results of the experiment or study, to persuade the audience to take some action (for example, give up smoking, eat fewer carbohydrates, or fund future research).

(3) The sources you use may be primary, secondary, or both.

As you proceed with research, be aware of whether your sources are primary or secondary. **Primary sources** for researching topics in the humanities are generally documents—such as old letters and records—and literary works. In the social sciences, primary sources can be field observations, case histories, and survey data. In the natural sciences, primary sources are generally empirical—field observations or measurements, experimental results, and the like.

Secondary sources are commentaries on primary sources. For example, a review of a new novel is a secondary source, as is a discussion of adolescence based on survey data. Experienced researchers usually consult both primary and secondary sources, read them critically, and draw on them carefully.

A report from an archaeological dig is considered a primary source.

Just as you consider your rhetorical situation when you write, the authors of the sources you use have responded to their rhetorical situations. They have specified a goal for their work, a group of readers who might be interested in their findings, and a document form that best expresses their ideas. Thinking about the rhetorical situations that underlie the sources you consider will help you locate those most useful to you, read them with a critical eye, and incorporate them into your paper appropriately.

BEYOND THE RULE

PRIMARY, SECONDARY, AND TERTIARY SOURCES

Descriptions of types of research sources vary. To see examples of various descriptions of primary, secondary, and even tertiary sources (those that draw on secondary sources), visit **www.harbrace.com**.

9b Finding books

Three types of books are commonly used in the research process. **Scholarly books** are written by experts to advance knowledge of a certain subject. Most include original research. Before being published, these books are reviewed by scholars in the same field as the author(s). **Trade books** may also be written by experts or scholars, though they may be authored by journalists or freelance writers instead. But the audience and purpose of trade books differ from those of scholarly books. Rather than addressing other scholars, authors of trade books write to inform a general audience of research that has been done by others. **Reference books** such as encyclopedias and dictionaries provide factual information. These secondary sources contain short articles or entries written and reviewed by experts in the field. Their audience includes both veteran scholars and those new to a field of study.

(1) An online catalog helps you locate books.

The easiest way to find books related to your research question is to consult your library's online catalog. Once you are logged on, navigate

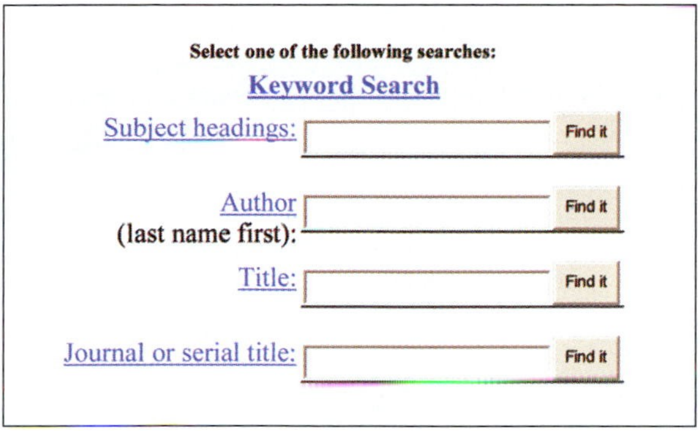

Fig. 9.1. Search boxes from a university library's Web page.

to the Web page with search boxes similar to those in fig. 9.1. When a research area is new to you, you can find many sources by doing either keyword searches or subject searches. To perform a **keyword search,** choose a word or phrase that you think might be found in the title of a book or in notes in the catalog's records. Some online catalogs allow users to be quite specific. The keyword search page in fig. 9.2 provides options for specifying a language, a location in the library, a type of book (or type of material other than a book, such as a brochure or government document), the way the results should be organized, the publisher, and the date of publication. The keyword search page in fig. 9.2 also provides some recommendations for entering words. By using a word or part of a word followed by asterisks, you can find all sources that include that root, even when suffixes have been added. For example, if you entered *environment**, you would find not only sources with *environment* in the title, subject headings, and content notes, but also sources with *environments, environmental,* or *environmentalist* in those locations. This search technique is called **truncation.**

You can also enter multiple keywords in search boxes by using **logical operators** such as *and, or, not,* and *near* (*and, or,* and *not* are sometimes called **Boolean operators**). These words narrow or broaden a search. They are used in electronic searches for books and for other documents such as articles and government brochures.

Although you will probably begin your research by using keyword searches, you may employ **subject searches** as well. To perform a successful subject search, you will have to enter words that correspond

Type the **WORD(S)** you want, then click Submit Search

Language: ANY

Material Type: ANY

Book/Serial: ANY

Location: ANY

Search and Sort: Date

Publisher:

Year: After _____ and Before _____

Search

SIMPLE
SEARCH

START
OVER

	Type in Words to search:	EXAMPLES
ADJACENCY	Multiple words are searched together as one phrase.	United States supreme court
TRUNCATION	Words may be right-hand truncated using an asterisk. Use a single asterisk * to truncate from 1-5 characters. Use a double asterisk ** for open-ended truncat ion.	environment* polic* fyodor dost**
OPERATORS	Use "and" or "or" to specify multiple words in any field, any order. Use "and not" to exclude words. Parentheses group words together when using Boolean operators.	(annotated bibliography) and child* (alaska or canada) and (adventure and not vacation)
PROXIMITY	Use "near" to specify words close to each other, in any order. Use "within #" to specify terms which occur within # words of each other in the record.	California near university america within 3 econom*

Fig. 9.2. Keyword search page from a university library's Web site.

LOGICAL OPERATORS

The words *and, or, not,* and *near* are the most common logical operators. However, online catalogs and periodical databases have various instructions for using them. If you have trouble following the guidelines presented here, check the instructions for the particular search box you are using.

and	narrows a search ("Starbucks **and** Vienna" returns only those records that contain both keywords.)
or	broadens a search ("Starbucks **or** Vienna" finds all records that contain information about either keyword.)
not	excludes specific items ("Starbucks **and** Austria **not** Vienna" excludes any records that mention Austria's capital city.)
near	finds records in which the two keywords occur in close proximity, within a preset number of words, and excludes those in which the keywords are widely separated ("Starbucks **near** globalization" lists only those records in which references to both *Starbucks* and *globalization* occur in close proximity.)

to the subject categories established by the Library of Congress. The best strategy for performing this type of search is to first enter words familiar to you. If, for some reason, the search does not yield any results, ask a reference librarian for a subject-heading guide. Author searches and title searches can also be useful, though only when you already have a particular author or title in mind.

Once you find the online catalog record for a book you would like to use, write down its **call number.** This number appears on the book itself and indicates where the book is shelved. The online record will reveal the status of the book, letting you know whether it is currently checked out or has been moved to a special collection. To find the book, consult the key to your library's shelving system, usually posted throughout the library. Library staff can also help you find books.

(2) Specialized reference books are listed in your library's online catalog.

A specialized encyclopedia or dictionary can often provide background information on people, events, and concepts related to the topic you

are researching. To find such sources using an online search page, enter the type of reference book and one or two keywords identifying your topic. For example, entering "encyclopedia of alcoholism" resulted in the following list of titles.

Encyclopedia of Drugs, Alcohol, and Addictive Behavior

Encyclopedia of Drugs and Alcohol

The Encyclopedia of Alcoholism

USEFUL REFERENCE BOOKS

For a detailed list of reference books and a short description of each, consult *Guide to Reference Books* by Robert Balay and *American Reference Books Annual* (*ARBA*). A few widely used reference books are listed here.

Special Dictionaries and Encyclopedias

- *Dictionary of American History*
- *Dictionary of Art*
- *Encyclopedia of Bioethics*
- *Encyclopedia of Higher Education*
- *Encyclopedia of Psychology*

Collections of Biographies

- *American National Biography*
- *Dictionary of Scientific Biography*
- *Notable American Women*
- *Who's Who in America*

---

(3) You may need to consult books not listed in your library's online catalog.

If you cannot find a particular book in your library, you have several options. Frequently, libraries have links to the catalogs of other libraries. By using such links, you can determine whether another library has the book you want and then order it through your library's interlibrary loan service. In addition, your library may have the database WorldCat, which locates books as well as images, sound recordings, and other materials. You may also access reference, fiction, and nonfiction books at **Bartleby.com**.

Exercise 2

Choose a research question, perhaps one you composed in exercise 1. Find the titles of a scholarly book, a trade book, and a reference book related to your choice.

9c Finding articles

Articles can be found in various **periodicals** (publications that appear at regular intervals). Because they are published daily, weekly, or monthly, periodicals offer information that is often more recent than that found in books. **Scholarly journals** usually contain reports of original research written by experts to an academic audience. **Trade magazines** feature articles written by staff writers or industry specialists. Because they are written for members of a particular trade, these articles address on-the-job concerns. **Popular magazines** and **newspapers** are generally written by staff writers for the general public. These periodicals carry a combination of news stories that attempt to be objective and essays that reflect the opinions of editors or guest contributors. The following are examples of the various types of periodicals.

> **Scholarly journals:** *The Journal of Developmental Psychology, The Journal of Business Communication*
>
> **Trade magazines:** *Farm Journal, Automotive Weekly*
>
> **Magazines (news):** *Time, Newsweek*
>
> **Magazines (public affairs):** *The New Yorker, National Review*
>
> **Magazines (special interest):** *National Geographic, Discover*
>
> **Newspapers:** *The New York Times, The Washington Post*

(1) An electronic database can help you find articles.

Your library's online catalog lists the titles of periodicals; however, it does not provide the titles of individual articles within these periodicals. The best strategy for finding print articles is to use an **electronic database,** which is a collection of articles compiled by a company that indexes them according to author, title, date, keywords, and other features. The electronic databases available in libraries are sometimes called **database subscription services, licensed databases,** or **aggregated databases.** Similar to an online catalog, an electronic database allows you to search for sources by author, title, keyword, and so on. However, such databases focus on specific subject areas.

A database search will generally yield an **abstract,** which is a short summary of an article. By scanning the abstract, you can determine whether to locate the complete text of the article, which can often be downloaded and printed. You can access your library's databases by using its computers or, if you have a password, by using an Internet link from a remote computer. College libraries subscribe to a wide variety of database services, but the following are the most common.

ERIC: Articles related to education

JSTOR: Articles from journals in the arts, humanities, ecology, and social sciences

PsycINFO: Articles related to psychology

You may be able to access the search boxes for databases directly, or you may have to access the databases through the search boxes of a vendor such as OCLC, InfoTrac, LexisNexis, or EBSCO. For example, OCLC's FirstSearch offers access to a number of databases (see fig. 9.3). To use this resource, you must first choose from a list of broad topics (such as

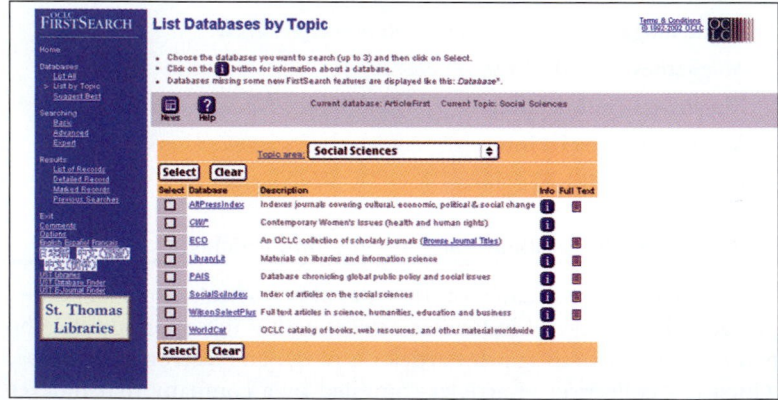

Fig. 9.3. Example of a screen from OCLC's FirstSearch.

"Arts and Humanities" and "Business and Economics") or specialized databases (such as MEDLINE and GeoRefS). FirstSearch also prompts you to enter keywords related to your topic.

If you were using FirstSearch to research the role of Starbucks in globalization, as Andy Pieper did for his paper (see **12c**), you could select one of the following topics: "General," "Business and Economics," or "Consumer Affairs and People." To research the status of African Americans in the U.S. military, as Nicole Hester did for her paper (see **14b**), you could select "General" or "Public Affairs and Law." To research the relationship between sleep and academic performance among college students, as Nikki Krzmarzick did for her paper (see **13c**), you could select "Life Sciences" or "Social Sciences." (Note that OCLC also provides access to books and Web resources through its WorldCat feature.)

The databases available through FirstSearch vary from one library to another. Similarly, the appearance of the opening screen for FirstSearch differs from one school to another. The example shown in fig. 9.3 is from the library system through which Nikki Krzmarzick conducted her search.

TIPS FOR CONDUCTING A SEARCH FOR PERIODICAL LITERATURE

- Identify keywords that clearly represent the topic.
- Determine the databases to be searched.
- Perform your search, using logical operators (see **9b(1)**).
- Refine your search strategy if the first search returned too many or too few citations, or (worse) irrelevant ones.
- Download and print the relevant articles.

(2) Print indexes provide essential information not found in electronic databases.

Before computers were widely used, researchers relied on **print indexes.** These bound volumes still provide essential backup when computers are out of service as well as access to older articles that may not be included in electronic databases. Some of the most useful print indexes, with their dates of beginning publication, are as follows.

Applied Science and Technology Index. 1958– .
Art Index. 1929– .

Biological and Agricultural Index. 1946– .

Business Periodicals Index. 1958– .

Cumulative Index to Nursing and Allied Health Literature (*CINAHL*). 1982– .

General Science Index. 1978– .

Humanities Index. 1974– .

Index to Legal Periodicals. 1908– .

Music Index. 1949– .

Philosopher's Index. 1967– .

Public Affairs Information Service (PAIS) Bulletin. 1915– .

Social Sciences Index. 1974– .

When they publish electronic versions of their indexes, some publishers change the title: *Current Index to Journals in Education* (*CIJE*) and *Resources in Education* (*RIE*) are the bound volumes for research in education, and ERIC is the electronic version. Consult the front of any bound volume for a key to the abbreviations used in individual entries.

(3) InfoTrac College Edition provides easy access to articles.

With InfoTrac College Edition and a passcode, you can conveniently search for articles with the Web browser on your own computer. You do not have to be networked to your library's Web site. InfoTrac College Edition indexes articles in over 3,800 journals and magazines and provides the full text of these articles. The InfoTrac screens in figs. 9.4 and 9.5 illustrate part of the research Nikki Krzmarzick conducted for her paper (see **13c**). Clicking in the box labeled "Mark" next to the article on the relationship between sleep and grade-point average, as shown in fig. 9.4, and then clicking on "text and full content retrieval choices" brought up the complete article, whose first page appears in fig. 9.5.

Exercise 3

Choose a research question, perhaps one from exercise 1. Find the titles of a scholarly article, a magazine article, and a newspaper article related to your choice.

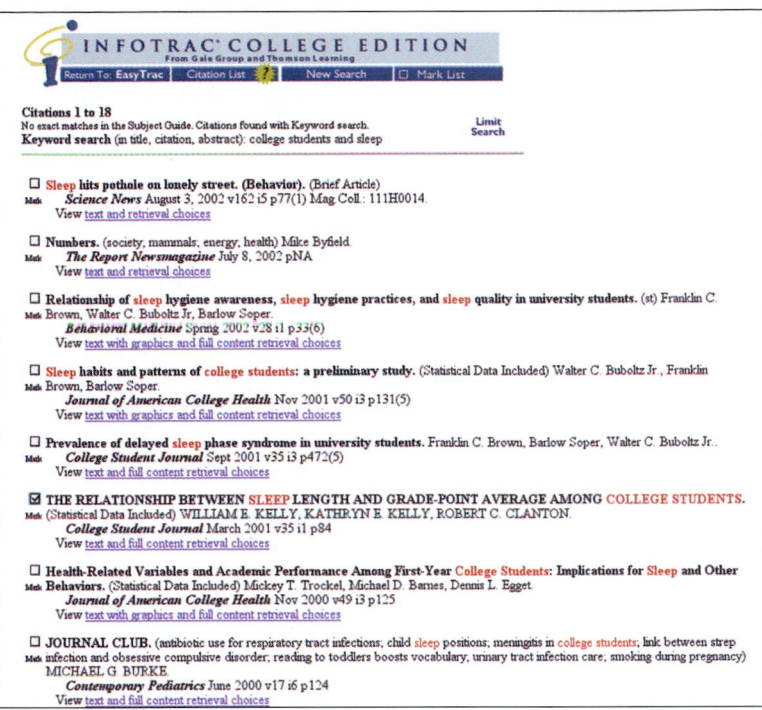

Fig. 9.4. Example of an InfoTrac screen.

9d Finding online sources

Through the Internet, you can find not only text files but also audio and video files. Most researchers start their online research by using search engines, meta-search engines, or subject directories. **Search engines** are electronic indexes of words and terms from Web pages. To use them effectively, you should understand their features. Always consult the Help feature to learn how to perform an advanced search so that you will not waste time weeding out results that are not of interest to you. Advanced searches with a search engine are performed in much the same way as searches in online catalogs and databases. You can

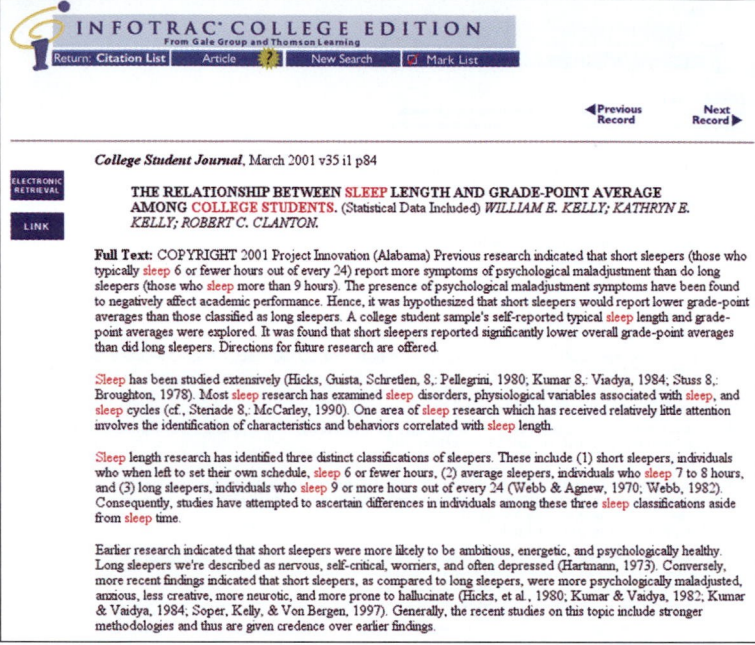

Fig. 9.5. First page of an article found through InfoTrac.

specify which words or phrases to use, how close words should be, which words should be excluded, and whether any word should be truncated. (See **9b(1)**.) The following are the addresses for some commonly used search engines.

Google	**www.google.com**
Infoseek	**infoseek.go.com**
Lycos	**www.lycos.com**
MSN Search	**search.msn.com**
WebCrawler	**www.webcrawler.com**

If you are looking solely for news stories, consider using the following.

Google News	**www.google.com/news**
TotalNEWS	**www.totalnews.com**

Meta-search engines are also useful research tools. *Meta-* means "transcending" or "more comprehensive." Meta-search engines check a number of search engines, including those previously listed. Try the following for starters.

Dogpile	**www.dogpile.com**
MetaCrawler	**www.metacrawler.com**

Unlike search engines, **subject directories** are collections of Web sources arranged topically. Yahoo! (**www.yahoo.com**) offers a subject directory under "Web Directory" on its home page: it includes categories such as "Arts," "Health," and "Education." Some researchers find subject directories easier to use because most of the irrelevant Web sites have been weeded out. The following are some other useful subject directories for academic and professional research.

Academic Info	**www.academicinfo.net**
The Internet Public Library	**www.ipl.org/ref**
Librarians' Index to the Internet	**lii.org**
The WWW Virtual Library	**vlib.org**

Although searching the Web is a popular research technique, it is not the only technique you should use. Search engines cover only the portion of the Internet that allows free access. You will not find library books or database materials through a Web search because library and database services are available only to paid subscribers (students fall into this category). When you search the Web, remember that no single search engine covers the entire Web and that surprisingly little overlap occurs when different search engines are used to find information on the same topic. Thus, using more than one search engine is a good idea.

(1) Knowing your location on the Web will help you keep track of your sources.

It is easy to get lost on the Web as you click from link to link. You can keep track of your location by looking at the Web address, or **URL (uniform resource locator),** at the top of your screen. Web addresses generally include the following information: server name, domain name, directory (and perhaps subdirectory) name, file name, and file type.

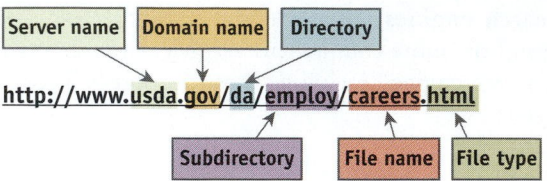

Sometimes when you click on a link, you will end up at a totally different Web site, so be sure to check the server and domain names when you are unsure of your location.

If you find that a URL has changed, which is likely if a site is regularly updated, you may still be able to find the site you are looking for by dropping the last part of the address and trying again. You may need to do this several times. If this strategy does not work, you can also run a search or look at the links on related Web sites.

Because sites change and even disappear, scholarly organizations such as the Modern Language Association (see chapter **12**) and the American Psychological Association (see chapter **13**) require that bibliographic entries for Web sites include both the **access date** (the date on which the site was visited) and the **posting date** (the date when the site was last modified or updated). When you print out material from the Web, the access date usually appears at the top or bottom of the printout. The posting date generally appears on the site itself. Some sites do not show a posting date, however, and printouts sometimes will not have an access date. Keeping a separate record of this information can help you when you need to verify information on a site or list it in a bibliography. If a site does not have a posting date, note that it is undated; doing so will establish that you did not accidentally omit a piece of information.

A convenient way to keep track of any useful Web site you visit is to create a **bookmark**—a record of a Web address you may want to return to in the future. The bookmarking function of a Web browser is usually labeled Bookmarks or Favorites.

Exercise 4

Perform a database search and a Web search using the same keywords for each. Print the first screen of the hits (results) you get for each type of search. Compare the two printouts, describing how the results of the two searches differ.

(2) The U.S. Government provides vast amounts of public information.

If you need information on particular federal laws, court cases, or population statistics, U.S. Government documents may be your best sources. You can find these documents by using online databases such as Congressional Universe, MARCIVE, LexisNexis Academic Universe, Census 2000, and STAT-USA. In addition, the following Web sites are helpful.

FirstGov	**www.firstgov.gov**
U.S. Government Printing Office	**www.gpoaccess.gov**
U.S. Courts	**www.uscourts.gov**
FedWorld	**www.fedworld.gov**

(3) Your rhetorical situation may call for the use of images.

If your rhetorical situation calls for the use of images, as did Andy Pieper's (see **12c**) and Nikki Krzmarzick's (**13c**), the Internet offers you billions from which to choose. However, if an image you choose is copyrighted, you will need to contact the author, artist, or designer for permission to use it. Figure 9.6 is an example of an image with a caption and a permission statement. You do

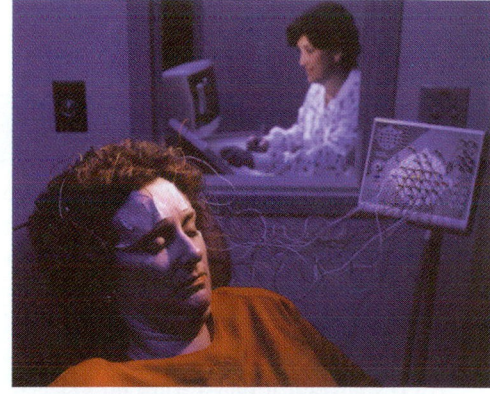

Fig. 9.6. A researcher monitors a participant's sleep patterns. (Photo reproduced courtesy of Charles Gupton/Corbis.)

not need to obtain permission to use public domain images or those that are cleared for reuse.

Many search engines allow you to search for images. On the search pages for Google and AltaVista, you must first click on the Image button. For MetaCrawler, you must choose Images from the pull-down menu. Collections of specific images are available at the following Web sites.

Advertisements

Ad*Access	scriptorium.lib.duke.edu/adaccess
Adflip	www.adflip.com
Advertising World	advertising.utexas.edu/world

Art

The Artchive	www.artchive.com
The Web Gallery of Art	www.wga.hu

Clip art

The Icon Browser	www.ibiblio.org/gio/iconbrowser
Webclipz	www.webclipz.com

Photography

The New York Public Library Picture Collection Online	digital.nypl.org/mmpco
Smithsonian Images	smithsonianimages.com

9e Field research

Although much of your research will consist of reading, viewing, or listening to sources, you may also find it helpful to conduct **field research**—to gather information in a natural setting. Interviews, discussions, questionnaires, and observations are the most common methods for such research.

(1) Consider interviewing an expert.

After you have consulted some sources on your topic, you may find that you still have questions that might best be answered by someone who has firsthand experience in the area you are researching. Consider contacting a teacher, government official, business owner, or other person with the relevant background to see whether it would be possible to schedule an interview. Most people welcome the opportunity to discuss their work, especially with a student who shows genuine interest. Because you will have done some reading on your topic before your meeting, you will be prepared to conduct a well-informed interview.

To arrange an interview, introduce yourself, briefly describe your project, and then explain your reasons for requesting the interview. Most people are busy, so try to accommodate the person you hope to interview by asking him or her to suggest an interview date. If you intend to tape your interview, ask for permission ahead of time.

Start preparing your list of questions before the day of the interview. Effective interviews usually contain a blend of open (or broad) questions and focused (or narrow) questions. Here are a few examples.

Open questions

What do you think about _____?

What are your views on _____?

Why do you believe _____?

Focused questions

How long have you worked as a/an _____?

When did you start _____?

What does _____ mean?

If you ask a question that elicits just a "yes" or "no," reformulate the question so that it begins with *why, when, what, who, where,* or *how.* By doing so, you give your interviewee a chance to elaborate. If you know that the person you are interviewing has published articles or a book on your topic, ask questions that will advance your knowledge, rather than questions that the author has already answered in print.

Preparing a list of questions before an interview is essential, but do not just recite your questions during the meeting. An interview is a special kind of conversation. Although you will be guiding it, the person you are speaking with is likely to say something you did not expect but would like to know more about. Do not be afraid to ask questions that are not on your list but come to mind during the interview. Along with your list of questions, be sure to bring pen and paper so that you can

take notes and a tape recorder with fresh batteries and an extra tape cassette if you will be recording the interview.

After the interview, take some time to review your notes. It will be hard to take down everything that is said during the interview, so expand on the notes you do have. If you recorded the interview, transcribe the relevant parts of the recording. The next step is to write extensively about the interview. Ask yourself what you found most important, most surprising, and most puzzling. You will find this writing especially worthwhile when you are able to use portions of it in your final paper.

(2) Consider participating in an online discussion group.

Less formal than an interview, a discussion with other people interested in your topic can also be useful. Online discussion groups, or forums (see **6c**), allow you to read messages posted to all the members of a group interested in a specific topic and to post messages or questions yourself. For instance, a writing teacher may belong to a specialized e-mail list, or **listserv,** that is operated by the Alliance for Computers and Writing and called ACW-L. Participants in this online forum discuss issues related to using computers to teach writing. Someone on the ACW-L list can send e-mail messages to the **listserv address,** which redistributes them to hundreds of other writing teachers around the world, and then receive replies from any of those teachers. You can find addresses of online discussion groups at either **www.forumone.com** or **groups.google.com**. Your instructor may even have created a discussion forum especially for your class.

(3) Consider using a questionnaire to gather information from a large number of people.

Whereas an interview elicits information from one person whose name you know, a questionnaire provides information from a number of anonymous people. To be effective, a questionnaire should be short and focused. If the list of questions is too long, people may not be willing to take the time to answer them all. If the questions are not focused on your research topic, you will find it difficult to integrate the results into your paper.

Questionnaires elicit information in a variety of ways, through several types of questions. The types of questions you decide to use depend on the purpose of your survey. The first four types of questions below are the easiest for respondents to answer. Open questions, which require much more time to answer, should be asked only when the other types of questions cannot elicit the information you want.

EXAMPLES OF TYPES OF SURVEY QUESTIONS

Questions that require a simple yes-or-no answer:

Do you commute to work in a car? (Circle one.)

Yes   No

Multiple-choice questions:

How many people do you commute with? (Circle one.)

0   1   2   3   4

Questions with answers on a checklist:

How long does it take you to commute to work? (Check one.)

___ 0–30 minutes   ___ 30–60 minutes   ___ 60–90 minutes   ___ 90–120 minutes

Questions with a ranking scale:

If the car you drive or ride in is not working, which of the following types of transportation do you rely on? (Rank the choices from 1 for most frequently used to 4 for least frequently used.)

___ bus   ___ shuttle van   ___ subway   ___ taxi

Open questions:

What aspect of commuting do you find most irritating?

Be sure to begin your questionnaire with an introduction stating what the purpose of the questionnaire is, how the results will be used, and how many questions it contains or approximately how long it should take to complete. In the introduction, you should also assure participants that their answers will remain confidential. To protect survey participants' privacy, colleges and universities have **institutional review boards (IRBs)** set up to review questionnaires. Before you

distribute your questionnaire, check with the institutional review board on your campus to make certain that you have followed its guidelines.

Administering a questionnaire can sometimes be problematic. Many questionnaires sent through the mail are never returned. If you do decide to mail out a questionnaire, provide a self-addressed envelope and directions for returning it. It is a good idea to send out twice as many copies as you would like returned because the proportion of responses is generally low. Questionnaires can sometimes be distributed in college dormitories or in classes, but this procedure must be approved by school officials. Listservs (**6c(1)**) can also be used to conduct surveys. Just remember that a survey limited to people who have a strong interest in a topic will not yield results representative of other groups, such as the students at your school or the citizens of your state.

Once the questionnaires have been completed and returned, tally the results for all but the open questions on an unused copy. To find patterns in the responses to the open questions, first read through them all; you might find that you can create categories for the responses. For example, the open question "What aspect of your commute do you find most irritating?" might elicit answers that fall into such categories as "length of time," "amount of traffic," or "bad weather conditions." By first creating categories, you will find it easier to tally the answers to the open questions.

CHECKLIST for Creating a Questionnaire

- Does each question relate directly to the purpose of the survey?
- Are the questions easy to understand?
- Are they designed to elicit short, specific responses?
- Are they designed to collect concrete data that can be analyzed easily?
- Have respondents been given enough space to write their answers to open questions?
- Do you have access to the group you want to survey?
- Have you asked a few classmates to "test-drive" your questionnaire?

10 EVALUATING PRINT AND ONLINE SOURCES

As you find sources that seem to address your research question, you have to evaluate them to determine how, or even whether, you can use them in your paper. In short, you need to establish whether the information they contain is credible, relevant, and timely. This chapter will help you

- assess an author's credibility (**10a**),
- evaluate a publisher's credibility (**10b**),
- evaluate online sources (**10c**), and
- determine the relevance and timeliness of a source (**10d**).

10a Credibility of authors

To be considered credible, authors must be trustworthy. They can attain such status by presenting information honestly, logically, fairly, and respectfully. That is, credible authors present facts accurately, support their opinions with evidence, connect their ideas reasonably, and demonstrate respect for any opposing views. To evaluate the credibility of the authors of your sources, find out what their credentials are, consider what worldview informs their ideas, and note how other readers respond to their work.

(1) Credentials help establish an author's credibility.

When evaluating sources, consider whether the authors have credentials that are relevant to the topics they address. Although many works have only one author, some are composed collaboratively, so be sure to take into account the credentials of all of the authors responsible for the material in the sources you use.

Credentials take various forms, including academic or professional training, publications, and experience. A college biology professor who specializes in genetics is likely to be credible when writing about genes, for example, and a civil engineer who specializes in bridges should have credibility when writing about how a particular bridge could be strengthened. However, given their areas of specialization, the biologist would not necessarily be considered a credible source of information on the foraging habits of black bears, and the engineer would not have credibility concerning the design of hydroelectric power plants.

To find information about the credentials of an author whose work you want to use, look

- on the jacket of a book,
- on a separate page near the front or back of the book,
- in the preface of the book,
- in a note at the bottom of the first or last page of an article in print, or
- on a separate page of a periodical or a Web page devoted to providing background on contributors.

As you read about an author, ask yourself the following questions.

CHECKLIST for Assessing an Author's Credentials

- Does the author's education or profession relate to the subject of the work?
- With what institutions, organizations, or companies has the author been affiliated (see **10b**)?
- What awards has the author won?
- What other works has the author produced?
- Do other experts speak of the author as an authority (see **10a(3)**)?

(2) An author's work reflects a specific worldview.

An author's values and beliefs about the world constitute his or her **worldview,** which underpins any article, book, or Web site he or she produces. To determine what these values and beliefs are, consider the author's purpose and intended audience.

It might be easiest to start by identifying the audience. For example, of the following four excerpts about malpractice lawsuits, excerpts 1 and 2 are intended for physicians, while 3 and 4 are written for patients.

1   Just as quickly as medical knowledge and disease treatment options increase, so too do advances in the strategies lawyers use to bring medical malpractice suits.

Last year, an Ohio jury awarded $3.5 million to the family of a man who died of a heart attack.

His family claimed that the physician didn't do enough to help the man lose weight and stop smoking, given that physicians now know how smoking and excess weight contribute to heart disease and given the significant advances in treatment.

—**TANYA ALBERT,** "Lawyers Try New Tacks in Malpractice Suits"

2   A new study led by Wendy Levinson, Professor in Medicine, suggests that the most important reason a patient with a bad outcome decides to sue his or her doctor for malpractice is not medical negligence but how the doctor talks with the patient.

—"Bad Rapport with Patients to Blame for Most Malpractice Suits,"
University of Chicago Chronicle

3   Medical malpractice suits are legal claims that are filed against a medical professional whose actions or negligence causes injury to a patient under [his or her] care. It is estimated that 800,000 people are the victims of medical malpractice every year, though only one in eight file medical malpractice suits. Medical malpractice suits can be filed against a medical professional whose actions range from negligence (or inaction/substandard action) that causes injury to the willful and malicious abuse of patients undergoing medical care.

—"Medical Malpractice Suits," **www.onlinelawyersource.com**

4   A growing number of doctors fed up with skyrocketing malpractice insurance premiums are calling on their patients to bear part of the burden.

Some physicians are requiring patients to sign waivers promising not to sue for "frivolous" reasons or, in some cases, for any reason at all. Others are billing for telephone consultations, paperwork and other services that once were free.

Perhaps the most controversial—and possibly illegal—approach is charging user, or administrative, fees. Patients increasingly are protesting paying more—on top of their copayments, deductibles and premiums—for medical services already covered by their health plans.

—**CAROLE FLECK,** "Doctors' Fees Try Their Patients"

Published on a news Web site for doctors, excerpt 1 focuses on the frivolous nature of some malpractice suits. The second excerpt, taken from a university newspaper (no author is identified), highlights the research of a medical professor at that university: her findings downplay the role of negligence in malpractice suits and highlight the role of doctor-patient rapport. In contrast to the first two excerpts, the next two are sympathetic toward patients. Appearing on a commercial Web site that helps patients locate medical malpractice lawyers, excerpt 3 emphasizes the large number of malpractice cases that go unfiled. In excerpt 4, taken from a news bulletin for retired people, the reporter questions whether doctors have the right to pass on the high costs of malpractice insurance to their patients.

As you read and use sources, keep in mind that they reflect the worldviews of the authors and often of the audience for whom they were written. By identifying these various values and beliefs, you can responsibly represent and report the information in your sources. When you find yourself referring to information that reveals economic, political, religious, or social biases, you should feel free to question or argue with the author, as does Natalie Angier when she questions the views of Robert Wright and a few other evolutionary psychologists.

5   Now, it makes sense to be curious about the evolutionary roots of human behavior. It's reasonable to attempt to understand our impulses and actions by applying Darwinian logic to the problem. We're animals. We're not above the rude little prods and jests of natural selection. But evolutionary psychology as it has been disseminated across mainstream consciousness is a cranky and despotic Cyclops, its single eye glaring through an overwhelmingly masculinist lens. I say masculinist rather than male because the view of male behavior promulgated by hardcore evolutionary psychologists is as narrow and inflexible as their view of womanhood is.

—**NATALIE ANGIER,** *Woman: An Intimate Geography*

The following questions may help you determine the worldview of an author whose work you hope to use.

> ## CHECKLIST for Determining an Author's Worldview
>
> - What is the author's educational and professional background?
> - What are the author's and publisher's affiliations; that is, with what types of organizations do they align themselves?
> - What is the editorial slant of the organization publishing the author's work? Where does it lie on the political spectrum from conservative to liberal?
> - Can you detect any signs of bias on the part of the author or the publisher?
> - Is the information purported to be factual? Objective? Personal?
> - Who advertises in the source?
> - To what types of Web sites do any links lead?
> - How can you use the source? As fact? Opinion? Support? Authoritative testimony? Material to be refuted?

(3) Online sources, book reviews, and texts written by other authors can provide additional information about an author.

You can learn more about authors by searching the Internet for information about them. For example, the Nobel e-Museum provides biographical information about Nobel laureates (see fig. 10.1). To find Internet sources, use a general search engine such as Google or AltaVista or a specialized search engine such as the People search option offered by Lycos (www.whowhere.lycos.com). Either type of engine will locate sites containing background information on the author or bibliographical information about his or her other works.

Book reviews, many of which are available online, often include information that is useful for determining whether an author is credible. When you read reviews, though, remember that a work by a credible author may get some negative responses. Look for the main point of a review, and decide whether that main point amounts to a positive or negative response to the book as a whole. For example, if an author is described as "entertaining but unreliable," the negative adjective is more important than the positive one. Or if an author is described as "dry but nevertheless informative," the praise outweighs the complaint. Being a credible source does not mean being a perfect source. However, dismiss from further consideration any writer whom more than one

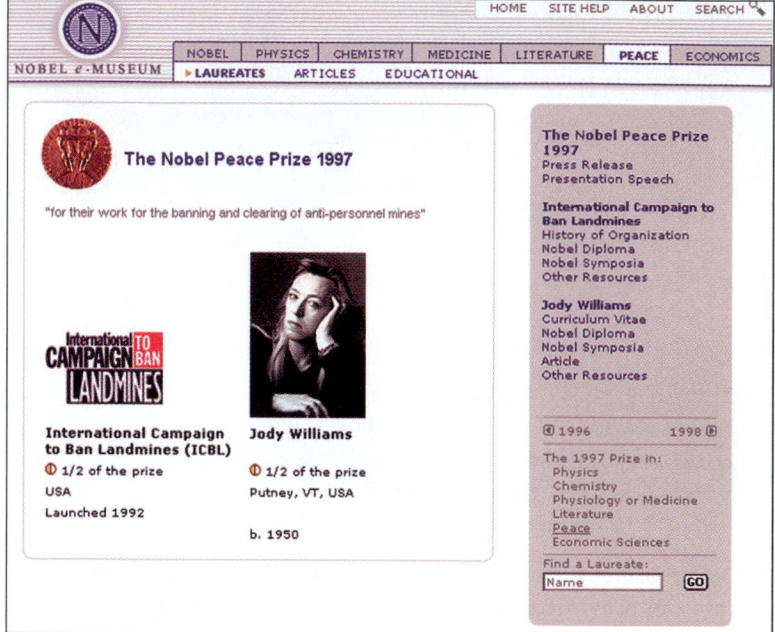

Fig. 10.1. Biographical information about Nobel laureates may be found on the Nobel e-Museum Web site.

reviewer characterizes as ill-informed, careless with facts, biased, or dishonest in any way. Keep in mind, though, that few writers please all reviewers all the time, so your responsibility is to read reviews critically.

As you research a topic, you will find that writers often refer to the work of other writers. To gain insight into how an author influences the work of others, keep track of who is being discussed or cited by whom. If several well-known writers offer negative evaluations of an author's work or do not mention the work at all, that author's contribution is likely considered insignificant or unreliable. If, on the other hand, several writers praise or build on the work of the author you are evaluating, you can be confident in the credibility of your source.

Exercise 1

Choose a book you plan to use for your research paper. Locate at least two reviews of this book. Then, write a one-page report of what the reviews have in common and how they differ.

10b Credibility of publishers

Credible sources are published by reliable institutions, organizations, and companies. When you are doing research, consider not only the credibility of authors but also the credibility of the media through which their work is made available to you. Some publishers hold authors accountable to higher standards than others do.

(1) Book publishers are either commercial or academic.

When evaluating books, you can usually assume that publishers associated with universities (university presses) demand a high standard of scholarship. Although some university presses have better reputations than others, the works such publishers produce are generally considered trustworthy—in great part because of the publishers' requirement that books be reviewed by experts before publication. Books published by commercial presses, in contrast, typically do not undergo the same type of review. Thus, to determine how a trade book has been received by others writing in the same area, you have to rely on book reviews (see **10a(3)**).

(2) Periodicals are written for an academic audience or for the general public.

Periodicals are published periodically—daily, weekly, or monthly (see **9c**). They include scholarly journals, magazines (trade, news, public affairs, and special interest), and newspapers. An article published in a scholarly journal is generally considered more credible than one published in a magazine because it has usually been both written and reviewed by an expert. Authors of these journal articles are expected to include both in-text citations and bibliographies so that other researchers can consult the sources used (see chapters **12–15**).

Articles that appear in magazines and newspapers may be reliable, but keep in mind that they are usually written quickly and chosen for publication by someone on the magazine's staff—not by an expert in the field. Because magazines and newspapers often report research results that were initially published elsewhere, you should try to find the original source to ensure the accuracy of their reports. This is not always an easy task, though, especially since in-text citations and

Forum defends right to know

By MIKE JOHNSTON
associate editor

Changes to the Clean Air Act

THE ASSOCIATED PRESS

Fig. 10.2. Examples of bylines for a staff writer of a local newspaper (left) and a wire service (right).

bibliographies are rarely provided in these periodicals. Your best bet for finding the original source is to use a search engine.

When evaluating an article in a magazine or newspaper, also take into account the reputation of the publication itself. To gauge the credibility of magazines and newspapers, you can examine several issues and consider the space devoted to various stories, the tone of the commentary on the editorial pages, and the extent to which staff members (as opposed to wire services) are responsible for stories. Figure 10.2 shows an example of a byline for a staff writer and an example of a byline for a wire service.

10c Online sources

If you are evaluating a periodical source that you obtained online, you can follow the guidelines for print-based sources (see **10a–b**). But if you are evaluating a Web site, you also need to consider the nature of the site and its sponsor. Although many sites are created by individuals working on their own, many others are sponsored by colleges or universities, professional or nonprofit organizations, and commercial enterprises. The type of sponsor is typically indicated in the site's address, or URL, by a suffix that represents the domain. Colleges and universities are indicated by the suffix **.edu**, government departments and agencies by **.gov**, professional and nonprofit organizations by **.org**, network sites by **.net**, and businesses by **.com**. Depending on the nature of your research paper, you can access any or all of the various types of sites. But, as you evaluate their content, remember that every site is shaped to achieve a specific purpose and to address a target audience.

Suppose, for example, you were writing a paper about how a corporate bankruptcy revealed serious irregularities in the practices of a major energy company. An education site could provide a scholarly analysis of the practices in question; a government site could contain data compiled by the Securities and Exchange Commission (SEC); an organization site could give you the viewpoint of an association of accountants; and a business site could convey information from the energy company in question. Each of these sites would offer different content, which would be shaped by the rhetorical situation as envisioned by each site's sponsor. For example, the SEC is an agency of the federal government that reports to the U.S. Congress, which, in turn, represents American citizens. Accordingly, the purpose of the SEC's Web site is to show its audience that the agency is providing careful oversight of business practices (see fig. 10.3). The commercial site of an energy company such as Enron, on the other hand, has a vested interest in making the company look good to current customers and potential clients.

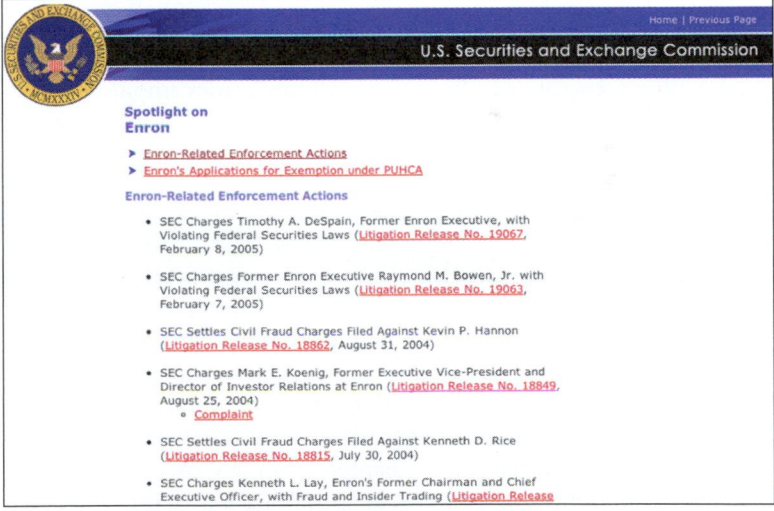

Fig. 10.3. The Securities and Exchange Commission site provides links to the details of the Enron case. If you visited www.enron.com you would get a more positive view of the company.

You can find out more about the sponsor of a Web site by using navigational buttons or links such as "About Us" or "Our Vision." The following is an excerpt from a Web page for National Public Radio, found by clicking on "About NPR" on the organization's home page (www.npr.org).

What is NPR?

NPR is an internationally acclaimed producer and distributor of noncommercial news, talk, and entertainment programming. A privately supported, not-for-profit, membership organization, NPR serves more than 770 independently operated, noncommercial public radio stations. Each member station serves local listeners with a distinctive combination of national and local programming.

This passage provides information not only on NPR's radio programming but also on its status as a nonprofit organization.

For a summary of criteria you can use to evaluate both online and print sources, see pages 242 and 243.

Exercise 2

Find Web sites that have three different kinds of sponsors but contain material relevant to a specific subject, such as global warming or disaster efforts. Explain the differences and similarities among the three sites you choose.

10d   Relevance and timeliness

A source is useful only when it is relevant to your research question. Given the huge and ever-growing amount of information available on most topics, you should be prepared to put aside a source that will not help you answer your research question or achieve your rhetorical purpose. There are plenty of other sources, which you can locate by using the search strategies discussed in chapter 9. Some writers get off track when they cannot bring themselves to abandon a source they like, even if it is no longer relevant—as often happens when their focus has changed during the process of conducting research, drafting the paper, and revising it. It is better to abandon an irrelevant source than to write a poorly focused paper.

You may reject some sources altogether. You are also likely to use only parts of others. Seldom will an entire book, article, or Web site be useful for a specific research paper. A book may have just a chapter or a section or two on your topic. The table of contents can lead you to these relevant chapters or sections, and the index can lead you to relevant pages. Web sites have hyperlinks or buttons that you can click on to locate relevant information. Once you find potentially useful material, read it with your research question and rhetorical purpose in mind.

Useful sources are also timely. You should always seek up-to-date information. However, if you are writing about a specific era in the past, you should also consult sources written during that period. To determine when a source was published, look for the date of publication. In books, it appears with other copyright information on the page following the title page (see page 279). Dates of periodicals appear on their covers and frequently on the top or bottom of pages throughout each issue (see page 284). The date on which a Web site was established or last updated frequently appears on the site, and the date on which you access it will usually appear on any hard copy you print out (see page 294). Do not confuse the access date with the posting date.

CHECKLIST for Establishing Relevancy and Timeliness

- Does the table of contents, index, or directory of the work include key words related to your research question?
- Does the abstract of a journal article contain information on your topic?
- If an abstract is not available, are any of the article's topic sentences relevant to your research question?
- Do the section heads of the source include words connected to your topic?
- On a Web site, are there hyperlinks or buttons that can lead you to relevant information?
- Is the work recent enough to provide up-to-date information?
- If you need a source from another time period, is the work from the right period?

Criteria for Evaluating Sources

TYPE OF SOURCE	PURPOSE	AUTHORS/PUBLISHERS
Scholarly books	To advance knowledge among experts	Experts/University presses
Trade books	To provide information of interest to the general public	Experts, journalists, professional writers/ Commercial presses
Reference books	To provide factual information	Experts/Commercial presses
Articles from scholarly journals	To advance knowledge among experts	Experts/Publishers associated with professions or universities
Articles from magazines or newspapers	To report current events or provide general information about current research	Journalists and professional writers (sometimes experts)/ Commercial presses
Editorials from newspapers	To state a position on an issue	Journalists/ Commercial presses
Sponsored Web sites	To report information	Often a group author
Interviews with experts	To report views of an expert	Professional or student writer reporting views of expert

SOURCES DOCUMENTED?	PRIMARY AUDIENCE	CHIEF ADVANTAGE
Yes	Other experts	Reliable because they are written and reviewed by experts
Sometimes	Educated public	Accessible because the language is not overly technical
Yes	Other experts and educated public	Reliable because the entries are written by experts
Yes	Other experts	Reliable because the entries are written and reviewed by experts
No	General public	Accessible because the language is not overly technical
No	General public	Current because they are published daily
No	General public	Accessible by computer
No	General public	Reliable because the interviewee is an expert

USING SOURCES EFFECTIVELY AND RESPONSIBLY

11

To use sources effectively, you need to remember that you are a *writer,* not simply a compiler of data. Yours is the most important voice in a paper that has your name on it. To use sources responsibly, you need to acknowledge others' ideas and words when you incorporate them into a paper you write. This chapter will help you

- consider your rhetorical situation (**11a**),
- organize notes effectively (**11b**),
- compose a working bibliography or an annotated bibliography (**11c**),
- integrate sources (**11d**),
- avoid plagiarism (**11e**), and
- respond to sources (**11f**).

11a The rhetorical situation and the research paper

Like any other paper, a research paper should originate in an exigence and have a purpose appropriate for a particular audience and context. It should not be a mere compilation of research findings or a list of works consulted. Rather, in a research paper, you discuss what others have discovered, thus creating a conversation in which you play an essential role: your sources interact with one another, and, because you yourself are a source, you talk back to them.

By studying the following introductory paragraphs to a research article, you can see how the author, Timothy Quinn, chooses words, sentence types, organization strategies, and citation conventions according to his rhetorical situation. In the first paragraph, he alludes to his exigence: the increasing presence of coyotes in areas inhabited by people and the lack of a clear explanation for this presence. Because he states a problem with no easy solution, Quinn finds his own research niche. At the end of the second paragraph, Quinn states his purpose: to document coyotes' typical diet and assess changes in that diet caused by human population and land use. Quinn shows his understanding of audience and context by citing other researchers' work according to the appropriate convention of providing the name(s) of author(s) and the year of publication.

Coyotes (*Canis latrans*) are becoming increasingly common in human-modified habitats throughout North America (Atkinson and Shackleton 1991, MacCracken 1982). One possible explanation for this trend is that human-dominated areas produce abundant food sources for coyotes. Coyotes living in urban habitats have relatively small home ranges (Atkinson and Shackleton 1991, Shargo 1988), which may indicate abundant food resources. However, little is known about the diet of coyotes in these areas. MacCracken's (1982) description of the annual diet of coyotes in residential habitats was based on a small number of scats ($n = 97$) collected during a single month. Atkinson and Shackleton (1991) described the diet of coyotes in an area that was mostly agricultural (>50% of the study area) and Shargo's (1988) description of urban coyote diet was based on 22 scats. Additionally, none of these studies looked at diet as a function of human density.

Coyotes may play an important role in human-modified landscapes. Soulé et al. (1988) suggested that coyotes may reduce the abundance of house cats (*Felis catus*) and other small mammalian carnivores that prey on songbirds and thus indirectly contribute to the maintenance of native avifauna. My objectives were to document the annual diet of coyotes in three types of urban habitat of western Washington and to qualitatively assess how coyote diets changed as a function of land use patterns and human density.

—**TIMOTHY QUINN**, "Coyote (*Canis latrans*) Food Habits and
Three Urban Habitat Types of Western Washington"

As you work toward providing an appropriate response to your rhetorical situation, be sure to present yourself as thoughtful and informed. Whether your audience consists of a single instructor or some larger group, you must establish that you are a credible author (see **10a**). By conducting research and citing sources, you demonstrate that you have

- educated yourself about your topic,
- drawn accurately on the work of others (including diverse points of view),
- understood what you have discovered,
- integrated research data into a paper that is clearly your own, and
- provided all the information readers will need to consult the sources you have used.

The rest of this chapter and chapters **12–15** will help you fulfill these responsibilities.

11b Organizing notes

Taking thorough and organized notes is critical when you are preparing to write a research paper in which you attribute specific words and ideas to others while taking credit for your own ideas. Some researchers are most comfortable taking notes in notebooks. Others like to write notes directly on pages they have photocopied or printed out from an online source (see **2d**). Still others write notes on index cards or type them into computer files—two methods that allow notes to be rearranged easily. Each method has advantages and disadvantages, and your choice should be guided by the requirements of your project and your own working style.

(1) Organizing notes in a ring binder or folder

When using a ring binder, you can combine pages of notes with photocopies or printouts of relevant source material. Moreover, you can add, remove, and rearrange material easily. Remember to identify the source on every page of notes and to use a fresh page for each new source. Be sure to distinguish direct quotations from paraphrases or summaries (see **11d**), and keep your working bibliography (**11c**) separate from your notes.

(2) Taking notes on photocopies and printouts

An easy way to take notes is to use photocopies of articles and excerpts from books or printouts of sources from the Web. On a printout or photocopy, you can mark quotable material while also jotting down your own ideas in the margins (see fig. 11.1). This method reduces the risk of including inaccurate quotations in your paper, because you have eliminated the step of copying quotes exactly as they appear in the original source. Make sure to record the source on a photocopy if this information is not shown on the original page(s). Printouts from the Web almost always indicate the source and the date of access, but you should also note the date on which the site was posted or last updated (see **9d(1)**).

It was the authors of the Declaration of Independence who stated the principles that all men are created equal in their rights, and that <u>it is to secure these rights that governments are instituted among men.</u>

= the purpose of gov't according to Truman

It was the authors of the Constitution who made it clear that, under our form of government, <u>all citizens are equal before the law,</u> and that the Federal Government has a duty to guarantee to every citizen equal protection of the laws.

= a radical idea for many Americans at the time

The Civil Rights Committee did more than repeat these great principles. It described a method to put these principles into action, and to make them a living reality for every American, regardless of his race, his religion, or his national origin.

background on the Civil Rights Committee link to Fahy

<u>When every American knows that his rights and his opportunities are fully protected and respected by the Federal, State, and local governments, then we will have the kind of unity that really means something.</u>

what Truman is after

Public Papers of the Presidents of the United States: Harry S. Truman, 1945–53, vol. 4 (Washington, D.C.: U.S. Government Printing Office, 1964), 923–5.

Fig. 11.1. Photocopied source with notes.

The example in fig. 11.1 comes from the work Nicole Hester did for her research paper on the desegregation of the U.S. military (see **14b**).

(3) Organizing notes in computer files

You may find it efficient to use a computer for taking notes—recording them quickly and storing them safely. Then, later, you can easily copy and paste information into various files and ultimately into a draft of your paper. Given the ease of computer use, though, it is important to remember to identify which records are direct quotations (see **11d(2)**), which are paraphrases (**11d(3)**), and which are your own thoughts. Always provide necessary bibliographic information so that you will not have trouble finding the source later. The following tips can help you use your computer efficiently when taking and filing notes for a research paper.

TIPS ON USING A COMPUTER TO ORGANIZE NOTES

- Create a separate master folder (or directory) for the paper.
- Create folders within the master folder for your bibliography, notes, and portions of drafts.
- Keep all the notes for each source in a separate file.
- Use a distinctive font or a different color to distinguish your own thoughts from the ideas of others (see fig. 11.2).
- Place direct quotations in quotation marks.
- When taking notes, record exactly where the information came from.
- When you discover new sources, add them to your working bibliography (see **11c**).
- Consider using the Annotation or Comment feature of your word-processing program to make notes on documents you have downloaded.

```
Scott, Alwyn
"Shot of Americana"
FI

Some coffee shops in Europe are Starbucks spin-offs. Some even
have American names—Chicago Coffee, San Francisco Coffee,
Coffee Shop. Scott says European imitators "suggest American
style,if not Seattle." Seems like traditional coffee cultures
are competing with Starbucks AND Starbucks imitators.
```

Fig. 11.2. The researcher used green to distinguish his response to a quotation from one of his sources.

(4) Arranging notes on note cards

Taking notes on index cards (also known as three-by-five cards) can be useful if you are working in a library without a laptop or if you prefer handwritten notes that you can rearrange as your research proceeds. Each index card should show the author's name (and a short title if the bibliography contains more than one work by that author), the exact page number(s) from which the information is drawn, and a brief comment on how you intend to use the information or a reflection on what you think about it. By putting a heading of two or three key words at the top of each card, you can easily arrange your cards as you prepare to draft your paper.

Whatever method you use to create your notes, consider the points in the following list.

TIPS FOR TAKING NOTES

- Identify the source for every note.
- Put the full bibliographic citation on the first page of every photocopy.
- Copy verbatim any useful passage you think you may quote. Put quotation marks around quoted words. In computer files, you can also use different fonts or different colors to identify quoted text.
- When a source has stimulated your thinking, identify both the source and the fact that the note is your own idea based on that source.

11c Working bibliography and annotated bibliography

A **working bibliography,** or preliminary bibliography, contains information (titles, authors, dates, and so on) about the materials you think you might use. Creating a working bibliography can help you evaluate the quality of your research. If you find that your most recent source is five years old, for example, or that you have relied exclusively on information from magazines or Web sites, you may need to find some other sources.

Some researchers find it convenient to put each bibliographic entry on a separate index card; this makes it easy to add or drop a card and to arrange the list alphabetically without recopying it. Others prefer to use a computer, which can sort and alphabetize automatically, making it easier to move material directly to the final draft.

It is also a good idea to follow the bibliographical format you have been instructed to use in your paper right from the start. This book covers the most common formats:

Modern Language Association (MLA), chapter **12**

American Psychological Association (APA), chapter **13**

The Chicago Manual of Style (CMS), chapter **14**

The Council of Science Editors (CSE), chapter **15**

The examples given in the rest of this chapter follow the MLA's bibliographical and documentation style.

If you are asked to prepare an **annotated bibliography,** you should list all your sources alphabetically according to the last name of the author. Then, at the end of each entry, summarize the content of the source in one or two sentences.

Zimmer, Carl. <u>Soul Made Flesh: The Discovery of the Brain—and How It Changed the</u> <u>World</u>. New York: Free, 2004. This book is a historical account of how knowledge of the brain developed and influenced ideas about the soul. It covers a span of time and place, beginning four thousand years ago in ancient Egypt and ending in Oxford, England, in the seventeenth century.

11d Integrating sources

You can integrate sources into your own writing in a number of ways— quoting exact words, paraphrasing sentences, and summarizing longer pieces of text or even entire texts. Whenever you borrow others' ideas in these ways, be careful to integrate the material—properly cited—into your own sentences and paragraphs. Once you have represented source material accurately and responsibly, you will be ready to respond to it.

(1) Writers introduce the sources they use.

When you borrow textual material, introduce it to readers by establishing the source, usually an author's name. You may also need to include additional information about the author, especially if the author's name is unfamiliar to your audience. For example, in a paper on medications given to children, the following statement becomes more credible if the audience is given the added information about Jerome Groopman's background.

professor of medicine at Harvard University,

According to Jerome Groopman, "Pediatricians sometimes adopt extraordinary measures to insure that their patients are not harmed by treatments that have not been adequately studied in children" (33).

Phrases such as *According to Jerome Groopman* and *from the author's perspective* are called **attributive tags** because they attribute, or ascribe, information to a source. Most attributive tags in academic writing consist of the name of an author (or a related noun or pronoun) and a verb in order to report what that author has said, written, thought, or felt. Verbs commonly found in attributive tags are listed below. For a list of the types of complements that follow such verbs, see **27d(3)**.

VERBS USED IN ATTRIBUTIVE TAGS

admit	disagree	observe
advise	discuss	point out
argue	emphasize	reject
believe	explain	reply
claim	find	state
concede	imply	suggest
conclude	insist	think
deny	note	

When you integrate sources, be sure to find out whether it is appropriate to add evaluative remarks. If your assignment requires that you be objective, refrain from injecting your own opinions when introducing the ideas of another writer. You can convey your opinion of the material when responding to it (see **11f**). If, on the other hand, your assignment allows you to voice your opinion when presenting ideas, you can easily add an adverb to one of the verbs on the list to indicate your attitude toward the material: *persuasively* argue, *strongly* oppose, *inaccurately* represent.

If you decide to integrate graphics as source material, you must label them as figures and assign them arabic numbers. You can then refer to them within the text of your paper in a parenthetical comment, as in this example: "The red and black bands of the Western coral snake are bordered by narrower bands of yellow or white (see fig. 11.3)." You may also want to include a title or caption with the figure number.

Fig. 11.3. Western coral snake.

(2) Direct quotations draw attention to key passages.

Include a direct quotation in a paper only if

- you want to retain the beauty or clarity of someone's words,
- you need to reveal how the reasoning in a specific passage is flawed or insightful, or
- you plan to discuss the implications of the quoted material.

Keep quotations as short as possible, and make them an integral part of your text.

Quote *accurately.* Any quotation of another person's words should be placed in quotation marks or, if longer than four lines, set off as an indented block. (See **12a(2)**.) If you need to clarify a quotation by changing it in any way, place square brackets around the added or changed words.

"In this role, he [Robin Williams] successfully conveys a diverse range of emotion."

If you want to omit part of a quotation, replace the deleted words with ellipsis points. (See **39h**.)

"Overseas markets . . . are critical to the financial success of Hollywood films."

When modifying a quotation, be sure not to alter its essential meaning.

CHECKLIST for Using Direct Quotations

- Have you copied all the words and punctuation accurately?
- Have you attributed the quotation to a specific source?
- Have you used ellipsis points to indicate anything you omitted? (See **39h**.)
- Have you used square brackets around anything you added to or changed in a direct quotation? (See **39g**.)
- Have you used quotations sparingly? Rather than using too many quotations, consider paraphrasing or summarizing the information instead.

(3) Paraphrases convey another person's ideas in different words.

A **paraphrase** is a restatement of someone else's ideas in approximately the same number of words. Paraphrasing allows you to demonstrate that you have understood what you have read; it also enables you to help your audience understand it. Paraphrase when you want to

- clarify difficult material by using simpler language,
- use another writer's idea but not his or her exact words,
- create a consistent tone (see **4a(3)**) for your paper as a whole, or
- interact with a point that your source has made.

Your paraphrase should be almost entirely in your own words and should accurately convey the content of the original passage.

(a) Use your own words and sentence structure when paraphrasing.

As you compare the source below with the paraphrases that follow, note the similarities and differences in both sentence structure and word choice.

Source

Zimmer, Carl. <u>Soul Made Flesh: The Discovery of the Brain—and How It Changed the World</u>. New York: Free, 2004. 7.

The maps that neuroscientists make today are like the early charts of the New World with grotesque coastlines and blank interiors. And what little we do know about how the brain works raises disturbing questions about the nature of our selves.

Inadequate paraphrase

The maps used by neuroscientists today resemble the rough maps of the New World. Because we know so little about how the brain works, we must ask questions about the nature of our selves (Zimmer 7).

If you simply change a few words in a passage, you have not adequately restated it. You may be committing plagiarism (see **11e**) if the wording of your version follows the original too closely, even if you provide a page reference for the source.

Adequate paraphrase

Carl Zimmer compares today's maps of the brain to the rough maps made of the New World. He believes that the lack of knowledge about the workings of the brain makes us ask serious questions about our nature (7).

In the second paraphrase, both vocabulary and sentence structure differ from those in the original. This paraphrase also includes an attributive tag ("Carl Zimmer compares") and a page reference.

(b) Maintain accuracy.

Any paraphrase must accurately maintain the sense of the original. If you unintentionally misrepresent the original because you did not understand it, you are being *inaccurate.* If you deliberately change the gist of what a source says, you are being *unethical.* Compare the original statement below with the paraphrases.

Source

Kolbert, Elizabeth. "Ice Memory." <u>New Yorker</u> 7 Jan. 2002: 37.

Humans are a remarkably resourceful species. We have spread into every region of the globe that is remotely habitable, and some, like Greenland, that aren't even that. The fact that we have managed this feat in an era of exceptional climate stability does not diminish the accomplishment, but it does make it seem that much more tenuous.

Inaccurate or unethical paraphrase

Human beings have to be resourceful in order to inhabit a wide range of remote areas. This accomplishment is remarkable in a time when our climate is constantly changing (Kolbert 37).

Accurate paraphrase

Elizabeth Kolbert believes that the spread of humans throughout the world, even to remote places like Greenland, demonstrates not only that we are resourceful but also that our achievement, however remarkable, has not yet been threatened by climate change (37).

Although both paraphrases include a reference to an author and a page number, the first focuses only on the greatness of the human achievement mentioned by Kolbert, failing to note its tenuous nature.

(4) Summaries convey ideas efficiently.

When you summarize, you condense the main point(s) of your source. Although a summary omits much of the detail the writer uses in the original, it accurately reflects the essence of that work. In most cases, then, a **summary** reports a writer's main idea (see **3c**) and the most important support given for it.

Whereas the length of a paraphrase (see **11d(3)**) is usually close to that of the original material, a summary is shorter than the material it reports. When you paraphrase, you restate an author's ideas in order to present or examine them in detail. When you summarize, you present just the gist of the author's ideas, without including background information and details. Summaries can include short quotations of key phrases or ideas, but you must always enclose another writer's exact words in quotation marks when you blend them with your own.

Source

Kremmer, Christopher. The Carpet Wars. New York: HarperCollins, 2002. 197.

Iraq was once, like the United States today, a country of firsts. Sedentary society emerged in Mesopotamia around 5000 BC when people learned to plant, irrigate and harvest crops. Three thousand years before Christ, writing based on abstract symbols was invented to label the fruits of agricultural surplus. When a potter's wheel was turned on its side and hitched to a horse, modern transportation was born. It was where time was first carved into sixty minutes and circles into three hundred and sixty degrees. When in the ninth century the Arab caliph Haroun al-Rashid wanted to demonstrate his society's superiority over Europe, he sent Charlemagne a clock.

Summary

Iraq was once a center of innovation, where new methods of agriculture, transportation, writing, and measurement were generated (Kremmer 197).

This example reduces six sentences to one, retaining the key idea but eliminating specific examples such as the clock. A writer who believes that the audience needs examples might decide to paraphrase the passage instead.

Exercise 1

Find a well-developed paragraph in one of your recent reading assignments. Rewrite it in your own words, varying the sentence structure of the original. Make your paraphrase approximately the same length as the original. Next, write a one-sentence summary of the same paragraph.

11e Avoiding plagiarism

The purpose of this chapter has been to help you use the work of others responsibly. To ensure that your audience can distinguish between the ideas of other writers and your own contributions, give credit for all information you gather through research. It is not necessary, however, to credit information that is **common knowledge,** which includes well-known events and other facts such as the following: "The *Titanic* hit an iceberg and sank on its maiden voyage." This event has been the subject of many books and movies, so some information about it has become common knowledge.

If, however, you are writing a research paper about the *Titanic* and wish to include the ship's specifications, such as its overall length and gross tonnage, you will be providing *un*common knowledge, which must be documented. After you have read a good deal about a given subject, you will be able to distinguish between common knowledge and the distinctive ideas or interpretations of specific writers. If you have been scrupulous about recording your own thoughts as you took notes, you should have little difficulty distinguishing between what you knew to begin with and what you learned through your research.

Taking even part of someone else's work and presenting it as your own leaves you open to criminal charges. In the film, video, music, and software businesses, this sort of theft is called **piracy.** In publishing and education, it is called **plagiarism.** Whatever it is called, it is illegal, and penalties range from failing a paper or course to being expelled from school. Never compromise your integrity or risk your future by submitting someone else's work as your own.

BEYOND THE RULE

PLAGIARISM

If you follow the news, you may be aware of cases in which well-established writers have been accused of plagiarism. These stories demonstrate that plagiarism is not just an academic problem. For information about some of these cases, visit **www.harbrace.com**.

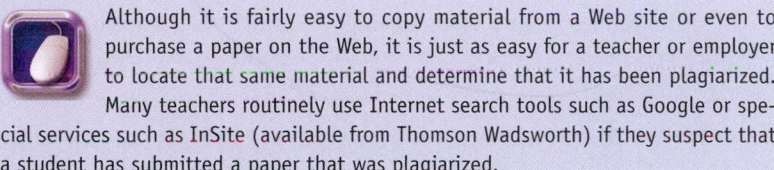
Although it is fairly easy to copy material from a Web site or even to purchase a paper on the Web, it is just as easy for a teacher or employer to locate that same material and determine that it has been plagiarized. Many teachers routinely use Internet search tools such as Google or special services such as InSite (available from Thomson Wadsworth) if they suspect that a student has submitted a paper that was plagiarized.

To review how to draw responsibly on the words and ideas of others, consider the following examples.

Source

McConnell, Patricia B. <u>The Other End of the Leash</u>. New York: Ballantine 2002. 142.

Status in male chimpanzees is particularly interesting because it is based on the formation of coalitions, in which no single male can achieve and maintain power without a cadre of supporting males.

Paraphrase with documentation

Patricia B. McConnell, an authority on animal training, notes that by forming alliances with other male chimpanzees, a specific male can enjoy status and power (142).

This example includes not only the original author's name but also a parenthetical citation, which marks the end of the paraphrase and provides the page number on which the source can be found.

Quotation with documentation

Patricia B. McConnell, an authority on animal training, argues that male chimpanzees achieve status "based on the formation of coalitions, in which no single male can achieve and maintain power without a cadre of supporting males" (142).

Quotation marks show where the copied words begin and end; the number in parentheses indicates the exact page on which those words appear. Again, the author is identified in the sentence, although her name could have been omitted at the beginning of the sentence and noted within the parenthetical reference instead:

An authority on animal training argues that male chimpanzees achieve status "based on the formation of coalitions, in which no single male can achieve and maintain power without a cadre of supporting males" (McConnell 142).

If, after referring to the following checklist, you cannot decide whether you need to cite a source, the safest policy is to cite it.

CHECKLIST of Sources That Should Be Cited

- Writings, both published and unpublished
- Opinions and judgments that are not your own
- Statistics and other facts that are not widely known
- Images and graphics, such as works of art, drawings, charts and graphs, tables, photographs, maps, and advertisements
- Personal communications, such as interviews, letters, and e-mail messages
- Public electronic communication, including television and radio broadcasts, motion pictures and videos, sound recordings, Web sites, and online discussion groups or forums

Exercise 2

After reading the source material, decide which of the quotations and paraphrases that follow it are written correctly and which would be considered problematic. Be prepared to explain your answers.

Source

Polsby, Daniel D. "Second Reading." <u>Reason</u> Mar. 1996: 33.

Generally speaking, though, it must be said that even among enthusiasts who think about the Second Amendment quite a lot, there has been little appreciation for the intricate and nuanced way in which constitutional analysis is practiced, and has to be practiced, by judges and lawyers.

1. People who care about the Second Amendment do not really understand how hard judges and lawyers have to work (Polsby 33).

2. Daniel Polsby has claimed that nobody understands the Second Amendment (33).

3. Daniel Polsby has claimed that public debate over the meaning of the Second Amendment seldom includes a deep understanding of the careful analysis judges and lawyers practice when interpreting the Constitution (33).

4. Those who tout the rights of the Second Amendment may not have a deep understanding of the careful analysis judges and lawyers practice when interpreting the Constitution (33).

5. According to Daniel Polsby, "there has been little appreciation for the intricate and nuanced way in which constitutional analysis is practiced, and has to be practiced, by judges and lawyers."

6. Few enthusiasts of the Second Amendment appreciate the nuanced ways in which constitutional analysis is practiced by judges and lawyers (33).

11f Responding to sources

When incorporating sources, not only will you summarize, paraphrase, quote, and document them, you will often respond to them as well. To prepare for interacting with your sources, you may find it useful to make notes in the margins of whatever you are reading. Next to relevant passages, jot down your agreement, disagreement, surprise, questions, and so on (see **2d**).

Readers of academic research papers or articles expect the authors of those works to be critical. They want to know whether facts are accurate or erroneous, whether logic is strong or weak, whether the organization is well planned or ill conceived, and whether conclusions are valid or doubtful. Researchers, therefore, critique the sources they use to ensure that their readers' concerns are being addressed. However, they also evaluate the strengths and weaknesses of sources in order to motivate a line of research. For example, they may try to show that previous research is insufficient in some way so that they can establish an exigence for their own research.

For your own paper, consider responding to your sources by examining their timeliness, coverage, reliability, and reasoning.

(1) Considering the currency of sources

Depending on the nature of your research, the currency of sources may be an important consideration. Using up-to-date sources is crucial when researching most topics. Historical research may call for sources from a specific period in the past as well. When you consider the currency of a source, start by looking for the date of its publication. Then, examine any data reported. Even though a source is published in the same year that you are doing research, it may include data that are several years old and thus possibly irrelevant. In the following example, the writer questions the usefulness of an out-of-date statistic mentioned in a source.

According to Jenkins, only 50% of all public schools have Web pages (23); however, this statistic is taken from a report published in 1997. A more recent count would likely yield a much higher percentage.

(2) Noting the thoroughness of research

Coverage refers to the comprehensiveness of research. The more comprehensive a study is, the more convincing are its findings. Similarly, the more examples an author provides, the more compelling are his or her conclusions. Claims that are based on only one instance are often criticized for being merely anecdotal or otherwise unsubstantiated. The writer of the following response suggests that the author of the source in question may have based his conclusion on too little information.

Johnson concludes that middle-school students are expected to complete an inordinate amount of homework given their age, but he bases his conclusion on research conducted in only three schools. To be more convincing, Johnson needs to conduct research in more schools, preferably located in different parts of the country.

(3) Checking the reliability of findings

Research, especially when derived from experiments or surveys, must be reliable (see **18b**). Experimental results are considered **reliable** if they can be reproduced by researchers using a similar methodology. Results that cannot be replicated in this way are unreliable because they are supported by only one experiment.

Reliability is also a requirement for reported data. Researchers are expected to report their findings accurately and honestly, not distorting them to support their own beliefs or claiming others' ideas as their own. To ensure the reliability of their work, researchers must also report all relevant information, not intentionally excluding any that weakens their conclusions. When studies of the same phenomenon give rise to disputes, researchers should discuss conflicting results or interpretations. The writer of the following response focuses on the problematic nature of her source's methodology.

Jamieson concludes from her experiment that a low-carbohydrate diet can be dangerous for athletes, but her methodology suffers from lack of detail. No one would be able to confirm her experimental findings without knowing exactly what and how much the athletes consumed.

(4) Examining the author's reasoning

When a source is logical, its reasoning is sound. Lapses in logic may be the result of using evidence that does not directly support a claim, appealing to the reader's emotions, or encouraging belief in false authority. Faulty reasoning is often discussed in terms of rhetorical fallacies. A list of these fallacies, along with examples, can be found on pages 191–196.

MLA DOCUMENTATION

12

The Modern Language Association (MLA) provides guidelines for documenting research in literature, languages, linguistics, and composition studies. The *MLA Handbook for Writers of Research Papers* is published specifically for undergraduates. Updates to the handbook's content can be found at **www.mla.org**. This chapter includes

- guidelines for citing sources within the text of a paper (**12a**),
- guidelines for documenting sources in the works-cited list (**12b**), and
- a sample student paper (**12c**).

12a MLA in-text citations

(1) In-text citations indicate that a writer has drawn material from other sources.

The citations you use within the text of a research paper refer your readers to the list of works cited at the end of the paper, tell them where to find the borrowed material in the original source, and indicate the boundaries between your ideas and those you have borrowed. In the following example, the parenthetical citation guides the reader to page 20 of the article by Doherty in the works-cited list.

In-text citation

Starbucks has now expanded its goals to include leading the world coffee shop market. With over 5,000 coffee shops already in operation—nearly 1,200 of which are located outside the United States—Starbucks hopes to reach revenues of $6 billion by 2005 (Doherty 20).

Works-cited entry

Doherty, Jacqueline. "Make It Decaf: Despite Heavy Revenue Gains, Starbucks' Earnings

Growth Is Slowing." <u>Barrons</u>. 20 May 2002: 20.

The MLA suggests reserving numbered notes for supplementary comments—for example, when you wish to explain a point further, but the subject matter is tangential to your topic. When numbered notes are used, superscript numbers are inserted in the appropriate places in the text, and the notes are gathered at the end of the paper on a separate page titled "Notes." You can create a superscript number in Microsoft Word by typing the number, highlighting it, pulling down the menu for Format, clicking on Font, and then clicking in the box next to Superscript. Other word-processing programs have similar procedures for creating superscript numbers.

In-text note number

To reach its goals, Starbucks will have to enter new markets in Africa, Asia,

and the Middle East,[1] and especially in Europe, where coffee is a staple of many

countries.

Notes entry

[1] It should be noted that in Saudi Arabia, Starbucks, along with other multinational

corporations, tries to conform to the existing cultural mores.

An in-text citation usually provides two pieces of information about borrowed material: (1) information that directs the reader to the relevant source on the works-cited list, and (2) information that directs the reader to a specific page or section within that source. An author's last name and a page number generally suffice. To create an in-text citation, either place both the author's last name and the page number in parentheses or introduce the author's name in the sentence and supply just the page number in parentheses.

Some recent union negotiations have been successful (Craig and Kaupa 234).

Craig and Kaupa describe recent successful union negotiations (234).

When referring to information from a range of pages, separate the first and last pages with a hyphen: (34-42). If the page numbers have the same hundreds or thousands digit, do not repeat it when listing the final page in the range: (234-42) or (1350-55) but (290-301) and (1395-1402). If you refer to an entire work, no page number is necessary.

The following examples are representative of the types of in-text citations you might be expected to use. For more details on the placement and punctuation of citations, including those following long quotations, see pages 269–271.

Directory of MLA Parenthetical Citations

1. Work by one author

Set on the frontier and focused on characters who use language sparingly, Westerns often reveal a "pattern of linguistic regression" (Rosowski 170).

OR

Susan J. Rosowski argues that Westerns often reveal a "pattern of linguistic regression" (170).

2. More than one work by the same author(s)

When your works-cited list includes more than one work by the same author(s), provide a shortened title in your in-text citation that identifies the relevant work. Use a comma to separate the name (or names) from the shortened title when both are in parentheses. For example, if you listed two works by Antonio Damasio on your works-cited page, then you would cite one of those within your text as follows:

According to one neurological hypothesis, "feelings are the expression of human flourishing or human distress" (Damasio, Looking for Spinoza 6).

OR

Antonio Damasio believes that "feelings are the expression of human flourishing or human distress" (Looking for Spinoza 6).

3. Work by two or three authors

Some environmentalists seek to protect wilderness areas from further development so that they can both preserve the past and learn from it (Katcher and Wilkins 174).

Use commas to separate the names of three authors: (Bellamy, O'Brien, and Nichols 59).

4. Work by more than three authors

Use either the first author's last name followed by the abbreviation *et al.* (from the Latin *et alii,* meaning "and others") or all the last names. (Do not italicize or underline the abbreviated Latin phrase.)

In one important study, women graduates complained more frequently about "excessive control than about lack of structure" (Belenky et al. 205).

OR

In one important study, women graduates complained more frequently about "excessive control than about lack of structure" (Belenky, Clinchy, Goldberger, and Tarule 205).

5. Works by different authors with the same last name

When your works-cited list includes works by different authors with the same last name, provide a first initial, along with the last name, in parenthetical citations, or use the author's first and last name in the text. For example, if your works-cited list included entries for works by both Richard Enos and Theresa Enos, you would cite the work of Theresa Enos as follows.

Pre-Aristotelian rhetoric still has an impact today (T. Enos 331-43).

OR

Theresa Enos mentions the considerable contemporary reliance on pre-Aristotelian rhetoric (331-43).

If two authors have the same last name and first initial, spell out each author's first name in a parenthetical citation.

6. Work by a corporate author

A work has a corporate author when individual members of the group that created it are not identified. If the corporate author's name is long, you may use common abbreviations for parts of it—for example, *Assn.* for "Association" and *Natl.* for "National."

Strawbale constructions are now popular across the nation (Natl. Ecobuilders Group 2).

7. Two or more works in the same citation

When two sources provide similar information or when you combine information from two sources in the same sentence, cite both sources, separating them with a semicolon.

Agricultural scientists believe that crop productivity will be adversely affected by solar dimming (Beck and Watts 90; Harris-Green 153-54).

8. Multivolume work

When you cite material from more than one volume of a multivolume work, include the volume number (followed by a colon and a space) before the page number.

Katherine Raine claims that "true poetry begins where human personality ends" (2: 247).

You do not need to include the volume number in a parenthetical citation if your list of works cited includes only one volume of a multivolume work.

9. Anonymous work

The Tehuelche people left their handprints on the walls of a cave, now called Cave of the Hands ("Hands of Time" 124).

Use the title of an anonymous work in place of an author's name. If the title is long, provide a shortened version. For example, the shortened title for "Chasing Down the Phrasal Verb in the Discourse of Adolescents" is "Chasing Down."

10. Indirect source

If you need to include material that one of your sources quoted from another work because you cannot obtain the original source, use the following format (*qtd.* is the abbreviation for "quoted").

The critic Susan Hardy Aikens has argued on behalf of what she calls "canonical

multiplicity" (qtd. in Mayers 677).

A reader turning to the list of works cited should find a bibliographic entry for Mayers, the source consulted, but not for Aikens.

11. Poetry, drama, and sacred texts

When you refer to poetry, drama, or sacred texts, you should give the numbers of lines, acts and scenes, or chapters and verses, rather than page numbers. This practice enables readers to consult an edition other than the one you have used. Act, scene, and line numbers (all arabic numerals) are separated by periods with no space before or after them. The MLA suggests that biblical chapters and verses be treated similarly, although some writers prefer to use colons instead of periods in such citations. In all cases, the progression is from larger to smaller units.

The following example illustrates a citation referring to lines of poetry.

Emily Dickinson alludes to her dislike of public appearance in "I'm Nobody! Who Are

You?" (lines 5-8).

Use *line* or *lines* in the first parenthetical citation; subsequent citations require only numbers. For more details on quoting poetry, see **16f(4)**.

The following citation shows that the famous "To be, or not to be" soliloquy appears in act 3, scene 1, lines 56–89 of *Hamlet.*

In Hamlet, Shakespeare presents the most famous soliloquy in the history of the English

theater: "To be, or not to be . . ." (3.1.56-89).

Citations of biblical material identify the book of the Bible, the chapter, and the pertinent verses. In the following example, the writer

refers to the creation story in Genesis, which begins in chapter 1 with verse 1 and ends in chapter 2 with verse 22.

The Old Testament creation story (New American Standard Bible, Gen. 1.1-2.22), told with remarkable economy, culminates in the arrival of Eve.

Mention in your first citation which version of the Bible you are using; list only book, chapter, and verse in subsequent citations. Note that the names of biblical books are neither underlined nor enclosed in quotation marks.

BEYOND THE RULE

ABBREVIATIONS FOR IN-TEXT CITATIONS

The MLA provides standard abbreviations for the works of Shakespeare and Chaucer, for certain other literary works, and for the parts of the Bible. You can find these abbreviations at **www.harbrace.com**.

12. Constitution

When referring to the Constitution, use these common abbreviations:

United States Constitution	US Const.
article	art.
section	sec.

The testimony of two witnesses is needed to convict anyone of treason (US Const., art. 3, sec. 3).

13. Works with numbered paragraphs or screens

If an electronic source does not have page numbers, provide paragraph or screen numbers instead. If paragraphs are numbered, cite the number(s) of the paragraph(s) after the abbreviation *par.* (for one paragraph) or *pars.* (for more than one). If a screen number is provided, cite that number after the word *screen* (or *screens* for more than one).

Alston describes three types of rubrics for evaluating customer service (pars. 2-15).

Hilton and Merrill provide examples of effective hyperlinks (screen 1).

If an electronic source includes no numbers distinguishing one part from another, you should cite the entire source. In this case, to establish that you have not accidentally omitted a number, avoid using a parenthetical citation by providing what information you have within the sentence that introduces the material.

Raymond Lucero's Shopping Online offers useful advice for consumers who are concerned about transmitting credit card information over the Internet.

(2) The MLA offers guidelines for placing and punctuating in-text citations and quotations.

(a) Placement of in-text citations

When you acknowledge your use of a source by placing the author's name and a relevant page number in parentheses, insert this parenthetical citation directly after the information you used, generally at the end of a sentence but *before* the final punctuation mark (a period, question mark, or exclamation point).

Oceans store almost half the carbon dioxide released by humans into the atmosphere (Wall 28).

However, you may need to place a parenthetical citation earlier in a sentence to indicate that only the first part of the sentence contains borrowed material. Place the citation after the clause containing the material but before a punctuation mark (a comma, semicolon, or colon).

Oceans store almost half the carbon dioxide released by humans into the atmosphere (Wall 28), a fact that provides hope for scientists studying global warming but that alarms scientists studying organisms living in the oceans.

(b) Lengthy quotations

When a quotation is more than four lines long, set it off from the surrounding text by indenting all lines one inch (or ten spaces) from the left margin. The first line should not be indented further than the others. The right margin should remain the same. Double-space the entire quotation.

In Nickel and Dimed, Barbara Ehrenreich describes the dire living conditions of the working poor:

> The lunch that consists of Doritos or hot dog rolls, leading to faintness before the end of the shift. The "home" that is also a car or a van. The illness

or injury that must be "worked through," with gritted teeth, because there's no sick pay or health insurance and the loss of one day's pay will mean no groceries for the next. These experiences are not part of a sustainable lifestyle, even a lifestyle of chronic deprivation and relentless low-level punishment. They are, by almost any standard of subsistence, emergency situations. And that is how we should see the poverty of millions of low-wage Americans—as a state of emergency. (214)

A problem of this magnitude cannot be fixed simply by raising the minimum wage.

Note that the period precedes the parenthetical citation at the end of an indented (block) quotation.

Rarely will you need to quote more than a paragraph, but if you do, distinguish between the paragraphs by indenting the first line of each an extra quarter of an inch (or three spaces).

(c) Punctuation

Punctuation marks clarify meaning in quotations and citations. The following list summarizes their common uses.

- A colon separates volume numbers from page numbers in a parenthetical citation.

  (Raine 2: 247)

- A comma separates the author's name from the title when it is necessary to list both in a parenthetical citation.

  (Kingsolver, Animal Dreams)

  A comma also indicates that page or line numbers are not sequential.

  (44, 47)

- Ellipsis points indicate an omission within a quotation.

  "They lived in an age of increasing complexity and great hope; we in an age of . . . growing despair" (Krutch 2).

- A hyphen indicates a continuous sequence of pages or lines.

  (44-47)

- A period separates acts, scenes, and lines of dramatic works.

  (3.1.56)

A period also distinguishes chapters from verses in biblical citations.

(Gen. 1.1)

■ A question mark placed inside the final quotation marks indicates that the quotation is a question. Notice that the period after the parenthetical citation marks the end of the sentence.

Peter Elbow asks, "What could be more wonderful than the pleasure of creating or appreciating forms that are different, amazing, outlandish, useless—the opposite of ordinary, everyday, pragmatic?" (542).

When placed outside the final quotation marks, a question mark indicates that the quotation is part of a question posed by the writer of the paper.

What does Kabat-Zinn mean when he advises people to practice mindfulness "as if their lives depended on it" (305)?

■ Square brackets enclose words that have been added to the quotation as clarification and are not part of the original material.

"The publication of this novel [Beloved] establishes Morrison as one of the most important writers of our time" (Boyle 17).

12b MLA list of works cited

All of the works you cite should be listed at the end of your paper, beginning on a separate page with the heading "Works Cited." Use the following tips as you prepare your list.

TIPS FOR PREPARING A LIST OF WORKS CITED

■ Center the heading "Works Cited" one inch from the top of the page.

■ Arrange the list of works alphabetically by the author's last name.

■ If a source has more than one author, alphabetize the entry according to the last name of the first author.

■ If you use more than one work by the same author, alphabetize the works by the first major word in each title. For the first entry, provide the author's complete name (last name given first), but substitute three hyphens (---) for the name in subsequent entries.

- For a work without an author, alphabetize the entry according to the first important word in the title.

- Type the first line of each entry flush with the left margin and indent subsequent lines one-half inch or five spaces (a hanging indent).

- Double-space equally throughout—between lines of an entry and between entries.

Directory of MLA-Style Entries for a Works-Cited List

BOOKS

ARTICLES

OTHER PRINT SOURCES

LIVE PERFORMANCES AND DIGITAL RECORDINGS

IMAGES

ONLINE BOOKS, ARTICLES, AND DOCUMENTS

ONLINE RECORDINGS AND IMAGES

WEB SITES

ADDITIONAL TYPES OF WORKS-CITED ENTRIES

For the following additional types of works-cited entries, visit
www.harbrace.com.

- Article in a series
- Article in a special issue of a journal
- Book with two publishers
- Course home page
- Home page for academic department
- Manuscript, print
- Musical composition
- Online book with editor
- Online book with translator
- Online letter to the editor
- Online manuscript
- Patent
- Personal photograph
- Synchronous communication
- Work from personal subscription service, such as America Online

When writing down source information for your bibliography, be sure to copy the information directly from the source (e.g., the title page of a book). (See fig. 12.1, on page 279.)

General Documentation Guidelines for Print-Based Sources

Author, Artist, or Editor

One author or artist. Place the last name before the first, separating them with a comma. Add any middle name or initial after the first name. Use another comma before any abbreviation or number that follows the first name. Indicate the end of this unit of the entry with a period.

Halberstam, David.
Johnston, Mary K.
King, Martin Luther, Jr.

Two or more authors or artists. List names in the same order used on the title page of the book. The first person's name is inverted (that is, the last name appears first); the others are not. Separate all names with commas, placing the word *and* before the final name.

West, Nigel, and Oleg Tsarev.
Green, Bill, Maria Lopez, and Jenny T. Graf.

Four or more authors or artists. List the names of all the authors or artists, or provide just the first person's name (inverted) and the abbreviation *et al.* (for *et alii*, meaning "and others").

Quirk, Randolph, Sidney Greenbaum, Geoffrey Leech, and Jan Svartvik.
OR
Quirk, Randolph, et al.

Corporate or group author. Omit any initial article *(a, an,* or *the)* from the name.

Institute of Medicine.
Department of Natural Resources.

Editor. If an editor or editors are listed instead of an author or authors, include the abbreviation *ed.* for "editor" or *eds.* for "editors."

Espinoza, Toni, ed.
Gibb, Susan, and Karen Enochs, eds.

Title

Underlined titles. Underline the titles of books, magazines, journals,

<u>Newsweek</u>.
<u>Hamlet</u>.

newspapers, plays, films, and Web sites. Capitalize all major words (nouns, pronouns, verbs, adjectives, adverbs, and subordinating conjunctions). Make underlining continuous, not separate under each word. Do not underline the period completing this unit of the entry.

<u>Weird English</u>.
<u>The Aviator</u>.

Titles in quotation marks. Use quotation marks to enclose the titles of short works such as journal or magazine articles, short stories, and songs. (See **38b**.)

"Three Days to See."
"Selling the Super Bowl."
"Generations."

Subtitles. Always include a subtitle if the work has one. Use a colon to separate a main title and a subtitle.

<u>Lost in Translation: Life in a New Language</u>.
"Silence: Learning to Listen."

Titles within titles. When an underlined title includes the title of another work normally underlined, do not underline the embedded title.

<u>Essays on</u> The Death of a Salesman.
BUT
<u>The Death of a Salesman</u>.

If the embedded title normally requires quotation marks, it should be underlined as well as enclosed in quotation marks.

<u>Understanding "The Philosophy of Composition" and the Aesthetic of Edgar Allan Poe</u>.
BUT
"The Philosophy of Composition."

When a title in quotation marks includes the title of another work normally underlined, retain the underlining.

"A Salesman's Reading of <u>The Death of a Salesman</u>."

If the embedded title is normally enclosed in quotation marks, use only single quotation marks.

"The European Roots of 'The Philosophy of Composition.' "

(continued on page 278)

Publication Data

City of publication. If more than one city is listed on the title page, mention only the first. Place a colon after the name of the city.

Boston:
New York:

If the work was published outside the United States and the city of publication is unfamiliar, add an abbreviation for the country or for the province if the work is Canadian.

Norwich, Eng.:
Prince George, BC:

Publisher's name. Provide a shortened form of the publisher's name, and place a comma after it. To shorten the name of the publisher, use the principal name.

Knopf (for Alfred A. Knopf)
Random (for Random House)

For books published by university presses, abbreviate *University* and *Press* without periods.

Harvard UP (for Harvard University Press)

If two publishers are listed, provide the city of publication and the name of the publisher for each. Use a semicolon to separate the two.

Manchester, Eng.: Manchester UP; New York: St. Martin's

Publisher's imprint. You will sometimes need to list both a publisher's name and an imprint. The imprint is usually listed above the publisher's name on the title page. In a works-cited entry, use a hyphen to separate the two names: imprint-publisher.

Quill-HarperCollins
Vintage-Random

Copyright date. Although the copyright date may be found on the title page, it is usually found on the next page—the copyright page (see fig. 12.2). Place a period after the date.

Fig. 12.1. The title page includes most, if not all, of the information needed for a bibliographic entry.

PROTECTING AMERICA'S HEALTH
Title

•

The FDA, Business, and One Hundred Years of Regulation
Subtitle

PHILIP J. HILTS
Author

Publisher (shorten to Knopf)   Alfred A. Knopf   New York   2003   Date of publication

City of publication

Fig. 12.2. If the title page does not give the book's date of publication, turn to the copyright page, which is usually on the back of the title page.

BOOKS

1. Book by one author

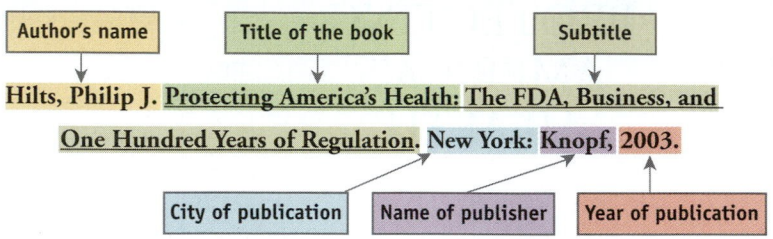

Author's name: Hilts, Philip J.
Title of the book: Protecting America's Health:
Subtitle: The FDA, Business, and One Hundred Years of Regulation.
City of publication: New York:
Name of publisher: Knopf,
Year of publication: 2003.

2. Book by two authors

West, Nigel, and Oleg Tsarev. The Crown Jewels: The British Secrets at the Heart of the KGB Archives. New Haven: Yale UP, 1999.

3. Book by three authors

Spinosa, Charles, Ferdinand Flores, and Hubert L. Dreyfus. Disclosing New Worlds: Entrepreneurship, Democratic Action, and the Cultivation of Solidarity. Cambridge: MIT P, 1997.

4. Book by more than three authors

Bullock, Jane A., George D. Haddow, Damon Cappola, Erdem Ergin, Lissa Westerman, and Sarp Yeletaysi. Introduction to Homeland Security. Boston: Elsevier, 2005.

OR

Bullock, Jane A., et al. Introduction to Homeland Security. Boston: Elsevier, 2005.

5. Book by a corporate author

Institute of Medicine. Blood Banking and Regulation: Procedures, Problems, and Alternatives. Washington: Natl. Acad., 1996.

6. Book by an anonymous author

Primary Colors: A Novel of Politics. New York: Warner, 1996.

Begin the entry with the title. Do not use *Anonymous* or *Anon.*

7. Book with an author and an editor

Stoker, Bram. Dracula. Ed. Glennis Byron. Peterborough, ON: Broadview, 1998.

Include both the name of the author and the name of the editor (preceded by *Ed.*). Note that this book was published in Ontario, Canada, so the abbreviation for the province is included (see page 278).

8. Book with an editor instead of an author

Kachuba, John B., ed. <u>How to Write Funny</u>. Cincinnati: Writer's Digest, 2000.

9. Edition after the first

Murray, Donald. <u>The Craft of Revision</u>. 4th ed. Boston: Heinle, 2001.

10. Introduction, preface, foreword, or afterword to a book

Olnos, Edward James. Foreword. <u>Vietnam Veteranos: Chicanos Recall the War</u>. By Lea

Ybarra. Austin: U of Texas P, 2004. ix-x.

The name that begins the entry is the author of the foreword or other section, not of the entire book. Instead of *Foreword*, type *Preface, Afterword,* or *Introduction* if you are citing from one of these sections.

11. Anthology (a collection of works by different authors)

Buranen, Lisa, and Alice M. Roy, eds. <u>Perspectives on Plagiarism and Intellectual</u>

<u>Property in a Postmodern World</u>. New York: State U of New York P, 1999.

Include the name(s) of the editor(s), followed by the abbreviation *ed.* (or *eds*). For individual works within an anthology, consult the following two models.

12. A work originally published in an anthology

Rowe, David. "No Gain, No Game? Media and Sport." <u>Mass Media and Society</u>. 3rd ed.

Ed. James Curran and Michael Gurevitch. New York: Oxford UP, 2000. 346-61.

Use this form for an article, essay, story, poem, or play that was published for the first time in the anthology you are using. Place the title of the anthology after the title of the individual work, noting the edition if it is not the first. Provide the name(s) of the editor(s) after the abbreviation *Ed.* for "edited by." List the publication data for the anthology and the range of pages on which the work appears. (See pages 283–284 for information on noting inclusive page numbers.)

If you cite more than one work from an anthology, provide only the name(s) of the author(s), the title of the work, the name(s) of the editor(s), and the inclusive page numbers in an entry for each work. Then, also provide an entry for the entire anthology, in which you include the relevant publication data (see the sample entry for an anthology in item 11).

Clark, Irene L. "Writing Centers and Plagiarism." Buranen and Roy 155-67.

Howard, Rebecca Moore. "The New Abolitionism Comes to Plagiarism." Buranen and Roy 87-95.

13. A work from a journal reprinted in a textbook or an anthology

Shaugnessy, Mina P. "Diving In: An Introduction to Basic Writing." <u>College Composition and Communication</u> 27.3 (1976): 234-39. Rpt. in <u>Cross-Talk in Comp Theory</u>. Ed. Victor Villanueva. Urbana: NCTE, 1997. 289-95.

Use the abbreviation *Rpt.* for "Reprinted."

14. A work from an edited collection reprinted in a textbook or an anthology

Brownmiller, Susan. "Let's Put Pornography Back in the Closet." <u>Take Back the Night: Women on Pornography</u>. Ed. Laura Lederer. New York: Morrow, 1980. 252-55. Rpt. in <u>Conversations: Readings for Writing</u>. 4th ed. By Jack Selzer. New York: Allyn, 2000. 578-81.

See item 12 for information on citing more than one work from the same anthology.

15. Translated book

Garrigues, Eduardo. <u>West of Babylon</u>. Trans. Nasario Garcia. Albuquerque: U of New Mexico P, 2002.

Place the abbreviation *Trans.* for "Translated by" before the translator's name.

16. Republished book

Alcott, Louisa May. <u>Work: A Story of Experience</u>. 1873. Harmondsworth, Eng.: Penguin, 1995.

Provide the publication date of the original work after the title.

17. Multivolume work

Young, Ralph F., ed. <u>Dissent in America</u>. 2 vols. New York: Longman-Pearson, 2005.

Cite the total number of volumes in a work when you have used material from more than one volume. Include the year the volumes were published. If the volumes were published over a span of time, provide inclusive dates: (1997-99) or (1998-2004).

If you have used only one volume, include that volume's number (preceded by the abbreviation *Vol.*) in place of the total number of volumes.

Young, Ralph F., ed. <u>Dissent in America</u>. Vol. 1. New York: Longman-Pearson, 2005.

Note that the publisher's name in this entry is hyphenated: the first name is the imprint; the second is the publisher.

18. Article in a multivolume work

To indicate a specific article in a multivolume work, provide the author's name and the title of the article in quotation marks. Note the page numbers for the article after the date of publication.

Baxby, Derrick. "Edward Jenner." <u>Oxford Dictionary of National Biography</u>. Ed.

H. C. G. Matthew and Brian Harrison. Vol. 30. Oxford: Oxford UP, 2004. 4-8.

If required by your instructor, include the number of volumes and the inclusive publication dates after the page numbers: 382-89. 23 vols. 1962-97.

19. Book in a series

Sumner, Colin, ed. <u>Blackwell Companion to Criminology</u>. Blackwell Companions to

Sociology 8. Malden: Blackwell, 2004.

When citing a book that is part of a series, provide the name of the series and, if one is listed, the number designating the work's place in it. The series name is not underlined. Abbreviate words in the series name according to the MLA guidelines; for example, the word *Series* is abbreviated *Ser.*

ARTICLES

A **journal** is a publication written for a specific discipline or profession; a **magazine** is written for the general public. You can find most of

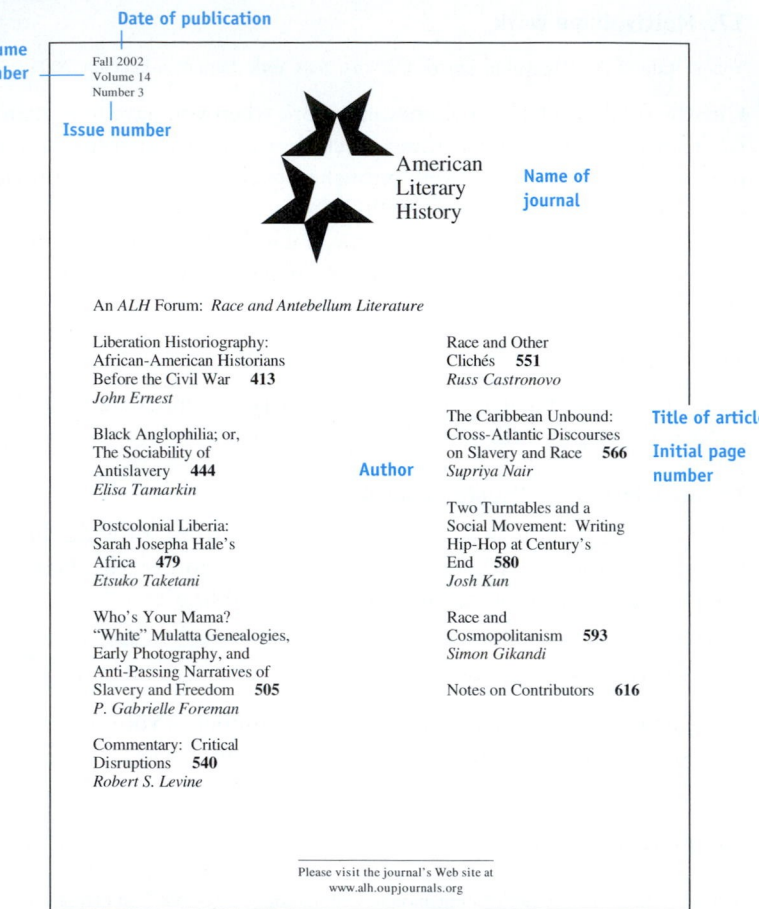

Fig. 12.3. First page of a journal.

the information required for a works-cited entry on the first page of the journal or sometimes in the footer of the article you are citing. (See fig. 12.3.)

Title of article and name of periodical

Put the article title in quotation marks with a period inside the closing quotation marks. Underline the name of the periodical. Capitalize all major words (nouns, pronouns, verbs, adjectives, adverbs, and subordinating conjunctions).

"Staring into the Political Abyss." <u>U.S. News and World Report</u>.

Volume and issue numbers

In an entry for an article from a journal, provide the volume number. For a journal with continuous pagination, include only the volume number after the name of the journal. For a journal whose issues are paginated separately, put a period after the volume number and add the issue number.

<u>Contemporary Review</u> 194   <u>Studies in the Literary Imagination</u> 26.3

A journal paginated *continuously* uses the number 1 to identify only the first page of the first issue in a volume. The first page of a subsequent issue in that volume is numbered to follow the last page of the first volume, and so on. In contrast, a journal paginated *separately* uses the number 1 to identify the first page of each issue in a volume.

Date

For journals, place the year of publication in parentheses after the volume or issue number. For magazines and newspapers, provide the date of issue after the name of the periodical. Note the day first (if provided), followed by the month (abbreviated except for May, June, and July) and year.

Journal	<u>Journal of Marriage and Family</u> 65 (2003)
Magazine	<u>Economist</u> 13 Aug. 2005
Newspaper	<u>Chicago Tribune</u> 24 July 2002

Page numbers

Use a colon to separate the date from the page number(s). Note all the pages on which the article appears, separating the first and last page with a hyphen: (21-39). If the page numbers have the same hundreds or thousands digit, do not repeat it when listing the final page in the range: (131-42) or (1680-99). Magazine and newspaper articles are often interrupted by advertisements or other articles. If the first part of an article appears on pages 45 through 47 and the rest on pages 92 through 94, give only the first page number followed by a plus sign: 45+.

20. Article in a journal with continuous pagination

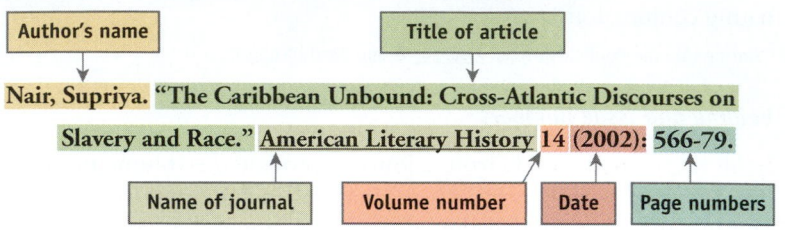

| Author's name |
| Title of article |

Nair, Supriya. "The Caribbean Unbound: Cross-Atlantic Discourses on

Slavery and Race." American Literary History 14 (2002): 566-79.

| Name of journal | Volume number | Date | Page numbers |

21. Article in a journal with each issue paginated separately

Andrews, William L. "Postmodern Southern Literature: Confessions of a Norton

Anthologist." Studies in the Literary Imagination 35.1 (2002): 105-12.

When you use an article from a journal paginated separately, include the issue number as well as the volume number. In this example, 35 is the volume number, and 1 is the issue number.

22. Article in a monthly magazine

Keizer, Garret. "How the Devil Falls in Love." Harper's Aug. 2002: 43-51.

23. Article in a weekly magazine or newspaper

Klotowitz, Alex. "The Trenchcoat Robbers." New Yorker 8 July 2002: 34-39.

24. Article in a daily newspaper

Moberg, David. "The Accidental Environmentalist." Chicago Tribune 24 Sept. 2002, final

ed., sec. 2: 1+.

When not part of the newspaper's name, the name of the city where the newspaper is published should be given in brackets after the title: Star Telegram [Fort Worth]. If a specific edition is not identifed on the masthead, put a colon after the date and then provide the page reference. Specify the section by inserting the section letter as it appears in the newspaper (A7 or 7A, for example).

25. Unsigned article or wire service article

"View from the Top." National Geographic July 2001: 140.

26. Editorial in a newspaper or magazine

Beefs, Anne. "Ending Bias in the Human Rights System." Editorial. New York Times 22

May 2002, natl. ed.: A27.

27. Book or film review in a magazine

Denby, David. "Horse Power." Rev. of <u>Seabiscuit</u>, dir. Gary Ross. <u>New Yorker</u> 4 Aug.

2003: 84-85.

Include the name of the reviewer, the title of the review (if any), the phrase *Rev. of* (for "Review of"), the title of the work being reviewed, and the name of the editor, author, or director.

28. Book or film review in a journal

Graham, Catherine. Rev. of <u>Questionable Activities: The Best</u>, ed. Judith Rudakoff.

<u>Canadian Theatre Review</u> 113 (2003): 74-76.

OTHER PRINT SOURCES

29. Encyclopedia entry

Robertson, James I., Jr. "Thomas Jonathan Jackson." <u>Encyclopedia of the American Civil</u>

<u>War: A Political, Social, and Military History</u>. Ed. David S. Heidler and Jeanne T.

Heidler. 5 vols. Santa Barbara: ABC-CLIO, 2000.

When the author of an encyclopedia article is indicated only by initials, check the table of contents for a list of contributors. If an article is anonymous, begin the entry with the article title.

Full publication information is not necessary for a well-known reference work that is organized alphabetically. Along with the author's name, the title of the article, and the name of the encyclopedia, list the edition and year of publication in one of two ways: 5th ed. 2004 or 2002 ed.

Petersen, William J. "Riverboats and Rivermen." <u>The Encyclopedia Americana</u>. 1999 ed.

30. Dictionary entry

When citing a specific dictionary definition for a word, use the abbreviation *Def.* (for "Definition"), and indicate which one you used if the entry has two or more.

"Reactive." Def. 2a. <u>Merriam-Webster's Collegiate Dictionary</u>. 10th ed. 2001.

31. Sacred text

Begin your works-cited entry for a sacred text with the title of the work, rather than information about editors or translators.

<u>New American Standard Bible</u>. Anaheim: Foundation, 1997.

<u>The Qur'an</u>. Trans. Muhammad A. S. Abdel Haleem. Oxford: Oxford UP, 2004.

32. Government publication

United States. Office of Management and Budget. <u>A Citizen's Guide to the Federal Budget</u>. Washington: GPO, 1999.

When citing a government publication, list the name of the government (e.g., United States or Minnesota) and the agency that issued the work. Underline the title of a book or pamphlet. Indicate the city of publication. Federal publications are usually printed by the Government Printing Office (GPO) in Washington, DC, but be alert for exceptions.

When the name of an author or an editor appears on a government publication, insert that name after the title and introduce it with the word *By* or the abbreviation *Ed.* to indicate the person's contribution.

33. Law case

Chavez v. Martinez. No. 01-1444. Supreme Ct. of the US. 27 May 2003.

Include the name of the first plaintiff, the abbreviation *v.* for "versus," the name of the first defendant, the case number preceded by the abbreviation *No.,* the name of the deciding court, and the date of the decision. Although law cases are underlined in the text of a paper, they are *not* underlined in works-cited entries.

34. Public law

No Child Left Behind Act of 2001. Pub. L. 107-110. 8 Jan. 2002. Stat. 115.1425.

Include the name of the act, its public law number, the date it was enacted, and its Statutes at Large cataloging number. Notice the use of abbreviations in the example.

Although no works-cited entry is needed for familiar sources such as the U.S. Constitution, an in-text citation should still be included (see page 268).

35. Pamphlet or bulletin

<u>Stucco in Residential Construction</u>. St. Paul: Lath & Plaster Bureau, 2000.

If the pamphlet has an author, begin with the author's name, as you would for a book.

36. Published dissertation

Fukuda, Kay Louise. <u>Differing Perceptions and Constructions of the Meaning of</u>
<u>Assessment in Education</u>. Diss. Ohio State U, 2001. Ann Arbor: UMI, 2002.

After the title of the dissertation, include the abbreviation *Diss.*, the name of the university granting the degree, the date of completion, and the publication information. In the example, *UMI* stands for "University Microfilms International," which publishes many dissertations.

37. Published letter

In general, treat a published letter like a work in an anthology, adding the date of the letter and the number (if the editor assigned one).

Helen Hunt Jackson. "To Thomas Bailey Aldrich." 4 May 1883. <u>The Indian Reform</u>
<u>Letters of Helen Hunt Jackson, 1879-1885</u>. Ed. Valerie Sherer Mathes. Norman: U
of Oklahoma P, 1998. 258-59.

LIVE PERFORMANCES AND DIGITAL RECORDINGS

38. Play performance

<u>Proof</u>. By David Auburn. Dir. Daniel Sullivan. Walter Kerr Theater, New York. 8 Oct. 2002.

Cite the date of the performance you attended.

39. Lecture or presentation

Guinier, Lani. Address. Barbara Jordan Lecture Series. Schwab Auditorium. Pennsylvania
State U., University Park. 4 Oct. 2004.

Scheiber, Andrew. Class lecture. English 215. Aquinas Hall, U of St. Thomas, St. Paul.
30 Apr. 2003.

Identify the site and the date of the lecture or presentation. Use the title if available; otherwise, provide a descriptive label.

40. Interview

Furstenheim, Ursula. Personal interview. 16 Jan. 2003.

Sugo, Misuzu. Telephone interview. 20 Feb. 2003.

For an interview you conducted, give only the name of the person you interviewed and the date of the interview. If the interview was conducted by someone else, add the name of the interviewer, as well as a title, if there is one, or a descriptive label, and the name of the source.

Harryhausen, Ray. Interview with Terry Gross. <u>Fresh Air</u>. Natl. Public Radio. WHYY,

Philadelphia. 6 Jan. 2003.

41. Film

<u>My Big Fat Greek Wedding</u>. Dir. Joel Zwick. IFC, 2002.

The company that produced or distributed the film (IFC, in this case) appears before the year of release. It is not necessary to cite the city in which the production or distribution company is based.

When you want to highlight the contribution of a specific person, list the contributor's name first. Other supplementary information may be included after the title.

Gomez, Ian, perf. <u>My Big Fat Greek Wedding</u>. Screenplay by Nia Vardalos. Dir. Joel

Zwick. IFC, 2002.

42. Radio or television program

When referring to a specific episode, place quotation marks around its title. Underline the title of the program.

" 'Barbarian' Forces." <u>Ancient Warriors</u>. Narr. Colgate Salsbury. Dir. Phil Grabsky.

Learning Channel. 1 Jan. 1996.

To highlight a specific contributor, begin the entry with that person's name.

Finch, Nigel, dir. "The Lost Language of Cranes." By David Leavitt. Prod. Ruth Caleb.

Great Performances. PBS. WNET, New York. 24 June 1992.

43. DVD

<u>A River Runs through It</u>. Dir. Robert Redford. Screenplay by Richard Friedenberg. 1992.

DVD. Columbia, 1999.

Cite relevant information about the title and director as you would for a film. Note the original release date of the film, the medium (i.e., DVD), and the release date for the DVD. If the original company producing the film did not release the DVD, list the company that released the DVD instead.

44. Multidisc DVD

More Treasures from American Film Archives, 1894-1931: 50 Films. Prod. Natl. Film

    Preservation Foundation. DVD. 3 discs. Image Entertainment, 2004.

List the number of discs after noting the medium. For a particular segment from a multidisc DVD, indicate the title of the work, relevant information about the author or director, and the date the work was initially released. In place of the number of discs, indicate the number of the disc used.

A Bronx Morning. By Jay Leyda. 1931. More Treasures from American Film Archives,

    1894-1931: 50 Films. Prod. Natl. Film Preservation Foundation. DVD. Disc 2.

    Image Entertainment, 2004.

45. Sound recording on CD

Franklin, Aretha. Amazing Grace: The Complete Recordings. Atlantic, 1999.

For a sound recording on another medium, identify the type (*Audiocassette* or *LP*).

Raitt, Bonnie. Nick of Time. Audiocassette. Capitol, 1989.

When citing a recording of a specific song, begin with the name of the performer, and place the song title in quotation marks. Identify the author(s) after the song title. If the performance is a reissue from an earlier recording, provide the original date of recording (preceded by *Rec.* for "Recorded").

Horne, Lena. "The Man I Love." By George Gershwin and Ira Gershwin. Rec. 15 Dec.

    1941. Stormy Weather. BMG, 1990.

IMAGES

46. Work of art

Gauguin, Paul. Ancestors of Tehamana. 1893. Art Institute of Chicago, Chicago.

Identify the artist's name, the title of the work (underlined), the organization or individual holding the work, and the city in which the work is located. The date of creation is optional but, if included, should follow the work's title. For a photograph of a work of art, provide publication information for its source after the name of the city in which the original is located.

47. Cartoon or comic strip

Cheney, Tom. Cartoon. <u>New Yorker</u> 9 June 2003: 93.

Trudeau, Garry. "Doonesbury." Comic strip. <u>Daily Record</u> [Ellensburg] 21
April 2005: A4.

After the creator's name, place the title of the work (if given) in quotation marks and include the descriptor *Cartoon* or *Comic strip*.

48. Map or chart

<u>Cincinnati and Vicinity</u>. Map. Chicago: RAND, 1996.

Include the title and the appropriate descriptor, *Map* or *Chart*.

49. Advertisement

Nu by Yves Saint Laurent. Advertisement. <u>Allure</u> June 2003: 40.

The name of the product and/or that of the company being advertised is followed by the designation *Advertisement*.

ONLINE BOOKS, ARTICLES, AND DOCUMENTS

Many of the guidelines for documenting online sources are similar to those for print sources. In fact, if a document exists in print as well as online, you must provide the information required for that type of print-based source before providing information about the document's online publication and access. For a source found only in electronic form, provide just the information about its online publication and access.

Electronic publication information

Indicate the title of an Internet site, the date of publication (or most recent update), and the site's sponsoring organization, usually found at the bottom of the site's home page. (See fig. 12.4.)

Title of site

Date of last update   Date of publication

Fig. 12.4. The home page for the Art Institute of Chicago indicates the title of the site (which is also the name of the sponsoring organization), the date of the last update, and the date of publication.

Access information

State the date of access and the URL (Internet address) for a Web site. You can find this information by printing out a page you are using. The date you accessed the site and the URL can be found at the top or the bottom of the printed page. (See fig. 12.5.)

By providing your readers with a complete URL, including the protocol, or access identifier (http, ftp, telnet, news), all punctuation marks, and both path and file names, you tell them how to locate the source.

<http://stanfordmag.org.marapril99/>

<ftp://beowulf.engl.uky.edu/pub/beowulf>

Fig. 12.5. When you print a page from a Web site, the URL and the date of access usually appear at the top or bottom of the page.

Place the address within angle brackets, < >, so that it is clearly separated from any other punctuation in your citation. Divide the address after a slash when it does not fit on a single line. Make sure that the address is accurate; Web browsers (such as Netscape) distinguish between uppercase and lowercase letters in a URL, and they will not be able to find a site if marks such as hyphens and underscores are missing. If the URL for the specific page you want to cite is extremely long, you may use the URL for the site's search page instead. If there is no search page, cite the site's home page, followed by the word *Path,* a colon, and the sequence of links you used. Separate the links with semicolons.

<http://www.essentialsofmusic.com>. Path: Eras; Classical; Composer; Mozart.

Also keep in mind that Internet addresses often change, so double-check the URLs you list before submitting your work. Because sites may disappear, it is wise to print out a hard copy of any material you use as a source.

BEYOND THE RULE

THE COLUMBIA GUIDE TO ONLINE STYLE

Recognizing that increasing numbers of writers conduct most of their research online, Columbia University Press published *The Columbia Guide to Online Style* (COS). You can find COS formatting guidelines, sample in-text citations, and sample bibliographic entries at **www.harbrace.com**.

50. Online book

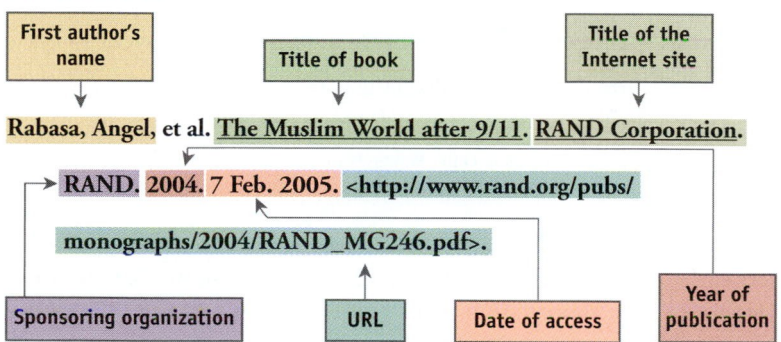

Because there are more than three authors, the abbreviation *et al.* has been used in the example, but listing all names is also acceptable: Rabasa, Angel, Cheryl Benard, Peter Chalk, C. Christine Fair, Theodore W. Karasik, Rollie Lal, Ian O. Lesser, and David E. Thaler. Note that in this example the name of the sponsoring organization is in the title of the Internet site.

When the book has an editor or a translator, list that name after the title. The name of a site editor follows the title of the site.

Flaubert, Gustave. <u>Madame Bovary</u>. Trans. Eleanor Marx Aveling. New York: Modern
    Library, 1918. <u>Electronic Text Center</u>. Ed. David Seaman. 2001. Alderman Lib., U of
    Virginia. 7 Jan. 2005 <http://etext.lib.virgina.edu/toc/modeng/public/FlaBova.html>.

51. Online book with separate date of print publication

Rohrbough, Malcolm J. <u>Days of Gold: The California Gold Rush and the American</u>
    <u>Nation</u>. Berkeley: U of California P, 1997. <u>History E-book Project</u>. American
    Council of Learned Societies. 2005. Scholarly Publication Office, U of Michigan
    Lib. 17 Feb. 2005 <http://name.umdl.umich.edu/HEB00571>.

52. Part of an online book

Strunk, William, Jr. "Elementary Rules of Usage." <u>The Elements of Style</u>. Ithaca:
    Humphrey, 1918. <u>Bartleby.com: Great Books Online</u>. Ed. Steven van Leeuwen.
    1999. 6 June 2003 <http://www.bartleby.com/141/strunk.html>.

53. Online encyclopedia entry

"Iran." <u>Encyclopaedia Britannica Online</u>. 2002. Encyclopaedia Britannica. 6 Mar. 2004
    <http://search.eb.com/>.

54. Encyclopedia entry from a library subscription service

Turk, Austin T. "Terrorism." <u>Encyclopedia of Crime and Justice</u>. 2nd ed. Ed. Joshua
    Dressler. 4 vols. New York: Macmillan Reference USA, 2002. <u>Gale Virtual</u>
    <u>Reference Library</u>. Thomson Gale. Pennsylvania State U, Pattee Lib., University
    Park. 7 Feb. 2005 <http://find.galegroup.com/gvrl/>.

Include the name of the service (Thomson Gale), the name of the subscriber (Pennsylvania State U, Pattee Lib.), and the subscriber's location
(include a state abbreviation if the state is not part of the subscriber's
name).

55. Online journal article

Harnack, Andrew, and Gene Kleppinger. "Beyond the MLA Handbook: Documenting
    Sources on the Internet." <u>Kairos</u> 1.2 (1996). 14 Aug. 1997 <http://www.english.ttu/
    acw/kairos/index.html>.

56. Article from a scholarly archival database

Winnett, Susan. "The Memory of Gender." <u>Signs: Journal of Women and Culture in</u>
<u>Society</u> 28.1 (2002): 462-63. <u>JSTOR</u>. 14 Nov. 2004 <http://www.jstor.org/search>.

Include the name of the database following all the information about the article. JSTOR and Project Muse are frequently used databases.

57. Online abstract

Landers, Susan J. "FDA Panel Findings Intensify Struggles with Prescribing of
Antidepressants." <u>American Medical News</u> 47.37 (2004): 1-2. Abstract. ProQuest
Direct. Washington State U Lib., Pullman. 7 Feb. 2005 <http://proquest.umi.com/>.

Add the word *Abstract* after the page numbers.

58. Online magazine article

Plotz, David. "The Cure for Sinophobia." <u>Slate</u> 4 June 1999. 15 June 1999 <http://
www.slate.com/StrangeBedfellow/99-06-04/StrangeBedfellow.asp>.

The first date is the publication date; the second is the date of access.

59. Online newspaper article

"Tornadoes Touch Down in S. Illinois." <u>New York Times on the Web</u> 16 Apr. 1998. 20
May 1998 <http://www.nytimes.com/aponline/a/AP-Illinois-Storms.html>.

When no author is identified, begin with the title of the article. If the article is an editorial, include *Editorial* after the title: "America's Promises." Editorial.

60. Review in an online newspaper

Parent, Marc. "A Father, a Son and an Ideal That's Painfully Tested." Rev. of <u>Scout's</u>
<u>Honor</u>, by Peter Applebome. <u>New York Times on the Web</u> 6 June 2003. 12 June
2003 <http://www.nytimes.com/2003/06/06/books/06BOOK.html>.

61. Article from a library subscription database

You can find most of the information you need for a works-cited entry on the abstract page of the article you select. (See fig. 12.6.)

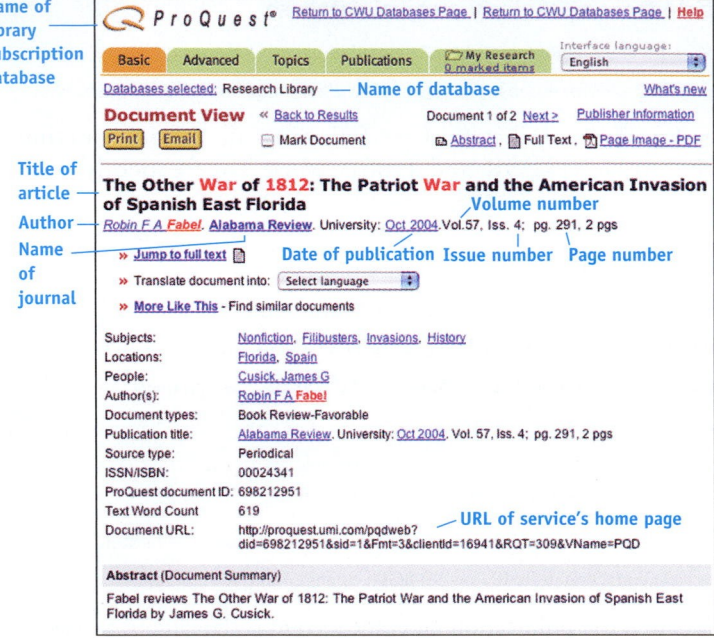

Fig. 12.6. Abstract page from a database.

a. ERIC

Holmes, Julie A. "The Least Restrictive Environment: Is Inclusion Best for All Special

Needs Students?" (1999): 1-12. ERIC. Inst. of Education Sciences, Dept. of

Education, Washington. ED437760. 6 Nov. 2004 <http://www.eric.ed.gov/>.

Be sure to include the ERIC database number.

b. EBSCO

Folks, Jeffrey J. "Crowd and Self: William Faulkner's Sources of Agency in The Sound

and the Fury." Southern Literary Journal 34.2 (2002): 30- . Academic Search

Premier. EBSCO. Wright State U, Dunbar Lib., Dayton, OH. 6 June 2003

<http://www.epnet.com/>.

For sources that list only the page number on which a work begins,
include that number and a hyphen. Leave a space before the period.

c. LexisNexis

Suggs, Welch. "A Hard Year in College Sports." The Chronicle of Higher Education 19

    Dec. 2003: 37. Academic Universe: News. LexisNexis. U of Texas at Austin, U

    Texas Lib., Austin. 17 July 2004 <http://www.lexis-nexis.com/>.

Provide the name of the LexisNexis database (e.g., Academic Universe or State Capitol) in which you found the article. Add a colon, and then indicate the path you followed for your search (e.g., News, Business, or Legal). Underline both name and path.

d. ProQuest

Fabel, Robin F. A. "The Other War of 1812: The Patriot War and the American Invasion of

    Spanish Florida." Alabama Review. AMA Titles. ProQuest. Central Washington U,

    Brooks Memorial Lib., Ellensburg. 8 Mar. 2005 <http://proquest.umi.com/>.

e. InfoTrac

Priest, Ann-Marie. "Between Being and Nothingness: The 'Astonishing Precipice' of

    Virginia Woolf's Day and Night." Journal of Modern Literature 26.2 (2002-03):

    66-80. InfoTrac College Edition. Gale. Alabama Virtual Library. 12 Jan. 2004

    <http://www.galegroup.com/>.

62. Online congressional document

United States. Cong. Senate. Special Committee on Aging. Global Aging: Opportunity or

    Threat for the U.S. Economy? 108th Cong., 1st sess. S. Hrg. 108-30. Washington:

    GPO, 2003. 7 Jan. 2005 <http://frwebgate.access.gpo.gov/cgibin/

    getdoc.cgi?dbname=108_senate_hearings&docid=f:86497.wais.pdf>.

Provide the number and session of Congress and the type and number of publication. (*S* stands for "Senate"; *H* or *HR* stands for "House of Representatives.")

Bills	S 41, HR 82
Reports	S. Rept. 14, H. Rept. 18
Hearings	S. Hrg. 23, H. Hrg. 25
Resolutions	S. Res. 32, H. Res. 52
Documents	S. Doc. 213, H. Doc. 123

63. Online document from a government office

United States. Dept. of State. Bur. of Democracy, Human Rights, and Labor. <u>Guatemala Country Report on Human Rights Practices for 1998</u>. Feb. 1999. 1 May 1999 <http://www.state.gov/www/global/human_rights/1998_hrp_report/guatemal.html>.

Begin with the name of the country, state, or city whose government is responsible for the publication and the department or agency that issued it. If a subdivision of the larger organization is responsible, name that subdivision. If an author is identified, provide the name between the title and the date of issue of the document. Place the word *By* before the author's name.

64. Online law case

Tennessee v. Lane. No. 02-1667. Supreme Ct. of the US. 17 May 2004. 28 Jan. 2005 <http://www.usdoj.gov/osg/briefs/2003/3mer/2mer/2002-1667.mer.aa.pdf>.

65. Online public law

Individuals with Disabilities Education Act. Pub. L. 105-17. 4 June 1997. Stat. 104.587-698. 29 Jan. 2005 <http://www.ed.gov/policy/spece/leg/idea/idea.pdf>.

66. Online sacred text

<u>Sama Veda</u>. Trans. Ralph T. H. Griffith. 1895. <u>Sacred-Texts.com</u>. Ed. John B. Hare. 2 Feb. 2005. 6 Mar. 2005 <http://www.sacred-texts.com>.

ONLINE RECORDINGS AND IMAGES

67. Online music

Moran, Jason. "Jump Up." <u>Same Mother</u>. Blue Note, 2005. 7 Mar. 2005 <http://www.bluenote.com/detail.asp?SelectionID=10376>.

68. Online speech

Malcolm X. "The Ballot or the Bullet." Detroit, 12 Apr. 1964. <u>American Rhetoric: Top One Hundred Speeches</u>. Ed. Michael E. Eidenmuller. 2005. 14 Jan. 2005 <http://www.americanrhetoric.com/speeches/malcomxballot.htm>.

mla **12b** 301

"12 Apr. 1964" is the date the speech was delivered, "2005" is the year of the speech's electronic publication, and "14 Jan. 2005" is the date of access.

69. Online video

Riefenstahl, Leni, dir. <u>Triumph of the Will</u>. 1935. <u>Movieflix.com</u>. 2005. 17 Feb. 2005

<http://www.movieflix.com/movie_info.mfx?movie_id=404>.

"1935" is the year in which the movie was originally released, "2005" is the year in which it was made available online, and "17 Feb. 2005" is the date of access.

70. Online television or radio program

"Religion and the American Election." Narr. Tony Hassan. <u>The Religion Report</u>. Radio

National. 3 Nov. 2004. Transcript. 18 Feb. 2005 <http://www.abc.net.au/rn/talks/

8.30/relrpt/stories/s1243269.htm>.

If the source is a transcript rather than the visual or audio broadcast, include the word *Transcript* between the date the program aired and the date of access.

71. Online interview

McLaughlin, John. Interview with Wolf Blitzer. <u>CNN</u>. 14 July 2004. 21 Dec. 2004

<http://www.cnn.com/2004/US/07/14/transcript.mclaughlin/index.html>.

72. Online work of art

Vermeer, Johannes. <u>Young Woman with a Water Pitcher</u>. c. 1660. Metropolitan Museum

of Art, New York. 2 Oct. 2002 <http://www.metmuseum.org/collection/

view1.asp?dep_11&item_89%2E15%2E21>.

73. Online photograph

Lange, Dorothea. <u>Migrant Mother</u>. 1936. Prints and Photographs Division, Lib. of

Congress, Washington. Digital id. fsa 8b29516. 9 Feb. 2005 <http://www.loc.gov/

rr/print/list/128_migm.html>.

The identification number for a photograph, such as "Digital id. fsa 8b29516" in the example, is included if it is available.

74. Online map or chart

"Virginia 1624." Map. <u>Map Collections 1544-1996</u>. Library of Congress. 26 Apr. 1999
<http://memory.loc.gov/cgibin/map_mp/_ammmem_8kk3::&title_Virginia++>.

"Daily Cigarette Smoking among High School Seniors." Chart. National Center for
Health Statistics. 27 Jan. 2005. Centers for Disease Control and Prevention, US
Dept. of Health and Human Services. 25 Feb. 2005 <http://www.cdc.gov/nchs/
images/hp2000/hdspr/hdslide13.gif>.

75. Online advertisement

Milk Processor Education Program. "Got Milk?" Advertisement. 16 Feb. 2005
<http://www.milkpep.org/programs/lebron.cfm>.

76. Online cartoon or comic strip

Cagle, Daryl. "Social Security Pays 3 to 2." Cartoon. <u>Slate.com</u>. 4 Feb. 2005. 5 Feb. 2005
<http://cagle.slate.msn.com/politicalcartoons/>.

WEB SITES

77. Web site

<u>The Rossetti Archive</u>. Ed. Jerome McGann. 2002. Institute for Advanced Technology in
the Humanities, U of Virginia. 4 June 2003 <http://www.iath.virginia.edu/
rossetti/index.html>.

Include the title of the site (underlined), the name of the editor or editors (if listed), the version number (if given), the date of publication or of the last update, the name of the sponsoring organization or institution, and the URL. (See pages 293–294.)

78. Web site with incomplete information

<u>Breastcancer.org</u>. 2 Feb. 2005. 5 Feb. 2005 <http://www.breastcancer.org/>.

If a Web site does not provide all the information usually included in a works-cited entry, list as much as is available.

79. Section of a Web site

Altman, Andrew. "Civil Rights." 3 Feb. 2003. <u>Stanford Encyclopedia of Philosophy</u>. Ed.
    Edward N. Zalta. Spring 2003 ed. Center for the Study of Lang. and Information,
    Stanford U. 12 June 2003 <http://plato.stanford.edu/archives/spr2003/entries/
    civilrights/>.

Mozart, Wolfgang Amadeus. Concerto No. 3 for Horn, K. 447. <u>Essentials of Music</u>. 2001.
    Norton and Sony. 18 Feb. 2005 <http://www.essentialsofmusic.com>. Path: Eras;
    Classical; Composer; Mozart.

If the URL does not vary for different pages of a site, indicate how you
accessed your source by listing the sequence of links after the word *Path*
and a colon.

80. Personal home page

Gladwell, Malcolm. Home page. 8 Mar. 2005 <www.gladwell.com>.

After the name of the site's creator, provide the title or include the
words *Home page*.

ONLINE COMMUNICATIONS

81. E-mail

Peters, Barbara. "Scholarships for Women." E-mail to Rita Martinez. 10 Mar. 2003.

The entry begins with the name of the person who created the
e-mail. Put the subject line of the e-mail message in quotation
marks. The recipient of the message is identified after the words
E-mail to. If the message was sent to you, use *the author* rather than
your name.

82. Discussion group or forum

Schipper, William. "Re: Quirk and Wrenn Grammar." Online posting. 5 Jan. 1995.
    Ansaxnet. 12 Sept. 1996 <http://www.mun.ca/Ansaxdat/>.

Provide the name of the forum (in this case, Ansaxnet) between the
date of posting and the date of access.

83. Newsgroup

May, Michaela. "Questions about RYAs." Online posting. 19 June 1996. 29 June 1996
   <news:alt.soc.generation-x>.

The name of a newsgroup (in angle brackets) begins with the prefix
news followed by a colon.

84. Web log (blog)

Cuthbertson, Peter. "Are Left and Right Still Alright?" Conservative Commentary.
   7 Feb. 2005. 18 Feb. 2005 <http://concom.blogspot.com/2005/02/
   are-left-and-right-still-alright.html>.

OTHER SOURCES ACCESSED BY COMPUTER

85. CD-ROM

"About Richard III." Cinemania 96. CD-ROM. Redmond: Microsoft, 1996.

Indicate which part of the CD-ROM you are using, and then provide
the title of the CD. Begin the entry with the name of the author if one
has been provided.

Jordan, June. "Moving Towards Home." Database of Twentieth-Century African American
   Poetry on CD-ROM. CD-ROM. Alexandria: Chadwyck-Healey, 1999.

86. Work from a periodically published database on CD-ROM

Parachini, John V. "Combating Terrorism: The 9/11 Commission Recommendations and
   the National Strategies." RAND Electronically Distributed Documents. CT-231-1.
   CD-ROM. Disc 8. RAND. 2004.

87. DVD-ROM

Klein, Norman M. Bleeding Through: Layers of Los Angeles, 1920-1986. DVD-ROM.
   Karlsruhe: ZKM Center for Art and Media, 2003.

88. Multidisc publication

CDA: The Contextual Data Archive. 2nd ed. CD-ROM. 7 discs. Los Altos: Sociometrics,
   2000.

12c Sample MLA-style paper

(1) Submit a title page if your instructor requires one.

The MLA recommends omitting a title page and instead providing the identification on the first page of the paper (see page 307). Some instructors require a final outline with a paper; this serves as a table of contents. If you are asked to include an outline, prepare a title page as well. A title page usually provides the title of the paper, the author's name, the instructor's name, the name of the course with its section number, and the date—all centered on the page. A sample title page is shown in fig. 12.7.

Starbucks in Vienna: Coffee Cultures at a Crossroads

Andy Pieper

Professor Miller

English 299, Section 1

27 November 2002

Fig. 12.7. Sample title page for an MLA-style paper.

(2) Studying a sample MLA-style paper prepares you to write your own.

Interested in the effects of globalization, Andy Pieper decided to focus his paper on what happens when Starbucks opens coffee shops overseas. As you study his paper, notice how he develops his thesis, considers more than one point of view, and observes the conventions for an MLA-style paper.

TIPS FOR PREPARING AN MLA-STYLE PAPER

- Number all pages (including the first one) with an arabic numeral in the upper-right corner, one-half inch from the top. Put your last name before the page number.
- On the left side of the page, one inch from the top, type your name, the name of your professor, the course number, and the date of submission.
- Double-space between the heading and the title of your paper, which should be centered on the page. If your title consists of two or more lines, double-space them and center each.
- Double-space between your title and the first line of text.
- Indent the first paragraph, and every subsequent paragraph, one-half inch (or five spaces).
- Double-space throughout.

The writer's
last name
and the
page number

1 inch

Andy Pieper   Heading

Professor Miller

English 299, Section 1

27 November 2002

Center the
title.

Starbucks in Vienna: Coffee Cultures at a Crossroads

From St. Paul to Sao Paulo, from Rome to Riyadh, and from Johannesburg

to Jakarta, world citizens are increasingly being pushed toward a global culture.

We are being affected internationally through the media we experience, the food

we eat, and the products we consume as multinational corporations act on a world

stage (Rothkopf 38). People with disposable incomes can watch MTV in India,

catch a Hollywood-produced movie in Australia, purchase a Mickey Mouse doll in

Oman, use an Icelandic cell phone to call a friend in Malaysia, send an e-mail

from an IBM computer in Russia, and purchase a bucket of Kentucky Fried

Chicken in Japan.

Double-space
throughout.

All of these examples are signs of globalization, a term coined to

describe the increasingly prominent role of large companies in the world

marketplace. At the forefront of globalization is the multinational corporation,

which David Korten, author of When Corporations Rule the World, defines as

a business that takes "on many national identities, maintaining relatively

autonomous production and sales facilities in individual countries, establishing

local roots and presenting itself in each locality as a good local citizen" (125).

Many of these multinationals originate and are headquartered in the United

States or other Western nations, but they have means of production or outlets in

countries all over the world.

Background
information

Use one-inch
margins on
both sides of
the page.

Proponents of globalization claim that this process is advantageous because

it makes business efficient and helps foster international ties. Opponents argue

that local cultures are damaged and that globalization primarily benefits wealthy

Indent
paragraphs
five spaces.

1 inch

Pieper 2

corporations in nations already rich. The Starbucks Coffee Corporation is one example of a multinational company involved in globalization. No matter what the long-term advantages or disadvantages of globalization prove to be,

Thesis investigating how a Western company like Starbucks establishes itself overseas shows that a multinational corporation can succeed in offering its own brand of culture, despite the strength or longevity of the local culture it enters. The introduction of Starbucks to Vienna illustrates this point because Starbucks offers an American-style coffee shop experience to a city that is already rich in its own coffee traditions.

Throughout the 1990s, Starbucks sought to dominate the American coffee shop market, and it succeeded. The company has skyrocketed since its stock debuted in 1992, and within ten years went from revenues of $92 million to $2.6 billion at the end of fiscal year 2001. Today, it has achieved status as an American brand that is nearly as familiar as Coca-Cola and McDonald's. Starbucks has now expanded its goals to include leading the world coffee shop market. With over 5,000 coffee shops already in operation--nearly 1,200 of which are located outside the United States--Starbucks hopes to reach revenues of $6 billion by 2005 (Doherty 20). In order to accomplish this, the coffee corporation intends to open an additional 5,000 stores worldwide (Scott 1). To reach its goals, Starbucks will have to enter new

A superscript number indicates an endnote. markets in Africa, Asia, and the Middle East,[1] and especially in Europe, where coffee is a staple of many countries. From the sidewalk cafés of Paris to the espresso bars of Venice, Europeans have maintained a long love affair with coffee--not only with the beverage itself, but also with their own coffeehouses. Therefore, the continent represents both a challenge and an opportunity for Starbucks.

As part of its expansion plan, Starbucks had already opened European outlets in Great Britain, Germany, and Switzerland by the time it opened a store

Pieper 3

in Vienna, the capital of Austria, in the spring of 2002. Under this plan, The writer connects a local issue to a worldwide concern.

Starbucks typically enters into a joint-venture agreement with a local firm,

initially holding a minority stake in the foreign operation, usually twenty percent.

This arrangement shields Starbucks from any large losses incurred when stores

are first opened. In this way, Starbucks presents itself as a local company, when in

fact it is a multinational with similar operations throughout the globe. The local

firm then sets up a few outlets, buying prime real estate and strategically placing

stores near symbols of historic and cultural significance[2]--as in Vienna, where the

first outlet opened across from the city's famous opera house. Once some success

is accomplished, Starbucks buys enough of the foreign-owned branch to control

the company, and proceeds to enlarge rapidly throughout the country (Burke, Citation of a work by three authors

Smith, and Wosnitza 47).

Vienna, considered by many to be the birthplace of the coffeehouse

tradition, is legendary for its coffee culture. The first Viennese coffeehouses

appeared after invading Turks left sacks of coffee outside the city walls as

they fled in 1683 (Pendergast 10). Intellectual life abounded in elegant cafés

by the nineteenth century, as they became meeting places for early modernists

such as Sigmund Freud and Gustav Klimt, as well as for notable exiles such

as Vladimir Lenin and Leon Trotsky. In Vienna, the people take pride in

the history and enjoy the culture that surrounds the coffeehouse tradition.

Austrians received the opening of Starbucks with mixed emotions:

> Many Viennese sniff that their culture has been infected, that Viennese Block quotation
> use their 1,900 or so coffee shops to linger and meet, smoke and
> drink, savor the wonders of pastries with cream and marzipan, ponder
> the world, write books and read free newspapers. They drink from
> china cups and order from a waiter, usually in a stained black dinner
> jacket. (Erlanger B3)

Skeptics found it difficult to believe that an American brand such as Starbucks could survive in an environment steeped in its own local history of coffee and pride in its heritage, but these skeptics seem to have underestimated Starbucks.

There are several fundamental differences between the Starbucks experience and the traditional experience found in Viennese coffeehouses. Instead of ordering through a server, Starbucks patrons order at an American-style coffee bar. As opposed to more traditional offerings such as Sachertorte and hot goulash, Starbucks sells American-style sweets like blueberry muffins and chocolate-chip cookies. Furthermore, patrons are not allowed to smoke in any Starbucks outlet in order to allow the aroma of coffee to fill each store. Smoking, however, is a large part of the European coffeehouse experience.

These differences add up to two coffee cultures at a crossroads in Vienna. Traditional American offerings are pitted against the offerings of Viennese coffeehouses that have conducted business for centuries. Both Starbucks and independent Viennese coffeehouses sell good coffee, so the primary product being sold is fairly similar. But two essentially different aesthetic experiences and cultures are involved, and they now compete within the same locality. If Austrians had wanted the Starbucks experience previously, they would have had to seek it in other countries. Now, the Viennese cannot help but notice Starbucks. The two coffee cultures have thus become intertwined--competing against each other across not oceans, but streets.

The writer describes and analyzes an image. Illustrating these differences is the following picture of a ticket seller for the opera house across from the first Viennese Starbucks. On break from work, the man is dressed in aristocratic attire from the eighteenth century, but he is sipping his Starbucks coffee out of a paper cup rather than from the kind of

Pieper 5

china cup he would have received in a traditional
Viennese coffeehouse. Moreover, he is smoking a
cigarette outside instead of inside the store, as is
customary in nearly all European coffeehouses.
At first glance, this image appears harmless; it is
a combination of new and old. Upon further
examination, however, it is more than that. The
Starbucks logo, the international symbol of the
American company, hangs above the young man,
with the angle of the photograph making him appear
to be in a Starbucks advertisement. The similar color
green in both the man's jacket and the Starbucks
logo melts the two together even further. Also, the

Photo courtesy of Roland Schlager.

reflection of another man dressed in a business suit can be seen facing the
subject of the photo. The businessman seems to be walking straight toward the
ticket seller. The image can be interpreted as a sign of the times: Starbucks and
its corporate chain of coffee shops, extending their reach and marching straight
into the traditional independent cultures of other countries. The photograph also
shows the apparent willingness of locals to embrace the products and service
Starbucks provides even if it means abandoning a long-established cultural
tradition of their own.

Starbucks has seen initial success in its Austrian operations with an
estimated 100,000 patrons in its first two months of operation (Erlanger A1).
This result is not uncommon since the market trend over the past decade has
worked overwhelmingly in Starbucks' favor. The company has not failed in any
of the markets into which it has introduced itself. A large part of the reason its
expansion plans are on schedule in Europe is that Starbucks represents

**Citation of a
newspaper
article**

Pieper 6

something different but nevertheless nonthreatening. In this case, a familiar product is being sold from one Western nation to another. The primary difference is in how that product is offered and what other products are offered along with it.

Starbucks also has played an inadvertent role in a movement that now exists throughout Europe, in which coffee shops are opening with an atmosphere noticeably reminiscent of Starbucks. Alwyn Scott, of the <u>Seattle Times</u>, writes, "For proof of Starbucks' impact, look no further than its army of European imitators. New coffee chains are springing up with names--Chicago Coffee, San Francisco Coffee, Coffee Shop--that suggest American style, if not Seattle" (F1). Therefore, the traditional coffee cultures that reside in countries like Austria, France, and Italy compete with American culture from two fronts: Starbucks and its imitators.

The writer examines an opposing claim and refutes it.

Competition alone is not necessarily bad. It is essential to capitalist economies. Without competition, there is no freedom of choice, and little innovation. People are left with the same options over and over again, while nothing new emerges. Free-market competition encourages companies to adapt to the changing needs and wants of populations. By opening stores in cities like Vienna, Starbucks could claim that it is simply offering the Viennese a choice that responds to their changing needs and that they are not compelled to accept this choice. It could even claim that it fosters diversity by increasing the options for consumers and creating an expanded coffee culture that includes not only the traditional coffeehouses but also the Americanized experience found in Starbucks and its imitators. However, Starbucks wields an immense amount of power in the regions where it establishes itself. This power is seen in its brand name--familiar from South Korea to Mexico--and in its wealth. Its coffee shops also present a powerful cultural experience, one that immerses the consumer in an

Pieper 7

American-style environment. By expanding its base to include countries all over the world, Starbucks is expanding the role of American culture abroad. This expansion diversifies the cultures of other countries, provides competition for existing coffee cultures, and offers new options to consumers. But, at some point, competition could become hegemony. In other words, the exportation of American culture occurs right along with the exportation of American products. Such expansion of American goods and services could overwhelm another culture, creating a more homogenous, Americanized culture that blurs the distinctiveness of the native one. Increasingly, foreign markets are becoming saturated with Western goods from multinational corporations, which have spread their products--whatever they may be--to places around the globe. Some suggest that this occurrence is working toward the establishment of a single global culture. According to Hugh Mackay, of the Open University, "that 'global culture' is not something which draws in any even or uniform way on the vast diversity of cultures in the world . . . but, rather, consists of the global dissemination of US or Western culture--the complete opposite of diversity" (60).

Three ellipsis points mark an omission.

So far, Starbucks has been able to coexist with the traditional coffee culture in Vienna; the city's architecture, art, and beauty are likely to remain intact no matter how many stores Starbucks opens there. Because a relatively familiar product is passing from one Western nation to another in this case, and people have both the means to buy it and the freedom to reject it, cultural change may be limited to the Viennese getting used to drinking coffee out of paper cups and standing in the street to smoke. The social and economic effects of globalization may be more serious, as Mackay suggests, when multinational corporations operate in developing nations and limited means give people fewer choices. The lasting effects of globalization have yet to be seen. But it is clear that

The writer's conclusion is drawn from research reported on previous pages.

the already ubiquitous green mermaid, like the pervasive golden arches, is going to become even easier to find. And if Starbucks can flourish in an environment with a well-established local coffee culture of its own, then it is feasible that other multinational corporations will export not only their products but also the cultural experience that accompanies those products, no matter how strong the local culture may be.

1 inch

Notes **Center the heading.**

[1]It should be noted that in Saudi Arabia, Starbucks, along with other

multinational corporations, tries to conform to the existing cultural mores. Upon

its introduction into Riyadh, Starbucks changed its logo (normally a crowned

mermaid in a green circle) to one that did not include a depiction of a female

since any representations of females are considered pornography (King,

"Sellout"). In addition, stores make women enter through separate doors as well

as drink their coffee in separate areas. The company has defended itself by stating,

"While Starbucks adheres to the local customs by providing separate entrances,

service and seating, all our stores provide equal amenities, service, menu and

seating to both men and women" (King, "Arabia's" A27).

[2]In the fall of 2000, Starbucks opened an outlet in Beijing's Forbidden City,

which was built early in the fifteenth century and listed as the world's largest

imperial palace. Administrators of the site agreed to rent space to the Starbucks

Chinese affiliate as a way of improving services. After news of the opening

spread, a survey indicated that "over 70 percent of nearly 60,000 people surveyed

were opposed to the café's entry . . . the main reason being the damaging effects to

Chinese cultural heritage and its atmosphere" ("Starbucks").

Numbers on notes match the superscript numbers in the body of the paper.

1 inch

Pieper 10

Center the heading. Works Cited

Alphabetize entries according to the authors' last names.

Burke, Greg, Stacey Vanek Smith, and Regine Wosnitza. "Whole Latte Shakin': Can U.S. Gourmet Coffee Chain Starbucks Convert Continental Europe's Café Society? It's Ready to Try." <u>Time International</u>. 9 Apr. 2001: 47.

Doherty, Jacqueline. "Make It Decaf: Despite Heavy Revenue Gains, Starbucks'

Indent subsequent lines of each entry one-half inch or five spaces.

Earnings Growth Is Slowing." <u>Barrons</u>. 20 May 2002: 20.

Erlanger, Steven. "An American Coffeehouse (or 4) in Vienna." <u>New York Times</u>. 1 June 2002: A1+.

King, Colbert I. "Saudi Arabia's Apartheid (Cont'd)." Editorial. <u>Washington Post</u>. 19 Jan. 2002, final ed.: A27.

Three hyphens indicate the same author as in the preceding entry.

---. "The Saudi Sellout." Editorial. <u>Washington Post</u>. 26 Jan. 2002, final ed.: A23.

Korten, David C. <u>When Corporations Rule the World</u>. West Hartford: Kumarian, 1995.

Mackay, Hugh. "The Globalization of Culture?" <u>A Globalizing World? Culture, Economics, Politics</u>. Ed. David Held. New York: Routledge, 2000. 47-84.

Pendergast, Mark. <u>Uncommon Grounds: The History of Coffee and How It Transformed Our World</u>. New York: Basic, 1999.

Rothkopf, David. "In Praise of Cultural Imperialism?" <u>Foreign Policy</u> 107 (1997): 38-52.

Scott, Alwyn. "A Shot of Americana; Starbucks Jolts Europe's Coffeehouses." <u>Seattle Times</u>. 19 May 2002: F1.

"Starbucks Café in Forbidden City Under Fire." <u>People's Daily Online</u>. 24 Nov.

Place a URL within angle brackets.

2000. 3 June 2002 <http://english.peopledaily.com.cn/200011/24/eng20001124_56044.html>.

13 APA DOCUMENTATION

The American Psychological Association (APA) publishes a style guide entitled *Publication Manual of the American Psychological Association.* Its documentation system (called an *author-date system*) is used for work in psychology and many other disciplines, including education, economics, and sociology. Updates to the style guide are provided at **www.apastyle.org**. This chapter includes

- guidelines for citing sources within the text of a paper (**13a**),
- guidelines for documenting sources in a reference list (**13b**), and
- a sample student paper (**13c**).

13a APA-style in-text citations

APA-style in-text citations usually include just the last name(s) of the author(s) of the work and the year of publication. However, be sure to specify the page number(s) for any quotations you use in your paper. The abbreviation *p.* (for "page") or *pp.* (for "pages") should precede the number(s). If you do not know the author's name, use a shortened version of the source's title instead. If your readers want to find more information about your source, they will look for the author's name, or in its absence, the title of the work, in the bibliography at the end of your paper.

You will likely consult a variety of sources for your research paper. The following examples are representative of the types of in-text citations you can expect to use.

1. Work by one author

A prominent neurologist has concluded, "Pushing back the age at which the widespread form of Alzheimer's strikes—from, say, age 70 to age 90—would be nearly tantamount to a cure" (Kosik, 1999, p. 17).

OR

Kosik (1999) maintains, "Pushing back the age at which the widespread form of Alzheimer's strikes—from, say, age 70 to age 90—would be nearly tantamount to a cure" (p. 17).

Use commas within a parenthetical citation to separate the author's name from the date and the date from the page number(s). Include a page number or numbers only when you are quoting directly from the source.

2. Work by two authors

Whether or not children spend time in day care, their development in early childhood is determined primarily by the nature of the care they receive from parents (Darvas & Walsh, 2002).

Use an ampersand (&) to separate the authors' names.

3. Work by more than two authors

The speech of Pittsburgh, Pennsylvania is called *Pittsburghese* (Johnstone, Bhasin, & Wittkofski, 2002).

For works with three to five authors, cite all the authors the first time the work is referred to, but in subsequent references give only the last name of the first author followed by *et al.* (meaning "and others"): Johnstone et al. For works with six or more authors, provide only the last name of the first author followed by *et al.*, even in the first citation.

4. Anonymous work

Use a shortened version of the title to identify an anonymous work.

Chronic insomnia often requires medical intervention ("Sleep," 2003).

This citation refers to an article identified in the bibliography as "Sleep disorders: Standard methods of treatment."

If the word *Anonymous* is used in the source itself to designate the author, it appears in place of an author's name.

The documents could damage the governor's reputation (Anonymous, 2001).

5. Two or more works by different authors in the same parenthetical citation

In informal conversation, a speaker might use the word *like* to focus the listener's

attention (Eriksson, 1995; Ferrar & Bell, 1995).

Use a semicolon to separate citations, and arrange them in alphabetical order.

6. Two or more works by the same author in the same parenthetical citation

The amygdala is active when a person experiences fear or anger (Carey, 2001, 2002).

Bayard (1995a, 1995b) discusses the acquisition of English in New Zealand.

Order the dates of publication of works by the same author from earliest to most recent; however, if the works have the same publication date, distinguish the dates with lowercase letters (*a, b, c,* and so on) assigned according to the order in which the entries for the works are listed in your paper's bibliography (see page 320).

7. Personal communication

State educational outcomes are often interpreted differently by teachers in the same

school (J. K. Jurgensen, personal communication, May 4, 2003).

Personal communications include letters, memos, e-mail messages, personal interviews, and telephone conversations. These sources are cited in the text only; they do not appear in the reference list.

13b APA-style reference list

All of the works you cite should be listed at the end of your paper, beginning on a separate page with the heading "References." The following tips will help you prepare your list.

TIPS FOR PREPARING A REFERENCE LIST

- Center the heading "References" one inch from the top of the page.
- Include only those sources you explicitly cited in your paper. Do not, however, include entries in your reference list for any personal communications you cited.
- Arrange the list of works alphabetically by the author's last name.
- If a source has more than one author, alphabetize by the last name of the first author.
- If you use more than one work by the same author(s), arrange them according to the date of publication, placing the entry with the earliest date first. If two or more works by the same author(s) have the same publication date, the entries are arranged so that the titles of the works are in alphabetical order, according to the first important word in each title; lowercase letters *a, b, c,* and so on are then added to the date to distinguish the works.
- When an author's name appears both in a one-author entry and first in a multiple-author entry, place the one-author entry first.
- For a work without an author, alphabetize the entry according to the first important word in the title.
- Type the first line of each entry flush with the left margin and indent subsequent lines one-half inch or five spaces (a hanging indent).
- Double-space throughout—between lines of each entry and between entries.

Whether you are submitting an APA-style paper in a college course or preparing a manuscript for publication, you can be guided by the format of the following sample entries. For additional types of entries, including those documenting sources found through InfoTrac, visit www.harbrace.com.

Directory of APA-Style Entries for the Reference List

The following guidelines are for books, articles, and most electronic sources. For additional guidelines for documenting electronic sources, see page 332.

When preparing entries for your reference list, be sure to copy the bibliographic information directly from the sources (e.g., the title page of a book). (See fig. 13.1, on page 326.)

General Documentation Guidelines for Print-Based Sources

Author or Editor

One author. Use the author's first initial and middle initial (if given) and his or her last name. Place the last name before the initials, and follow it with a comma. Include a space between the first and middle initials. Any abbreviation or number that is part of a name, such as *Jr.* or *II*, is placed after a comma following the initials. Indicate the end of this information unit with a single period.

Walters, D. M.
Thayer-Smith, M. S.
Villa, R. P., Jr.

Two to six authors. Invert the last names and initials of all authors. Use a comma to separate names from initials, and use an ampersand (&) (in addition to the comma) before the last name of the last author.

Vifian, I. R., & Kikuchi, K.
Kempf, A. R., Cusack, R., & Evans, T. G.

Seven or more authors. List the names of the first six authors, but substitute *et al.* for the remaining names.	Bauer, S. E., Berry, L., Hacket, N. P., Bach, R., Price, T. M., Brown, J. B., et al.
Corporate or group author. Provide the author's full name.	Hutton Arts Foundation. Center for Neuroscience.
Editor. If a work has an editor or editors instead of an author or authors, include the abbreviation *Ed.* for "editor" or *Eds.* for "editors" in parentheses after the name(s).	Harris, B. E. (Ed.). Stroud, D. F., & Holst, L. F. (Eds.).

Publication Date

Books and journals. Provide the publication date in parentheses, placing a period after the closing parenthesis. For books, this date can be found on the copyright page, which is the page following the title page (see fig. 13.2, on page 327). For journals, the publication date can be found at the bottom of the first page of the article (see fig. 13.3, on page 328). For a work that has been accepted for publication but has not yet been published, place *in press* in parentheses. For a work without a date of publication, use *n.d.* in parentheses.	(2004). (in press). (n.d.).
Magazines and newspapers. For monthly publications, provide both the year and the month, separated by a comma. For daily publications, provide the year, month, and day. Use a comma between the year and the month.	(2005, January). (2004, June 22).
Conferences and meetings. If a paper presented at a conference, symposium, or professional meeting is published, the publication date is given as the year only, in parentheses.	(2004). (2004, September).

(continued on page 324)

Publication Date *(continued from page 323)*

For unpublished papers, provide the year and the month in which the gathering occurred, separated by a comma.

Title

Books. Capitalize only the first word and any proper nouns in a book title. Italicize the entire title, and place a period at the end of this information unit.

Language and the mind.
Avoiding work-related stress.

Journals, magazines, or newspapers. Capitalize all major words in the name of a journal, magazine, or newspaper. Italicize the entire name and place a comma after it.

Journal of Child Psychology,
Psychology Today,
Los Angeles Times,

Articles and chapters. Do not italicize the titles of short works such as journal articles or book chapters. In a bibliographic entry, titles of articles and chapters appear before book titles and the names of journals, magazines, or newspapers. Capitalize only the first word of the title and any proper nouns.

Treating posttraumatic stress disorder.

Subtitles. Always include any subtitle provided for a source. Use a colon to separate a main title and a subtitle. Capitalize only the first word of the subtitle and any proper nouns.

Reading images: The grammar of visual design.
Living in Baghdad: Realities and restrictions.

Volume, Issue, Chapter, and Page Numbers

Journal volumes and issue numbers. A journal paginated *continuously* designates only the first page of the first issue in a volume as page 1. The first page of a subsequent issue in the same volume is given the page number that follows the last page number of the previous issue. In contrast, each issue of a journal paginated

Journal of Applied Social Psychology, 32,
Behavior Therapy, 33(2),

separately begins with page 1. When you use an article from a journal paginated continuously, provide only the volume number (italicized). When you use an article from a journal paginated separately, include the issue number (placed in parentheses) as well as the volume number. Only the volume number is italicized. A comma follows this unit of information.

Book chapters. Provide the numbers of the first and last pages of the relevant chapter preceded by the abbreviation *pp.* (for "pages"). Use an en dash (a short dash) between the page numbers, and place them in parentheses after the title of the book.

New communitarian thinking (pp. 126–140).

Articles. List the page numbers after the comma that follows the volume or issue number.

TESOL Quarterly, 34(2), 213–238.

Publication Data

City and state. Identify the city in which the publisher of the work is located. If two or more cities are given on the title page, use the first one listed. Add the two-letter U.S. Postal Service abbreviation for the state unless the city is one of the following: Baltimore, Boston, Chicago, Los Angeles, New York, Philadelphia, or San Francisco. If the publisher is a university press whose name mentions a state, do not include the state abbreviation. When a work has been published in a city outside the United States, add the name of the country unless the city is Amsterdam, Jerusalem, London, Milan, Moscow, Paris, Rome,

Boston:

Lancaster, PA:

University Park: Pennsylvania State University Press.

Oxford, England:

(continued on page 326)

Publication Data *(continued from page 325)*

Stockholm, Tokyo, or Vienna—in
these cases, the name of the city
alone is sufficient.

Publisher's name. Provide only
enough of the publisher's name so
that it can be identified clearly. Omit
words such as *Publishers* and abbreviations such as *Inc.* However, include
Books and *Press* when they are part of
the publisher's name. The publisher's
name follows the city and state or
country, after a colon. A period ends
this unit of information.

New Haven, CT: Yale University
Press.

New York: Harcourt.

Cambridge, England: Cambridge
University Press.

Title	Working with People with Learning Disabilities
Subtitle	Theory and Practice
Authors	*David Thomas and Honor Woods*

Publisher	Jessica Kingsley Publishers
Cities of publication	London and New York

Fig. 13.1. The title page of a book provides most of the information necessary for creating a bibliographic entry for a research paper.

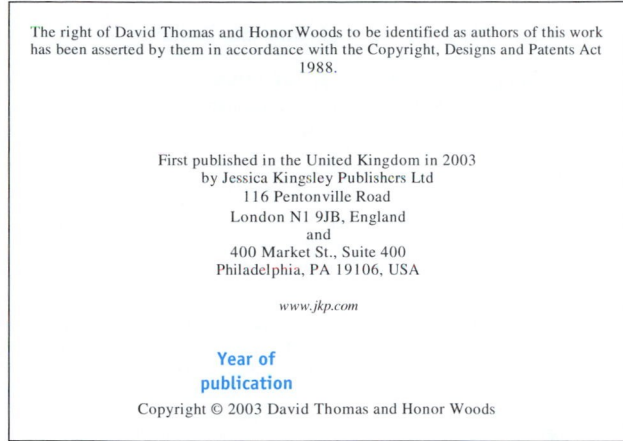

Fig. 13.2. Look for a book's date of publication on the copyright page, which follows the title page.

BOOKS

1. Book by one author

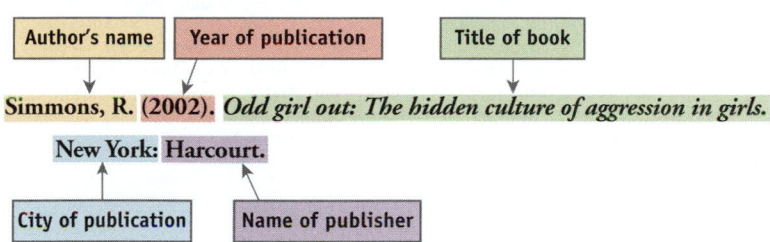

2. Book by two or more authors

Thomas, D., & Woods, H. (2003). *Working with people with disabilities: Theory and*

practice. London: Jessica Kingsley.

If there are more than six authors, list the first six names and use the abbreviation *et al.* in place of the remaining names (see page 323).

Title **Work Attitudes of American Indians**

Author CHARLES N. WEAVER[1]
School of Business and Administration
St. Mary's University

Analysis of 22 samples representative of the labor force of the continental United States shows few differences in 13 work attitudes between American Indians (n = 732) and European Americans (n = 12,810). American Indians were more insecure in their jobs and were less satisfied with their financial situation. They were more likely to prefer a job that offers a high income and chances for promotion. As their increasing earnings reach parity and the effects of discrimination and prejudice lessen, these few differences should diminish.

There are many remarkable features about American Indians that could attract the attention of social scientists. Their population fell by an astonishing 97% from 10 million in 1492 (Dobyns, 1976) to less than 250,000 in 1900 (U.S. Census Bureau, 1993), leading many to believe that they were on the verge of extinction (Office of American Indian Trust, 1999). But, their numbers grew slowly to 377,000 in 1950 (U.S. Census Bureau, 1993), at which time they were the worst fed, worst clad, worst housed, and worst schooled, and received the poorest medical care and government services of any racial group in the United States (Embry, 1956). In 1950, life expectancy was 68 years for Whites and 60 years for Blacks, but only 17 years for reservation Indians (Embry, 1956). Then, from 1950 to 1990, their population accelerated to almost 2 million (U.S. Census Bureau, 1993), and from 1990 to 1997, it grew 12% to 2.3 million, making them the fastest growing segment of the United States population (U.S. Census Bureau, 1997). "Today, [they] are in a period of social, cultural, economic, and political revitalization" (Office of American Indian Trust, 1999, p.1). Their number is expected to be 4.4 million by 2050 (U.S. Census Bureau, 1997).

The main source of demographic and labor force information about American Indians is the federal government. Since the first complete census of American Indians in 1890 (U.S. Census Bureau, 1993), they have been classified for reporting purposes in various ways, such as the 25 largest tribes; American Indians, Eskimos, and Aleuts; and American Indians and Alaska Natives. From reports based on these various methods of classification, a unique and interesting profile of today's American Indian emerges. About half of them live on either side of

[1]Correspondence concerning this article should be addressed to Charles N. Weaver, School of Business and Administration, One Camino Santa Maria, St. Mary's University, San Antonio, TX 78228-8607.

Year of publication

Name of journal

Volume number

432

Issue number

Journal of Applied Social Psychology, 2003, 33, 2, pp. 432-443. Page numbers

Fig. 13.3. The first page of a journal article provides the information needed to complete a bibliographic entry for that source.

3. Book with editor(s)

Antony, M. M., Rachman, S., Richter, M. A., & Swinson, R. P. (Eds.). (1998). *Obsessive-compulsive disorder*. New York: Guilford Press.

4. Book with a corporate or group author

U.S. War Department. (2003). *Official military atlas of the Civil War*. New York: Barnes & Noble.

When the author and the publisher of a book are the same, use the publisher's name at the beginning of the entry and *Author* at the end.

American Psychiatric Association. (1995). *American Psychiatric Association capitation handbook*. Washington, DC: Author.

5. Edition after the first

Cember, H. (1996). *Introduction to health physics* (3rd ed.). New York: McGraw-Hill.

Identify the edition in parentheses immediately after the title. Use abbreviations: *2nd, 3rd,* and so on for the edition number and *ed.* for "edition."

6. Translation

Freud, S. (1999). *The interpretation of dreams* (J. Crick, Trans.). New York: Oxford University Press. (Original work published 1899)

A period follows the name of the publisher but not the parenthetical note about the original publication date.

7. Multivolume work

Doyle, A. C. (2003). *The complete Sherlock Holmes* (Vols. 1 & 2). New York: Barnes & Noble.

If the multivolume work was published over a period of more than one year, use the range of years for the publication date.

Hawthorne, Nathaniel. (1962–1997). *The centenary edition of the works of Nathaniel Hawthorne* (Vols. 1–23). Columbus: Ohio University Press.

8. Government report

Executive Office of the President. (2003). *Economic report of the President, 2003* (GPO Publication No. 040-000-0760-1). Washington, DC: U.S. Government Printing Office.

9. Selection from an edited book

Wolfe, A. (1996). Human nature and the quest for community. In A. Etzioni (Ed.), *New communitarian thinking* (pp. 126–140). Charlottesville: University Press of Virginia.

Italicize the book title but not the title of the selection.

10. Selection from a reference book

Wickens, D. (2001). Classical conditioning. In *The Corsini encyclopedia of psychology and behavioral science* (Vol. 1, pp. 293–298). New York: John Wiley.

ARTICLES IN PRINT

11. Article with one author in a journal with continuous pagination

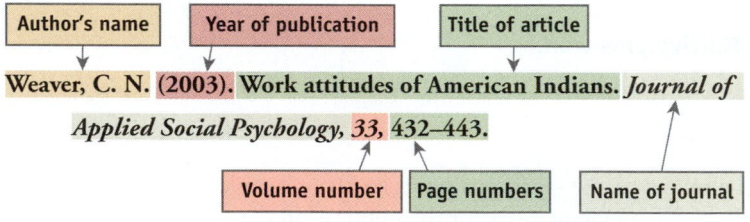

Figure 13.3 (on page 328) shows where the information for this type of entry is found on the first page of an article.

12. Article with two authors in a journal with each issue paginated separately

Rudisill, J. R., & Edwards, J. M. (2002). Coping with job transitions. *Consulting Psychology Journal, 54*(1), 55–62.

13. Article with three to six authors

Frost, R. O., Steketee, G., & Williams, L. (2002). Compulsive buying, compulsive hoarding, and obsessive-compulsive disorder. *Behavior Therapy, 33*(2), 201–213.

14. Article with more than six authors

Reddy, S. K., Arora, M., Perry, C. L., Nair, B., Kohli, A., Lytle, L. A., et al. (2002). Tobacco and alcohol use outcomes of a school-based intervention in New Delhi. *American Journal of Health Behavior, 26,* 173–181.

15. Article in a monthly, biweekly, or weekly magazine

Winson, J. (2002, June). The meaning of dreams. *Scientific American, 12,* 54–61.

For magazines published weekly or biweekly, add the day of the issue: (2003, May 8).

16. Article in a newspaper

Liptak, A. (2002, June 16). Polygamist's custody fight raises many issues. *The New York Times,* p. A20.

Include the letter indicating the section with the page number.

17. Letter to the editor

Mancall, M. (2002, June 17). Answer to cynicism [Letter to the editor]. *The New York Times,* p. A20.

After the title, indicate within brackets that the work is a letter to the editor.

18. Book review

Kamil, M. L. (2002). The state of reading research [Review of the book *Progress in*

understanding reading: Scientific foundations and new frontiers]. *American*

Journal of Psychology, 115, 451–458.

SOURCES PRODUCED FOR ACCESS BY COMPUTER

The APA guidelines for electronic sources are similar to those for print sources. Exceptions are explained after the sample entries that follow. Information about when and how the source was retrieved appears at the end. Notice that the period that normally ends an entry is omitted after a URL because trailing periods can cause difficulty in retrieving files. If a URL has to continue on a new line, break it before a period or after a slash.

19. Article in a journal published only online

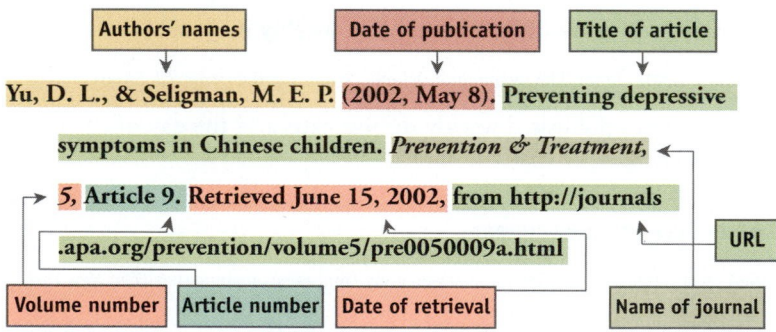

20. Online article based on a print source

Lindsay, D. S., & Poole, D. A. (2001). Children's eyewitness reports after exposure to

misinformation from parents [Electronic version]. *Journal of Experimental*

Psychology: Applied, 7(1), 27–50.

The words in square brackets indicate that the article came from the electronic version of a journal that is also published in print.

21. Article in an online newspaper

McGrath, C. (2002, June 15). Father time. *New York Times.* Retrieved June 15, 2002, from

http://nytimes.com/pages/science/index.html

22. Message posted to a newsgroup

Korniejczuk, V. (2002, June 11). Clinical psychology and psychiatry—what's the

difference? [Msg 4]. Message posted to news://sci.psychology.theory

Provide the message number within square brackets after the message title.

23. Message posted to a forum or discussion group

Vellenzer, G. (2004, January 24). Synonyms of entreaty [Msg 2]. Message posted to

http://groups.google.com/groups?selm=MPG.1a7cacccd54e9c27989b95%40news

.CIS.DFN.DE&output=gplain

24. Article from a database

Kim, Y., & Seidlitz, L. (2002). Spirituality moderates the effect of stress on emotional and

physical adjustment. *Personality & Individual Differences, 32*(8), 1377–1390.

Retrieved December 6, 2004, from PsycINFO database.

Most of the information you will need for documenting an article from a database can be found on the abstract page (see fig. 13.4). Do not confuse the vendor of the database (EBSCO), also referred to as a library subscription service, with the name of the database (PsycINFO).

25. Authored document from a Web site

Harvey, S. (1994, September). *Dynamic play therapy: An integrated expressive arts*

approach to the family treatment of infants and toddlers. Retrieved December 28,

2003, from http://www.zerotothree.org/aboutus/dialogue.html

When the document is from a large Web site, such as one sponsored by a university or government body, provide the name of the host organization before the URL.

Darling, C. (2002). *Guide to grammar and writing*. Retrieved September 12, 2003, from

Capital Community College Web site: http://cctc2.commnet.edu/grammar/

modifiers.htm

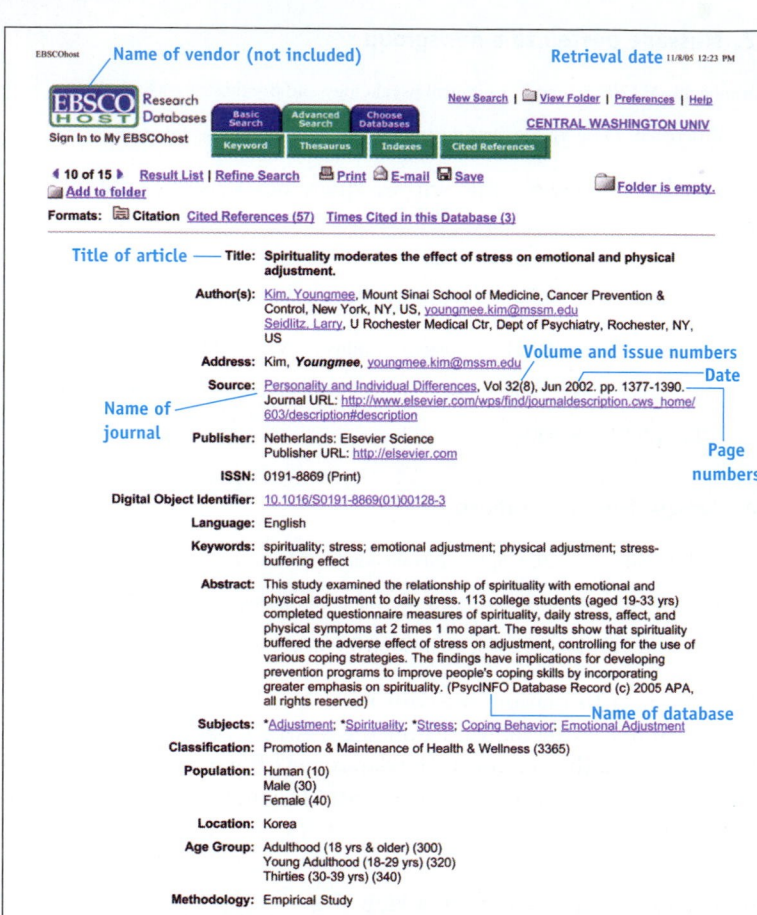

Fig. 13.4. Computer printout of an abstract page.

26. Document with no identified author from a Web site

American School Counselor Association. (2004). *Ethical standards for school*

counselors. Retrieved December 6, 2004, from http://www.schoolcounselor.org/

content.asp?contentid=173

Use the name of the organization hosting the Web site as the author of the document. In fig. 13.5, the name of the organization appears in the upper-left corner. If a date is provided (as there is on the printout in fig. 13.5, just before the preamble), place it in parentheses. If there is no date listed, use the abbreviation *n.d.* The date of retrieval and the URL are located at the bottom of the computer printout in fig. 13.5, but they will sometimes appear at the top.

27. Online government publication from GPO Access database

U.S. General Accounting Office. (2000, April). Federal prisons: Containing health care

costs for an increasing inmate population (Publication No. GAO/T-GGD-00-112).

Retrieved August 24, 2005, from General Accounting Office Reports Online via

GPO Access: http://www.gpoaccess.gaoreports/index/html

28. Personal communication

Personal communications such as e-mail messages, letters, telephone conversations, and personal interviews do not appear in the reference list but should be cited in the text as follows: (S. L. Johnson, personal communication, September 3, 2003).

OTHER SOURCES

29. Motion picture

Smith, M. (Producer/Writer), & Gaviria, M. (Producer/Director). (2001). *Medicating kids*

[Motion picture]. (Available from the Public Broadcasting Service, 1320 Braddock

Place, Alexandria, VA 22314)

Begin with the primary contributor(s), identifying the nature of the contribution. Follow with the release date, the title, and the descriptive label in square brackets. For a film with limited distribution, provide,

Fig. 13.5. Computer printout of a Web document with no identified author.

within parentheses, information about how it can be obtained. For a widely distributed film, indicate the country where it was produced and the name of the studio, after the descriptive label: [Motion picture]. United States: Paramount Pictures.

30. Television program

Holt, S. (Producer). (2002, October 1). *The mysterious lives of caves* [Television

broadcast]. Alexandria, VA: Public Broadcasting Service.

Give the title of the program in italics. If citing an entire series (e.g., *Nova* or *The West Wing*), cite the producer for the series as a whole, and use the descriptive label *Television series* in the square brackets.

13c APA-style student paper

The APA recognizes that a paper may have to be modified so that it adheres to an instructor's requirements. The following boxes offer tips for preparing a title page and an abstract page for a typical student paper. For tips on preparing a reference list, see page 320.

APA Documentation

↕ ½ inch

Place the page header five spaces from the page number.

Running Head: SLEEP AND MEMORY

The running head includes no more than fifty characters.

←——————→

Use 1-inch margins on both sides of the page.

If required, the course name and number replace the affiliation.

The Sleep and Memory Connection

Nikki Krzmarzick

University of St. Thomas

TIPS FOR PREPARING THE TITLE PAGE OF AN APA-STYLE PAPER

- Place the number 1 (to indicate that this is the first page) an inch from the right side of the paper and a half inch from the top.

- Place a **manuscript page header** (the first two or three words of the title) in the upper-right corner, five spaces before the page number. The manuscript page header should appear on all subsequent pages along with the appropriate page number.

- Below the page header but on the left side of the page, list the **running head,** a shortened version of the title (no more than fifty characters). Use *all* uppercase letters for the running head.

- Place the title in the center of the page, with your name below it. You may include your affiliation and a course name or number if your instructor requests one. Double-space these lines.

1 inch

½ inch
Sleep and Memory   2

Abstract

Current research indicates that sleep plays a role in learning and memory. Results of research cited within the paper suggest that sleep affects the acquisition of knowledge and skills needed to perform perceptual, critical, and creative-thinking tasks. This topic's relevance to college students is addressed, and practical applications of findings to that end are discussed. Further research is necessary to establish how the brain acquires, consolidates, and organizes information for later retrieval.

Center the heading.

The maximum length for an abstract is 120 words.

TIPS FOR PREPARING THE ABSTRACT AND THE BODY OF AN APA-STYLE PAPER

- Place the number 2 an inch from the right side of the paper and a half inch from the top on the abstract page.
- Place a manuscript page header five spaces to the left of the page number.
- Center the word *Abstract* one inch from the top of the paper.
- Be sure that the abstract (a short summary) is no more than 120 words. For advice on summarizing, see **11d(4)**.
- Double-space throughout the body of the abstract. Do not indent the first line of the abstract.
- Place the number 3 on the first page of the body of the paper, along with the manuscript page header.
- Center the title of the paper one inch from the top of the page.
- Use one-inch margins on both the left and right sides of your paper.
- Double-space throughout the body of the paper, indenting each paragraph one-half inch or five to seven spaces.

Center the title.

The Sleep and Memory Connection

Double-space throughout.

It is finals week. In 24 hours, Kyle Rosemount has a biology exam. He is not sure he is on track to pass the class, so a good grade is essential. He regrets not starting earlier in the week but has resolved to stay up all night reviewing course material. This method will afford him almost 16 hours of study time. Rosemount reasons that this amount of time will be sufficient and is almost positive he would not have spent more hours with the material had he started exam preparations the previous week.

Use 1-inch margins on both sides.

This scenario is all too familiar to college students, and many have used the same logic as Rosemount in thinking that the total number of hours spent studying is more critical than when that studying takes place. It seems to make sense that the more time one spends studying the subject matter, the better one will retain the information. But current research on the possibility of a relationship between sleep and memory suggests that this assumption is not necessarily true. In fact, irregular sleep patterns and cram sessions may actually be sabotaging students' efforts.

Thesis and background information

If there is a connection between sleep and memory, then getting regular sleep may be essential for memory consolidation and for optimal performance on both critical- and creative-thinking tasks. An exploration of this possibility requires a basic understanding of the sleep cycle. To an observer, a sleeping person appears passive, unresponsive, and essentially isolated from the rest of the world and its barrage of stimuli. While it is true that humans are unaware of most of what is happening around them during sleep, the brain is far from inactive. It can be as active during sleep as in a waking state. When it is asleep, the rate and type of neuronal firings (electrical activity) change. The brain cycles through four sleep stages before moving into REM sleep. All of this occurs at relatively predictable intervals while a person is asleep. Generally, it takes about 90 minutes to cycle through the four stages of sleep and one REM episode, each with distinct neuronal characteristics (Hobson, 1989). Figure 1 graphs these stages for an 8-hour sleep period.

Citation of a work by one author

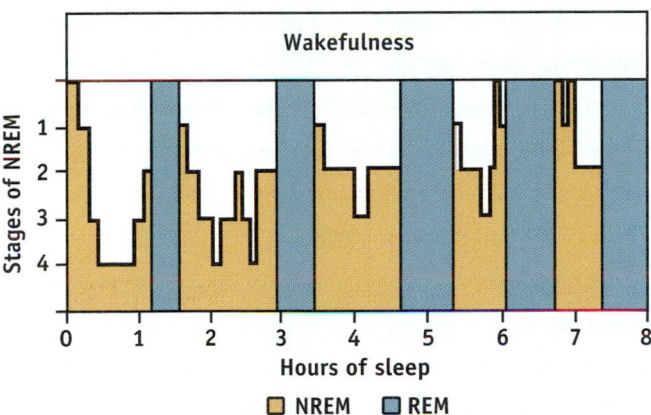

Figure 1. Sleep stages. *Note.* From *Good sleep, good learning, good life,* by Piotr Wozniak, July 2000. Retrieved September 19, 2002, from http://www.supermemo.com/articles/sleep.htm. Reprinted with permission.

The writer contacted the copyright holder for permission to reproduce this figure.

The first two stages of sleep are characterized by high-amplitude, low-frequency neural waves, aptly named slow-wave sleep. During these phases, the brain is relatively inactive and fires at a baseline rate. Wave III and wave IV sleep are known as fast-wave sleep, recognized on an electroencephalogram readout by low-amplitude, high-frequency neuronal activity. REM sleep is characterized by rapid motion of the eyes beneath closed lids. This is the stage of sleep associated with vivid dreams, and it is thus sometimes called dream sleep. Some dreams may occur within other stages as well, but they lack the rich visual and emotional content of REM dreams. The function of this fascinating phenomenon remains at least a partial mystery.

Current research examines links between sleep, or stages of sleep, and memory or learning. Some studies suggest that all-night cram sessions, such as the one Rosemount is planning, do not improve performance and may even have the opposite effect (Kelly, Kelly, & Clanton, 2001; Pilcher & Walters, 1997). The idea that sleep is linked to learning is supported by studies showing that certain types of

The writer focuses on a specific problem.

A semicolon separates sources. All five authors are listed in the first citation of their work.

learning are hampered by sleep disruption or deprivation (Horne, 1988; Karni, Tanne, Rubenstein, Askenasy, & Sagi, 1994).

Discussion of research findings

Some studies implicate REM sleep as having a particularly important role in memory consolidation (Karni et al., 1994). Early research showed the importance of REM sleep for rats. Hunt (1989) summarizes a few of these early studies that indicate the importance of the timing of REM sleep:

A quotation of forty or more words is set off as a block quotation.

> Over the past few years Carlyle Smith (1981) has studied the REM augmentation following learning in rats over several days and has found that these increases occur as regular "windows" that climb steadily over a six-day period (Smith and Lapp, 1984). Deprivation of REM during these specific windows of augmentation was at its most effective in disrupting prior learning between 48 and 60 hours after training (Smith and Kelly, 1986). (p. 28)

The writer uses *et al.* in a subsequent reference to a five-author source.

Research involving human participants has yielded similar results. Karni et al. (1994) showed that performance on a procedural task improves "neither during nor immediately after practice but rather 8 to 10 hours after a training session has ended" (p. 679). Hunt reports confirmation of the "window" phenomenon by noting that in 1985 Epstein found participants in his study reporting life events as dream content 2 or 3 days after the experiences (Hunt, 1989). Epstein's findings differ in nature from those of Karni et al. (1994) in that they are more difficult to quantify because his data depend on dream recall, which is subjective. While Epstein's observations are not the most scientifically sound support for optimal timing of REM sleep, they are worth noting and could be significant when pooled with other findings supporting the idea that the brain processes new information and experiences over the course of a few days. In addition to the timing of sleep following training, the amount of REM sleep may play a role. Toward the end of the entire sleep cycle, time spent in REM sleep increases. When people are deprived of REM sleep, their brains react by going into REM sleep more frequently or by staying at the REM stage longer during a sleep-recovery phase (Hobson, 1989).

Authors' names followed by publication dates in parentheses

Although there is no definitive answer as to which type of sleep is needed for memory consolidation, studies show that lack of sleep hinders learning in various ways. Pilcher and Walters (1997) noted its negative impact on participant performance on a test of cognitive ability. Horne (1988) found that participants performed creative-thinking tasks at a decreased capacity when compared with a control group. Karni et al. (1994) observed the damaging effect of sleep deprivation on perceptual learning.

Some studies include a self-report measure for perceived effort, concentration and the like (e.g., Buboltz, Brown, & Soper, 2001; Pilcher & Walters, 1997). Participants are asked to report how confident they are in their performance and to rate that performance. Findings from these self-report measures are somewhat disturbing. It appears that the tendency exists, when a person is sleep deprived, to overestimate performance. Surprisingly, although Pilcher and Walters (1997) noted that sleep deprivation negatively affected the ability of participants to perform on a test, the participants overestimated their performance. They also rated themselves as having expended more effort than participants in the control group did. Perhaps such skewed perception partially explains why college students often deprive themselves of sleep. If their perception is that performance is not hindered, there is no incentive to make sleep a priority.

The studies outlined above illustrate multiple types of learning and memory that may be affected by sleep. It is noteworthy that many of these studies used variables and methodologies that are realistic: They involve tasks similar to those that college students are asked to perform. For example, it is common for students to be asked to employ creative problem-solving skills in a classroom setting. Visual discrimination tasks, too, are common in college courses. Most students have experienced tests in which they must recognize a painting or a literary passage and then name its painter or author. This line of research offers an obvious link between science and real-life situations.

Clearly there is a need for more research on this topic. The fact that an adequate amount of sleep is necessary for a person's health and well-being is well established. We now have sufficient evidence to warrant a closer look at just how important the role of sleep is. Further research may find that all stages of sleep play an important role in optimal functioning, or that one or two stages are particularly important. The exact relationship between sleep and memory is not yet known.

Application of findings to research question

College students have notoriously bad sleeping habits, often because they are attempting to balance schoolwork, part-time jobs, extracurricular activities, and a social life. Known for their irregular sleep patterns, they are often sleep-deprived and/or suffer from some type of disturbed sleep (e.g., difficulty falling, or staying, asleep) (Hicks, Fernandez, & Pellegrini, 2001).

Based on the current body of research literature, it appears that there is a link between sleep and optimal functioning. For this reason, it is important for college students to manage their time in a way that allows them to study material over a period of a couple of days or longer and to have adequate sleep time in order to maximize retention. The consequences of inadequate sleep go beyond simply feeling sleepy. It is alarming that the self-reported sleep habits and quality of sleep of over 1,500 college students have worsened over the last decade (Hicks et al., 2001), indicating that necessary precautions are not being taken to ensure that at the very least students are educated regarding the importance of sleep.

Conclusion

It is evident that Kyle Rosemount is not doing himself any favors by delaying his studying until the last minute. Ideally, Rosemount should have studied in shorter blocks of time over a week, or at least a couple of days, allowing more time to process the information and commit it to memory. It may be that the sleep deprivation college students inflict upon themselves, particularly around finals time, may lead them to overestimate performance while actually hindering it.

1 inch

½ inch

Sleep and Memory   8

References

Buboltz, W. C., Brown, F. C., Jr., & Soper, B. (2001). Sleep habits and patterns of
college students: A preliminary study. *Journal of American College Health,
50*(3), 131–135.

Hicks, R. A., Fernandez, C., & Pellegrini, R. J. (2001). The changing sleep habits
of university students: An update. *Perceptual and Motor Skills, 93*(3), 648.

Hobson, J. A. (1989). *Sleep.* New York: Scientific American Library.

Horne, J. A. (1988). Sleep loss and divergent thinking ability. *Sleep, 11*(6),
528–536.

Hunt, H. T. (1989). *The multiplicity of dreams: Memory, imagination, and
consciousness.* New Haven, CT: Yale University Press.

Karni, A., Tanne, D., Rubenstein, B. S., Askenasy, J. M., & Sagi, D. (1994, July
29). Dependence on REM sleep of overnight improvement of a perceptual
skill. *Science, 265*, 679–682.

Kelly, W. E., Kelly, K. E., & Clanton, R. C. (2001). The relationship between sleep
length and grade-point average among college students. *College Student
Journal, 35*, 84–86.

Pilcher, J. J., & Walters, A. S. (1997). How sleep deprivation affects psychological
variables related to college students' cognitive performance. *Journal of
American College Health, 46*(3), 121–126.

Wozniak, P. (2000, July). *Good sleep, good learning, good life.* Retrieved
September 19, 2002, from http://www.supermemo.com/articles/sleep.htm

Center the
heading.

Alphabetize
the entries
according to
the first
author's last
name.

Indent
subsequent
lines of each
entry one-
half inch or
five spaces.

No period
follows a
URL.

CMS DOCUMENTATION

14

The Chicago Manual of Style (CMS), published by the University of Chicago Press, provides guidelines for writers in history and other subject areas in the arts and humanities. The manual recommends documenting sources by using either footnotes or endnotes and, for most assignments, a bibliography. Updates to the manual can be found at **www.press. uchicago.edu/Misc/Chicago/cmosfaw/cmosfaq.html**. For questions about college-level papers unanswered in the manual, the editors of CMS direct the reader to Kate L. Turabian's *Manual for Writers of Term Papers, Theses, and Dissertations*. This chapter includes

- guidelines for citing sources within a CMS-style research paper and documenting sources in a bibliography (**14a**) and
- a sample student paper (**14b**).

14a CMS note and bibliographic forms

According to CMS style, in-text citations take the form of sequential numbers that refer to **footnotes** (notes at the bottom of each page) or **endnotes** (notes at the end of the paper). The information in these notes is condensed if a bibliography lists all the sources used in the paper. The condensed, or short, form for a note includes only the author's last name, the title (shortened if longer than four words), and the relevant page number(s): Eggers, *Court Reporters,* 312–15.

When no bibliography is provided for a paper, the full note form is used. For either footnotes or endnotes, a superscript number is placed in the text wherever documentation of a source is necessary. The number should be as close as possible to whatever it refers to, following the punctuation that appears at the end of the direct quotation or paraphrase. You can create a superscript number in Microsoft Word by highlighting the number, pulling down the menu for Format, clicking on Font, and then placing a checkmark next to Superscript. Other word-processing programs perform this function similarly.

TIPS FOR PREPARING FOOTNOTES

- Most word-processing programs will footnote your paper automatically. In Microsoft Word, pull down the Insert menu and choose Footnote. A superscript number will appear next to the relevant text. A box will also appear at the bottom of your page, in which you can insert the requisite information.

- If you do not have access to a word-processing program, be sure to leave enough space for footnotes on the bottom of the page to which they refer. After the last line of text on that page, create a separator—a solid line that stretches across one-third of the page. Leave one line space after the separator before typing the footnote.

- Each note begins with a full-size number followed by a period and a space.

- Use the abbreviation *Ibid.* (not italicized) to indicate that the source cited in an entry is identical to the one in the preceding entry. Include page numbers if they differ from those in the preceding entry: Ibid., 331–32.

- Indent the first line of a note five spaces.

- Single-space lines within a footnote.

- Double-space between footnotes when more than one appears on a page.

- No bibliography is necessary when the footnotes provide complete bibliographic information for all sources.

TIPS FOR PREPARING ENDNOTES

- Place endnotes on a separate page, following the last page of the body of the paper and preceding the bibliography (if one is included).

- Center the word *Notes* (not italicized) at the top of the page.

- Use the abbreviation *Ibid.* (not italicized) to indicate that a source cited in an entry is identical to the one in the preceding entry. Include page numbers if they differ from those in the preceding entry: Ibid., 331–32.

- Indent the first line of a note five spaces.

- Single-space between lines of an endnote and leave one blank line between endnotes.

- No bibliography is necessary when the endnotes provide complete bibliographic information for all sources used in the paper.

TIPS FOR PREPARING A BIBLIOGRAPHY

- Start the bibliography on a separate page, following the last page of the body of the paper if footnotes are used or following the last page of endnotes.
- Center the word *Bibliography* (not italicized) at the top of your paper. Some instructors may prefer that you use *Works Cited*.
- Alphabetize entries in the bibliography according to the author's last name.
- If a source has more than one author, alphabetize by the last name of the first author.
- For a work without an author, alphabetize the entry according to the first important word in the title.
- To indicate that a source has the same author(s) as in the preceding entry, begin an entry with a three-em dash (———) instead of the name(s) of the author(s). (If you do not know how to create this mark, search for *em dash,* using the Help function on your word processor.)
- Indent the second and subsequent lines of an entry five spaces.
- Single-space between lines of an entry and leave one blank line between entries.

Directory of CMS Note and Bibliographic Forms

BOOKS

General Documentation Guidelines for Print-Based Sources

The following guidelines are for books and articles. Both full note forms and bibliographic forms are provided. Remember that a short note form consists of just the author's last name, the title (shortened if longer than four words), and relevant page numbers.

Author or Editor

One author—note form. Provide the author's full name, beginning with the first name and following the last name with a comma. For the short note form, use only the last name(s) of author(s) or editor(s).

Full note form
1. Jamie Desler,

One author—bibliographic form. Invert the author's name so that the last name appears first. Place a period after the first name.

Bibliographic form
Desler, Jamie.

Two authors—note form. Use the word *and* between the names.

Full note form
1. Pauline Diaz and Edward Allan,

(continued on page 350)

Author or Editor *(continued from page 349)*

Two authors—bibliographic form. Invert the first author's name only. Place a comma and the word *and* after the first author's name. A period follows the second author's name.

Bibliographic form
Diaz, Pauline, and Edward Allan.

Three authors—note form. Use commas after the names of the first and subsequent authors. Include *and* before the final author's name.

Full note form
2. Joyce Freeland, John Bach, and Derik Flynn,

Three authors—bibliographic form. Invert the order of the first author's name only. Place a comma after this name and after the second author's name. Use *and* before the final author's name.

Bibliographic form
Freeland, Joyce, John Bach, and Derik Flynn.

Corporate or group author— note and bibliographic forms. Provide the full name of the group in all forms—full note, short note, and bibliographic.

Note form
3. Smithsonian Institution,
Bibliographic form
Smithsonian Institution.

Editor—note and bibliographic forms. Place the abbreviation *ed.* after the editor's name.

Full note form
4. Peggy Irmen, ed.,
Bibliographic form
Irmen, Peggy, ed.

Titles

Italicized titles. Italicize the titles of books, magazines, journals, newspapers, and films. Capitalize all major words (nouns, pronouns, verbs, adjectives, adverbs, and subordinating conjunctions). A book title is followed by a comma in a note form and by a period in the bibliographic form. In the short note form, a title

Full note form
The Great Design of Henry IV from the Memoirs of the Duke of Sully,
Short note form
Great Design of Henry IV,
Bibliographic form
The Great Design of Henry IV from the Memoirs of the Duke of Sully.

longer than four words is shortened by omitting any article at its beginning and using only important words from the rest of the title.

Titles in quotation marks. Use quotation marks to enclose the titles of journal or magazine articles, selections from anthologies, and other short works. (See **38b**.) In the note form, a title of a short work is followed by a comma. In the bibliographic form, it is followed by a period.

Full note form
"The Humor of New England,"

Bibliographic form
"The Humor of New England."

Subtitles. Include subtitles in the full note and bibliographic forms but not in the short note form.

Full note form
Appreciations: Painting, Poetry, and Prose,

Bibliographic form
Appreciations: Painting, Poetry, and Prose.

Journal volume and issue numbers. Whenever possible, include both the volume number and the issue number for any journal article you use. The volume number should appear after the title, and the issue number should appear after the volume number (preceded by the abbreviation *no.*). Use a comma to separate the two numbers.

American Naturalist 154, no. 2

Publication Data

List the city of publication, publisher's name, and date. A colon follows the city of publication, and a comma follows the publisher's name. In the full note form, this information should be placed within parentheses. No

Full note form
(New York: Alfred A. Knopf, 2005),

Bibliographic form
New York: Alfred A. Knopf, 2005.

(continued on page 352)

Publication Data *(continued from page 351)*

parentheses are needed for the bibliographic form. The short note form does not include publication data.

For a journal, place the year of publication in parentheses after the volume or issue number. For a magazine, provide the full date of publication.

International Social Work 47 (2004)
Journal of Democracy 14, no. 1 (2003)
Time, January 24, 2005

City and state. Identify the city of publication. If the city is not widely known, add a two-letter state abbreviation (or, for a city outside the United States, a province or country abbreviation). If the city of publication is Washington, include the abbreviation for the District of Columbia, *DC.* When two cities are listed on the title page, use only the first in the bibliographic entry unless both are located in the same state.

Baltimore
Carbondale, IL
Waterloo, ON
Harmondsworth, UK
Carbondale and Edwardsville: Southern Illinois Press

Publisher's name. Provide either the full name of each publisher, as given on the title page, or an abbreviated version. The style chosen must be consistent throughout the notes and bibliography. Even when the full name is provided, some words may be omitted: an initial *The* and words such as *Company* or *Corporation* or abbreviations such as *Co.* or *Inc.* The word *University* may be abbreviated to *Univ.*

Univ. of Chicago Press
Penguin Books
HarperCollins

Page Numbers

If you are citing information from a specific page or pages of a book or article, place the page number(s) at the end of the footnote or endnote. If you are citing more than one page, separate the first and last page with an en dash (or short dash): 35–38. If the page numbers have the same hundreds or thousands digit, do not repeat it when listing the final page in the range: 123–48. Page numbers are not included in a bibliographic entry for a book. A bibliographic entry for an article ends with the range of pages on which the article appears.

The following list contains entries for the full note form and the bibliographic form. The short note form is provided only for a book with one author. For more examples of short forms, see the endnotes of the sample student paper (pages 372–373).

BOOKS

1. Book with one author

Full note form

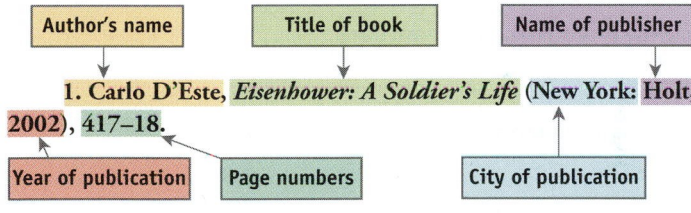

Short note form

1. D'Este, *Eisenhower*, 417–18.

Bibliographic form

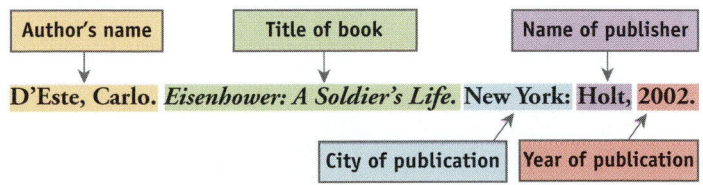

2. Book with two authors
Full note form

2. Cathy Scott-Clark and Adrian Levy, *The Stone of Heaven* (Boston: Little, Brown, 2001), 28.

Bibliographic form

Scott-Clark, Cathy, and Adrian Levy. *The Stone of Heaven.* Boston: Little, Brown, 2001.

3. Book with three authors
Full note form

3. Xue Litai, John W. Lewis, and Sergei N. Goncharov, *Uncertain Partners: Stalin, Mao, and the Korean War* (Palo Alto, CA: Stanford Univ. Press, 1993).

Bibliographic form

Litai, Xue, John W. Lewis, and Sergei N. Goncharov. *Uncertain Partners: Stalin, Mao, and the Korean War.* Palo Alto, CA: Stanford Univ. Press, 1993.

4. Book with more than three authors
Full note form

4. Mike Palmquist and others, *Transitions: Teaching Writing in Computer-Supported and Traditional Classrooms* (Greenwich, CT: Ablex, 1998), 153.

In the note form, just the first person's name is used, followed by *and others*. The bibliographic form should include all the authors' names.

Bibliographic form

Palmquist, Mike, Kate Kiefer, James Hartvigsen, and Barbara Goodlew. *Transitions: Teaching Writing in Computer-Supported and Traditional Classrooms.* Greenwich, CT: Ablex, 1998.

5. Book with an editor

Full note form

> 5. Hanna Schissler, ed., *The Miracle Years* (Princeton, NJ: Princeton Univ. Press, 2001).

Bibliographic form

Schissler, Hanna, ed. *The Miracle Years.* Princeton, NJ: Princeton Univ. Press, 2001.

6. Book with an author and an editor

Full note form

> 6. Ayn Rand, *The Art of Fiction,* ed. Tore Boeckmann (New York: Plume, 2000).

Use the abbreviation *ed.* for "edited by."

Bibliographic form

Rand, Ayn. *The Art of Fiction.* Edited by Tore Boeckmann. New York: Plume, 2000.

Write out the words *Edited by.*

7. Translated book

Full note form

> 7. Murasaki Shikibu, *The Tale of Genji,* trans. Royall Tyler (New York: Viking, 2001).

Use the abbreviation *trans.* for "translated by."

Bibliographic form

Shikibu, Murasaki. *The Tale of Genji.* Translated by Royall Tyler. New York: Viking, 2001.

Write out the words *Translated by.*

8. Edition after the first
Full note form

8. Edward O. Wilson, *On Human Nature,* 14th ed. (Cambridge: Harvard Univ. Press, 2001).

Bibliographic form

Wilson, Edward O. *On Human Nature.* 14th ed. Cambridge: Harvard Univ. Press, 2001.

9. One volume in a multivolume work
Full note form

9. Thomas Cleary, *Classics of Buddhism and Zen,* vol. 3 (Boston: Shambhala Publications, 2001), 116.

Bibliographic form

Cleary, Thomas. *Classics of Buddhism and Zen.* Vol. 3. Boston: Shambhala Publications, 2001.

10. Government document
Full note form

10. U.S. Bureau of the Census, *Statistical Abstract of the United States,* 120th ed. (Washington, DC, 2000), 16.

Bibliographic form

U.S. Bureau of the Census. *Statistical Abstract of the United States.* 120th ed. Washington, DC, 2000.

11. Selection from an anthology

Full note form

> 11. Elizabeth Spencer, "The Everlasting Light," in *The Cry of an Occasion,* ed. Richard Bausch (Baton Rouge: Louisiana State University Press, 2001), 171–82.

Bibliographic form

Spencer, Elizabeth. "The Everlasting Light." In *The Cry of an Occasion,* edited by

> Richard Bausch, 171–82. Baton Rouge: Louisiana State University Press, 2001.

When only one selection from an anthology is used, inclusive page numbers precede the publication data in the bibliographic entry.

12. Published letter

Full note form

> 12. Lincoln to George McClellan, Washington, DC, 13 October 1862, in *This Fiery Trial: The Speeches and Writings of Abraham Lincoln,* ed. William E. Gienapp (New York: Oxford Univ. Press, 2002), 178.

Bibliographic form

Lincoln, Abraham. Abraham Lincoln to George McClellan, Washington DC, 13 October

> 1862. In *This Fiery Trial: The Speeches and Writings of Abraham Lincoln,* ed.
> William E. Gienapp, 178. New York: Oxford Univ. Press, 2002.

13. Indirect (secondary) source

Full note form

> 13. Toni Morrison, *Playing in the Dark* (New York: Vintage, 1992), 26, quoted in Jonathan Goldberg, *Willa Cather and Others* (Durham, NC: Duke Univ. Press, 2001), 37.

Bibliographic form

Morrison, Toni. *Playing in the Dark,* 26. New York: Vintage, 1992. Quoted in Jonathan

> Goldberg, *Willa Cather and Others* (Durham, NC: Duke Univ. Press, 2001), 37.

Cite both the original work and the secondary source in which you found it quoted. Begin with the name of the author you have quoted, and provide information about the work (which should be available in the notes or bibliography of the indirect source you used). Then provide information about the secondary source.

ARTICLES

14. Article in a journal

Full note form

> 14. A. Schedler, "The Menu of Manipulation," *Journal of Democracy* 13, no. 2 (2002): 48.

Use initials for an author's first and/or middle names only when they are used in the original publication.

Bibliographic form

Schedler, A. "The Menu of Manipulation." *Journal of Democracy* 13, no. 2 (2002): 36–50.

15. Article in a popular (general-circulation) magazine

Full note form

> 15. John O'Sullivan, "The Overskeptics," *National Review,* June 17, 2002, 23.

For a magazine published monthly, include only the month and the year, with no comma between them.

Bibliographic form

O'Sullivan, John. "The Overskeptics." *National Review,* June 17, 2002, 22–26.

16. Article from an online journal

Full note form

> 16. Lars Wik and others, "Quality of Cardiopulmonary Resuscitation during Out-of-Hospital Cardiac Arrest," *Journal of the American Medical Association* 293, no. 3 (2005), http://jama.ama-assn.org/cgi/content/full/293/3/299 (accessed January 28, 2005).

Place the URL along with the date of access (in parentheses) after the date of publication.

Bibliographic form

Wik, Lars, Jo Kramer-Johansen, Helge Myklebust, Hallstein Sorebo, Leif Svensson, Bob
    Fellows, and Petter Andreas Steen. "Quality of Cardiopulmonary Resuscitation
    during Out-of-Hospital Cardiac Arrest." *Journal of the American Medical
    Association* 293, no. 3 (January 19, 2005), http://jama.ama-assn.org/cgi/content/
    full/293/3/299 (accessed January 28, 2005).

Include the full date of publication as well as the date of access.

17. Article from a journal database

Full note form

17. Samuel Guy Inman, "The Monroe Doctrine and Hispanic America," *Hispanic
America Historical Review* 4, no. 4 (1921): 635, http://links.jstor.org/sici?sici=0018
-2168%28192111%294%3A4%3C635%ATMDAHA%3E2.0.CO%3B2-8.

A URL that runs onto a second line may be broken *after* a single or
double slash or *before* a comma, a period, a hyphen, a question mark, a
percent symbol, a number sign (#), a tilde (~), or an underscore (_). It
can be broken either before or after an ampersand (&) or an equals
sign. Include an access date in parentheses between the URL and the
final period if the material you are using is time-sensitive or if an access
date is required by your discipline.

Bibliographic form

Inman, Samuel Guy. "The Monroe Doctrine and Hispanic America." *Hispanic America
    Historical Review* 4, no. 4 (1921): 635–81. http://links.jstor.org/sici?sici=0018
    -2168%28192111%294%3A4%3C635%ATMDAHA% 3E2.0.CO%3B2-8.

18. Article from an online magazine

Full note form

18. Mark Frank, "Judge for Themselves: Why a Supreme Court Ruling on
Sentencing Guidelines Puts More Power Back on the Bench," *Time*, January 24, 2005,
http://www.time.com/time/magazine/printout/0,8816,1018063,00.html.

Bibliographic form

Frank, Mark. "Judge for Themselves: Why a Supreme Court Ruling on Sentencing Guidelines Puts More Power Back on the Bench." *Time*, January 24, 2005. http://www.time.com/time/magazine/printout/0,8816,1018063,00.html.

19. Newspaper article

Full note form

19. Rick Bragg, "An Oyster and a Way of Life, Both at Risk," *New York Times,* June 15, 2002, national edition, sec. A.

If the city of publication is not part of the newspaper's name, it should be added at the beginning and italicized as if part of the name: *St. Paul Pioneer Press*. If the city is not well known or could be confused with another city with the same name, add the state name or abbreviation within parentheses after the city's name. If the paper is a well-known national one, such as the *Wall Street Journal,* it is not necessary to add the city of publication.

Bibliographic form

Bragg, Rick. "An Oyster and a Way of Life, Both at Risk." *New York Times.* June 15, 2002, national edition, sec. A.

If the name of the newspaper and the date of publication are mentioned in the text of the paper, no bibliographic entry is needed.

OTHER SOURCES

20. Interview

Full note form

20. Yoko Ono, "Multimedia Player: An Interview with Yoko Ono," interview by Carolyn Burriss-Krimsky, *Ruminator Review,* no. 10 (Summer 2002): 28.

Bibliographic form

Ono, Yoko. "Multimedia Player: An Interview with Yoko Ono." By Carolyn Burriss-

Krimsky. *Ruminator Review,* no. 10 (Summer 2002): 26–29.

If you are required to list interviews, each entry should include the name of the person being interviewed, the title of the interview, the name of the person who conducted it, and any available publication data.

21. Videocassette or DVD

Full note form

21. *Araby,* VHS, produced and directed by Dennis J. Courtney (Los Angeles:

American Street Productions, 1999).

Bibliographic form

Araby. VHS. Produced and directed by Dennis J. Courtney. Los Angeles: American Street

Productions, 1999.

Place *VHS* (for videocassette) or *DVD* after the title.

14b CMS-style paper

The following student paper addresses an important development in the Civil Rights movement. Because it includes a full bibliography, the endnotes are written in short form (see page 346). Although CMS does not provide guidelines for a title page for a student paper, one is shown in fig. 14.1 as a sample.

RACE IN THE U.S. ARMY:

AN EXECUTIVE ORDER FOR HOPE

BY

NICOLE HESTER

AMERICAN HISTORY 257

DR. MELISSA HILL

DECEMBER 6, 2002

Figure 14.1. Sample title page for a CMS-style paper.

1

RACE IN THE U.S. ARMY: AN EXECUTIVE ORDER FOR HOPE

While students of the Civil Rights movement are often familiar with the Supreme Court decision *Brown v. The Board of Education,* which acknowledged the inherent inequality in separate but equal practices, that decision would not happen until 1955, nearly eight years after President Harry S. Truman issued an executive order to integrate the federal government and, in particular, the United States military. Although the earlier Thirteenth (1865), Fourteenth (1868), and Fifteenth (1870) Amendments redefined freedom, citizenship, and voting, these amendments were diluted by Supreme Court decisions in the nineteenth and early twentieth centuries. In cases like *Plessy v. Ferguson,* the court established the precedent of "separate but equal," which legally allowed the separation of races in public facilities.[1] Thus, Truman's executive order in 1948 became an important step in the long-term struggle for civil rights.

Like American schools, the United States Army was segregated, and this segregation remained in place until after the Second World War (1941–1945). In July of 1948, by executive order, President Truman demanded equal treatment and equal opportunity in the armed forces, setting into motion a series of events that would force change, however slow it might be:

> It is hereby declared to be the policy of the President that there shall be equality of treatment and opportunity for all persons in the armed services without regard to race, color, religion or national origin. This policy shall be put into effect as rapidly as possible, having due regard to the time required to effectuate any necessary changes without im-pairing efficiency or morale.[2]

With such language as "all persons" and "as rapidly as possible," Truman showed that his statement was more than a publicity stunt. While understanding the scale of the change he was demanding, Truman was also aware of the sentiment of the American people and numerous government officials. Examining the desegregation of

President Truman reviews Black troops.

the Army from the viewpoints of those who sought to keep the races segregated and those who wanted integration leads to understanding how the law can begin to secure the pathways to justice and freedom.[3] Truman's executive order in 1948 illustrates how the government can be a vehicle for social change.

Historically, approximately 200,000 Blacks enlisted to fight in the Civil War, but their involvement was strongly influenced by the need for manpower.[4] After the Civil War, the Army maintained only four Black regiments. Although there were 380,000 Blacks in the Army during the First World War, no more than 42,000 actually served in combat units; most Blacks served as laborers.[5] The end of the First World War ushered in a time of analysis and redefinition of the roles of Blacks in the armed forces. The Selective Service Act of 1940 would forbid discrimination because of race with regard to enlisting and being inducted into the armed forces.[6] However, in October 1940, Robert P. Patterson, the Secretary of War, stated that the Selective Service Act would not eliminate segregation within the armed forces; instead, it would allow Blacks to serve in segregated units:[7]

> The policy of the War Department is not to intermingle colored and white enlisted personnel in the same regimental organizations. This policy has been proven satisfactory over a long period of years and to make changes would produce situations destructive to morale and detrimental to the preparations for national defense.[8]

Patterson's statement followed the idea of "separate but equal" and ultimately undercut any effect the Selective Service Act could have had on integration. The enlistment of Blacks was increasing, but their advancement was not, no doubt because they were restricted to separate units. The existence of segregation, stemming from earlier war practices and later defined by War Department policy, would become the norm in the Second World War. From the perspective of those in the War Department, the policy was working effectively, and to "experiment" with its segregated structure would be detrimental to all within military ranks.[9]

These beliefs were reinforced by unreliable data. Supporting the policy outlined by the War Department, results from the U.S. Army General Classification Tests (AGCT), which tested general learning ability, showed 45 percent of Blacks and only 5 percent of Whites in the lowest class of exam scores. However, the War Department did not assess any reasons *why* the test results showed the deficit. Because of the "differences in opportunity and background," Blacks generally did not receive the same level of educational opportunity as Whites, so a difference in overall level of performance in standardized testing was bound to exist.[10] Although the Army was correct in its statement about the difference in test results, it ignored the direct effect that segregation and social constraints were having on the academic performance of Black Americans.

The testing issue, however, was only an excuse for preventing integration. For those who believed that segregation was *right*, allowing Blacks equal opportunities in the armed services would enable them to "achieve equality in America by force."[11] Simply put, separatists were afraid that the growing political power of Blacks would lead to a revolt, bringing about the end of segregation, which threatened what separatists thought was right. More importantly, the Army did not believe the government should intervene, forcing desegregation within an otherwise segregated nation. In January 1948, nearly seven months before Truman's executive order, a Gallup poll showed that 81 percent of Southerners had heard of Truman's civil rights plan, and 58 percent felt that it should *not* be passed in Congress, compared to the 14 percent in the New England and Middle Atlantic region who felt

4

that Truman's civil rights initiative should not be passed. In the same survey, Southern Whites responded 5-to-1 in an overwhelming show of support for segregation.[12] In a memorandum from December 1941, when the United States entered the Second World War, Chief of Staff General George C. Marshall reflected the sentiment that existed in the country and explained the Army's resistance to promote social change. In his words, integrating the U.S. Army

> would be tantamount to solving a social problem which has perplexed the American people throughout the history of this nation. The army cannot accomplish such a solution, and should not be charged with the undertaking. The settlement of vexing racial problems cannot be permitted to complicate the tremendous task of the War Department and thereby jeopardize discipline and morale.[13]

When Truman asked for the equal treatment of soldiers regardless of "race, color, religion, or national origin,"[14] he was essentially asking the government to ignore the widespread sentiment of White Americans. Undoubtedly, there were significant numbers of Blacks, Whites, and others craving freedom, but the nation as a whole was not ready for what Truman demanded. After so many years of segregation and prejudice, Truman was fighting a widely supported status quo.

Knowing the greatness of the change he had demanded, Truman established a committee that would be known as the Fahy Committee. Named after its chairman, Charles H. Fahy, the multiracial committee consisted of seven men, including Black leader Lester Granger and the executive secretary of the Urban League, John H. Sengstacke, who were responsible for examining the existing procedures and practices of the armed forces to devise a way to carry out the president's new policy.[15] The Fahy Committee set out to show the ways in which segregation was hurting the "effectiveness" of the armed forces and to establish the positive results that would follow from integrating the armed forces, particularly the Army.[16]

5

The Fahy Committee wrestled tirelessly with the Army to put an end to the quota system, which limited the number of Black enlistees to 10 percent, as well as the segregation that prevented the advancement of Blacks within the Army.[17] Essentially the Army needed to use every individual within its ranks as effectively as possible, regardless of race, but the quota system and segregation made this impossible.[18] Because the skills of Black soldiers could be used only in Black units, White units sometimes had to leave essential positions unfilled.

When the Army could no longer deny the statistical and practical truth that segregation was inefficient and ineffective, Adjutant General of the Army Edward F. Witsell finally announced on March 27, 1950, that *all* appointments would be open to *all* applicants without regard to race or color.[19] As Mershon and Schlossman discuss in *Foxholes and Color Lines,* by assessing the integration of the armed forces, the Fahy Committee helped Truman to fight segregation and essentially prepare Americans for change.[20] Having the law on their side, Blacks were encouraged in their pursuit of equal opportunity. They began to hope that the equality being fostered in the federal government would eventually affect state practices, and that prejudice and bigotry would soon fade.

However, changing the minds of individuals is an entirely different task from changing the laws. Lee reports the statement of an unnamed White officer requesting relief in 1945 from the Ninety-Second Division, an engineer battalion where Black troops worked with Whites:

> Although I can still find such interest in a few specific individuals, for the rank and file I can feel only disgust for their inherent slovenliness, and their extreme indolence, indifference and frequent insolence. . . . I am likewise convinced that with few exceptions colored officers with whom I have come into contact are thoroughly incompetent, and for the most part are to be viewed in a light little different from enlisted men.[21]

6

This statement shows that while the law can create an environment in which freedom can exist, the law cannot change racist hearts and minds.

Knowing that legal equality was far off and that a deeply changed society was a hope for the distant future, Blacks in the military were then faced with daunting questions about their dual role as Blacks and as Americans. From their perspective, they enlisted to defend a country that would not defend them. For what reason should Blacks then enlist? What were they fighting for? Who were they really fighting against? The simplified answer to these questions came for Blacks in what would become known as the Double V Campaign: victory abroad and victory at home. In early 1942, this campaign was explained in the Black newspaper the *Courier* as a "struggle to remove the contradiction between the claims of American democratic ideology and the racial inequalities evident in American life."[22] Blacks were fighting for what they knew America was capable of, and ultimately created for, even while being bound by the racial policies of the Army; they still had a larger vision of what America could truly be. Fighting on the battlefields of foreign countries for a nation that rejected them in so many ways, the pursuit of freedom and equality came at a high emotional cost for Blacks in the Army. Hubert Humphrey used a quotation by James Baldwin, who served in the Second World War, to exemplify the Black experience and struggle:

> You must put yourself in the skin of a man who is wearing a uniform of his country, is a candidate for death in its defense, and who is called a "nigger" by his comrades-in-arms and his officers . . . and who watches German prisoners of war being treated by Americans with more human dignity than he has ever received at their hands. And who, at the same time, as a human being, is far freer in a strange land than he has even been at home. HOME! The very word begins to have a despairing and diabolical ring. You must consider what happens to this citizen, after all he has endured, when he returns—home; search, in his

7

> shoes, for a job, for a place to live; ride, in his skin, on segregated
> buses; see, with his eyes, the signs saying "White" and "Colored," and
> especially the signs that say "White Ladies" and "Colored Women" . . .
> imagine yourself being told to "Wait." And all of this happening in the
> richest and freest country in the world, and in the middle of the
> twentieth century.[23]

Between fighting for the freedom of others in the war and hoping justice would permeate the policies and social hierarchies in America, Black soldiers had an immense struggle that would not end after the war.

However, Blacks were not alone, there were others fighting along with them, and President Truman was certainly one of them. By issuing executive order 9981 in 1948, Truman clearly established his position concerning racial bias within the government by "tak[ing] significant unilateral action to alter the stance of the federal government toward minority groups . . . demonstrat[ing] dedication to the legal equality for racial minorities without waiting for congressional approval."[24] In short, Truman's order required action within the armed forces to end racial bias and to do so within a reasonable amount of time.[25] Sidestepping a conservative Congress and the prejudice of many Americans, Truman supported Blacks in their struggle for advancement and equality in the armed forces, even though he moved the law to a place where the American people were not necessarily ready to follow.

Understanding Truman's order concerning segregation, we are left to wonder why he would take such a political risk. Why should Truman be any different from other government officials or separatists that surrounded him? What could Truman gain from alienating himself from the legislative branch? Of course, Truman undoubtedly gained the support of Black voters because of his bold stance concerning race, but could that be the entirety of his motivations? What Truman *really* thought or felt is something we can never know, but in

8

October 1948 in an address in Harlem, New York, where he would receive the Franklin Roosevelt Award, Truman had this to say:

> It was the authors of the Declaration of Independence who stated the principle that all men are created equal in their rights, and that it is to secure these rights that governments are instituted among men.
>
> It was the authors of the Constitution who made it clear that, under our form of government, all citizens are equal before the law, and that the Federal Government has a duty to guarantee to every citizen equal protection of the laws.[26]

In his own words, Truman stated what the founding documents of this nation intended, and he was determined to see those principles put into action. Truman's biographer, David McCullough, describes Truman as "the kind of president the founding fathers had in mind for this country."[27] Yet Truman himself reveals that growing international concerns such as the Cold War were also influencing him:

> Today the democratic way of life is being challenged all over the world. Democracy's answer to the challenge of totalitarianism is its promise of equal rights and equal opportunities for all mankind.
>
> The fulfillment of this promise is among the highest purposes of government.
>
> Our determination to attain the goal of equal rights and equal opportunity must be resolute and unwavering.
>
> For my part, I intend to keep moving toward this goal with every ounce of strength and determination that I have."[28]

Simply, Truman effected the change in government because he was compelled by the same truth that compelled individuals in the Civil Rights movement and that compels individuals today to stand against injustice and discrimination.

9

Despite politics and despite the prevailing attitudes of many Americans, Truman initiated change. Beginning a process that would affect the Civil Rights movement, Truman established the grounds by which the government could step beyond the stance of most White Americans. Truman's executive order in 1948 showed how the action of one president can work against injustice and encourage those in the midst of a growing struggle for freedom. Legally free to advance in all branches of the armed forces, Blacks were able to prove the truth that they had been proclaiming for so long—that equality in humanity transcends racial differences.

10

Notes

1. *Plessy v. Ferguson,* 163 U.S. 537 (1896).

2. Merrill, *Documentary History,* 11:741.

3. It is beyond the scope of my paper to discuss all the non-Whites who were affected by Truman's order. In this essay, I focus on the effect of Truman's order on people whom I refer to as Black.

4. Lee, *Employment of Negro Troops*, 4.

5. Ibid., 73–74.

6. Mershon and Schlossman, *Foxholes and Color Lines*, 44–45.

7. Ibid., 73–77.

8. Nalty and MacGregor, *Blacks in the Military*, 108.

9. Ibid.

10. Lee, *Employment of Negro Troops,* 141.

11. Reddick, "Negro Policy," 12.

12. Gallup, *Public Opinion 1935–1971,* 2:782–83.

13. Nalty and MacGregor, *Blacks in the Military,* 114–15.

14. Merrill, *Documentary History,* 11:741.

15. Gardner, *Truman and Civil Rights*, 114.

16. Billington, "Freedom to Serve," 273.

17. Mershon and Schlossman, *Foxholes and Color Lines,* 209.

18. Nalty and MacGregor, *Blacks in the Military,* 289.

19. Ibid., 269.

20. Mershon and Schlossman, *Foxholes and Color Lines,* 217.

21. Lee, *Employment of Negro Troops,* 187.

22. Osur, *Blacks in the Army Air Forces*, 11–12.

23. Quoted in Hubert H. Humphrey, *Beyond Civil Rights*, 19. Humphrey provides no indication of the source of Baldwin's statement, and I have been unable to track it down.

11

24. Mershon and Schlossman, *Foxholes and Color Lines,* 167–68.

25. Mayer, *Stroke of a Pen*, 4.

26. Truman, *Public Papers*, 4:923–25.

27. McCullough, *Truman*, 991.

28. Truman, *Public Papers,* 4:923–25.

Bibliography

Billington, Monroe. "Freedom to Serve: The President's Committee on Equality of Treatment and Opportunity in the Armed Forces, 1949–1950." *Journal of Negro History* (1966): 262–74. http://links.jstor.org/ sici?sici500222992%28196610%2951%3A4%3C262%3AFTSTPC%.

Gallup, George H. *The Gallup Poll: Public Opinion 1935–1971.* Vol. 2. New York: Random House, 1972.

Gardner, Michael R. *Harry Truman and Civil Rights: Moral Courage and Political Risks.* Carbondale and Edwardsville: Southern Illinois Univ. Press, 2002.

Humphrey, Hubert H. *Beyond Civil Rights: A New Day of Equality.* New York: Random House, 1968.

Lee, Ulysses. *The Employment of Negro Troops.* Washington, DC: Center of Military History, 1963.

Mayer, Kenneth. *With the Stroke of a Pen: Executive Orders and Presidential Power.* Princeton: Princeton Univ. Press, 2001.

McCullough, David. *Truman.* New York: Simon & Schuster, 1992.

Merrill, Dennis, ed. *Documentary History of the Truman Presidency.* Vol. 11. Bethesda, MD: University Publishers of America, 1996.

Mershon, Sherie, and Steven Schlossman. *Foxholes and Color Lines.* Baltimore: Johns Hopkins University Press, 1998.

Nalty, Bernard C., and Morris J. MacGregor. *Blacks in the Military.* Wilmington, DE: Scholarly Resources, 1981.

Osur, Alan M. *Blacks in the Army Air Forces During World War II.* Washington, DC: Office of Air Force History, 1941.

Plessy v. Ferguson, 163 U.S. 537 (1896).

Reddick, L. D. "The Negro Policy of the United States Army, 1775–1945." *Journal of Negro History* 34, no. 1 (1949): 9–29. http://www.jstor.org/ search/8dd55340.10427454971/110?configsortorder5SCORE& frame5noframe&dpi53&config5jstor.

Truman, Harry. *Public Papers of the Presidents of the United States: Harry S. Truman, 1945–53.* Vol. 4. Washington, DC: GPO, 1964.

15

CSE DOCUMENTATION

The Council of Science Editors (CSE), formerly the Council of Biology Editors (CBE), has established guidelines for writers in the life sciences, the physical sciences, and mathematics. The CSE/CBE manual—*Scientific Style and Format: The CBE Manual for Authors, Editors, and Publishers*—covers both general style conventions for spelling, punctuation, capitalization, and so forth and specific scientific conventions for such items as chemical names and formulas. In addition, the manual presents two formats for citing and documenting research sources: the citation-sequence system and the name-year system. You can find updates to the manual's contents at **www.cbe.org**. This chapter includes

- guidelines for citing sources within a CSE-style research paper and documenting sources on the references list (**15a**) and
- a sample student paper (**15b**).

15a CSE citation-sequence and name-year systems

As you prepare to write your paper, be sure to find out which format your instructor prefers—the citation-sequence system or the name-year system. Because these systems differ significantly, it is important to know which you will be expected to use before you get started. Once you know your instructor's preference, follow the guidelines in one of the following boxes as you prepare your in-text citations and references list.

TIPS FOR PREPARING CITATION-SEQUENCE IN-TEXT CITATIONS

- Place a superscript number after each mention of a source or each use of material from it. This number corresponds to the number assigned to the source on the references list.
- Be sure to place the number immediately after the material used or the word or phrase indicating the source: Herbert's original method[1] was used.
- Use the same number each time you use material from or refer to the source.
- Order the numbers according to the sequence in which sources are introduced: Both Li[1] and Holst[2] have shown. . . .
- If a phrase refers to more than one source, use commas to separate the corresponding numbers; note that there is no space after each comma. Use an en-dash between two numbers to indicate a sequence of sources: The early studies[1,2,4–7]. . . .

TIPS FOR PREPARING NAME-YEAR IN-TEXT CITATIONS

- Place the author's last name and the year of publication in parentheses after the mention of a source: In a more recent study (Karr 2002), these findings were not replicated. Using the author's last name, the reader will be able to find the corresponding entry in the references list.
- Omit the author's name from the parenthetical citation if it appears in the text preceding it: In Karr's study (2002), these findings were not replicated.
- Use semicolons to separate multiple citations within a set of parentheses. Order these citations chronologically when the year differs but alphabetically when the years are the same: (Li 1998; Holst 2001) but (Lamont 1998; Li 1998).

TIPS FOR PREPARING A REFERENCES LIST

- Place the heading "References" or "Cited References" next to the left margin.
- If you are using the citation-sequence system, list the sources in the order in which they were introduced in the text. See page 387 for an example.

- If your paper employs the name-year system, your references list should be ordered alphabetically according to the author's last name. See page 384 for an example.

- Entries for the two types of references lists differ only in the placement of the year of publication: the name-year system calls for the date to be placed after the author's name; the citation-sequence system calls for the date to be placed after the publisher's name in entries for books and after the periodical's name in entries for articles.

Use the following directory to find sample bibliographic entries for the citation-sequence system.

Directory of CSE Citation-Sequence Bibliographic Entries

BOOKS

ARTICLES

ELECTRONIC SOURCES

General Documentation Guidelines

The following guidelines are for both books and articles.

Author or Editor

One author. Begin the entry with the author's last name and the initials for the first and middle name (if one is given) and then a period. Notice that there is no comma after the last name and no period or space between initials.

Klemin TK.
Laigo MS.

Two or more authors. Invert the names and initials of all authors, using commas to separate the authors' names.

Stearns BL, Sowards JP.
Collum AS, Dahl PJ, Steele TP.

Organization as author. Whenever possible, use an abbreviation or acronym for the name of the organization.

AMA.
UNICEF.
Canadian Society for Chemistry.

Editor. Add the word *editor* or *editors* after the last name.

Walter PA, editor.
Mednick VB, Henry JP, editors.

Titles

Books. Use the title given on the book's title page. Titles are neither underlined nor italicized. Capitalize only the first word of the title and any proper nouns or adjectives. Subtitles are not capitalized.

The magpies: the ecology and behaviour of black-billed and yellow-billed magpies.

If the book is a second or subsequent edition, follow the title with a period and then the number of the edition: 3rd ed.

Genetics. 5th ed.

Journals, magazines, and newspapers. For journal titles of more than one word, use standard abbreviations

J Mamm (for *Journal of Mammology*)
National Geographic
New York Times

(for example, *Sci Am* for *Scientific American*). Standard abbreviations are listed in Appendix 1 of *Scientific Style and Format*. They can also be found at **www.library.uq.edu.au/faqs/endnote/biosciences.txt**. Use full names of magazines and newspapers, omitting any initial *The*.

Publication Data

Books. Include the place of publication, the publisher's name, and the year of publication. The place of publication can usually be found on the title page. If more than one city is mentioned, use the first one listed. If the city is not well known, clarify the location by including an abbreviation for the state, province, or country in parentheses after the name of the city. The publisher's name should be listed next, separated from the place of publication by a colon and one space. (Standard abbreviations for publishing companies may be used. These are listed in Appendix 2 of *Scientific Style and Format*.) After the publisher's name, if you are using the citation-sequence system, list the year of publication, separating it from the publisher's name with a semicolon and one space.

London: Chatto & Windus; 2004.
Orlando (FL): Harcourt; 2005.

Journals. Use one space after the journal title; then indicate the date of publication and the volume and issue numbers. Place a semicolon between the date of publication and the volume number. Put the issue number in parentheses. An issue number is not required for articles in journals with continuous pagination.

Journal with separate pagination
Nature 2002;420(6911)
Journal with continuous pagination
Am Nat 2004;164

(Continued on page 380)

Publication Data *(continued from page 379)*

Note that there are no spaces separating the year, the volume number, and the issue number.

Magazines and newspapers.
Place the year, month, and day of publication (if any) after the name of the magazine or newspaper.

Magazine
National Geographic 2002 Nov
Newspaper
New York Times 2004 Oct 26

Page Numbers

Books. At the end of the entry, provide the total number of pages, excluding preliminary pages with roman numerals. Use the abbreviation *p* for *pages*: 431 p.

Journals and magazines. Page numbers should be expressed as a range, with the second number shortened as much as possible: 237–45 or 430–4.

Newspapers. Include the section letter, the page number, and the column number: Sect A:2(col 1).

Electronic Sources

Because the CSE manual was last published in 1994, it refers users who need guidance in documenting electronic sources to another scientific manual: *National Library of Medicine Recommended Formats for Bibliographic Citation.* According to this guide, entries for electronic sources are similar to those for books and articles; however, they include three additional pieces of information:

Ollerton J, Johnson SD, Cranmer L, Kellie S. The pollination ecology of an assemblage of grassland asclepiads in South Africa. Ann Bot [Internet]; 2003 [cited 2005 May 13];92(6): 807–34. Available from: http://aob.oupjournals.org/cgi/content/full/92/6/807

See pages 382–383 for other examples.

1. The word *Internet* is placed in square brackets after the title of the book or the name of the journal to indicate that the work is an online source.
2. The date of access, preceded by the word *cited*, is given in square brackets after the date of publication.
3. The Internet address (URL) is included at the end of the entry.

BOOKS

1. Book with one author

Citation-sequence system

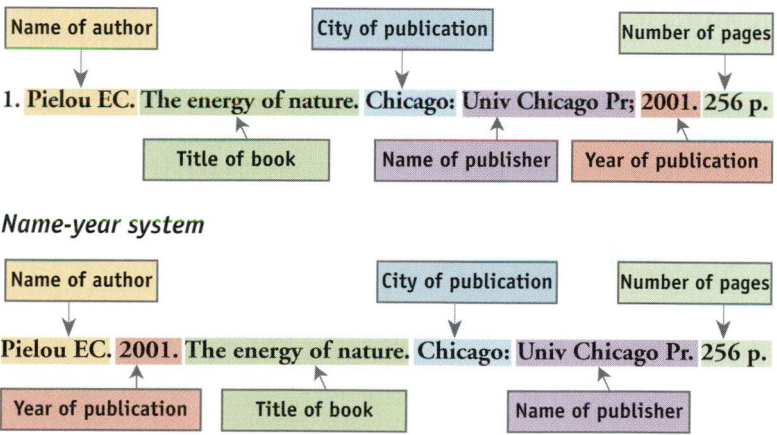

2. Book with two or more authors

2. McPherson GR, DeStefano S. Applied ecology and natural resource management.

    Cambridge: Cambridge Univ Pr; 2002. 180 p.

3. Book with an organization (or organizations) listed as author

3. Seattle Times. Natural wonders: the flora, fauna & formations of Washington. Seattle:

    Seattle Times; 2003. 150 p.

4. Book with editor(s)

4. Pimentel D, Westra L, Noss RF, editors. Ecological integrity. Washington: Island Pr; 2000. 428 p.

5. Chapter or part of an edited book

5. Hall SJ, Raffaelli DG. Food web patterns: what do we really know? In: Gange AC, Brown VK, editors. Multitrophic interactions in terrestrial systems. Oxford: Blackwell Science; 1997. p 395–418.

ARTICLES

6. Article in a journal with continuous pagination

6. Crickett A, Morgan D, Gulik S. New insights into chimpanzees, tools, and termites from the Congo Basin. Am Nat 2004;164:567–81.

7. Article in a journal with issues paginated separately

7. Milad MR, Quirk GJ. Neurons in medial prefrontal cortex signal memory for fear extinction. Nature 2002;420(6911):70–3.

8. Article in a popular (general-circulation) magazine

8. Morell V. Kings of the hill? National Geographic 2002 Nov:100–20.

9. Article in a newspaper

9. O'Connor A. Heart attack risk linked to time spent in traffic. New York Times 2004 Oct 26;Sect F:9(col 4).

ELECTRONIC SOURCES

10. Online book

10. Nielsen C. Interrelationships of the living phyla [Internet]. New York: Oxford Univ Pr; 1995 [cited 2002 Oct 30]. 467 p. Available from: http://emedia.netlibrary.com/reader/reader.asp?product_id522950

11. Article in an online journal

11. Van Lunteren E, Torres A, Moyer M. Effects of hypoxia on diaphragm relaxation rate during fatigue. J Appl Physiol [Internet] 1997 [cited 2002 Dec 2]; 82(5):1472–8. Available from: http://jap.physiology.org/cgi/content/full/82/5/1472

12. Article in an online newspaper

12. Forero J. As Andean glaciers shrink, water worries grow. New York Times on the Web [Internet] 2002 Nov 23 [cited 2002 Dec 7]:[about 31 paragraphs]. Available from: http://www.nytimes.com/2002/11/24/international/americas/ 24BOLI.html?pagewanted51

13. Web site

13. Corvus corax [Internet]. Bay Shore (NY): Long Island Ravens MC; c2000–2002 [updated 2001 Dec 3; cited 2003 Jan 3]. Available from: http://www.liravensmc.org/ About/about_ravens.htm

14. Listserv posting

14. Reed T. Patient Safety News. In: MEDLIB-L [Internet]. [Chicago: Medical Library Assoc]; 2002 Nov 18, 9:46am [cited 2002 Nov 30]:[1 paragraph]. Available from: MEDLIB-L@LISTSERV.ACSU.BUFFALO.EDU

Name-year system

The following sample entries for a references list in the name-year format correspond to those listed in the section on the citation-sequence system. However, the list is ordered alphabetically. The individual entries for books and articles differ from those in citation-sequence format only in the placement of the date. According to the name-year system, the date follows the author's name. Because the National Library of Medicine provides only one format for online sources, the entries for these sources are not repeated in this list.

References

Crickett A, Morgan D, Gulik S. 2004. New insights into chimpanzees, tools, and termites from the Congo Basin. Am Nat 164:567–81.

Hall SJ, Rafaelli DG. 1997. Food web patterns: what do we really know? In: Gange AC, Brown VK, editors. Multitrophic interactions in terrestrial systems. Oxford: Blackwell Scientific. p 395–418.

McPherson GR, DeStefano S. 2002. Applied ecology and natural resource management. Cambridge: Cambridge Univ Pr. 180 p.

Milad MR, Quirk GJ. 2002. Neurons in medial prefrontal cortex signal memory for fear extinction. Nature 420(6911):70–3.

Morell V. 2002 Nov. Kings of the hill? National Geographic:100–20.

O'Connor A. 2004 Oct 26. Heart attack risk linked to time spent in traffic. New York Times;Sect F:9(col 4).

Pielou EC. 2001. The energy of nature. Chicago: Univ Chicago Pr. 256 p.

Pimental D, Westra L, Noss RF, editors. 2000. Ecological integrity. Washington: Island Press. 428 p.

Seattle Times. 2003. Natural wonders: the flora, fauna & formations of Washington. Seattle: Seattle Times. 150 p.

15b CSE-style paper

Papers written for courses in the natural sciences often take the form of reports of study results and are generally divided into six main sections: **abstract, introduction, methods and materials, results, discussion,** and **references** (see **18c(2)** and **18d**). The following sample report, written by Geoff Rutledge for a course in comparative anatomy and physiology, includes excerpts from his abstract and introduction along with the references list. Because the CSE guidelines were not intended to be applied to undergraduate papers, you should follow your instructor's directions for formatting a title page similar to the one shown here. To read the complete report, visit **www.harbrace.com**.

The Effect of Nicotine Chewing Gum on Cardiovascular Function in Nonsmokers

Geoff Rutledge

Comparative Anatomy and Physiology 350

April 26, 2002

1

Abstract

Nicotine, the primary addictive substance in tobacco, affects cardiovascular function primarily through its binding to sympathetic postganglionic nicotinic acetylcholine receptors. This binding stimulates the release of norepinephrine, which in turn stimulates heart rate, ventricle contraction strength, and vasoconstriction of blood vessels. This study examined the cardiovascular effects in nonsmokers who chewed gum containing 4 mg of nicotine for 20 min.

[The abstract continues.]

2

Introduction

Nicotine, the primary addictive substance found in tobacco,[1] is a drug known to have both stimulant and depressant impacts, thus producing complex changes in the body.[2] However, in most clinical settings, nicotine's sympathetic impact has been found to strongly dominate any parasympathetic activity.[3] Nicotine's stimulatory mode of action involves activating a release of catecholamines directly through the adrenal medulla and also stimulating postganglionic sympathetic nerve endings.[3] These postganglionic sympathetic nerve endings are normally stimulated by a release of acetylcholine (Ach) from the preganglionic neuron. However, nicotine mimics Ach and binds to the nicotinic acetylcholine receptors, thus stimulating the release of the sympathetic neurotransmitter norepinephrine (Nor) into the body.[3] In addition to producing this release of Nor from the sympathetic nervous system, nicotine also produces a release of Nor and the sympathetic neurotransmitter epinephrine (Epi) from the adrenal medulla, thus strengthening the stimulatory mode of action.[2]

[Text omitted.]

This experiment tested the effects of nicotine chewing gum on cardiovascular function in nonsmoking individuals. Previous studies have shown significant increases in heart rate, systolic blood pressure, and diastolic blood pressure of smokers within 30 min of being exposed to nicotine from cigarettes, oral snuff, chewing tobacco, and nicotine gum.[5] This study investigated the effect of nicotine chewing gum on nonsmokers, in order to determine the effects of isolated nicotine (free from other toxins present in cigarette smoke) on human cardiovascular systems not acclimated to its presence. Because of the stimulatory effects of nicotine on the sympathetic release of Nor and Epi, the hypothesis tested was that individuals exposed to nicotine would experience increases from normal testing values in both heart rate and blood pressure.

[The introduction continues and is followed by the remainder of the paper.]

11

References

1. Tanus-Santos JE, Toledo JCY, Cittadino M, Sabha M, Rocha, JC, Moreno H. Cardiovascular effects of transdermal nicotine in mildly hypertensive smokers. Am J Hypertens 2001;14:610–4.

2. Goodman LS, Gilman A. The pharmacological basis of therapeutics. 5th ed. New York: Macmillan; 1975. 1704 p.

3. Haass M, Kuhler W. Nicotine and sympathetic neurotransmission. Cardiovasc Drug Ther 1997;10:657–65.

4. Silverthorn DU. Human physiology: an integrated approach. 2nd ed. Upper Saddle River (NJ): Prentice Hall; 2001. 816 p.

5. Benowitz NL, Porchet H, Sheiner L, Jacob P. Nicotine absorption and cardiovascular effects with smokeless tobacco use: comparison with cigarettes and nicotine gum. Clin Pharmacol Ther 1988;44:23–8.

6. Nyberg G, Panfilov V, Sivertsson R, Wilhelmsen L. Cardiovascular effects of nicotine chewing gum in healthy nonsmokers. Eur J Clin Pharmacol 1982;23:303–7.

7. Benowitz NL, Gourlay SG. Cardiovascular toxicity of nicotine: implications for nicotine replacement therapy. J Am Coll Cardiol 1997;29:1422–31.

Researchers in the social and natural sciences often collect data through observation.

16 WRITING TO INTERPRET LITERATURE

You have been interpreting and writing about literature—talking about plot, characters, and setting—ever since you wrote your first book report. When you write about literature in college—whether the work is fiction, drama, poetry, essays, manifestos, or memoirs—you will still discuss plot, characters, and setting. But you will also apply many of the same strategies you use when writing about other topics: you will respond to an exigence, explore and focus your subject, formulate a thesis statement that can be supported from the literary work itself, address an audience, and arrange your thoughts in the most effective way. In short, you will respond to the rhetorical situation.

Figure 16.1 (on page 392) shows how the elements of the rhetorical situation apply to a specific piece of writing about literature: an article on Henry James by literary critic Sarah A. Wadsworth. In response to the accepted belief that James invented the character type described as "the American woman abroad" in his novel *Daisy Miller,* Wadsworth argues that James's portrayal reshaped rather than invented the type.

This chapter will help you

- recognize the various genres of literature (**16a**),
- use the specialized vocabulary for discussing literature (**16b**),
- employ various critical approaches for interpreting literature (**16c**),
- realize the value of a careful reading (**16d**),
- understand specific terms that define the purpose of an interpretation (**16e**), and
- apply the special conventions for writing about literature (**16f–g**).

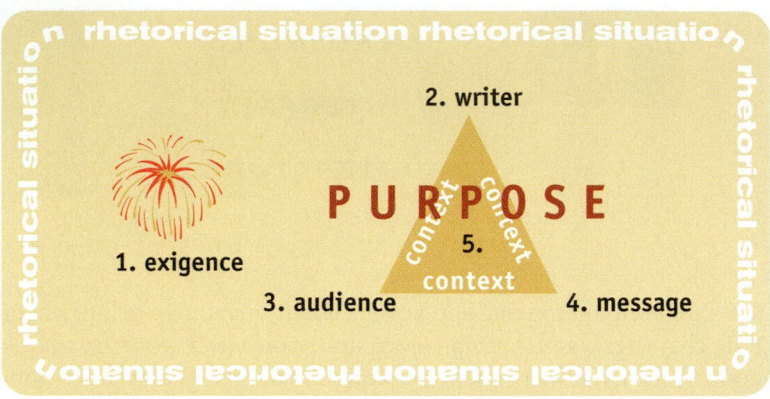

1. Recognition of the character type "the American woman abroad" in works prior to *Daisy Miller*
2. Sarah A. Wadsworth, Ph.D.
3. Scholars interested in Henry James and nineteenth-century women's issues and female characters in literature
4. *Daisy Miller* reshaped rather than reinvented the character type "the American woman abroad."
5. Dispute over James's place in the nineteenth-century literary canon

Fig. 16.1. Sample rhetorical situation for literature.

16a Literature and its genres

Like all specialized fields, literature can be divided into categories, which are referred to as **genres.** A genre can be identified by its particular features or conventions. Some genres are timeless and universal (drama and poetry, for instance); while others are context-specific and develop within a specific culture (detective fiction is a recent Western cultural phenomenon).

Just as you can recognize film genres—action, suspense, horror, comedy, animated, Western, and science fiction—you can identify various literary genres: from poetry and drama to essays and narratives. Just as film genres sometimes overlap (for example, when an action film is partially animated), so do literary genres: some poems are referred to as prose poems, whereas some plays are written in poetic verse. But even when genres overlap, the identifiable features of each genre are still evident.

Some of the most widely studied literary genres are fiction, drama, and poetry, though many forms of nonfiction (including personal essays and memoirs, literacy narratives, and manifestos) are being studied in college courses on literature. All imaginative literature can be characterized as fictional, but the term **fiction** is applied specifically to novels and short stories.

Drama differs from all other imaginative literature in one specific way: it is meant to be performed—whether on stage, on film, or on television—with the director and actors imprinting the lines with their own interpretations. In fact, the method of presentation distinguishes drama from fiction, even though the two genres share many of the same elements (setting, character, plot, and dialogue). In a novel, you often find extensive descriptions of characters and setting, as well as passages revealing what characters are thinking. In a play, you learn what a character is thinking when he or she shares thoughts with another character in dialogue or presents a **dramatic soliloquy** (a speech delivered to the audience by an actor alone on the stage). And like fiction, nonfiction, and poetry, drama can be read; in which case, you bring your interpretative abilities to the printed page rather than to a performance of the work.

Poetry shares many of the components of fiction and drama. It, too, may have a narrator with a point of view. Dramatic monologues and narrative poems sometimes have a plot, a setting, and characters. But poetry is primarily characterized by its extensive use of connotative language, imagery, allusions, figures of speech, symbols, sound, and rhythm.

16b Vocabulary for discussing literature

Like all specialized fields, literature has a unique vocabulary, which describes the various features of literary texts and concepts of literary analysis. As you learn this vocabulary, you will learn more than just a list of terms: you will learn how to understand, interpret, and write about literature.

(1) Characters carry the plot forward.

The **characters** are the humans or humanlike personalities (aliens, creatures, robots, animals, and so on) who carry the plot forward; they

Understanding how a particular character moves the plot forward will help you interpret the work as a whole.

usually include a main character, called a **protagonist,** who is in external conflict with another character or an institution or in internal conflict with himself or herself. This conflict usually reveals the **theme,** or the central idea of the work (see **16b(7)**).

Because writing about literature often requires character analysis, you need to understand the characters in any work you read. You can do so by paying close attention to their appearance, their language, and their actions. You also need to pay attention to what the narrator or other characters say about them. Whether you are writing about characters in a novel, in a play, or in a poem, you will want to concentrate on what those characters do and say—and why.

(2) Imagery is conveyed by descriptive language.

The imagery in a piece of literature is conveyed by **descriptive language,** or words that describe a sensory experience. Notice the images in "Portrait," a prose poem by Pinkie Gordon Lane that focuses on the life—and death—of a mother.

> My mother died walking along a dusty road on a Sunday morning in New Jersey. The road came up to meet her sinking body in one quick embrace. She spread out like an umbrella and dropped into oblivion before she hit the ground. In that one swift moment all light went out at the age of forty-nine. Her legacy: the blackened knees of the scrub-woman who ransomed her soul so that I might live, who bled like a tomato whenever she fought to survive, who laughed fully when amused—her laughter rising in one huge crescendo—and whose wings soared in dark despair. . . .
>
> —**PINKIE GORDON LANE,** *Girl at the Window*

The dusty road, the sinking body, the quick embrace—these images convey the loneliness and swiftness of death. The blackened knees, bleeding tomato, and rising laughter, in contrast, are images of a life of work, struggle, and joy.

(3) The narrator tells the story.

The **narrator** of a literary work tells the story, and this speaking voice can be that of a specific character (or of characters taking turns), can seem to be that of the work's author (referred to as the **persona,** which should not be confused with the author), or can be that of an all-knowing presence (referred to as an **omniscient narrator**) that transcends both characters and author. Whatever the type of voice, the narrator's tone reveals his or her attitude toward events and characters and even, in some circumstances, toward readers. By determining the tone and the impact it has on you as a reader, you can gain insight into the author's purpose. (See **4a(3)**.)

Through the voices of her characters, her narrators, and herself, prominent American author Alice Walker speaks to the importance of preserving Black culture.

(4) Plot is the sequence of events and more.

The **plot** is what happens in the story, the sequence of events (the narrative)—and more. The plot establishes how events are patterned or related in terms of conflict and resolution. Narrative answers "What comes next?" and plot answers "Why?" Consider this example:

Narrative	The sister returned home to visit her family and left again.
Plot	The city sister visited her country family, for whom she had no respect, and they were relieved when she left again.

Plot usually begins with a conflict, an unstable situation that sets events

In Alice Walker's "Everyday Use," Dee and her boyfriend come to the country to visit her mother and sister.

in motion (for instance, the state of tension or animosity between the city sister and her country family). In what is called the **exposition,** the author introduces the characters, setting, and background—the elements that not only constitute the unstable situation but also relate to the events that follow. The subsequent series of events leads to the **climax,** the most intense event in the narrative. The climax is also referred to as the **turning point** because what follows is **falling action** (or **dénouement**) that leads to a resolution of the conflict and a stable situation.

(5) Setting involves place and time.

Setting involves place—not just the physical setting, but also the social setting (the morals, manners, and customs of the characters). Setting also involves time—not only historical time, but also the length of time

This nineteenth-century street scene, illustrating a time when both people and vehicles moved more slowly, suggests the spirit of early San Francisco.

covered by the narrative. Setting includes atmosphere, or the emotional response to the situation, often shared by the reader with the characters. For example, San Francisco in the nineteenth century is a markedly different setting from the same city in the twenty-first century. Not only has the physical appearance of the city changed, but so has the social setting and the atmosphere. Being aware of the features of the setting will help you better understand the story, whether it is written as fiction, drama, or poetry.

(6) Symbols resonate with broader meaning.

Frequently used by writers of literature, a **symbol** is an object, usually concrete, that stands for something else, usually abstract. For example, at the beginning of *A Streetcar Named Desire,* a play by Tennessee Williams, one of the main characters buys a paper lantern to cover a naked light bulb. During the scenes that follow, she frequently talks about light, emphasizing her preference for soft lighting. At the end of the play, another character tears off the lantern, and a third character tries to return the ruined lantern to the main character as she is being taken away to a mental hospital. Anyone seeing this play performed or reading it carefully would note that the paper lantern is a symbol. It is an object that is part of the setting and the plot, but it also stands for something more than it is (a character's avoidance of harsh truths).

When you write about a particular symbol, first note where it appears in the literary work. To determine what the symbol might mean, consider why it appears in those places and to what effect. Once you have an idea about the meaning, trace the incidents in the literary work that reinforce it.

(7) The theme is the main idea of a literary work.

The main idea of a literary work is its **theme.** Depending on how they interpret a work, different readers may identify different themes. To test whether the idea you have identified is central to the work in question, check to see if it is supported by the setting, plot, characters, and symbols. If you can relate these components to the idea you are considering, then that idea can be considered the work's theme. The most prominent literary themes arise out of conflict: person versus person, person versus self, person versus nature, or person versus society.

When you believe you have identified the theme, state it as a sentence—and be precise. A theme conveys a specific idea; it should not be confused with a topic.

Topic	family heritage
Vague theme	Alice Walker's "Everyday Use" is about family heritage.
Specific theme	"Everyday Use" reveals a conflict between a sister who puts her heritage on display and a sister who puts her heritage to use, every day.

BEYOND THE RULE

OTHER USEFUL LITERARY TERMS

As you draft and revise your essays about literature, you may want to use some of the literary terms, such as *antagonist, local color,* and *climax,* defined at **www.harbrace.com**.

CHECKLIST for Interpreting a Literary Work

- From whose point of view is the story told?
- Who is the protagonist? How is his or her character developed?
- With whom or what is the protagonist in conflict?
- How are the other characters depicted and distinguished through dialogue?
- What is the theme? How does the author use setting, plot, characters, and symbols to establish that theme?
- What symbols, images, or figures of speech does the author use? To what effect?

16c Approaches to interpreting literature

Writing a paper about a literary work usually requires you to focus on the work itself and to demonstrate that you have read it carefully—a process known as **close reading.** (Compare close reading with reading rhetorically; see chapter 2.) Through close reading, you can offer an **interpretation,** an explanation of what you see in a work. An interpretation can be shaped by your personal response to what you have read, a specific type of literary theory, or the views of other readers, whom you wish to support or challenge.

Literary theory, the scholarly discussion of how the nature and function of literature can be determined, ranges from approaches that focus almost exclusively on the text itself (its language and structure) to approaches that show how the text relates to author, reader, language, society, culture, economics, or history. Familiarity with literary theory enriches your reading of literature as well as your understanding of the books and essays about literature that you will discover when you do research (see chapter 9). Literary theory can also help you decide how you want to focus your writing about literature.

Although the most popular theoretical approaches to literature overlap somewhat, each has a different primary focus: the reader, some feature of the social or cultural context, the text itself, or the author or characters. Interpreting literature involves a responsible reliance on one or more of these approaches—*for whatever your interpretation, the text should support it.*

(1) Reader-response theory focuses on the reader.

According to **reader-response theory,** readers construct meaning as they read and interact with the elements within a text, with each reader bringing something different (intellectual values and life experiences) to the text on every reading. Thus, meaning is not fixed *on* the page; it depends on what each reader brings *to* the page. Furthermore, the same reader can have different responses to the same literary work when rereading it after a number of years: a father of teenagers might find Gwendolyn Brooks's "we real cool" more disturbing than it had seemed when he first read it in high school. Although a reader-response approach to literature encourages diverse interpretations, you cannot simply say, "Well, that's what this work means to me" or "That's my interpretation." You must demonstrate to your audience how each element of the work supports your interpretation.

(2) Both feminist and gender-based literary theories focus on issues related to gender and sexuality.

The significance of sex, gender, or sexual orientation within a particular social context is the interpretive focus of **feminist** and **gender-based literary theories.** These theories enable a reader to analyze the ways in which a work (through its characters, theme, or plot) promotes or challenges the prevailing intellectual or cultural assumptions of its day regarding issues related to gender and sexuality, including patriarchy and compulsory heterosexuality. For instance,

Like the early suffragists, many feminist literary critics focus on prevailing social and cultural constraints affecting women.

Edith Wharton's *The Age of Innocence* compares two upper-class nineteenth-century women in terms of the specific social pressures that shaped and constricted their lives and loves. A feminist critic might emphasize the oppression of these women and the repression of their sexuality. On reading Henry James's *The Bostonians,* another critic, using a gender-based approach, might focus on the positive features of the domestic relationship between the financially independent Olive and Verena. That same critic might also try to explain why Jake Barnes in Ernest Hemingway's *The Sun Also Rises* bonds with some men and is contemptuous of others.

(3) Race-based literary theory focuses on issues related to race relations.

Frederick Douglass's *Narrative* details his encounters with racism, both as a victim of slavery and as a free man.

A useful form of race-based literary criticism, **critical race theory** focuses on the significance of race relations (race, racism, and power) within a specific historical and social setting in order to explain the experience and literary production of any people whose history is characterized by political, social, and psychological oppression. Not only does this theoretical approach seek out previously neglected literary works, but it also illuminates the ways in which race, ethnicity, and the imbalance of power inform many works. Previously neglected works such as Zora Neale Hurston's *Their Eyes Were Watching God,* Rudolpho Anaya's *Bless Me, Ultima,* and Frederick Douglass's *Narrative,* which demonstrate how racism affects the characters' lives, have taken on considerable cultural value in the last twenty years. **African American literary criticism,** for example, has been particularly successful in invigorating the study of great African American writers, whose works can be more fully appreciated when readers consider how literary elements of some of these works have been informed by the social forces that helped produce them. Closely associated with critical race theory is **postcolonial theory,** which takes into account the relationship of the colonized with the colonizer and the challenge a text can direct at the dominant powers at a particular time and place, asserting a drive toward the liberation of oppressed social groups. Joseph Conrad's *Heart of Darkness,* Jean Rhys's *Wide Sargasso Sea,* Daniel Defoe's *Robinson Crusoe,* and E. M. Forster's *A Passage to India* can all be read productively through the lens of postcolonial theory.

(4) Class-based literary theory focuses on socioeconomic issues.

To explain the conflict between literary characters or between a character and a community or institution, **class-based literary theory** draws on the work of Karl Marx, Terry Eagleton, and others who have addressed the implications of social hierarchies and the accompanying economic tensions. These theorists argue that differences in socioeconomic class—in the material conditions of daily life—divide people in profoundly significant ways, more so than differences in race, ethnicity, culture, and gender. Thus, a class-based approach can be used to explain why Emma Bovary is unhappy, despite her "good" (that is, financially advantageous) marriage, in Gustave Flaubert's *Madame Bovary*, why Bigger Thomas gets thrown into such a confused mental state in Richard Wright's *Native Son*, or why a family loses its land in John Steinbeck's *The Grapes of Wrath*.

(5) Text-based literary theory focuses on the work itself.

Text-based literary theory demands concentration on the piece of literature itself; with this approach, only the use of concrete, specific examples from the text validates an interpretation. The reader must pay careful attention to the elements within the literary work—plot, characters, setting, tone, dialogue, imagery, and so on—to evaluate their interaction, overall effect, and meaning. Nothing more than what is contained within the text itself—not information about the author's life or about his or her culture or society—is needed to understand and appreciate the text's unchanging meaning. Readers may change, but the meaning of the text does not. A close reading of the work is essential, then, in order to account for all of its particularities, including the ways in which the language and the structure fit within a specific literary genre.

(6) Context-based literary theory focuses on the time and place in which a work was created.

Context-based literary theory considers the historical period during which a work was written and the cultural and economic patterns that prevailed during that period. For example, recognizing that Willa Cather published *My Ántonia* during World War I can help account for the darker side of that novel about European immigrants' harsh life in the American West; similarly, understanding that Arthur Miller wrote *The Crucible* in response to the accusations of the House Un-American Activities Committee in the 1950s helps explain why that play generated so much excitement when it was first produced. Critics who use a context-based and class-based approach known as **cultural studies** consider how a literary work interacts with economic conditions, socioeconomic classes, and other cultural artifacts (such as songs or fashion) from the period in which it was written.

(7) Psychoanalytic theories focus on psychological factors affecting the writing and the reading of literature.

This ancient stone sculpture, called the **Venus of Willendorf**, represents an archetype known as the earth mother.

By focusing on the psychological states of the author and the characters as well as the reader, **psychoanalytic theories** seek to explain human experience and behavior in terms of sexual impulses and unconscious motivations (drives, desires, fears, needs, and conflicts). When applied to literature, these theories (based on the work of Nancy Chodorow, Hélène Cixous, Sigmund Freud, Melanie Klein, and Jacques Lacan, among others) help readers discern the motivations of characters, envision the psychological state of the author as implied by the text, and evaluate the psychological reasons for their own interpretations. Readers may apply the psychoanalytic approach to explain why Hamlet is deeply disturbed by his mother's remarriage, why Holden Caulfield rebels at school (in J. D. Salinger's *The Catcher in the Rye*), or why Rochester is blinded (in Charlotte Brontë's *Jane Eyre*).

Theorists who use the work of psychiatrist Carl Jung to explore **archetypes** (meaningful images that arise from the human unconscious and that appear as recurring figures or patterns in literature) are also using a psychoanalytic approach to interpret literature, whether the literary form is a fairy tale, fable, epic poem, Greek drama, postmodern novel, or movie script. Archetypal figures include the hero, the earth mother, the scapegoat, the outcast, and the cruel stepmother; archetypal patterns include the quest, the initiation, the test, and the return.

16d   Active reading and literary interpretation

As you read, trust your own reactions. Were you amused, moved, or confused? Which characters interested you? Were you able to follow the plot? Did the work remind you of any experience of your own? Did it introduce you to a different world in terms of historical or geographical setting, or did you encounter a familiar cast of characters? These first impressions can provide the seeds from which strong essays will grow, especially when they are later modified as you consider the work further.

(1) You can understand your response by considering how it is shaped by your identity.

When reflecting on your response to some element of a work of literature, you can consider how your reading might be shaped by the factors that make you who you are. For example, if you find yourself responding positively or negatively to a character in a novel or play, you could ask yourself whether this response has anything to do with your

- psychological makeup,
- political beliefs,
- gender or sexual orientation,
- race,
- social class,
- religion,
- geographic location, or
- conscious or unconscious theoretical approach.

Thinking along these lines can help you decide how to focus your essay and prepare you for using one or more theoretical approaches as the basis for your interpretation.

(2) After choosing a topic, develop it, based on evidence in the text.

If you are choosing your own topic, your first step is to reflect on your personal response, focusing on that response as you formulate a tentative thesis statement. Next, consider what specific evidence from the text will best explain and support your interpretation and thesis statement.

Because most readers will be interested in what *you* think, you need to discover a way to demonstrate your originality in terms of a topic you can develop adequately, by applying one or more rhetorical methods (see **3g**). You might define why you consider a character heroic, classify a play as a comedy of manners, or describe a setting that anchors a work's meaning. Perhaps you can compare and contrast two poems on a similar subject or explore cause-and-effect relationships in a novel. Why, for example, does an apparently intelligent character make a bad decision? Or you might show how the description of a family's house in a novel defines that family's values or reveals the effects of an underlying conflict.

(3) Research can reveal the ways other readers have responded to a literary work.

You will undoubtedly anchor your essay in your personal response or interpretation. But if you read works of literary theory, visit online discussion groups or forums (see **6c**), participate in class discussions, or become active in a book club, you can engage in a dialogue that can enrich your own ideas. Many instructors prefer that you advance your own ideas at the same time as you use and give credit to outside sources. Although it is tempting to lean heavily on the interpretations of experts, remember that your readers are mainly interested in your interpretation and in your use of the sometimes conflicting interpretations of others (including the other members of your class) to support your own points.

To locate material on a specific writer or work, consult your library's catalog (see **9b–c**) and *The MLA International Bibliography*, an index of books and articles about literature that is an essential resource for literary studies and that can be consulted in printed volumes or online.

In addition to having books and articles about specific writers, your school or public library also possesses a number of reference books that provide basic information on writers, books, and literary theory. Works such as *Contemporary Authors, The Oxford Companion to English Literature,* and *The New Princeton Handbook of Poetic Terms* can be useful when you are beginning your research or when you have encountered terms you need to clarify.

16e Types of literary interpretation

An interpretation that attempts to explain the meaning of one feature of a literary work is called an **analysis.** To analyze a work of literature, a writer focuses on one of its elements, such as the setting or the main character, and determines how that one element contributes to the work's overall meaning. A common form of analysis is **character**

analysis, in which a writer interprets one or more aspects of a single character. An analysis can also focus on a single scene, symbol, or theme.

An interpretation that attempts to explain every element in a literary work is called an **explication** and is usually used only with poetry. When explicating William Wordsworth's "A Slumber Did My Spirit Seal," a writer might note that the *s* sound reinforces the hushed feeling of sleep and death in the poem. But it would also be necessary to consider the meanings of *slumber, spirit,* and *seal.*

An **evaluation** of a work gauges how successful the author is in communicating meaning to readers. The most common types of evaluation are book, theater, and film reviews. A writer can also evaluate a work by focusing on how successfully one of its parts contributes to the meaning conveyed by the others. Like any other interpretation, an evaluation is a type of argument in which a writer cites evidence to persuade readers to accept a clearly formulated thesis. (See chapters **3** and **8.**) An evaluation of a literary work should provide evidence of its strengths as well as its weaknesses, if any.

 Although summarizing a literary work can be a useful way to make sure you understand it, do not confuse a summary with an analysis, an explication, or an evaluation. Those who have read the work do not need to read a summary of it. Do not submit one unless your instructor has asked for it.

Exercise 1

Attend a film, a play, or a poetry reading at your school or in your community. Write a two- to three-page essay evaluating the work, using one of the theoretical approaches discussed in this chapter.

16f Conventions for writing about literature

Writing about literature involves adhering to several conventions.

(1) The first person is typically used.

When writing your analysis of a piece of literature, you can use the first-person singular pronoun, *I:*

Although some critics believe Anaya's novel to be about witchcraft, I think it is about the power of belief.

By doing so, you indicate that your opinion about a work differs from a popular one. To own an opinion, belief, or interpretation, though, you must support it with specific evidence from the text itself.

(2) The present tense is used in discussions of literary works.

Use the present tense when discussing a literary work, since the author of the work is communicating to the reader at the present time. (See **26b(1)**.)

In "A Good Man Is Hard to Find," the grandmother reaches out to touch her killer just before he pulls the trigger.

Similarly, use the present tense when reporting how other writers have interpreted the work you are discussing.

As Henry Louis Gates demonstrates in his analysis of . . . .

(3) Documentation of sources follows certain formats.

When writing about a work assigned by your instructor, you may not need to give the source and publication information. However, if you are using an edition or translation that may be different from the one your audience is using, you should indicate this. One way of doing so is to use the MLA format for listing works cited, as explained in section **12b**, although your bibliography in this case will consist of only a single work—the one you are discussing. An alternative way of providing documentation for a single source is by acknowledging the first quotation from the work in an explanatory note on a separate page at the end of your paper and then giving parenthetical page numbers in the body of the paper for all subsequent references to the work.

[1]Dorothy Allison, "Believing in Literature," *Skin: Talking about Sex, Class, and Literature* (Ithaca: Firebrand, 1994) 165-82. All subsequent references to this work will be identified with page numbers within the text.

If you use this note form, you may not need to repeat the bibliographical information on a list of works cited, nor will you need to include the author's name in subsequent parenthetical references. Check with your instructor about the format he or she prefers.

When you use a bibliography to provide publication data, you must indicate specific references whenever you quote a line or passage. According to MLA style, such bibliographic information should be placed in the text in parentheses directly after the quotation, and a period, a semicolon, or a comma should follow the parentheses. (See **12a(1)** and **38d(1)**.) Quotations from short stories and novels are identified by the author's name and page number.

"A man planning to spend money on me was an experience rare enough to feel odd" (Gordon 19).

Quotations from poems are referred to by line number.

"O Rose, thou are sick!" (Blake 1).

And quotations from plays require act, scene, and line numbers.

"How much better it is to weep at joy than to joy at weeping" (*Ado* 1.1.28).

This reference indicates that the line quoted is from act I, scene I, line 28 of Shakespeare's play *Much Ado about Nothing*.

(4) Quoting poetry involves several conventions.

For poems and verse plays, type quotations involving three or fewer lines in the text and insert a slash (see **39i**) with a space on each side to separate the lines.

"Does the road wind uphill all the way? / Yes, to the very end" (Rossetti 1-2). Christina Rossetti opens her poem "Uphill" with this two-line question and answer.

Quotations of more than three lines should be indented one inch from the left-hand margin and double-spaced. Do not use slashes at the ends of lines, and make sure to follow the original text for line breaks, special indenting, or spacing. For this type of block quotation, place your citation outside the final punctuation mark.

(5) Authors' names are referred to in standard ways.

Use the full name of the author of a work in your first reference and only the last name in all subsequent references. For instance, refer to

"Charles Dickens" or "Willa Cather" the first time, and after that, use "Dickens" or "Cather." Never refer to a female author differently than you do a male author. For example, use "Robert Browning and Elizabeth Barrett Browning" or "Browning and Barrett Browning" (not "Browning and Mrs. Browning" or "Browning and Elizabeth").

16g A student essay interpreting a work of literature

In the following essay, undergraduate English major Kaitlyn Andrews-Rice analyzes Alice Walker's short story "Everyday Use." In addition to reading the story, she watched a dramatization of it on DVD. Andrews-Rice had the opportunity to choose her own topic, so she focused (see 3b) on the ways two sisters use their heritage, showing that everyday use is the best way.

Kaitlyn Andrews-Rice

Dr. Glenn

English 100

7 March 2005

Honoring Heritage with Everyday Use

"Everyday Use," one of the short stories in Alice Walker's <u>In Love & Trouble:</u>
<u>Stories of Black Women</u>, vividly demonstrates how three women, Mrs. Johnson and her
two daughters, regard their heritage.[1] Through the eyes of Mrs. Johnson, the story
unfolds when her older daughter returns to her country home, mother, and sister.
Throughout the story, Walker emphasizes the shared heritage of these three women and
the different ways they use it. In "Everyday Use," an authentic appreciation of heritage
does not come from showcasing fashionable artifacts or practices; rather, it comes from
embracing that heritage every day.

Walker's physical description of the sisters illustrates the different ways each
puts her heritage to use. The beautiful, sophisticated Dee embraces her heritage
by showcasing the fashionable Afrocentric sentiment of the time. Her mother
describes her as wearing "a dress so loud it hurts my eyes. There are yellows and
oranges enough to throw back the light of sun," and her hair "stands straight up like
the wool on a sheep" (52). But in addition to her African style, Dee also has "neat-
looking" feet, "as if God himself had shaped them with a certain style" (52). That
she's stylish comes as no surprise, for even before she appears in the story, the
reader is told that "at sixteen, she had a style of her own, and knew what style was"
(50). Dee is a book-smart city woman, who uses her knowledge of fashion and style
to enhance her physical attributes: she is "lighter than [her sister] Maggie, with nicer
hair and a fuller figure" (49). Maggie, on the other hand, replicates her Southern
black heritage every day, by helping her mother clean up the dirt yard (raking,
lifting, sweeping), in preparation for Dee's homecoming. In addition, Maggie works

hard churning butter, cooking over a wood-burning stove, and using the outhouse. She's darker skinned, "homely and ashamed of the burn scars down her arms and legs" (47), and her simple country clothes, "pink skirt and red blouse" (49), are in sharp contrast with Dee's fancy garb.

The filmed version of the story allows the viewer to see Dee arrive home with her boyfriend, Hakim-a-barber, both in their African clothes, exchanging glances of superiority and amusement as they take Polaroid snapshots of the unsophisticated mother

Dee wants to capture the living conditions of her mother and sister.

and sister and their shabby house, as though Dee was completely separated from such living conditions, that heritage, her family.

Another way that Walker illustrates the divide between Dee's understanding of her heritage and her family's is through the use of names. When Dee arrives, she announces that she is "Not 'Dee,' Wangero Leewanika Kemanjo!" (53). According to the interview with Walker that accompanies the Wadsworth Original Film Series in Literature's filmed version of "Everyday Use," the changing of one's name to a more Afrocentric name was common during this time (Everyday Use). In Dee's mind, this fashionable African name is yet another way she is honoring her roots, embracing her heritage, and she tells her family that she "couldn't bear it any longer, being named after the people who oppress [her]" (53). Ironically, her given name carried with it a rich inheritance, that of a long line of Dees or Dicies. Yet Dee is the daughter who denies her Southern heritage and is embarrassed by her Southern family, especially by Maggie, who has taken no steps to "make something of [herself]" (59) other than a wife to local John Thomas Dee. At this point in the story, though, Mrs. Johnson and Maggie agree to go along with Dee's ways and continue to try to please her, even if they do not understand her. It is not until later in Dee's visit that they come to realize the way Dee has embraced a heritage she does not fully understand or appreciate.

To further emphasize the differences among the ways these women understand their heritage, Walker focuses on their educations. Mrs. Johnson describes the way Dee would read to them before she left for college: "She washed us in a river of make-believe, burned us with a lot of knowledge we didn't necessarily need to know" (50). Even though she's somewhat puzzled by Dee's knowledge, she maintains pride in her daughter, especially since Mrs. Johnson never had an education, and Maggie "knows she is not bright" and can read only by "stumbling along good-naturedly" (50). But when Dee accuses Maggie of being "backward," Mrs. Johnson realizes how little Dee's education has taught her about appreciating her heritage.

The focus on family-made quilts at the end of the story shines light on Walker's final take on how heritage is used differently by these women. Mrs. Johnson explains that Dee was offered these quilts before she left for college but refused them because they were "old-fashioned, out of style" (57). Now that the quilts are stylish, Dee wants them in her life. She wants to hang them on her walls, displaying them alongside the butter churn top that she plans to use as a "centerpiece on the alcove table" and dasher that she will do "something artistic" (56) with. For Dee, these artifacts should be on display, not used. But for Maggie and her mother, the quilts represent not only a direct link with their ancestors but a distinct form of African American expression. These particular quilts are made from scraps of Grandma Dee's dresses and from a scrap of fabric from Great Grandpa Ezra's uniform "that he wore in the Civil War" (56). The piecing together of these scraps to form a quilt is a testament to their importance in the heritage of this family. As Dee holds the quilts, she repeats "Imagine!" (57), as if it is so difficult to think of a time when all the stitching was done by hand, something that Maggie is capable of doing every day because "it was Grandma Dee and Big Dee who taught her how to quilt"

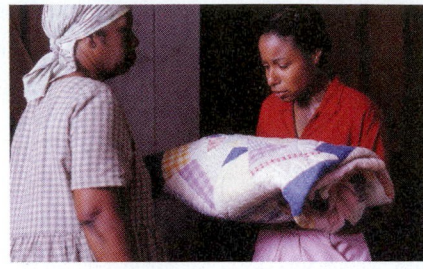

Every time Maggie uses the quilts, she feels connected to her family.

(58). When Dee asks to take some quilts back to the city to hang on the wall, her mother resists, saying that Maggie planned to use them. Only then does Dee reveal her prejudices, accusing her sister of being "backward enough to put them [the quilts] to everyday use" (57), right before she storms out of the house.

At this point, when she's been denied the quilts, Dee accuses her family of not understanding their true heritage, saying "It's really a new day for us. But from the way you and Mama still live you'd never know it" (59). She considers herself to be forward looking, because of her African style and name, her education, her cultural displays. In Dee's eyes, her "backward" family does not understand their heritage because they do not display the quilts or the butter churn, they *use* them every day. As Dee drives away, Maggie smiles, and it is "a real smile, not scared" (59), because she knows she embraces, lives, and understands her heritage in a very intimate way.

Andrews-Rice 5

Notes

[1]Alice Walker, "Everyday Use," In Love & Trouble: Stories of Black Women (New York: Harcourt, 1973) 47-59. All subsequent quotations from this work will be identified by page numbers.

Andrews-Rice 6

Works Cited

Everyday Use. Dir. Bruce Schwartz. Perf. Karen ffolkes, Rachel Luttrell, and
    Lyne Odums. 2003. DVD. Thomson Wadsworth, 2005.

Walker, Alice. In Love & Trouble: Stories of Black Women. New York: Harcourt,
    1973. 47-59.

Exercise 2

Based on your reading of Kaitlyn Andrews-Rice's paper on "Everyday Use," what personal or political values do you think she brought to her interpretation of that text? Which of the theoretical approaches to literature did she use as the basis for her interpretation (see **16c**)? Write a one- to two-page paper analyzing her interpretation of the story.

The **social sciences** include psychology, sociology, political science, economics, business, education, and some areas of environmental science. Researchers in the social sciences primarily study how humans behave as members of groups—families, peer groups, ethnic communities, political parties, and many others. Their goal is to state how and why a person or a group tends to behave in a certain way under a particular set of circumstances. Some social scientists, however, study the behavior of animals other than humans.

In courses in the social sciences, you will most often be asked to write observation reports, applications of theory, and library research reports. Given this variety of possible assignments, you will find it beneficial to analyze each rhetorical situation before you start writing. Figure 17.1 illustrates how the elements of the rhetorical situation underpin "What Makes You Who You Are," a newspaper article written in the context of the nature versus nurture debate. Claiming that both nature (genes) and nurture (environment) have a role in shaping human behavior, Matt Ridley describes how genetic and environmental influences interact.

This chapter will help you

- determine the audience, purpose, and research question for a paper in the social sciences (**17a**),
- decide which types of evidence, sources, and reasoning to use in such a paper (**17b**), and
- follow appropriate style, formatting, and documentation conventions when writing the paper (**17c–d**).

1. A newspaper article in which environmental influences were said to be more important than genetic make-up
2. Matt Ridley, author of *Nature via Nurture*
3. Lay readers interested in understanding human behavior
4. Genes and environmental influences interact.
5. The debate over the impacts of nature (genetic make-up) and nurture (environmental influences) on human behavior

Fig. 17.1. Sample rhetorical situation for the social sciences.

17a Audience, purpose, and the research question

The first step to take in completing a writing assignment for a course in the social sciences is to determine your audience and purpose. Your audience will always include your instructor, but it could include students in your class as well. You may also be writing for others outside your class. For example, you may have the opportunity to present your work at a student research conference. Identifying your audience will help you decide how much background information to present, how much technical language to include, and what types of reasoning and evidence (sources) to use.

Most researchers in the social sciences write either to inform or to persuade. If they are simply reporting the results of a study, their purpose is informative. However, if they urge their audience to take some action, their purpose is persuasive. Once you know what your purpose is and to whom you are writing, you can craft a research question that will help you find sources, evaluate them, and use them responsibly (chapters **9–11**). Here are some examples of different types of research questions that could be posed about the topic of community service by students:

Questions about causes
Why do students perform community service?

Questions about consequences
What do students believe they have learned through their community service activities?

Questions about process
How do college instructors set up community-service opportunities?

Questions about definitions or categories
What does community service entail?

Questions about values
What values do instructors hope to cultivate by offering community-service opportunities?

17b   Evidence, sources, and reasoning

Because researchers in the social sciences try to explain behavior, they commit themselves to observing the activities of humans and other animals, either as individuals or in groups. In order to make accurate observations, these researchers either design controlled laboratory experiments or conduct field research. Interviews and surveys are the two most common techniques for gathering data in the field, although observations and interviews are also widely used. (See **9e**.) Both laboratory experiments and field research yield data that social science researchers can use as evidence to make statements (or claims) about human behavior.

Researchers in the social sciences distinguish between quantitative studies and qualitative studies. **Quantitative studies,** such as laboratory experiments and surveys, yield data that can be presented in numerical form, as statistics. Using statistical data and formulas, researchers show how likely it is for a behavior or consequences of the behavior to occur. If you decide to undertake a quantitative study, you should turn your research question into a **hypothesis,** a prediction of what the results of your experiment or survey will be. The study you design, then, will be based on this hypothesis, which should be as objective as possible. Obviously, you cannot entirely eliminate the influence of your own preconceptions, but you can strive to be impartial by avoiding any value judgments. The results of your study will either prove or disprove your hypothesis. Be prepared to provide possible explanations for either result.

Researchers who perform **qualitative studies,** such as observations and interviews, are interested in interpreting behavior by first watching, listening to, or interacting with individuals or a group. If you decide to conduct a qualitative study, you will not reason *from* a hypothesis; you will reason *to* a hypothesis. You will observe a phenomenon and note what you see or hear. Then, instead of reporting numbers as evidence, you will provide detailed descriptions and discuss their significance. Although you may not be able to demonstrate the degree of impartiality prescribed for quantitative research, you should still strive to maintain an objective stance.

Researchers in the social sciences recognize that some studies, such as the field report in 17d, contain both quantitative and qualitative features. They also expect to use both primary and secondary sources (see 9a(3)) in many research projects. Primary sources comprise data derived from experiments, observations, surveys, or interviews. Secondary sources are articles or case studies written about a research topic.

17c Special conventions for reports in the social sciences

(1) Writers in the social sciences follow conventions specified by the style manuals they use.

The language and grammatical structures you use will depend on the style manual prescribed by the discipline in which you are writing. Most of the social sciences follow the guidelines presented in the

Publication Manual of the American Psychological Association (APA; see chapter **13**). This manual stresses the importance of writing prose that is clear, concise, unbiased, and well organized. The following specific tips can help you write in the style recommended by the APA manual.

TIPS FOR PREPARING A PAPER IN THE SOCIAL SCIENCES

- Use the active voice as often as possible, although the passive voice may be acceptable for describing methodology. (See page 589.)
- Choose verb tenses carefully. Use the present tense to discuss results and present conclusions (as in "The findings suggest . . ."). Reserve the past tense for referring to specific events in the past and for describing your procedures (as in "Each participant signed a consent form . . .").
- Use a first-person pronoun rather than referring to yourself or to any coauthor(s) and yourself in the third person.

 I
 ~~The experimenter~~ described the procedure to each participant.
 ∧

 We
 ~~The experimenters~~ retested each participant after a rest period.
 ∧

- Clarify noun strings by placing modifiers after the main noun.

 the method for testing literacy NOT the literacy testing method

---

(2) Information is presented in a specific order.

Writing assignments in the social sciences require you to state a research question, thesis, or hypothesis, to discuss research that has already been published about your topic, and, then, in many cases, to describe your methodology and present your conclusions or results. Specific formats are discussed in the following sections.

(a) Library research report

Writing a library research report requires that you read a wide variety of sources on a specific topic and then summarize, critique, and integrate those sources (see chapter **11**). These reports generally include the following elements, in this order:

- Statement of the research question or thesis
- Presentation of background information, using sources
- Discussion of major findings presented in the sources
- Application of those findings to the specific research question
- Conclusions
- References

An excerpt from a library research report is shown in fig. 17.2. Author P. A. Blissitt includes an abstract and uses headings to identify the sections of her report. Notice that Blissitt maintains a neutral stance that conveys an impression of impartiality, although she clearly and strongly states her point of view. Another example of a library research report is Nikki Krzmarzick's paper on sleep and memory (see **13c**).

Abstract: The relationship of sleep to memory and learning is complex. Sleep affects memory, and memory must be present for learning to occur. A number of studies have been conducted to increase our understanding of their relationship. In addition to the numerous scientific investigations of each concept separately, sleep, memory, and learning have been studied together to determine (a) the effect of sleep on memory and learning, (b) the effect of sleep deprivation in general on memory and learning, (c) the effect of rapid eye movement (REM) sleep deprivation on memory and learning, (d) the effect of memory and learning on REM sleep, and (e) the effect of non-REM sleep loss on memory and learning. Neuro-anatomic correlates have been pursued as well with most attention to the hippocampus. Despite considerable efforts to date, many of the studies reveal contradictory or inconclusive findings. Much remains unknown, and additional work is needed. Implications for nursing include those that have a direct effect on the patient, the nurse, and nursing science.

Sleep, memory, and learning are most often studied as individual concepts. As separate unrelated concepts, much remains unknown about each of them. Yet, despite our lack of knowledge about each individually, the relationship of sleep to memory and learning has been and continues to be investigated in animals and humans. As result of these studies, our knowledge of the relationship of sleep to memory and learning is increasing. This article reviews knowledge about the relationship of sleep to memory, including (a) the effect of sleep on learning and memory, (b) the relationship of sleep deprivation in general to memory, (c) the effect of rapid eye movement (REM) sleep deprivation on memory, (d) the effect of memory and learning on REM sleep, (e) the effect of non-REM sleep deprivation on memory and learning, (f) neuro-anatomic correlates, and (g) implications for nursing practice and research. Only human studies are included. Studies conducted on patients with insomnia are not included because their pattern of cognitive deficits may be different [27]

Sleep, Memory, and Learning

Sleep, memory, and learning are each complex multidimensional biobehavioral systems. Sleep, for example consists of several distinct phases: Stage 1--transitional sleep, Stage 2--light sleep, Stages 3 and 4--slow wave sleep, and Stage 5--REM sleep. Together, Stages 1-4 are called non-REM sleep. Non-REM sleep often is compared with REM sleep. Each of these stages occurs five to six times nightly with a complete cycle of stages lasting 60-90 minutes. One sleep cycle consists of a progression from Stage 1 through Stage 4 of non-REM sleep followed by a return to Stages 3 or 2 of non-REM sleep, then REM sleep. [38, 42] The amount, type, timing, and quality of sleep are all important considerations.

Fig. 17.2. Excerpt from a library research report.

(b) Application of theory

When your assignment calls for an **application of theory,** you will use a specific theory to interpret the behavior of some person or group. Your report should include these sections:

- Introduction to the research question
- Discussion of previous research
- Description of the theory to be applied
- Identification of the participant(s) in the study
- Discussion of how the theory applies to the behavior of the participant(s)
- Concluding statement about the participant(s) and/or the theory

(c) Observation report

An **observation report** such as Mike Demmon's field report on diving ducks (see **17d**) contains certain standard elements. If you write an observation report, include the sections described below; however, check with your instructor to see whether you should make any modifications.

Many researchers in the social sciences collect data through observation.

- Introduction: The writer establishes the need for the current study and presents a hypothesis.
- Methodology: The writer describes how the study was performed (so that other researchers can replicate it). This section may include subsections that describe the participants, the materials used, and so forth.
- Results: The writer presents findings, often using charts or graphs.
- Discussion: The writer discusses the significance of the findings, relating them to the original hypothesis and to other research done on the topic.

(3) A reference list provides detailed information about the sources used.

At the end of any paper you write for a course in the social sciences, you should include a list of all the sources you used. By doing so, you provide your readers with the details they need to consult these sources on their own. You can find guidelines for creating a reference list in **13b**.

17d Sample student field report

Mike Demmon's field report for an advanced environmental science course is an example of a paper that presents original research. (Environmental science is often considered a natural science, but Demmon's report is included here because it is a report on animal behavior.) His report includes a description of the research objectives and procedures, a table listing the data, and a discussion of the findings. Because Demmon's work was original field research, he was not required to use secondary sources, so his report does not include a reference list. Although Demmon calls his report a quantitative analysis, it includes some qualitative elements as well. For example, his subjective voice is evident when he uses the word *surprisingly* to qualify his observation about how late it was when the ducks began to be active. As you read Demmon's report, you may note that the headings and order differ from those described on page 420. Demmon adjusted the headings and organization to accommodate his instructor's directions.

Avian Ecology   1

Mike Demmon

Avian Ecology and Management

December 11, 2000

Quantitative Analysis of Diving Ducks

Statement of method

Methodology

Follow a specific duck for a 10-minute time period and record diving patterns, times, and frequency of dives. Stagger the species being watched to create an equal representation of each species within the data. Try not to follow the same duck in any two 10-minute intervals.

Statement of goals

Objectives

To determine whether any of the species have evolved to share limited resources of the environment. To look for evidence of these species having evolved within the same environment.

Description of procedure

Procedures

During the class field trip to Eagle Lake, I participated in a quantitative evaluation of several diving duck species. During this time we monitored several different variables to see whether feeding practices were staggered between species, whether frequencies of dives were different between species, and whether any of the species interacted with each other. The three species we studied were the Ruddy Duck (*Oxyura jamaicensis*), the Redhead Duck (*Aytheya americana*), and the Bufflehead Duck (*Bucephala albeola*).

Avian Ecology 2

Data						*Summary of data*

Time	Species	Sex	Number of Dives	Dive Time (seconds, respectively)	Other Activities
8:30–8:40	Bufflehead	Male	0	N/A	Preening & sleeping
8:45–8:55	Bufflehead	Female	1	Lost after 4 minutes	Preening & followed by 2 males
9:00–9:10	Ruddy	Female	4	21, 27, 33, 19 lost after 5 minutes	Paired with 2 females, ran males off, preening
9:15–9:25	Redhead	Male	13	45, 46, 13, 49, 17, 13, 24, 14, 33, 47, 49	N/A
9:30–9:40	Ruddy	Male	3	6, 33, 17	Following a female
9:45–9:55	Bufflehead	Female	7	9, 13, 11, 22, 20, 29, 19	Followed by 2 males
10:00–10:10	Redhead	Female	8	12, 14, 14, 13, 18, 21, 18, 26	N/A
10:15–10:25	Redhead	Female	11	17, 13, 14, 22, 19, 20, 17, 21, 24, 23, 19	Following 2 males
10:30–10:40	Bufflehead	Female	3	21, 11, 17	Sleeping & following 1 male
10:45–10:55	Ruddy	Male	7	9, 12, 22, 27, 16, 11, 15	N/A
11:00–11:10	Redhead	Male	10	10, 18, 22, 11, 19, 27, 10, 31, 17, 14	N/A
11:15–11:25	Ruddy	Female	6	15, 13, 21, 29, 18	Preening
11:30–11:40	Bufflehead	Male	4	12, 18, 15, 19	Followed a female

Discussion of data

Conclusions

As the data above show, there is no evidence that these species practice any variation in diving time or frequency of dives, or that any of the species directly and intentionally interact. Surprisingly, the data do seem to show that activities do not begin until mid-morning. When we arrived, about 8 a.m., a large percentage of the birds were still sleeping. Once the birds awaken, it appears as though they ritually preen themselves before feeding. With the exception of human-induced movements, it appeared that there were no significant interactions between any of the species. As may have been expected, the Buffleheads also appeared to be courting at times. The data above also show that the majority of the birds that were paired or followed by the other sex were Buffleheads.

Discussion of possibilities for further research

Adjustments for Future Research

In order to refine this study, it would be advantageous to develop a better, easier method to follow each individual bird. I found that it was very difficult to follow a diving duck for prolonged periods of time. Also, looking through a monocular spotting scope for 10-minute segments can be very aggravating. It would also be advantageous to get closer to the birds being observed. Finally, the study time is possibly too long. It should be possible to observe more specimens and get a better sampling in half the time.

18 WRITING IN THE NATURAL SCIENCES

The **natural sciences** include mathematics, the biological sciences (botany and zoology), the physical sciences (chemistry and physics), and the earth sciences (geology and astronomy). The natural sciences also include **applied sciences** such as medicine and allied health studies, engineering, and computer science. The natural sciences are problem-solving disciplines that report results derived from meticulous observation and experimentation. Common writing assignments in science courses are laboratory reports, literature reviews, and critiques of journal articles. To fulfill any of these assignments successfully, start by examining your rhetorical situation. Figure 18.1 (on page 426) illustrates how a group of researchers addressed their rhetorical situation in producing an article on popular diets for *The Journal of the American Medical Association.*

This chapter will help you

- determine the audience, purpose, and research question for a paper in the natural sciences (**18a**),
- decide which types of evidence, sources, and reasoning to use in such a paper (**18b**), and
- follow appropriate style, formatting, and documentation conventions when writing the paper (**18c–d**).

18a Audience, purpose, and the research question

Before you start working on a writing assignment for a course in the natural sciences, be sure to determine your audience and your purpose. Your instructor will always be one of your readers, but you may be asked to share your work with other readers as well. If you are enrolled

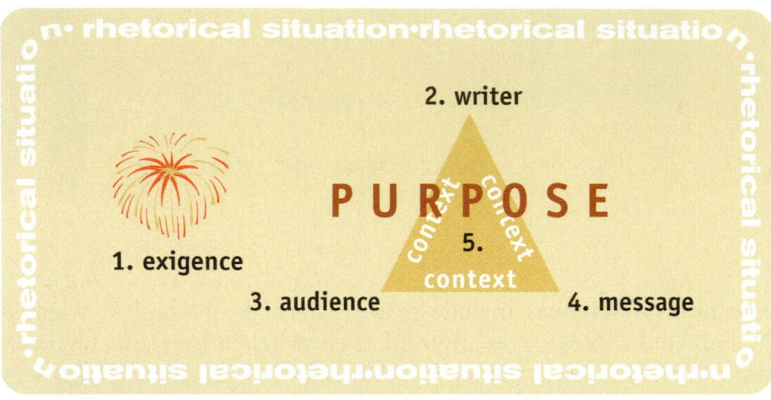

1. Lack of data on the health effects of popular diets (Atkins, Ornish, Weight Watchers, and Zone)
2. Michael L. Dansinger, Joi Augustine Gleason, John L. Griffith, Harry P. Selker, and Ernest J. Schaefer
3. Physicians
4. Each diet helped participants reduce their weight and their cardiac risk factor; the degree of adherence to the diet was correlated with the reductions in weight and cardiac risk factor.
5. The widespread use of popular diets, some of which depart from conventional medical recommendations

Fig. 18.1. Sample rhetorical situation for the natural sciences.

in an advanced class, you may be expected to present your work at a local, regional, or national conference. By knowing who your audience is, you will be able to gauge how much background information is adequate, how much technical language is appropriate, and what types of evidence and reasoning are necessary.

Researchers in the sciences generally write to inform their readers by discussing studies pertaining to a specific topic or by reporting the results of an experiment. However, their purpose may be evaluative if they are critiquing a journal article or argumentative if they are encouraging readers to take a specific action. After you have determined your purpose and audience, craft a research question that will guide you to sources and help you use them responsibly (see chapters **9–11**). The following examples of research questions focus on global warming.

Questions about cause
What causes global warming?

Questions about consequences
What are the effects of global warming?

Questions about process
How can global warming be stopped?

Questions about definitions or categories
What types of greenhouse gases are responsible for global warming?

Questions about values
What are a scientist's responsibilities to the public in the face of global warming?

Research questions in the sciences are often narrowed to enable precise measurements.

Questions about length, distance, frequency, and so on
How far has Mendenhall Glacier receded each year for the past decade, and do the values show any trend?

Questions about comparisons and correlations
How are emission intensities related to the total amount of emissions?

18b Evidence, sources, and reasoning

Researchers in the natural sciences attempt to quantify and understand phenomena in the world around them. They look for **empirical evidence**—facts that can be measured or tested—to support their claims. Most of their investigations, then, are set up as experiments. If you conduct an experiment for a course in the natural sciences, you will be expected to start with a **hypothesis,** a prediction that serves as a basis for experimentation. To test the hypothesis, you will follow a procedure, either one established in another study or specified by your instructor or one designed by yourself. The results of your experiment will either validate your hypothesis or show it to be in error. This systematic way of proceeding from a hypothesis to verifiable results is called the **scientific method.** Consisting of six steps, this method helps ensure the objectivity and accuracy of experimental findings.

THE SCIENTIFIC METHOD

1. *State a problem*: When you state the problem, you establish the exigence (the reason for your writing).

2. *Collect evidence*: Close observation is the most important skill for collecting evidence. Be sure to record all details as accurately as you can. Alternatively, you may read the reports of other researchers who have addressed a problem similar to yours. If you draw on observations and experiments, you are using primary sources; if you use scientific articles and statistical charts, you are using secondary sources.

3. *Form a hypothesis*: A hypothesis is a tentative claim, or prediction, about the phenomenon you are studying.

4. *Test the hypothesis*: Although you have conducted some research before formulating the hypothesis, you now continue that research through additional observation or experimentation.

5. *Analyze the results*: Look at your results in light of your hypothesis. Attempt to find patterns, categories, or other relationships.

6. *State the conclusion*: If you have validated your hypothesis, explain why it accounts for *all* of your data. If your hypothesis is disproved, suggest revisions to it or offer a new one.

18c Special conventions for reports in the natural sciences

(1) Writers in the natural sciences follow conventions specified by the style manuals they use.

Scientific writing consists mainly of the clear and accurate presentation of facts, each with a specific source—your own experiments, studies published by other researchers, surveys, and so on. Scientific writing is also objective, keeping the writer's actions and responses in the background. In this way, the focus of the writing remains on the data (as in "The data reveal . . . ") instead of on the researcher (as in "I found . . . ").

The conventions you will follow in writing a paper for a science course, especially when documenting your sources, depend on the style manual used in the specific discipline. The following list presents a few of the most common manuals.

Style Books and Manuals for the Sciences

American Chemical Society. *The ACS Style Guide: A Manual for Authors and Editors.* 2nd ed. Washington DC: American Chemical Society, 1998.

American Institute of Physics. *AIP Style Manual.* 4th ed. New York: American Institute of Physics, 1990.

American Mathematical Society. *A Manual for Authors of Mathematical Papers.* Rev. ed. Providence, RI: American Mathematical Society, 1990.

American Medical Association. *American Medical Association Manual of Style.* 9th ed. Baltimore: Williams, 1997.

Council of Biology Editors. *Scientific Style and Format: The CBE Manual for Authors, Editors, and Publishers.* 6th ed. New York: Cambridge University Press, 1994.

United States Geological Society. *Suggestions to Authors of the Reports of the United States Geological Survey.* 7th ed. Washington, DC: US Government Printing Office, 1991.

You can find a sampling of the documentation requirements of the Council of Science Editors (formerly the Council of Biology Editors) in chapter **15**. This group of editors expects scientific writing to be "accurate, clear, economical, fluent, and graceful" (p. 101 of *The CBE Manual*). The Council of Science Editors also addresses the difficulty that nonspecialists may have in reading scientific prose: the solution is to avoid the excessive use of abstract nouns, long noun phrases, abbreviations, undefined technical vocabulary, and conversational jargon (for example, using *reefer* instead of *refrigerator*).

BEYOND THE RULE

OBJECTIVITY AND SUBJECTIVITY

Researchers today hesitate to claim that any reporting can be completely objective. Everything we do is affected by our perception of ourselves, others, and the world around us. Although scientists want to control their experimental methods to filter out as much bias as possible, even that desire is subjective in some respects. For more information, visit **www.harbrace.com**.

(2) The format of a laboratory report reflects the scientific method.

The most frequent writing assignment in the natural sciences is the **laboratory report** (or perhaps a **lab summary,** an informal version of a laboratory report). The format of this type of report follows the steps of the scientific method by starting with a problem and a hypothesis and concluding with a statement proving, modifying, or disproving the hypothesis.

- The **abstract** states the problem and summarizes the results. (You may not have to include an abstract if your report is short or if your instructor does not require it.)
- The **introduction** states the research question or hypothesis clearly and concisely, explains the scientific basis for the study, and provides brief background material on the subject of the study and the techniques to be used. The introduction usually includes citations referring to relevant sources.
- The **methods and materials** section is a narrative that describes how the experiment was conducted. It lists the materials that were used, identifies where the experiment was conducted, and describes the procedures that were followed. (Your lab notes should help you remember what you did. Anyone who wants to repeat your work should be able to do so by following the steps described in this section.)
- **Results** are reported by describing (but not interpreting) major findings and supporting them with properly labeled tables or graphs showing the empirical data.
- The **discussion** section analyzes the results, showing how they are related to the goals of the study and commenting on their significance. This section also reports any problems encountered and offers suggestions for further testing of the results.
- **References** are listed at the end of the paper. The list includes only works that were referred to in the report. The comprehensiveness and the accuracy of this list allow readers to evaluate the quality of the report and put it into a relevant context.

An example of scientific writing (Heather Jensen's lab report for a first-year biology course) appears in the next section. This paper is representative of a report based on an experiment outlined in a lab manual. It includes section headings and graphics—drawings of the various stages of mitosis and a graph showing the results. The Council of

Science Editors approves two documentation formats (see chapter **15**): the citation-sequence format and the name-year format. Jensen uses the citation-sequence format.

18d Sample student laboratory report

A specific format is used for a laboratory report so that the various parts of an experiment can be easily located and so that the experiment can be **replicated** (repeated in order to verify the results). When you write a laboratory report for a science course, you will likely follow a format created by your instructor or other scientists. The grade you receive for your work will depend on how well you execute the experiment, follow the prescribed format, and maintain impartiality. Study Heather Jensen's report to get a sense of the style and format generally expected.

Observations and Calculations of Onion Root Tip Cells

Heather Jensen

Biology 101

June 7, 2002

Summary of experiment

ABSTRACT

This laboratory experiment examined *Allium* (onion) root tip cells in the five stages of mitosis. The five stages of mitotic division were identified and recorded, and a 50-cell sample was chosen for closer examination. Of those 50 cells, 64% were found to be in interphase, 20% in prophase, 6% in metaphase, 6% in anaphase, and only 4% in telophase. The results showed that onion root tip cells spend the majority of their life cycle in a rest period (interphase). Prophase was calculated to be the longest phase of active division, while telophase was the shortest. These results were consistent with the experiments completed by other students and scientists.

Introduction describing the purpose of the experiment

INTRODUCTION

This lab report outlines a laboratory experiment on mitosis, the division of the nucleus of a cell to form two new cells with the same number of chromosomes as the parent cell. Mitotic cell division consists of five visually identifiable stages: interphase, prophase, metaphase, anaphase, and telophase. The purpose of this laboratory experiment was to identify and observe cells in each phase of mitosis, as well as to calculate an estimation of the real time involved in each stage of mitosis in an onion root tip cell. The onion root tip was chosen for this experiment because of

Superscript number referring to the first source

easy availability and rapid growth. Rapid root growth resulted in an easy opportunity to observe multiple cells in the phases of mitosis in a small sample, on one or two slides. Onion root cells complete the entire cycle of division in 80 minutes,[1] and it

1

was expected that larger numbers of cells would be found in interphase because the majority of a life cycle is spent performing normal cell functions.

MATERIALS AND METHODS

The materials required for this experiment include a compound microscope and prepared slides of a longitudinal section of *Allium* (onion) root tip. First, the slides were placed on a compound microscope under low power, a 40x magnification level. The end of the root tip was located; then the cells immediately behind the root cap were examined. These cells appeared as a darker area under low power. This area of cells was identified as the apical meristem,[1] an area of rapid growth and division in the onion root tip. This area of cells was examined while keeping the microscope on low power, to find and identify cells in interphase, prophase, metaphase, anaphase, and telophase.[2] Then high power, a 400x magnification, was used to further examine and record the appearance of these cells.

After the multiple phases of mitosis were observed, a large area of 50 cells in mitosis was selected for further examination. This area was located under low power in order to assess rows of cells in an easily countable space. Then the number of cells in each stage of mitosis was counted. These numbers were divided by the total number of cells examined, or 50 cells, and multiplied by 100 in order to calculate the percentage of cells in each phase of mitosis. For example, if 10 cells were observed in interphase, then $10/50 = 0.20$ and $0.20 \cdot 100 = 20\%$ of cells were in interphase. The actual time of each phase of mitosis in this sample of cells was calculated by multiplying the percentage by the total time of the division cycle, 80 minutes for the onion root tip cell.[1] For example, if 20% of the cells were observed in interphase, then 20% $(20/100) \cdot 80$ minutes $= 16$ minutes total time spent in interphase.

Margin notes:

List of materials and description of methodology

Superscript number referring again to the first source

Superscript number referring to the second source

2

RESULTS

Drawings and Observations

INTERPHASE

This phase lasts from the completion of a division cycle to the beginning

of the next cycle. All regular cell functions occur in this phase (except reproduction).[3]

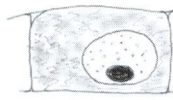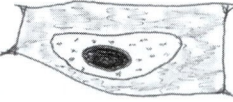

Figure 1   Two cells observed in interphase

PROPHASE

Technically the first phase of mitosis, this stage is marked by the thickening

and shortening of chromosomes, which makes them appear visible under a

compound microscope. The nucleus appears grainy at first and then the

chromosomes appear more clearly defined as prophase progresses.

Figure 2   Two cells observed in prophase

METAPHASE

This phase is identified by the lining up of double chromosomes along the

center line, the equator, of the cell.

3

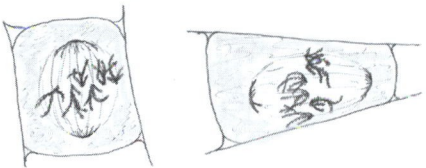

Figure 3   Two cells observed in metaphase

ANAPHASE

This phase is classified by the separation of the double chromosomes. They will begin to pull apart to opposite poles of the cell.

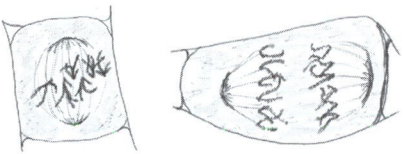

Figure 4   Two cells observed in anaphase

TELOPHASE

In telophase, the chromosomes have reached the opposite poles of the cell, and the connection between the chromosomes begins to break down as the nuclear membrane begins to form around each chromosomal clump. At the end of telophase, cytokinesis, or the division of the cytoplasm, takes place. In plant cells, a cell plate begins to form in the center of the cell and then grows outward to form a new cell wall, completely dividing the old cell into two new cells, both with a complete set of chromosomes.

Figure 5   Two cells observed in telophase

Table 1 shows the number of cells found in each phase of mitosis.

Table summarizing findings

Table 1   Number of cells in each phase

Interphase	Prophase	Metaphase	Anaphase	Telophase
32 cells	10 cells	3 cells	3 cells	2 cells

Table 2 shows the calculated percentage of cells in each phase of mitosis.

Table 2   Percentage of cells in each phase

Interphase	Prophase	Metaphase	Anaphase	Telophase
64% of cells	20% of cells	6% of cells	6% of cells	4% of cells

Figure 6 shows the actual time cells spent in each phase of mitosis.

Graph of data

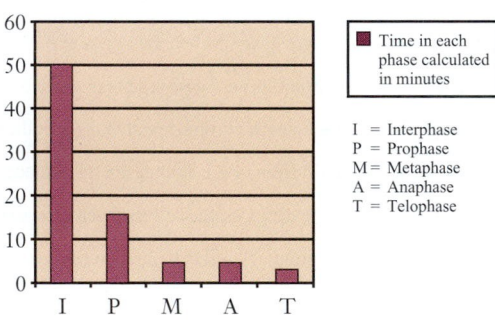

Figure 6   Time spent in each phase of mitosis

DISCUSSION

This laboratory experiment provided firsthand experience with the phases of cell division. The five phases became more easily recognizable as each cell was examined and classified. Cells often looked like they could be classified in interphase or prophase or like they were between phases. Observation led to the confirmation that mitosis is a fluid process and not just a series of distinct phases. During the experiment, difficulties with overdyed and gray areas caused uncertainty because visual indications of phase were impossible to detect. This problem was lessened through the careful selection of clear patches of cells for observation. The expectation that a large number of cells would be found in interphase was confirmed by the numbers of cells counted in the cell sample of the onion root tip. Online comparison of the results of this experiment to those of other similar experiments confirmed the results found here as typical of an onion (*Allium*) root tip.[4] This indicated that the careful selection of clear patches of cells for sampling proved an effective method for eliminating error that might have been caused by the incorrect labeling of cells or the poor visibility of cells in overdyed or gray areas. Further studies might include larger samples of cells. Experiments with larger numbers of cells would offer additional evidence to confirm the results found in this experiment.

Explanation of how the experiment's results fulfilled its purpose

Description of a problem that was encountered

Superscript number referring to the fourth source

6

List of references in citation-sequence format

REFERENCES

1. Schraer WD, Stoltze H. Biology: the study of life. 4th ed. Needham (MA): Prentice Hall; 1991. Mitosis and asexual reproduction. p 397–415.

2. Smith DW, Maier CGA. Plant biology lab manual. Dubuque (IA): Kendall/Hunt; 1995. Topic 5, The plant cell. p 52–66.

3. Alexander GM, Goodson P, Hanneman PJ, Melear, CT. Scott, Foresman biology. Glenview (IL): Scott, Foresman; 1985. Information storage and transfer in cells. p 117–43.

4. Yesnik A, Jaster K. The bio 1 super virtual lab book [Internet]. Washington DC: Sidwell Friends School; 1998 [modified 2002; accessed 2002 Jun 7]. Mitosis lab. Available from: http://www.sidwell.edu/us/science/vlb/mitosis/.

7

19 WRITING IN BUSINESS

Writing in business requires the same attention to audience, purpose, and context as does writing in any other situation or discipline. However, the nature of authorship differs: although you are the writer, you must project both your own image and that of your employer as credible and reliable. To do so, you need to follow the conventions and formats expected by the business community.

If you take business courses, you will receive a variety of assignments; letters, memos, business plans, and grant proposals are some of the more common. To complete such assignments successfully, start by analyzing the rhetorical situation. Figure 19.1 (on page 440) illustrates the rhetorical situation addressed by Yuka Hayashi in writing an article for the *Wall Street Journal,* titled "Fund Firms Get High-Level Rebuke—SEC's Campos Says They Acted Nonchalantly Despite Stock Scandals."

This chapter will help you

- recognize the stylistic conventions of standard business writing (**19a**),
- write a business letter (**19b**),
- prepare a business memo (**19c**),
- compose a résumé and a letter of application (**19d–e**), and
- develop a business plan (**19f**).

A sample grant proposal and information on how to write one can be found at **www.harbrace.com**.

19a Stylistic conventions of business writing

Whether you are writing e-mail messages, memos, letters, or a business plan, you need to meet fixed as well as unexpected deadlines. You might even find yourself working to meet several deadlines at once. The

rhetorical situation·rhetorical situation

2. writer

PURPOSE

1. exigence

5. context

3. audience

4. message

rhetorical situation·rhetorical situation

1. Decreasing confidence in the stock market following corporate scandals
2. Yuka Hayashi, correspondent for the *Wall Street Journal*
3. Readers who buy and sell mutual funds
4. The Securities and Exchange Commissioner has told the mutual funds industry that measures need to be taken to protect investors.
5. The current discourse regarding business ethics and corporate responsibility

Fig. 19.1. Sample rhetorical situation for business writing.

strategies described in this section will help you produce comprehensive and well-organized documents on time.

(1) Consider your purpose and audience.

Determine what, exactly, your piece of writing should do; then, focus your attention on fulfilling that obligation. For example, if you are writing a recommendation letter for an employee seeking promotion, describe the employee's accomplishments, strengths, and limitations, but avoid using valuable time and space to write about the company's philosophy or your own role in mentoring the employee. If you have questions about a writing assignment, make the inquiries necessary to form a clear picture of what you are being asked to write, for whom—and why.

(2) Determine the format for your writing.

Business writing follows established formats. Business letters, résumés and letters of application, and business plans all conform to certain formats (see **19b–f**). You may be able to save time if you keep beside you a sample of the kind of writing you are doing so that you can use it as a model for your own document.

(3) State points clearly.

Business writing conforms to basic formats, primarily so that it can be read efficiently. By stating your main points clearly, and sometimes emphatically, you will be able to achieve that goal. Whether you make your main points in an introductory abstract, in topic sentences, or in bulleted lists, they should stand out from the rest of your text.

19b Business letters

Business letters serve a variety of purposes—to inquire, to inform, to complain, to respond. (For letters of application, see **19e**.) Regardless of the purpose, a business letter usually fits onto a single sheet of paper, single-spaced.

TIPS FOR COMPOSING BUSINESS DOCUMENTS

Be direct.

- State the purpose of your document in your opening sentence or paragraph.
- Write straightforward sentences, beginning with a subject and an active verb (see **26d(2)**).
- Use technical language sparingly, unless the document is intended for a specialized audience (see **32c(4)**).

Be concise.

- Compose direct sentences that are neither too long nor too complicated.
- Include only necessary details.
- Use numbers, bullets, or descriptive headings that help readers locate information easily.
- Use graphs, tables, and other visual elements that convey information succinctly.

Use conventional formatting.

- Follow the standard formats developed for your type of business or for your company, or use those outlined in this chapter (**19b–f**).
- Avoid using informal language, unless you know that a casual tone is acceptable.

It also follows a standard block format: each element is typed flush with the left margin, with no indentations to indicate new paragraphs. A paragraph break is indicated by double-spacing between paragraphs.

ELEMENTS OF A STANDARD BUSINESS LETTER

- **Return address.** Your employer may require that you use letterhead stationery. If not, type your mailing address one inch from the top of the paper, flush left on a one-inch margin, and single-spaced.

- **Date.** Type the date beneath your return address. If you are using letterhead stationery, type the date one or two lines below the letterhead's last line.

- **Recipient's name and address.** Provide the full name and address of the recipient. Single-space these lines, and allow an extra line space above them. If you do not know the person's name, try to find it by checking the company's Web site or phoning the company. If you cannot find the recipient's name, use an appropriate title such as *Personnel Director* or *Customer Service Manager*.

- **Greeting.** Type your greeting two lines below the last line of the recipient's address. The conventional greeting is *Dear* _____ followed by a colon. If you and the recipient use first names to address each other, use the person's first name. Otherwise, use *Mr., Ms., Mrs.,* or *Miss* and the last name. (Choose *Ms.* when you do not know a woman's preference.) If you do not know the recipient's name, you can use an appropriate title, such as *Personnel Director*.

- **Body of the letter.** Begin the first paragraph two lines below the greeting. Single-space lines within a paragraph; double-space between paragraphs. If your letter runs onto a second page, provide the recipient's last name, the date, and the page number in three single-spaced lines at the top left on the second page.

- **Closing.** Close your letter two lines after the end of the body with an expression such as *Sincerely* or *Cordially* followed by a comma.

- **Signature.** Type your full name four lines below the closing. Then, in the space above your typed name, sign your full name, using blue or black ink. If you have addressed the recipient by his or her first name, sign just your first name.

- **Additional information.** If you are enclosing extra material such as a résumé, type *Enclosure* or the abbreviation *Enc.* two lines below your name. If you would like the recipient to know the names of people receiving copies of the letter, use the abbreviation *cc* (meaning "copies") and a colon followed by the other recipients' names. Place this element on the line directly below the enclosure line or, if there is no enclosure, two lines below your name.

The following sample **letter of inquiry** (a letter designed to elicit information) contains all the parts of a typical business letter.

Letter of inquiry

550 First Avenue
Ellensburg, WA 98926
February 4, 2004

Mr. Mark Russell
Bilingual Publications
5400 Sage Avenue
Yakima, WA 98907

Dear Mr. Russell:

I am a junior in the Bilingual Education Program at Central Washington University. For my coursework in bilingual careers, I am investigating positions in publishing that include the use of two languages. Your name and address were given to me by my instructor, Marta Cole, who worked for you from 1999 through 2004.

I have consulted your Web site to see what kind of publishing you do. I am most interested in your publication of dual documents—one in English and one in Spanish. Could you please send me samples of such documents so that I can have a better idea of the types of publications you produce?

I am also interested in finding out what qualifications I would need to work for a business like yours. I am fluent in both Spanish and English and have taken a course in translation. If possible, I would like to ask you a few questions about your training and experience. Would you have time for an interview?

Sincerely,
Chris Humphrey
Chris Humphrey

19c   Business memos

A **memo** (short for *memorandum*) is a short document sent within a business to announce a meeting, set a schedule, or request information or action. Because it is circulated internally, a memo is usually less formal than a letter, but it should still be direct and concise. The following guidelines for formatting a memo are fairly standard, but note that a particular organization may establish its own format.

ELEMENTS OF A STANDARD BUSINESS MEMO

- **Heading.** On four consecutive lines, type *To* followed by a colon and the name(s) of the recipient(s), *From* followed by a colon and your name and title (if appropriate), *Date* followed by a colon and the date, and *Subject* followed by a colon and a few words identifying the memo's subject. (The abbreviation *Re,* for "regarding," is sometimes used instead of *Subject*.) This information should be single-spaced. If you are sending copies to individuals whose names are not included in the *To* line, place those names on a new line beginning with *cc* and a colon.

- **Body.** Use the block format (see **19b**), single-spacing lines within each paragraph and double-spacing between paragraphs. Double-space between the heading and the body of the memo.

Business memo

Heading

To: Intellectual Properties Committee
From: Leo Renfrow, Chair of Intellectual Properties Committee
Date: March 15, 2005
Subject: Review of Policy Statement

Body of memo

At the end of our last meeting, we decided to have our policy statement reviewed by someone outside our university. Clark Beech, chair of the Intellectual Properties Committee at Lincoln College, agreed to help us. Overall, as his review shows, the format of our policy statement is sound. Dr. Beech believes that some of the content should be further developed, however. It appears that we have used some ambiguous terms and included some conditions that would not hold up in court.

Early next week, my assistant will deliver a copy of Dr. Beech's review to each of you. Please look it over by our next meeting, on March 29. If you have any questions or comments before then, please call me at ext. 1540.

19d Résumés

A **résumé** is essentially an argument (chapter **8**) designed to emphasize a person's job qualifications by highlighting his or her experience and abilities. Along with its accompanying letter of application (see **19e**), a résumé should command attention. If you create and save your résumé as a word-processing file, you can easily tailor it for each position you seek.

 You may find it helpful to use a software program that allows you to select the kind of résumé you need and then prompts you to complete the various sections. Such software also allows you to view your completed document in its entirety and redesign any or all of it.

The first step in writing a résumé is listing the jobs you have had, the activities and clubs you have participated in, and the offices you have held. Be sure to include dates, job titles, and responsibilities. Omit tangential information, such as a list of hobbies. You can organize your résumé in two ways. A **chronological résumé** lists positions and activities in *reverse* chronological order; that is, your most recent experience comes first. This format works well if you have a steady job history and want to emphasize your most recent experience because it is closely related to the position for which you are applying. An alternative way to organize a résumé is to list experience in terms of job skills rather than jobs held. This format, called an **emphatic résumé,** is especially useful when you have the required skills but your work history in the particular field is modest or you are just starting your career.

Regardless of the design and format you choose, remember that your résumé is, in effect, going to someone's office for a job interview. Make sure that it is dressed for success. If possible, design the résumé to fit on a single page. Use good-quality paper (preferably white or off-white) and a laser printer. Use boldface type for headings. Resist the impulse to make the design unnecessarily complicated, however. When in doubt, opt for simplicity.

Emphatic résumé

Karen Tran
10363 East 10th Avenue
Little Rock, AR 72204
(501) 328-6974
ktran@hotmail.com

CAREER OBJECTIVE:
A full-time management position specializing in food and beverage services.

MANAGEMENT SKILLS:
Familiarity with all contemporary models of effective management; good writing and communication skills; experience with planning and evaluating food service operations; experience with operating a coffee shop.

EXPERIENCE IN FOOD SERVICE:
Assisted in the transfer of data on development of new restaurant locations for a major restaurant development firm; developed and provided customer service information to employees; worked for three years in food service.

ADDITIONAL EXPERIENCE:
Worked with students, parents, and faculty at Western Ozark University as an information specialist; helped edit the yearbook; gave campus tours.

EDUCATION:
Western Ozark University, B.S. with honors, 2002; majored in Business Administration with an emphasis in Management; minor in Nutrition; Phi Beta Kappa.

EXTRACURRICULAR:
Active in Management Club and yearbook.

References available on request.

BEYOND THE RULE

ONLINE RÉSUMÉS

Some job applicants create Web-based versions of their résumés, which may include links to their relevant work. They also create non-Web versions that can be downloaded and then printed out or scanned into a résumé database. To learn about writing online résumés, visit **www.harbrace.com**.

TIPS FOR RÉSUMÉ WRITING

- Include your name, address, telephone number, and an e-mail address or fax number, if available.
- Identify your career or job objective simply, without elaborating on future goals. Reserve details about your plans until asked about them during an interview. Try to match your qualifications to the employer's needs.
- List your college or university degree and any pertinent areas in which you have had special training.
- Do not include personal data such as age and marital status.
- Even if an advertisement or posting asks you to state a salary requirement, any mention of salary should usually be deferred until an interview.
- Whenever possible, establish a clear relationship between jobs you have had and the job you are seeking.
- The names and addresses of **references** (people who have agreed to speak or write on your behalf) are not usually listed on a résumé. Instead, job candidates are advised to take a list of references to interviews. Make sure that the individuals on your list understand the nature of the position you are seeking. The list should include their names and addresses as well as their telephone numbers and/or e-mail addresses.
- To show that you are well organized and thoughtful, use a clean, clear format.
- Proofread your résumé before sending it. Errors in spelling, punctuation, word choice, or grammar can ruin your chances of getting an interview.

BEYOND THE RULE

THE APPLICATION PACKAGE

An application package consists of a résumé and a letter of application. Both of these documents are important for any job search. To see a sample chronological résumé and get further information on application letters, résumés, and interviews, visit **www.harbrace.com**.

19e Letters of application

Writing a letter of application is an essential step in applying for a job. A prospective employer gets a first impression of you from your letter of application. Because this letter usually accompanies a résumé (see **19d**), it should do more than simply repeat information that can be found there. Your letter of application provides you with the chance to sound articulate, interesting, and professional. Make the most of it.

Address your letter to a specific person. If you are responding to an advertisement that mentions a department without giving a name, call the company and find out who will be doing the screening and how that person spells his or her name. If you cannot obtain a specific name, use an appropriate title such as *Human Resource Director*. You can assume that the recipient will be screening many applications, so try to keep your letter to one page.

Model letter of application

10363 East 10th Avenue
Little Rock, AR 72204
April 19, 2003

Ms. Roxanne Kirkwood
Roxy's Coffee Shop
1819 South University Avenue
Little Rock, AR 72204

Dear Ms. Kirkwood:

I am writing to apply for the position of Business Manager of Roxy's Coffee Shop
advertised in this morning's *Arkansas Democrat-Gazette*. My education and experience
are well suited to this position; I'd welcome the chance to work full-time at making a
new business successful.

As you can see from my résumé, I majored in Business Administration with an
emphasis in management; I am continuing my education by pursuing an MBA at
UALR. Whenever possible, I have found campus activities and jobs that would give me
experience in working with people. As an assistant in the Admissions Office at Western
Ozark University, I worked successfully with students, parents, alumni, and faculty. The
position required both a knowledge of university regulations and an understanding of
people with different needs.

I also benefited from working as an intern last summer for Brinker Enterprises, a
firm that has established many different restaurant chains around the country. While
an employee there, I helped develop a new template for customer service. More
important, I improved my knowledge of what it takes to make a food service business
successful.

I am interested in putting my training to use at Roxy's because it is close to school
and I can draw upon skills I already have. The location makes it possible for me to
fulfill two objectives at the same time. I hope that we can schedule an interview
sometime during the next few weeks. I will be here in Little Rock except for the week
of May 7, but I will be checking my phone and e-mail messages daily when I am out
of town. You should have no difficulty reaching me.

Sincerely,

Karen Tran

Karen Tran

Enc.

In your opening paragraph, you should identify the position you are applying for, explain how you learned about it, and—in a single sentence—state why you believe you are qualified to fill it. In the paragraphs that follow, describe the experience and abilities that qualify you for the job. If your experience is extensive, establish that fact and then focus on how you excelled in one or two specific situations. Mention that you are enclosing a résumé, but do not summarize it. Your goal is to get a busy person, who will not want to read the same information twice, to look at your résumé.

In addition to stating your qualifications, your letter of application can also indicate why you are interested in working for the company or organization to which you are applying. Demonstrating that you already know something about it will help you appear to be a serious candidate. Extensive information on most companies is available in their annual reports. You can also find information by searching the Web (see **9d**).

In your closing paragraph, offer any additional useful information, and make a direct request for an interview. Be sure to specify how and where you can be reached. Indicate that you would enjoy the opportunity to exchange information.

19f Business plans

Business plans have three main purposes: (1) to ensure that the writer of the plan has considered all the potential risks as well as benefits of the business venture, (2) to persuade lenders and potential investors that their money will be safely invested because the writer has planned realistically and has sufficient expertise, and (3) to help the new business stay on track during its early development. To fulfill these purposes adequately, a business plan should be well researched, clearly written, and complete—that is, it should provide all the information a loan officer or investor might need.

When Roxanne Kirkwood received an assignment in a management course that required her to research and write a proposal for an actual business, she chose to write about opening a coffee shop where people could order coffee and something light to eat. Because the plan was a course assignment, she was not required to include her personal worth in the financial data or to supply the supporting documents that would be important elements of an actual plan. Though brief, her business plan contains all of the other required elements. With minor modifications, it could be used as part of a loan application.

ELEMENTS OF A BUSINESS PLAN

- **Cover page.** Include the name and address of the business.

- **Table of contents**

- **Executive summary.** State briefly the objectives of the business plan, and describe the business. Indicate who will own the business and under what form of ownership (partnership, corporation, or sole proprietorship). Finally, explain why the business will be successful. Write the summary *after* you have completed the following sections.

- **Description of business.** Identify the kind of business (service or retail), explain why the business is distinctive, and briefly describe its market.

- **Business location.** Discuss lease or sale terms, the need for and costs of renovation, and features of the neighborhood.

- **Licenses and permits.** Explain what kinds of licenses and permits must be obtained and whether the business name is registered.

- **Management.** Include information about managers' experience and education, the organizational structure, proposed salaries and wages, and any other pertinent management resources (accountant, attorney, and so on).

- **Personnel.** List the personnel needed—full-time or part-time, skilled or unskilled—and explain whether training will be required and how it will be provided.

- **Insurance.** Describe insurance needs and potential risks.

- **Market.** Characterize the market—its size and potential for growth and the typical customers. Describe how the business will attract customers—advertising, pricing, product quality, and/or services.

- **Competition.** Analyze competitors, and describe how the business addresses a market need.

- **Financial data.** Include a current balance sheet and income statement and projected (or actual) income statements by month and quarter for two years, as well as cash flow and balance sheet projections.

- **Supporting documents.** Include résumés, financial statements, and letters of reference for the owner(s) as well as letters of intent from suppliers, leases, contracts, deeds, and other legal documents.

Roxy's   1

BUSINESS PLAN

FOR

ROXY'S COFFEE SHOP

1819 South University Avenue

Little Rock, AR 72204

Roxanne Kirkwood
Telephone number: (501) 847-2539
Fax number: (501) 847-2540
E-mail address: roxys@aol.com

Roxy's   2

Table of Contents

Executive Summary

Overview of the business plan

Roxy's Coffee Shop will provide a desirable service for students, staff, and faculty at the University of Arkansas at Little Rock (UALR) as well as for area residents. The purpose of this business plan is to secure financial backing for the shop's first year of operation. Roxanne Kirkwood will be the sole proprietor of the business and will be the general manager. She will hire an experienced coffee shop manager to oversee the actual operation of the business.

Students, staff, and faculty at UALR have requested an establishment like Roxy's for many years. The UALR campus is near a main shopping area and several working-class neighborhoods that are being revitalized. There is also a major hospital a block away on University Avenue. Roxanne Kirkwood is asking for a loan of $60,000 to open the shop and help with operating expenses until it makes a profit. The loan will be repaid in monthly installments beginning in the first month of the second year of business and will be secured using the borrower's home as collateral. Roxy's Coffee Shop will offer a useful, desirable service to a university community that continues to grow as well as to a revitalized neighborhood that has the potential for providing more consumers.

Roxy's will offer a somewhat limited menu. Focusing on coffee as the main sale item will allow for the greatest amount of profit. Serving a few other high-demand hot and cold drinks, as well as some desserts, will support the main focus on coffee. The shop will intentionally be kept small to provide the best service with the lowest prices while offering excellent quality. The research carried out for this proposal shows that Roxy's has an ideal location, a practical plan, and a product that is in demand.

Detailed
description
of the
business

Description of Business

Roxy's will be a small, independently owned coffee shop serving regular and specialty coffee. Although juice, smoothies, hot chocolate, tea, bottled water, carbonated beverages, fruit, and desserts such as pie, cake, cookies and brownies will also be served, premium quality, fair trade coffee will be marketed at a reasonable price as the primary menu item. Although Little Rock has a number of coffee shops, none are easily accessible from the UALR campus.

Roxy's primary market will be UALR students, faculty, and staff, since the restaurants on campus all close by 7:00 in the evening and the campus coffee kiosk closes at 2:00 in the afternoon. People who live close to the campus in the surrounding neighborhoods will form a secondary market. These people will benefit from having a place nearby to enjoy coffee. In addition, Roxy's will appeal to shoppers and businesspeople frequenting the nearby malls and businesses. Situated on University Avenue, Roxy's will have an ideal location on a main thoroughfare going through the center of UALR campus, so it is convenient for morning commuter traffic.

Once financial backing for the company has been secured, all suppliers are willing to begin delivery. Restaurant supplies will be obtained through AbestKitchen.com, and a merchant account will be provided by Redwood Internet.

Details
about the
location of
the
business

Business Location

Roxy's will be located at 1819 S. University Avenue, a main thoroughfare in Little Rock. This location is one block from the main campus on University Avenue, near Highway 630, which runs through the heart of Little Rock. This location is ideal because UALR students, staff, and faculty can walk to the coffee shop from campus. In addition, tourists and businesspeople can find the location easily and park without trouble. Roxy's will be open most of the hours that the UALR library is open.

The 250-square-foot space will be leased for one year at $2,500 a month, with the option to renew and renegotiate terms at the end of that time. No walls will be moved, and electrical service and plumbing lines are to be left as they are. Renovations will involve only surface changes such as wall treatments, decorations, and furniture. The estimated cost for these changes, as noted in the financial data section of this business plan, is projected to be $5,000. Although the rent may seem high, the location of the building—only a couple of blocks from a major intersection in Little Rock offering access to traffic and potential customers—makes the cost worthwhile. This freestanding building with an adjacent parking lot is located directly on the street. The building is convenient not only for UALR students, staff, and faculty, but also for shoppers from the two major malls in Little Rock as well as for staff and visitors from a major hospital located on University Avenue. On either side of University Avenue are neighborhoods consisting of mostly working-class homes. Owners are struggling to rejuvenate these neighborhoods and keep them from being overtaken by commercial and business properties. Homeowners, attempting to keep a neighborhood feel, should welcome a local spot such as Roxy's as a place to meet socially.

Licenses and Permits

All necessary licenses and permits will be obtained. The State of Arkansas leaves most decisions up to the county in which the business is located. The Little Rock Small Business Administration is gathering information on licenses and permits.

Description of managers' responsibilities and compensation

Management

Roxy's general manager will be Roxanne Kirkwood. A business manager will be hired to assist with business operation and marketing. The general manager will work 40 hours a week for an annual salary of $30,000. The general manager will alternate day and night shifts with the business manager Monday through Friday. The business manager will work 40 hours a week for an annual salary of $25,000. Salaries will increase only when the business becomes clearly profitable.

Summary of personnel requirements

Personnel

Other than the managers, Roxy's will hire two part-time employees who will work 15 hours per week at $8.00 an hour. These employees will be responsible for the shop 16 hours on Saturdays and 14 hours on Sundays, including getting ready to open and cleaning up before closing. Managers will be on call.

Description of insurance coverage

Insurance

Roxy's will have the standard liability and property insurance. Although exact numbers are still being negotiated, costs are estimated at $100 per month. Roxy's main insurance needs include liability coverage for any accident on the property affecting customers or employees and coverage for property losses resulting from fire, theft, or vandalism. The business will not provide health insurance for employees.

Identification of the market for the new business

The Market

Roxy's target market is UALR students, staff, and faculty. Although the campus has on-site food vendors, including a coffee vendor, these vendors close early. A large portion of UALR's student body attends night classes, which begin

Roxy's 7

long after the coffee vendor's closing time of 2:00 in the afternoon. Many of these students visit the library, which is open until 11:00 on weeknights. In addition, a large neighborhood surrounds the campus, and a main street borders the campus, moving a large amount of traffic right past Roxy's. Because of Roxy's location near the intersection of Highway 630 and University Avenue, the ability to attract shoppers, tourists, and hospital staff and visitors is guaranteed.

Competition

Little Rock has not yet been inundated with coffee shops as many American cities have. There is one chain, Coffey Beanery, which has a stand in one mall and one shop halfway across town in West Little Rock, off Chenal. There are no Starbucks and only a few independently owned establishments. The other independently owned shops are located in neighborhoods nowhere near UALR or University Avenue.

Identification of competing businesses

Table summarizing projected financial data for the first year of operation

Financial Data

Table 1

Estimated Expenses for First Year of Operation

Expense	Startup Only	Monthly	Yearly
Equipment including crockery	X		$15,000
Furniture, fixtures and remodeling	X		10,000
Inventory including coffee beans and food		$2,000	24,000
Rent		2,500	30,000
Insurance		100	1,200
Advertising	$800	100	2,000
Utilities		1,000	12,000
Licenses and permits			500
Miscellaneous		200	2,400
General manager			30,000
Business manager		2,083.33	25,000
Part-time employees		960	11,520
Total needed for first year	$800	$8,943.33	$163,620
Total needed for startup costs		$80,000	(approximately 3 months operating costs, plus a small emergency reserve)
Total supplied by borrower		$20,000	
Total supplied by lender		$60,000	

Package directions often include abbreviated sentences.

USING A GRAMMAR CHECKER

Most word-processing programs have features that help writers identify grammar errors as well as problems with usage and style. But these grammar checkers have significant limitations. Because they are programmed according to specific rules, they search for violations of those rules. A grammar checker will usually identify

- fused sentences, sometimes called run-on sentences (chapter **23**),
- some misused prepositions (**33c**),
- wordy or overly long sentences (chapters **28** and **34**), and
- missing apostrophes in contractions (**37b**).

However, a grammar checker will frequently miss subtle stylistic problems as well as

- sentence fragments (chapter **22**),
- problems with adverbs or adjectives (**24a**),
- dangling or misplaced modifiers (**24c–d**),
- problems with pronoun-antecedent agreement (**25c**),
- errors in subject-verb agreement (**26f**), and
- misused or missing commas (chapter **35**).

Since these problems can weaken your credibility as a writer, you should never rely solely on a grammar checker to find them. Furthermore, grammar checkers cannot distinguish between true errors and choices you make deliberately to suit your rhetorical situation. As a result, they often flag words or phrases that you have chosen intentionally.

Used carefully, a grammar checker can be a helpful tool, but keep the following advice in mind.

- Use a grammar checker only in addition to your own editing and proofreading. When in doubt, consult the appropriate chapters in this handbook.
- Always evaluate any sentences flagged by a grammar checker to determine whether there is, in fact, a problem.
- Carefully review the revisions proposed by a grammar checker before accepting them. Sometimes the proposed revisions create entirely new errors.
- Adjust the settings on your grammar checker to look only for errors you make frequently. (However, even if used in this way, a grammar checker may miss some errors.)

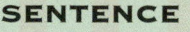

SENTENCE ESSENTIALS 20

When you think of the word *grammar,* you might also think of the word *rule*—a regulation that you must obey unless you are prepared to get into trouble. But *rule* has another meaning: "a description of what is true in most cases." A grammar rule, then, is a statement of how language is commonly or conventionally used. However, language use, as you know, varies according to the rhetorical situation. You are probably already aware of varying your own speech or writing for a special audience or occasion. Because language allows such variety, you have many options to consider as you draft and revise—a number of words and word arrangements at your disposal. By learning some basic grammatical terminology and concepts, you will understand what your options are and how to make the most of them. This chapter will help you

- identify the parts of speech (**20a**),
- recognize the essential parts of a sentence (**20b**),
- identify predicates (**20c**),
- identify subjects and complements (**20d**), and
- recognize basic sentence patterns (**20e**).

20a Parts of speech

When you look up a word in the dictionary, you will often find it followed by one or more of these labels: *adj., adv., conj., interj., n., prep., pron.,* and *v.* (or *vb.*). These are the abbreviations for the traditional eight parts of speech: *adjective, adverb, conjunction, interjection, noun, preposition, pronoun,* and *verb.* The definition of a word depends on which of these labels applies to the word. For example, when labeled as a noun, the word *turn* has several meanings, one of which is "curve": We were surprised by the *turn* in the road. When *turn* is labeled as a verb, one of its possible meanings is "to change color": The leaves have *turned*.

By learning the eight parts of speech, not only will you be able to use a dictionary effectively, you will also better understand the feedback your teacher, supervisor, or peers give you as well as provide fellow writers with specific recommendations. Someone reading your work, for example, may suggest that you use more action verbs. And you may note, as you read another's work, that it would be improved by balancing abstract nouns such as *nutrition* with concrete nouns such as *spinach*.

BEYOND THE RULE

COUNTING PARTS OF SPEECH

Prior to the eighteenth century, only two parts of speech—nouns and verbs—were counted. Now, in addition to the eight traditional parts of speech established in that century, others such as *determiners* and *expletives* are widely recognized. To learn more about the history of the parts of speech, visit **www.harbrace.com**.

(1) Verbs usually express action or being.

Thousands of verbs are **action verbs.** Just think of everything you do in one day: wake, eat, drink, wash, walk, drive, study, work, laugh, smile, talk, and so on. In contrast, only a few verbs express being or experiencing. Called **linking verbs,** these include *be, seem, become,* and the sensory verbs *look, taste, smell, feel,* and *sound.* Both action verbs and linking verbs are frequently accompanied by **auxiliary verbs**—verbs that add meaning to a main verb, such as information about time, ability, or certainty (*have studied, will study, can study, must be studying*). These verbs are sometimes called **auxiliaries** or **helping verbs.**

The base form of most action verbs fits into this frame sentence:

We should _____ (it). [With some verbs, *it* is not used.]

The base form of most linking verbs fits into this frame sentence:

It should _____ good (terrible, fine).

Writers of travel brochures often choose action verbs to create images of fun-filled vacations.

THINKING RHETORICALLY ABOUT

VERBS

Decide which of the following sentences evokes a clearer image.

The team captain **was** absolutely ecstatic.

Grinning broadly, the team captain **shot** both her arms into the air.

You probably chose the sentence with the action verb (*shot*) rather than the sentence with *was*. Most writers avoid using the verb *be* in any of its forms (*am, is, are, was, were,* or *been*) when their rhetorical situation calls for vibrant imagery. Instead, they use vivid action verbs. For more information on choosing effective words, see chapters 32–34.

(2) Nouns usually name people, places, things, and ideas.

Proper nouns are specific names and are capitalized: *Bill Gates, Redmond, Microsoft Corporation.* **Common nouns,** also called **generic nouns,** refer to any member of a class or category: *person, city, company.* Common nouns that have singular and plural forms are called **count nouns** because the entities they name can be counted: *book, books; car, cars.* **Noncount nouns** have only one form because they name things that cannot be counted: *furniture, air.* **Collective nouns** such as *team, committee,* and *faculty,* which comprise individual members, are either singular or plural, depending on the context (see 26f(7)).

Most nouns fit into this frame sentence:

(The) _____ is (are) important (unimportant, interesting, uninteresting).

THINKING RHETORICALLY ABOUT

NOUNS

Nouns like *entertainment* and *nutrition* are **abstract nouns.** They refer to concepts. Nouns like *guitar* and *tofu* are **concrete nouns.** They refer to things perceivable by the senses. When your rhetorical situation calls for the use of abstractions, balance them with tangible details conveyed through concrete nouns. For example, if you use the abstract nouns *impressionism* and *cubism* in an art history paper, also include concrete nouns that will enable your readers to see the colors and brushstrokes of the paintings you are discussing. To learn more about how your choice of nouns can enhance your writing, see chapters **32** and **33**.

(3) A pronoun usually takes the place of a previously mentioned noun or noun phrase.

Most **pronouns** are words that substitute for nouns or noun phrases (see **21a(1)**). The nouns or noun phrases to which pronouns refer are called **antecedents.** *Dan* and *the old, decrepit house* are the antecedents in the following sentences.

Dan said **he** will have the report done by Friday.

They bought the old, decrepit house because they thought **it** had charm.

A pronoun and its antecedent may be in either the same sentence or separate, but usually adjacent, sentences.

The students worked in the field for an entire semester. At the end of the school year, **they** presented their findings at the Undergraduate Research Conference.

The pronouns in the preceding examples are called **personal pronouns.** However, there are other types of pronouns as well: indefinite, possessive, relative, interrogative, intensive, and reflexive. For a detailed description of pronouns, see chapter **25**.

THINKING RHETORICALLY ABOUT

PRONOUNS

Why is the following passage somewhat unclear?

> The study found that students succeed when they have clear directions, consistent and focused feedback, and access to help. This led administrators to create a tutoring center at our university.

The problem is that the pronoun *this* at the beginning of the second sentence could refer to all of the information provided by the study or just to the single finding that students need access to help. If you discover that the referent for a pronoun you have used is vague, replace it with clarifying information:

> **The results of this study** led administrators to create a tutoring center at our university.

(4) An adjective modifies a noun or a pronoun.

Adjectives most commonly modify nouns: *spicy* food, *cold* day, *special* price. Sometimes they modify pronouns: *blue* ones, anyone *thin*. Most adjectives answer one of these questions: Which one? What kind of . . . ? How many? What color (or size or shape, and so on)? Although adjectives usually precede the nouns they modify, they occasionally follow them: *enough* time, time *enough*. Adjectives may also follow linking verbs (such as *be, seem,* and *become*):

The <u>moon</u> is **full** tonight.

<u>He</u> seems **shy.**

When an adjective follows a linking verb, it modifies the subject of the sentence (see **20d(3)**).

Nouns sometimes function as adjectives.

> The **marble** is from Italy. [*Marble* is a noun functioning as a noun.]

> An incredible **marble** statue was hidden in the basement. [*Marble* is a noun functioning as an adjective.]

Most adjectives fit into one of these frame sentences:

He told us about a/an _____ dog (person, object, idea).

The dog (person, object, idea) is very _____.

Articles, classified either as **determiners** (see Glossary of Terms) or as a subclass of adjectives, indicate that the word that follows is a noun. English has three articles: *a, an,* and *the.*

ARTICLE USAGE

Indefinite Articles, *a* and *an*

The indefinite articles *a* and *an* classify the singular nouns they precede. Use *a* before a consonant sound (*a* yard, *a* university). Use *an* before a vowel sound (*an* apple, *an* hour). Indefinite articles are used for classification (that is, to refer to a certain type or class) in the following common contexts.

■ With the first mention of a noun. Use an indefinite article when you introduce a singular noun for the first time.

> I bought **a** writing journal for my English class. It was not very expensive.

■ With the expletive *there.* Use an indefinite article when you introduce a topic that includes a singular noun.

> There is **a** good reason for using a journal to improve your English.

■ For a generalization. When you are referring to a singular noun in a general way, use an indefinite article.

> **A** writing journal is a notebook in which you can write down ideas without worrying about grammar.

If a noun is plural or if it cannot be counted, then no article is needed.

> **Journals** are useful. **Writing** is an important skill.

Definite Article, *the*

The definite article *the* can precede singular or plural nouns as well as noncount nouns. It is used for identification in the following common contexts.

■ For a subsequent mention. Once a noun has been introduced, use the definite article before it later in the same sentence or paragraph.

> I wrote about two of my favorite possessions—a guitar and a flute. I received **the** guitar as a gift from my parents.

A subsequent mention does not always include exact repetition of a noun. However, the noun chosen must be close in meaning to a word or phrase in the previous clause or sentence.

> The teacher **grades** us on each assignment, but **the grade** isn't based solely on grammatical correctness. [The noun *grade* is close in meaning to the verb *grades*.]

■ For something that is unique. When referring to something that is unique in everyone's shared experience, use the definite article.

> One teacher asked her students to write about **the** moon in their journals.

Other nouns like *moon* include *universe, solar system, sun, earth,* and *sky.* A noun may be considered unique as long as the audience will recognize the referent. For example, *airport* may be preceded by *the* when only one airport would come to mind in the specific context.

> My friend wrote about her experience at **the** airport.

■ For an abstract class. *The* is used with a noun that refers to an abstract class.

> **The** writer's journal has become a mainstay in the composition classroom.

(5) Adverbs modify verbs, adjectives, and other adverbs.

Adverbs most frequently modify verbs. They provide information about time, manner, place, and frequency, thus answering one of these questions: When? How? Where? How often?

The conference <u>starts</u> **tomorrow.** [time]

I **rapidly** <u>calculated</u> the cost. [manner]

We <u>met</u> **here.** [place]

They **often** <u>work</u> late on Thursdays. [frequency]

Adverbs that modify verbs can often move from one position in a sentence to another. Compare the positions of *yesterday* and *carefully* in the following sentences.

> **Yesterday** the team traveled to St. Louis.
>
> The team traveled to St. Louis **yesterday.**
>
> He **carefully** removed the radio collar.
>
> He removed the radio collar **carefully.**

Most adverbs that provide information about how an action is performed fit into this frame sentence:

> They _____ moved (danced, walked) across the room.

Adverbs also modify adjectives and other adverbs by intensifying or otherwise qualifying the meanings of those words.

> I was **somewhat** <u>surprised</u>. [modifying an adjective]
>
> He was **unusually** <u>generous</u>. [modifying an adjective]

> The changes occurred **quite** <u>rapidly</u>. [modifying an adverb]
>
> The team played **surprisingly** <u>well</u>. [modifying an adverb]

For more information on adverbs, see **24a**.

THINKING RHETORICALLY ABOUT

ADVERBS

What do the adverbs add to the following sentences?

> The scientist **delicately** places the slide under the microscope.
>
> "You're late," he scolded **vehemently.**
>
> She is **wistfully** hopeful.

Adverbs like these can help you portray an action, indicate how someone is speaking, and add detail to a description.

(6) Prepositions set up relationships between words.

A **preposition** combines with a pronoun, noun, or noun phrase to create a **prepositional phrase.** A prepositional phrase functions as an adjective or an adverb.

> The tour **of the old city** has been postponed. [adjectival, modifying *the tour*]
>
> The editor wrote comments **in the margin.** [adverbial, modifying *wrote*]

Common one-word prepositions are *on, in, at, to, for, over,* and *under.* Common **phrasal prepositions** (prepositions consisting of more than one word) are *except for, because of, instead of,* and *according to.* For a list of prepositions and more information on prepositional phrases, see **21a(4).**

(7) Conjunctions are connectors.

Coordinating conjunctions connect similar words or groups of words; that is, a coordinating conjunction generally links a noun to a noun, an adjective to an adjective, a phrase to a phrase, and so on.

> The game was dangerous **yet** appealing. [connecting adjectives]
>
> They foraged for food at dawn **and** at dusk. [connecting prepositional phrases]

There are seven coordinating conjunctions. Use the made-up word *fanboys* to help you remember them.

F	A	N	B	O	Y	S
for	*and*	*nor*	*but*	*or*	*yet*	*so*

Correlative conjunctions, or **correlatives,** consist of two parts. The most common correlatives are *both . . . and, either . . . or, neither . . . nor,* and *not only . . . but also.*

> The defeat left me feeling **both** sad **and** angry. [connecting adjectives]
>
> **Either** Pedro **or** Jeanie will introduce the guest speaker. [connecting nouns]

For more information on coordinating and correlative conjunctions, see **21c(1–2).**

A **subordinating conjunction** introduces a clause that depends on a main (independent) clause.

The river rises **when** <u>the snow melts</u>.

Common subordinating conjunctions are *because, although, when,* and *if.* For a longer list of subordinating conjunctions and more information on independent and dependent clauses, see **21b(2)** and **21c(3)**. To learn how to use coordination and subordination to improve sentences, see chapter **28**.

(8) Interjections are expressions of surprise or strong feeling.

Interjections are most commonly used either before a sentence or at the beginning of a sentence to indicate surprise, dread, or some other strong emotion. Interjections are generally followed by an exclamation point or a comma.

Wow! Your design is astounding.

Oh no, you can't be telling the truth.

Exercise 1

Identify the part of speech for each word in the sentences below.

1. After we finished lunch, we piled into a minivan and explored the valley.
2. A narrow river runs through it.
3. The tour guide drove very slowly because the road was old and rutted.
4. We stopped at a roadside stand for fresh figs. Oh, were they good!
5. While we were there, we bought flowers for the guide.

20b   Subjects and predicates

A sentence consists of two parts:

SUBJECT + PREDICATE

The **subject** is generally someone or something that either performs an action or is described. The **predicate** expresses the action initiated by the subject or gives information about the subject.

> **The <u>quarterback</u> + <u>passed</u> the ball to his wide receiver.**
>
> **The <u>landlord</u> + <u>has renovated</u> the apartment.**
>
> [The subject performs an action; the predicate expresses that action.]

> **<u>He</u> + <u>is</u> talented.**
>
> **Their <u>plans</u> + <u>had sounded</u> reasonable.**
>
> [The subject is described; the predicate gives information about the subject.]

The central components of the subject and the predicate are often called the **simple subject** (the main noun or pronoun) and the **simple predicate** (the main verb and any auxiliary verbs). They are underlined in the example sentences above. Compound subjects and compound predicates include a connecting word (a conjunction) such as *and, or,* or *but.*

> **The Republicans <u>and</u> the Democrats** are debating the issues. [compound subject]

> The candidate **stated his views on abortion <u>but</u> did not discuss stem-cell research.** [compound predicate]

THINKING RHETORICALLY ABOUT

SUBJECTS AND PREDICATES

Generally, sentences have the pattern subject + predicate. However, writers often vary this pattern to provide emphasis or cohesion.

> He + elbowed his way into the lobby and paused. [subject + predicate]
>
> From a far corner came + shrieks of laughter. [predicate + subject]

In the second sentence, the predicate contains information related to the first sentence and is thus placed at the beginning. The placement of the subject at the end of the second sentence puts emphasis on the information it conveys. To learn how writers commonly vary sentence structure, see chapters **31** and **32**.

Exercise 2

Identify the subject and the predicate in each sentence, noting any compound subjects or compound predicates.

1. Magicians are in our oceans.
2. They are octopuses.
3. Octopuses can become invisible.
4. They just change color.
5. They can also change their shape.
6. These shape-changers look frightening.
7. Octopuses can release poisons and produce spectacles of color.
8. The blue-ringed octopus can give an unsuspecting diver an unpleasant surprise.
9. Researchers consider the poison of the blue-ringed octopus one of the deadliest in the world.
10. Octopuses and their relatives have been living on Earth for millions of years.

20c Predicates

The central part of the predicate is the verb. A verb may be a single word, or it may consist of a main verb accompanied by one or more auxiliary verbs. The most common auxiliaries are *be (am, is, are, was, were, been)*, *have (has, had)*, and *do (does, did)*. Others, including *can, may*, and *might*, are called **modal auxiliaries.**

They **work** as volunteers. [single-word verb]

They **have been working** as volunteers. [verb with two auxiliaries]

They **might work** as volunteers. [verb with modal auxiliary]

Occasionally, an adverb intervenes between the auxiliary and the main verb.

They **have <u>always</u> worked** as volunteers.

Have you <u>ever</u> **volunteered?**

Exercise 3

Review the sentences in exercise 2, identifying all main verbs and auxiliary verbs.

20d Subjects and complements

Subjects and complements take different positions in a sentence. In most sentences, the subject refers to someone or something performing an action or being described. It usually appears before the verb.

The <u>chair</u> of the committee presented his plans for the new year.

Complements are parts of a sentence required by the verb to make the sentence complete. For example, the sentence *The chair of the committee presented* is incomplete without the complement *his plans.* There are four types of complements: direct objects, indirect objects, subject complements, and object complements.

Subjects and complements are generally pronouns, nouns, or noun phrases. Because a pronoun can replace an entire noun phrase, you can use an easy pronoun test to help you recognize noun phrases that are subjects or complements: simply substitute a pronoun for the corresponding group of words. Common pronouns used for this test are *he, she, it, they, him, her, them, this,* and *that.*

The chair of the committee introduced **the members.**

(1) Subjects are usually pronouns, nouns, or noun phrases.

Grammatically complete sentences contain a subject, which generally takes the form of a pronoun, noun, or noun phrase. An imperative sentence, however, is written without the understood subject, *you.*

My best friend is a nutritionist. [noun phrase]

She works at a clinic. [pronoun]

Eat plenty of fruits and vegetables. [understood *you*]

To identify the subject of a sentence, find the verb and then use it in a question beginning with *who* or *what,* as shown in the following examples.

Jennifer works at a clinic.

Verb: **works**

WHO works? **Jennifer**

[not the clinic] **works.**

Subject: **Jennifer**

Meat contains cholesterol.

Verb: **contains**

WHAT contains? **Meat**

[not cholesterol] **contains.**

Subject: **Meat**

Some sentences begin with an **expletive**—*there* or *it.* Such a word occurs in the subject position, forcing the true subject to follow the verb.

There were **no exercise machines.**

A subject following the expletive *it* is often a clause rather than a phrase. You will learn more about clauses in chapter **21**.

It is essential **that children learn about nutrition at an early age.**

Beginning a Sentence with *There*

In sentences beginning with the expletive *there,* the verb comes before the subject. The verb *are* is often hard to hear when it follows *there*, so be careful that you do not omit it.

      are

There ⌃ many good books on nutrition.

(2) Direct and indirect objects are usually pronouns, nouns, or noun phrases.

Objects complete the meaning begun by the subject and verb.

My roommate writes **movie scripts.** [The object *movie scripts* completes the meaning of the sentence.]

Whether an object is required in a sentence depends on the meaning of the verb. Some sentences have no objects at all; others have one or even two objects.

> The robins are migrating. [A sentence with no object.]
>
> She lent **me** her **laptop.** [*Me* is one object; *laptop* is another.]

(a) Direct objects

The **direct object** of an action verb either receives the action or shows the result of the action.

> I. M. Pei designed **the East Building of the National Gallery.**
>
> Steve McQueen invented **the bucket seat** in 1960.

Compound direct objects include a connecting word, usually *and.*

> Thomas Edison patented **the phonograph <u>and</u> the microphone.**

To identify a direct object, find the subject and the verb and then use them in a question ending with *what* or *whom.*

Marie Curie discovered radium.	They hired a new engineer.
Subject and verb:	Subject and verb:
Marie Curie discovered	**They hired**
Marie Curie discovered WHAT?	They hired WHOM?
radium	**a new engineer**
Direct object: **radium**	Direct object: **a new engineer**

Some direct objects are clauses (see **21b**).

> Researchers found **that patients responded favorably to the new medication.**

(b) Indirect objects

Some sentences can have both a direct object and an **indirect object.** Indirect objects are typically pronouns, nouns, or noun phrases that name the recipient of the direct object. Indirect objects commonly appear after the verbs *bring, buy, give, lend, offer, sell,* and *send.*

> The supervisor gave **the new employees** computers.
>
> She sent **them** contracts in the mail.

Like subjects and direct objects, indirect objects can be compound.

> She offered **Elena and Octavio** a generous benefits package.

(3) Subject and object complements are usually pronouns, nouns, noun phrases, adjectives, or adjectival phrases.

Complements can be pronouns, nouns, or noun phrases; however, they can also be adjectives or **adjectival phrases**—phrases in which the main word is an **adjective** (a word that classifies or describes a noun or pronoun). The adjective may be accompanied by a word that softens or intensifies its meaning (such as *somewhat, very,* or *quite*).

(a) Subject complements

A **subject complement,** which identifies, classifies, or describes the subject, follows a linking verb (see **20a(1)**). The most common linking verb is *be* (*am, is, are, was, were, been*). Other linking verbs are *become, seem, appear,* and the sensory verbs *feel, look, smell, sound,* and *taste.*

> The game is **a test of endurance.** [noun phrase]

> The winner is **you.** [pronoun]

> The game rules sound **quite complicated.** [adjectival phrase]

(b) Object complements

An **object complement** identifies or describes the direct object. Object complements help complete the meaning of verbs such as *call, elect, leave, make, name,* and *paint.*

> Sports reporters called the rookie **the best player of the year.** [noun phrase]

> News of the strike left the fans **somewhat disappointed.** [adjectival phrase]

Exercise 4

In the sentences in exercise 2, identify all direct objects, indirect objects, subject complements, and object complements.

20e Basic sentence patterns

Understanding basic sentence patterns and variations will help you recognize subjects and complements. The six basic sentence patterns presented in the following box are based on three verb types. You have already been introduced to linking verbs (such as *be, seem, sound,* and *taste*). These verbs are followed by a subject complement or an adverbial phrase, such as a prepositional phrase indicating place. Verbs that are not linking are either transitive or intransitive (see **26d(1)**). Notice that *trans* in the words *transitive* and *intransitive* means "over or across." Thus, the action of a **transitive verb** carries across to an object, but the action of an **intransitive verb** does not. Intransitive verbs have no complements, although they are often followed by adverbs or adverbial phrases.

BASIC SENTENCE PATTERNS

Pattern 1   SUBJECT + INTRANSITIVE VERB

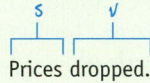

Prices dropped.

Prices dropped precipitously.

Pattern 2   SUBJECT + TRANSITIVE VERB + DIRECT OBJECT

He writes detective stories.

Pattern 3   SUBJECT + TRANSITIVE VERB + INDIRECT OBJECT + DIRECT OBJECT

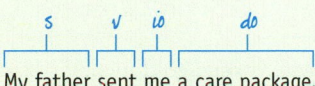

My father sent me a care package.

(Continued on page 480)

(Continued from page 479)

Pattern 4 SUBJECT + TRANSITIVE VERB + DIRECT OBJECT + OBJECT COMPLEMENT

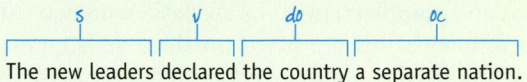

The new leaders declared the country a separate nation.

Pattern 5 SUBJECT + LINKING VERB + SUBJECT COMPLEMENT

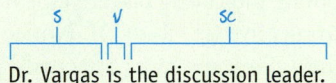

Dr. Vargas is the discussion leader.

Pattern 6 SUBJECT + LINKING VERB + ADVERBIAL PHRASE

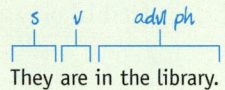

They are in the library.

Word Order

Some languages, such as French and Cantonese, have sentence patterns similar to those you have learned for English. These languages are called **SVO (subject-verb-object) languages,** even though not all sentences have objects. The patterns for other languages vary. SOV (subject-object-verb) languages and VSO (verb-subject-object) languages are also common. Keep the SVO pattern in mind to help you understand English sentences.

When declarative sentences, or statements, are turned into questions, the subject and the auxiliary verb are sometimes inverted; that is, the auxiliary verb is moved to the front of the sentence, before the subject.

Statement: A Chinese skater (has) won a gold medal.

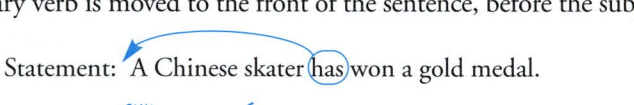

Question: Has a Chinese skater won a gold medal?

Often, a question word such as *what* or *why* opens an interrogative sentence. As long as the question word is the object of the sentence, the auxiliary verb comes before the subject.

Question: What has a Chinese skater won?

If a statement does not include an auxiliary verb or a form of the linking verb *be,* then a form of *do* is added to create the corresponding question. Once again, the auxiliary verb (in this case, *do*) is placed in front of the subject.

Statement: A Chinese skater won a gold medal.

Question: Did a Chinese skater win a gold medal?

You have learned six basic sentence patterns in this section. However, as you study sentences more closely, you will find other patterns as well. For example, some patterns require mention of a destination or location. The sentence *I put the documents* is incomplete without a phrase such as *on your desk.* Other sentences have phrases that are not essential but do add pertinent information. These phrases can sometimes be moved. For example, the phrase *on Friday* can be placed either at the beginning or at the end of a sentence.

I finished my assignment **on Friday.**

On Friday, I finished my assignment.

To learn how to write effective sentences by varying their structure, see chapter **31.**

Inverting the Subject and the Verb in Questions
English is one of a few languages in which the subject and the verb are inverted in questions. Most languages rely on intonation to indicate that a question is being asked, without a change in word order. (English speakers occasionally use uninverted questions to ask for clarification or to indicate surprise.) In many languages other than English, an option for making a statement into a question is to add a particle, such as the Japanese *ka.*

THINKING RHETORICALLY ABOUT

SENTENCE PATTERNS WITH DIRECT OBJECTS

If you want to intensify a feeling or emphasize a contrast, alter the sentence pattern by placing the direct object at the beginning of the sentence. A comma is sometimes used after the direct object in such sentences.

They loved the queen. They despised **the king.**

They loved the queen. **The king,** they despised.

I acquired English at home. I learned **French** on the street.

I acquired English at home. **French** I learned on the street.

Exercise 5

a. Identify the basic pattern of each sentence in exercise 2.
b. Write a question corresponding to each of the sentences in exercise 2. Put a check mark next to the questions in which a subject and a verb are inverted.

Exercise 6

Shift the emphasis in each of the underlined sentences by moving the direct object to the front of the sentence.

1. Leah considers her medical studies her priority. <u>She calls her rock band a hobby</u>.
2. He learned to play the clarinet when he was eight. <u>He mastered the saxophone later on</u>.
3. They renovated the state house. <u>They condemned the old hotel</u>.
4. We played volleyball in the fall. <u>We played basketball in the winter</u>.
5. They named their first child Theodore. <u>They named their second child Franklin</u>.

21   PHRASES AND CLAUSES IN SENTENCES

Within a sentence, groups of words form phrases and clauses. Like single words, these larger units function as specific parts of speech: nouns, verbs, adjectives, or adverbs. By understanding how word groups function, you will be able to make your sentences clear, concise, and complete. You will also be able to vary sentence structure so that your paragraphs are rhythmic and cohesive. This chapter will help you

- recognize phrases (**21a**),
- recognize clauses (**21b**),
- recognize words that connect words, phrases, and clauses (**21c**), and
- identify sentence forms and functions (**21d–e**).

BEYOND THE RULE

DEFINITION OF *PHRASE*

There are two definitions of the word *phrase*. The traditional definition is that a **phrase** is a sequence of grammatically related words without a subject, a predicate, or both. However, linguists define a **phrase** as a unit that has one word as its main part. The traditional definition allows only multiword groupings to be phrases; the linguists' definition also allows single-word phrases. In most composition handbooks, including this one, the traditional definition is used. For more information on phrases, visit **www.harbrace.com**.

21a Phrases

(1) A noun phrase consists of a main noun and its determiners and modifiers.

Noun phrases serve as subjects and complements. They can also be objects of prepositions, such as *in, of, on, at,* and *to.* (See **21a(4)** for a longer list of prepositions.)

> **The heavy frost** killed **many fruit trees.** [subject and direct object]
>
> **My cousin** is **an organic farmer.** [subject and subject complement]
>
> **His farm** is in **eastern Oregon.** [subject and object of the preposition *in*]

THINKING RHETORICALLY ABOUT

NOUN PHRASES

In the sentences above, the articles *the* and *an* as well as the adjectives *heavy, organic,* and *eastern* add specificity. For example, the noun phrase *an organic farmer* tells the reader more than the word *farmer* alone would. By choosing nouns and noun phrases carefully, you will make your sentences more precise and cohesive.

Much of Greenland lies within the Arctic Circle. ~~The area~~ This large island is owned by Denmark. Its native name is Kaballit Nunaat.

[*The area* could refer to either Greenland or the area within the Arctic Circle. *This large island* clearly refers to Greenland. *Its native name* is more precise than just *Its name.*]

Nouns and Determiners
The determiners *a*, *an*, *this*, and *that* are used with singular nouns. Other determiners, such as *some*, *few*, *these*, and *those*, are used with plural nouns.

an/that opportunity [determiners and singular count noun]
some/few/those opportunities [determiners and plural count noun]

The determiners *less* and *much* precede noncount nouns.

less time, **much** energy [determiners used with noncount nouns]

Abstract and plural generic nouns are rarely preceded by determiners.

Patience is a virtue. [abstract noun]
Customers can be demanding. [plural generic noun]

In other languages, determiners may not be used as they are in English. For example, in Italian, the definite article, equivalent to the English *the*, is used with abstract nouns.

La pazienza è una virtù. [The definite article *la* precedes the noun *pazienza*.]

---

(2) A verb phrase is essential to the predicate.

The predicate says something about the subject and contains a word that expresses action or state of being—a verb (see **20a(1)**). Besides a main verb, a **verb phrase** also includes an auxiliary, or helping verb, such as *be, have, do, will,* or *should*.

The flight **is arriving.** [auxiliary verb + main verb]
The passengers **have deplaned.** [auxiliary verb + main verb]

For a complete discussion of verb structure, see chapter **26**. For more information on using verbs to convey meaning effectively, see **27d(3)**, **30e**, and **31c**.

(3) Verbals may be used as nouns or as modifiers.

Verb forms used as nouns or modifiers (adjectives or adverbs) are called **verbals.** Because of their origin as verbs, verbals in phrases often have their own objects and modifiers.

> He wanted **to finish the task quickly.**
> [The object of the verbal *to finish* is *the task. Quickly* is a modifier.]

Phrases with verbals are divided into three types: gerund phrases, participial phrases, and infinitive phrases.

Central to a **gerund phrase** is the *-ing* verb form (see **26a(1)**). A gerund phrase functions as a noun, usually serving as the subject or object in a sentence.

> **Writing a bestseller** was her only goal. [subject]
>
> My neighbor enjoys **writing about distant places.** [object]

Because gerund phrases act as nouns, pronouns can replace them.

> **That** was her only goal.
>
> My neighbor enjoys **it.**

THINKING RHETORICALLY ABOUT

GERUNDS

What is the difference between the following sentences?

> They bundle products together, which can often result in higher consumer costs.
>
> Bundling products together can often result in higher consumer costs.

In the first sentence, the actor, *they,* is the focus. In the second sentence, the action of the gerund phrase, *bundling products together,* is the focus. As you revise sentences, ask yourself whether you want to emphasize actors or actions.

Participial phrases include either a present participle (*-ing* form) or a past participle (*-ed* form for regular verbs or another form for irregular verbs). (See **26a** for more information on verb forms.)

> **Planning her questions carefully,** she was able to hold fast-paced and engaging interviews. [present participle]

<u>**Known** for her interviewing skills,</u> she was asked to host her own radio program. [past participle]

Participial phrases function as modifiers. They may appear at various points in a sentence: beginning, middle, or end.

<u>**Fearing** a drought,</u> all the farmers in the area used less irrigation water.

All the farmers in the area, <u>**recognizing the signs of drought,**</u> used less irrigation water.

Farmers used less irrigation water, <u>**hoping to save it for later in the season.**</u>

The commas setting off the participial phrases in the preceding examples signal that the phrases are not essential for readers to understand who is using less irrigation water. Instead, the phrases add descriptive details or reasons to the sentences. Sometimes, however, a participial phrase provides additional information that specifies who or what is being discussed. In this case, the phrase is not set off by commas.

The reporter **providing the most accurate account of the war** was once a soldier. [The participial phrase distinguishes this reporter from others.]

For more advice on using punctuation with phrases containing verbals, see **35b(2)** and **35d(1)**.

THINKING RHETORICALLY ABOUT

PARTICIPIAL PHRASES

If some of your sentences sound monotonous or choppy, try combining them by using participial phrases.

The ecstatic fans crowded along the city streets. They were celebrating their team's first state championship.

REVISED:

Crowded along the city streets, the ecstatic fans celebrated their team's first state championship.

OR

Celebrating their team's first state championship, the ecstatic fans crowded along the city streets.

A present participle (*-ing* form) cannot function alone as the main verb in a sentence. When an *-ing* form is the main verb, it is generally preceded by a form of *be* (*am, is, are, was,* or *were*).

> *are*
> They ∧ **thinking** about the future.

Infinitive phrases serve as nouns or as modifiers. The form of the **infinitive** is distinct—the infinitive marker *to* followed by the base form of the verb.

> The company intends **to hire twenty new employees.** [direct object]

> **To attract customers,** the company changed its advertising strategy. [modifier of the verb *changed*]

> We discussed his plan **to use a new packing process.** [modifier of the noun *plan*]

BEYOND THE RULE

SPLIT INFINITIVES

Some instructors advise against putting words between the infinitive marker *to* and the base form of the verb.

> *carefully*
> Be sure to ~~carefully~~ proofread your paper ∧.

This is good advice to remember if the intervening words create an awkward sentence.

> *Under the circumstances, the*
> ∧ ~~The~~ jury was unable to~~, under the circumstances,~~ convict the defendant.

However, most writers today recognize that an adverb splitting an infinitive can provide emphasis.

> He never planned to actually publish his work.

For more information on split infinitives, visit **www.harbrace.com**.

VERBS FOLLOWED BY GERUNDS OR INFINITIVES

Some verbs in English are followed by a gerund, some are followed by an infinitive, and some are followed by either.

Verbs Followed by a Gerund

admit   avoid   consider   deny   dislike   enjoy   finish   suggest

Example: She **enjoys playing** the piano.

Verbs Followed by an Infinitive

agree   decide   deserve   hope   need   plan   promise   seem

Example: She **promised to play** the piano for us.

When an infinitive follows a form of *make* or sometimes a form of *have,* the marker *to* is omitted.

Example: The teacher **had** the student **repeat** the song.

Verbs Followed by a Pronoun, Noun, or Noun Phrase and an Infinitive

advise	encourage	order	require
cause	invite	persuade	teach

Example: Her father **taught** her **to play** the piano.

Verbs Followed by Either a Gerund or an Infinitive

begin	like	prefer	stop
continue	love	remember	try

Examples: She **likes to play** the piano. She **likes playing** the piano.

Although both gerund phrases and infinitive phrases can serve as direct objects, their meanings may be different.

We **stopped discussing** the plan. [The discussion has ended.]

We **stopped to discuss** the plan. [The discussion has not yet started.]

Good dictionaries provide information on the use of gerunds and infinitives (see **32e(1)** for a list of recommendations).

(4) Prepositional phrases are generally used as modifiers.

Prepositional phrases provide information about time, place, cause, manner, and so on.

With great feeling, Martin Luther King expressed his dream **of freedom.**
[*With great feeling* describes the way the speech was delivered, and *of freedom* specifies the topic of the dream.]

King delivered his most famous speech **at a demonstration in Washington, DC.**
[Both *at a demonstration* and *in Washington, DC* provide details about place.]

A **prepositional phrase** consists of a **preposition** (a word such as *around, at,* or *near*) and a noun, noun phrase, or pronoun (**object of the preposition**). A prepositional phrase generally modifies another element in the sentence.

The professor's lecture **on censorship** stirred controversy.

Everyone **in the class** was upset.

Some students met the professor **after class.**

A prepositional phrase occasionally serves as a subject.

After supper is too late!

When the object of the preposition is a pronoun such as *whom* or *what,* the preposition may follow rather than precede its object, especially in questions.

What was the book **about?** [The object of the preposition is *what.* COMPARE: The book was about what?]

SOME COMMON PREPOSITIONS

about	behind	except	of	to
above	beside	for	on	toward
after	between	from	out	under
around	by	in	over	until
as	despite	into	past	up
at	down	like	since	via
before	during	near	through	with

Phrasal prepositions consist of more than one word.

Except for the last day, it was a wonderful trip.

The postponement was **due to** inclement weather.

PHRASAL PREPOSITIONS

according to	due to	in spite of
apart from	except for	instead of
as for	in addition to	out of
because of	in case of	with regard to
by means of	in front of	with respect to

Prepositions in Collocations
Some verbs, adjectives, and nouns combine with prepositions to form **collocations** (see also **33c**).

verb + preposition	adjective + preposition	noun + preposition
apply to	fond of	interest in
rely on	similar to	dependence on
trust in	different from	fondness for

For other information about prepositions, consult the **Glossary of Usage** or a specialized dictionary (see **32e(1)**).

(5) An appositive can expand the meaning of a noun or a noun phrase.

Appositives (usually nouns or noun phrases) identify, explain, or supplement the meaning of other nouns or noun phrases. Thus, they add detail and variety to sentences.

When an appositive provides essential information, no commas are used.

Jonathan Weiner's book ***The Beak of the Finch*** won a Pulitzer Prize. [The appositive identifies the book being referred to.]

When an appositive provides extra details, commas set it off.

The Beak of the Finch, **a book by Jonathan Weiner,** won a Pulitzer Prize. [The appositive provides an extra detail about the book.]

For more information on how to punctuate nonessential appositives, see **35d(2)**.

(6) Absolute phrases provide descriptive details or express causes or conditions.

An **absolute phrase** is usually a noun phrase modified by a participial phrase or a prepositional phrase.

She left town at dawn, **all her belongings packed into a Volkswagen Beetle.**

Her guitar in the front seat, she pulled away from the curb.

The preceding absolute phrases provide details; the following absolute phrase expresses cause.

More vaccine having arrived, the staff scheduled its distribution.

To learn how to punctuate absolute phrases, see **35b(2)** and **35d(3)**.

Exercise 1

Label the underlined phrases in the following sentences as noun phrases, verb phrases, prepositional phrases, or verbal phrases. For verbal phrases, specify the type: gerund, participial, or infinitive. Next, identify any appositive phrases or absolute phrases in the sentences.

1. <u>Most museums</u> acquire, preserve, and exhibit objects <u>with artistic, historical, or scientific value</u>.

2. <u>Nontraditional museums</u> abound <u>in the United States and Canada</u>.

3. <u>Established in 1849</u>, the Mutter Museum in Philadelphia displays <u>pathological specimens</u>.

4. Some of the paintings in <u>the Museum of Bad Art</u> <u>were donated</u>.

5. You <u>can learn</u> the history of <u>the potato</u> <u>at The Food Museum Online</u>.

6. For those interested in various methods for <u>making toast</u>, the Cyber Toaster Museum can be visited <u>via the Internet</u>.

7. <u>Located within the Science Museum of Minnesota</u>, the Museum of Questionable Medical Devices displays objects <u>ranging from weight-reduction glasses to the age-reversing McGregor Rejuvenator</u>.

8. <u>To learn more about funeral vehicles</u>, consider <u>visiting the National Museum of Funeral History</u>, <u>a museum dedicated to providing the public with information on a common cultural ritual</u>.

9. A large collection <u>of footwear</u>, including a pair <u>of Queen Victoria's ballroom slippers</u>, is on display at <u>the Bata Shoe Museum</u>.

10. <u>Their curiosity piqued</u>, some tourists travel <u>great distances</u> <u>to see</u> <u>collections of unusual objects</u>.

Exercise 2

Add details to the following sentences by adding prepositional phrases, verbal phrases, appositive phrases, or absolute phrases. After you finish, label the phrases you added.

1. The students filed into the classroom.
2. My friend delivered the bad news.
3. The driver stopped abruptly.
4. I attended the lecture.
5. Jennifer clicked Send.

21b Clauses

(1) An independent clause can stand alone as a complete sentence.

A **clause** is a group of related words that contains a subject and a predi-cate. An **independent clause,** sometimes called a **main clause,** has the same grammatical structure as a simple sentence: both contain a sub-ject and a predicate. (See **20b**.)

The students earned high grades.

Other clauses can be added to independent clauses to form longer, more detailed sentences.

(2) A dependent clause is attached to an independent clause.

A **dependent clause** also has a subject and a predicate. However, it can-not stand alone as a complete sentence because of the word introducing it—usually a relative pronoun or a subordinating conjunction.

The athlete **who placed first** grew up in Argentina.
[relative pronoun]

She received the gold medal **because she performed flawlessly.**
[subordinating conjunction]

If it is not connected to an independent clause, a dependent clause is considered a sentence fragment (see **22c**).

(a) Dependent clauses can be used as subjects or objects.

Dependent clauses that serve as subjects or objects are called **noun clauses** (or **nominal clauses**). They are introduced by *if, that,* or a *wh-*word such as *why, what,* or *when.* Notice the similarity in usage between noun phrases and noun clauses.

Noun phrases	Noun clauses
The testimony may not be true. [subject]	**What the witness said** may not be true. [subject]
We do not understand **their motives.** [direct object]	We do not understand **why they did it.** [direct object]
Send the money to **a charity.** [object of the preposition]	Send the money to **whoever needs it most.** [object of the preposition]

When no misunderstanding would result, *that* can be omitted.

> The scientist said **she was moving to Australia.** [*that* omitted]

However, *that* should always be retained when there are two noun clauses.

> The scientist said **that she was moving to Australia** and **that her research team was planning to accompany her.** [*that* retained in both noun clauses]

(b) Dependent clauses can be used as modifiers.

Two types of dependent clauses—adjectival (relative) clauses and adverbial clauses—serve as modifiers. An **adjectival clause,** or **relative clause,** answers one of these questions about a noun or pronoun: Which one? What kind of . . . ? Such clauses, which nearly always follow the words they modify, usually begin with a **relative pronoun** (*who, whom, that, which,* or *whose*) but sometimes start with a **relative adverb** (*when, where,* or *why*). Notice the similarity in usage between adjectives and adjectival clauses.

Adjectives	Adjectival clauses
Nobody likes **malicious** gossip. [answers the question "What kind of gossip?"]	Nobody likes news reports **that pry into someone's private life.** [answers the question "What kind of news reports?"]
Some **diligent** students begin their research early. [answers the question "Which students?"]	Students **who have good study habits** begin their research early. [answers the question "Which students?"]
The **public** remarks were troubling. [answers the question "Which remarks?"]	The remarks **that were made public** were troubling. [answers the question "Which remarks?"]

THINKING RHETORICALLY ABOUT

ADJECTIVAL CLAUSES

If your sentences sound monotonous or choppy, try using an adjectival clause to combine them.

> *Dub* is a car magazine. It appeals to drivers with hip-hop attitudes.
>
> *Dub* is a car magazine **that appeals to drivers with hip-hop attitudes.**
>
> A Hovercraft can go where many vehicles cannot. It is practically amphibious.
>
> A Hovercraft, **which can go where many vehicles cannot,** is practically amphibious.

Relative pronouns can be omitted as long as the meaning of the sentence is still clear.

> Mother Teresa was a woman **the whole world admired.**
> [*Whom,* the object in the adjectival clause, is omitted.]
>
> She was someone **who cared more about serving than being served.**
> [*Who,* the subject in the adjectival clause, cannot be omitted.]

The relative pronoun is not omitted when the clause is set off by commas.

> Mother Teresa, **whom the whole world admired,** cared more about serving than being served.

Although writers have traditionally used *that* at the beginning of restrictive clauses, *which* has become acceptable if, as in the following example, it does not cause confusion. Grammar checkers, however, do not recognize this option and will instruct you to change *which* to *that.*

The committee opposes spending which would increase the deficit.

An **adverbial clause** usually answers a question about a verb: Where? When? How? Why? In what manner? Adverbial clauses are introduced by subordinating conjunctions such as *because, although,* and *when.* (For a list of subordinating conjunctions, see **21c(3).**) Notice the similarity in usage between adverbs and adverbial clauses.

Adverbs	Adverbial clauses
Occasionally, the company hires new writers. [answers the question "How frequently does the company hire new writers?"]	**When the need arises,** the company hires new writers. [answers the question "How frequently does the company hire new writers?"]
She acted **selfishly.** [answers the question "How did she act?"]	She acted **as though she cared only about herself.** [answers the question "How did she act?"]

THINKING RHETORICALLY ABOUT

ADVERBIAL CLAUSES

In an adverbial clause that refers to time or establishes a fact, both the subject and any form of the verb *be* can be omitted. Using such **elliptical clauses** will make your writing more concise.

While fishing, he saw a rare owl.
[COMPARE: **While he was fishing,** he saw a rare owl.]

Though tired, they continued to study for the exam.
[COMPARE: **Though they were tired,** they continued to study for the exam.]

Be sure that the omitted subject of an elliptical clause is the same as the subject of the independent clause. If not, revise either the adverbial clause or the main clause.

While ∧ *I was* reviewing your report, a few questions occurred to me.

OR

While reviewing your report, ∧ *I thought of* a few questions ~~occurred to me~~.

For more information on the use of elliptical constructions, see **34c.**

21c Conjunctions and conjunctive adverbs

(1) Coordinating conjunctions join words, phrases, or clauses.

In the following examples, note that coordinating conjunctions (see **20a(7)**) link grammatical elements that are alike. Each conjunction, though, signals a specific meaning.

> tired **yet** excited [*Yet* joins two adjectives and signals contrast.]
>
> in the boat **or** on the pier [*Or* joins two phrases and marks them as alternatives.]
>
> We did not share a language, **but** somehow we communicated. [*But* joins two independent clauses and signals contrast.]

Coordinating conjunctions also join independent clauses standing alone as sentences.

> In the more open places are little lavender asters, and the even smaller-flowered white ones that some people call beeweed or farewell-summer. **And** in low wet places are the richly flowered spikes of great lobelia, the blooms an intense startling blue, exquisitely shaped.
>
> —**WENDELL BERRY**, *Home Economics*

(2) Correlative conjunctions also join words, phrases, or clauses.

Correlative conjunctions (see **20a(7)**), consisting of two or more words, join single words, phrases, or clauses. However, they do not join sentences.

> **either** you **or** I [*Either . . . or* joins two words and marks them as alternatives.]
>
> **neither** on Friday **nor** on Saturday [*Neither . . . nor* joins two phrases and marks them both as false or impossible.]
>
> **Not only** did they run ten miles, **but** they **also** swam twenty laps. [*Not only . . . but also* joins two independent clauses and signals addition.]

Generally, a correlative conjunction links similar structures. The following sentence has been revised because the correlative conjunction was linking a phrase to a clause.

> **Not only** ~~saving~~ *did he save* the lives of the accident victims, **but** he **also** prevented many spinal injuries.

(3) Subordinating conjunctions introduce dependent clauses.

A subordinating conjunction introduces a dependent clause and carries a specific meaning. For example, it may indicate cause, concession, condition, or purpose.

> She studied Spanish **so that** she would be able to work in Costa Rica.
> [*So that* signals a purpose.]

> **Unless** the project receives more funding, the research will stop.
> [*Unless* signals a condition.]

SUBORDINATING CONJUNCTIONS

after	how	than
although	if	though
as if	in case	unless
as though	in that	until
because	insofar as	when, whenever
before	once	where, wherever
even if	since	whether
even though	so that	while

(4) Conjunctive adverbs link independent clauses.

Conjunctive adverbs—such as *however, nevertheless, then,* and *therefore*—link independent clauses. These adverbs signal relationships such as cause, condition, and contrast. All conjunctive adverbs can be used at the beginning of an independent clause. Some may appear in the middle or at the end of a clause.

> Heat the oil; **then,** add the onions. [*Then* begins the clause and signals another step in a sequence.]

> He made copies of the report for members of the committee. He **also** sent copies to the city council. [*Also* appears in the middle of the clause and signals an additional action.]

> My mother and father have differing political views. They rarely argue, **however.** [*However* ends the clause and signals contrast.]

For more about the use of conjunctive adverbs, see **23c**. For information on punctuating linked independent clauses, see **35a** and **36a**.

Exercise 3

First, identify the dependent clauses in the following paragraph; then, identify all coordinating conjunctions, correlative conjunctions, subordinating conjunctions, and conjunctive adverbs.

1With the goal of crossing both the North Pole and the South Pole alone, Børge Ousland started his 1,240-mile trek on March 3, 2001. **2**He had already crossed the South Pole in 1997, so this time he planned to walk, ski, and swim across the North Pole. **3**When he left Cape Arkticheskiy in Russia, he weighed 214 pounds. **4**When he reached Ward Hunt Island in Canada on March 23, he weighed only 177 pounds. **5**Although Ousland had prepared for the most grueling triathlon imaginable, he had no way of predicting what he would have to endure. **6**One night huge chunks of ice forced upward from the packed surface almost destroyed his camp, and the next morning he had to search hard for snow that he could melt into fresh water. **7**About a week into his trip, Ousland's sledge started to break down. **8**Ousland considered canceling his trip at that point, but instead he steeled himself and ordered a new sledge, which did not arrive until several days later. **9**Ousland also had to swim across leads, shoot at approaching polar bears, and endure the pain of frostbite and strained tendons. **10**Despite all the misery, Ousland continually took cues from his surroundings. **11**Whenever he came to a lead, he asked himself what a polar bear would do. **12**When crossing treacherous pack ice, he thought as a fox would, making each step count. **13**Ousland said the most important lesson from the journey was perseverance. **14**He never gave up.

21d Sentence forms

You can identify the form of a sentence by noting the number and kind of each clause it contains.

(1) A simple sentence consists of a single independent clause.

ONE INDEPENDENT CLAUSE

A **simple sentence** is equivalent to one independent clause. Essentially, then, it must have a subject and a predicate.

The lawyer presented her final argument.

However, you can expand a simple sentence by adding one or more prepositional phrases or verbal phrases.

> The lawyer presented her final argument **in less than an hour.**
> [A prepositional phrase adds information about time.]
>
> **Encouraged by the apparent sympathy of the jury,** the lawyer presented her final argument. [A verbal phrase adds detail.]

(2) A compound sentence consists of at least two independent clauses but no dependent clauses.

INDEPENDENT CLAUSE + INDEPENDENT CLAUSE

The independent clauses of a compound sentence are most commonly linked by a coordinating conjunction. However, punctuation may sometimes serve the same purpose. (See **36a** and **39d**.)

> The Democrats proposed a new budget, **but** the Republicans opposed it. [The coordinating conjunction *but* links two independent clauses and signals contrast.]
>
> The Democrats proposed a new budget; the Republicans opposed it. [The semicolon serves the same purpose as the coordinating conjunction.]

(3) A complex sentence has one independent clause and at least one dependent clause.

INDEPENDENT CLAUSE + DEPENDENT CLAUSE

A dependent clause in a complex sentence can be a noun clause, an adjectival clause, or an adverbial clause.

> **Because he was known for architectural ornamentation,** no one predicted **that the house <u>he designed for himself</u> would be so plain.** [This sentence has three dependent clauses. *Because he was known for architectural ornamentation* is an adverbial clause. *That the house he designed for himself would be so plain* is a noun clause, and *he designed for himself* is an adjectival clause within the noun clause. The relative pronoun *that* has been omitted from the beginning of this adjectival clause.]

(4) A compound-complex sentence consists of at least two independent clauses and at least one dependent clause.

INDEPENDENT CLAUSE + INDEPENDENT CLAUSE +

DEPENDENT CLAUSE

The combination of a compound sentence and a complex sentence is called a **compound-complex sentence.**

> **Because it snowed heavily in October that year,** the ski resorts opened early, **and** the skiers flocked to them. [*Because* introduces the dependent clause; *and* connects the two independent clauses.]

THINKING RHETORICALLY ABOUT

SENTENCE FORMS

If one of your paragraphs has as many simple sentences as the one below, try combining some of those sentences into compound, complex, or compound-complex sentences. As you do, you might need to add extra detail as well.

> I rode the school bus every day. I didn't like to, though. The bus smelled bad. And it was always packed. The worst part was the bumpy ride. Riding the bus was like riding in a worn-out sneaker.

REVISED:

> As a kid, I rode the school bus every day, but I didn't like to. I hated the smell, the crowd, and the ride itself. Every seat was filled, and many of the kids took their shoes off for the long ride home down a road so bumpy you couldn't even read a comic book. Riding that bus was like riding inside a worn-out sneaker.

Exercise 4

Identify each sentence in the paragraph in exercise 3 as simple, compound, complex, or compound-complex.

Exercise 5

Vary the sentence forms in the following paragraph. Add details as needed.

We arrived at the afternoon concert. We were late. We couldn't find any seats. It was hot, so we stood in the shade. We finally found seats under an umbrella. The shade didn't help, though. We could feel our brains melting. The music was cool, but we weren't.

21e Sentence functions

Sentences serve a number of functions. Writers commonly state facts or report information with **declarative sentences.** They give instructions with **imperative sentences.** They use questions, or **interrogative sentences,** to elicit information or to introduce topics. And they express emotion with **exclamatory sentences.**

Declarative   The runners from Kenya won the race.

Imperative   Check their times.

Interrogative   Wasn't it an incredible race?

Taking note of end punctuation can help you identify sentence types. Generally, a period marks the end of a declarative or an imperative sentence, and a question mark ends an interrogative sentence. An exclamation point indicates that a sentence is exclamatory.

Exclamatory   The runners from Kenya won the race! Check their times! What an incredible race!

Imperatives are also easy to identify because the subject is always understood to be *you.* Because an imperative is directed to another person or to other people, the subject *you* is implied:

Look over here! [COMPARE: You look over here.]

Advertisers often use imperatives to draw in readers.

BEYOND THE RULE

SENTENCE FUNCTIONS

Each type of sentence can be used for a variety of purposes. For example, imperative sentences are used not only to give directions, but also to make suggestions ("Try using a different screwdriver."), to issue invitations ("Come in."), to extend wishes ("Have a good time."), and to warn others ("Stop there."). Furthermore, a single purpose, such as getting someone to do something, can be accomplished in more than one way.

Imperative	Close the window, please.
Declarative	We should close the window.
Interrogative	Would you please close the window?

For further discussion of the connection between the form and the function of sentences, see **www.harbrace.com**.

THINKING RHETORICALLY ABOUT

SENTENCE TYPES

One type of interrogative sentence, the **rhetorical question,** is not a true question because an answer is not expected. Instead, like a declarative sentence, a rhetorical question is used to state an opinion. However, a positive rhetorical question can correspond to a negative assertion, and vice versa.

Rhetorical questions	Equivalent statements
Should we allow our rights to be taken away?	We shouldn't allow our rights to be taken away.
Isn't it time to make a difference?	It's time to make a difference.

Because they are more emphatic than declarative sentences, rhetorical questions focus the reader's attention on major points.

Exercise 6

Identify the function of each of these sentences.

1. Who is going to the concert?
2. Go early to get good seats.
3. The concert was six hours long.
4. What an amazing song that was!

22

SENTENCE

FRAGMENTS

As its name suggests, a **sentence fragment** is only a piece of a sentence; it is not complete. This chapter can help you

- recognize sentence fragments (**22a**) and
- revise fragments resulting from incorrectly punctuated phrases and dependent clauses (**22b–c**).

Do not rely on a grammar checker to flag all the fragments in your writing. The grammar checker used in producing this chapter recognized only half of the fragments serving as examples. Instead of relying on a grammar checker, use the methods described in this chapter. Also refer to **Using a Grammar Checker** on page 461.

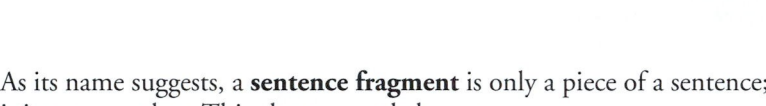

22a Recognizing sentence fragments

A complete sentence consists of a subject and a predicate (see **20b**), but a fragment may be missing either or both of these parts and thus require revision.

Magazines often include articles about alternative medicine. ~~Usually~~ *, usually* covering both the benefits and the drawbacks of particular methods.

Sometimes, alternative medical treatment includes hypnosis. ~~The~~ *, the* placement of a patient into a sleeplike state.

Alternatively, a fragment may have the essential sentence components but begin with a subordinating conjunction or a relative pronoun (see **21b(2)**).

Subordinating conjunction beginning a fragment

Most people can be hypnotized easily~~.~~, although ~~**Although**~~ **the depth of the trance for each person varies greatly.**

Relative pronoun beginning a fragment

Hypnosis is usually induced by a hypnotist~~.~~, who ~~**Who**~~ **gives repetitive, monotonous commands.**

Note that imperative sentences (see **21e**) are not considered fragments. In these sentences, the subject, *you,* is not stated explicitly. Rather, it is implied. In fact, the subject of an imperative sentence is often called the **understood you.**

Find out as much as you can about alternative treatments.
[COMPARE: *You* find out as much as you can about alternative treatments.]

Subject Pronouns

In some languages, subject pronouns are dropped when there is no risk of misunderstanding. In Japanese, a sentence such as *Sushi o tabemasu* ("Eat sushi") is permissible when the subject pronoun can be determined from the context. In Spanish, the verb form reveals information about the subject; unless needed for clarity or emphasis, a subject pronoun can be omitted, as in *Trabajo en un banco* ("I work in a bank"). In English, however, subject pronouns must be included in all except imperative sentences.

FOUR METHODS FOR IDENTIFYING FRAGMENTS

Fragments may be difficult to find within the context of neighboring sentences. If you have trouble recognizing fragments, try one or more of these methods:

1. Read each paragraph backwards, sentence by sentence. When you read your sentences out of order, you may more readily note the incompleteness of a fragment.
2. Locate the essential parts of each sentence. First, find the main verb and any accompanying auxiliary verbs. Remember that verbals cannot function

(Continued on page 508)

(Continued from page 507)

as main verbs (see **26a(5)**). After you find the main verb, find the subject by asking "Who?" or "What?" (see **20d(1)**). Finally, check to see that the sentence does not begin with a relative pronoun or a subordinating conjunction (see **21b(2)**).

Test sentence: Striving to provide educational opportunities for African Americans.

Test: Main verb? *None.* "Striving" and "to provide" are both verbals.

Subject? *None.*

[Because there is no subject or main verb, this test sentence is a fragment.]

Test sentence: Striving to provide educational opportunities for African Americans, Mary McLeod Bethune opened a small school in 1904.

Test: Main verb? *Opened.*

Subject? *Mary McLeod Bethune.*

Relative pronoun or subordinating conjunction? *None.*

[This test sentence contains a subject and a verb, and it does not begin with a relative pronoun or subordinating conjunction. It is therefore complete.]

3. Put any sentence you think might be a fragment into this frame:

    They do not understand the idea that _____.

    Only a full sentence will make sense in this frame. If a test sentence, other than an imperative, does not fit into the frame, it is a fragment.

    Test sentence: Depending on availability of food.

    Test: They do not understand the idea that *depending on availability of food.*

    [The sentence does not make sense, so the test sentence is a fragment.]

    Test sentence: The number of tiger sharks grows or shrinks depending on availability of food.

    Test: They do not understand the idea that *the number of tiger sharks grows or shrinks depending on availability of food.*

    [The sentence does make sense, so the test sentence is complete.]

4. Rewrite any sentence you think might be a fragment as a yes/no question. Only full sentences can be rewritten this way.

    Test sentence: Which is made from the leaves of the foxglove plant.

Test: *Is which made from the leaves of the foxglove plant?*

[The question does not make sense, so the test sentence is a fragment.]

Test sentence: Some heart patients take digitalis, which is made from the leaves of the foxglove plant.

Test: *Do some heart patients take digitalis, which is made from the leaves of the foxglove plant?*

[The question does make sense, so the test sentence is complete.]

Exercise 1

Identify the sentence fragments in the following paragraph. Be prepared to explain how you identified each fragment. Revise the fragments by attaching them to related sentences or by recasting them as full sentences.

¹One of the most versatile American sculptors of the twentieth century, Alexander Calder (1898–1976) is best known for his mobiles. ²Playfully balanced arrangements of abstract or organic forms. ³As a young man, Calder first studied mechanical engineering. ⁴Even though he came from a family of sculptors. ⁵It was not until four years after he earned his degree that he enrolled in an art school. ⁶Shortly thereafter, Calder moved to Paris. ⁷Where his wire sculptures won him worldwide recognition. ⁸During the 1930s, he began to experiment with motion. ⁹Eventually developing the mode of sculpture that most people think of when they hear the name *Calder*.

22b Phrases as sentence fragments

A phrase (see 21a) may be mistakenly written as a sentence fragment. You can revise such a fragment by attaching it to a related sentence, usually the one preceding it. This method creates a strong link between the fragment and the independent clause it follows. If you are unsure of the correct punctuation to use with phrases, see **35b** and **35d**.

Verbal phrase as fragment

Early humans valued color. *, creating* ~~Creating~~ **permanent colors with natural pigments.**

Prepositional phrase as fragment

For years, the Scottish have dyed sweaters with soot. *, originally* ~~Originally~~ **from the chimneys of peat-burning stoves.**

Compound predicate as fragment

Arctic foxes turn white when it snows. *and* ~~And~~ **thus conceal themselves from prey.**

Appositive phrase as fragment

During the Renaissance, one of the most highly valued pigments was ultramarine. *—an* ~~An~~ **extract from lapis lazuli.**

Appositive list as fragment

In order to derive dyes, we have always experimented with what we find in nature. *: shells,* ~~Shells,~~ **roots, insects, flowers.**

Absolute phrase as fragment

The deciduous trees of New England are known for their brilliant autumn color. *, sugar* ~~Sugar~~ **maples dazzling tourists with their deep orange and red leaves.**

Instead of attaching a fragment to the preceding sentence, you can recast the fragment as a full sentence. This method of revision elevates the importance of the information conveyed in the fragment.

Fragment: Early humans valued color. **Creating permanent colors with natural pigments.**

Revision: Early humans valued color. They created permanent colors with natural pigments.

Fragment: Humans painted themselves for a variety of purposes. **To attract a mate, to hide themselves from game or predators, or to signal aggression.**

Revision: Humans used color for a variety of purposes. For example, they painted themselves to attract a mate, to hide themselves from game or predators, or to signal aggression.

Exercise 2

Revise each fragment by attaching it to a related sentence or by recasting it as a full sentence.

1. The first person to produce an artificial dye commercially was William Perkin. A nineteen-year-old Englishman.

2. At one time in Europe, mummy was a popular pigment. Made by crushing the remains of Egyptian mummies.

3. Many food producers package their products in red. Believing that it attracts consumers.

4. Red causes the release of adrenaline in humans. As well as in other animal species.

5. Crayola assigns the colors of crayons unusual names. Including Outer Space and Pig Pink.

6. There are three colors on the Italian flag. Green on the left side, red on the right side, and white in the center.

7. One of Marie Antoinette's favorite shades was puce. The French word for "flea."

8. At times, the pigment saffron was quite popular. And worth its weight in gold.

9. The pigment carmine was in high demand. Spanish conquistadors making vast fortunes on its production.

10. Sir Isaac Newton showed that white light comprised all the visible colors of the spectrum. By passing a beam of sunlight through a prism.

22c Dependent clauses as sentence fragments

Dependent clauses that are punctuated as if they were independent clauses are sentence fragments. An adverbial clause or an adjectival clause (see **21b(2)**) is a common culprit. Such a fragment can be revised by attaching it to a related sentence, usually the sentence preceding it. By linking the fragment to the independent clause, you explicitly indicate their relationship—cause and effect, for example.

Adverbial clause as fragment

because

The iceberg was no surprise. ~~**Because**~~ the *Titanic's* wireless operators had received reports of ice in the area.

Adjectival clause as fragment

, which

More than two thousand people were aboard the *Titanic.* ~~**Which**~~ was the world's largest ocean liner in 1912.

, which

The shipbuilders first constructed the keel. ~~**Which**~~ was considered the backbone of the ship.

Two other methods can be used to revise these types of fragments. You can recast the fragment as a full sentence by removing the subordinating conjunction or relative pronoun and supplying any missing elements. This method of revision draws more attention to the information conveyed in the fragment. Compare the following revised sentences with those above.

Revision: The iceberg was no surprise. The *Titanic's* wireless operators had received reports of ice in the area.

Revision: More than two thousand people were aboard the *Titanic.* In 1912, this ocean liner was the world's largest.

You can also reduce the fragment to a phrase (see **21a**) and then attach the phrase to a related sentence. When you link a phrase to a sentence, you establish a certain relationship between the two. Unlike clauses, however, participial and appositive phrases suggest relationships less directly because they do not include subordinating conjunctions or relative pronouns.

Revision: The shipbuilders first constructed the keel—considered the backbone of the ship. [dependent clause reduced to a participial phrase]

Revision: More than two thousand people were aboard the *Titanic,* the world's largest ocean liner in 1912. [dependent clause reduced to an appositive phrase]

If you are unsure of the correct punctuation to use with phrases or dependent clauses, see chapter **35**.

THINKING RHETORICALLY ABOUT

FRAGMENTS

When used judiciously, fragments—like short sentences—emphasize ideas, add surprise, or enhance the rhythm of a paragraph. Fragments are not appropriate for all types of writing, however. They are generally permitted only when the rhetorical situation allows the use of an intimate or playful tone.

The room is full of sunlight. **Yellow. Cream. Gold. White.** These colors cover two-thirds of its surface, which is also awash with lavenders and reds falling in sun-filled stripes from the curtains, the walls, the man, the table, the chair, the dresser.   —**ELAINE SCARRY**, *On Beauty and Being Just*

Narrow, shoulderless highway 61 looked as if a tar pot had overturned at the summit and trickled a crooked course down. **A genuine white-knuckled road.**
—**WILLIAM LEAST HEAT-MOON**, *Blue Highways*

BEYOND THE RULE

ABBREVIATED SENTENCES

You encounter sentence fragments every day—in conversations, in e-mail messages, and even in some instructional materials. In conversation, someone might ask you, "Going anywhere tonight?" And you might respond, "Maybe."

(Continued on page 514)

(Continued from page 513)

To end an e-mail message, you might write, "See you later." When preparing a meal, you have probably read instructions similar to these: "Just heat and serve." "Cook to golden brown." The writers of such instructions expect you to know what is to be heated or browned. These kinds of fragments, in which words that can be understood from the context are omitted, are called **abbreviated sentences.** For other examples of abbreviated sentences, visit **www.harbrace.com**.

Package directions often include abbreviated sentences.

Exercise 3

Revise each fragment by attaching it to a related sentence or by recasting it as a full sentence.

1. The iceberg was hard to see. Because there was no wind causing waves to splash against it.
2. The lookouts on the *Titanic* did not spot the iceberg. Until it was too late.

3. The name given to the large ocean liner was *Titanic*. Which means "of great size."
4. One of the most reliable eyewitnesses was Jack Thayer. Who gave his report shortly after he was rescued.
5. Moviegoers raved about the film *Titanic*. Which was based on the ship's story.

Exercise 4

Advertisements often contain sentence fragments. Find a newspaper or magazine advertisement that contains several fragments. Rewrite the advertisement so that it consists of complete sentences; then, write a short paragraph explaining why you think the advertiser may have used the fragments.

Exercise 5

Follow the guidelines in this chapter to locate and revise the fragments in the following passage. If you find it necessary, make other changes to enhance the paragraph as well. Be prepared to explain your revisions.

[1]A giant hairy animal has caught the fascination of many people. [2]Including normally skeptical citizens and scientists. [3]They are all interested in the phenomenon of Sasquatch. [4]Also commonly called Big Foot. [5]*Sasquatch* comes from the Salish word *saskehavas.* [6]The North American Sasquatch has a counterpart. [7]The Himalayan Yeti. [8]Both have been studied by cryptozoologists. [9]Who research undiscovered animals. [10]In our country, most sightings of Sasquatch occur in the Pacific Northwest. [11]From northern California to central Alaska. [12]Although reports have come from almost every state. [13]During the settlement of the United States, stories of hairy ape-men were told by Native Americans. [14]And later on by trappers. [15]Teddy Roosevelt recorded one such story.

COMMA SPLICES

AND

FUSED SENTENCES

23

Comma splices and fused sentences are sentence-level mistakes resulting from incorrect or missing punctuation. Both are punctuated as one sentence when they should be punctuated as two sentences (or two independent clauses). By revising comma splices and fused sentences, you indicate sentence boundaries and connections and thus make your writing more coherent. This chapter will help you

- review the rules for punctuating independent clauses (**23a**),
- recognize comma splices and fused sentences (**23b**), and
- learn ways to revise them (**23c–d**).

A **comma splice,** or **comma fault,** refers to the incorrect use of a comma between two independent clauses (see **36a**).

Most stockholders favored the merger,$_\wedge$ *but* the management did not.

This kind of error can be easily fixed. Because a comma is a weak mark of punctuation, usually placed between words or phrases (see chapter **35**), it is not conventionally used to join independent clauses. For this purpose, you should use connecting words, stronger marks of punctuation, or both.

A **fused sentence** consists of two independent clauses run together without any punctuation at all. This type of sentence is sometimes called a **run-on sentence.**

The first section of the proposal was approved$_\wedge$ *;however,* the budget will have to be resubmitted.

Revising a fused sentence is also easy. All you have to do is include appropriate punctuation and any necessary connecting words.

23a   Punctuating independent clauses

In case you are unfamiliar with or unsure about the conventions for punctuating independent clauses, here is a short review.

A comma and a coordinating conjunction can join two independent clauses (see **35a**). The coordinating conjunction indicates the relationship between the two clauses. For example, *and* signals addition, whereas *but* and *yet* signal contrast. The comma precedes the conjunction.

> INDEPENDENT CLAUSE, **and** INDEPENDENT CLAUSE.

The new store opened this morning, **and** the owners greeted everyone at the door.

A semicolon can join two independent clauses that are closely related. A semicolon generally signals addition or contrast.

> INDEPENDENT CLAUSE; INDEPENDENT CLAUSE.

One of the owners comes from this area; the other grew up in Costa Rica.

A semicolon may also precede an independent clause that begins with a conjunctive adverb such as *however* or *nevertheless*. Notice that a comma follows this type of connecting word.

The store will be open late on Fridays and Saturdays; **however,** it will be closed all day on Sundays.

BEYOND THE RULE

PUNCTUATION IN SENTENCES CONTAINING CONJUNCTIVE ADVERBS

A comma used to set off a conjunctive adverb is sometimes omitted when there is no risk of misreading.

(Continued on page 518)

(Continued from page 517)

The sea was unusually hot; **thus** the coral turned white.
[No misreading is possible, so the comma can be omitted.]

He was so nervous that his stomach was churning; **however,** he answered the question calmly and accurately.
[The comma is needed. Without it, *however* might be interpreted as meaning "in whatever way" rather than "in contrast." COMPARE: However he answered the question, he would offend someone.]

For more examples, visit **www.harbrace.com**.

A colon can join two independent clauses. The second clause usually explains or elaborates the first.

INDEPENDENT CLAUSE: INDEPENDENT CLAUSE.

The owners extended a special offer: anyone who makes a purchase during the opening will receive a 10 percent discount.

A period separates clauses into distinct sentences.

INDEPENDENT CLAUSE. INDEPENDENT CLAUSE.

The store is located on the corner of Pine Street and First Avenue. It was formerly an insurance office.

Occasionally, commas are used between independent clauses, but only when the clauses are short, parallel in form, and unified in meaning.

They came, they shopped, they left.

Commas are also used to separate a statement from an attached question (also called a **tag question**).

You went to the grand opening, **didn't you?**

For more information on punctuating sentences, see chapters **35**, **36**, and **39**.

| **23b** | **Two methods for identifying comma splices and fused sentences** |

If you have trouble recognizing comma splices or fused sentences, try one of the following methods.

1. Locate a sentence that might have one of these problems. It may have a comma or no punctuation at all. Put the sentence in this frame:

   They do not understand the idea that _____.

   Only complete sentences will make sense in the frame. If just part of a test sentence fits into the frame, you have probably located a comma splice or a fused sentence.

   Test sentence: The wild Bactrian camel, a two-humped camel living in the Gobi Desert, can drink salt water.

   Test: They do not understand the idea that *the wild Bactrian camel, a two-humped camel living in the Gobi Desert, can drink salt water.*

   [The sentence makes sense. No revision is necessary.]

   Test sentence: Male proboscis monkeys have oddly shaped large noses, they also have unusual webbed paws.

   Test: They do not understand the idea that *male proboscis monkeys have oddly shaped large noses, they also have unusual webbed paws.*

   [The sentence does not make sense because there are two sentences completing the frame, rather than one, so the test sentence needs to be revised.]

   Revision: *Male proboscis monkeys have oddly shaped large noses. They also have unusual webbed paws.*

2. Try to rewrite a possibly incorrect sentence as a question that can be answered with *yes* or *no.* If just part of the sentence makes sense, you have likely found a comma splice or a fused sentence.

   Test sentence: The Arctic tern migrates from the Arctic to Antarctica.

   Test: *Does the Arctic tern migrate from the Arctic to Antarctica?*

   [The question makes sense. No revision is necessary.]

   Test sentence: Meerkats use their claws to forage for food they frequently prey on scorpions.

   Test: *Do meerkats use their claws to forage for food they frequently prey on scorpions?*

[The question does not make sense because only one of the two sentences has been made into a question. The test sentence should be revised.]

Revision: *Meerkats use their claws to forage for food. They frequently prey on scorpions.*

Once you have identified a problematic sentence, you can simply correct it (see **23c**), or you can deepen your analysis by determining whether the problem is a comma splice or a fused sentence. To make such a determination, follow these steps.

1. Notice how many pairs of grammatical subjects and verbs are in the sentence (see **20b**).
   a. Find the verbs.
   b. Match verbs to subjects.

   (1) Male proboscis monkeys[S] have[V] oddly shaped large noses, they[S] also have[V] unusual webbed paws. [two pairs]

   (2) Meerkats[S] use[V] their claws to forage for food they[S] frequently prey[V] on scorpions. [two pairs]

2. Look for the punctuation that separates the pairs of subjects and verbs (if there are at least two). Sentence (1) has a comma. Sentence (2) has no punctuation.
3. If no punctuation separates the pairs, you have found a fused sentence, unless there is a dependent clause present (see **21b(2)**). Sentence (2) is a fused sentence.

   Meerkats use their claws to forage for food ~~they~~ [. They] frequently prey on scorpions.

   Notice, however, that the following sentence includes a dependent clause and thus is not fused.

   Meerkats use their claws to forage for food, which frequently consists of scorpions and beetles.

4. If a comma separates the pairs of subjects and verbs, you may have found a comma splice.

a. If the comma is followed by a coordinating conjunction or a nonessential (nonrestrictive) dependent clause (see 35d), the sentence does not contain a comma splice.

Male proboscis monkeys have oddly shaped large noses, and they also have unusual webbed paws.

A male proboscis monkey has an oddly shaped large nose, whose size may attract mates.

b. If there is neither a coordinating conjunction nor a nonrestrictive dependent clause, as in sentence (1), the sentence contains a comma splice.

Male proboscis monkeys have oddly shaped large noses~~, they~~ ^. They also have unusual webbed paws.

You can also find comma splices and fused sentences by remembering that they commonly occur in certain circumstances:

- With transitional words and phrases such as *however, therefore,* and *for example* (see also 23c)

  Comma splice: The director is not able to meet with you this week~~,~~ ^; however ^, next week she will have time on Monday and Tuesday.

  [Notice that a semicolon replaces the comma.]

- When an explanation or an example is given in the second sentence

  Fused sentence: The cultural center has a new collection of spear points ^. ~~many~~ Many of them were donated by a retired anthropologist.

- When a positive clause follows a negative clause

  Comma splice: A World Cup victory is not just an everyday sporting event~~, it~~ ^. It is a national celebration.

- When the subject of the second clause is a pronoun whose antecedent is in the preceding clause

  Fused sentence: Lake Baikal is located in southern Russia ^. ~~it~~ It is 394 miles long.

23c Revising comma splices and fused sentences

If you find comma splices or fused sentences in your writing, try one of the following methods to revise them.

(1) Use a comma and a coordinating conjunction to link clauses.

By linking clauses with a comma and a coordinating conjunction (such as *and* or *but*), you signal the relationship between them (addition or contrast, for example).

> Fused sentence: Joseph completed the first experiment ∧ he will complete the other by Friday.
>
> *, and*

> Comma splice: Some diplomats applauded the treaty, ∧ others opposed it vehemently.
>
> *but*

(2) Use a semicolon or a colon to link clauses or a period to separate them.

When you link independent clauses with a semicolon (see chapter **36**), you signal their connection indirectly. There are no explicit conjunctions to use as cues. The semicolon usually indicates addition or contrast. When you link clauses with a colon (see **39d(1)**), the second clause serves as an explanation or an elaboration of the first. A period (see **39a(1)**) indicates that each clause is a complete sentence, distinct from surrounding sentences.

> Comma splice: Our division's reports are posted on our Web page, hard copies are available by request.
>
> Revision 1: Our division's reports are posted on our Web page; hard copies are available by request.
>
> Revision 2: Our division's reports are posted on our Web page. Hard copies are available by request.

> Fused sentence: His choice was difficult ∧ he would either lose his job or betray his ethical principles.
>
> :

(3) Rewrite one clause as a phrase or as a dependent clause.

A dependent clause (**21b(2)**) includes a subordinating conjunction such as *although* or *because*, which indicates how the dependent and independent clauses are related (in expressing cause and effect, for example). Phrases that do not include prepositions (see **21a**) suggest relationships less directly because they do not include explicit connecting words.

> Comma splice: The wind had blown down trees and power lines, the whole city was without electricity for several hours.

> Revision 1: **Because of the downed power lines,** the whole city was without electricity for several hours. [using a phrase]

> Revision 2: **Because the wind had blown down power lines,** the whole city was without electricity for several hours. [using a dependent clause]

(4) Integrate one clause into the other.

When you integrate clauses, you generally retain the important details but omit or change some words.

> Fused sentence: The proposal covers all but one point it does not describe how the project will be assessed.

> Revision: The proposal covers all the points except assessment procedures.

(5) Use transitional words or phrases to link independent clauses.

Another way to revise comma splices and fused sentences is to use transitional words (conjunctive adverbs) or transitional phrases (see the lists that follow). You can use these words or phrases to begin new sentences.

> Fused sentence: Sexual harassment is not just an issue for women. After all, men can be sexually harassed too.

You can also use them to join two clauses into one sentence.

> Comma splice: The word *status* refers to relative position within a group; however, it is often used to indicate only positions of prestige.

CONJUNCTIVE ADVERBS

also	however	next
anyhow	incidentally	otherwise
anyway	indeed	similarly
besides	instead	still
consequently	likewise	then
finally	meanwhile	therefore
furthermore	moreover	thus
hence	nevertheless	

TRANSITIONAL PHRASES

after all	even so	in fact
as a result	for example	in other words
at any rate	in addition	on the contrary
at the same time	in comparison	on the other hand
by the way	in contrast	that is

A transitional word or phrase may either begin an independent clause or take another position within it. When it appears within the clause, the transitional word or phrase is generally set off by commas.

She believed that daily exercise has many benefits**; however,** she couldn't fit it into her schedule. [The conjunctive adverb begins the second independent clause and is positioned after a semicolon and before a comma (see also **36a**).]

She believed that daily exercise has many benefits. She couldn't, **however,** fit it into her schedule. [The conjunctive adverb appears later in the second clause. In this position, it is set off by commas.]

The following checklist will help you find and fix comma splices and fused sentences.

CHECKLIST for Comma Splices and Fused Sentences

1 **Common Sites for Comma Splices or Fused Sentences**

- With transitional words or phrases such as *however, therefore,* and *for example*
- When an explanation or an example occurs in the second sentence
- When a positive clause follows a negative clause
- When the subject of the second clause is a pronoun whose antecedent is in the preceding clause

2 **How to Identify a Comma Splice or a Fused Sentence**

a. Notice how many pairs of subjects and verbs (see **20b**) are in the sentence.

  (1) Find the verbs.

  (2) Match the verbs to their subjects.

b. Look for the punctuation that separates the pairs of subjects and verbs (if there are at least two).

c. If no punctuation separates the pairs and no dependent clause is present, you have found a fused sentence.

d. If a comma separates the pairs, you may have found a comma splice.

  (1) If there is a coordinating conjunction or a nonessential dependent clause, there is no comma splice.

  (2) If there is no coordinating conjunction or nonessential dependent clause, there is a comma splice.

3 **How to Fix Comma Splices and Fused Sentences**

- Link the clauses with a comma and a coordinating conjunction.
- Link the clauses, using a semicolon or a colon.
- Separate the clauses by punctuating each as a sentence.
- Make one clause dependent.

(Continued on page 526)

(Continued from page 525)

- Reduce one clause to a phrase.
- Rewrite the sentence, integrating one clause into the other.
- Use transitional words or phrases to link the clauses.

As you edit fused sentences and comma splices, you will refine the connections between your sentences, making them clearer and more coherent. By taking the time to revise, you will be helping your readers follow your train of thought. For more information on joining clauses, see chapter **28**.

Exercise 1

Connect each pair of sentences in two of the following ways: (a) join them with a semicolon or colon, (b) join them with a coordinating conjunction, (c) reduce one to a phrase or dependent clause (see **21c(3)** for a list of subordinating conjunctions), or (d) integrate one clause into the other.

1. Our national parks offer a variety of settings. They attract millions of visitors every year.
2. The Grand Teton National Park includes a sixteen-peak mountain range. It offers extensive hiking trails and wildlife-viewing opportunities.
3. Yellowstone National Park is generally full of tourists. The geysers and cliffs are worth the visit.
4. Hikers especially enjoy their vacations at Yellowstone National Park. The park consists of two million acres of backcountry perfect for hiking.
5. Vacationers enchanted by cascading water should visit Yosemite National Park. The waterfalls at Yosemite reach heights of more than two thousand feet.

Exercise 2

Connect each pair of sentences by including a transitional word or phrase and any necessary punctuation.

1. Discoveries in neuroscience have yielded many benefits. Researchers have developed medication for schizophrenia and Tourette's syndrome.
2. The average human brain weighs about three pounds. The average brain of a sperm whale weighs seventeen pounds.
3. Researchers studying brain hemispheres have found that many professional musicians process music in their left hemisphere. The notion that musicians and artists depend on the right side of their brain is considered outmoded.
4. The brain needs water to function properly. Dehydration commonly leads to lethargy and hinders learning.
5. The body of a brain cell can move. Most brain cells stay put, extending axons outward.

23d Divided quotations

When you divide quotations (see also **11d** and chapter **38**) with attributive tags such as *he said* or *she asked,* be sure to use a period between independent clauses.

Comma splice: "Beauty brings copies of itself into being," states Elaine

Scarry, "it makes us draw it, take photographs of it, or describe it to other

people."

[Both parts of the quotation are complete sentences, so the attributive tag is attached to the first, and the sentence is punctuated with a period. The second sentence stands by itself.]

A comma separates two parts of a single quoted sentence.

> "Musing takes place in a kind of meadowlands of the imagination," writes
> Rebecca Solnit, "a part of the imagination that has not yet been plowed,
> developed, or put to any immediately practical use." [Because the divided
> quotation is a single sentence, a comma is used.]

Exercise 3

Revise the following paragraph so that no comma splices remain.
Some sentences may not need revision.

[1]In the introduction to his book of true stories, *I Thought My
Father Was God,* Paul Auster describes how he was able to collect these
accounts of real and sometimes raw experience. [2]In October 1999,
Auster, in collaboration with National Public Radio, began the
National Story Project, during an interview on the radio program
Weekend All Things Considered, he invited listeners to send in their
stories about unusual events—"true stories that sounded like fiction."
[3]In just one year, over four thousand stories were submitted, Auster
read every one of them. [4]"Of the four thousand stories I have read,
most have been compelling enough to hold me until the last word,"
Auster affirms, "Most have been written with simple, straightforward
conviction, and most have done honor to the people who sent them
in." [5]Some of the stories Auster collected can now be read in his
anthology, choosing stories for the collection was difficult, though.
[6]"For every story about a dream or an animal or a missing object,"
explains Auster, "there were dozens of others that were submitted,
dozens of others that could have been chosen."

24

MODIFIERS

Modifiers are words, phrases, or clauses that modify; that is, they qualify or limit the meaning of other words. For example, if you were to describe a sandwich as "humdrum" or "lacking sufficient mustard" or as something "that is eaten only under duress," you would be using modifiers. Modifiers enliven writing with details; if they are not placed correctly, however, they can disrupt coherence. As you revise, be sure to place your modifiers close to the words they modify. This chapter will help you

- recognize modifiers (**24a**),
- use conventional comparative and superlative forms (**24b**),
- place modifiers effectively (**24c–d**), and
- revise double negatives (**24e**).

24a Recognizing modifiers

The most common modifiers are adjectives and adverbs. **Adjectives** modify nouns and pronouns; **adverbs** modify verbs, adjectives, and other adverbs. (See **20a(4–5)**.) You can distinguish an adjective from an adverb, then, by determining what type of word is being modified.

Adjectives	**Adverbs**
She looked **curious.** [modifies pronoun]	She looked at me **curiously.** [modifies verb]
productive meeting [modifies noun]	**highly** productive meeting [modifies adjective]
a **quick** lunch [modifies noun]	**very** quickly [modifies adverb]

In addition, consider the form of the modifier. Many adjectives end with one of these suffixes: *-able, -al, -ful, -ic, ish, -less,* or *-y.*

accept**able**   rent**al**   event**ful**   angel**ic**   sheep**ish**   effort**less**   sleep**y**

Adjective Suffixes in Other Languages

In some languages, adjectives and nouns agree in number. In Spanish, for example, when a noun is plural, the adjective is plural as well: *vistas claras.* In English, however, adjectives do not have a plural form: *clear views.*

Present and past participles are most frequently used in verb phrases (see **26a(5)**), but they can also be used as adjectives.

a **determining** factor
[present participle]

a **determined** effort
[past participle]

Be sure to include the complete *-ed* ending of a past participle.

Please see the ~~enclose~~ *enclosed* documents for more details.

THINKING RHETORICALLY ABOUT

ADJECTIVES

When your rhetorical situation calls for vivid images or emotional intensity, choose appropriate adjectives to convey these qualities. That is, instead of describing a movie that you did not like with the overused adjective *bad* or *boring,* you could say that it was *tedious* or *mind-numbing.* When you sense that you might be using a lackluster adjective, search for an alternative in a thesaurus. If any of the words listed there are unfamiliar, be sure to look them up in a dictionary so that you do not misuse them.

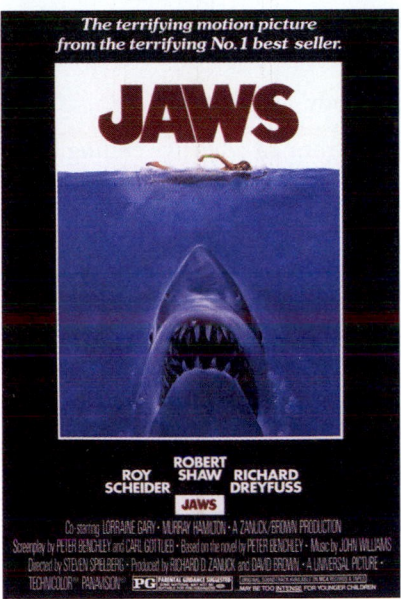

Movie ads include descriptive adjectives.

Using Participles as Adjectives

Both present participles and past participles are used as adjectives; however, they cannot be used interchangeably. For example, when you want to indicate an emotion, use a present participle with a noun referring to someone or something that is the cause of the emotion. In the phrase *the exciting tennis match,* the tennis match is the cause of the excitement. Use a past participle with a noun referring to someone who experiences an emotion. In the phrase *the excited crowd,* the crowd is experiencing the excitement.

Here is a list of commonly confused participles:

annoying, annoyed	frustrating, frustrated
boring, bored	interesting, interested
confusing, confused	surprising, surprised
embarrassing, embarrassed	tiring, tired

The easiest type of adverb to identify is the **adverb of manner** (see **20a(5)**). It is formed by adding *-ly* to an adjective.

careful**ly**   unpleasant**ly**   silent**ly**

If an adverb is formed from an adjective ending in *-y,* the *y* is changed to *i* before *-ly* is added.

eas**y** [adjective]   eas**ily** [adverb]

If the adverb is formed from an adjective ending in *-le,* the *-e* is changed to *-y.*

simp**le** [adjective]   simp**ly** [adverb]

However, not all adverbs end in *-ly.* Adverbs that indicate time or place (*today, tomorrow, here,* and *there*) do not have the *-ly* ending. In addition, not all words that end in *-ly* are adverbs. Certain adjectives that are formed from nouns have the *-ly* ending (*cost, costly; friend, friendly*).

A few words—*fast* and *well,* for example—can function as either adjectives or adverbs.

They like **fast** cars. [adjective]

They ran **fast** enough to catch the bus. [adverb]

(1) Nouns can be modifiers.

Adjectives and adverbs are the most common modifiers, but nouns can also be modifiers (***movie** critic, **reference** manual*).

Noun Modifiers
In noun combinations, the first noun is the modifier. Different word orders produce different meanings.

A *company phone* is a phone that belongs to the company.

A *phone company* is a company whose business involves phones.

(2) Phrases and clauses can be modifiers.

Participial phrases, prepositional phrases, and some infinitive phrases are modifiers (see **21a(3–4)**).

> **Growing in popularity every year,** mountain bikes now dominate the market. [participial phrase]

> Mountain bikes first became popular **in the 1980s.** [prepositional phrase]

> Some people use mountain bikes **to commute to work.** [infinitive phrase]

Both adjectival clauses and adverbial clauses are modifiers.

> BMX bicycles have frames **that are relatively small compared to those of other types of bikes.** [adjectival clause]

> **Although mountain bikes are designed for off-road use,** many people ride them on city streets. [adverbial clause]

Exercise 1

Underline the modifiers in the following paragraph.

1Although it seems unbelievable, there once was a race of little people. **2**The first skeleton of *Homo floresiensis* was found in September 2003 on an island near Bali. **3**Archaeologists working in the area excavated the skeleton from a limestone cave. **4**They believe that this species of human is a version of *Homo erectus*, who arrived on the island and became small to adapt to its conditions.

(3) Adjectives and adverbs are sometimes confused.

An adjective used after a sensory linking verb (such as *look, smell, taste, sound,* or *feel*) modifies the subject of the sentence. A common error is to use an adverb after this type of linking verb.

> bad
> I felt ~~badly~~ about missing the rally. [The adjective *bad* modifies *I.*]

These sensory verbs are confusing because they can be either linking verbs, as in the previous example, or action verbs. When they are action verbs, they should be modified by adverbs.

She looked ∧angry at the referee. [The adverb *angrily* modifies *looked*.] *(angrily inserted, angry struck)*

BUT She looked angry. [The adjective *angry* modifies *she*.]

Good and *well* are easy to confuse. In academic rhetorical situations, *good* is considered an adjective and so is not used with action verbs.

The whole team played ∧good. *(well inserted, good struck)*

Another frequent error is the dropping of *-ly* endings from adverbs. Although you may not hear the ending in spoken sentences, be sure to include it when you write.

We were looking for the ∧local known island protected as a wildlife refuge. *(locally inserted, local struck)*

Exercise 2

Revise the following sentences to use adverbs considered conventional in academic writing.

1. My brother said he was real nervous.
2. He did not think he could drive good enough to pass the driver's test.
3. I told him that to pass he would just have to drive reasonable well.
4. He looked calmly as he got into the tester's car.
5. As I knew he would, my brother passed his test easy.

24b Comparatives and superlatives

Many adjectives and adverbs change form to show degrees of quality, quantity, time, distance, manner, and so on. The **positive form** of an adjective or adverb is the word you would look for in a dictionary: *hard, urgent, deserving*. The **comparative form,** which either ends in *-er* or is preceded by *more* or *less*, compares two elements: I worked *harder* than I ever had before. The **superlative form,** which either ends in *-est* or is preceded by *most* or *least*, compares three or more elements: Jason is the *hardest* worker I have ever met.

Positive	Comparative	Superlative
hard	harder	hardest
urgent	more/less urgent	most/least urgent
deserving	more/less deserving	most/least deserving

The following guidelines can help you decide when to add the suffix *-er* or *-est* to show degree and when to use *more/less* or *most/least*.

GUIDELINES FOR FORMING COMPARATIVES AND SUPERLATIVES

- One-syllable words generally take *-er* and *-est* endings: *fast, faster, fastest.*

- Two-syllable adjectives ending in a consonant and *-y* also generally take *-er* and *-est* endings, with the *y* changed to an *i: noisy, noisier, noisiest.*

- Two-syllable adjectives ending in *-ct, -nt,* or *-st* are preceded by *more/less* or *most/least: less exact, least exact; more recent, most recent; more honest, most honest.*

- Adverbs of manner ending in *-ly* are preceded by *more/less* or *most/least: more fully, most fully.*

- Two-syllable adjectives with the suffix *-ous, -ish, -ful, -ing,* or *-ed* are preceded by *more/less* or *most/least: more/most famous; more/most squeamish; less/least careful; more/most lasting; less/least depressed.*

- Two-syllable adjectives ending in *-er, -ow,* or *-some* take either *-er* and *-est* or one of the preceding qualifiers: *tenderer, tenderest, more/less tender, most/least tender; narrower, narrowest, more/less narrow, most/least narrow; handsomer, handsomest, more/less handsome, most/least handsome.*

- Words of three or more syllables are preceded by *more/less* or *most/least: less/least fortunate; more/most intelligent.*

- Some modifiers have irregular comparative and superlative forms:

  little, less, least

  good/well, better, best

(Continued on page 536)

(Continued from page 535)

> bad/badly, worse, worst
>
> far, further/farther, furthest/farthest

(See also the **Glossary of Usage**.)

(1) Effective comparisons are complete and logical.

When you use the comparative form of an adjective or adverb, be sure to indicate what two elements are being compared. The revision of the following sentence makes it clear that the metropolitan area is currently bigger than it was in the past.

The metropolitan area is much **bigger** ∧ *now than it was five years ago*.

Without this revision, the reader may wonder whether the metropolitan area is bigger than a rural area or some other area. Occasionally, the second element in a comparison is implied. The word *paper* does not have to be repeated after *second* in the sentence below.

> She wrote two papers, and the instructor gave her a **better** grade on the second.

A comparison should also be logical. The following example illogically compares *population* and *Wabasha*.

> The **population** of Winona is larger than **Wabasha.**

This faulty comparison can be revised in three ways:

- Repeat the word that names what is being compared.

  The **population** of Winona is larger than the **population** of Wabasha.

- Use a pronoun that corresponds to the first element in the comparison.

  The **population** of Winona is larger than **that** of Wabasha.

- Use possessive forms.

  Winona's population is larger than **Wabasha's.**

(2) A double comparative or superlative is redundant.

Use either an ending or a preceding adverb, not both, to form a comparative or superlative.

The first bridge is **more narrower** than the second.

The **most narrowest** bridge is in the northern part of the state.

BEYOND THE RULE

ABSOLUTE MODIFIERS

Dictionaries list comparative forms of many adjectives or adverbs that have absolute meanings, as in *a more perfect society, the deadest campus,* and *less completely exhausted.* Such comparisons are rarely found in academic writing. For more information, visit **www.harbrace.com**.

Exercise 3

Provide the correct comparative or superlative form of each modifier within parentheses.

1. Amphibians can be divided into three groups. Frogs and toads are in the (common) group.
2. Because they do not have to maintain a specific body temperature, amphibians eat (frequently) than mammals do.
3. Reptiles may look like amphibians, but their skin is (dry).
4. During the Devonian period, (close) ancestors of amphibians were fish with fins that looked like legs.
5. In general, amphibians have (few) bones in their skeletons than do other animals with backbones.
6. Color markings on amphibians vary, though the back of an amphibian is usually (dark) than its belly.

24c Placement of modifiers

Your modifiers will be effective if you choose those with precise meanings and place them so that they add to the clarity and coherence of your sentences. A modifer whose placement confuses the meaning of a sentence is called a **misplaced modifier.**

(1) Place a modifier as close as possible to the relevant word or word group.

Modifiers such as *almost, even, hardly, just,* and *only* are clearest when they are placed right before the words they modify. Altering placement can alter meaning.

The committee can **only** nominate two members for the position.
[The committee cannot appoint or elect the two people to the position.]

The committee can nominate **only** two members for the position.
[The committee cannot nominate more than two members.]

Only the committee can nominate two members for the position.
[No person or group other than the committee can nominate members.]

(2) Place prepositional phrases and adjectival clauses as close as possible to the word or word group they modify.

Readers expect phrases and clauses to modify the nearest grammatical element. Misplaced phrases and clauses cause confusion.

She recorded the song from the movie that was her favorite.
her favorite

OR

She recorded a song from her favorite movie.

The following sentence is fine as long as Jesse wrote the proposal, not the review. If he wrote the review, the modifying clause should be moved, or the sentence should be recast.

I have not read the review of the proposal Jesse wrote.

I have not read the review ∧of the proposal ~~Jesse wrote~~.

Jesse wrote

OR

I have not read ∧~~the~~ review of the proposal ~~he wrote~~.

Jesse's

(3) Revise squinting modifiers so that they modify only one element.

A **squinting modifier** is one that might be interpreted as modifying either what precedes it or what follows it. Sentences containing such modifiers can confuse readers. To avoid such lack of clarity, reposition the modifier and/or provide appropriate punctuation.

Even though Erikson lists some advantages **overall** his vision of a successful business is faulty.

Revision: Even though Erikson lists some **overall** advantages**,** his vision of a successful business is faulty. [word repositioned; punctuation added]

Revision: Even though Erikson lists some advantages**, overall,** his vision of a successful business is faulty. [punctuation added]

Ordering Adjectives That Modify the Same Noun
In English, two or more adjectives modifying the same noun are used in a particular order based on their meanings. (The use of more than three consecutive adjectives is rare.) The following list shows the usual order of adjectives and gives examples.

Size	*large, small, tiny, miniscule*
Evaluator	*fascinating, painful, content*
Shape	*square, round, triangular*
Age	*young, old, aged, newborn, antique*
Color	*black, white, green, brown*
Nationality or geography	*Arabian, Cuban, Peruvian, Slavic*
Religion	*Jewish, Catholic, Protestant, Buddhist*
Material	*silk, paper, plastic, steel*

(Continued on page 540)

(Continued from page 539)

> We visited a **fascinating Italian** village.
>
> Marquita showed us her **new black** scarves.

Adverbs of Frequency
Adverbs of frequency (such as *always, never, sometimes,* and *often*) appear before one-word verbs.

> He **rarely** <u>goes</u> to horror movies.

However, these adverbs appear after a form of *be* when it is the main verb.

> Movies based on Stephen King novels <u>are</u> **always** popular.

When a sentence contains more than one verb in a verb phrase, the adverb of frequency is placed after the first auxiliary verb.

> My friends <u>have</u> **never** <u>seen</u> *The Shining.*
>
> I <u>have</u> **seldom** <u>been</u> frightened by a movie.

Exercise 4

Improve the clarity of the following sentences by moving the modifiers. Some sentences may not require editing.

1. In 1665, Sir Isaac Newton devised three laws about moving objects that are still discussed today.
2. According to one of the laws, an object only moves when force is applied.
3. Once in motion, something must force an object to slow down or to speed up; otherwise, it will continue at a constant speed.
4. Another law explains the variables affecting an object's movement.
5. Another of Newton's contributions is the law about action and reaction that engineers use to plan rocket launchings.
6. Scientists still use the laws of motion formulated by Newton over three hundred years ago to understand moving objects.

24d Revising dangling modifiers

Dangling modifiers are words, phrases, or reduced clauses that lack an appropriate noun, noun phrase, or pronoun to modify. To avoid including dangling modifiers in your essays, look carefully at any sentence that begins with a modifier. Be sure that the noun, noun phrase, or pronoun being modified is the subject of the sentence. Sometimes, a dangling modifier contains a form of an action verb, but the sentence has no clear actor performing that action or the actor is not in the subject position. Other times, a dangling modifier consists of adjectives that are modifying an object in the sentence rather than the subject. You can revise sentences that contain dangling modifiers in one of these ways:

■ Provide a noun or pronoun.

Working overtime, *we increased* our earnings ~~increased~~ dramatically.

[According to the original sentence, the earnings worked overtime.]

■ Move the modifier

The ~~Crouched and ugly, the~~ young boy gasped at the *crouched and ugly* phantom moving across the stage.

[According to the original sentence, the young boy was crouched and ugly.]

■ Reword the modifier.

After Richie gave his speech, ~~After listening to Richie's speech,~~ the mood in the room changed.

[According to the original sentence, the mood listened to the speech.]

Sentence modifiers and absolute phrases are not considered to be dangling.

Marcus played well in the final game, **on the whole.**

Considering all she's been through this year, Marge is remarkably cheerful.

Exercise 5

Revise the following sentences to eliminate misplaced and dangling modifiers. Some sentences may not require editing.

1. Climbing a mountain, fitness becomes all-important.
2. Getting to the top must be in doubt to make the climb a true adventure.
3. Having set their goals, the mountain must challenge the climbers.
4. In determining an appropriate challenge, considering safety precautions is necessary.
5. Taking care to stay roped together, accidents are less likely to occur.
6. Even when expecting sunny weather, rain gear should be packed.
7. Knowing how to rappel is necessary before descending a cliff.
8. Although adding extra weight, climbers should not leave home without a first-aid kit.
9. Climbers should not let themselves become frustrated if they are not immediately successful.
10. By taking pains at the beginning of a trip, agony can be averted at the end of a trip.

24e Double negatives

Most words that express negation are modifiers. The term **double negative** refers to the use of two negative words within a clause to express a single negation.

> He did**n't** keep ~~no~~ *any* records.

OR

> He ~~didn't keep~~ *kept* **no** records.

Because *hardly, barely,* and *scarcely* denote severely limited or negative conditions, using *not, nothing,* or *without* with any of these modifiers creates a double negative.

I couldn't **hardly** ~~quit~~ in the middle of the job.

OR

I could**n't** ~~**hardly**~~ quit in the middle of the job.

The motion passed with ~~**not**~~ **scarcely** a protest.

OR

The motion passed with ~~**not scarcely**~~ a protest.

[handwritten: little inserted before "not scarcely"]

Occasionally, emphasis requires the use of two negatives in a sentence. Such a construction is not considered a double negative.

It would**n't** be safe **not** to install smoke detectors. [This construction is permissible when *not* is being emphasized. Otherwise, the sentence should be revised. COMPARE: It would be dangerous not to install smoke detectors.]

Negation in Other Languages
The use of two negative words in one sentence is common in languages such as Spanish:

Yo **no** compré **nada.** [I didn't buy anything.]

If your native language allows this type of negation, be especially careful to check for and revise any double negatives you find in your English essays.

Exercise 6

Using what you have learned in this chapter, revise the following sentences to remove modifier errors.

1. As a woman in the twentieth century, the life of Gertrude Bell was unusual.
2. Young, wealthy, and intelligent, many people were impressed by the red-headed Bell.
3. Among the first women to graduate from Oxford, she couldn't hardly be satisfied with domestic life.

4. Instead, Bell traveled to what were considered the most remotest countries in the world, saw the wonders of the Ottoman Empire, and explored the desert of Iraq.

5. Several of the Arab sheiks who knew Bell thought that she acted bold.

6. The war in Iraq didn't give Bell no time to pursue her research.

7. She became an Arab rebellion supporter.

8. While traveling in Iraq, meetings with important politicians took place.

9. In 1921, Winston Churchill invited Bell to a conference in the Middle East because the other Great Britain conference participants knew little about Iraq.

10. When the photo of the conference participants was taken, Bell looked elegantly in her feathered hat and silk dress among the thirty-six black-suited males.

25

PRONOUNS

When you use pronouns effectively, you add clarity and coherence to your writing. However, if you do not provide the words, phrases, or clauses that make the pronoun reference clear, you might unintentionally cause confusion. As you revise your work, be on the lookout for pronouns that do not have conventional forms or specific antecedents. This chapter will help you

- recognize various types of pronouns (**25a**),
- determine the forms of pronouns (**25b**),
- make sure that pronouns agree with their antecedents (**25c**), and
- provide clear pronoun references (**25d**).

25a Recognizing pronouns

A **pronoun** is commonly defined as a word that refers to either a noun or a word group acting as a noun. The noun, noun phrase, or noun clause being referred to by a pronoun may be in the same sentence or in nearby sentences. English has several types of pronouns: personal, relative, interrogative, and reflexive/intensive pronouns.

(1) Personal pronouns are identified according to person, number, and case.

To understand the uses of personal pronouns, you must first be able to recognize person, number, and case. **Person** indicates whether a pronoun refers to the writer (**first person**), the reader (**second person**), or any other entity being discussed (**third person**). **Number** reveals whether a pronoun is singular or plural (see also **26b**). **Case** refers to the form a pronoun takes depending on its function in the sentence. Pronouns can be subjects, objects, or possessives. When they function as subjects (see **20d(1)**), they are in the subjective case; when they function as objects (see **20d(2)**), they are in the objective case; and when they are possessives, they are in the possessive case (see **37a**). Possessives can be divided into two groups based on whether they are followed by nouns. The possessive determiners *my, your, his, her, its, our,* and *their* are all followed by nouns; the possessive pronouns *mine, yours, his, hers, ours,* and *theirs* are not.

> **Their** budget is higher than **ours.** [*Their* is a possessive determiner; *ours* is a possessive pronoun.]

CASE:	Subjective		Objective		Possessive	
NUMBER:	Singular	Plural	Singular	Plural	Singular	Plural
First person	I	we	me	us	my mine	our ours
Second person	you	you	you	you	your yours	your yours
Third person	he, she, it	they	him, her, it	them	his, her, hers, its	their theirs

THINKING RHETORICALLY ABOUT

PRONOUNS

As you write, consider which pronouns are called for by your rhetorical situation. In some situations, you will be expected to use *I*; in others, you will not. In some situations, you will address the reader as *you* (as is done in this handbook), but in others, you will avoid addressing the reader directly. Whatever pronouns you decide to use, be sure to use them consistently.

First, ~~one~~ you must determine your priorities.

OR

First, one must determine one's priorities.

(2) A relative pronoun usually relates an adjectival clause to a noun or noun phrase in the main clause.

An adjectival clause (or relative clause) ordinarily begins with one of these relative pronouns: *who, whom, which, that,* or *whose.* To provide a link between this type of dependent clause and the main clause, the relative pronoun corresponds to a word or words in the main clause called the **antecedent.**

ant   *rel pro*

The students talked to **a reporter who** had just returned from overseas.

Notice that if you rewrite the dependent clause as a separate independent clause, you use the antecedent in place of the relative pronoun:

A reporter had just returned from overseas.

Who, whose, and *whom* ordinarily refer to people; *which* refers to things; *that* refers to either people or things. The possessive pronoun *whose* (used in place of the awkward *of which*) sometimes refers to things.

The poem, **whose** author is unknown, has recently been set to music.

	Refers to people	Refers to things	Refers to either
Subjective	who	which	that
Objective	whom	which	that
Possessive			whose

Knowing the difference between an essential clause and a nonessential clause will help you decide whether to use *which* or *that.* A clause that a reader needs in order to identify the antecedent correctly is an **essential clause.**

ant   *ess cl*

The person who presented the award was last year's winner.

If the essential clause were omitted from this sentence, you would not know which person was last year's winner.

A **nonessential clause** is *not* needed for correct identification of the antecedent and is thus set off by commas. A nonessential clause often follows a proper noun (a specific name).

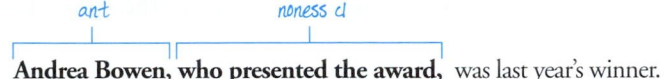

Andrea Bowen, who presented the award, was last year's winner.

Notice that even if the nonessential clause were removed from this sentence, you would still know who last year's winner was.

According to a traditional grammar rule, *that* is used in essential adjectival clauses, and *which* is used in nonessential adjectival clauses.

I need a job **that** pays well.

I took a job, **which** pays well enough.

However, some professional writers do not follow both parts of this rule. Although they will not use *that* in nonessential clauses, they will use *which* in essential clauses.

According to Trask, *nonverbal communication* refers to "any aspect of communication **which** does not involve words."

(3) Interrogative pronouns introduce questions.

Interrogative pronouns are question words that appear in the same positions that nouns do. *What* and *which* can be either subjects or objects. *Who* is used as a subject, and its counterpart, *whom*, is used as an object. *Whose* is a possessive interrogative pronoun.

Subjective interrogative pronoun	**Who** won the award?
Objective interrogative pronoun	**Whom** did you consult?
Possessive interrogative pronoun	**Whose** is it?

(4) Reflexive pronouns direct the action back to the subject; intensive pronouns are used for emphasis.

Myself, yourself, himself, herself, itself, ourselves, yourselves, and *themselves* are used as either **reflexive pronouns** or **intensive pronouns.** Both types of pronouns are objects and must be accompanied by subjects. Reflexive pronouns are used when the actor and the recipient of the action are the same. Intensive pronouns are used to provide emphasis.

Reflexive pronoun   **He** was always talking to **himself.**

Intensive pronoun   **I, myself,** delivered the letter.

Avoid using a reflexive pronoun as a subject. A common error is using *myself* in a compound subject.

Ms. Palmquist and ~~myself~~ *I* discussed our concern with the senator.

Hisself and *theirselves* are inappropriate in college or professional writing. Instead, use *himself* and *themselves.* Attempts to create a gender-neutral singular reflexive pronoun have resulted in such forms as *themself;* these forms are also inappropriate in college or professional writing.

Each student completed a project by ~~themself~~ *himself or herself*.

25b Pronoun case

The term *case* refers to the form a pronoun or determiner takes to indicate its relationship to other words in a sentence. There are three cases: subjective, objective, and possessive. The following sentence includes all three.

He [subjective] wants **his** [possessive] legislators to help **him** [objective].

(1) Pronouns in the subject or subject complement position are in the subjective case.

A pronoun that is the subject of a sentence, even when it is part of a compound subject (see **20b**), is in the subjective case. To determine which pronoun form is correct in a compound subject, say the sentence using the pronoun alone, omitting the noun. For the following sentence, notice that "*Me* solved the problem" sounds strange.

                      and I
~~Me and~~ Marisa ⌄ solved the problem.

Also, remember that when you use the pronoun *I* in a compound subject, you should place it last in the sequence. If the compound subject contains two pronouns, test each one by itself to ensure that you are using the appropriate case.

He
⌄ ~~Him~~ and I joined the club in July.

A subject complement renames the subject (see **20d(3)**). Pronouns functioning as subject complements should also be in the subjective case.

                              I
The first to arrive were Kevin and ⌄ ~~me~~.

In conversational English, "It's *me*" (or *him, her, us,* or *them*) is acceptable.

Noun or Pronoun as Subject
In some languages, a noun in the subject position may be followed by a pronoun. In Standardized English, though, such a pronoun should be omitted.

My roommate ~~he~~ works in the library for three hours a week.

(2) Pronouns functioning as objects are in the objective case.

Whenever a pronoun is an object—a direct object, an indirect object, or the object of a preposition—it takes the **objective case.**

Direct object	Miguel loves **her**.
Indirect object	Miguel gave **her** his love.
Object of a preposition	Miguel cares deeply for **her**.

Pronouns in compound objects are also in the objective case.

                        me
They will appoint you or ⌄ ~~I~~. [direct object]

me
They lent Tom and ~~I~~ money for tuition. [indirect object]

me
He gets nowhere by scolding Jane or ~~I~~. [direct object of the gerund]

me
Dad wanted Sheila and ~~I~~ to keep the old car. [direct object of the sentence; subject of the infinitive phrase (see **25b(c)**)]

me
Janice sat between my brother and ~~I~~. [object of the preposition]

To determine whether to use the subjective or objective case, remember to say the sentence with just the pronoun. Notice that "Dad wanted *I* to keep the old car" does not sound right. Another test is to substitute *we* and *us*. If *we* sounds natural, use the subjective case. If *us* sounds better, use the objective case, as in "Janice sat between *us*."

(3) Possessive forms are easily confused with contractions.

Its, their, and *whose* are possessive forms. Be sure that you do not confuse them with common contractions: *it's* (*it is*), *they're* (*they are*), and *who's* (*who is*).

(4) Appositive pronouns are in the same case as the nouns they rename.

If the noun that an appositive pronoun renames is in the subjective case, the appositive pronoun should be in the subjective case.

I
The red team—Rebecca, Leroy, and ~~me~~—won by only one point.

Likewise, if the noun is in the objective case, the appositive pronoun should be in the objective case.

me
A trophy was presented to the red team—Rebecca, Leroy, and ~~I~~.

When the order is reversed and a pronoun is followed by a noun, the pronoun still must be in the same case as the noun.

We
~~Us~~ students need this policy.

us
The director told ~~we~~ extras to go home.

To test the case of a pronoun that is followed by an appositive, remove the appositive.

We need this policy.

The director told **us** to go home.

Grammar checkers often provide minimal help in identifying case errors. A grammar checker found nothing wrong with this sentence: Carol and me agree that Mark is a good athlete. In addition, grammar checkers miss as many errors involving *who/whom* as they find (see **25b(5)**), and they almost never find problems with pronoun-antecedent agreement (**25c**). See **Using a Grammar Checker** on page 461.

Exercise 1

Revise the following paragraph, using appropriate cases for pronouns. Some sentences may not require editing.

¹When I was twelve, my family lived in Guatemala for a year. ²My parents taught English at a university; me and my younger brother went to a local school. ³Although the Spanish language was new to both Sam and I, we learned to speak it quickly. ⁴At first, we couldn't understand much at all, but with the help of a tutor, who we met every day after school, we started learning "survival" Spanish. ⁵Sam had better pronunciation than me, but I learned vocabulary and grammar faster than him. ⁶After we learned to ask and answer some basic questions, we started making friends, whom eventually introduced us to they're own version of Spanish. ⁷They taught us slang words that our tutor didn't even know. ⁸However, though Sam and me benefited from all our Spanish lessons, we learned the language so quickly because, unless we were with our parents or by ourself, we listened to it, read it, wrote it, and spoke it all day long.

(5) *Who/whoever* and *whom/whomever* are often misused.

You may be able to avoid confusion about the correct usage of *who/whoever* and *whom/whomever* if you remember that the case of these pronouns is determined by their grammatical function in a dependent clause. A pronoun functioning as the subject in a dependent clause takes the subjective case, even if the whole clause is used as an object.

> I remembered **who** won the Academy Award that year. [*Who* is the subject of the clause *who won the Academy Award that year.* The clause is the object of the verb *remembered.*]

> She offered help to **whoever** needed it. [*Whoever* is the subject of the clause *whoever needed it.* The clause is the object of the preposition *to.*]

When the pronoun is an object in a dependent clause, use w*hom* or *whomever*.

> They helped **whom** they liked. [direct object]

> Gabriel happily greeted **whomever** he met that day. [direct object]

> No one knew for **whom** the song was written. [*Whom* is the object of the preposition *for.*]

Whom may be omitted in sentences where no misunderstanding would result.

> The friend he relied on moved away. [*Whom* has been omitted after *friend.*]

Such expressions as *I think, he says, she believes,* and *we know* can follow either *who* or *whom.* The case of the pronoun still depends on its grammatical function in the clause. To make sure that you have used the correct form, delete the intervening phrase.

> Walter picked Jan, **who** he knows speaks well.
> [*Who* is the subject of the verb *speaks.*]

> Walter picked Jan, **whom** he knows we all respect.
> [*Whom* is the object of the verb *respect.*]

BEYOND THE RULE

WHO/WHOEVER OR *WHOM/WHOMEVER*

Although many writers still prefer *whom* or *whomever* as object pronouns, dictionaries have also approved the use of *who* or *whoever* in informal contexts.

I wonder **who** she voted for.

Give the campaign literature to **whoever** you see.

Who do you plan to vote for?

In college writing, though, it is better to use *whom* or *whomever* as the object pronoun.

Whom will they elect president?

For additional information, visit **www.harbrace.com**.

Exercise 2

Following the guidelines for college and professional writing, choose the appropriate form of each pronoun in parentheses.

1. Separate the white chess pieces from the black pieces, and decide (who/whom) will play with the white pieces.
2. The opening move is made by (whoever/whomever) has received the white game pieces.
3. (Whoever/Whomever) the black pieces were given to makes the following move.
4. The player (who/whom) can put the other player's king in check is close to becoming the winner.
5. (Whoever/Whomever) is unable to free his king must concede the game.

(6) Pronouns in the objective case precede and follow infinitives; possessive determiners precede gerunds.

A pronoun grouped with an infinitive, either as its subject or as its object, takes the objective case.

The director wanted **me** to help **him**.

A **gerund** (-*ing* verb form functioning as a noun) is preceded by a possessive determiner.

I appreciated **his** helping Denise. [COMPARE: I appreciated **Tom's** helping Denise.]

Notice that the possessive case is used before a gerund, but not before a **present participle** (-*ing* verb form functioning as an adjective).

I saw **him** helping Diane.

(7) Knowing what is omitted in elliptical constructions is essential in choosing pronoun case.

The words *as* and *than* frequently introduce **elliptical constructions**—clauses in which the writer intentionally omits words. To check whether you have used the correct case in an elliptical construction, read the written sentence aloud, inserting any words that have been omitted from it.

She admires Clarice as much as **I.** [subjective case]
Read aloud: She admires Clarice as much as *I do.*

She admires Clarice more than **I.** [subjective case]
Read aloud: She admires Clarice more than *I do.*

She admires Clarice more than **me.** [objective case]
Read aloud: She admires Clarice more than *she admires me.*

Exercise 3

Revise the following sentences, using appropriate pronouns and determiners. Some sentences may not require editing.

1. The board of directors has asked you and I to conduct a customer survey.
2. They also recommended us hiring someone with extensive experience in statistical analysis.
3. You understand statistics better than me.
4. Although the board asked me to be in charge, I would like you to recruit and interview candidates.
5. The directors recognize your expertise and will surely approve of you taking the lead.

25c Pronoun-antecedent agreement

A pronoun and the word or word group to which it refers, the antecedent, agree in number (both are either singular or plural).

> The **supervisor** said that **he** would help.
> [Both antecedent and pronoun are singular.]
>
> My **colleagues** said that **they** would help.
> [Both antecedent and pronoun are plural.]

A pronoun also agrees with its antecedent in gender (masculine, feminine, or neuter).

> **Joseph** claims that **he** can meet the deadline. [masculine antecedent]
>
> **Anna** claims that **she** can meet the deadline. [feminine antecedent]
>
> The **committee** claims that **it** can meet the deadline. [neutral antecedent]

Possessive Determiners

A possessive determiner (*his, her, its, their, my, our,* or *your*), traditionally labeled a possessive pronoun, agrees with its antecedent, not with the noun it precedes.

> Ken Carlson brought ~~her~~ *his* young daughter to the office today.
>
> [The possessive determiner *his* agrees with the antecedent, *Ken Carlson,* not with the following noun, *daughter.*]

(1) Indefinite pronouns can serve as antecedents.

Although most antecedents for pronouns are nouns, they can be **indefinite pronouns.** Most indefinite pronouns are considered singular.

anyone	anybody	anything
everyone	everybody	everything
someone	somebody	something
no one	nobody	nothing
each	either	neither

Notice that an indefinite pronoun takes a singular verb form.

Everyone **has** [not *have*] the right to an opinion.

Difficulties arise, however, because *everyone* seems to refer to more than one person. Thus, the definition of grammatical number and our everyday notion of number conflict. In conversation and informal writing, a plural pronoun or determiner is often used with the singular *everyone*. Nonetheless, when you write for an audience that expects you to follow traditional grammar rules, make sure to use a third-person singular pronoun or determiner.

Each of these companies has ~~their~~ *its* books audited.

Everyone has the combination to ~~their~~ *his or her* private locker.

You can avoid the awkwardness of using *his or her* by using an article instead, by making the antecedent noun and the possessive determiner both plural, or by rewriting the sentence using the passive voice (see **26d(3)**).

Everyone has the combination to **a** private locker. [article]

Students have combinations to **their** private lockers. [plural antecedent]

The combination to a private locker **is issued** to everyone. [passive voice]

(2) An antecedent sometimes refers to both genders.

When an antecedent is a noun that can refer to people of either gender, rewrite the sentence to make the noun plural or, if not too cumbersome, use *he or she* or *his or her.*

Plural	**Lawyers** represent their clients.
Singular	A lawyer represents the clients **he or she** has accepted.
	A lawyer represents **his or her** clients.

(See **32d** for more information on using inclusive language.)

 Be careful not to introduce errors into your writing when you are trying to avoid sexist language. (See **32d(1)**.)

> $\overset{\textit{drivers let}}{\text{Whenever}}$ ~~a driver lets~~ their $\overset{\textit{licenses}}{\sim}$ ~~license~~ expire, they have to take a driving test.

(3) The pronoun agrees with the nearer of two antecedents joined by *or* or *nor*.

If a singular and a plural antecedent are joined by *or* or *nor,* place the plural antecedent second and use a plural pronoun.

> Either Jennifer **or** her <u>roommates</u> will explain how <u>they</u> chose their majors.

> Neither the president **nor** the <u>senators</u> stated that <u>they</u> would support the proposal.

(4) When a collective noun is the antecedent, the number of the pronoun depends on the meaning of the noun.

When an antecedent is a collective noun, determine whether you intend the noun to be understood as singular or plural. Then, make sure that the pronoun agrees in number with the noun.

> The choir decided that $\overset{\textit{it}}{\text{~~they~~}}$ would tour during the winter rather than in the spring. [Because the choir decided as a unit, *choir* should be considered singular. The singular form, *it*, replaces the plural, *they*.]

> The committee may disagree on methods, but $\overset{\textit{they}}{\sim}$ ~~it~~ must agree on basic aims. [Because the committee members are behaving as individuals, *committee* is regarded as plural. The plural form, *they*, replaces the singular, *it*.]

Exercise 4

Revise the following sentences so that pronouns or determiners agree with their antecedents.

1. A researcher relies on a number of principles to help him make ethical decisions.
2. Everyone should have the right to participate in a study only if she wants to.
3. A team of researchers should provide its volunteers with informed-consent forms, in which they describe to the volunteers the procedures and risks involved in participation.
4. Every participant should be guaranteed that the information they provide will remain confidential.
5. Institutions of higher education require that a researcher address ethical issues in their proposal.

25d Clear pronoun reference

The main rhetorical principle to keep in mind regarding pronoun reference is clarity. In the following sentence, the pronoun *they* clearly refers to the noun *cattle*—its antecedent.

> Our ranching operation keeps **cattle** year-round in the same pastures where **they** are bred, born, and raised.

A pronoun may refer to two or more antecedents.

> **Jack and I** knew **we** were late.

Sometimes a pronoun refers to a noun that follows it.

> When **she** turned nineteen, **Cindy** decided to leave home.

The meaning of each pronoun in a sentence should be immediately obvious.

(1) Ambiguous or unclear pronoun references can confuse readers.

When a pronoun can refer to either of two antecedents, the ambiguity may confuse readers. To make the antecedent clear, replace the pronoun with a noun or rewrite the sentence.

Mr. Anderson told Mr. Eggers that *Mr. Eggers* he would be in charge of the project.

OR

Mr. Anderson put Mr. Eggers in charge of the project.
[In the unrevised sentence, it is not clear who will be in charge of the project.]

(2) Remote or awkward references can cause readers to misunderstand.

To help readers understand your meaning, place pronouns as close to their antecedents as possible. The following sentence needs to be revised so that the relative pronoun *that* is close to its antecedent, *poem.*

The **poem** *that was originally written in 1945* has been published in a new book ~~that was originally written in 1945~~.

Notice, however, that a relative pronoun does not always have to follow its antecedent directly. In the following example, there is no risk of misunderstanding.

We slowly began to notice the **changes** in our climate **that** were forecast several years ago.

(3) Broad or implied references can make writing vague.

Pronouns such as *it, this, that,* and *which* may refer to a specific word or phrase or to the sense of a whole clause, sentence, or paragraph.

The weight of the pack was manageable, once I became used to **it.**
[*It* refers specifically to *weight.*]

Large corporations may seem stronger than individuals, but **that** is not true.
[*That* refers to the sense of the whole first clause.]

When used carelessly, broad references can interfere with clear communication. Unless the meaning is clear, avoid reference to the general idea of a preceding clause or sentence. Instead, state clearly what *this* or *that* refers to.

> When class attendance is compulsory, some students feel that education is being forced on them. This *perception* is unwarranted. [*This* has no clear antecedent.]

Remember to express an idea explicitly rather than merely implying it.

> My father is a music teacher. *Teaching music* ~~It~~ is a profession that requires much patience. [*It* has no expressed antecedent.]

Be especially careful to provide clear antecedents when you are referring to the work or possessions of others. In the following sentence, the possessive noun *Jen Norton's* might seem like it could be an antecedent for *she*; however, because it is a modifier and not a noun, it does not qualify as a true antecedent.

> In *her* ~~Jen Norton's~~ article, *Jen Norton* ~~she~~ argues that workplace conditions need improvement.

(4) The use of the expletive *it* can result in wordiness or ambiguity.

The expletive *it* does not have a specific antecedent (see **20d(1)**). Instead, it is used to postpone, and thus give emphasis to, the subject of the sentence. A sentence that begins with this expletive can sometimes be wordy or awkward. Revise such a sentence by replacing *it* with the postponed subject.

> *Trying to repair the car* *useless* ~~It was no use~~ ~~trying to repair the car~~.

Avoid placing one *it* near another *it* with a different meaning.

> *Staying in the old apartment* ~~It~~ would be simpler ~~to stay in the old apartment~~, but it is too far from my job. [The first *it* is an expletive (see the **Glossary of Terms**); the second *it* refers to *apartment*.]

Exercise 5

Edit the following sentences to make all references clear. Some sentences may not require editing.

1. It is remarkable to read about Lance Armstrong's victories.

2. A champion cyclist, a cancer survivor, and a humanitarian, it is no wonder that Lance Armstrong is one of the most highly celebrated athletes in the world.

3. Armstrong's mother encouraged his athleticism, which led to his becoming a professional triathlete by age sixteen.

4. Though you might not believe it, Armstrong was only a senior in high school when he started training for the Olympic developmental team.

5. By the time he was twenty-five, Armstrong was ranked as the top cyclist in the world.

6. Not long afterward, because of intense pain, he sought medical attention, and they told him he had testicular cancer.

7. The cancer had spread to his lungs and brain; thus, they said his chances for recovery were slim.

8. Armstrong underwent dramatic surgery and aggressive chemotherapy; this eventually helped him recover.

9. Armstrong started training five months after their diagnosis and went on to win major championships, including the Tour de France.

10. For Lance Armstrong, it hasn't been only about racing bikes; he has become a humanitarian as well, creating the Lance Armstrong Foundation to help cancer patients and to fund cancer research around the world.

26

VERBS

Choosing verbs to convey your message precisely is the first step toward writing clear and effective sentences. The next step is to ensure that the verbs you choose conform to the conventions your audience expects you to follow. This chapter will help you

- identify conventional verb forms (**26a**),
- use verb tenses to provide information about time (**26b**),
- use verb tenses consistently (**26c**),
- distinguish between the active voice and the passive voice (**26d**),
- use verbs to signal the factuality or likelihood of an action or event (**26e**), and
- ensure that subjects and verbs agree in number and person (**26f**).

26a Verb forms

Most English verbs have four forms, following the model for *walk.*

walk, walks, walking, walked

However, English also includes irregular verbs, which may have as few as three forms or as many as eight:

let, lets, letting   *be, am, is, are, was, were, being, been*

(1) Regular verbs have four forms.

A regular verb has a **base form.** This is the form you find in a dictionary. *Talk, act, change,* and *serve* are all base forms.

The second form of a regular verb is the **-s form.** To derive this form, add to the base form either *-s* (*talks, acts, changes, serves*) or, in some cases, *-es* (*marries, carries, tries*). See **40d** for information on spelling changes that accompany the addition of *-es*.

The third form of a regular verb is the *-ing* **form,** also called the **present participle.** It consists of the base form and the ending *-ing* (*talking, acting*). Depending on the verb, spelling changes may occur (*changing, chatting*). (See **40d**.)

The fourth form of a regular verb consists of the base form and the ending *-ed* (*talked, acted*). Again, spelling may vary when the suffix is added (*changed, served, chatted*). (See **40d**.) The *-ed* form has two names. When it is used without the auxiliary verb *have* or *be*, it is called the **past form** (We *talked* about the new plan). In contrast, when the *-ed* form is used with one of these auxiliary verbs, it is called the **past participle** (We *have talked* about it several times. A committee *was formed* to investigate the matter).

Verb Forms of Regular Verbs

Base Form	-s Form (Present Tense, Third Person, Singular)	-ing Form (Present Participle)	-ed Form (Past Form and Past Participle)
work	works	working	worked
watch	watches	watching	watched
apply	applies	applying	applied
stop	stops	stopping	stopped

When verbs are followed by words with similar sounds, you may find the verb endings (*-s* and *-ed*) difficult to hear. In addition, these verb endings may seem unfamiliar because your dialect does not have them. Nonetheless, you should use *-s* and *-ed* when you write for an audience that expects you to include these endings:

seems
She **seem** satisfied with the report.

supposed
We were **suppose** to receive the results yesterday.

(2) Irregular verbs have from three to eight forms.

Most irregular verbs, such as *write,* have forms similar to some of those for regular verbs: base form (*write*), -*s* form (*writes*), and -*ing* form (*writing*). However, the past form (*wrote*) and the past participle (*written*) vary from the regular forms. In fact, some irregular verbs have two acceptable past forms and/or past participles (see *awake, dive, dream,* and *get* in the following chart). Other irregular verbs have only three forms because the same form serves as the base form, the past form, and the past participle (see *set* in the chart). If you are unsure about verb forms not included in the chart, consult a dictionary.

Verb Forms of Irregular Verbs

Base Form	-*s* Form (Present Tense, Third Person, Singular)	-*ing* Form (Present Participle)	Past Form	Past Participle
arise	arises	arising	arose	arisen
awake	awakes	awaking	awaked, awoke	awaked, awoken
bear	bears	bearing	bore	borne, born
begin	begins	beginning	began	begun
bite	bites	biting	bit	bitten
break	breaks	breaking	broke	broken
bring	brings	bringing	brought	brought
buy	buys	buying	bought	bought
choose	chooses	choosing	chose	chosen
come	comes	coming	came	come
dive	dives	diving	dived, dove	dived
do	does	doing	did	done
dream	dreams	dreaming	dreamed, dreamt	dreamed, dreamt

(Continued on page 566)

(Continued from page 565)

Base Form	-s Form (Present Tense, Third Person, Singular)	-ing Form (Present Participle)	Past Form	Past Participle
drink	drinks	drinking	drank	drunk
drive	drives	driving	drove	driven
eat	eats	eating	ate	eaten
fall	falls	falling	fell	fallen
forget	forgets	forgetting	forgot	forgotten
forgive	forgives	forgiving	forgave	forgiven
get	gets	getting	got	gotten, got
give	gives	giving	gave	given
go	goes	going	went	gone
hang (suspend)	hangs	hanging	hung	hung
hang (execute)	hangs	hanging	hanged	hanged
hold	holds	holding	held	held
keep	keeps	keeping	kept	kept
know	knows	knowing	knew	known
lay (see the **Glossary of Usage**)	lays	laying	laid	laid
lead	leads	leading	led	led
lie (see the **Glossary of Usage**)	lies	lying	lay	lain

Base Form	-s Form (Present Tense, Third Person, Singular)	-ing Form (Present Participle)	Past Form	Past Participle
lose	loses	losing	lost	lost
pay	pays	paying	paid	paid
rise (see the **Glossary of Usage**)	rises	rising	rose	risen
say	says	saying	said	said
see	sees	seeing	saw	seen
set (see the **Glossary of Usage**)	sets	setting	set	set
sink	sinks	sinking	sank	sunk
sit (see the **Glossary of Usage**)	sits	sitting	sat	sat
speak	speaks	speaking	spoke	spoken
spend	spends	spending	spent	spent
stand	stands	standing	stood	stood
steal	steals	stealing	stole	stolen
swim	swims	swimming	swam	swum
take	takes	taking	took	taken
teach	teaches	teaching	taught	taught
tell	tells	telling	told	told
throw	throws	throwing	threw	thrown
wear	wears	wearing	wore	worn
write	writes	writing	wrote	written

The verb *be* has eight forms.

be	**Be** on time!
am	I **am** going to arrive early tomorrow.
is	Time **is** of the essence.
are	They **are** always punctual.
was	The meeting **was** scheduled for 10 a.m.
were	We **were** only five minutes late.
being	He is **being** delayed by traffic.
been	How long have we **been** here?

Omission of Forms of *Be* in Other Languages
Forms of the verb *be* can be omitted in some languages.
In English, however, they are necessary.

Sentence without an auxiliary verb: The population ˄is growing.

Sentence without a linking verb: It ˄is quite large.

(3) A phrasal verb consists of a main verb and a particle.

A **phrasal verb** is a combination of a verb and a particle such as *up, out,* or *on.* Such a verb + particle unit is often idiomatic, conveying a meaning that differs from the common meanings of the individual words. For example, the definitions that first come to mind for the words *blow* and *up* are not likely to help you understand the phrasal verb *blow up* when it means "to enlarge": She *blew up* the photograph so that she could see the faces better. However, the meanings of other phrasal verbs are similar to common definitions; the particles just add a sense of completion: They *finished up* the report by six o'clock. The particle *up* in *finish up* does not refer to a direction; instead, it emphasizes the completion of the report. Still other phrasal verbs retain the common meanings of the verb and the particle: The protesters *hung up* a banner.

The parts of most phrasal verbs may be separated by a short noun phrase or a pronoun.

> She **called** the meeting **off.**
> The student **turned** it **in** yesterday.

Some phrasal verbs are not separable, however.

> The group **went over** the proposal.
> I **came across** an interesting fact.

Particles that add little meaning are often deleted, especially if they seem redundant.

> I **sent** ~~out~~ the invitations.

Phrasal Verbs
If you cannot find phrasal verbs in a conventional dictionary, use a specialized dictionary that provides both definitions and information about the separability of these verbs. See **32e** for a list of dictionaries.

---

(4) Auxiliary verbs combine with main verbs.

The auxiliary verbs *be, do,* and *have* combine with main verbs, both regular and irregular:

be	*am, is, are, was, were surprised*
	am, is, are, was, were writing
do	*does, do, did call*
	doesn't, don't, didn't spend
have	*has, have, had prepared*
	has, have, had read

When you combine auxiliary verbs with main verbs, you alter the meanings of the main verbs in some subtle ways. The resulting verb combinations may provide information about time, emphasis, or action in progress. (See **26b**.)

Be, do, and *have* are not just auxiliary verbs, though. They may be used as main verbs as well.

be   I **am** from Texas.

do   He **does** his homework early in the morning.

have   They **have** an apartment near a park.

A sentence may even include one of these verbs as both an auxiliary and a main verb.

They **are being** careful.

Did you **do** your taxes by yourself?

She **has** not **had** any free time this week.

Another type of auxiliary verb is called a **modal auxiliary.** By combining a modal auxiliary such as *will, should,* or *could* with the base form of a main verb, you can make a request (*could* you help), give an instruction (you *should* attend), or express certainty (we *shall* overcome), necessity (she *must* sleep), obligation (they *should* laugh), possibility (you *can* dream), or probability (it *could* happen).

Modal Auxiliaries and Main Verbs

Although English verbs are often followed by the infinitive marker *to* (as in *want to go* and *plan to leave*), modal auxiliaries do not follow this pattern.

We **should** ~~to~~ finish our report by Friday.

Each modal auxiliary has more than one meaning. For example, *may* can indicate permission or probability.

The instructor said we **may** have an extension. [permission]

The weather **may** improve by tomorrow. [probability]

The following list provides examples of the common meanings conveyed by modal auxiliaries.

COMMON MEANINGS OF MODAL AUXILIARIES

Meaning	Modal Auxiliary +	Main Verb	Example
Ability	can, could	afford	They *can afford* to buy a small house.
Certainty	will	leave	We *will leave* tomorrow.
Obligation	must	return	You *must return* your books by the due date.
Advice	should	talk	He *should talk* with his counselor.
Permission	may	use	You *may use* the computer in the main office.

When a modal auxiliary occurs with the auxiliary *have* (*must have forgotten, should have known*), *have* frequently sounds like the word *of*. When you proofread, be sure that modal auxiliaries are not followed by *of*.

                 have
They **could ︿of taken** another route.

Writers generally do not combine modal auxiliaries unless they want to portray a regional dialect.

                 be able to
We **might ︿could** plan the meeting for after the holidays.

Phrasal Modals

English also has **phrasal modals,** or auxiliary verbs consisting of more than one word. They have meanings similar to those of one-word modals.

be able to (ability): We **were able to** find the original document.

have to (obligation): You **have to** report your test results.

(Continued on page 572)

(Continued from page 571)

Other common phrasal modals are *be going to, be supposed to, had better, used to,* and *ought to.* Most of these auxiliary verbs have more than one form (*am able to, is able to, were able to*). Only *had better, ought to,* and *used to* have a single form.

(5) Participles are accompanied by auxiliary verbs.

Present participles (*-ing* verb forms) are used with the auxiliary verb *be:* We *were waiting* for the next flight. Depending on the intended meaning, past participles can be used with either *be* or *have:* We *have waited* for an hour. The first flight *was canceled.* If a sentence contains only a participle, it is probably a fragment (see **22b**).

I sit on the same bench every day. ~~Dreaming~~ , *dreaming* of far-off places.

When a participle is part of a verbal phrase, it often appears without an auxiliary verb (see **21a(3)**).

> **Swatting** at mosquitoes and **cursing** softly, the campers quickly packed up their gear.

Exercise 1

Supply the correct form of each verb in parentheses.

1. I (awake) early that morning.
2. Jason said we were (suppose) to leave at 5:00 a.m.
3. I wasn't (use) to getting up before dark, but I (manage) to be at the bus stop on time.
4. The sun was just (begin) to rise.
5. My backpack (be) heavy, so I (lay) it next to the other gear that was (lie) in a heap.
6. Without my pack on, though, I (be) cold.
7. I had (forget) how chilly mornings (be) in the desert.
8. Jason (see) me shivering and (lend) me his jacket.
9. "(Be) you okay?" he (ask).
10. "Yes," I (lie). It (be) early, it (be) cold, and I (be) nervous.

Exercise 2

Revise the following sentences. Explain any changes you make.

1. Any expedition into the wilderness suffer its share of mishaps.
2. The Lewis and Clark Expedition began in May 1804 and end in September 1806.
3. The Fates must of smiled on Meriwether Lewis and William Clark, for there were no fatalities under their leadership.
4. Lewis and Clark lead the expedition from St. Louis to the Pacific Ocean and back.
5. President Thomas Jefferson commission the expedition in 1803 in part because he was interest in finding the Northwest Passage— a hypothetical waterway connecting the Atlantic and Pacific Oceans.
6. By 1805, the Corps of Discovery, as the expedition was call, included thirty-three members.
7. The Corps might of lost all maps and specimens had Sacajawea, a Native American woman, not fish them from the Missouri River.
8. Sacajawea could of went off with her own people in Idaho, but she accompany Lewis and Clark to the Pacific.
9. When the Mandans had finish inspecting York, William Clark's African American servant, they assume he was the expedition's leader.
10. The success of the expedition depend on its members' willingness to help one another.

26b Verb tenses

Verb tenses provide information about time. For example, the tense of a verb may indicate that an action took place in the past or that an action is ongoing. Verb tenses are labeled as present, past, or future; they are also labeled as simple, progressive, perfect, or perfect progressive. The chart shows how these labels apply to the tenses of *walk*.

Verb Tenses

	Present	Past	Future
Simple	walk, walks	walked	will walk
Progressive	am, is, are walking	was, were walking	will be walking
Perfect	has, have walked	had walked	will have walked
Perfect progressive	has, have been walking	had been walking	will have been walking

   Some of the tenses have more than one form because they depend on the person and number of the subject. **Person** refers to the role of the subject. First person (*I, we*) indicates that the subject of the verb is the writer or writers. Second person (*you*) indicates that the subject is the audience. Third person (*he, she, it, they*) indicates that the subject is someone or something other than the writer or audience. **Number** indicates whether the subject is one or more than one (*I/we, building/buildings*). In the following subsections, conjugation tables are used to show how person and number influence the forms of the regular verb *work*.

(1) Simple tenses have many uses, not all related to specific points in time.

The conjugation for the simple present tense includes two forms of the verb: the base form and the *-s* form. Notice that the third-person singular form is the only form with the *-s* ending.

Simple Present Tense

	Singular	Plural
First person	I **work**	We **work**
Second person	You **work**	You **work**
Third person	He, she, it **works**	They **work**

Tense is not the same as time. Although the words *present, past,* and *future* may lead you to think that these tenses refer to actions happening now, in the past, and in the future, this strict separation does not always hold. For example, the simple present tense is used to indicate a current state, a habitual action, or a general truth.

We **are** ready. [current state]

Dana **uses** common sense. [habitual action]

The sun **rises** in the east. [general truth]

The simple present tense is also commonly used to add a sense of immediacy to historical actions and to discuss literary and artistic works (see fig. 26.1).

Fig. 26.1. In his painting *Sun Rising through Vapor,* J. M. W. Turner divides the canvas into areas of light and dark. (Notice the use of the simple present tense—"divides"—to describe an artistic work.)

In 1939, Hitler's armies **attack** Poland. [historical present]

Joseph Conrad **writes** about what he sees in the human heart. [literary present]

On occasion, the simple present tense is used to refer to a future event.

My bus **leaves** in twenty minutes.

The simple past tense of regular verbs has only one form: the base form with the *-ed* ending. The past tense for irregular verbs varies (see 26a(2)).

Simple Past Tense

	Singular	Plural
First person	I **worked**	We **worked**
Second person	You **worked**	You **worked**
Third person	He, she, it **worked**	They **worked**

The simple past tense is used to refer to completed past actions or events.

He **traveled** to the Philippines. [past action]

The accident **occurred** several weeks ago. [past event]

The simple future tense also has only one form: the base form accompanied by the auxiliary *will*.

Simple Future Tense

	Singular	Plural
First person	I **will work**	We **will work**
Second person	You **will work**	You **will work**
Third person	He, she, it **will work**	They **will work**

The simple future tense refers to future actions or states.

I **will call** you after work today. [future action]

The video **will be** ready by Friday. [future state]

(2) Progressive tenses indicate that events have begun but have not been completed.

The present progressive tense of a verb consists of a form of the auxiliary verb *be* and the present participle (*-ing* form) of the main verb.

Present Progressive Tense

	Singular	Plural
First person	I **am working**	We **are working**
Second person	You **are working**	You **are working**
Third person	He, she, it **is working**	They **are working**

Notice that the present participle remains the same regardless of person and number, but the auxiliary *be* appears in three forms: *am* for first-person singular, *is* for third-person singular, and *are* for the other person-number combinations.

The present progressive tense signals an activity in progress or a temporary situation.

> The doctor **is attending** a conference in Nebraska. [activity in progress]
>
> We **are living** in a yurt right now. [temporary situation]

The present progressive tense can refer to a future event when it occurs with a word or phrase indicating future time.

> Tomorrow we **are leaving** for Alaska. [*Tomorrow* indicates a time in the future.]

Like the present progressive, the past progressive tense is a combination of the auxiliary verb *be* and the present participle (*-ing* form) of the main verb. However, the auxiliary verb is in the past tense, rather than in the present tense.

Past Progressive Tense

	Singular	Plural
First person	I **was working**	We **were working**
Second person	You **were working**	You **were working**
Third person	He, she, it **was working**	They **were working**

The past progressive tense signals an action or event that occurred in the past and was repeated or ongoing.

The new member **was** constantly **interrupting** the discussion. [repeated past action]

We **were eating** dinner when we heard the news. [ongoing past action]

The future progressive tense has only one form. Two auxiliaries, *will* and *be,* are used along with the *-ing* form of the main verb.

Future Progressive Tense

	Singular	Plural
First person	I **will be working**	We **will be working**
Second person	You **will be working**	You **will be working**
Third person	He, she, it **will be working**	They **will be working**

The future progressive tense refers to actions that will occur over some period of time in the future.

She **will be giving** her report at the end of the meeting. [future action]

Verbs Not Used in the Progressive Form
Some verbs that do not express actions but rather mental states, emotions, conditions, or relationships are not used in the progressive form. These verbs include *believe, belong, contain, cost, know, own, prefer,* and *want.*

contains
The book ~~is containing~~ many Central American folktales.

knows
He ~~is knowing~~ many old myths.

(3) Perfect tenses indicate action performed prior to a particular time.

The present perfect tense is formed by combining the auxiliary *have* with the past participle of the main verb.

Present Perfect Tense

	Singular	Plural
First person	I **have worked**	We **have worked**
Second person	You **have worked**	You **have worked**
Third person	He, she, it **has worked**	They **have worked**

The participle remains the same regardless of person and number; however, the auxiliary has two forms: *has* (for third-person singular) and *have* (for the other person-number combinations). The present perfect tense signals a time prior to the present. It can refer to a situation originating in the past but continuing into the present. It can also refer to a past action that has current relevance.

> They **have lived** in New Zealand for twenty years. [situation originating in the past and still continuing]

> I **have read** that book already. Do you have another? [past action that is completed but currently relevant]

The past perfect tense is also formed by combining the auxiliary *have* with the past participle. However, the auxiliary is in the past tense. There is only one form of the past perfect for regular verbs.

Past Perfect Tense

	Singular	Plural
First person	I **had worked**	We **had worked**
Second person	You **had worked**	You **had worked**
Third person	He, she, it **had worked**	They **had worked**

The past perfect tense refers to an action completed at a time in the past prior to another past time or past action.

> Before 1990, he **had worked** in a shoe factory. [past action prior to a given time in the past]

> I **had studied** geology before I transferred to this school. [past action prior to another past action]

The future perfect tense consists of two auxiliaries, *will* and *have,* along with the past participle of the main verb. There is only one form of the future perfect tense.

Future Perfect Tense

	Singular	Plural
First person	I **will have worked**	We **will have worked**
Second person	You **will have worked**	You **will have worked**
Third person	He, she, it **will have worked**	They **will have worked**

The future perfect tense refers to an action that is to be completed prior to a future time.

> By this time next year, I **will have finished** medical school.

(4) Perfect progressive tenses combine the forms and meanings of the progressive and the perfect tenses.

The present perfect progressive tense consists of two auxiliaries, *have* and *be,* plus the present participle (*-ing* form) of the main verb.

Present Perfect Progressive Tense

	Singular	Plural
First person	I **have been working**	We **have been working**
Second person	You **have been working**	You **have been working**
Third person	He, she, it **has been working**	They **have been working**

The form of the auxiliary *have* varies with person and number. The auxiliary *be* appears as the past participle. The present perfect progressive signals that an action, state, or event originating in the past is ongoing or incomplete.

> I **have been feeling** tired for a week. [ongoing state]
>
> We **have been organizing** the conference since April. [incomplete action]

The past perfect progressive tense follows the pattern *had* + *been* + present participle (*-ing* form) of the main verb. The auxiliary *have* is in the past tense.

Past Perfect Progressive Tense

	Singular	Plural
First person	I **had been working**	We **had been working**
Second person	You **had been working**	You **had been working**
Third person	He, she, it **had been working**	They **had been working**

The past perfect progressive tense refers to a situation or action occurring over a period of time in the past and prior to another past action or time.

She **had been living** so frugally all year that she saved enough money for a new car. [past situation prior to another action in the past]

The future perfect progressive tense follows the pattern *will* + *have* + *been* + present participle (*-ing* form) of the main verb.

Future Perfect Progressive Tense

	Singular	Plural
First person	I **will have been working**	We **will have been working**
Second person	You **will have been working**	You **will have been working**
Third person	He, she, it **will have been working**	They **will have been working**

The future perfect progressive tense refers to an action that is occurring in the present and will continue to occur for a specific amount of time.

In one more month, I **will have been working** on this project for five years.

(5) The auxiliary verb *do* is used to question, negate, or emphasize.

Unlike *be* and *have,* the auxiliary verb *do* is not used with other verbs to indicate tense. Instead, it is used to question, negate, or emphasize.

> **Do** you have any questions? [question]
>
> I **do** not have any questions. [negation]
>
> I **do** have a few questions. [emphatic sentence]

The auxiliary *do* occurs only in the simple present (*do, does*) and the simple past (*did*).

Exercise 3

Explain what the verb tenses used in the following paragraph reveal about the time or duration of the actions expressed by the main verbs.

[1]Professor Alex Cohen and his literature students are leaving on Friday for Oxford University. [2]While there, they will study Keats and Wordsworth. [3]Although they have been studying these poets since September, Professor Cohen believes that the students will gain greater insight into English poetry because they will have access to important archives. [4]Professor Cohen studied in Oxford when he was an undergraduate, earning a degree in English and classics. [5]This is the first trip he has planned for students. [6]However, with the help of a university grant, he will be planning many more. [7]He is already exploring the possibility of taking students from his mythology class to Greece next year.

Exercise 4

For each sentence, explain how the meaning of the sentence changes when the verb tense changes.

1. In "Fiji's Rainbow Reef," Les Kaufman (describes/described) the coral reefs of Fiji and (discusses/discussed) the factors affecting their health.

2. Rising water temperatures (damaged/have damaged/did damage) the reefs in 2000 and 2002.

3. The algae that (provide/provided) color (do not survive/did not survive) in the warmer water.

4. The lack of algae (has left/had left) the coral "bleached."

5. Strangely, though, new life (is flourishing/was flourishing/has been flourishing) in some of these areas.

6. Scientists (study/will study) this area to understand its resilience.

Exercise 5

In a paragraph from one of your recent writing assignments, underline all the verbs and identify the tenses you used. Explain why they are appropriate.

---

(6) Tense forms help convey the duration or time sequence of actions or events.

When you use more than one tense form in a single sentence, you give readers information about how actions or events are related in time and duration.

Whenever he **calls** on me, I **stutter** nervously. [Both forms indicate habitual actions.]

When the speaker **had finished,** everyone **applauded.** [The past perfect tense *had finished* indicates a time before the action expressed by *applauded*.]

Infinitives and participles (see **21a(3)**) can be used to express time relations within a sentence. The present infinitive (*to* + base form) of a verb generally expresses action occurring later than the action expressed by the main verb.

They **want to design** a new museum. [The action of designing will take place in the future.]

The perfect infinitive (*to* + *have* + past participle) signals that an action, state, or event is potential or hypothetical or that it did not occur.

> She **hopes to have earned** her degree by the end of next year.
>
> The governor **would like to have postponed** the vote. [The postponement did not occur.]

The present participle (*-ing* form) indicates simultaneous or previous action.

> **Laughing** loudly, the old friends **left** the restaurant arm in arm. [The friends were laughing as they were leaving.]
>
> **Hearing** that she was distressed, I **rushed** right over. [The action of hearing occurred first.]

The perfect participle (*having* + past participle) expresses action completed before that conveyed by the main verb.

> **Having learned** Spanish at an early age, she **spoke** to the Mexican diplomats in their native language.

The past participle can be used to express either simultaneous action or previous action.

> **Led** by a former Peace Corps worker, the volunteers **provided** medical assistance. [Both actions occurred simultaneously.]
>
> **Encouraged** by job prospects, he **moved** to Atlanta. [The encouragement preceded the move.]

Exercise 6

Revise the following sentences so that all verbs express the appropriate time sequences.

1. We expected the storm to have bypassed our town, but it didn't.
2. We would like to have prior notice; however, even the police officers were taken by surprise.
3. Not having known much about flooding, the emergency crew was at a disadvantage.
4. Having thrown sandbags all day, the volunteers had been exhausted by 5 p.m.
5. They went home, succeeding in preventing a major disaster.

26c Consistency of verb tenses

The tenses of a verb have two features: time frame and aspect. **Time frame** refers to whether the tense is present, past, or future. **Aspect** refers to whether it is simple, progressive, perfect, or perfect progressive. (See **26b**.) Consistency in the time frame of your verbs, though not necessarily in their aspect, ensures that your sentences link together logically. In the following paragraph, notice that the time frame remains the past, but the aspect is either the simple, the perfect, or the progressive.

past perfect

In the summer of 1983, I **had** just **finished** my third year of architecture

simple past   *past perfect (compound predicate)*

school and **had** to find a six-month internship. I **had grown** up and **gone**

past perfect

through my entire education in the Midwest, but I **had been** to New York

simple past   *simple past*

City once on a class field trip and I **thought** it **seemed** like a pretty good

simple past

place to live. So, armed with little more than an inflated ego and my school

portfolio, I **was** off to Manhattan, oblivious to the bad economy and the fact

past progressive

that the city **was overflowing** with young architects.

—**PAUL K. HUMISTON,** "Small World"

If you do need to shift to another time frame, you can signal the change in tense by using a time marker:

now, then, today, yesterday
in two years, during the 1920s
after you finish, before we left

For example, in the following paragraph, the time frame shifts back and forth between present and past—between today, when Edward O. Wilson is studying ants in the woods around Walden Pond, and the nineteenth century, when Thoreau lived there. The time markers are circled.

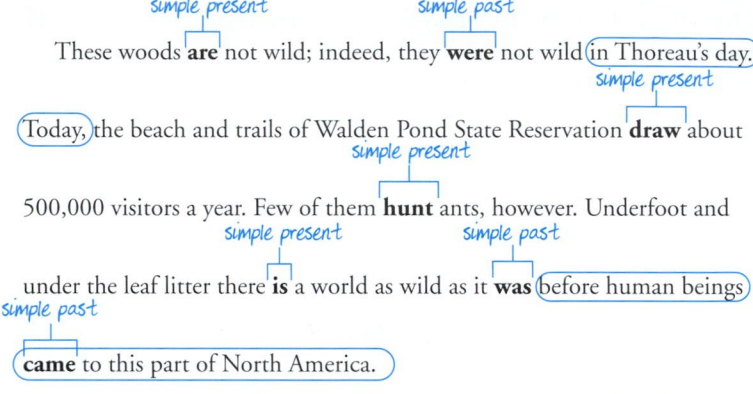

—**JAMES GORMAN,** "Finding a Wild, Fearsome World beneath Every Fallen Leaf"

On occasion, a shift in time is indicated implicitly—that is, without an explicit time marker. A writer may change tenses without including a time marker for any of these reasons: (1) to explain or support a general statement with information about the past, (2) to compare and contrast two different time periods, and (3) to comment on a topic. Why do you think the author of the following paragraph varies the verb tenses?

> Thomas Jefferson, author of the Declaration of Independence, **is** considered one of our country's most brilliant citizens. His achievements **were** many, as **were** his interests. Some historians **describe** his work as a naturalist, scientist, and inventor; others **focus** on his accomplishments as an educator and politician. Yet Jefferson **is** best known as a spokesman for democracy.

Except for the two uses of *were* in the second sentence, all verbs are in the present tense. The author uses the past tense in the second sentence to provide evidence from the past that supports the topic sentence.

Exercise 7

Determine whether the shifts in tense in the following paragraph are effective. Be prepared to explain your reasoning.

[1]The statement that clothing **is** a language, though occasionally made with the air of a man finding a flying saucer in his backyard, **is** not new. [2]Balzac, in *Daughter of Eve* (1839), **observed** that for a woman dress **is** "a continual manifestation of intimate thoughts, a language, a symbol." [3]Today, as semiotics **becomes** fashionable, sociologists **tell** us that fashion too **is** a language of signs, a nonverbal system of communication. . . .   —ALISON LURIE, "Clothing as a Sign System"

26d Voice

Voice indicates the relationship between a verb and its subject. When a verb is in the **active voice,** the subject is generally a person or thing performing an action. When a verb is in the **passive voice,** the subject is the *receiver* of the action.

> Susan Sontag **wrote** the essay. [active voice]
>
> The essay **was written** by Susan Sontag. [passive voice]

(1) Transitive verbs, but not linking or intransitive verbs, can be used in the passive voice.

A **linking verb** relates the subject and a word referring to the subject (the complement). (See **20d(3).**) A linking verb may be a verb referring to the senses (such as *feel, look, smell, sound,* or *taste*) or a verb that indicates being (*be*), seeming (*seem, appear*), remaining (*remain, keep, stay*), or becoming (*become, grow, turn*).

> Morgan **is** studious.
>
> He **sounds** authoritative.
>
> He **seems** responsible.

Linking verbs are used only in the active voice.

An **intransitive verb** does not take an object. In other words, there is no noun or pronoun following the verb and receiving its action.

> Claudia **studies** hard.

Like linking verbs, intransitive verbs are used only in the active voice.

In contrast, a **transitive verb** takes a direct object; that is, a noun or pronoun follows the verb and receives its action.

Claudia **wrote** the prize-winning essay.

Transitive verbs can usually be used in either the active or the passive voice. When the voice is passive, the recipient of the action expressed by the verb is the subject, not the direct object, of the sentence.

The prize-winning essay **was written** by Claudia.

(2) Sentences in the active voice emphasize actors and actions.

Sentences in the active voice are generally clearer and more vigorous than their passive counterparts. To use the active voice for emphasizing an actor and an action, first make the actor the subject of the sentence, and then choose a verb that will help your readers see what the actor is doing.

Passive voice   The graduation ceremony was planned by a group of students. A well-known columnist was invited to give the graduation address.

Revised   A group of students planned the graduation ceremony. They invited a well-known columnist to give the graduation address.

For more information on using the active voice to write forceful sentences, see **30e**.

(3) The passive voice highlights the recipient of the action.

The passive voice differs from the active voice in three ways. First, the subject in a passive sentence is the recipient of the action, not the actor.

The **construction** of the Guggenheim Museum was finished in 1959.

Second, if an actor is mentioned, that noun or pronoun is placed in a prepositional phrase beginning with the preposition *by*.

The Guggenheim Museum was designed by **Frank Lloyd Wright.**

Finally, the verb form is different. A verb in the passive voice consists of a form of the auxiliary verb *be* and the past participle. Depending on the verb tense, the auxiliaries *have* and *will* may appear as well. The following are the most common tense forms of the passive voice for *call.*

Simple present: *am called, is called, are called*
Simple past: *was called, were called*
Simple future: *will be called*
Present progressive: *am being called, is being called, are being called*
Past progressive: *was being called, were being called*
Present perfect: *has been called, have been called*
Past perfect: *had been called*
Future perfect: *will have been called*

THINKING RHETORICALLY ABOUT

THE PASSIVE VOICE

Use the passive voice when you want to stress the recipient of an action, rather than the actor, or when the actor's identity is unimportant or unknown. For example, you could use the passive voice to emphasize the topic of a discussion.

Tuition increases **will be discussed** at the next board meeting.

Or you could use it when you do not know who performed some action.

The lights **were left on** in the building last night.

Writers of scientific prose often use the passive voice to highlight the conditions of an experiment rather than the experimenter.

Alcohol use **was defined** as the number of days (during the past 30 days) that respondents drank alcohol. Shorter recall periods have yielded more reliable and valid self-reports when assessing behavior (Kauth, St. Lawrence, & Kelly, 1991); thus, a retrospective 30-day period **was selected.**

—CATHERINE DAVIS, student

Grammar checkers cannot distinguish between a true passive construction, such as *have been seen,* and a form of *be* followed by an adjective, such as *have been healthy.* Thus, they incorrectly flag the latter as a passive construction. In addition, they cannot tell when passive constructions are appropriate and so generally advise writers to "correct" them. For more information about grammar checkers, see **Using a Grammar Checker** on page 461.

Exercise 8

Identify the voice in each sentence as active or passive.

1. In a recent *National Geographic* report, Tom O'Neill describes the discovery of ancient art in Guatemala.
2. Archaeologist William Saturno recently discovered the oldest known Maya mural.
3. The mural was found in a tunnel used by looters.
4. The tunnel was actually a small room attached to a pyramid.
5. The small room was covered with debris; its exact dimensions were hard to gauge.
6. The archaeologist found the mural by accident.
7. The mural was dated to about 150 years before the beginning of the Maya Classic Period.
8. For protection from further looting, the research crew posted guards outside the small room.
9. Pigments and wall plaster were gathered for analysis.
10. The details of the mural have not yet been interpreted.

Exercise 9

Rewrite the sentences in exercise 8, making active verbs passive and passive verbs active. Add or delete actors when necessary. If one version of a sentence is better than the other, explain why.

26e Mood

The **mood** of a verb expresses the writer's attitude toward the factuality of what is being expressed. The **indicative mood** is used for statements and questions regarding fact or opinion. The **imperative mood** is used to give commands or directions. The **subjunctive mood** is used to state requirements, make requests, express wishes, and signal hypothetical situations.

Indicative   We will be on time.

Imperative   Be on time!

Subjunctive   The director insists that we be on time.

By using moods correctly, you can show your readers how you feel about the content of your sentences—certain, confident, doubtful, hesitant, ambivalent, and so on.

(1) Verb forms signal moods.

Verb forms for the indicative mood are described in **26b**. The verb form for the imperative is simply the base form. A verb in the subjunctive mood can be present subjunctive, past subjunctive, or perfect subjunctive. The **present subjunctive** is the base form of the verb.

> The doctor recommended that he **go** on a diet.

> The curator requested that I **be** at the museum by five o'clock.

In the passive voice, the present subjunctive form consists of *be* and the past participle of the main verb.

> We demanded that you **be reimbursed.**

The **past subjunctive** has the same form as the simple past (for example, *had, offered, found,* or *wrote*). However, the past subjunctive form of *be* is *were,* regardless of person or number.

> If they **offered** me the job, I would take it.

> She acts as if she **were** the employer rather than the employee.

The past subjunctive form in the passive voice consists of *were* and the past participle.

> Even if he **were given** a large amount of money, he would not change his mind.

Although it is called "past," the past subjunctive refers to the present or the future.

The **perfect subjunctive** has the same form as the past perfect tense: *had* + past participle. The perfect subjunctive signals that a statement is not factual.

I wish I **had known** about the scholarship competition.

To use the passive voice of a perfect subjunctive form, add the past participle of the main verb to the auxiliaries *had been*.

If she **had been awarded** the scholarship, she would have quit her part-time job.

(2) The subjunctive mood is mainly used in dependent clauses.

Although you may not use the subjunctive mood when speaking with your friends, using it in your writing shows your readers how you feel about your claims. In addition, your audience may expect you to follow the conventions for formal writing. The following guidelines should help you avoid pitfalls in the use of the subjunctive.

TIPS FOR USING THE SUBJUNCTIVE

- In clauses beginning with *as if* and *as though,* use the past subjunctive or the perfect subjunctive.

  He acts as if he ∧**was** the owner.
  were

  She looked at me as though she ∧**heard** this story before.
  had

- In nonfactual dependent clauses beginning with *if,* use the past subjunctive or the perfect subjunctive. Avoid using *would have* in the *if* clause.

  If I ∧**was** rich, I would buy a yacht.
  were

  If the driver ∧**would have checked** his rearview mirror, the accident would not have happened.
  had

  Note that *if* does not always mark a clause as nonfactual.

If it is sunny tomorrow, I'm going fishing. [indicative mood]

■ In dependent clauses following verbs that express wishes, requirements, or requests, use the past subjunctive or the perfect subjunctive.

were
I wish I ∧**was** taller.

had
My brother wishes he ∧**studied** harder years ago.

B E Y O N D   T H E   R U L E

DECLINE OF THE SUBJUNCTIVE

Some linguists believe that certain subjunctive forms are disappearing from the English language. For more information, visit **www.harbrace.com**.

Exercise 10

Use subjunctive verb forms to revise the following sentences.

1. The planners of *Apollo 13* acted as if the number 13 was a lucky number.
2. Superstitious people think that if NASA changed the number of the mission, the astronauts would have had a safer journey.
3. They also believe that if the lunar landing would have been scheduled for a day other than Friday the Thirteenth, the crew would not have encountered any problems.
4. The crew used the lunar module as though it was a lifeboat.
5. If NASA ever plans a space mission on Friday the Thirteenth again, the public would object.

26f Subject-verb agreement

A verb must agree with its subject in number. That is, when a subject is plural, the verb must have a plural form; when the subject is singular, the verb must have a singular form. The subject and verb must also agree in person. First-person subjects require first-person verb forms, second-person subjects require second-person verb forms, and third-person subjects require third-person verb forms. Notice in the following examples that the singular third-person subject takes a singular verb (*-s* form) and that the plural third-person subject takes a plural verb (base form). (If you cannot easily recognize verbs and their subjects, see **20b–d**.)

Singular The **car** in the lot **looks** new. [*Car* and *looks* are both singular.]

Plural The **cars** in the lot **look** new. [*Cars* and *look* are both plural.]

You can refer to the following subsections for guidance on ensuring subject-verb agreement in particular situations:

- when words come between the subject and the verb (**26f(1)**),
- when two or more subjects are joined by conjunctions (**26f(2)–(3)**),
- when word order is inverted (**26f(4)**),
- when the subject is a relative pronoun (**26f(5)**), an indefinite pronoun (**26f(6)**), or a collective noun or measurement word (**26f(7)**),
- when the subject is a noun that is plural in form but singular in meaning (**26f(8)**),
- when the subject is singular but its complement is plural (**26f(9)**), and
- when the subject is a noun clause beginning with *what* (**26f(10)**).

Adding *-s* to Nouns and Verbs

Standardized English requires the addition of *-s* to mark most nouns as plural but most verbs as third-person singular in the present tense. (Modal auxiliaries are the exception.) Be careful not to confuse the verb ending and the noun ending.

The **students** need attention. [noun + *-s*]

The student **needs** attention. [verb + *-s*]

Except for *be,* verbs have different forms to indicate third-person singular and third-person plural only in the simple present tense.

Simple present tense of *be*: *am, is, are*

Simple past tense of *be*: *was, were*

Simple present tense of other verbs: base form or base form + *s* or *-es,* as in *read/reads* or *push/pushes*

When the third-person singular verb form (*-s* form) is confused with the third-person plural form (base form), the subject and verb will not agree in number. As you edit your writing, watch for the potential pitfalls described in the following subsections.

(1) Agreement errors are likely when other words come between the subject and the verb.

The **rhythm** of the pounding waves **is** calming. [*Waves* is not the subject; it is the object of the preposition *of.*]

Certain phrases commonly occur between the subject and the verb; however, they do not affect the number of the subject or the form of the verb:

accompanied by	as well as	not to mention	including
along with	in addition to	no less than	together with

Her **salary,** together with tips, **is** just enough to live on.

Tips, together with her salary, **are** just enough to live on.

(2) Subjects joined by *and* usually take a plural verb.

Writing on a legal pad and writing with a computer are not the same at all.

A compound subject that refers to a single person or thing takes a singular verb.

The **founder and president** of the art association **was** elected to the board of the museum.

Red beans and rice is the specialty of the house.

(3) Agreement errors are common when subjects are joined by *or* or *nor*.

When singular subjects are linked by *or, either . . . or,* or *neither . . . nor,* the verb is singular as well.

> The **provost or** the **dean** usually **presides** at the meeting.
>
> **Either** his **accountant or** his **lawyer has** the will.
>
> **Neither** the **car nor** the **motorcycle is** for sale.

If one subject is singular and one is plural, the verb agrees in number with the subject closer to the verb.

> Neither the basket nor the **apples were** expensive. [plural]
>
> Neither the apples nor the **basket was** expensive. [singular]

The verb also agrees in person with the nearer subject.

> Either Frank or **you were** going to make the announcement. [second person]
>
> Either you or **Frank was** going to make the announcement. [third person]

(4) Inverted word order may lead to agreement errors.

In most sentences, the subject precedes the verb.

> S   V
>
> The large **cities** of the Northeast **were** the hardest hit by the storm.

The subject and verb can sometimes be inverted for emphasis; however, they must still agree.

> V   S
>
> Hardest hit by the storm **were** the large **cities** of the Northeast.

When the expletive *there* begins a sentence, the subject and verb are also inverted; the verb still agrees with the subject, which follows it (see **20d(1)**).

> V   S
>
> There **are** several **cities** in need of federal aid.

(5) Clauses with relative pronouns are common sites for agreement errors.

In an adjectival (relative) clause (see **21b(2)**), the subject is generally a relative pronoun (*that, who,* or *which*). To determine whether the relative pronoun is singular or plural, you must find its antecedent (the word or words it refers to). When the antecedent is singular, the relative pronoun is singular; when the antecedent is plural, the relative pronoun is plural. In essence, the verb in the adjectival clause agrees with the antecedent.

sing ant   sing

The person who reviews proposals is out of town this week.

pl ant   pl v

The director met with the **students who are** studying abroad next quarter.

pl ant   pl v

The Starion is one of **the new models that include** air conditioning as standard equipment.

BEYOND THE RULE

ONE AS A POSSIBLE ANTECEDENT

According to traditional grammar rules, in sentences containing the pattern *one* + *of* + plural noun + adjectival clause (such as the sentence just before this box), the antecedent for the relative pronoun (*that,* in this case) is the plural noun (*models*). The verb in the adjectival clause is thus plural as well. However, professional writers often consider *one,* instead of the plural noun, to be the antecedent of the relative pronoun and thus make the verb singular:

The Starion is **one** of the new models **that includes** air conditioning as standard equipment.

For more information on this variation, visit **www.harbrace.com**.

(6) Agreement errors frequently occur with indefinite pronouns.

The indefinite pronouns *each, either, everybody, one,* and *anyone* are considered singular and so require singular verb forms.

Either of them **is willing** to lead the discussion.

Each has bought a first-class ticket.

Everybody in our apartment building **has** a parking place.

Other indefinite pronouns, such as *all, any, some, none, half,* and *most,* can be either singular or plural, depending on whether they refer to a unit or quantity (singular) or to individuals (plural).

My sister collects **books; some are** quite valuable.

My sister collects **jewelry; some** of it **is** quite valuable.

Singular subjects that are preceded by *every* or *each* and joined by *and* require a singular verb.

Every cat **and** dog in the county **has** to be vaccinated.

Each fork **and** spoon **has** to be polished.

However, placing *each* after a plural subject does not affect the verb form. The verb should agree with the plural subject.

Colleges and vocational schools **each have** their advantages.

When an indefinite pronoun is followed by a prepositional phrase beginning with the preposition *of* (see **21a(4)**), the verb agrees in number with the object of the preposition.

None of **those are** spoiled.

None of **it is** spoiled.

More than **half** of the **population** in West Texas **is** Hispanic.

More than **half** of the **people** in West Texas **are** Hispanic.

BEYOND THE RULE

AGREEMENT WITH *NONE*

Some grammarians reason that, like *no one, none* is singular and thus should be followed by a singular verb:

None of the grant requests **has** been rejected.

Nonetheless, many reputable writers have used *none* with plural verbs, leading to the widespread acceptance of this usage:

None of the grant requests **have** been rejected.

For more information, visit **www.harbrace.com**.

(7) Collective nouns and measurement words often cause agreement difficulties.

Collective nouns and measurement words require singular verbs when they refer to groups or units. They require plural verbs when they refer to individuals or parts.

Singular (regarded as a group or unit)	Plural (regarded as individuals or parts)
The **majority rules.**	The **majority** of us **have voted** already.
Ten million gallons of oil **is** more than enough.	**Ten million gallons** of oil **were spilled.**
The **number is** insignificant.	A **number** of workers **were** absent.

Although the use of *data* and *media* as collective nouns has gained currency, treat *data* and *media* as plural in most academic writing. (See the **Glossary of Usage**.)

> The data **are** in the appendix.

> The media **have** shaped public opinion.

(8) Words ending in -s are sometimes singular.

Individual titles that are plural in form are treated as singular because they refer to a single book, movie, recording, or other work.

> *Coffee and Cigarettes* **is** now available on DVD.

A reference to a word is also considered singular.

> *Beans* **is** a slang word for "a small amount": I don't know beans about football.

A few nouns ending in *-s* are actually singular. Examples are *linguistics, news,* and *Niagara Falls.*

> The **news is** encouraging.

Some nouns (such as *athletics, politics, electronics, measles,* and *deer*) can be either singular or plural, depending on their meanings.

Singular	Plural
Statistics is an interesting subject.	**Statistics are** often misleading.

(9) Verbs agree with subjects, not with subject complements.

Some sentences may have a singular subject and a plural subject complement, or vice versa. In either case, the verb agrees with the subject.

> Her primary **concern is** rising health-care **costs.**

> **Croissants are** the bakery's **specialty.**

THINKING RHETORICALLY ABOUT

AGREEMENT OF RELATED SINGULAR AND PLURAL NOUNS

When a sentence has two or more nouns that are related, use either the singular form or the plural form consistently.

> The **student** raised her **hand.**

> The **students** raised their **hands.**

Occasionally, you may have to use a singular noun to retain an idiomatic expression or to avoid ambiguity.

> **They** kept their **word.**

> The **participants** were asked to name their favorite **movie.**

(10) An agreement error may occur when the subject of a sentence is a noun clause beginning with *what*.

In noun clauses, *what* may be understood as either "the thing that" or "the things that." If it is understood as "the thing that," the verb in the main clause is singular.

> What we need **is** a new policy. [*The thing that* we need is a policy.]

If *what* is understood as "the things that," the verb in the main clause is plural.

> What we need **are** new guidelines. [*The things that* we need are guidelines.]

Often the main noun in the subject complement of a sentence in which *what* is used in this way will help you determine whether a singular or a plural verb should be used. In the example sentences above, *policy* and *is* are singular; *guidelines* and *are* are plural.

BEYOND THE RULE

WHAT IN NOUN CLAUSES AND VERB AGREEMENT

According to traditional grammar rules, a singular verb should be used in both the noun clause containing *what* and the main clause.

What **is** needed **is** new guidelines.

However, many current writers and editors consider this rule outmoded. For more information, see **www.harbrace.com**.

Although grammar checkers do flag agreement errors, they are only occasionally correct, and they frequently flag acceptable sentences and recommend incorrect alternatives. For instance, one grammar checker flagged the sentence "What I think is my own business," suggesting that *is* should be changed to *am* to agree with *I*. Because a grammar checker cannot distinguish separate clauses, it first compares *think* to *I* and finds agreement, but then compares *is* with *I* as well and finds a problem. For more information about grammar checkers, see **Using a Grammar Checker** on page 461.

Exercise 11

In each sentence, choose the correct form of the verb in parentheses. Make sure that the verb agrees with its subject according to the conventions for academic and professional writing.

1. There (is/are) at least two good reasons for changing motor oil: risk of contamination and danger of additive depletion.
2. Reasons for not changing the oil (include/includes) the cost to the driver and the inconvenience of the chore.
3. What I want to know (is/are) the number of miles I can drive before changing my oil.
4. My best friend and mechanic (says/say) three thousand miles.

5. But my brother says every three thousand miles (is/are) too often.
6. Each of the car manuals I consulted (recommends/recommend) five-thousand-mile intervals.
7. Neither the automakers nor the gas station attendants (know/knows) how I drive, however.
8. Recommendations for changing oil (is/are) based on the assumption that normally we all drive between 40 and 65 mph on good highways when it is not too hot or too cold.
9. I am one of those drivers who on hot days (speeds/speed) along at 70 mph on interstates or (bumps/bump) along at 45 mph on a dusty road.
10. I need an oil-life monitor that (tells/tell) me when it is time to change my oil.

Exercise 12

Complete the following sentences, making sure that subjects and verbs agree.

1. Applying for college and enrolling in courses . . .
2. Erik is one of the students who . . .
3. Either of them . . .
4. Neither the president nor the senators . . .
5. The list of volunteers . . .
6. There . . .
7. Hidden beneath the stairs . . .
8. The teacher, along with her students, . . .
9. Ten months . . .
10. Politics . . .
11. Their hope for the future . . .
12. What we requested . . .

EFFECTIVE SENTENCES

S

Variety adds interest to texts and images.

THINKING RHETORICALLY ABOUT

SENTENCE STYLE

Most professional writers and readers use the following words to describe effective sentences.

- *Exact.* Precise words and word combinations ensure exactness and enable readers to come as close as they can to a full understanding of the writer's message.
- *Conventional.* Sentences are conventional when they conform to the usage expectations of a particular community. For most academic assignments, you will be expected to use Standardized English.
- *Consistent.* A consistent writing style is characterized by the use of the same types of words and grammatical structures throughout a piece of writing. A style that is inconsistent jars the readers' expectations.
- *Parallel.* Related to consistency, parallelism refers to the placement of similar ideas into similar grammatical structures.
- *Concise.* Concise prose is free of meaningless redundancies.
- *Coherent.* Coherence refers to clear connections between adjacent sentences and paragraphs.
- *Varied.* To write appealing paragraphs, a writer uses both short and long sentences. When sentences vary in length, they usually also vary in structure, rhythm, and emphasis.

In the following chapters, you will learn to identify the rhetorical options considered effective by most academic and professional writers. Remember, though, that expectations as to what is appropriate may vary across rhetorical situations. You may find that it does not make sense to apply a general rule such as "Use the active voice" in all circumstances. For example, you may be expected to write a vigorous description of an event, detailing exactly what happened, but find that you need to use the passive voice when you do not know who was responsible for the event: Several of the campaign signs *were defaced*. Or, as another example, you may need to set aside the rule calling for Standardized English if you are writing dialogue in which the speakers use regional dialects. By analyzing your rhetorical situation, rather than always following general rules, you will write sentences that make sense to you and to your audience.

SENTENCE

UNITY

27

Effective academic and professional writing comprises sentences that are consistent, clear, and complete. By carefully crafting your sentences, you demonstrate concern for your audience and thus have a better chance of achieving your rhetorical purpose. This chapter can help you

- choose and arrange details (**27a**),
- include necessary words (**27b**),
- revise mixed metaphors (**27c**),
- relate sentence parts (**27d**), and
- complete comparisons (**27e**) and intensifiers (**27f**).

27a Choosing and arranging details

Well-chosen details add interest and credibility to your writing. As you revise, you may occasionally notice a sentence that would be clearer and more believable with the addition of a phrase or two about time, location, or cause.

Missing important detail	An astrophysicist from the Harvard-Smithsonian Center has predicted a galactic storm.
With detail added	An astrophysicist from the Harvard-Smithsonian Center has predicted **that** a galactic storm **will occur within the next 10 million years.**

Without the additional information about time, most readers would wonder when the storm was supposed to hit. Knowing that the storm is predicted for millions of years in the future will help them accept the information presented.

Missing important detail	The cataclysm in the Milky Way will result in radiation levels capable of killing nearby organisms, but it will not affect Earth.
With detail added	The cataclysm in the Milky Way will result in radiation levels capable of killing nearby organisms, but it will not affect Earth, **which is 25,000 light-years away.**

The additional information in the second sentence about location helps readers understand why the Earth will be unaffected by a cataclysm in the Milky Way.

The details you choose will help your readers understand your message. If you provide too many details within a single sentence, though, your readers may lose sight of your main point. When you revise, be sure that the details you included in your first draft are still meaningful. The writer of the following sentence deleted the mention of her uncle as she revised because this detail was irrelevant to the main idea of her essay.

> When I was only sixteen, I left home to attend a college in California ~~that my uncle had graduated from twenty years earlier~~.

When considering how much detail to include, you may sometimes want to write a long and fairly complex sentence. Just be sure that every detail contributes to the central thought, as in the following excerpt.

> A given mental task may involve a complicated web of circuits, which interact in varying degrees with others throughout the brain—not like the parts in a machine, but like the instruments in a symphony orchestra combining their tenor, volume, and resonance to create a particular musical effect.
> —JAMES SHREEVE, *Beyond the Brain*

By using parallel structures (see chapter **29**) and careful punctuation, this writer has created a long, yet coherent, sentence.

Besides choosing details purposefully, you also need to indicate a clear connection between the details and the main idea of your sentence.

Unrelated	Many tigers facing possible extinction live in India, **where there are many people.**
Related	Many tigers facing possible extinction live in India, **where their natural habitat is shrinking because of population pressure.**

Exercise 1

Rewrite the following sentences so that the details clearly support the main idea. You may need to combine sentences or add words.

1. Firefighting is a dangerous job, but there are many high-tech devices and fire-resistant materials.

2. Wildfires can trap firefighters. Fire shelters are being developed to withstand temperatures as high as 2,000 degrees.

3. NASA developed Uninhabited Aerial Vehicles. Firefighters need to get accurate information fast.

4. Firefighters have difficulty seeing through smoke. A thermal imaging camera detects differences in heat and distinguishes between humans and surrounding objects.

5. Opticom is a traffic-control system, so firefighters can get to a fire quickly. They can change a red light to green from 2,000 feet away.

27b | Including necessary words

When we speak or write quickly, we often omit small words. As you revise, be sure to include all necessary articles, prepositions, verbs, and conjunctions. Without the added article, the following sentence is incomplete.

> *an*
> The ceremony took place in ⌃auditorium.

Even though prepositions are sometimes omitted in speech, they should always be included in writing.

> *of*
> We discussed a couple ⌃issues at the meeting.

When a sentence has a **compound verb** (two verbs linked by a conjunction), you may need to supply a different preposition for each verb to make your meaning clear.

> *in*
> He neither **believes** ⌃nor **approves of** exercise.

All verbs, both auxiliary and main (see **26a(4)**), should be included to make sentences complete.

> *has*
> She ˄ seen the movie three times.

> *been*
> Voter turnout has never ˄ and will never be 100 percent.

In sentences with two short clauses in which the second verb is exactly the same as the first, the second can be omitted.

> The wind **was** fierce and the thunder [was] deafening.

Include the word *that* before a clause when it makes the sentence easier to read. Without the added *that* in the following sentence, a reader may stumble over *discovered the fossil* before understanding that *the fossil* is linked to *provided.*

> *that*
> The paleontologists discovered ˄ the fossil provided a link between the dinosaur and the modern bird.

That should always be retained when a sentence has two parallel clauses.

> The graph indicated **that the population had increased** but **that the number of homeowners had not.**

A grammar checker will sometimes alert you to a missing word, but it will just as often fail to do so. It may also tell you that a word is missing when it is not. You are better off proofreading your work yourself.

27c Revising mixed metaphors

When you use language that evokes images, make sure that the images are meaningfully related. Unrelated images are called **mixed metaphors.** The following sentence includes incompatible images.

> *incurred a large*
> As he climbed the corporate ladder, he ˄ ~~sank into a sea of~~ debt.

The combination of two images—climbing a ladder and sinking into a sea—could create a picture in the reader's mind of a man hanging onto a ladder as it disappears into the water. The easiest way to revise such a sentence is to replace the words evoking one of the conflicting images.

27d   Relating sentence parts

(1) Mixed constructions are illogical.

A sentence that begins with one kind of grammatical structure and shifts to another is a **mixed construction.** To untangle a mixed construction, make sure that the sentence includes a conventional subject—a noun, a noun phrase, a gerund phrase, an infinitive phrase, or a noun clause. Prepositional phrases and adverbial clauses are not typical subjects.

> *Practicing*
> ^~~By practicing~~ a new language daily will help you become proficient.
> [A gerund phrase replaces a prepositional phrase.]

> *Her scholarship award*
> ^~~Although she won a scholarship~~ does not give her the right to skip classes.
> [A noun phrase replaces an adverbial clause.]

If you find a sentence that has a mixed construction, you can either revise the subject, as in the previous examples, or leave the beginning of the sentence as a modifier and add a new subject after it.

> By practicing a new language daily, **you** will become more proficient.
>
> Although she won a scholarship, **she** does not have the right to skip classes.

(2) Sentence parts are linked together logically.

When drafting, writers sometimes compose sentences in which the subject is said to be something or to do something that is not logically possible. This breakdown in meaning is called **faulty predication.** Similarly, mismatches between a verb and its complement can obscure meaning.

(a) Mismatch between subject and verb
The joining of a subject and a verb must create a meaningful idea.

Mismatch	The absence of detail screams out at the reader.
	[An *absence* cannot scream.]
Revision	The reader immediately notices the absence of detail.

(b) Illogical equation with *be*

When a form of the verb *be* joins two parts of a sentence (the subject and the subject complement), these two parts should be logically related.

Speed
~~The importance of speed~~ is essential when you are walking on thin ice.

[*Importance* cannot be essential.]

(c) Mismatches in definitions

When you write a formal definition, be sure that your subject and predicate (see **20b**) fit together grammatically. The term being defined should be followed by a noun or a noun phrase, not an adverbial clause. Avoid using *is when* or *is where*.

Ecology is ~~when you~~ the study of the relationships among living organisms and between living organisms and their environment.

Exploitative competition is ~~where~~ the contest between two or more organisms ~~vie~~ vying for a limited resource such as food.

(d) Mismatch of *reason* with *is because*

You can see why *reason* and *is because* are a mismatch by looking at the meaning of *because*: "for the reason that." Saying "the reason is for the reason that" is redundant. Thus, revise any sentence containing the construction *the reason is . . . because*.

The ~~reason the~~ old train station was closed ~~is~~ because it had fallen into disrepair.

(e) Mismatch between verb and complement

A verb and its complement should fit together meaningfully.

Mismatch	Only a few students used the incorrect use of *there*.
	[To "use an incorrect use" is not logical.]
Revision	Only a few students used *there* incorrectly.

To make sure that a relative pronoun in the object position is connected logically to a verb, replace the pronoun with its antecedent. In the following sentence, *the inspiration* is the antecedent for *that.*

Mismatch	The inspiration that the author created touched young writers. [To "create an inspiration" is not logical.]
Revision	The author inspired young writers.

(3) Verbs used to integrate information are followed by specific types of complements.

Attributive tags are phrases used to identify sources of information (see **11d(1)**). Most verbs in attributive tags are followed by a noun clause beginning with *that* or a *wh-* word (**21b(2)**). A few common verbs and their typical complements are listed below. (Some verbs such as *explain* fall into more than one category.)

VERBS FOR ATTRIBUTION AND THEIR COMPLEMENTS

Verb + *that* **noun clause**

agree	claim	explain	report	suggest
argue	demonstrate	maintain	state	think

Example: The researcher **reported that the weather patterns had changed.**

Verb + noun phrase + *that* **noun clause**

convince	persuade	remind	tell

Example: He **told the reporters that he was planning to resign.**

Verb + *wh-* **noun clause**

demonstrate	discuss	report	suggest
describe	explain	state	wonder

Example: She **described what had happened.**

Exercise 2

Revise the following sentences so that each verb is followed by a conventional complement.

1. The committee chair discussed that funding requests had specific requirements.
2. He persuaded that mass transit was affordable.
3. The two groups agreed how the problem could be solved.
4. Brown and Edwards described that improvements had been made to the old building.
5. They wondered that such a catastrophe could happen.

27e Completing comparisons

A comparison has two parts: someone or something is compared to someone or something else. As you revise your writing, make sure that your audience knows who or what is being compared. To revise incomplete comparisons, add necessary words, phrases, or clauses.

Printers today are quite different . *from those sold in the early 1990s*

His first novel was better . *than the one just published*

After you are sure that your comparisons are complete, check to see that they are also logical.

Her test scores are higher than *those of* the other students.

In the original sentence, *scores* were being compared to *students*. You could also rewrite this sentence as follows:

Her test scores are higher than the other students'.

Because *test scores* have already been mentioned, it is clear that *students'* (with an apostrophe) is short for *students' test scores.*

27f Completing intensifiers

In speech, the intensifiers *so, such,* or *too* are used to mean "very," "unusually," or "extremely."

> That movie was **so** funny.

In academic and professional writing, however, the intensifiers *so, such,* and *too* require a completing phrase or clause.

> That movie was **so** funny **that I watched it twice.**
> Julian has **such** a hearty laugh **that it makes everyone else laugh with him.**
> The problem is just **too** complex **to solve in one day.**

Exercise 3

Revise the following sentences to make them clear and complete.

1. By studying the villains' faces in the *Star Wars* movies can reveal popular notions about the look of evil.
2. To design the character of Darth Maul for *The Phantom Menace,* Iain McCaig started by illustrating a picture of his worst nightmare.
3. He drew generic male face with metal teeth and long red ribbons of hair falling in front of it.
4. Ralph McQuarrie sketched designs for R2D2 and Darth Vader, including his mask. McCaig wanted to create something scarier.
5. When after arriving at many dead ends, McCaig finally had an idea of what he wanted to do.
6. He designed a face that looked as though it been flayed.
7. The evil visage of Darth Maul was so horrible. To balance the effect, McCaig added elegant black feathers.
8. However, the need to add beauty was not shared by others on the production team, and the feathers eventually became small horns.

28

SUBORDINATION

AND

COORDINATION

Subordination and coordination both refer to the joining of grammatical structures. **Subordination** is the linking of grammatically unequal structures (usually a dependent clause to an independent clause). **Coordination** is the linking of structures that have the same grammatical rank (two independent clauses, for example). By using subordination and coordination, you indicate connections between ideas as well as add variety to your sentence style (see chapter **31**). This chapter will help you

- use subordination effectively (**28a**),
- use coordination effectively (**28b**), and
- avoid faulty or excessive subordination and coordination (**28c**).

28a Using subordination effectively

Subordinate means "being of lower rank." A subordinate grammatical structure cannot stand alone; it is dependent on the main (independent) clause. The most common subordinate structure is the dependent clause (see **21b(2)**), which usually begins with a subordinating conjunction or a relative pronoun.

(1) Subordinating conjunctions

A **subordinating conjunction** specifies the relationship between a dependent clause and an independent clause. For example, it might signal a causal relationship.

The painters finished early **because they work well together.**

Here are a few of the most frequently used subordinating conjunctions:

Cause	*because*
Concession	*although, even though*
Condition	*if, unless*
Effect	*so that*
Sequence	*before, after*
Time	*when*

By using subordinating conjunctions, you can combine short sentences and indicate how they are related.

After the   *, we*
~~The~~ crew leader picked us up early on Friday~~.~~ ~~We~~ ate breakfast together at a local diner.

If the subjects of the two clauses are the same, the dependent clause can often be shortened.

eating
After ~~we ate~~ our breakfast, we headed back to the construction site.

(2) Relative pronouns

A **relative pronoun** (*who, whom, which, that,* or *whose*) introduces a dependent clause that, in most cases, modifies the pronoun's antecedent. (See **25a(2)**.)

The temple has a <u>portico</u> **that faces west.**

By using a **relative clause**—that is, a dependent clause introduced by a relative pronoun—you can embed details into a sentence without sacrificing conciseness.

, which has sold well in the United States
Japanese automakers have produced a hybrid car.

A relative clause can be shortened, as long as the meaning of the sentence remains clear.

The runner ~~who was~~ from Brazil stumbled just before the finish line.

A relative clause beginning with *which* sometimes refers to an entire independent clause rather than modifying a specific word or phrase. Because this type of reference can be vague, you should avoid it if possible.

As
He is a graduate of a top university, ~~which should provide~~ him with many *he should have* opportunities.

28b Using coordination effectively

Coordinate means "being of equal rank." Coordinate grammatical elements have the same form. For example, they may be two words that are both adjectives, two phrases that are both prepositional, or two clauses that are both dependent or both independent.

a **stunning** and **satisfying** conclusion [adjectives]

in the attic or **in the basement** [prepositional phrases]

so that everyone would be happy and **so that no one would complain** [dependent adverbial clauses]

The company was losing money, yet **the employees suspected nothing.** [independent clauses]

To indicate the relationship between coordinate words, phrases, or clauses, choose an appropriate coordinating conjunction.

Addition	*and*
Alternative	*or, not*
Cause	*for*
Contrast	*but, yet*
Result	*so*

By using coordination, you can avoid unnecessary repetition and thus make your sentences more concise.

The hike to the top of Angels Landing has countless switchbacks *and* ~~. It also has~~ long drop-offs.

Choosing Conjunctions

In English, use either a coordinating conjunction or a subordinating conjunction, but not both, to signal a connection between clauses.

Even though I took some aspirin, ~~but~~ I still have a sore shoulder.

Because he had a severe headache, ~~so~~ he went to the health center.

Alternatively, the clauses in these two example sentences can be connected with coordinating conjunctions, rather than subordinating conjunctions.

I took some aspirin, **but** I still have a sore shoulder.

He had a severe headache, **so** he went to the health center.

Exercise 1

Using subordination and coordination, revise the sentences in the following paragraph so that they emphasize the ideas you think are important.

1The Lummi tribe lives in the Northwest. **2**The Lummis have a belief about sorrow and loss. **3**They believe that grief is a burden. **4**According to their culture, this burden shouldn't be carried alone. **5**After the terrorist attack on the World Trade Center, the Lummis wanted to help shoulder the burden of grief felt by others. **6**Some of the Lummis carve totem poles. **7**These carvers crafted a healing totem pole. **8**They gave this pole to the citizens of New York. **9**Many of the citizens of New York had family members who were killed in the terrorist attacks. **10**The Lummis escorted the totem pole across the nation. **11**They made stops for small ceremonies. **12**At these ceremonies, they offered blessings. **13**They also offered songs. **14**The Lummis don't believe that the pole itself heals. **15**Rather, they believe that healing comes from the prayers and songs said over it. **16**For them, healing isn't the responsibility of a single person. **17**They believe that it is the responsibility of the community.

28c Avoiding faulty or excessive subordination and coordination

(1) Precise conjunctions enhance readability.

Effective subordination requires choosing subordinating conjunctions carefully. In the following sentence, the use of *as* is distracting because it can mean either "because" or "while."

> *Because*
> ⟨As time was running out, I randomly filled in the remaining circles on the exam sheet.

Sometimes you may need to add a subordinating conjunction to a phrase for clarity. Without the addition of *although* in the revision of the following sentence, the connection between being a new player and winning games is unclear.

> *Although* *he won*
> ⟨Chen was a new player, ⟨~~winning~~ more than half of his games.

Your choice of coordinating conjunction should also convey your meaning precisely. For example, to indicate a cause-and-effect relationship, *so* is more precise than *and*.

> *so*
> The rain continued to fall, ~~and~~ the concert was canceled.
> ⟨

(2) Excessive subordination and coordination can confuse readers.

As you revise your writing, make sure that you have not overused subordination or coordination. In the following ineffective sentence, two dependent clauses compete for the reader's focus. The revision is clearer because it eliminates one of the dependent clauses.

Ineffective

Although researchers used to believe that ancient Egyptians were the first to domesticate cats, they now think that cats may have provided company for humans 5,000 years earlier **because** the intact skeleton of a cat has been discovered in a Neolithic village on Cyprus.

Revised

Although researchers used to believe that ancient Egyptians were the first to domesticate cats, they now think that cats may have provided company for humans 5,000 years earlier. They base their revised estimate on the discovery of an intact cat skeleton in a Neolithic village on Cyprus.

Overuse of coordination results in a rambling sentence in need of revision.

Ineffective

The lake was surrounded by forest, and it was large and clean, so it looked refreshing.

Revised

Surrounded by forest, the large, clean lake looked refreshing.

Exercise 2

Revise the following sentences to eliminate faulty or excessive coordination and subordination. Be prepared to explain why your sentences are more effective than the originals.

1. The Duct Tape Guys usually describe humorous uses for duct tape, providing serious information about the history of duct tape on their Web site.

2. Duct tape was invented for the U.S. military during World War II to keep the moisture out of ammunition cases because it was strong and waterproof.

3. Duct tape was originally called "duck tape" as it was waterproof and ducks are like that too and because it was made of cotton duck, which is a durable, tightly woven material.

4. Duck tape was also used to repair jeeps and to repair aircraft, its primary use being to protect ammunition cases.

5. When the war was over, house builders used duck tape to connect duct work together, and the builders started to refer to duck tape as "duct tape" and eventually the color of the tape changed from the green that was used during the war to silver, which matched the ducts.

29

PARALLELISM

Parallelism is the use of grammatically equivalent structures to clarify meaning and to emphasize ideas. Parallel structures often occur in a series.

> Their goals are **to raise awareness of the natural area, to build a walking path near the creek running through it,** and **to construct a nature center at the east end of the parking lot.**

This chapter will help you

- recognize parallel elements (**29a**),
- create parallelism by repeating words and grammatical forms (**29b**),
- use parallel elements to link sentences (**29c**),
- link parallel elements with correlative conjunctions (**29d**), and
- use parallelism for emphasis in introductions and conclusions (**29e**).

29a Recognizing parallel elements

Two or more elements are considered parallel when they have similar grammatical forms—for example, when they are all nouns or all prepositional phrases. Parallel elements are frequently joined by a coordinating conjunction (*and, but, or, yet, so, nor,* or *for*). In the examples that follow, the elements in boldface have the same grammatical form.

Words   The dean is both **determined** and **dedicated.**

Phrases   She emphasized her commitment to **academic freedom, professional development, cultural diversity,** and **social justice.**

Phrases	Her goals include **publicizing student and faculty research, increasing the funding for that research, and providing adequate research facilities.**
Clauses	Our instructor explained **what the project had entailed** and **how the results had been used.** He said **that we would conduct a similar project** but **that we would likely get different results.**
Sentences	**When I interviewed for the job, <u>I tried not to sweat.</u>** **When I got the job, <u>I managed not to shout.</u>**

Exercise 1

Write two sentences that illustrate each of the following structures: parallel words, parallel phrases, parallel clauses, and parallel sentences. Use the examples in this section as models.

29b Repeating words and grammatical forms

(1) The repetition of words often creates parallel elements.

By repeating a preposition, the infinitive marker *to,* or the introductory word of a clause, you can create parallel structures that will help you convey your meaning clearly, succinctly, and emphatically.

Preposition	For about fifteen minutes, I have been pacing in my office, hands **on** my hips, a scowl **on** my face, and a grudge **on** my mind. My embarrassment stemmed not **from** the money lost but **from** the notoriety gained.
Infinitive marker *to*	She wanted her audience **to remember** the protest song and **to understand** its origin.
Introductory word of a clause	The team vowed **that** they would support each other, **that** they would play their best, and **that** they would win the tournament.

(2) Parallel structures can be created through the repetition of form only.

Sometimes parallel structures are similar in form even though no words are repeated. The following example includes the *-ing* form (present participle) of three different verbs.

> People all around me are **buying, remodeling,** or **selling** their houses.

The next example includes a compound dependent clause, each part of which has a two-word subject and a one-word predicate.

> Whether **mortgage rates rise** or
> > **building codes change,** the real estate market should remain strong this spring.

29c Linking two or more sentences

Repeating a pattern emphasizes the relationship of ideas. The following two sentences come from the conclusion of "Letter from Birmingham Jail."

> **If I have said anything** in this letter that overstates the truth and indicates an unreasonable impatience, **I beg you to forgive me. If I have said anything** that understates the truth and indicates my having a patience that allows me to settle for anything less than brotherhood, **I beg God to forgive me.** —MARTIN LUTHER KING, JR.

Almost every structure in the second sentence is parallel to a structure in the first. To create this parallelism, King repeats words and uses similar grammatical forms. But the second sentence would still be parallel with the first even if more of its words were different. For example, substituting *written* for *said* and *reveals* for *indicates* ("If I have written anything that understates the truth and reveals my having a patience . . . ") would result in a sentence that was still parallel with the first sentence. Such changes, though, would lessen the impact of this particular passage because they would detract from the important substitution of "God" for "you" in the second sentence.

THINKING RHETORICALLY ABOUT

PARALLELISM

Parallel elements make your writing easy to read. But consider breaking from the parallel pattern on occasion to emphasize a point. For example, to describe a friend, you could start with two adjectives and then switch to a noun phrase.

My friend Alison is **kind, modest,** and **the smartest mathematician in the state.**

29d Using correlative conjunctions

Correlative conjunctions (or **correlatives**) are pairs of words that link other words, phrases, or clauses (see **20a(7)** and **21c(2)**).

both . . . and
either . . . or
neither . . . nor
not only . . . but also
whether . . . or

Notice how the words or phrases following each conjunction in the pair are parallel.

He will major in **either** <u>biology</u> **or** <u>chemistry</u>.

Whether <u>at home</u> **or** <u>at school</u>, he is always busy.

Be especially careful when using *not only . . . but also.*

His team not only practices
~~Not only practicing~~ at 6 a.m. during the week~~,~~ but ~~his team~~ also scrimmages on Sunday afternoons.

OR

does his team practice   it
Not only ~~practicing~~ at 6 a.m. during the week, but ~~the team~~ also scrimmages on Sunday afternoons.

29e Emphasizing key ideas in introductions and conclusions

By expressing key ideas in parallel structures, you emphasize them. However, be careful not to overuse parallel patterns, or they will lose their impact. Parallelism is especially effective in the introduction to a paragraph or an essay. The following passage from the introduction to a chapter of a book on advertising contains three examples of parallel forms.

> While **men are encouraged to fall in love with their cars, women are more often invited to have a romance,** indeed an erotic experience, with **something closer to home, something that truly does pump the valves of our hearts**—the food we eat. And the consequences become even more severe as we enter into the territory of **compulsivity** and **addiction.**
>
> —JEAN KILBOURNE, *Deadly Persuasion*

Parallel structures can also be effective in the conclusion to an essay.

> **Because these men work** with **animals,** not **machines, because they live** outside in landscapes of torrential beauty, **because they are confined** to **a place** and **a routine** embellished with awesome variables, **because calves die** in the arms that pulled others into life, **because they go** to the mountains as if on a pilgrimage to find out what makes a herd of elk tick, **their strength** is also **a softness, their toughness, a rare delicacy.**
>
> —GRETEL EHRLICH, "About Men"

BEYOND THE RULE

PARALLELISM AND POLITICS

Because parallelism helps make ideas easy to grasp and remember, it is frequently used by politicians when giving speeches. Some parallel structures have been used so often that they have become clichés. But others have helped to win elections or defined important moments in world history. For examples, visit **www.harbrace.com**.

Exercise 2

Make the structures in each sentence parallel. In some sentences, you may have to use different wording.

1. Helen was praised by the vice president, and her assistant admired her.

2. Colleagues found her genial and easy to schedule meetings with.

3. When she hired new employees for her department, she looked for applicants who were intelligent, able to stay focused, and able to speak clearly.

4. At meetings, she was always prepared, participating actively yet politely, and generated innovative responses to department concerns.

5. In her annual report, she wrote that her most important achievements were attracting new clients and revenues were higher.

6. When asked about her leadership style, she said that she preferred collaborating with others rather than to work alone in her office.

7. Although dedicated to her work, Helen also recognized that parenting was important and the necessity of cultivating a life outside of work.

8. She worked hard to save money for the education of her children, for her own music lessons, and investing for her retirement.

9. However, in the coming year, she hoped to reduce the number of weekends she worked in the office and spending more time at home.

10. She would like to plan a piano recital and also have the opportunity to plan a family vacation.

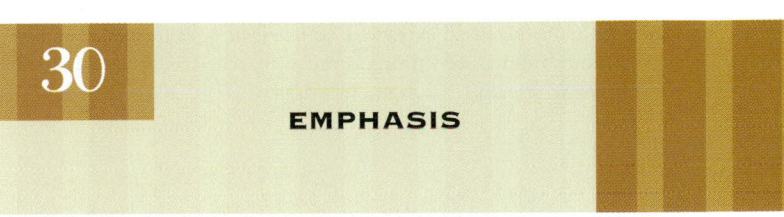

30

EMPHASIS

In any rhetorical situation, some of your ideas will be more important than others. You can direct the reader's attention to these ideas by emphasizing them. This chapter will help you

- place words where they receive emphasis (**30a**),
- use cumulative and periodic sentences (**30b**),
- arrange ideas in climactic order (**30c**),
- repeat important words (**30d**),
- choose between active voice and passive voice (**30e**),
- invert word order in sentences (**30f**), and
- use an occasional short sentence (**30g**).

You can also emphasize ideas by using subordination and coordination (chapter **28**), parallelism (chapter **29**), and exact word choice (chapter **33**).

30a Placing words for emphasis

Words at the beginning or the end of a sentence—especially the end—receive emphasis. Notice how the revision of the following sentence adds emphasis to the beginning to balance the emphasis at the end.

~~In today's society, most good~~ *Good* jobs *today* require a college education.

You can also emphasize an important idea by placing it after a colon or a dash. (See also **39d–e**.)

By "power" I mean precisely the capacity to do what force always does**:** coerce assent.   —**CYNTHIA OZICK**

By 1857, miners had extracted 760 tons of gold from these hills—and left behind more than ten times as much mercury, as well as devastated forests, slopes and streams.   —REBECCA SOLNIT

Exercise 1

Find the most important idea in each set of sentences. Then combine each set into one sentence so that the most important idea is emphasized. Be prepared to explain your changes.

1. Snowboarding is a new sport. It debuted at the Olympics in 1998. The Olympics were held in Nagano, Japan, that year.

2. Snowboarders came from around the world. Some competed in the giant slalom. Others participated in the halfpipe.

3. Snowboarding has increased in popularity. Each year, more and more people go snowboarding. It attracted 50 percent more participants in 2000 than it did in 1999.

4. Snowboarding is a fast-growing sport. The number of snowboards sold each year has increased dramatically.

5. However, the inventor of the snowboard is hard to identify. People have been sliding down hills on sleds for a long time.

6. Some sources credit M. M. "Jack" Burchet. Burchet tied his feet to a piece of plywood in 1929.

7. Sherman Poppen is most frequently cited as the inventor of the snowboard. His Snurfer went into production in 1966. (The name is a combination of the words *snow* and *surfer*.)

8. Poppen created the Snurfer for his daughter. He bound two skis together. He also fixed a rope at the front end.

9. Snowboarding originated as a sport for kids. It eventually became a competitive sport.

10. The United States snowboarding team won two medals in the 1998 Olympic Games. The team won five medals in the 2002 Olympic Games.

30b Using cumulative and periodic sentences

In a **cumulative sentence,** the main idea (the independent clause) comes first; less important ideas or supplementary details follow.

> **The day was hot for June,** a pale sun burning in a cloudless sky, wilting the last of the irises, the rhododendron blossoms drooping.
>
> —ADAM HASLETT

In a **periodic sentence,** however, the main idea comes last, just before the period.

> In a day when movies seem more and more predictable, when novels tend to be plotless, baggy monsters or minimalist exercises in interior emotion, **it's no surprise that sports has come to occupy an increasingly prominent place in the communal imagination.** —MICHIKO KAKUTANI

Both of these types of sentences can be effective. Because cumulative sentences are more common, however, the infrequently encountered periodic sentence tends to provide more emphasis.

30c Ordering ideas from least to most important

By arranging your ideas in **climactic order**—from least important to most important—you build up suspense. If you place your most important idea first, the sentence may seem to trail off. If you place it in the middle, readers may not recognize its full significance. If, however, you place it at the end of the sentence, it will not only receive emphasis but also provide a springboard to the next sentence. In the following example, the writer emphasizes a doctor's desire to help the disadvantaged and then implies that this desire has been realized through work with young Haitian doctors.

> While he was in medical school, the soon-to-be doctor discovered his calling: to diagnose infectious diseases, to find ways of curing people with these diseases, and **to bring the lifesaving knowledge of modern medicine to the disadvantaged.** Most recently, he has been working with a small group of young doctors in Haiti.

THINKING RHETORICALLY ABOUT

CLIMACTIC ORDER

Placing the least important idea at the end of the sentence can be effective when you are trying to be humorous, as in the following example:

> Contemporary man, of course, has no such peace of mind. He finds himself in the midst of a crisis of faith. He is what we fashionably call "alienated." He has seen the ravages of war, he has known natural catastrophes, he has been to singles bars. **—WOODY ALLEN**

30d Repeating important words

Although effective writers avoid unnecessary repetition, they also understand that deliberate repetition emphasizes key words or ideas.

> We **forget** all too soon the things we thought we could never **forget.** We **forget** the loves and betrayals alike, **forget** what we whispered and what we screamed, **forget** who we are. **—JOAN DIDION**

In this case, the emphatic repetition of *forget* reinforces the author's point—that we do not remember many things that once seemed impossible to forget. If you decide to repeat a word for emphasis, make sure that the word you choose conveys one of your central ideas.

30e Choosing between the active voice and the passive voice

(1) Sentences in the active and passive voices differ in form.

A sentence in the **active voice** emphasizes an actor and an action by having the actor as the subject. The **passive voice** emphasizes the receiver or the result of the action, with the actor often omitted entirely. (See **26d.**) If a reference to an actor is included in a passive sentence, this reference appears in a prepositional phrase beginning with *by.* The verb phrase in the passive voice also differs from its active counterpart: it includes the auxiliary verb *be* and the past participle of the main verb.

Active   Bob Dylan wrote that song.

Passive   That song **was written by** Bob Dylan.

(2) Sentences in the active voice highlight actors and actions.

The author of the following excerpt uses the active voice to describe the passage of an airplane and the passengers inside it.

> [1]The tiny red light of an airplane **passes** through the sky. [2]It **soars** past a low cloud, the North Star, the bold white W of Cassiopeia—vanishing and reappearing, winking in a long ellipsis. [3]Inside, its passengers **read** glossy periodicals, **summon** flight attendants, and **unhitch** the frames of their safety belts. [4]They **gaze** from the panes of double windows and **float** away in a tight red arc.   —KEVIN BROCKMEIER, "Space"

Notice how much less effective the third sentence is when written in the passive voice, with the emphasis on the actors removed.

> Inside, glossy periodicals **are read,** flight attendants **are summoned,** and the frames of safety belts **are unhitched.**

(3) Sentences in the passive voice emphasize recipients or objects of actions.

In a paragraph from a government-sponsored Web page that warns against the use of illicit drugs, the passive voice is used to discuss the drug methamphetamine. Paragraphs on users and producers of the drug are written primarily in the active voice, but the paragraph about the drug itself and the various ways in which it is used is written in the passive voice. Drug users and producers are not mentioned in this paragraph because the drug itself is the focus.

> Methamphetamine **can be ingested, inhaled,** or **injected.** It **is sold** as a powder or in small chunks which resemble rock candy. It **can be mixed** with water for injection or sprinkled on tobacco or marijuana and smoked. Chunks of clear, high-purity methamphetamine ("ice," "crystal," "glass") **are smoked** in a small pipe, much as "crack" cocaine **is smoked.**
> —UTAH ATTORNEY GENERAL'S OFFICE

Because whoever or whatever is responsible for the action is not the subject of a sentence in the passive voice, such a sentence is often imprecise. Politicians sometimes favor the passive voice because it allows them to avoid responsibility by saying, for example, "Taxes will have to be raised" or "A few miscalculations were made."

Grammar checkers flag all uses of the passive voice they find, usually suggesting that they be changed to the active voice. Be sure to determine for yourself whether the active voice or the passive voice is more appropriate for your rhetorical situation.

30f Inverting word order

Most sentences begin with a subject and end with a predicate. When you move words out of their normal order, you draw attention to them.

<u>At the back of the crowded room</u> sat **a newspaper reporter.**
[COMPARE: **A newspaper reporter** sat <u>**at the back of the crowded room.**</u>]

<u>Fundamental to life in New York</u> is **the subway.**
[COMPARE: **The subway** is <u>**fundamental to life in New York.**</u>]

A sentence with inverted word order will stand out in a paragraph containing other sentences with standard word order. Notice the inverted word order in the second sentence of the following passage.

[1]The Library Committee met with the City Council on several occasions to persuade them to fund the building of a library annex. [2]So successful were their efforts that a new wing will be added by next year. [3]This wing will contain archival materials that were previously stored in the basement.

The modifier *so successful* appears at the beginning of the sentence, rather than in its normal position, after the verb: Their efforts were *so successful* that . . . . The inverted word order emphasizes the committee's accomplishment.

Inverting Word Order

English sentences are inverted in various ways. Sometimes the main verb in the form of a participle is placed at the beginning of the sentence. The subject and the auxiliary verb(s) are then inverted.

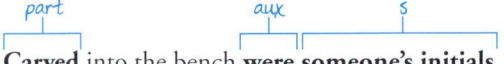

Carved into the bench **were someone's initials.**

[COMPARE: Someone's initials were carved into the bench.]

An adjective may also begin a sentence. In this type of sentence, the subject and the linking verb are inverted.

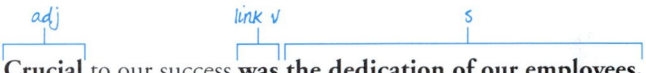

Crucial to our success **was the dedication of our employees.**

[COMPARE: The dedication of our employees was crucial to our success.]

In other inverted sentences, the auxiliary verb comes before the subject. Sentences beginning with a negative adverb (such as *never, seldom,* or *rarely*) require this type of inversion.

Rarely have we experienced such bad weather!

30g Using an occasional short sentence

In a paragraph of mostly long sentences, try using a short sentence for emphasis. To optimize the effect, lead up to the short sentence with an especially long sentence.

> After organizing the kitchen, buying the groceries, slicing the vegetables, mowing the lawn, weeding the garden, hanging the decorations, and setting up the grill, I was ready to have a good time when my guests arrived. **Then the phone rang.**

Exercise 2

Add emphasis to each of the following sentences by using the strategy indicated. You may have to add some words and/or delete others.

1. (climactic order) In the 1960 Olympics, Wilma Rudolph tied the world record in the 100-meter race, she tied the record in the 400-meter relay, she won the hearts of fans from around the world, and she broke the record in the 200-meter race.

2. (periodic sentence) Some sports reporters described Rudolph as a gazelle because of her beautiful stride.

3. (inversion) Rudolph's Olympic achievement is impressive, but her victory over a crippling disease is even more spectacular.

4. (final short sentence) Rudolph was born prematurely, weighing only four and one-half pounds. As a child, she suffered from double pneumonia, scarlet fever, and then polio.

5. (cumulative sentence) She received help from her family. Her brothers and sister massaged her legs. Her mother drove her to a hospital for therapy.

6. (inversion) Her siblings' willingness to help was essential to her recovery, as were her mother's vigilant care and her own determination.

7. (periodic sentence) Her passions became basketball and track after she recovered, built up her strength, and gained self-confidence.

8. (climactic order) Rudolph set a scoring record in basketball, she set the standard for future track and field stars, and she set an Olympic record in track.

9. (active voice) Many female athletes, including Florence Griffith Joyner and Jackie Joyner-Kersee, have been inspired by Wilma Rudolph.

31

VARIETY

To make your writing lively and distinctive, include a variety of sentence types and lengths. Notice how the sentences in the paragraph below vary in length (short and long), form (simple, compound, and compound-complex), and type (statements, questions, and commands). This assortment of sentences makes this paragraph about pleasure pleasurable to read.

> Start with the taste. Imagine a moment when the sensation of honey or sugar on the tongue was an astonishment, a kind of intoxication. The closest I've ever come to recovering such a sense of sweetness was secondhand, though it left a powerful impression on me even so. I'm thinking of my son's first experience with sugar: the icing on the cake at his first birthday. I have only the testimony of Isaac's face to go by (that, and his fierceness to repeat the experience), but it was plain that his first encounter with sugar had intoxicated him—was in fact an ecstasy, in the literal sense of the word. That is, he was beside himself with the pleasure of it, no longer here with me in space and time in quite the same way he had been just a moment before. Between bites Isaac gazed up at me in amazement (he was on my lap, and I was delivering the ambrosial forkfuls to his gaping mouth) as if to exclaim, "Your world contains *this?* From this day forward I shall dedicate my life to it." (Which he basically has done.) And I remember thinking, this is no minor desire, and then wondered: Could it be that sweetness is the prototype of *all* desire?   —**MICHAEL POLLAN**, *The Botany of Desire*

This chapter will help you

- revise sentence length and form (**31a**),
- vary sentence openings (**31b**), and
- use an occasional question, command, or exclamation (**31c**).

If you have difficulty distinguishing between various types of sentence structures, review the fundamentals in chapters **20** and **21**.

31a Revising sentence length and form

(1) Combine short sentences.

To avoid the choppiness of a series of short sentences, consider using one of the following methods to combine some of the sentences into longer sentences.

(a) Use coordinate or correlative conjunctions.

Try combining ideas using coordinate conjunctions (*and, but, or, for, nor, so,* and *yet*) or correlative conjunctions (*both . . . and, either . . . or, neither . . . nor,* and *not only . . . but also*).

Simple sentences	Minneapolis is one of the Twin Cities. St. Paul is the other. They differ in many ways.
Combined	Minneapolis **and** St. Paul are called the Twin Cities, **but** they differ in many ways.
Simple sentences	The company provides health insurance. It also provides dental insurance.
Combined	The company provides **both** health insurance **and** dental insurance.

(b) Use relative pronouns or subordinating conjunctions.

The relative pronouns *who, which, whose,* and *that* can be used to combine simple sentences.

Simple sentences	Today, lawmakers discussed some new legislation. This legislation would promote the safety of rocket passengers.
Combined	Today, lawmakers discussed some new legislation **that** would promote the safety of rocket passengers.

You can also use subordinating conjunctions such as *because, so that,* and *even though* to join simple sentences. For a full list, see page 499.

Simple sentences	Legislation on space tourism has not been passed. Plans for a commercial rocket service are going forward anyway.
Combined	**Although** legislation on space tourism has not been passed, plans for a commercial rocket service are going forward anyway.

You may also decide to use both a subordinating and a coordinating conjunction.

Simple sentences	Private rockets have been involved in very few accidents. Legislators are discussing safety issues, though. They have not agreed on any regulations yet.
Combined	**Although** private rockets have been involved in very few accidents, legislators are discussing safety issues, **but** they have not agreed on regulations yet.

Although a grammar checker will flag long sentences, it cannot determine whether they contribute to variety. You will have to decide whether you have used them effectively. See **Using a Grammar Checker** on page 461.

THINKING RHETORICALLY ABOUT

SHORT SENTENCES

Occasionally, a series of brief sentences produces an intended effect. For example, a writer may have a rhetorical reason for conveying a sense of abruptness; thus, what might seem choppy in one situation could be considered dramatic in another. The short sentences in the following passage capture the quick actions taking place as an accident is about to occur.

"There's a truck in your lane!" my friend yelled. I swerved toward the shoulder. "Watch out!" she screamed. I hit the brakes. The wheel locked. The back of the car swerved to the right.

Exercise 1

Convert each set of short sentences into a single longer sentence. Use no more than one coordinating conjunction in the revised sentence.

1. It was the bottom of the ninth inning. The score was tied. The bases were loaded. There were two outs.

2. A young player stepped up to the plate. This was his first season. He had hit a home run yesterday. He had struck out his last time at bat.

3. He knew the next pitch could decide the game. He took a practice swing. The pitcher looked him over.

4. The pitch came in high. The batter swung low. He missed this first pitch. He also missed the second pitch.

5. He had two strikes against him. The young player hit the next ball. It soared over the right-field fence.

(2) Avoid the overuse of coordinating conjunctions.

In early drafts, some writers overuse the coordinating conjunctions *and* and *but*, so the pattern of long compound sentences becomes tedious. The use of coordinating conjunctions can also be ineffective if the relationship the writer is signaling is vague. The following strategies should help you revise ineffective uses of coordinating conjunctions.

(a) Use a more specific subordinating conjunction or conjunctive adverb.

You can often replace *and* with a more specific subordinating conjunction or conjunctive adverb (see **21c**).

I worked all summer to earn tuition money, ~~and I didn't~~ *so that I wouldn't* have to work during the school year.

OR

I worked all summer to earn tuition money and **thus** didn't have to work during the school year.

(b) Use a relative clause to embed information.

Seafood ~~is nutritious, and it is low in fat, and it~~ *, which is nutritious and low in fat,* has become available in greater variety.

(c) Allow two or more verbs to share the same subject.

Marie quickly grabbed a shovel, ~~and then she~~ ran to the edge of the field, and ~~then she~~ put out the fire before it could spread to the trees.

(d) Place some information in an appositive phrase.

Karl Glazebrook *, a researcher in astronomy at Johns Hopkins University,* ~~is a researcher in astronomy at Johns Hopkins University,~~ ~~and he~~ has questioned the conventional theory of galaxy formations.

(e) Place some information in a prepositional or verbal phrase.

In the thick snow,
~~The snow was thick, and~~ we could not see where we were going.

After pulling ~~The plane pulled~~ away from the gate on time, *the plane* ~~and then it~~ sat on the runway for two hours.

OR

The plane, after pulling away from the gate on time, sat on the runway for two hours.

In the last example, the subject, *plane,* and the verb, *sat,* are separated. Although it is usually best to keep the subject next to the verb so that the relationship between them is clear, breaking this pattern on occasion can add variety without sacrificing clarity.

Exercise 2

Revise the following paragraph, using any of the methods for revising the ineffective use of coordinating conjunctions.

[1]Onions are pungent, they are indispensable, and they are found in kitchens everywhere. [2]China is the leading producer of this vegetable. [3]Libya is the leading consumer, and on average a Libyan eats over sixty-five pounds of onions a year. [4]One hundred billion pounds of

onions are produced each year, and they make their way into a variety of foods. **⁵**Raw onions add zest to salads, but they also add zest to burgers and salsas. **⁶**Cooked onions give a sweetness to pasta sauces, and they can also be added to soups and curries. **⁷**The onion is a ubiquitous ingredient, yet its origin remains unknown.

31b Varying sentence openings

Most writers begin more than half of their sentences with the subject. Although this pattern is common, relying on it too heavily can make writing sound dull. Experiment with the following alternatives for beginning your sentences.

(1) Begin with an adverb or an adverbial clause.

Immediately, the dentist stopped drilling and asked me how I was doing. [adverb]

When the procedure was over, he explained that I should not eat or drink anything for an hour. [adverbial clause]

(2) Begin with a prepositional or verbal phrase.

In the auditorium, voters waited in silence before casting their ballots. [prepositional phrase]

To win, candidates need to convey a clear message to voters. [infinitive phrase]

Reflecting on the election, we understood clearly how the incumbent defeated the challenger. [participial phrase]

(3) Begin with a connecting word or phrase.

In each of the following examples, the connecting word or phrase shows the relationship between the ideas in the pair of sentences. (See also **4d**.)

Many restaurants close within a few years of opening. **But** others, which offer good food at reasonable prices, become well established.

Difficulty in finding a place to park keeps some people from going out to lunch downtown. **However,** that problem may be alleviated with the construction of a new underground parking garage.

Independently owned restaurants struggle to get started for a number of reasons. **First of all,** they have to compete against successful restaurant chains.

(4) Begin with an appositive or absolute phrase.

A town of historic interest, Santa Fe also has many art galleries. [appositive phrase]

History, art, and the color of the sky—these drew her to Santa Fe. [appositive series]

Her face turned to the sky, she absorbed the warmth of the sun. [absolute phrase]

(5) Begin with a direct object or a predicate adjective.

I was an abysmal football player. **Soccer,** though, I could play well. [direct object]

Vital to any success I had were my mother's early lessons. [predicate adjective]

Exercise 3

Rewrite each sentence so that it does not begin with a subject.

1. John Spilsbury was an engraver and mapmaker from London who made the first jigsaw puzzle in about 1760.

2. He pasted a map onto a piece of wood and used a fine-bladed saw to cut around the borders of the countries.

3. The jigsaw puzzle was first an educational toy and has been a mainstay in households all over the world ever since its invention.

4. The original puzzles were quite expensive because the wooden pieces were cut by hand.

5. Most puzzles are made of cardboard today.

31c Using questions, commands, and exclamations

When you have written a long series of declarative statements, you can vary the paragraph by introducing another type of sentence: a question, a command, or an exclamation (see **21e**). The sentence that varies from the others will catch the reader's attention.

(1) Raise a question or two for variety.

If people could realize that immigrant children are better off, and less scarred, by holding on to their first languages as they learn a second one, then perhaps Americans could accept a more drastic change. What if every English-speaking toddler were to start learning a foreign language at an early age, maybe in kindergarten? What if these children were to learn Spanish, for instance, the language already spoken by millions of American citizens, but also by so many neighbors to the South?

—ARIEL DORFMAN

Just as variety in the elements of an image draws the viewer's attention, variety in sentences catches the reader's attention.

You can either answer the question or let readers answer it for themselves, in which case it is called a **rhetorical question** (see **21e**).

(2) Add an exclamatory sentence for variety.

But at other moments, the classroom is so lifeless or painful or confused—and I so powerless to do anything about it—that my claim to be a teacher seems a transparent sham. Then the enemy is everywhere: in those students from some alien planet, in the subject I thought I knew, and in the personal pathology that keeps me earning my living this way. What a fool I was to imagine that I had mastered this occult art—harder to divine than tea leaves and impossible for mortals to do even passably well!

—PARKER PALMER, *The Courage to Teach*

Although you can make your sentences emphatic without resorting to the use of exclamation points (see chapter **30**), the introduction of an exclamatory sentence can break up a regular pattern of declarative sentences.

(3) Include a command for variety.

> Now I stare and stare at people shamelessly. Stare. It's the way to educate your eye. —**WALKER EVANS**

In this case, a one-word command, "Stare," provides variety.

Exercise 4

Explain how questions and commands add variety to the following paragraph. Describe other ways in which this writer varies his sentences.

1The gods, they say, give breath, and they take it away. **2**But the same could be said—couldn't it?—of the humble comma. **3**Add it to the present clause, and, of a sudden, the mind is, quite literally, given pause to think; take it out if you wish or forget it and the mind is deprived of a resting place. **4**Yet still the comma gets no respect. **5**It seems just a slip of a thing, a pedant's tick, a blip on the edge of our consciousness, a kind of printer's smudge almost. **6**Small, we claim, is beautiful (especially in the age of the microchip). **7**Yet what is so often used, and so rarely recalled, as the comma—unless it be breath itself?

—**PICO IYER,** "In Praise of the Humble Comma"

UNITED COLORS
OF BENETTON.

An inclusive advertisement appeals to a diverse audience.

32

GOOD USAGE

Using the right words at the right time can make the difference between having your ideas taken seriously and seeing them brushed aside. In academic or professional writing, it is important to sound well informed and respectful. In conversation with friends, it is just as important to sound casual; otherwise, your friends may think that you are cold or snobbish. Whatever the occasion, choosing the right words will help you connect with your audience. This chapter will help you

- understand how word choice is related to the rhetorical situation (**32a**),
- write in a clear, straightforward style (**32b**),
- choose words that are appropriate for your audience, purpose, and context (**32c**),
- use inclusive language (**32d**), and
- realize the benefits of dictionaries (**32e**) and thesauruses (**32f**).

32a Usage and the rhetorical situation

The words you use vary from situation to situation. How you talk to a loan officer differs from how you talk to your best friend. A discussion with a loan officer is likely to be relatively formal, while a conversation with a friend will be less so. Understanding such differences in tone and making word choices that reflect them are essential in writing because readers cannot see your body language, hear the inflections of your voice, or interrupt to say that they are having trouble following you. Instead, readers respond to the words on the page or the screen. You can help them understand your ideas by choosing words that they know or that you can explain to them. When drafting, use words that come immediately to mind. Some of these words will be good choices. Others you can replace as you revise. Remembering your rhetorical situation will help you use the right word at the right time.

32b Clear style

Although different styles are appropriate for different situations, you should strive to make your writing clear and straightforward. An ornate and wordy style takes more time to read and could make you seem stuffy or pretentious. To achieve a clear style, first choose words that your audience understands and that are appropriate for the occasion.

Ornate   The majority believes that achievement derives primarily from the diligent pursuit of allocated tasks.

Clear   Most people believe that success results from hard work.

When you write clearly, you show your readers that you are aware of the time and effort it takes to read closely. If you want readers to take your writing seriously, you must show them respect by not using obscure words when common words will do and by not using more words than necessary. Using words that are precise (see **33a**) and sentences that are concise (see chapter **34**) can also help you achieve a clear style.

Exercise 1

Revise the following sentences for an audience that prefers a clear, straightforward style.

1. Expert delineation of character in a job interview is a task that is not always possible to achieve.

2. In an employment situation, social pleasantries may contribute to the successful functioning of job tasks, but such interactions should not distract attention from the need to complete all assignments in a timely manner.

3. Commitment to an ongoing and carefully programmed schedule of physical self-management can be a significant resource for stress reduction in the workplace.

32c Appropriate word choice

Unless you are writing for a specialized audience and have good reason to believe that this audience will welcome slang, colloquial expressions, or jargon, the following advice can help you determine which words to use and which to avoid.

(1) Slang is effective in only a few rhetorical situations.

The term **slang** covers a wide range of words or expressions that are considered casual, facetious, or fashionable by people in a particular age group, locality, or profession. Although such words are often used in private conversation or in writing intended to mimic conversation, they are usually out of place in academic or professional writing. If your rhetorical situation does call for the use of slang, be sure that the words or expressions you choose are not so new that your audience will be unable to understand what you mean and not so old that your use of them makes you seem out of touch with popular culture.

(2) Conversational (or colloquial) words are usually too informal for academic and professional writing.

Words labeled *colloquial* in a dictionary are fine for casual conversation and for written dialogues or personal essays on a light topic. Such words are sometimes used for special effect in academic writing, but you should usually replace them with more appropriate words. For example, conversational words such as *dumb* and *kid around* could be replaced by *illogical* and *tease*.

 Because contractions (such as *you'll* for "you will" and *she's* for "she is") reflect the sound of conversation, you can use them in some types of writing to create a friendly tone. However, some of your instructors or supervisors may consider them too informal for academic or professional writing.

(3) Regionalisms can make writing vivid.

Regionalisms—such as *tank* for "pond" and *sweeper* for "vacuum cleaner"—can make writing lively and distinctive, but they are effective only when the audience can understand them in a specific context.

Moreover, many readers consider regionalisms too informal for use in academic and professional writing. Consider your rhetorical situation before using regionalisms.

(4) Technical words are essential when writing for specialists.

When writing for a diverse audience, an effective writer will not refer to the need for bifocals as *presbyopia*. However, technical language is appropriate when the audience can understand it (as when one physician writes to another) or when the audience would benefit by learning the terms in question.

Jargon is technical language tailored specifically for a particular occupation. Jargon can be an efficient shortcut for conveying specialized concepts, but you should use it only when you are sure that you and your readers share an understanding of the terms. *Splash,* for example, does not always refer to water or an effect (as in *making a splash*); the word also signifies a computer screen that can appear after you click on a Web site but before you view its opening page.

BEYOND THE RULE

FROM JARGON TO ACCEPTABILITY

Terms that originate as jargon sometimes enter mainstream usage because nonspecialists begin to use them. As computer use has grown, for example, technical terms such as *download* and *mouse* have become commonly understood. For additional examples of widely adopted jargon, visit **www.harbrace.com**.

32d Inclusive language

By making word choices that are inclusive rather than exclusive, you invite readers into your writing. Advertisers follow a similar principle when they choose images that appeal to a diverse audience. Prejudiced or derogatory language has no place in academic or professional writing; using it undermines your authority and credibility as a writer.

Even if you are writing for one person you think you know well, do not assume that you know everything about that person. A close colleague at work might have an uncle who is gay, for example, or his sister might be married to someone of a different race or religion. Do not try to justify demeaning language on the grounds that you meant it as a joke. Take responsibility for the words you use.

An inclusive advertisement appeals to a diverse audience.

(1) Nonsexist language indicates respect for both men and women.

Effective writers show equal respect for men and women. For example, they avoid using *man* to refer to people in general because they feel that the word excludes women.

> Achievements [OR Human achievements]
> **Man's** ~~achievements~~ in science are impressive.

Sexist language has a variety of sources, such as contempt for the opposite sex and unthinking repetition of words used by others. Stereotyping can also lead to sexist language. Women, like men, can be *firefighters* or *police officers*—words that are increasingly used as gender-neutral alternatives to *firemen* and *policemen*.

A grammar checker can find sexist words ending in *-ess (authoress)* or *-man (policeman)* and almost always flags *mankind*. Unfortunately, grammar checkers also erroneously identify as sexist many appropriate uses of the words *female, woman,* and *girl,* but not similar uses of *male, man,* and *boy.*

Being alert for sexist language and knowing how to revise it will help you gain acceptance from your audience, whatever its demographics. Use the following tips to ensure that your writing is respectful.

TIPS FOR AVOIDING SEXIST LANGUAGE

When you review your drafts, revise the following types of sexist language.

- **Generic *he:*** A doctor should listen to *his* patients.

  A doctor should listen to **his or her** patients. [use of the appropriate form of *he or she*]

  Doctors should listen to **their** patients. [use of plural forms]

  By listening to patients, **doctors obtain important diagnostic information.** [elimination of *his* by revising the sentence]

- **Occupational stereotype:** Glenda James, a *female* engineer at Howard Aviation, won the best-employee award.

  Glenda James, an engineer at Howard Aviation, won the best-employee award. [removal of the unnecessary gender reference]

- **Terms such as *man* and *mankind* or those with *-ess* or *-man* endings:** Labor laws benefit the common *man. Mankind* benefits from philanthropy. The *stewardess* brought me some orange juice.

  Labor laws benefit **working people.** [replacement of the stereotypical term with a gender-neutral term]

  Everyone benefits from philanthropy. [use of an indefinite pronoun]

  The **flight attendant** brought me some orange juice. [use of a gender-neutral term]

- **Stereotypical gender roles:** I was told that the university offers free tuition to faculty *wives.* The minister pronounced them *man* and wife.

  I was told that the university offers free tuition to faculty **spouses.** [replacement of the stereotypical term with a gender-neutral term]

The minister pronounced them **husband** and wife. [use of a term equivalent to *wife*]

■ **Inconsistent use of titles:** *Mr. Holmes* and his *wife,* Mary, took a long trip to China.

Mr. and Mrs. [or Ms.] Holmes took a long trip to China. [consistent use of titles]

OR **Peter and Mary Holmes** took a long trip to China. [removal of titles]

OR **Peter Holmes** and **Mary Wolfe** took a long trip to China. [use of full names]

■ **Unstated gender assumption:** Have your *mother make your costume* for the school pageant.

Have your **parents provide you with a costume** for the school pageant. [replacement of the stereotypical words with gender-neutral ones]

Exercise 2

Make the following sentences inclusive by eliminating sexist language.

1. The ladies met to discuss the company's current operating budget.
2. The old boys run the city's government.
3. Mothers should read to their small children.
4. Some fans admired the actress because of her movies; others praised her for her environmental activism.
5. For six years, he worked as a mailman in a small town.

(2) Nonracist language promotes social equity.

Rarely is it necessary to identify anyone's race or ethnicity in academic or professional writing. However, you may need to use appropriate racial or ethnic terms if you are writing a demographic report, an argument against existing racial inequities, or a historical account of a particular event involving ethnic groups. Determining which terms a particular group prefers can be difficult because preferences sometimes vary within a group and change over time. One conventional way to refer to Americans of a specific descent is to include an adjective before the word *American*: *African American, Asian American, European*

American, Latin American, Mexican American, Native American. These words are widely used; however, members of a particular group may identify themselves in more than one way. In addition to *African American* and *European American, Black* (or *black*) and *White* (or *white*) have long been used. People of Spanish-speaking descent may prefer *Chicano/Chicana, Hispanic, Latino/Latina, Puerto Rican,* or other terms. Members of cultures that are indigenous to North America may prefer a specific name such as *Cherokee* or *Haida,* though some also accept *American Indian.* An up-to-date dictionary that includes notes on usage can help you choose appropriate terms.

(3) Writing about any type of difference should be respectful.

If a writing assignment requires you to distinguish people based on age, ability, geographical area, religion, or sexual orientation, show respect to the groups or individuals you discuss by using the terms they prefer.

(a) Referring to age

Although some people object to the term *senior citizen,* a better alternative has not been provided. When used respectfully, the term refers to a person who has reached the age of retirement (but may not have decided to retire) and is eligible for certain privileges granted by society. However, if you know your audience would object to this term, find out which alternative is preferred.

(b) Referring to disabilities or illness

A current recommendation for referring to disabilities and illnesses is "to put the person first." In this way, the focus is placed on the individual rather than on the limitation. Thus, *persons with disabilities* is preferred over *disabled persons.* For your own writing, you can find out whether such person-first expressions are preferred by noting whether they are used in the articles and books (or by the people) you consult. Be aware, though, that some writers and readers think that these types of expressions sound unnatural, and others maintain that they do not serve their intended purpose because the last word in a phrase can carry the greater weight, especially at the end of a sentence.

(c) Referring to geographical areas

Certain geographical terms need to be used with special care. Though most frequently used to refer to people from the United States, the term *American* may also refer to people from Canada, Mexico, and Central or South America. If your audience may be confused by this term, use *people from the United States* or *U.S. citizens* instead.

The term *Arab* refers to people who speak Arabic. If you cannot use specific terms such as *Iraqi* or *Saudi Arabian,* be sure you know that a country's people speak Arabic and not another language. Iranians, for example, are not Arabs because they speak Farsi.

British, rather than *English,* is the preferred term for referring to people from the island of Great Britain or from the United Kingdom.

(d) Referring to religion

Reference to a person's religion should be made only if it is relevant to your rhetorical situation. If you must mention religious affiliation, use only those terms considered respectful. Because religions have both conservative and liberal followers, be careful not to make generalizations about political stances (see **8i(12)**).

(e) Referring to sexual orientation

If your rhetorical situation calls for identifying sexual orientation, choose terms used by the people you are discussing. The words *gay*, *lesbian*, and *bisexual* are generally used as adjectives. Their use as nouns to refer to specific people may be considered offensive.

CHECKLIST for Assessing Usage within a Rhetorical Situation

- Do your words convey the meaning you intend?
- Can your audience understand the words you have used?
- Do you explain any words your audience might not understand?
- Have you used any words that could irritate or offend members of your audience?
- Do any of your words make you sound too casual or too formal?
- Do your words help you to fulfill your rhetorical purpose?
- Are your words appropriate for the context in which you are writing?
- Are your words appropriate for the context in which they will be read?

32e Dictionaries

A good dictionary is an indispensable tool for writers. Desk dictionaries such as *The American Heritage Dictionary* and *Merriam-Webster's Collegiate Dictionary* do much more than provide the correct spellings of words; they also give meanings, parts of speech, plural forms, and verb tenses, as well as information about pronunciation and origin. In addition, a reliable dictionary also includes labels that can help you decide whether words are appropriate for the purpose, audience, and context of your writing. Words labeled *dialect, slang, colloquial, nonstandard,* or *unconventional,* as well as those labeled *archaic* or *obsolete* (meaning that they are no longer in common use), are generally inappropriate for college and professional writing. If a word has no label, you can safely assume that it can be used in writing for school or work. But whether the word is appropriate depends on the precise meaning a writer wants to convey (see **33a**). Because language is constantly changing, it is important to choose a desk dictionary with a recent copyright date. Many dictionaries are available—in print, online, or on CD-ROM. Pocket dictionaries, which are useful for checking spellings and definitions, omit important information on usage and derivation. The dictionaries incorporated into most word-processing programs are equivalent to pocket dictionaries and may provide insufficient information.

(1) Consulting an unabridged or special dictionary can enhance your understanding of a word.

An **unabridged dictionary** provides a comprehensive survey of English words, including detailed information about their origins. A **specialized dictionary** presents words related to a specific discipline or to some aspect of usage.

Unabridged Dictionaries

The Oxford English Dictionary. 2nd ed. 20 vols. 1989– . CD-ROM. 1994.

Webster's Third New International Dictionary of the English Language. CD-ROM. 2003.

Specialized Dictionaries

The American Heritage Dictionary of Idioms. 1997.

The American Heritage Guide to Contemporary Usage and Style. 2005.

The BBI Dictionary of English Word Combinations. 1997.

The New Fowler's Modern English Usage. 3rd ed. 2000.

Merriam-Webster's Dictionary of English Usage. 1994.

Dictionaries and Other Resources

The following dictionaries are recommended for nonnative speakers of English.

Collins Cobuild New Student's Dictionary. 2002.

Longman Advanced American English. 2000.

Heinle's Newbury House Dictionary of American English. 4th ed. 2003.

Two excellent resources for ESL students are the following:

Longman Language Activator. 2003. (A cross between a dictionary and a thesaurus, this book supplies definitions, usage guidelines, and sample sentences.)

Swan, Michael. *Practical English Usage.* 3rd ed. 2005. (This is a practical reference guide to problems encountered by those who speak English as a second language.)

(2) Dictionary entries provide a range of information.

Figure 32.1 shows sample entries from the tenth edition of *Merriam-Webster's Collegiate Dictionary.* Notice that *move* is listed twice—first as a verb, then as a noun. The types of information these entries provide can be found in almost all desk dictionaries, though sometimes in a different order.

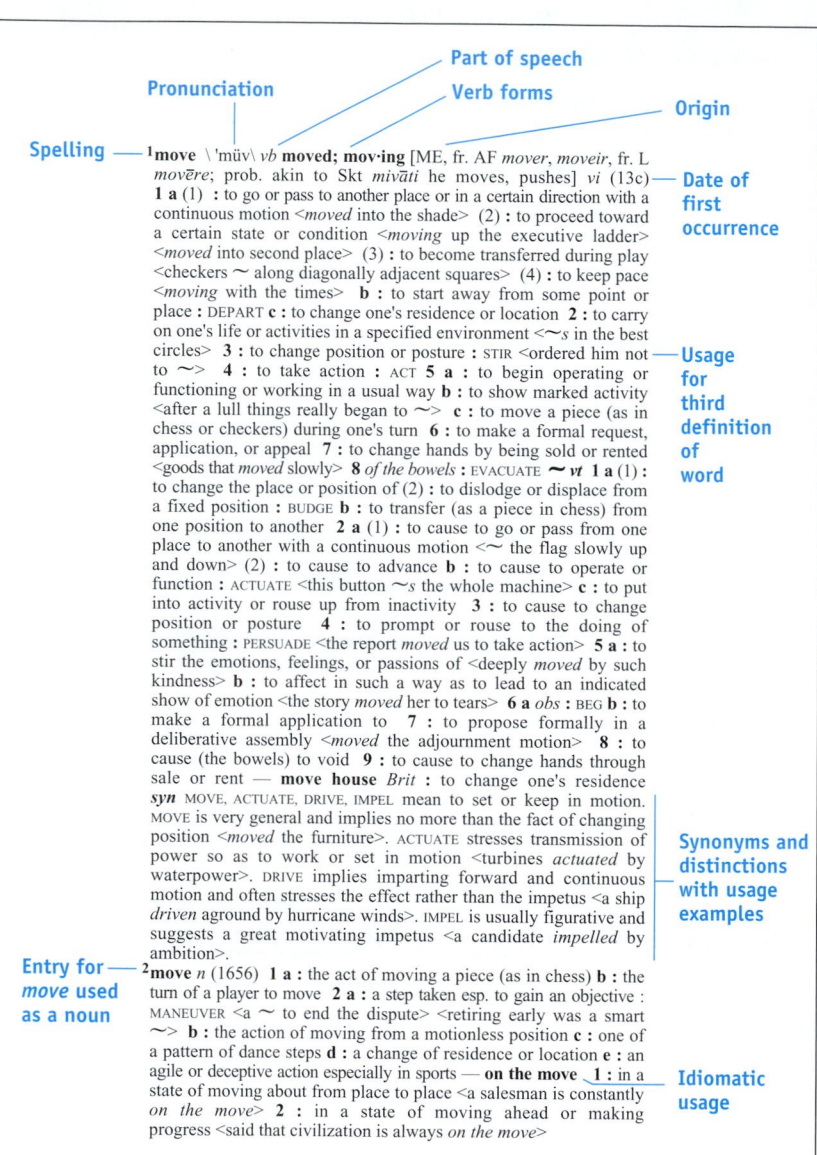

Spelling — ¹**move** \\'müv\\ *vb* **moved; mov·ing** [ME, fr. AF *mover, moveir*, fr. L *movēre*; prob. akin to Skt *mivāti* he moves, pushes] *vi* (13c) **1 a** (1) : to go or pass to another place or in a certain direction with a continuous motion <*moved* into the shade> (2) : to proceed toward a certain state or condition <*moving* up the executive ladder> <*moved* into second place> (3) : to become transferred during play <checkers ~ along diagonally adjacent squares> (4) : to keep pace <*moving* with the times> **b** : to start away from some point or place : DEPART **c** : to change one's residence or location **2** : to carry on one's life or activities in a specified environment <~s in the best circles> **3** : to change position or posture : STIR <ordered him not to ~> **4** : to take action : ACT **5 a** : to begin operating or functioning or working in a usual way **b** : to show marked activity <after a lull things really began to ~> **c** : to move a piece (as in chess or checkers) during one's turn **6** : to make a formal request, application, or appeal **7** : to change hands by being sold or rented <goods that *moved* slowly> **8** *of the bowels* : EVACUATE ~ *vt* **1 a** (1) : to change the place or position of (2) : to dislodge or displace from a fixed position : BUDGE **b** : to transfer (as a piece in chess) from one position to another **2 a** (1) : to cause to go or pass from one place to another with a continuous motion <~ the flag slowly up and down> (2) : to cause to advance **b** : to cause to operate or function : ACTUATE <this button ~s the whole machine> **c** : to put into activity or rouse up from inactivity **3** : to cause to change position or posture **4** : to prompt or rouse to the doing of something : PERSUADE <the report *moved* us to take action> **5 a** : to stir the emotions, feelings, or passions of <deeply *moved* by such kindness> **b** : to affect in such a way as to lead to an indicated show of emotion <the story *moved* her to tears> **6 a** *obs* : BEG **b** : to make a formal application to **7** : to propose formally in a deliberative assembly <*moved* the adjournment motion> **8** : to cause (the bowels) to void **9** : to cause to change hands through sale or rent — **move house** *Brit* : to change one's residence *syn* MOVE, ACTUATE, DRIVE, IMPEL mean to set or keep in motion. MOVE is very general and implies no more than the fact of changing position <*moved* the furniture>. ACTUATE stresses transmission of power so as to work or set in motion <turbines *actuated* by waterpower>. DRIVE implies imparting forward and continuous motion and often stresses the effect rather than the impetus <a ship *driven* aground by hurricane winds>. IMPEL is usually figurative and suggests a great motivating impetus <a candidate *impelled* by ambition>.

²**move** *n* (1656) **1 a** : the act of moving a piece (as in chess) **b** : the turn of a player to move **2 a** : a step taken esp. to gain an objective : MANEUVER <a ~ to end the dispute> <retiring early was a smart ~> **b** : the action of moving from a motionless position **c** : one of a pattern of dance steps **d** : a change of residence or location **e** : an agile or deceptive action especially in sports — **on the move 1** : in a state of moving about from place to place <a salesman is constantly *on the move*> **2** : in a state of moving ahead or making progress <said that civilization is always *on the move*>

Labels around the entry (left and right):
- Pronunciation
- Part of speech
- Verb forms
- Origin
- Date of first occurrence
- Usage for third definition of word
- Synonyms and distinctions with usage examples
- Entry for *move* used as a noun
- Idiomatic usage

Fig. 32.1. Examples of dictionary entries.

TYPES OF INFORMATION PROVIDED BY DICTIONARY ENTRIES

- **Spelling, syllabication (word division), and pronunciation**
- **Parts of speech and word forms.** Dictionaries identify parts of speech— for instance, with *n* for "noun" or *vi* for "intransitive verb." Meanings will vary depending on the part of speech identified. Dictionaries also identify irregular forms of verbs, nouns, and adjectives: *fly, flew, flown, flying, flies; child, children; good, better, best.*
- **Word origin**
- **Date of first occurrence**
- **Definition(s).** Generally, the oldest meaning is given first. However, meanings can also be ordered according to common usage.
- **Usage.** Quotations show how the word can be used in various contexts. Sometimes a comment on usage problems is placed at the end of the entry.
- **Idioms.** When the word is part of a common idiom (see **33c**), the idiom is listed and defined, usually at the end of the entry.
- **Synonyms.** Some dictionaries provide explanations of subtle differences in meaning among a word's synonyms.

Exercise 3

Study the definitions for the pairs of words in parentheses. Then choose the word you think best completes each sentence. Be prepared to explain your answers.

1. Sixteen prisoners on death row were granted (mercy/clemency).
2. The outcome of the election (excited/provoked) a riot.
3. The young couple was (covetous/greedy) of their neighbors' estate.
4. While she was traveling in Muslim countries, she wore (modest/chaste) clothing.
5. The president of the university (authorized/confirmed) the rumor that tuition would be increasing next year.

32f Thesauruses

A **thesaurus** provides alternatives for frequently used words. Unlike a dictionary, which explains what a word means and how it evolved, a thesaurus provides only a list of words that serve as possible synonyms for each term it includes. A thesaurus can be useful, especially when you want to jog your memory about a word you know but cannot recall. You may, however, use a word incorrectly if you simply pick it from a list in a thesaurus. If you find an unfamiliar yet intriguing word, make sure that you are using it correctly by looking it up in a dictionary. Several print thesauruses are available. Among them are *Roget's International Thesaurus* (2002) and *Merriam-Webster's Collegiate Thesaurus* (1994). Most word-processing programs include a thesaurus, and other thesauruses are available online.

Exercise 4

Review two or three of your recent papers, and find a word you used frequently. Look up that word in a thesaurus, and then check each possible synonym in a dictionary. Use one of these synonyms appropriately in a sentence, and explain why your usage is correct.

33

EXACTNESS

Make words work for you. By choosing the right word and putting it in the right place, you can communicate exactly what you mean and make your writing memorable. When drafting, choose words that express your ideas and feelings. Then, when revising, make those words precise and fresh. Use the words that you already know effectively, but add to your vocabulary regularly so that you can pick the exact words to suit your purpose, audience, and context. This chapter will help you

- master the denotations and connotations of words (**33a**),
- use fresh, clear expressions (**33b**),
- understand how to use idioms and collocations (**33c**),
- use the first- and second-person pronouns appropriately (**33d**), and
- compose clear definitions (**33e**).

33a Accurate and precise word choice

(1) A denotation is the literal meaning of a word.

Denotations are definitions of words, such as those that appear in dictionaries. For example, the noun *beach* denotes a sandy or pebbly shore. Select words whose denotations convey your point exactly.

Yosemite National Park ~~is really great.~~ *astounds even an indifferent tourist like me.*

[Because *great* can mean "extremely large" as well as "outstanding" or "powerful," its use in this sentence is imprecise.]

The speaker _inferred_ that the team attracted many new fans this year. *(implied)*

[*Imply* means "to suggest," so *implied* is the exact word for this sentence. *Infer* means "to draw a conclusion from evidence": From the figures before me, I *inferred* that the team attracted many new fans this year.]

(2) A connotation is the indirect meaning of word.

Connotations are the associations evoked by a word. *Beach,* for instance, may connote natural beauty, surf, shells, swimming, tanning, sunburn, and/or crowds. The context in which a word appears affects the associations it evokes. In a treatise on shoreline management, *beach* has scientific and geographic connotations; in a fashion magazine, this word is associated with bathing suits, sunglasses, and sunscreen. Most readers carry with them a wealth of personal, often emotional, associations that can influence how they respond to the words on a page. The challenge for writers is to choose the words that are most likely to spark the appropriate connotations in their readers' minds.

Mr. Kreuger's _relentlessness_ has earned praise from his supervisors. *(persistence)*

[*Relentlessness* has negative connotations, which make it an unlikely quality for which to be praised.]

I love the _odor_ of freshly baked bread. *(aroma)*

[Many odors are unpleasant; *aroma* sounds more positive, especially in association with food.]

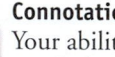

Connotations
Your ability to recognize connotations will improve as your vocabulary increases. When you learn a new word that seems to mean exactly what another word means, study the context in which each word is used. Then, to help yourself remember the new word, create a phrase or a sentence in which that word is used in the context you studied. If you are confused about the connotations of specific words, consult an ESL dictionary (see page 659).

(3) Specific, concrete words provide readers with helpful details.

A **general word** is all-inclusive, indefinite, and sweeping in scope. A **specific word** is precise, definite, and limited in scope.

General	Specific	More Specific/Concrete
food	fast food	cheeseburger
entertainment	film	*The Aviator*
place	city	Atlanta

An **abstract word** refers to a concept or idea, a quality or trait, or anything else that cannot be touched, heard, or seen. A **concrete word** signifies a particular object, a specific action, or anything that can be touched, heard, or seen.

Abstract	democracy, evil, strength, charity
Concrete	mosquito, hammer, plastic, fog

Some writers use too many abstract or general words, making their writing vague and lifeless. As you select words to fit your context, you should be as specific and concrete as you can. For example, instead of the word *bad,* consider using a more precise adjective.

bad neighbors: rowdy, snobby, nosy, fussy, sloppy, threatening

bad meat: tough, tainted, overcooked, undercooked, contaminated

bad wood: rotten, warped, scorched, knotty, termite-ridden

To test whether or not a word is specific, you can ask one or more of these questions about what you want to say: Exactly who? Exactly what? Exactly when? Exactly where? Exactly how? In the following examples, notice what a difference concrete words can make in expressing an idea and how adding details can expand or develop it.

Vague	She has kept no reminders of performing in her youth.
Specific	She has kept no sequined costume, no photographs, no fliers or posters from that part of her youth. —LOUISE ERDRICH
Vague	He realized that he was running through the cold night.
Specific	He found himself hurrying over creaking snow through the blackness of a winter night. —LOREN EISELEY

As these examples show, sentences with specific details are often longer than sentences without them. But the need to be specific does not necessarily conflict with the need to be concise. (See chapter **34**.) Sometimes substituting one word for another can make it far easier for your readers to see, hear, taste, or smell what you are hoping to convey.

> I ~~had an accident~~ *fell out of a canoe* while trying to ~~catch a fish~~ *land a muskie*.

Writers use general and abstract words successfully when such words are vital to communicating ideas, as in the following sentence about what happens when a plague comes to an end.

> We expect a catharsis, but we merely find a transition; we long for euphoria, but we discover only relief, tinged with, in some cases, regret and depression.
> —ANDREW SULLIVAN

(4) Figurative language contributes to exactness.

Figurative language is the use of words in an imaginative rather than a literal sense. Similes and metaphors are the chief **figures of speech.** A **simile** is a comparison of dissimilar things using *like* or *as.* A **metaphor** is an implied comparison of dissimilar things, without *like* or *as.*

Similes

He was **like a piece of rare and delicate china which was always being saved from breaking and finally fell.**   —ALICE WALKER

She sat **like a great icon** in the back of the classroom, tranquil, guarded, sealed up, watchful.   —REGINALD MCKNIGHT

Metaphors

His **money was a sharp pair of scissors** that snipped rapidly through tangles of red tape.   —HISAYE YAMAMOTO

The injured **bird was a broken handled flag** waving in the grass.
—TRACY YOUNGBLOM

Single words can be used metaphorically.

> These roses must be **planted** in good soil. [literal]
> Keep your life **planted** wherever you can put down the most roots. [metaphorical]

Similes and metaphors are especially valuable when they are concrete and describe or evoke essential relationships that cannot otherwise be communicated. Similes or metaphors can be extended throughout a paragraph of comparison, but be careful not to mix them. (See 27c.)

Exercise 1

Study the passsage below, and prepare to discuss in class your response to the author's use of exact and figurative language to communicate her ideas.

[1]The kitchen where I'm making dinner is a New York kitchen. [2]Nice light, way too small, nowhere to put anything unless the stove goes. [3]My stove is huge, but it will never go. [4]My stove is where my head clears, my impressions settle, my reporter's life gets folded into *my* life, and whatever I've just learned, or think I've learned—whatever it was, out there in the world, that had seemed so different and surprising—bubbles away in the very small pot of what I think I know and, if I'm lucky, produces something like perspective.   —JANE KRAMER, "The Reporter's Kitchen"

Exercise 2

Choose five of the items below, and use them as the bases for five original sentences containing figurative language.

1. the look on someone's face
2. a cold rainy day
3. studying for an exam
4. your favorite food
5. buying textbooks
6. a busy street
7. waiting in a long line for a movie
8. the way someone talks

33b Evocative language

Fresh expressions can capture the attention of readers, but when forced or overused, they lose their impact. Sometimes writers coin expressions as substitutes for words and phrases that have coarse or indelicate connotations. These expressions are called **euphemisms;** they occasionally become standardized. To talk about death or dying, for example, you might use words such as *pass away* or *being terminally ill*. However, although euphemisms may be pleasant sounding, they have a dark side.

They can be used by writers who want to obscure facts or avoid negative reactions by others. Euphemisms such as *revenue enhancement* for *tax hike* and *collateral damage* for *civilian deaths during a war* are considered insincere or deceitful.

BEYOND THE RULE

DOUBLESPEAK

In his novel *1984*, George Orwell coined the term *doublespeak* to refer to language used intentionally to obscure the facts surrounding bad news. William Lutz has continued in Orwell's steps, keeping track of language used to sugarcoat harsh realities. To find current examples of doublespeak, visit **www.harbrace.com**.

The expressions *bite the dust, breath of fresh air,* and *smooth as silk* were once striking and thus effective. Excessive use, though, has drained them of their original force and made them **clichés.** Newer expressions such as *put a spin on something* and *think outside the box* have also lost their vitality because of overuse. Nonetheless, clichés are so much a part of the language, especially the spoken language, that nearly every writer uses them from time to time. But effective writers often give a fresh twist to an old saying.

> I seek a narrative, a fiction, to order days like the one I spent several years ago, on a gray June day in Chicago, when I took a roller-coaster ride on the bell curve of my experience. —**GAYLE PEMBERTON**

> [Notice how much more effective this expression is than frequent references elsewhere to "being on an emotional roller coaster."]

Variations on familiar expressions from literature, many of which have become part of everyday language, can often be used effectively in your writing.

> Now is the summer of my great content. —**KATHERINE LANPHER**

> [This statement is a variation on Shakespeare's "Now is the winter of our discontent . . . ."]

Good writers, however, do not rely too heavily on the words of others; they choose their own words to communicate their ideas.

BEYOND THE RULE

CLICHÉS

Some scholars have defended clichés on the grounds that they convey widely accepted ideas in a direct way and can thus help writers to communicate effectively with certain readers in specific rhetorical situations. For information about this position, visit **www.harbrace.com**.

Exercise 3

From the following list of overused expressions, select five that you often use or hear and suggest creative replacements. Then, use each replacement in a sentence.

EXAMPLE

beyond the shadow of a doubt   *undoubtedly* OR *with total certainty*

1. an axe to grind
2. hit the nail on the head
3. see the light
4. business as usual
5. climb the walls

6. eat like a pig
7. beat around the bush
8. bite the bullet
9. breathe down someone's neck
10. strong as an ox

33c Idioms and collocations

Idioms are fixed expressions whose meanings cannot be entirely determined by knowing the meanings of their parts—*bear in mind, fall in love, in a nutshell, stand a chance*. **Collocations** are combinations of words that frequently occur together. Unlike idioms, they have meanings that *can* be determined by knowing the meanings of their parts—*depend on, fond of, little while, right now*. Regardless of whether you are using an idiom or a collocation, if you make even a small inadvertent change to the expected wording, you may distract or confuse your readers.

She tried to keep a ~~small~~ *low* profile.

They had ~~an invested~~ *a vested* interest in the project.

As you edit your writing, keep an eye out for idioms or collocations that might not be worded correctly. Then check a general dictionary, a dictionary of idioms (see page 659), or the **Glossary of Usage** at the end of this book to ensure that your usage is appropriate. Writers sometimes have trouble with the following collocations, all of which contain prepositions.

CHOOSING THE RIGHT PREPOSITION

Instead of	Use
abide **with**	abide **by** the decision
according **with**	according **to** the source
accused **for**	accused **of** the crime
bored **of**	bored **by** it
comply **to**	comply **with** rules
conform **of/on**	conform **to/with** standards
differ **to**	differ **with** them
in accordance **to**	in accordance **with** policy
independent **to**	independent **of** his family
happened **on**	happened **by** accident
plan **on**	plan **to** go
superior **than**	superior **to** others
type **of a**	type **of** business

 **Understanding and Using Idioms**

The context in which an idiom appears can often help you understand the meaning. For example, if you read "When they learned that she had accepted illegal campaign contributions, several political commentators raked her over the coals," you would probably understand that *to rake over the coals* means "to criticize severely." As you learn new idioms from your reading, make a list of those you might want to use in your own writing. If you are confused about the meaning of a particular idiom, check a dictionary of idioms (see page 659).

Exercise 4

Write a sentence using each of the following idioms and collocations correctly.

1. pass muster, pass the time
2. do one's best, do one's part, do one's duty
3. in a pinch, in a rut, in a way
4. cut down, cut back, cut corners
5. make time, make sure, make sense

33d First-person and second-person pronouns

Using *I* is appropriate when you are writing about personal experience. In academic and professional writing, the use of the first-person singular pronoun is also a clear way to distinguish your own views from those of others or to make a direct appeal to readers. However, if you frequently repeat *I feel* or *I think,* your readers may suspect that you do not understand much beyond your own experience or that you are more interested in talking about yourself than about your topic.

We, the first-person plural pronoun, is trickier to use correctly. When you use it, make sure that your audience can tell which individuals are included in this plural reference. For example, if you are writing a paper for a college course, does *we* mean you and the instructor, you and your fellow students, or some other group (such as all Americans)? If you are using *we* in a memo to co-workers, are you intending to include the entire company, your group within it, or you and a specific individual? Because you may inadvertently use *we* in an early draft to refer to more than one group of people, as you edit, check to see that you have used the first-person plural pronoun consistently.

BEYOND THE RULE

WHO IS PART OF *WE*?

Writing specialists have been discussing how the use of *we* can blind writers to differences of gender, race, religion, region, class, and sexual orientation. Readers sometimes feel excluded from works in which the first-person plural pronoun has been used carelessly. For more information about this debate, visit **www.harbrace.com**.

If you decide to address readers directly, you will undoubtedly use the second-person pronoun *you* (as has been done frequently in this book). There is some disagreement, though, over whether to permit the use of the indefinite *you* to mean "a person" or "people in general." Check with your instructor about this usage. If you are told to avoid using the indefinite *you*, recast your sentences. For example, use *one* instead of *you*.

Even in huge, anonymous cities, ~~you find~~ *one finds* community spirit.

However, owing to the formality of *one*, it might not always be the best choice. Changing the word order is another possibility.

Community spirit can be found even in huge, anonymous cities.

If you are unsatisfied with either of these strategies, use different words.

Community spirit arises even in huge, anonymous cities.

For additional advice on using pronouns, see chapter **25**.

Exercise 5

Revise the following paragraph to eliminate the use of the first- and second-person pronouns.

¹In my opinion, some animals should be as free as we are. **²**For example, I think orangutans, African elephants, and Atlantic bottle-nose dolphins should roam freely rather than be held in captivity. **³**We should neither exhibit them in zoos nor use them for medical research. **⁴**If you study animals such as these you will see that, like us, they show emotions, self-awareness, and intention. **⁵**You might even find that some use language to communicate. **⁶**It is clear to me that they have the right to freedom.

33e Clear definitions

Because words often have more than one meaning, you must clearly establish which meaning you have in mind in a particular piece of writing. By providing a definition, you set the terms of the discussion.

> In this paper, I use the word *communism* **in the Marxist sense of social organization based on the holding of all property in common.**

A **formal definition** first states the term to be defined, then puts it into a class, and finally differentiates it from other members of that class.

> A *phosphene* [term] is **a luminous visual image** [class] that **results from applying pressure to the eyeball** [differentiation].

A short dictionary definition may be adequate when you need to convey a special meaning that may be unfamiliar to readers.

> Here, *galvanic* means **"produced as if by electric shock."**

Giving a synonym may also clarify the meaning of a term. Such synonyms are often used as appositives.

> *Machismo,* **confidence with an attitude,** can be a pose rather than a reality.

Writers frequently show—rather than tell—what a word means by giving examples.

> Many homophones (**such as** *be* **and** *bee,* *in* **and** *inn,* **or** *see* **and** *sea*) are not spelling problems.

You can also formulate your own definition of a concept you wish to clarify.

Clichés could be defined as **thoughts that have hardened.**

When writing definitions, do not confuse readers by placing a predicate with a subject that is not logically connected to it. (See **27d**.) Constructions that combine *is* or *are* with *when, where,* or *because* are often illogical because forms of *be* signify identity or equality between the subject and what follows.

Faulty	The Internet is when you look at text and images from across the world.
Revised	The Internet allows you to look at text and images from across the world.

Exercise 6

Using your own words, define any four of the following terms in full sentences.

1. collaboration
2. honesty
3. party
4. style
5. globalization
6. terrorism

34

CONCISENESS

To facilitate readers' understanding, effective writers generally convey their thoughts clearly and efficiently. This does not mean that they always write short sentences; rather, they use each word wisely. This chapter will help you

- make each word count (**34a**),
- avoid unnecessary repetition (**34b**), and
- use elliptical constructions (**34c**).

34a Eliminating wordiness and other redundancies

After writing a first draft, review your phrasing to make sure that you have not been vague or repetitive. If you draft quickly or if you are worried about the length requirement for the assignment, you may write rambling sentences that obscure your message rather than clarify it.

(1) Redundancy contributes to wordiness.

Restating a key point in different words can help readers understand it. But there is no need to rephrase readily understood terms. If you do, your work will suffer from **redundancy**—repetition for no good reason.

Ballerinas auditioned ~~in the tryouts~~ for *The Nutcracker.*

Each student had a unique talent ~~and ability that he or she uses in his or her~~ for acting.

You should also avoid grammatical redundancy, as in double subjects (*my sister [she] is*), double comparisons (*[more] easier than*), and double negatives (*could[n't] hardly*).

Using Relative Pronouns
Review your sentences to make sure that no clause includes both a personal pronoun (**25a(1)**) and a relative pronoun (**25a(2)**) referring to the same antecedent (**25c**).

The drug **that** we were testing ~~it~~ has not been approved by the Food and Drug Administration.

The principal investigator, **whom** we depended on ~~her~~ for guidance, had to take a medical leave before the project was completed.

(2) Delete unnecessary words, and recast wordy phrases.

One exact word often says as much a several inexact ones.

spoke in a low and hard-to-hear voice	**mumbled**
a person who gives expert advice	**consultant**

Some unscrupulous brokers are ~~taking money and savings from~~ _{*cheating*} elderly people ~~who need that money because they planned to use it as a retirement~~ _{*out of their pensions.*} ~~pension.~~

As you edit a draft, delete words that add no significant meaning to adjacent words, and replace wordy expressions with single words whenever possible.

If ~~In the event that~~ taxes are raised, ~~expect complaints on the part of the voters.~~ *voters will complain.*

In addition, watch for empty or vague words such as *area, aspect, element, factor, feature, field, kind, situation, thing,* and *type*. They may signal wordiness.

Effective ~~In an employment situation, effective~~ communication is essential at work.

USELESS WORDS IN COMMON PHRASES

yellow [in color]

at 9:45 A.M. [in the morning]

[basic] essentials

bitter[-tasting] salad

connect [up together]

because [of the fact that]

[really and truly] fearless

circular [in shape]

return [back]

rich [and wealthy] nations

small[-size] potatoes

[true] facts

was [more or less] hinting

by [virtue of] his authority

REPLACEMENTS FOR WORDY EXPRESSIONS

at this moment (point) in time	now, today
due to the fact that	because
in view of the fact that	because
for the purpose of	for
it is clear (obvious) that	clearly (obviously)
there is no question that	unquestionably, certainly
without a doubt	undoubtedly
beyond the shadow of a doubt	certainly, surely
it is my opinion that	I think (believe)
in this day and age	today
in the final analysis	finally

(3) The constructions *there are* and *it is* can often be deleted.

There or *it* followed by a form of *be* is an **expletive**—a word that signals that the subject of the sentence will follow the verb. (See **20d(1)**.) Writers use expletives to create a sentence rhythm that emphasizes words that would not be emphasized in the typical subject-verb order. Notice the difference in rhythm between the following two sentences:

> Three children were playing in the yard.

> There were three children playing in the yard.

However, expletives are easily overused. If you find that you have drafted several sentences that begin with expletives, look for ways to revise a few of them.

> Hundreds *were*
> ~~There were hundreds~~ of fans crowding onto the field.

> Joining the crowd
> It was frightening ~~to join the crowd~~.
>
> OR
>
> I was afraid to join the crowd.

(4) Some relative pronouns can be deleted.

When editing a draft, check whether the relative pronouns *who, which,* and *that* can be deleted from any of your sentences. If a relative pronoun is followed by a form of the verb *be* (*am, is, are, was,* or *were*), you can often omit both the relative pronoun and the verb.

> The change ~~that~~ the young senator proposed yesterday angered most legislators.

> Bromo, ~~which is~~ Java's highest mountain, towers above its neighbors.

> The Endangered Species Act, ~~which was~~ passed in 1973, protects the habitat of endangered plants and animals.

When deleting a relative pronoun, you might have to make other changes to a sentence as well.

> handling
> The Tsukiji fish market, ~~which handles~~ 2,000 tons of seafood a day, rates as the world's largest.

Rewrite the sentences below to make them less wordy.

1. He put in an application for every job offered.
2. Prior to the time of the ceremony, he had not received an award.
3. The library is located in the vicinity of the post office.
4. The fans who were watching television made a lot of noise.
5. There was nobody home.
6. The release of certain chemicals, which are called *pheromones*, is a very primitive form of communication.
7. It is important to register early.
8. The road was closed because of the fact that there were so many accidents.

34b Avoiding unnecessary repetition

Repetition is useful only when it contributes to emphasis, clarity, or coherence.

~~One week was like the next week.~~ Each week was as boring as the last.

She hoped Alex understood that ^*her complaint did not reflect her feelings about him.* ~~the complaint she made did not mean she was complaining because she disliked him.~~

In the preceding examples, repetition serves no useful purpose; in the following example, however, it provides emphasis.

We will not rest until we have pursued **every** lead, inspected **every** piece of evidence, and interviewed **every** suspect. [The repetition of *every* is effective because it emphasizes the writer's determination.]

Instead of repeating a noun or substituting a synonym, you can use a pronoun as long as the reference is clear.

Teddy Roosevelt earned a reputation as the "conservation President."

During his two terms, ^*he* ~~Roosevelt~~ designated over 200 million acres as public land.

34c Using elliptical constructions

An **elliptical construction** is one that deliberately omits words that can be understood from the context. In the following sentence, the word group *is the goal* can be taken out of the second and third clauses without affecting the meaning. The revised sentence is more concise than the original.

> Speed is the goal for some swimmers, endurance ~~is the goal~~ for others, and relaxation ~~is the goal~~ for still others.

Sometimes, as an aid to clarity, commas mark omissions in elliptical constructions.

> My family functioned like a baseball team: my mom was the coach; my brother, the pitcher; and my sister, the shortstop. [Be sure to use semicolons to separate items with internal commas (see **36b**).]

As these examples show, parallelism reinforces elliptical constructions. (See chapter **29**.)

Exercise 2

Revise this paragraph to eliminate wordiness and needless repetition.

[1]When I look back on my high school career, I realize that I was not taught much about international affairs in the world in spite of the fact that improved communications, the media, the Internet, travel, trading with different foreign countries, and immigration have made the world smaller. [2]Nonetheless, because both international affairs and business interest me, I decided to major in political science now that I am in college and to study marketing as my minor. [3]There are advantages to this combination of a major and a minor in my job situation at work as well, for I am now currently working part-time twenty hours a week for a company that imports merchandise into the United States and exports products to other countries. [4]Eventually, at some future time, when I have graduated and received my bachelor's degree, I may go on to law school and pursue my interest in politics, unless, on the other hand, my supervisor makes the recommendation that I develop my skills in marketing by spending time overseas in one of the company's foreign offices. [5]The opportunity to work overseas would provide me with a knowledge, an understanding, and an appreciation of the world economy. [6]Such an understanding is essential for anyone hoping to succeed in business.

Serving our country as the tip of the spear

Smart. Tough. Elite.

The United States Marines

The use of the period, a strong mark of punctuation, with the words
"Smart. Tough. Elite." reinforces the strength of the image.

35

THE COMMA

Punctuation signals meaning. It lends to written language the flexibility that facial expressions, pauses, and variations in voice pitch give to spoken language. For instance, a pause after *called* in the first of the following examples would make it clear that the spoken sentence refers to only two people: the recruiter and Kenneth Martin. In the second example, a pause after *Kenneth* would let the listener know that the sentence refers to three people: the recruiter, Kenneth, and Martin. In written text, the same meanings can be established by commas.

When the recruiter called**,** Kenneth Martin answered.

When the recruiter called Kenneth**,** Martin answered.

But pauses are not a reliable guide for comma use because commas are often called for where speakers do not pause, and pauses can occur where no comma is necessary. A better guide is an understanding of some basic principles of comma usage.

This chapter will help you use commas to

- separate independent clauses joined by coordinating conjunctions (**35a**),
- set off introductory words, phrases, and clauses (**35b**),
- separate items in a series (**35c**),
- set off nonessential (nonrestrictive) elements (**35d**),
- set off geographical names and items in dates and addresses (**35e**), and
- set off direct quotations (**35f**),

as well as help you to

- recognize unnecessary or misplaced commas (**35g**).

35a Before a coordinating conjunction linking independent clauses

Use a comma before a coordinating conjunction (*and, but, for, nor, or, so,* or *yet*) that links two independent clauses. An **independent clause** is a group of words that can stand as a sentence (see **21b(1)**).

INDEMENDENT CLAUSE**,** **CONJUNCTION** INDEPENDENT CLAUSE.

	and	
	but	
	for	
Subject + predicate**,**	**nor**	subject + predicate.
	or	
	so	
	yet	

> Most Southwestern pottery comes from Arizona and New Mexico**,** **but** some also comes from Nevada, Utah, Colorado, and Texas.
>
> Studying such pottery seemed simple at first**,** **yet** it has challenged archaeologists and art historians for decades.

No matter how many clauses are in a sentence, a comma comes before each coordinating conjunction.

> No one knows exactly how many types of Southwestern pottery there are**,** **nor** is there a list of even the most common**,** **but** scientists are working to change that.

When the independent clauses are short, the comma is often omitted before *and, but,* or *or.*

> I collect pottery **and** my sister collects jewelry.

If a coordinating conjunction joins two parts of a compound predicate, the conjunction is not normally followed by a comma. (See **20b** and **35g(3)**.)

Archaeologists have developed a classification system, and have established a comprehensive time line for pottery production.

Sometimes a semicolon, instead of a comma, follows a conjunction separating two independent clauses, especially when the second clause already contains commas or when it reveals a contrast. (See also **36b**.)

Most archaeologists study the pottery of just one culture; **but** it should be possible, according to Russell, to study one type of pottery across several cultures.

Exercise 1

Combine each of the following pairs of sentences by using coordinating conjunctions and inserting commas where appropriate. (Remember that coordinating conjunctions do not always link independent clauses and that *but, for, so,* and *yet* do not always function as coordinating conjunctions.) Explain why you used each of the conjunctions you chose.

1. Dinosaurs lived for 165 million years. Then they became extinct.
2. No one knows why dinosaurs became extinct. Several theories have been proposed.
3. Some theorists believe that a huge meteor hit the earth. The climate may have changed dramatically.
4. Another theory suggests that dinosaurs did not actually become extinct. They simply evolved into lizards and birds.
5. Yet another theory suggests that they just grew too big. Not all of the dinosaurs were huge.

35b After introductory words, phrases, or clauses

(1) A comma follows an introductory dependent clause.

If you begin a sentence with a dependent (subordinate) clause, you should place a comma after it to set it off from the independent (main) clause.

> **INTRODUCTORY DEPENDENT CLAUSE,** INDEPENDENT CLAUSE.

Although the safest automobile on the road is expensive, the protection it offers makes the cost worthwhile.

(2) A comma often follows an introductory phrase.

By placing a comma after an introductory phrase, you set it off from the independent clause.

> **INTRODUCTORY PHRASE,** INDEPENDENT CLAUSE.

(a) Introductory prepositional phrases

Despite a downturn in the national economy, the number of students enrolled in this university has increased.

If you begin a sentence with a short introductory prepositional phrase, you may omit the comma as long as the resulting sentence is not difficult to read.

In 2006 the enrollment at the university increased.

BUT

In 2006, 625 new students enrolled in courses.

[A comma separates two numbers.]

A comma is not used after a phrase that begins a sentence in which the subject and predicate are inverted.

With travel came responsibilities.

[COMPARE: Responsibilities came with travel.]

(b) Other types of introductory phrases

If you begin a sentence with a participial phrase or an absolute phrase, place a comma after it.

Having traveled nowhere, she believed the rest of the world was like her own small town; **having read little,** she had no sense of how other people think. [participial phrases]

The language difference aside, life in Germany did not seem much different from life in the United States. [absolute phrase]

(3) A comma often follows an introductory word.

> **INTRODUCTORY WORD,** INDEPENDENT CLAUSE.

Use a comma to set off words such as interjections, **vocatives** (words used to address someone directly), or transitional words.

Oh, I forgot about the board meeting. [interjection]

Bob, your design impressed everyone on the board. [vocative]

Moreover, the new design will increase efficiency in the office. [transitional word]

Some adverbs and transitional words do not need to be set off by a comma if the omission does not affect the reader's understanding (see also **36a**).

Sometimes even a good design is rejected by the board. [A comma is not necessary.]

Exercise 2

Insert commas wherever necessary in the following paragraph, and explain why each comma is needed. Some sentences may not require editing.

¹If you had to describe sound would you call it a wave? ²Although sound cannot be seen people have described it this way for a long time. ³In fact the Greek philosopher Aristotle believed that sound traveling through air was like waves in the sea. ⁴Envisioning waves in the air he hypothesized that sound would not be able to pass through a vacuum because there would be no air to transmit it. ⁵Aristotle's hypothesis was not tested until nearly two thousand years later. ⁶In 1654 Otto von Guericke found that he could not hear a bell ringing inside the vacuum he had created. ⁷Thus Guericke established the necessity of air for sound transmission. ⁸However although most sound reaches us through the air it travels faster through liquids and solids.

35c Separating elements in a series

A **series** contains three or more parallel elements. To be parallel, elements must be grammatically equal; for example, all must be phrases, not combinations of phrases and clauses. (See chapter **29**.)

(1) Commas separate words, phrases, or clauses in a series.

A comma appears after each item in a series except the last one.

> Ethics are based on **moral, social,** or **cultural** values. [words]

> The code of ethics includes **seeking criticism of work, correcting mistakes,** and **acknowledging the contributions of everyone.** [phrases]

> Several circumstances can lead to unethical behavior: **people are tempted by a desire to succeed, they are pressured into acting inappropriately by others,** or **they are simply trying to survive.** [clauses in a series]

If elements in a series contain internal commas, you can prevent misreading by separating the items with semicolons.

> A researcher's code of ethics calls for disclosing all results, without omitting any data**;** indicating various interpretations of the data**;** and making the data and methodology available to other researchers, some of whom may choose to replicate the study.

THINKING RHETORICALLY ABOUT

COMMAS AND CONJUNCTIONS IN A SERIES

How do the following sentences differ?

> We discussed them all: life**,** liberty**, and** the pursuit of happiness.
> We discussed them all: life **and** liberty **and** the pursuit of happiness.
> We discussed them all: life**,** liberty**,** the pursuit of happiness.

The first sentence follows conventional guidelines; that is, a comma and a conjunction precede the last element in the series. The second and third sentences, because they veer from convention, do more than convey information. Having two conjunctions and no commas, the second sentence slows the pace of the reading, causing stress to be placed on each of the three elements in the series. Lacking any conjunctions, the third sentence speeds up the reading, as if to suggest that the rights listed do not need to be stressed because they are so familiar. To get a sense of how your sentences will be read and understood, try reading them aloud to yourself.

(2) Commas separate coordinate adjectives.

Two or more adjectives that modify the same noun are called **coordinate adjectives.** To test whether adjectives are coordinate, either interchange them or put *and* between them. If the meaning does not change, the adjectives are coordinate and so should be separated by a comma or commas.

> Crossing the **rushing, shallow** creek, I slipped off a rock and fell into the water.
> [COMPARE: a rushing and shallow creek OR a shallow, rushing creek]

The adjectives in the following sentence are not separated by a comma. Notice that they cannot be interchanged or joined by *and*.

> Sitting in the water, I saw an **old wooden** bridge.
> [NOT a wooden old bridge OR an old and wooden bridge]

Exercise 3

Using commas where necessary, write sentences in which coordinate adjectives modify any five of the following words.

EXAMPLE

metric system   *Most countries use the familiar, sensible metric system to measure distances.*

1. bagel
2. music
3. truck
4. painting
5. software
6. college

35d With nonessential elements

Nonessential (nonrestrictive) elements provide supplemental information, that is, information not needed to understand the central meaning of a sentence. Use commas to set off a nonessential word or word group: one comma separates a nonessential element at the end of a sentence; two commas set off a nonessential element in the middle of a sentence.

> The Feast and Fest Party**,** **planned for the last day of school,** should attract many students.

In this sentence, the phrase placed between commas conveys nonessential information: the reader does not need to know when the party will occur to realize which party is being referred to because the name of the party is given. Note, however, that in the following sentence, the same phrase is necessary for identification of the party. It specifies that the party is the one planned for the last day of school (not one planned for any other day).

> The party **planned for the last day of school** should attract many students.

In this sentence, the phrase is an **essential (restrictive) element** because the reader needs the information it provides in order to know which party the writer has in mind. Essential elements are not set off by commas; they are integrated into the sentence.

(1) Commas set off nonessential elements used as modifiers.

(a) Adjectival clauses
Nonessential modifiers are often **adjectival (relative) clauses**—those clauses introduced by relative pronouns (see **21b**). The most common relative pronouns are *who*, *which*, and *that*. In the following sentence, a comma sets off the adjectival clause because the content of that clause is not needed to identify the mountain.

> We climbed Mt. McKinley**,** **which is over 20,000 feet high.**

(b) Participial phrases
Nonessential modifiers also include **participial phrases**—those phrases introduced by present or past participles. (See also **21a(3)**.)

Mt. McKinley**,** **towering above us,** brought to mind our abandoned plan for climbing it. [participial phrase beginning with a present participle]

My sister**,** **slowed by a knee injury,** rarely hikes anymore. [participial phrase beginning with a past participle]

(c) Adverbial clauses

An adverbial clause beginning with a subordinating conjunction signaling cause (*because*), consequence (*so that*), or time (*when, after,* or *before*) is usually considered essential and is thus not set off by commas when it appears at the end of a sentence.

Dinosaurs may have become extinct **because their habitat was destroyed.**

In contrast, an adverbial clause that provides nonessential information, such as an extra comment, should be set off from the main clause. (See also **21b(2)**.)

Dinosaurs are extinct**,** **though they are alive in many people's imaginations.**

(2) Commas set off nonessential appositives.

Nonessential appositives provide extra details about nouns or pronouns. In the following sentence, the name of the person is mentioned, so the appositive is not essential for the reader to identify him. Thus, the appositive is set off by commas.

Even Milo Papadupolos**,** **my friend,** let me down.

If *my friend* precedes the specific name, that name is an appositive and might be necessary for identifying the particular friend. In this case, the appositive is essential and so is not set off by commas.

Even my friend **Milo Papadupolos** let me down.

Abbreviations of titles or degrees after names are treated as nonessential appositives.

Was the letter from Frances Evans**,** PhD**,** or from Francis Evans**,** MD?

Increasingly, *Jr.* and *Sr.* are being treated as part of a name, rather than as appositives, and so the comma after the name is occasionally omitted.

William Homer Barton**,** Jr.   OR   William Homer Barton Jr.

Exercise 4

Set off nonessential clauses, phrases, and appositives with commas.

1. Maine Coons long-haired cats with bushy tails have adapted to a harsh climate.
2. These animals which are extremely gentle despite their large size often weigh twenty pounds.
3. Most Maine Coons have exceptionally high intelligence which enables them to recognize language and even to open doors.
4. Unlike most cats Maine Coons will play fetch with their owners.
5. According to a legend later proven to be false Maine Coons developed from interbreeding between wildcats and domestic cats.

(3) Commas set off absolute phrases.

An **absolute phrase** (the combination of a noun and a modifying word or phrase) provides nonessential details and so should be separated from the rest of the sentence by a comma or commas. (See also **21a(6)**.)

> The actor**,** **his hair wet and slicked back,** began his audition.

> The director stared at him**,** **her mind flipping through the photographs she had viewed earlier.**

(4) Commas set off transitional expressions and other parenthetical elements.

Commas customarily set off transitional words and phrases such as *for example, that is,* and *namely.*

> An airline ticket**,** **for example,** can be delivered electronically.

Because they generally indicate little or no pause in reading, transitional words and phrases such as *also, too, at least,* and *thus* need not be set off by commas.

> My dislike of travel has **thus** decreased in recent years.

Use commas to set off other parenthetical elements, such as words or phrases that provide commentary you wish to stress.

> Over the past year, my flights have**,** **miraculously,** been on time.

(5) Commas set off contrasted elements.

Commas set off sentence elements in which words such as *never* and *unlike* express contrast.

A planet**,** **unlike** a star**,** reflects rather than generates light.

In sentences in which contrasted elements are introduced by *not only . . . but also,* place a comma before *but* if you want to emphasize what follows it. Otherwise, you can omit the comma.

Planets not only vary in size**,** **but also** travel at different speeds. [comma added for emphasis]

35e With geographical names and items in dates and addresses

Use commas to make geographical names, dates, and addresses easy to read.

(1) City and state

Nashville, Tennessee, is the largest country-and-western music center in the United States.

(2) Day and date

Martha left for Peru on **Wednesday, February 12, 2006,** and returned on March 12.

OR

Martha left for Peru on **Wednesday, 12 February 2006,** and returned on 12 March.

In the style used in the second example (which is not as common in the United States as the style in the first example), one comma is omitted because *12* precedes rather than follows *February*.

(3) Addresses

Although the name of the person or organization, the street address, and the name of the town or city are all followed by commas, the abbreviation for the state is not.

The codes were sent to **Ms. Melanie Hobson, Senior Analyst, Hobson Computing, 2873 Central Avenue, Orange Park, FL 32065.**

Exercise 5

Explain the reason for each comma used in the following sentences.

1. Alvar Nuñez Cabeza de Vaca, unlike most other Spanish conquistadors, came to perceive Native Americans as equals.
2. On February 15, 1527, Cabeza de Vaca was appointed to an expedition headed for the mainland of North America.
3. The expedition landed near what is now Tampa Bay, Florida, sometime in March 1528.
4. Devastated by misfortune, the expedition dwindled rapidly; Cabeza de Vaca and three other members, however, survived.
5. His endurance now tested, Cabeza de Vaca lived as a trader and healer among Native Americans of the Rio Grande Basin, learning from them and eventually speaking on their behalf to the Spanish crown.

35f With direct quotations accompanied by attributive tags

Many sentences containing direct quotations also contain attributive tags (see **11d(2)**). Use commas to set off these tags whether they occur at the beginning, in the middle, or at the end of a sentence.

(1) Attributive tag at the beginning of a sentence

Place the comma directly after the attributive tag, before the quotation marks.

> According to Jacques Barzun **,** "It is a false analogy with science that makes one think latest is best."

(2) Attributive tag in the middle of a sentence

Place the first comma inside the quotation marks that precede the attributive tag; place the second comma directly after the tag, before the next set of quotation marks.

> "It is a false analogy with science **,** " claims Jacques Barzun **,** "that makes one think latest is best."

(3) Attributive tag at the end of a sentence

Place the comma inside the quotation marks before the attributive tag.

> "It is a false analogy with science that makes one think latest is best," claims Jacques Barzun.

35g Unnecessary or misplaced commas

Although a comma may signal a pause, not every pause calls for a comma. As you read the following sentence aloud, you may pause naturally at several places, but no commas are necessary.

> Heroic deeds done by ordinary people inspire others to act in ways that are not only moral but courageous.

(1) A comma does not separate a subject and its verb or a verb and its object.

Although speakers often pause after the subject or before the object of a sentence, such a pause should not be indicated by a comma.

> In this climate, rain at frequent intervals⌀produces mosquitoes. [no separation between subject (*rain*) and verb (*produces*)]

> The forecaster said⌀that rain was likely. [no separation between verb (*said*) and direct object (the noun clause *that rain was unlikely*)]

(2) A comma does not follow a coordinating conjunction.

Avoid using a comma after a coordinating conjunction (*and, but, for, nor, or, so,* or *yet*).

> We worked very hard on her campaign for state representative, but⌀the incumbent was too strong in the northern counties.

(3) A comma does not generally separate elements in a compound predicate.

Avoid using a comma between two elements of a compound predicate.

> I read the comments carefully⌀and then started my revision.

If you want to slow the reading in order to place stress on the second element in a compound predicate, you can place a comma after the first element. Use this option sparingly, however, or it will lose its effectiveness.

I read the comments word by word**,** and despaired.

(4) Commas set off words, phrases, and clauses only if they are clearly nonessential.

In the following sentences, the elements in boldface are clearly essential and so should not be set off by commas. (See also **35d**.)

Zoe was born **in Chicago in 1985.**

Perhaps the thermostat is broken.

Everyone **who has a mortgage** is required to have fire insurance.

Someone **wearing an orange wig** greeted us at the door.

(5) A comma does not precede the first item of a series or follow the last.

Make sure that you place commas only between elements in a series, not before or after the series.

She was known for her photographs**,** sketches**,** and engravings.

The exhibit included her most deliberate**,** exuberant**,** and expensive photographs.

Exercise 6

Explain the use of each comma in the following paragraph.

[1]Contrails, which are essentially artificial clouds, form when moisture in the air condenses around particles in jet exhaust. [2]Like ordinary clouds, contrails block incoming sunlight and trap heat radiated from Earth's surface. [3]This process reduces daytime highs and increases nighttime lows, narrowing the temperature range. [4]Multiple contrails can cluster together and obscure an area as large as Iowa, Illinois, and Missouri combined, magnifying the effect. [5]Although they may not alter the overall climate, contrails could still have environmental consequences. —LAURA CARSTEN, "Climate on the Wing"

36

THE SEMICOLON

When you use a semicolon—instead of a comma or a period—you are making a rhetorical choice; you are clarifying the relationship you want readers to make between ideas in your sentence. The semicolon most frequently connects two independent clauses when the second clause supports or contrasts with the first. The semicolon also separates grammatically equal elements that contain internal commas. This chapter will help you understand that semicolons

- link closely related independent clauses (**36a**) and
- separate parts of a sentence containing internal commas (**36b**), but
- do not connect independent clauses with phrases or dependent clauses (**36c**).

36a Connecting independent clauses

A semicolon placed between two independent clauses indicates that they are closely related. The second of the two clauses generally supports or contrasts with the first.

> For many cooks, basil is a key ingredient; it appears in recipes worldwide. [support]
>
> Sweet basil is used in many Mediterranean dishes; Thai basil is used in Asian and East Indian recipes. [contrast]

Although a coordinating conjunction (preceded by a comma) can also signal these kinds of relationships between independent clauses, consider using an occasional semicolon for variety.

Sometimes, a transitional expression such as *for example* or *however* (see **4d(3)**) accompanies the semicolon and further establishes the exact relationship between the ideas.

Basil is omnipresent in the cuisine of some countries**;** **for example,** Italians use basil in salads, soups, and many vegetable dishes.

The culinary uses of basil are well known**;** **however,** this herb also has medicinal uses.

A comma is usually inserted after a transitional word; however, it can be omitted if doing so will not lead to a misreading.

Because *basil* comes from a Greek word meaning "king," it suggests royalty; **indeed** some cooks accord basil royal status among herbs and spices.

36b   Separating elements that contain commas

In a series of phrases or clauses containing commas, semicolons indicate where each phrase or clause ends and the next begins.

To survive, mountain lions need a large, open area in which to range**;** a steady supply of deer, skunks, raccoons, foxes, and opossums**;** and the opportunity to find a mate, establish a den, and raise a litter.

In this sentence, the semicolons help the reader distinguish the three separate phrases.

Exercise 1

Revise the following sentences, using semicolons to separate independent clauses or elements that contain internal commas.

1. Homelessness used to be typical only of the chronically unemployed, it is becoming more frequent among the working poor, some of whom earn just the minimum hourly wage of $5.15.
2. The last time the minimum wage was raised was in 1997, however, housing costs went up an average of about 20 percent in one year, which means they could have doubled since the last time the minimum wage was increased.
3. In some homeless families, even though both adults work full-time, their pay is low, they often cannot afford even the least

expensive housing, and they require state assistance, a form of welfare, to provide minimum shelter in a motel room for their children.

4. Such families are very crowded, living four, five, or six to a room, rarely having more than two double beds, a chair, and perhaps a roll-away bed, and lacking a place to keep the children's toys and school books.

5. These families eat at soup kitchens, they have no money for anything other than rent and basic clothing.

36c   Revising common semicolon errors

Semicolons do not set off phrases or dependent clauses. (See **21a** and **21b(2)**.) Use commas for these purposes.

We consulted Alinka Kibukian; **,** the local horticulturalist.
                                    ∧

Needing summer shade; **,** we planted two of the largest trees we could afford.
                         ∧

We learned that young trees need care; **,** which meant we had to do some extra chores after dinner each night.   ∧

Our trees have survived; **,** even though we live in a harsh climate.
                            ∧

Exercise 2

Replace any semicolon used to set off a phrase or a dependent clause. Do not change properly used semicolons.

1. Every morning I take vitamins; a multivitamin and sometimes extra vitamin C.

2. I used to believe that I could get my vitamins from a balanced diet; then I found out that diet may not provide enough of some vitamins, such as folic acid.

3. By eating a balanced diet, getting plenty of exercise, and keeping stress to a minimum; I thought I would stay healthy.
4. New research suggests that multivitamins are beneficial; when our diets do not provide all the recommended amounts of every vitamin every day; our health can suffer.
5. Although taking one multivitamin tablet a day is a healthy habit; we do not need to buy the most potent or most expensive vitamins available.

Exercise 3

Find or compose one sentence to illustrate each of the following uses of the semicolon.

1. To link two related independent clauses
2. To separate clauses in a sentence containing a conjunctive adverb such as *however* or *therefore*
3. To separate phrases or clauses that contain commas

37

THE APOSTROPHE

Apostrophes serve a number of purposes. For example, you can use them to show that someone owns something *(my neighbor's television)*, that someone has a specific relationship with someone else *(my neighbor's children),* or that someone has produced or created something *(my neighbor's recipe).* Apostrophes are also used in contractions *(can't, don't)* and in certain plural forms *(B.A.'s, M.D.'s).* This chapter will help you use apostrophes to

- indicate ownership and other relationships (**37a**),
- mark omissions of letters or numbers (**37b**), and
- form certain plurals (**37c**).

37a Indicating ownership and other relationships

An apostrophe most commonly indicates ownership or origin.

Fumi's computer, the photographer's camera [ownership]

Einstein's ideas, the student's decision [origin]

An apostrophe indicates other relationships as well. For example, you use an apostrophe to show how people are related or what physical or psychological traits they possess.

Linda's sister, the employee's supervisor [human relationships]

Mona Lisa's smile, the team's spirit [physical or psychological traits]

An apostrophe also indicates traits or features of animals, plants, objects, and abstract nouns.

the dog's ears, the tree's branches, the chair's legs, tyranny's influence

Words used to identify certain tools, buildings, events, and other things also include apostrophes.

> tailor's scissors, driver's license, bachelor's degree
>
> St. John's Cathedral, Parkinson's disease, Valentine's Day

You can also use an apostrophe with some forms of measurement.

> a day's wages, an hour's delay, five dollars' worth of chocolates

A noun usually follows a word with an apostrophe. However, occasionally, the noun is omitted when it is understood from the context.

> Is this Ana's or LaShonda's? [COMPARE: Is this Ana's book or LaShonda's book?]

Word with Apostrophe and _s_ or Phrase Beginning with _of_
In many cases, you can use either a word with an apostrophe and an _s_ or a prepositional phrase beginning with _of._

> Louise Erdrich's novels OR the novels **of** Louise Erdrich
>
> the plane's arrival OR the arrival **of** the plane

However, the ending -'_s_ is more commonly used with nouns referring to people, and the prepositional phrase is used with most nouns referring to location.

> my **uncle's** workshop, **Jan's** car, the **student's** paper [nouns referring to people]
>
> the **end of** the movie, the **middle of** the day, the **front of** the building [nouns referring to location]

(1) Most singular nouns, indefinite pronouns, abbreviations, and acronyms require -'s to form the possessive case.

> the dean's office Yeats's poems anyone's computer
>
> Walter Bryan Jr.'s letter [To avoid confusion, no comma precedes _Jr.'s_ here. _Jr._ is sometimes set off by a comma, however; see **35d(2)**.]
>
> the NFL's reputation OPEC's price increase

Unlike the possessive forms of nouns and indefinite pronouns, possessive pronouns and determiners *(my, mine, our, ours, your, yours, his, her, hers, its, their, theirs,* and *whose)* are not written with apostrophes (see **25b(3)**).

Japanese democracy differs from **ours.**

The committee concluded **its** discussion.

 Be careful not to confuse possessive pronouns and determiners with contractions. Whenever you write a contraction, you should be able to substitute the complete words for it without changing the meaning.

Possessive pronoun	**Contraction**
Its motor is small.	**It's** [It is] a small motor.
Whose turn is it?	**Who's** [Who is] representing us?

To form the possessive of most singular proper nouns, you add an apostrophe and an *s: Iowa's governor.* When a singular proper noun already ends in *-s,* though, you need to consult the publication guide for the discipline in which you are writing. The *MLA Handbook for Writers of Research Papers* recommends always using *-'s,* as in *Illinois's legislature, Dickens's novels, Ms. Jones's address,* and *Descartes's reasoning. The Chicago Manual of Style,* however, notes some exceptions to this rule. An apostrophe without an *s* is used under the following circumstances: (1) when a name ends in a syllable pronounced "eez" *(Sophocles' poetry),* (2) when a singular common noun ends in *-s (physics' contribution),* and (3) when the name of a place or organization ends in *-s* but refers to a single entity *(United States' foreign aid).*

(2) Plural nouns ending in -s require only an apostrophe for the possessive form.

the boys' game	the babies' toys	the Joneses' house

Plural nouns that do not end in *-s* need both an apostrophe and an *s.*

men's lives	women's health	children's projects

An apostrophe is not needed to make a noun plural. To make most nouns plural, add *-s* or *-es*. Add an apostrophe only to signal ownership, origin, and other similar relationships.

protesters
The ~~protesters'~~ met in front of the conference center.

The protesters' meeting was on Wednesday.

Likewise, to form the plural of a family name, use *-s* or *-es*, not an apostrophe.

Johnsons
The ~~Johnson's~~ participated in the study. [COMPARE: The Johnsons' participation in the study was crucial.]

Jameses
The trophy was given to the ~~James's~~. [COMPARE: The Jameses' trophy is on display in the lobby.]

(3) To show collaboration or joint ownership, add -'s or an apostrophe to the second noun only.

the carpenter and the **plumber's** decision [They made the decision collaboratively.]

the Becks and the **Lopezes'** cabin [They own one cabin jointly.]

(4) To show separate ownership or individual contributions, add -'s or an apostrophe to each noun.

the **Becks'** and the **Lopezes'** cars [Each family owns a car.]

the **carpenter's** and the **plumber's** proposals [They each made a proposal.]

(5) Add -'s to the last word of a compound noun.

my brother-in-**law's** friends, the attorney **general's** statements [singular]

my brother**s**-in-**law's** friends, the attorney**s** **general's** statements [plural]

To avoid awkward constructions such as the last two, writers often rephrase them using a prepositional phrase beginning with *of: the statements of the attorneys general.*

(6) Add -'s or an apostrophe to a noun that precedes a gerund.

> Lucy**'s having** to be there seemed unnecessary. [singular noun preceding gerund]
>
> The family appreciated the lawyers**' handling** of the matter. [plural noun preceding gerund]

Sometimes you may find it difficult to distinguish between a gerund and a participle (see **21a(3)**). A good way to tell the difference is to note whether the emphasis is on an action or on a person. In a sentence containing a gerund, the emphasis is on the action; in a sentence containing a participle, the emphasis is on the person.

> Our successful completion of the project depends on **Terry's providing** the illustrations. [gerund]
>
> I remember my **brother telling** me the same joke last year. [participle]

Gerund Phrases

When a gerund appears after a noun that ends with -'s or with just an apostrophe, the noun is the subject of the gerund phrase.

Lucy's having to be there [COMPARE: **Lucy** has to be there.]

The lawyers' handling of the matter [COMPARE: **The lawyers** handled the matter.]

The gerund phrase may serve as the subject or the object in the sentence (see **20d**).

> ⎡――――s――――⎤
> **Lucy's having to be there** seemed unnecessary.

> ⎡――――obj――――⎤
> The family appreciated **the lawyers' handling of the matter.**

(7) Follow an organization's preference for its name or the name of a product; follow local conventions for a geographical location.

Consumers Union	Actors' Equity	Shoppers Choice	Taster's Choice
Devil's Island	Devils Tower	Devil Mountain	

Whether an apostrophe is used in a brand name is determined by the organization owning the name.

Following the pattern of the examples, change the modifier after each noun to a possessive form that precedes the noun.

EXAMPLES

proposals made by the committee   *the committee's proposals*

poems written by Keats   *Keats's poems*

1. the day named after St. Patrick
2. a leave of absence lasting six months
3. the position taken by HMOs
4. the report given by the eyewitness
5. the generosity of the Lees
6. an article coauthored by Gloria and Alan
7. the weights of the children
8. the spying done by the neighbors
9. the restaurants in New Orleans
10. coffee roasted by Starbucks

37b Marking omissions of letters or numbers

Apostrophes mark omissions in contractions, numbers, and words mimicking speech.

they're [they are]   class of '06 [class of 2006]
y'all [you all]   singin' [singing]

Contractions are not always appropriate for formal contexts. Your audience may expect you to use full words instead (for example, *cannot* instead of *can't* and *will not* instead of *won't*).

 A grammar checker will often flag possessives, marking them as "possible" errors but not telling you whether the apostrophe goes before the *s* or after it, or if an added *s* is needed at all. A grammar checker is usually right, however, about missing apostrophes in contractions such as *can't* and *don't*.

37c Forming certain plurals

Although an apostrophe was used in the past for forming the plurals of numbers, abbreviations, and words used as words, it is used only rarely for this purpose today. These plurals are generally formed by simply adding -s.

1990s   fours and fives   YWCAs   two *and*s   the three Rs

Apostrophes are still used, however, with lowercase letters and with abbreviations that include internal periods or a combination of uppercase and lowercase letters.

x's and *y*'s   B.A.'s   Ph.D.'s

The MLA differs from this style in recommending the use of apostrophes for the plurals of uppercase letters (*A*'s and *B*'s).

Exercise 2

Insert apostrophes where needed in the following sentences. Be prepared to explain why they are necessary.

1. Whose responsibility is it to see whether its working?
2. Hansons book was published in the early 1920s.
3. They hired a rock n roll band for their wedding dance.
4. NPRs fund drive begins this weekend.
5. Youll have to include the ISBNs of the books youre going to purchase.
6. Only three of the proposals are still being considered: yours, ours, and the Wilbers.
7. Few students enrolled during the academic year 98–99.
8. There cant be more *x*s than there are *y*s in the equation.
9. The students formed groups of twos and threes.
10. The M.D.s disagreed on the patients prognosis.

Exercise 3

Add the apostrophes that are missing from the following paragraph.

[1]In his book *A Day in the Life: The Music and Artistry of the Beatles*, Mark Hertsgaard describes what he found in the archives of Londons Abbey Road Studios. [2]Although the Beatles released barely eleven hours worth of music in their eight-year studio career, the archives contain over four hundred hours of recordings from the 1960s, including a master tape of each song put out by EMI Records. [3]Also found in the archives are the working tapes that reveal each songs evolution. [4]For instance, to Hertsgaard, the first run-through of the song "A Day in the Life" sounds more like a folk ballad than the art song it became. [5]Used as the title of the book, this song is notable in other regards as well. [6]Hertsgaard shows how it reveals the collaboration of John Lennon and Paul McCartney. [7]Though the song could be called Johns because he came up with the narrative and its melody, it was Paul who made it a complete composition by providing the middle passage. [8]Yet perhaps the song is most significant because

of its message. [9]When the British Broadcasting Corporation (BBC) accused the Beatles of promoting drugs and refused to play the recording, Paul McCartney responded to the BBCs ban by saying that the groups purpose was to turn people on "to the truth" rather than to drugs. [10]According to Hertsgaard, in "A Day in the Life," the Beatles were expressing their belief that the world could be released from the hold of power and greed: it could be rejuvenated.

QUOTATION MARKS

38

Quotation marks enclose sentences or parts of sentences that play a special role. For example, quotation marks indicate that you are quoting someone else's words or that you are using a word or phrase in an unconventional way. This chapter will help you use quotation marks

- with direct quotations (**38a**),
- with titles of short works (**38b**),
- for words or phrases used ironically or unconventionally (**38c**), and
- in combination with other punctuation (**38d**).

38a Direct quotations

Double quotation marks set off direct quotations, including those in dialogue. Single quotation marks enclose a quotation within a quotation.

(1) Double quotation marks enclose direct quotations.

Quotation marks enclose only the quotation, not any expression such as *she said* or *he replied*. When a sentence ends with quoted material, place the period inside the quotation marks. For guidelines on comma placement, see **38d(1)**.

> "Like branding steers or embalming the dead," writes David Sedaris, "teaching was a profession I had never seriously considered."

When using direct quotations, reproduce all quoted material exactly as it appears in the original, including capitalization and punctuation. To learn how to set off long quotations as indented blocks, see **12a(2)** and **16f(4)**.

(2) Quotation marks are not used for indirect quotations.

An indirect quotation is a restatement of what someone else has said or written.

> David Sedaris claims that he never wanted to become a teacher, any more than he wanted to become a cowboy or a mortician.

(3) Single quotation marks enclose quotations within quotations.

If the quotation you are using includes another direct quotation, use single quotation marks for the embedded quotation.

> According to Anita Erickson, "when the narrator says, 'I have the right to my own opinion,' he means that he has the right to his own delusion."

However, if a quotation appears in a block quotation, use double quotation marks.

> Anita Erickson claims that the narrator uses the word *opinion* deceptively.
>
> > Later in the chapter, when the narrator says, "I have the right to my own opinion," he means that he has the right to his own delusion. Although it is tempting to believe that the narrator is acting according to a rational belief system, his behavior suggests that he is more interested in deception. With poisonous lies, whose concoction he savors, he has already deceived his business partner, his wife, and his children.

(4) Dialogue is enclosed in quotation marks.

When creating or reporting a dialogue, enclose in quotation marks what each person says, no matter how short. Use a separate paragraph for each speaker, beginning a new paragraph whenever the speaker changes. Expressions such as *he said,* as well as related narrative details, can be included in the same paragraph as a direct quotation.

> Farmer looked up, smiling, and in a chirpy-sounding voice he said, "But that feeling has the disadvantage of being . . ." He paused a beat. "Wrong."
> "Well," I retorted, "it depends on how you look at it."
>
> —**TRACY KIDDER,** *Mountains Beyond Mountains*

When quoting more than one paragraph by a single speaker, put quotation marks at the beginning of each paragraph. However, do not place closing quotation marks at the end of each paragraph—only at the end of the last paragraph.

(5) Thoughts are enclosed in quotation marks.

Quotation marks set off thoughts that resemble speech.

> "His silence on this topic has surprised everyone," I thought as I surveyed the faces of the other committee members.

Thoughts are usually marked by such phrases as *I thought, he felt*, and *she believed*. Remember, though, that quotation marks are not used with thoughts that are reported indirectly (see **38a(2)**).

> I wondered why he didn't respond.

(6) Short excerpts of poetry included within a sentence are enclosed in quotation marks.

When quoting fewer than four lines of poetry, enclose them in quotation marks and use a slash to indicate the line division (see also **39i**).

> After watching a whale swim playfully, the speaker in "Visitation" concludes, "What did you think, that joy / was some slight thing?"

To learn how to treat longer quotations of poetry, see **16f(4)**.

38b Titles of short works

Quotation marks enclose the title of a short work, such as a story, essay, poem, or song. The title of a larger work, such as a book, magazine, newspaper, or play, should be italicized (or underlined if you are using MLA style).

> "The Green Shepherd" first appeared in *The New Yorker*.

Short story	"The Lottery"	"The Fall of the House of Usher"
Essay	"Living Like Weasels"	"Play-by-Play"
Article	"Disneyland with the Death Penalty"	"Arabia's Empty Quarter"
Book chapter	"The Neurologist Vanishes"	"Spirits of Blood, Spirits of Air"

Short poem	"Orion"	"Mending Wall"
Song	"Lazy River"	"The Star-Spangled Banner"
TV episode	"An Englishman Abroad"	"The Last Time"

Use double quotation marks around the title of a short work embedded in a longer italicized (or underlined) title.

> *Interpretations of* "*A Good Man Is Hard to Find*" [book about a short story]

Use single quotation marks for a shorter title within a longer title that is enclosed in double quotation marks.

> "Irony in 'The Sick Rose'" [article about a poem]

Differing Uses of Quotation Marks

If you read a book published in Great Britain, you will notice that the use of quotation marks differs in some ways from the style presented here. For example, single quotation marks are used to set off the titles of short works, and a period is placed outside a quotation mark ending a sentence. Nevertheless, when writing in the United States, follow the rules for American English.

| **British usage** | In class, we compared Wordsworth's 'Upon Westminster Bridge' with Blake's 'London'. |
| **American usage** | In class, we compared Wordsworth's "Upon Westminster Bridge" with Blake's "London." |

38c For ironic tone or unusual usage

Writers sometimes use quotation marks to indicate that they are using a word or phrase ironically. The word *gourmet* is used ironically in the following sentence.

> His "gourmet" dinner turned out to be processed turkey and instant mashed potatoes.

Avoid using quotation marks around words that may not be appropriate for your rhetorical situation. Instead, take the time to choose suitable words. The revised sentence in the following pair is more effective than the first.

Ineffective   He is too much of a "wimp" to be a good leader.

Revised   He is too indecisive to be a good leader.

Similarly, putting a cliché (see **33b**) in quotation marks could make readers conclude that you do not care enough about expressing your meaning to think of a fresh expression.

38d With other punctuation marks

To decide whether to place some other punctuation mark inside or outside quotation marks, identify the punctuation mark and note whether it is part of the quotation or part of the surrounding context.

(1) With commas and periods

Quoted material is usually accompanied by an attributive tag such as *she said* or *he replied*. When your sentence starts with an attributive tag, place a comma after it to separate the tag from the quotation.

> She replied, "There's more than one way to slice a pie."

If your sentence starts with the quotation instead, place the comma inside the closing quotation marks.

> "There's more than one way to slice a pie," she replied.

Place the period inside closing quotation marks, whether single or double, if the quotation ends the sentence.

> Jason admitted, "I didn't understand 'An Algorithm for Life.'"

When quoting material from a source, provide the relevant page number(s). If you are following MLA guidelines, note the page number(s) in parentheses after the final quotation marks, and place the period that ends the sentence after the final parenthesis, unless the quotation is a block quotation. (See **12a(2)**.)

According to Diane Ackerman, "Love is a demanding sport involving all the muscle groups, including the brain" (86).

(2) With semicolons and colons

Place semicolons and colons outside quotation marks.

His favorite song was "Cyprus Avenue"; mine was "Astral Weeks."

Because it is repeated, one line stands out in "The Conductor": "We are never as beautiful as now."

(3) With question marks, exclamation points, and dashes

If the direct quotation includes a question mark, an exclamation point, or a dash, place that punctuation *inside* the closing quotation marks.

Jeremy asked, "What is truth?"

Gordon shouted "Congratulations!"

Laura said, "Let me tell—" Before she could finish her sentence, Dan walked into the room.

Use just one question mark inside the quotation marks when a question ends with a quoted question.

Why do children keep asking "Why?"

If the punctuation is not part of the quoted material, place it *outside* the closing quotation marks.

Who wrote "The Figure a Sentence Makes"?

You have to read "Awareness and Freedom"!

She called me a "toaster head"—understandable under the circumstances.

Exercise 1

Insert quotation marks where they are needed in the following sentences. Do not alter sentences that are written correctly.

1. Have you read Ian Buruma's essay The Joys and Perils of Victimhood?

2. Buruma writes, The only way a new generation can be identified with the suffering of previous generations is for that suffering to be publicly acknowledged, over and over again.

3. When my reading group met to talk about this essay, I started our discussion by noting that the word *victim* is defined in my dictionary as anyone who is oppressed or mistreated.

4. So how can we tell who the real victims are? asked Claudia.

5. Cahit responded, I think that both the Israelis and the Palestinians are victims of violence.

6. Yes, agreed Claudia, I worry especially about the women and children in that part of the world. I wish I could say to them, Do not give up hope!

7. According to Tony, the situation in the Middle East would improve if people could learn to live and let live.

8. Using the events of September 11, 2001, as an example, Kyle argued that victims can be of any race, nationality, religion, or gender.

9. Rachel agreed but added that victims can be of different ages as well, pointing out that child abuse is a growing concern.

10. I see many victims of abuse when I volunteer at the Center for the Family, Mai explained, but we must be careful not to confuse abuse with discipline.

39 THE PERIOD AND OTHER PUNCTUATION MARKS

To indicate the end of a sentence, you can use one of three punctuation marks: the period, the question mark, or the exclamation point. Your choice depends on the meaning you wish to convey.

Everyone passed the exam.

Everyone passed the exam? [informal usage]

Everyone passed the exam!

Other punctuation marks also clarify meaning and ease reading. Colons, dashes, parentheses, square brackets, ellipsis points, and slashes help your readers understand the message you want to convey. (For use of the hyphen, see **40f**.)

This chapter will help you use

- end punctuation marks (the period, the question mark, and the exclamation point) (**39a–c**),
- the colon (**39d**),
- the dash (**39e**),
- parentheses (**39f**),
- square brackets (**39g**),
- ellipsis points (**39h**), and
- the slash (**39i**).

To accommodate computerized typesetting, both CMS and the APA style manual call for only one space after a period, a question mark, an exclamation point, a colon, and each of the periods in ellipsis points. According to these manuals, there should be no space preceding or following a hyphen or a dash. The MLA style manual recommends using only one space after end punctuation marks but allows two spaces if they are used consistently.

39a The period

(1) A period marks the end of a sentence.

Use a period at the end of a declarative sentence.

> Many adults in the United States are overfed yet undernourished.
> Soft drinks account for 7 percent of their average daily caloric intake.

In addition, place a period at the end of an instruction or recommendation written as an imperative sentence (see **21e**).

> Eat plenty of fruits and vegetables. Drink six to eight glasses of water a day.

Indirect questions are phrased as statements, so be sure to use a period, rather than a question mark, at the end of such a sentence.

> I wonder why people eat so much junk food.
> [COMPARE: Why do people eat so much junk food?]

(2) Periods follow some abbreviations.

> Dr.   Jr.   a.m.   p.m.   vs.   etc.   et al.

Only one period follows an abbreviation that ends a sentence.

> The tour begins at 1:00 p.m.

Periods are not used with many common abbreviations (for example, *MVP, mph,* and *FM*). (See chapter **43**.) A dictionary lists the conventional form of an abbreviation as well as any alternatives.

39b The question mark

Place a question mark after a direct question.

> How does the new atomic clock work? Who invented this clock?

Use a period, instead of a question mark, after an indirect question—that is, a question embedded in a statement.

> I asked whether the new atomic clock could be used in cell phones.
> [COMPARE: Can the new atomic clock be used in cell phones?]

Indirect Questions
Indirect questions are written as declarative sentences. The subject and verb are not inverted as they would be in the related direct question.

We do not know when ~~will~~ the meeting _will_ end.

[COMPARE: When will the meeting end?]

Place a question mark after each question in a series of related questions, even when they are not full sentences.

Will the new atomic clock be used in cell phones? Word processors? Car navigation systems?

If a direct quotation is a question, place the question mark inside the final quotation marks.

Tony asked, "How small is this new clock?"

In contrast, if you include quoted material in a question of your own, place the question mark outside the final quotation marks.

Is the clock really "no larger than a sugar cube"?

If you embed in the middle of a sentence a question not attributable to anyone in particular, place a comma before it and a question mark after it.

When the question, how does the clock work? arose, the researchers described a technique used by manufacturers of computer chips.

The first letter of such a question should not be capitalized unless the question is extremely long or contains internal punctuation.

To indicate uncertainty about a fact such as a date of birth, place a question mark inside parentheses directly after the fact in question.

Chaucer was born in 1340 (?) and died in 1400.

39c The exclamation point

An exclamation point often marks the end of a sentence, but its primary purpose is rhetorical—to create emphasis.

Whoa! What a game!

When a direct quotation ends with an exclamation point, no comma or period is placed immediately after it.

"Get a new pitcher**!**" he yelled.

He yelled, "Get a new pitcher**!**"

Use the exclamation point sparingly so that you do not diminish its value. If you do not intend to signal strong emotion, place a comma after an interjection and a period at the end of the sentence.

Well**,** no one seriously expected this victory**.**

Exercise 1

Compose and punctuate brief sentences of the following types.

1. a declarative sentence containing a quoted exclamation
2. a sentence beginning with an interjection
3. a direct question
4. a declarative sentence containing an indirect question
5. a declarative sentence containing a direct question

39d The colon

A colon calls attention to what follows. It also separates numbers in time references and in parts of scriptural references and titles from subtitles. Leave only one space after a colon.

(1) A colon directs attention to an explanation, a summary, or a quotation.

When a colon appears between two independent clauses, it signals that the second clause will explain or expand on the first.

For I had no brain tumor, no eyestrain, no high blood pressure, nothing wrong with me at all**:** I simply had migraine headaches, and migraine headaches were, as everyone who did not have them knew, imaginary.

—JOAN DIDION

A colon is also used after an independent clause to introduce a direct quotation.

> Marcel Proust explained the importance of mindfulness this way: "The true journey of discovery consists not in seeking new landscapes but in having fresh eyes."

 The rules for using an uppercase or a lowercase letter to begin the first word of an independent clause that follows a colon vary across style manuals.

MLA	The first letter should be lowercase unless (1) it begins a word that is normally capitalized, (2) the independent clause is a quotation, or (3) it begins a rule or principle.
APA	The first letter should be uppercase.
CMS	The first letter should be lowercase unless (1) it begins a word that is normally capitalized, (2) the independent clause is a quotation, or (3) two or more sentences follow the colon.

Although an independent clause should always precede the colon, a phrase may sometimes follow it.

> I was finally confronted with what I had dreaded for months: the due date for the final balloon payment on my car loan.

All of the style manuals advise using lowercase letters for the first letter of a phrase following a colon.

(2) A colon may signal that a list follows.

Writers frequently use colons to introduce lists.

> Three students received internships: Asa, Vanna, and Jack.

Avoid placing a colon between a verb and its complement or after the words *including* and *such as*.

> The winners were ⊖: Asa, Vanna, and Jack.

> Many vegetarians do not eat dairy products such as ⊖: butter and cheese.

(3) A colon separates a title and a subtitle.

Use a colon between a work's title and its subtitle.

Collapse: How Societies Choose to Fail or Succeed

(4) Colons are used in certain numbers.

Colons are used between numbers in time designations and scriptural references.

11:45 a.m.   3:00 p.m.

Psalms 3:5   Gen. 1:1

However, MLA requires the use of periods in numbers referring to scripture.

Psalms 3.5   Gen. 1.1

(5) Colons have specialized uses in business correspondence.

A colon follows the salutation of a business letter and any notations.

Dear Dr. Horner: Dear Maxine: enc:

A colon introduces the headings in a memo.

To: From: Subject: Date:

Exercise 2

Insert colons where they are needed in the following sentences.

1. Before we discuss marketing, let's outline the behavior of consumers consumer behavior is the process individuals go through as they select, buy, or use products or services to satisfy their needs and desires.

2. The process consists of six stages recognizing a need or desire, finding information, evaluating options, deciding to purchase, purchasing, and assessing purchases.

3. Many consumers rely on one popular publication for product information *Consumer Reports*.

4. When evaluating alternatives, a consumer uses criteria; for example, a house hunter might use some of the following criteria price, location, size, age, style, and landscaping design.

5. The postpurchase assessment has one of two results satisfaction or dissatisfaction with the product or service.

39e The dash

A dash (or em dash) marks a break in thought, sets off a nonessential element for emphasis or clarity, or follows an introductory list or series. You can use your keyboard to form such a dash by typing two hyphens with no spaces between, before, or after the hyphens. Most word-processing programs can be set to convert these hyphens automatically to an em dash. Dashes signal a specific meaning, so use them purposefully rather than as mere substitutes for commas, semicolons, or colons. (For use of the short dash, or en dash, see **43g**.)

(1) A dash marks a break in the normal flow of a sentence.

Use a dash to indicate a shift in thought or tone.

> I was awed by the almost superhuman effort Stonehenge represents—but who wouldn't be?

(2) A dash or a pair of dashes sets off a nonessential element for emphasis or clarity.

> Dr. Kruger's specialty is mycology—the study of fungi.

> The trail we took down into the Grand Canyon—steep, narrow, winding, and lacking guardrails—made me wonder whether we could call a helicopter to fly us back out.

(3) A dash follows an introductory list or series.

If you decide to place a list or series at the beginning of a sentence in order to emphasize it, the main part of the following sentence (after the dash) should sum up the meaning of the list or series.

> Eager, determined to succeed, and scared to death—all of these describe how I felt on the first day at work.

THINKING RHETORICALLY ABOUT

COMMAS, DASHES, AND COLONS

Although commas, dashes, and colons may be followed by explanations, examples, or illustrations, is their rhetorical impact the same?

> He never failed to mention what was most important to him**,** the bottom line.

> He never failed to mention what was most important to him——the bottom line.

> He never failed to mention what was most important to him**:** the bottom line.

The comma, one of the most common punctuation marks, barely draws attention to what follows it. The dash, in contrast, signals a longer pause and so causes more emphasis to be placed on the information that follows. The colon is more direct and formal than either of the other two punctuation marks.

39f Parentheses

Use parentheses to set off information that is not closely related to the main point of a sentence or paragraph but that provides an interesting detail, an explanation, or an illustration. Parentheses used for this purpose indicate that the material they contain is an aside.

> If we refuse to talk "like a lady," we are ridiculed and criticized for being unfeminine. ("She thinks like a man" is, at best, a left-handed compliment.)
>
> —ROBIN LAKOFF

In addition, place parentheses around an acronym or abbreviation when introducing it after its full form.

> The Search for Extraterrestrial Intelligence (SETI) uses the Very Large Array (VLA) outside Sicorro, New Mexico, to scan the sky.

If you use numbers or letters in a list within a sentence, set them off by placing them within parentheses.

Your application should include (1) a current résumé, (2) a statement of purpose, and (3) two letters of recommendation.

For information on the use of parentheses in bibliographies and in-text citations, see chapters **12–15**.

THINKING RHETORICALLY ABOUT

DASHES AND PARENTHESES

Dashes and parentheses are both used to set off a nonessential element in a sentence, but they differ in the amount of emphasis they signal. Whereas dashes call attention to the material they set off, parentheses usually deemphasize the information they enclose.

Sylvia——an avid video-game player——is in front of her computer when she is not at her controls.

Sylvia (an avid video-game player) is enrolled in the flight technology program.

39g Square brackets

Square brackets set off additions or alterations used to clarify quotations. In the following example, the bracketed name specifies who "he" is.

Parker Pilgrim has written, "If he [Leonard Aaron] ever disapproved of any of his children's friends, he never let them know about it."

If your rhetorical situation calls for the exact replication of directly quoted material, use square brackets to indicate that a letter has been changed from uppercase to lowercase, or vice versa.

[I]f the network was ever going to become more than a test bed . . . , word of its potential had to spread.   —**KATIE HAFNER** AND **MATTHEW LYON**

To avoid the awkwardness of using brackets in such a way, consider rewording the sentence so that no change in capitalization is needed.

Hafner and Lyon note that "if the network was ever going to become more than a test bed . . . , word of its potential had to spread."

Square brackets are also used within parentheses to avoid the confusion of having two sets of parentheses.

Not every expert agrees. (See, for example, Katie Hafner and Matthew Lyon's *Where Wizards Stay Up Late* [New York: Simon, 1996].)

Angle brackets (< >) are often used to enclose Web addresses so that punctuation in the sentence is not confused with the dot(s) in the URL: <http://www.harbrace.com>.

39h Ellipsis points

Ellipsis points indicate an omission from a quoted passage or a reflective pause or hesitation.

(1) Ellipsis points mark an omission within a quoted passage.

Whenever you omit anything from material you quote, replace the omitted material with ellipsis points—three equally spaced periods. Be sure to compare your quoted sentence to the original, checking to see that your omission does not change the meaning of the original. The following examples illustrate how to use ellipsis points in quotations from a passage by Patricia Gadsby.

Original

Cacao doesn't flower, as most plants do, at the tips of its outer and uppermost branches. Instead, its sweet white buds hang from the trunk and along a few fat branches, popping out of patches of bark called cushions, which form where leaves drop off. They're tiny, these flowers. Yet once pollinated by midges, no-see-ums that flit in the leafy detritus below, they'll make pulp-filled pods almost the size of rugby balls.

—**PATRICIA GADSBY,** "Endangered Chocolate"

Omission within a quoted sentence

Patricia Gadsby notes that cacao flowers "once pollinated by midges . . . make pulp-filled pods almost the size of rugby balls."

Omission at the beginning of a quoted sentence

Do not use ellipsis points to indicate that you have deleted words from the beginning of a quotation, whether it is run into the text or set off in a block. The first word of the original sentence has been omitted in the following quotation.

> According to Patricia Gadsby, cacao flowers will become "pulp-filled pods almost the size of rugby balls."

Note that the first letter of the integrated quotation is not capitalized.

Omission at the end of a quoted sentence

To indicate that you have omitted words from the end of a sentence, put a space after the last word and before the three spaced ellipsis points. Then add the end punctuation mark (a period, a question mark, or an exclamation point). If the quoted material is followed by a parenthetical source or page reference, the end punctuation comes after the second parenthesis.

> Claiming that cacao flowers differ from those of most plants, Patricia Gadsby describes how "the sweet white buds hang from the trunk and along a few fat branches . . . ." OR "branches . . ." (2).

Omission of a sentence or more

To signal the omission of a sentence or more (even a paragraph or more), place an end punctuation mark (usually a period) before the ellipsis points.

> Patricia Gadsby describes the flowering of the cacao plant: "its sweet white buds hang from the trunk and along a few fat branches, popping out of patches of bark called cushions, which form where leaves drop off. . . . Yet once pollinated by midges, no-see-ums that flit in the leafy detritus below, they'll make pulp-filled pods almost the size of rugby balls."

If, in addition to omitting a full sentence, you omit part of another and that part ends in a comma, colon, or semicolon, place the relevant punctuation mark before the ellipsis points.

> Patricia Gadsby describes the flowering of the cacao plant: "its sweet white buds hang from the trunk and along a few fat branches, . . . Yet once pollinated by midges, no-see-ums that flit in the leafy detritus below, they'll make pulp-filled pods almost the size of rugby balls."

To signal the omission of a full line or more in quoted poetry, use spaced periods covering the length of either the line above it or the omitted line.

The yellow fog that rubs its back upon the window-panes,

· ·

Curled once about the house, and fell asleep.

> —**T. S. ELIOT**, "The Love Song of J. Alfred Prufrock"

To avoid excessive use of ellipses, replace some of the direct quotations with paraphrases. (See **11d(3)**.)

(2) Ellipsis points show that a sentence has been intentionally left incomplete.

Read aloud the passage that begins "The yellow fog **. . .**"

(3) Ellipsis points can mark a reflective pause or a hesitation.

Keith saw four menacing youths coming toward him **. . .** and ran.

A dash can also be used to indicate this type of a pause.

39i The slash

A slash between words, as in *and/or* and *he/she*, indicates that either word is applicable in the given context. There are no spaces before and after a slash used in this way. Because extensive use of the slash can make writing choppy, consider using *or* instead. (If you are following MLA conventions, avoid using the slash in formal prose.)

A slash is also used to mark line divisions in quoted poetry. A slash used in this way is preceded and followed by a space.

Wallace Stevens refers to the listener who, "nothing himself, beholds **/** Nothing that is not there and the nothing that is."

Exercise 3

Add dashes, parentheses, square brackets, and slashes at appropriate places in the following sentences. Be ready to explain the reason for every mark you add.

1. Researchers in an exciting field Artificial Intelligence AI are working on devices to assist the elderly.

2. One such device is Pearl a robotic nurse that helps around the house.

3. Another application is cooking software that checks for missing and or incorrect ingredients.

4. Researchers are even investigating Global Positioning Systems GPS as a way to track Alzheimer's patients' daily routines.

5. The actual cost of such devices expensive now but more affordable later is yet to be determined.

Exercise 4

Punctuate the following sentences with appropriate end marks, commas, colons, dashes, and parentheses. Do not use unnecessary punctuation. Give a justification for each mark you add, especially where more than one type of mark (for example, commas, dashes, or parentheses) is acceptable.

1. Many small country towns are very similar a truck stop a gas station a crowded diner and three bars

2. The simple life a nonexistent crime rate and down-home values these are some of the advantages these little towns offer

3. Why do we never see these quaint examples of pure Americana when we travel around the country on the interstates

4. Rolling across America on one of the big interstates I-20 I-40 I-70 I-80 or I-90 you are likely to pass within a few miles of a number of these towns

5. These towns almost certainly will have a regional or perhaps an ethnic flavor Hispanic in the southwest Scandinavian in the north

6. When I visit one of these out-of-the-way places I always have a sense of well really a feeling of safety

7. There's one thing I can tell you small-town life is not boring

8. My one big question however is what do you do to earn a living in these towns.

MECHANICS

M

Advertisers frequently use capitalization to highlight important words.

40 SPELLING, THE SPELL CHECKER, AND HYPHENATION

When you first draft a paper, you might not pay close attention to spelling words correctly. After all, the point of drafting is to generate and organize ideas. However, proofreading for spelling mistakes is essential as you near the end of the writing process. Your teachers, employers, or supervisors will expect you to submit polished work.

You can train yourself to be a good proofreader by checking a dictionary every time you question the spelling of a word. If two spellings are listed, such as *fulfill* and *fulfil*, either form is correct, although the first option provided is generally considered more common. Whatever spelling you choose in such cases, use it consistently. You can also learn to be a better speller by studying a few basic strategies. This chapter will help you

- use a spell checker (**40a**),
- spell words according to pronunciation (**40b**),
- spell words that sound alike (**40c**),
- understand how prefixes and suffixes affect spelling (**40d**),
- use *ei* and *ie* correctly (**40e**), and
- use hyphenation to link and divide words (**40f**).

40a Spell checker

The spell checker is a wonderful invention, but it does not relieve you of the responsibility for spelling words correctly. A spell checker finds errors by checking the words in a document against the words in its dictionary. When it finds a word that does not match any words in its dictionary, it flags that word as misspelled.

A spell checker will usually catch

- misspellings of common words,
- some commonly confused words (such as *affect* and *effect*), and
- obvious typographical errors (such as *tge* for *the*).

However, a spell checker generally will *not* catch

- specialized vocabulary or foreign words not in its dictionary,
- typographical errors that are still correctly spelled words (such as *was* for *saw*), and
- misuses of words that sound alike but are not on the spell checker's list of words commonly confused (such as *here* and *hear*).

The following strategies can help you use a spell checker effectively.

TIPS FOR USING A SPELL CHECKER

- Keep a separate file of words you tend to misspell. When you edit a document, use the Find feature of your word-processing program to search for and correct any misspellings of these words.
- If a spell checker regularly flags a word (or a name) that is not in its dictionary but is spelled correctly, add that word to its dictionary by clicking on the Add button. From that point on, the spell checker will accept the word you added.
- Reject any offers the spell checker makes to correct all instances of a particular error.
- Use a dictionary to evaluate the alternative spellings the spell checker provides because some of them may be erroneous.
- Always proofread your writing yourself; never rely on a spell checker to locate all of your spelling errors.

40b Spelling and pronunciation

Many words in English are not spelled the way they are pronounced, so pronunciation is not a reliable guide to correct spelling. Sometimes, people skip over an unstressed syllable, as when *February* is pronounced "Febwary," or they slide over a sound that is hard to articulate, as when *library* is pronounced "libary." Other times, people add a sound—for instance, when they pronounce *athlete* as "athalete." And people also switch sounds around, as in "irrevelant" for *irrelevant.* Such mispronunciations can lead to misspellings.

You can help yourself remember the spellings of some words by considering the spellings of their root words—for example, the root word for *irrelevant* is *relevant.* You can also teach yourself the correct spellings of words by pronouncing them the way they are spelled, that is, by pronouncing each letter mentally so that you "hear" even silent letters. You are more likely to remember the *b* in *subtle* if you pronounce it when spelling that word. Here are a few words typically misspelled because they include unpronounced letters:

condem*n*   foreign   lab*o*ratory   mus*c*le   solem*n*

Here are a few more that include letters that are often not heard in rapid speech, though they can be heard when carefully pronounced:

can*d*idate   diff*e*rent   enviro*n*ment   gover*n*ment   sep*a*rate

The words *and, have,* and *than* are often not stressed in speech and are thus misspelled. A spell checker will not catch these misspellings.

        have   *than*   *and*
They would rather ^of written two papers ^then taken midterm ^an final exams.

40c Words that sound alike

Pairs of words such as *forth* and *fourth* or *sole* and *soul* are **homophones:** they sound alike but have different meanings and spellings. Some words that have different meanings sound exactly alike (*break/brake*), others sound alike in certain dialects (*marry/merry*), and still others are only similar in sound, especially in rapid speech (*believe/belief*). A spell checker cannot identify words that are correctly spelled but incorrectly used. If you are unsure about the difference in meaning between any two words that sound alike, consult a dictionary. A number of frequently confused words are listed with explanations in this hand-book's **Glossary of Usage**.

Single words and two-word phrases that consist of the same letters but have different meanings can also be troublesome. The following are examples.

Everyday life was grueling.	She attended class **every day.**
They do not fight **anymore.**	They could not find **any more** evidence.

Other examples are *awhile/a while, everybody/every body, everyone/every one, maybe/may be, sometime/some time,* and *nobody/no body.*

A lot and *all right* are still spelled as two words. *Alot* is always considered incorrect; *alright* is also considered incorrect except in some newspapers and magazines. (See the **Glossary of Usage**.)

Singular nouns ending in *-nce* and plural nouns ending in *-nts* are easily confused.

Assistance is available.	I have two **assistants.**
His **patience** wore thin.	Some **patients** waited for hours.

Contractions, possessive pronouns, and possessive determiners are also often confused. In contractions, an apostrophe indicates an omit-ted letter (or letters). In possessive pronouns or determiners, there is no apostrophe. (See also **25b** and **37a(1)**.)

Contraction	Possessive
It's my turn next.	Each group waited **its** turn.
You're next.	**Your** turn is next.
There's no difference.	**Theirs** is no different.

TIPS FOR SPELLING WORDS THAT SOUND ALIKE

- Be on the lookout for words that are commonly confused (*accept/except*).
- Distinguish between similar sounding single words and two-word phrases (*maybe/may be*).
- Use *-nts,* not *-nce,* for plural words (*instants/instance*).
- Mark contractions, but not possessive pronouns, with apostrophes (*who's/whose*).

40d Prefixes and suffixes

When a prefix is added to a base word (often called the **root**), the spelling of the base word is unaffected.

necessary, **un**necessary   moral, **im**moral

Adding a suffix to the end of a base word often changes the spelling.

beauty, beaut**iful**   describe, descri**ption**   BUT   resist, resist**ance**

Although spellings of words with suffixes are irregular, they follow certain conventions.

(1) Dropping or retaining a final *e* depends on whether the suffix begins with a vowel.

- If a suffix begins with a vowel, the final *e* of the base word is dropped: bride, brid**al;** come, com**ing;** combine, combin**ation;** prime, prim**ary.**
- If a suffix begins with a consonant, the final *e* of the base word is retained: entire, entire**ly;** rude, rude**ness;** place, place**ment;** sure, sure**ly.** Some exceptions are *argument, awful, ninth, truly,* and *wholly.*
- To keep the /s/ sound in *ce* or the /j/ sound in *ge*, retain the final *e* before *-able* or *-ous:* courage**ous,** manage**able,** notice**able.**

(2) A final consonant is usually doubled when a suffix begins with a vowel.

- If the consonant ends a one-syllable word with a single vowel or a stressed syllable with a single vowel, double the final consonant: stop, sto**pped,** sto**pping;** omit, omi**tted,** omi**tting.**
- If there are two vowels before the consonant, the consonant is not doubled: loop, loop**ed,** loop**ing;** remain, remain**ed,** remain**ing.**
- If the final syllable is not stressed, the consonant is not doubled: edit, edit**ed,** edit**ing;** picket, picket**ed,** picket**ing.**

(3) A final *y* is changed or retained depending on whether it is preceded by a vowel.

- Change a final *y* to *i* when adding a suffix (except *-ing*): defy, def**ies,** def**ied,** def**iance** BUT defy**ing;** modify, modif**ies,** modif**ied,** modif**ier** BUT modify**ing.**

- Retain the final *y* when it is preceded by a vowel: stay, stay**s**, stay**ed**; obey, obey**s**, obey**ed**; gray, gray**ish**.
- Some verb forms are irregular and thus can cause difficulties: *lays, laid; pays, paid*. For a list of irregular verbs, see page 565.

(4) A final *l* is retained when *-ly* is added.

cool, cool**ly**   formal, formal**ly**   real, real**ly**   usual, usual**ly**

Exercise 1

Add the specified suffixes to the words that follow. Be prepared to explain the reason for the spelling of each resulting word.

EXAMPLE

-ly: late, casual, psychological   *lately casually psychologically*

1. -ing: put, admit, write, use, try, play
2. -ment: manage, commit, require, argue
3. -ous: continue, joy, acrimony, libel
4. -ed: race, tip, permit, carry, pray
5. -able: desire, read, trace, knowledge
6. -ly : true, sincere, normal, general

(5) A noun is made plural by adding *-s* or *-es* to the singular.

- If the sound in the plural form of a noun ending in *f* or *fe* changes from /f/ to /v/, change the ending to *-ve* before adding *-s:* thie**f**, thie**ves**; li**fe**, li**ves** BUT roof, roof**s**.
- Add *-es* to most nouns ending in *s, z, ch, sh,* or *x:* box, box**es**; peach, peach**es**.
- If a noun ends in a consonant and *y*, change the *y* to *i* and add *-es:* company, compan**ies**; ninety, ninet**ies**; territory, territor**ies**.
- If a noun ends in a consonant and *o*, add *-es:* hero, hero**es**; potato, potato**es**. However, note that sometimes just *-s* is added (photo, photo**s**; memo, memo**s**) and other times either an *-s* or *-es* suffix can be added (motto**s**, motto**es**; zero**s**, zero**es**).
- Certain nouns have irregular plural forms: woman, wom**en**; child, child**ren**; foot, f**eet**.

■ Add -*s* to most proper nouns: the Lee**s**; the Kennedy**s.** Add -*es* to most proper nouns ending in *s, z, ch, sh,* or *x:* the Rodriguez**es,** the Jones**es** BUT the Bachs.

BEYOND THE RULE

WORDS BORROWED FROM OTHER LANGUAGES

Words borrowed from Latin or Greek generally form their plurals as they did in the original language.

| **Singular** | criterion | alumnus, alumna | analysis | datum | species |
| **Plural** | criteri**a** | alumn**i,** alumn**ae** | analys**es** | dat**a** | species |

When a word with such an origin is in the process of changing, two different forms will be listed as acceptable in the dictionary: *syllabus/syllabuses, syllabi.* For further information, visit **www.harbrace.com.**

Exercise 2

Provide the plural forms for the following words. If you need extra help, check a dictionary.

1. virus
2. committee
3. phenomenon
4. copy
5. delay
6. embargo
7. self
8. belief
9. foot
10. portfolio
11. cactus
12. census

40e Confusion of *ei* and *ie*

An old rhyme will help you remember the order of letters in most words containing *e* and *i:*

Put *i* before *e*
Except after *c*
Or when sounded like *a*
As in *neighbor* and *weigh.*

Words with *i* before *e:* bel**ie**ve, ch**ie**f, pr**ie**st, y**ie**ld

Words with *e* before *i,* after *c:* conc**ei**t, perc**ei**ve, rec**ei**ve

Words with *ei* sounding like *a* in *cake:* **ei**ght, r**ei**n, th**ei**r, h**ei**r

Words that are exceptions to the rules in the rhyme include *either, neither, species, foreign*, and *weird*.

 **American and British Spelling Differences**
Spelling systems originating in the United States and Great Britain differ in a few minor ways. Spelling in other English-speaking countries varies according to the system adopted in each. Although most words are spelled the same in both systems, there are some differences, including the following.

American	check	realize	color	connection
British	cheque	realise	colour	connexion

Use the American spelling system when writing for an audience in the United States.

40f Hyphens

Hyphens link two or more words functioning as a single word, separate word parts to clarify meaning, and divide words at the ends of lines. They also have many conventional uses in numbers, fractions, and measurements. Do not confuse the hyphen with the em dash, which is keyboarded as a double hyphen with no spaces before and after, or the en dash, which is keyboarded by hitting Option and the hyphen. (See **39e** and **43f**.)

(1) Hyphens sometimes link two or more words that form a compound.

Some compounds are listed in the dictionary with hyphens (*eye-opener, cross-examine*), others are written as two words (*eye chart, cross fire*), and still others are written as one word (*eyewitness, crossbreed*). If you have questions about the spelling of a compound word, a dictionary is a good resource. However, it is also helpful to learn a few basic patterns.

- If two or more words serve as a single adjective before a noun, they should be hyphenated. If the words follow the noun, they are not hyphenated.

  You submitted an **up-to-date** report. The report was **up to date.**

  A **well-known** musician is performing tonight. The musician is **well known.**

- When the second word in a hyphenated expression is omitted, the first word is still followed by a hyphen.

  They discussed both **private-** and **public-sector** partnerships.

- A hyphen is not used after adverbs ending in *-ly* (*poorly planned event*), in names of chemical compounds (*sodium chloride solution*), or in modifiers with a letter or numeral as the second element (*group C homes, type IV virus*).

(2) Hyphens can be used to separate words into parts to clarify meaning.

- To avoid ambiguity or an awkward combination of letters or syllables, place a hyphen between the base word and its prefix: *anti-intellectual, de-emphasize, re-sign the petition* [COMPARE: *resign the position*].
- Place a hyphen between a prefix and a capital letter and between two or more related words: *anti-American, non-self-promoting.*
- Place a hyphen after the prefix *all-, e-, ex-,* or *self-: all-inclusive, e-commerce, ex-husband, self-esteem.* Otherwise, most words with prefixes are not hyphenated.

(3) Hyphens are frequently used in numbers, fractions, and units of measure.

- Place a hyphen between two numbers when they are spelled out: *thirty-two, ninety-nine.* However, no hyphen is used before or after the words *hundred, thousand,* and *million: five hundred sixty-three, forty-one million.*
- Hyphenate fractions that are spelled out: *three-fourths, one-half.*
- When you form a compound modifier that includes a number and a unit of measurement, place a hyphen between them: *twenty-first-century literature, twelve-year-old boy, ten-year project.*

Grammar checkers can identify many compound words and suggest correct spellings, such as *double-space* instead of *doublespace*. Grammar checkers can also alert you to missing hyphens in most fractions (*one-fourth*) and compound numbers (*twenty-seven*) but not to those missing from a compound noun or adjective (*mother-in-law, high-quality*) or to those used to avoid ambiguity (*re-cover* versus *recover*).

Exercise 3

Convert the following word groups into hyphenated compounds.

EXAMPLE

a movie lasting two hours   *a two-hour movie*

1. a man who is fify years old
2. a seminar that lasted all day
3. a street that runs only one way
4. history from the twentieth century
5. roads that are covered by ice and snow
6. a paper that is well written

Exercise 4

Edit the following paragraph to correct mistakes in spelling and the usage of hyphens. Be prepared to explain any changes you make.

[1]Profesor Alan S. Brown, from Southern Methodist University, is studying the phenomena of déjà vu—the allusion of having seen some thing or been some where before. [2]As part of his research in to such second time around experiences, Brown read both literary and psychlogical accounts from the Victorian era. [3]Some of these nineteenth century explanations, he beleives, are still relevent today. [4]Brown also describes a few curius findings about the people most likly to experience déjà vu. [5]For instants, people who travel are more likly to have déjà vu then those who stay at home, political librals report déjà vu more often then conservetives, and as people age déjà vu ocurs less frequently. [6]Brown admits that all the experiences that fall under the

label of déjà vu may actualy be five or six phenomenon and thus have varius causes. [7]He is currantly testing hypothesis that may shed some light on what is happenning in are brains when we feel that uncanny sense of familarity. [8]His results may make us re-consider notions about the nature of our preceptions and memorys.

CAPITALS

41

When you look at an advertisement, an e-mail message, or even a paragraph in this book, you can easily pick out capital letters. These beacons draw your attention to significant details—for example, the beginnings of sentences or the names of particular people, places, and products. Although most capitalization conventions apply to any rhetorical situation, others are specific to a discipline or a profession. In this chapter, you will learn the conventions expected in most academic and professional settings. This chapter will help you

- use capitals for proper names (**41a**),
- capitalize words in titles and subtitles of works (**41b**),
- capitalize the first letter of a sentence (**41c**),
- use capitals for computer keys, menu items, and icon names (**41d**), and
- avoid unnecessary capitalization (**41e**).

BEYOND THE RULE

CAPITALIZATION STYLES

You may have noticed that different capitalization styles are used in various types of publications. For instance, the word *president* is always capitalized in documents published by the U.S. Government Printing Office, but it is capitalized in most newspapers only when it is followed by a specific name:

The delegates met with **P**resident Truman.

The delegates met with the **p**resident.

To learn more about capitalization styles, visit **www.harbrace.com**.

Advertisers frequently use capitalization to highlight important words.

41a Proper names

When you capitalize a word, you emphasize it. That is why names of people and places are capitalized, even when they are used as modifiers (*Mexico, Mexican*). Some words, such as *college, company, park,* and *street,* are capitalized only if they are part of a name (*a university* but *Oregon State University*). The following names and titles should be capitalized.

(1) Names of specific persons or things

Zora Neale Hurston	Flight 224	Honda Accord
John Paul II	Academy Award	USS *Cole*
Skylab	Nike	Microsoft Windows

A word denoting a family relationship is capitalized only when it substitutes for the person's proper name.

I told **Mom** about the event. [I told Catherine about the event.]

I told my **mom** about the event. [NOT I told my Catherine about the event.]

(2) Titles accompanying proper names

A title is capitalized when it precedes the name of a person but not when it follows the name or stands alone.

Governor Peter Dunn	Peter Dunn, the governor
Captain Ray Machado	Ray Machado, our captain
Uncle Rory	Rory, my uncle
President Lincoln	Abraham Lincoln, the president of the United States

(3) Names of ethnic or cultural groups and languages

Asians	African Americans	Latinos/Latinas	Poles
Arabic	English	Korean	Spanish

(4) Names of bridges, buildings, monuments, and geographical features

Golden Gate Bridge	Empire State Building	Lincoln Memorial
Arctic Circle	Mississippi River	Grand Canyon

When referring to two or more geographical features, however, do not capitalize the generic term: *Lincoln and Jefferson memorials, Yellowstone and Olympic national parks.*

(5) Names of organizations, government agencies, institutions, and companies

B'nai B'rith	National Endowment for the Humanities
Phi Beta Kappa	Internal Revenue Service
Howard University	Ford Motor Company

When used as common nouns, *service, company,* and *university* are not capitalized. However, some institutions, such as universities or corporations, capitalize their shortened names.

> The policies of Hanson **U**niversity promote the rights of all individuals to equal opportunity in education. The **U**niversity complies with all applicable federal, state, and local laws.

(6) Names for days of the week, months, and holidays

Wednesday	August	Fourth of July

The names of the seasons—spring, summer, fall, winter—are not capitalized.

Capitalizing Days of the Week
Capitalization rules vary according to language. For example, in English, the names of days and months are capitalized, but in some other languages, such as Spanish and Italian, they are not.

(7) Designations for historical documents, periods, events, and movements

Declaration of Independence	New Deal	Renaissance
Impressionism	Stone Age	World Series

A historical period that includes a number is not capitalized unless it is considered a proper name.

twentieth century	the Roaring Twenties
the eighteen hundreds	the Gay Nineties

(8) Names of religions, their adherents, holy days, titles of holy books, and words denoting the Supreme Being

Buddhism, Christianity, Islam, Judaism

Buddhist, Christian, Muslim, Jew

Bodhi Day, Easter, Ramadan, Yom Kippur

Sutras, Bible, Koran, Talmud BUT biblical, talmudic

Buddha, God, Allah, Yahweh

Some writers always capitalize personal pronouns and possessive determiners referring to the Supreme Being; others capitalize such words only when capitalization is needed to prevent ambiguity:

> The Lord commanded the prophet to warn His people.

(9) Words derived from proper names

Americanize [verb]   Orwellian [adjective]   Marxism [noun]

When a proper name becomes the name of a general class of objects or ideas, it is no longer capitalized. For example, *zipper*, originally a capitalized trademark, now refers to a class of fastening devices and is thus written with a lowercase letter. A word derived from a brand name, such as *Xerox*, *Kodak*, or *Kleenex*, should be capitalized. Because the corporations that own these brand names object to their use for generic purposes, use *photocopy, camera,* or *tissue* instead. If you are not sure whether a proper name or derivative has come to stand for a general class, look up the word in a dictionary.

(10) Abbreviations and acronyms

These forms are derived from the initial letters of capitalized word groups:

AMEX AT&T CBS CST JFK NFL OPEC UNESCO YMCA

(See also 39a(2) and chapter 43.)

(11) Military terms

Names of forces and special units are capitalized, as are names of wars, battles, revolutions, and military awards.

United States Army   Marine Corps   Eighth Air Force   Green Berets
Russian Revolution   Gulf War   Operation Overlord   Purple Heart

Military words such as *army*, *navy,* and *war* are not capitalized when they stand alone.

> My sister joined the navy in 2002.

STYLE SHEET FOR CAPITALIZATION

Capitals	No capitals
the West [geographical region]	driving west [compass point]
a Chihuahua [a breed of dog named after a state in Mexico]	a poodle [a breed of dog]
Washington State University [a specific institution]	a state university
Revolutionary War [a specific war]	an eighteenth-century war
U.S. Army [a specific army]	a peacetime army
Declaration of Independence [title of a document]	a declaration of independence
May [specific month]	spring [general season]
Memorial Day [specific day]	a holiday
two Democratic candidates [refers to a political party]	democratic procedures [refers to a form of government]
a Ford tractor [brand name]	a farm tractor
Parkinson's disease [a disease named for a person]	flu, asthma, leukemia
Governor Clay [a person's title]	the governor of our state

41b Titles and subtitles

The first and last words in titles and subtitles are capitalized, as are major words—that is, all words other than articles (*a, an,* and *the*), coordinating conjunctions (*and, but, for, nor, or, so,* and *yet*), prepositions (see the list on page 490), and the infinitive marker *to.* (See also **38b** and **42a.**)

From Here to Eternity

"To Be a Student or Not to Be a Student"

APA guidelines differ slightly from other style guidelines: the APA recommends capitalizing any word in a title, including a preposition, that has four or more letters.

> *Southwestern Pottery from Anasazi to Zuni* [MLA and CMS]
>
> *Southwestern Pottery From Anasazi to Zuni* [APA]

MLA, APA, and CMS advise capitalizing all words in a hyphenated compound, except for articles, coordinating conjunctions, and prepositions.

> "The Arab-Israeli Dilemma" [compound proper adjective]
>
> "Stop-and-Go Signals" [lowercase for the coordinating conjunction]

However, when a hyphenated compound containing a prefix appears in a title or subtitle, MLA and APA advise capitalizing both elements when (1) the second element is a proper noun or adjective (*Pre-Columbian*) or (2) the compound contains a doubled letter that could be hard to read (*Anti-Intellectual*). CMS recommends capitalizing the second element only if the word is a proper noun or adjective.

> "Pre-Columbian Artifacts in Peruvian Museums" [MLA, APA, and CMS]
>
> "Anti-Independence Behavior in Adolescents" [MLA and APA]
>
> "Anti-independence Behavior in Adolescents" [CMS]

41c Beginning a sentence

It is not difficult to remember that a sentence begins with a capital letter, but there are certain types of sentences that deserve special note.

(1) Capitalizing the first word in a quoted sentence

If a direct quotation is a full sentence, the first word should be capitalized.

> When asked to name the books she found most influential, Nadine Gordimer responded, "**In** general, the works that mean most to one—change one's thinking and therefore maybe one's life—are those read in youth."

Even if you interrupt the quoted sentence with commentary, just the first letter should be capitalized.

> "**O**ddly," states Ved Mehta, "like my earliest memories, the books that made the greatest impression on me were the ones I encountered as a small child."

However, if you integrate someone else's sentence into a sentence of your own, the first letter should be lowercase.

> Nadine Gordimer believes that "**i**n general, the works that mean most to one—change one's thinking and therefore maybe one's life—are those read in youth."

(2) Capitalizing the first word in a freestanding parenthetical sentence

If you place a full sentence inside parentheses, and it is not embedded in a sentence of your own, be sure to capitalize the first word.

> Lance Armstrong has won the Tour de France a record-breaking seven times. (**P**revious record holders include Jacques Anquetil, Bernard Hinault, Eddy Merckx, and Miguel Indurain.)

If the sentence inside the parentheses occurs within a sentence of your own, the first word should not be capitalized.

> Lance Armstrong has won the Tour de France a record-breaking seven times (**p**reviously, he shared the record with four other cyclists).

(3) Lowercasing or capitalizing the first word in an independent clause following a colon

According to *The Chicago Manual of Style*, if there is only one independent clause (see **21b**) following a colon, the first word should be in lowercase. However, if two or more independent clauses follow the colon, the first word of each clause is capitalized.

> The ear thermometer is used quite frequently now: **t**his type of thermometer records a temperature more accurately than a glass thermometer.

> Two new thermometers are replacing the old thermometers filled with mercury: **T**he digital thermometer uses a heat sensor to determine body temperature. **T**he ear thermometer is actually an infrared thermometer that detects the temperature of the eardrum.

APA and MLA provide different style guidelines for this kind of situation. The APA manual recommends capitalizing the first word of any independent clause following a colon. The MLA manual advises capitalizing the first word only if the independent clause is a rule or principle.

> Think of fever as a symptom, not as an illness: **I**t is the body's response to infection. [APA]

> He has two basic rules for healthy living: **E**at sensibly, and exercise strenuously at least three times a week. [APA and MLA]

A grammar checker will flag a word at the beginning of a sentence that should be capitalized, but it will not be able to determine whether a word following a colon should be capitalized.

(4) Capitalizing the first word of an abbreviated question

When a series of abbreviated questions follows an introductory element, the first words of all questions are capitalized when the intent is to draw attention to the questions. Otherwise, such questions begin with lowercase letters.

> How do we distinguish the legal codes for families? For individuals? For genetic research?

> Are interest rates on car loans down to six percent? five? three?

41d   Computer keys, menu items, and icon names

When referring to specific computer keys, menu items, and icon names, capitalize the first letter of each.

> To find the thesaurus, press Shift and the function key F7.

> Instead of choosing Copy from the Edit menu, you can press Ctrl+C.

> For additional information, click on Resources.

41e Unnecessary capitals

(1) Unnecessary capitalization of common nouns

The same noun can be either common or proper, depending on the context. A **proper noun** names a specific entity. A **common noun,** which is usually preceded by a determiner such as *the, a, an, this,* or *that,* is not capitalized.

a speech course in theater and television
[COMPARE: Speech 324: Theater and Television]

a university, this high school
[COMPARE: University of Michigan, Hickman High School]

(2) Overusing capitalization to signal emphasis

Occasionally, a common noun is capitalized for emphasis.

The motivation of many politicians is Power.

If you use capitals for emphasis, do so sparingly; overuse will weaken the effect. For other ways to achieve emphasis, see chapter **30**.

(3) Signaling emphasis online

For online writing in academic and professional contexts, capitalize as you normally do. Be careful not to capitalize whole words for emphasis because your reader may think that you are SHOUTING—the term used to indicate the rudeness of this practice.

Exercise 1

Write a sentence using each of the following words correctly.

1. president	4. Company	7. street	10. Republican
2. President	5. east	8. Street	11. river
3. company	6. East	9. republican	12. River

Exercise 2

Edit the capitalization errors in the following paragraph. Be prepared to explain any changes that you make.

[1]Diana taurasi (Her teammates call her dee) plays basketball for the Phoenix mercury. [2]She has all the skills she needs to be a Star Player: She can pass and shoot, as well as rebound, block, and steal. [3]While playing for university of connecticut huskies, she won the Naismith award twice and ranked in the majority of the big east's statistical categories. [4]Shortly after the huskies won their third straight ncaa title, taurasi was drafted first overall by the Phoenix mercury. [5]In april of 2004, taurasi played on the u.s. national team against japan, and, in the Summer of 2004, she made her olympic debut in Athens.

42

ITALICS

When you use italics, you let readers know that you are treating a word or a group of words in a special way. For example, the following sentence is ambiguous.

The linguistics students discussed the word stress.

Does this sentence mean that the students discussed a particular word or that they discussed the correct pronunciation of words? By italicizing *stress,* the writer indicates that it was the word, not an accent pattern, that the students discussed.

The linguistics students discussed the word *stress.*

This chapter will help you use italics for

- the titles of separate works (**42a**),
- foreign words (**42b**),
- the names of legal cases (**42c**),
- the names of ships, submarines, aircraft, spacecraft, and satellites (**42d**),
- words, letters, or figures used as such or as statistical symbols or variables in algebraic expressions (**42e**), and
- words receiving emphasis (**42f**).

Word-processing programs make it easy to use italics. In handwritten or typewritten documents, you can indicate italics by underlining.

Edward P. Jones's novel <u>The Known World</u> won a Pulitzer Prize.

Although the use of italics instead of underlining is widely accepted in business writing, conventions for academic writing vary. MLA recommends underlining, but APA and CMS prefer italics. Remember that in e-mail and on Web pages, an underlined word or phrase often indicates a hyperlink. If you are not able to format your e-mail or other electronic text with italics, use an underscore before and after words you would normally italicize.

> Edward P. Jones's novel _The Known World_ won a Pulitzer Prize.

42a Titles of works published or produced separately

Italics indicate the title of a work published or produced as a whole rather than as part of a larger work. A newspaper, for example, is a separate work, but an editorial in a newspaper is not; thus, different conventions are used for indicating the title of the newspaper and the title of the editorial. (See also **38b**.) These conventions help readers realize the nature of a work and sometimes its relationship to another work.

> Helen Keller's "Three Days to See" originally appeared in the *Atlantic Monthly.* [an essay in a magazine]

The titles of the following kinds of separate works are italicized.

Books	*The Hours*	*The God of Small Things*
Magazines	*Wired*	*National Geographic*
Newspapers	*USA Today*	*Wall Street Journal*
Plays, films, videotapes	*Death of a Salesman*	*Master and Commander*
Television and radio shows	*American Idol*	*A Prairie Home Companion*
Recordings	*Kind of Blue*	*Great Verdi Overtures*
Works of art	*American Gothic*	*David*
Long poems	*Paradise Lost*	*The Divine Comedy*
Pamphlets	*Saving Energy*	*Tips for Gardeners*
Comic strips	*Peanuts*	*Doonesbury*

When an italicized title includes the title of a separate work within it, the embedded title is not italicized.

> The class read various selections from *Modern Interpretations of* Paradise Lost. [COMPARE: We studied various interpretations of *Paradise Lost.*]

Titles should not be placed in italics or between quotation marks when they stand alone on a title page, a book cover, or a newspaper masthead. Likewise, neither italics nor quotation marks are necessary for titles of major historical documents, religious texts, or Web sites.

> The Bill of Rights contains the first ten amendments to the U.S. Constitution.

> The Bible, a sacred text just as the Koran or the Torah is, begins with the Book of Genesis.

> Instructions for making a cane-and-reed basket can be found at Catherine Erdly's Web site, Basket Weaving.

According to MLA and CMS guidelines, an initial *the* in a newspaper or periodical title is not italicized. It is not capitalized either, unless it begins a sentence.

> The story was leaked to a journalist at the *New York Times*.

Also recommended is the omission of an article (*a, an,* or *the*) at the beginning of such a title when it would make a sentence awkward.

> The report will appear in Thursday's ~~the~~ *Wall Street Journal*.

42b   **Foreign words**

Use italics to indicate foreign words.

> Side by side, hunched low in the light rain, the two outcasts dip up *tsampa,* the roasted maize or barley meal, ground to powder and cooked as porridge or in tea, that is subsistence food in the Himalaya.   —PETER MATTHIESSEN

A foreign word used frequently in a text should be italicized only once—at its first occurrence.

> The Latin words used to classify plants and animals according to genus and species are italicized.

> *Homo sapiens*   *Rosa setigera*   *Ixodes scapularis*

Countless words borrowed from other languages have become part of English and are therefore not italicized.

> bayou (Choctaw)   karate (Japanese)   arroyo (Spanish)

If you are not sure whether a word has been accepted into English, look for it in a standard dictionary (see **32e**).

42c Legal cases

Italics identify the names of legal cases.

>   *Miranda v. Arizona*   *Roe v. Wade*

The abbreviation *v.* (for "versus") may appear in either italic or nonitalic type, as long as the style is used consistently. Italics are also used for the shortened name of a well-known legal case.

>   According to the *Miranda* decision, suspects must be informed of their right to remain silent and their right to legal advice.

Italics are not used to refer to a case by other than its official name.

>   All the major networks covered the O. J. Simpson trial.

42d Names of ships, submarines, aircraft, spacecraft, and satellites

Italicize the names of specific ships, submarines, aircraft, spacecraft, and satellites.

>   USS *Enterprise*   USS *Hawkbill*   *Enola Gay*   *Atlantis*   *Aqua*

The names of trains and the trade names of aircraft are not italicized.

>   Orient Express   Boeing 747   Concorde

42e Words, letters, or figures referred to as such and letters used in mathematical expressions

When you discuss a specific word, letter, or figure as itself, not as its referent, you should italicize it.

>   The word *love* is hard to define.
>   The *p* in *ptarmigan* is silent.
>   The *8* on the sign has faded, and the *5* has disappeared.

Statistical symbols and variables in algebraic expressions are also italicized.

The Pythagorean theorem is expressed as $a^2 + b^2 = c^2$.

42f Words receiving emphasis

Used sparingly, italics can emphasize words. When you think a sentence may be misunderstood, italicize words that you want readers to stress.

These *are* the right files. [*Are* receives more stress than it normally would.]

Italics can also emphasize emotional content.

We have to go *now.* [The italicized word signals urgency.]

If overused, italics will lose their impact. Instead of italicizing words, substitute more specific words (see chapter **33**) or vary sentence structures (chapter **31**).

Exercise 1

Identify all words that should be italicized in the following sentences. Explain why italics are necessary in each case.

1. Information about museum collections and exhibits can be found in art books, museum Web sites, and special sections of magazines and newspapers such as Smithsonian Magazine and the New York Times.
2. The Web site for the Metropolitan Museum of Art has pictures of Anthony Caro's sculpture Odalisque and Charles Demuth's painting The Figure 5 in Gold.
3. The title page of William Blake's Songs of Innocence is included in Masterpieces of the Metropolitan Museum of Art.
4. This book includes a photograph of a beautiful script used in the Koran; the script is known as the maghribi, or Western, style.
5. The large Tyrannosaurus rex discovered by Sue Hendrickson in South Dakota is on display at the Field Museum.

6. The International Museum of Cartoon Art provides information about the designers of such comic strips as Blondie, Peanuts, Mutt and Jeff, and Li'l Abner.

7. The Great Train Robbery, It Happened One Night, and Grand Illusion are in the collection at the Celeste Bartos Film Preservation Center.

8. In 1998, the Songwriters Hall of Fame honored John Williams, who has written music for such movies as Jaws, Star Wars, and E.T.

9. The Smithsonian Institution's National Air and Space Museum houses an impressive collection of aircraft and spacecraft, including Spirit of St. Louis and Gemini 4.

10. The digital collection listed on the Web site Experience Music Project includes music from the albums Fresh Cream and Bluesbreakers with Eric Clapton.

43 ABBREVIATIONS, ACRONYMS, AND NUMBERS

Abbreviations, acronyms, and numbers facilitate easy recognition and effective communication in both academic papers and business documents. An **abbreviation** is a shortened version of a word or phrase: *assn.* (association), *dept.* (department), *et al.* (*et alii* or "and others"). An **acronym** is formed by combining the initial letters and/or syllables of a series of words: *AIDS* (**a**cquired **i**mmune **d**eficiency **s**yndrome), *sonar* (**so**und **na**vigation **r**anging). This chapter will help you learn

- how and when to abbreviate (**43a–d**),
- when to explain an acronym (**43e**), and
- whether to spell out a number or use numerals (**43f–g**).

43a Proper names

Some abbreviations, such as *Ms., Mr.,* and *Mrs.,* appear before proper names.

Ms. Gretel Lopez	Mrs. Adrienne Marcus	St. Peter
Mr. Julio Rodriguez	Dr. Thomas Redshaw	Prof. Sue Li
Capt. Margaret Hoffner	Sen. Edward Kennedy	Rev. Kevin Burns

Others, such as *Jr., Sr., III,* and *MD,* appear after proper names.

Samuel Levy, Jr.	Deborah Hvidsten, MD	Henry VIII
Mark Ngo, Sr.	Erika C. Schuerer, PhD	Putman Amory III

In the past, periods were customarily used in abbreviations for academic degrees, but MLA and CMS now recommend omitting periods from abbreviations such as *MA, PhD,* and *MD.*

Abbreviated brand names create instant recognition for products.

Avoid redundant designations.

Dr. Carol Ballou OR Carol Ballou, MD [NOT Dr. Carol Ballou, MD]

Most abbreviations form plurals by adding *-s* alone, without an apostrophe: *Drs. Ballou and Hvidsten.* Exceptions are made when adding *-s* would create a different abbreviation, such as for *Mr.* and *Mrs.*

43b Addresses in correspondence

The names of states and words such as *Street, Road, Company,* and *Corporation* are usually written out when they appear in a letter, including in the address at the top of the page. However, they are abbreviated when used in the address on an envelope.

Sentence	Derson Manufacturing Company is located on Madison Street in Watertown, Minnesota.
Address	Derson Manufacturing Co. 200 Madison St. Watertown, MN 55388

When addressing correspondence within the United States, use the abbreviations designated by the U.S. Postal Service for the names of the states. (No period follows these abbreviations.)

POSTAL ABBREVIATIONS

Facilitating efficient delivery, the abbreviations of states' names required for U.S. mail consist of just two characters. Connecticut, for example, is CT, not Conn. For a list of these abbreviations, visit **www.harbrace.com**.

43c Abbreviations in source documentation

MLA, APA, and CMS all provide lists of abbreviations for writers to use when citing research sources in bibliographies, footnotes, and endnotes. Common abbreviations include the following (not all citation styles accept all of these abbreviations).

Bibliographies and Notes

anon., Anon.	anonymous, Anonymous
biog.	biography, biographer, biographical
bull.	bulletin
c. or ca.	circa, about (for example, *c. 1920*)
col., cols.	column, columns
cont.	contents OR continues, continued
et al.	*et alii* ("and others")
fig.	figure
fwd.	foreword, foreword by
illus.	illustrated by, illustrator, illustration
inc., Inc.	including; incorporated, Incorporated
intl.	international
introd.	introduction, introduction by
ms., mss.	manuscript, manuscripts

(Continued on page 764)

(Continued from page 763)

natl.	national
n.d.	no date
n.p.	no page number
no., nos.	number, numbers
p., pp.	page, pages
P, Pr.	Press
pref.	preface
pt., pts.	part, parts
trans. or tr.	translation, translated by
U, Univ.	University

Computer Terms

FTP	file transfer protocol
HTML	hypertext markup language
HTTP	hypertext transfer protocol
MB	megabyte
MOO	multiuser domain, object-oriented
URL	uniform resource locator

Divisions of Government

Cong.	Congress
dept.	department
div.	division
govt.	government
GPO	Government Printing Office
HR	House of Representatives

For abbreviations of Latin terms used in writing, see 43d(7).

43d Acceptable abbreviations in academic and professional writing

Abbreviations are usually too informal for use in sentences, but some have become so familiar that they are considered acceptable substitutes for full words.

(1) Using abbreviations for special purposes but not in sentences

The names of months, days of the week, and units of measurement are usually written out (not abbreviated) when they are included in sentences, as are words such as *Street* and *Corporation*.

> On a Tuesday in September, we drove ninety-nine miles to San Francisco, California, where we stayed in a hotel on Market Street.

In bibliographies, the months May, June, and July are never abbreviated. Except for September, the remaining months are abbreviated to their first three letters (*Jan., Mar., Dec.*). September is abbreviated as *Sept.*

Similarly, words such as *volume, chapter,* and *page* are written out within sentences, even though they are abbreviated in bibliographies and in citations of research sources.

> I read the introductory chapter and pages 82–89 in the first volume of the committee's report.

(2) Abbreviations in place names and of titles of address

Some abbreviations are commonly used in sentences: *St.* for Saint (*St. Louis*) or *Mt.* for mount or mountain (*Mt. Hood*), and *Mr., Mrs., Ms.,* and similar titles of address.

(3) Clipped forms

Because it functions as a word, a **clipped form** does not end with a period. Some clipped forms—such as *rep* (for representative), *exec* (for executive), and *info* (for information)—are too informal for use in college writing. Others—such as *exam, lab,* and *math*—have become acceptable because they have been used so frequently that they no longer seem like shortened forms.

(4) Abbreviations for time periods and zones

> 82 BC [OR BCE] for before Christ [OR before the common era]
>
> AD 95 [OR 95 CE] for *anno Domini*, "in the year of our Lord" [OR the common era]
>
> 7:40 a.m. for *ante meridiem*, before noon
>
> 4:52 EST for Eastern Standard Time

Words designating units of time, such as *minute* and *month,* are written out when they appear in sentences. They can be abbreviated in tables or charts.

sec.   min.   hr.   wk.   mo.   yr.

(5) The abbreviation for the United States (U.S. or US) as an adjective

the U.S. Navy, the US economy [COMPARE: The United States continues to enjoy a strong economy.]

The abbreviation *U.S.* or *US* should be used only as an adjective in academic and professional writing. When using *United States* as a noun, spell it out. The choice of U.S. or US will depend on the discipline in which you are writing: MLA lists US as the preferred form, but APA uses U.S., and CMS accepts either form.

(6) Individuals known by their initials

JFK   LBJ   E. B. White   B. B. King

In most cases, however, first and last names should be written out in full.

Oprah Winfrey   Tiger Woods

(7) Some abbreviations for Latin expressions

Certain abbreviations for Latin expressions are common in academic writing.

cf. [compare]   et al. [and others]   i.e. [that is]
e.g. [for example]   etc. [and so forth]   vs. OR v. [versus]

43e Acronyms

The ability to identify a particular acronym will vary from one audience to another. Some readers will know that NAFTA stands for the North American Free Trade Agreement; others may not. By spelling out acronyms the first time you use them, you are being courteous and clear.

Introduce the acronym by placing it in parentheses after the group of words it stands for.

> The Federal Emergency Management Administration (FEMA) was criticized by many after Hurricane Katrina.

Using Articles with Abbreviations, Acronyms, or Numbers
When you use an abbreviation, an acronym, or a number, you sometimes need an indefinite article. Choose *a* or *an* based on the pronunciation: use *a* before a consonant sound and *an* before a vowel sound.

A picture of **a UN** delegation is on the front page of today's newspaper. [*UN* is pronounced as two letters.]

I have **an IBM** computer. [*IBM* is pronounced as three letters.]

The reporter interviewed **a NASA** engineer. [*NASA* is pronounced as one word.]

My friend drives **a 1964** Mustang. [*1964* is pronounced "nineteen sixty-four."]

Exercise 1

Place a check mark next to those forms that are appropriate for use in the sentences of a college essay. Correct those that are not.

1. after 8 p.m.
2. 457 *anno Domini*
3. on St. Clair Ave.
4. two blocks from Water Street
5. in Aug.
6. in the second mo. of the yr.
7. in Calif.
8. at the UN
9. Ms. Lydia Snow
10. for a prof.

43f General uses of numbers

Depending on their uses, numbers are treated in different ways. In general, MLA and CMS recommend spelling out numbers from one through one hundred (*nine employees, ninety-one employees*). If one of these numbers is followed by a word such as *hundred, thousand,* or *million,* it may also be spelled out (*nine hundred years, ninety-one million years*). Use a numeral for any other number, unless it begins a sentence.

The register recorded 164 names.

APA advises spelling out only numbers below ten. All three of these style manuals recommend using words rather than numerals at the beginning of a sentence.

One hundred sixty-four names were recorded in the register. [Notice that *and* is not used in numbers greater than one hundred. NOT One hundred and sixty-four names . . . .]

In a discussion of related items involving both single- and double- or triple-digit numbers, use numerals for all numbers.

Only 5 of the 134 delegates attended the final meeting.

In scientific or technical writing, use numerals before measurement abbreviations (*2 L, 30 cc*).

43g Special uses of numbers

(1) Expressing specific times of day in either numerals or words

Numerals or words can be used to express times of day. They should be used consistently.

4 p.m. OR four o'clock in the afternoon

9:30 a.m. OR half-past nine in the morning OR nine-thirty in the morning [Notice the use of hyphens.]

(2) Using numerals and words for dates

In a text, months are written as words, years are written as numerals, and days and decades are written as either words or numerals.

May 20, 1976 OR 20 May 1976 [NOT May 20th, 1976]

the fourth of December OR December 4

the fifties OR the 1950s

from 1999 to 2003 OR 1999–2003 [Use an en dash, not a hyphen, in number ranges.]

 **Different Ways of Writing Dates**
Many cultures invert the numerals for the month and the day: *14/2/2006* or *14 February 2006.* In publications from the United States, the month generally precedes the day: *2/14/2006* or *February 14, 2006.*

(3) Using numerals in addresses

Numerals are commonly used in street addresses and zip codes.

25 Arrow Drive, Apartment 1, Columbia, MO 78209
OR, for an envelope, 25 Arrow Dr., Apt. 1, Columbia, MO 78209

(4) Using numerals for identification

A numeral may be used as part of a proper noun.

Channel 10   Edward III   Interstate 40   Room 311

(5) Referring to pages and divisions of books and plays

Numerals are used to designate pages and other divisions of books and plays.

page 15   chapter 8   part 2 in act 2, scene 1 OR in Act II, Scene I

(6) Expressing decimals and percentages numerically

Numerals are used to express decimals and percentages.

a 2.5 average   12 percent   0.853 metric ton

(7) Using numerals for large fractional numbers

Numerals with decimal points can be used to express large fractional numbers.

5.2 million inhabitants   1.6 billion years

(8) Different ways of writing monetary amounts

Monetary amounts should be spelled out if they occur infrequently in a piece of writing. Otherwise, numerals and symbols can be used.

two million dollars	$2,000,000
ninety-nine cents	99¢ OR $0.99

Commas and Periods with Numerals
Cultures differ in their use of the period and the comma with numerals. In American usage, a decimal point (period) indicates a number or part of a number that is smaller than one, and a comma divides large numbers into units of three digits.

7.65 (seven and sixty-five one-   10,000 (ten thousand)
hundredths)

In some other cultures, these usages of the decimal point and the comma are reversed.

7,65 (seven and sixty-five one-   10.000 (ten thousand)
hundredths)

Exercise 2

Edit the following sentences to correct the usage of abbreviations and numbers.

1. A Natl. Historic Landmark, Hoover Dam is located about 30 miles s.e. of Las. Vegas, Nev.
2. The dam is named after Herbert Hoover, the 31st pres. of the U.S.
3. It is administered by the U.S. Dept. of the Interior.
4. Built by the fed. gov. between nineteen thirty-three and 1935, this dam is still considered one of the greatest achievements in the history of civ. engineering.
5. Construction of the dam became possible after several states in the Southwest (namely, AZ, CA, CO, NV, NM, UT, and WY) agreed on a plan to share water from the river.

6. The concrete used in the dam would have built a highway 16 ft. wide, stretching all the way from San Francisco to NYC.

7. 3,500 men worked on the dam during an average month of construction; this work translated into a monthly payroll of $500,000.

8. Spanning the Colorado River, Hoover Dam created Lake Mead—a reservoir covering 247 sq. miles.

9. A popular tourist attraction, Hoover Dam was closed to the public after terrorists attacked the U.S. on 9/11/01.

10. Today, certain pts. of the dam remain closed to the public as part of the effort to improve U.S. security.

The term *usage* refers to the ways words are used in specific contexts. As you know from speaking and writing every day, the words you choose depend on your audience and your purpose. For example, you might use *guys* when you are at lunch with your friends but choose *people, class-mates, employees,* or another more formal or precise word when you are writing a report. By learning about usage in this glossary, you will increase your ability to use words effectively. Many of the entries are context-specific; others distinguish between words that sound or look similar.

The definitions and guidelines in this glossary will help you write clear and precise prose. Nonetheless, you should be aware that the idea of standard usage potentially carries with it the assumption that words not considered standard are inferior. Words labeled "nonstandard" are commonly condemned, even though they may be words some people have grown up hearing and using. A better way to discuss usage is to label what is conventional, or accepted practice, for a specific context. Thus, words commonly used in one context may not be appropriate in another. The following labels will help you choose appropriate words for your rhetorical situation.

Conventional	Words or phrases listed in dictionaries without special usage labels; generally considered appropriate in academic and professional writing.
Conversational	Words or phrases that dictionaries label *informal, slang,* or *colloquial;* although often used in informal speech and writing, not generally appropriate for formal writing assignments.
Unconventional	Words or phrases not generally considered appropriate in academic or professional writing and often labeled *nonstandard* in dictionaries; best avoided in formal contexts.

Agreement on usage occurs slowly, often after a period of debate. In this glossary, entries are marked with an asterisk (*) when new usages have been reported by dictionary editors but may not yet be accepted by everyone.

 Grammar checkers may identify some common usage errors (such as *its* instead of *it's*), but they will not find more subtle problems. Grammar checkers also rarely distinguish between words that are spelled similarly but have different meanings. For example, a grammar checker found nothing wrong with the following sentence, even though *capitol* is used incorrectly: The capitol of Minnesota is St. Paul.

a lot of *A lot of* is conversational for *many, much,* or *a great deal of:* They do not have ~~a lot of~~ **much** time. *A lot* is sometimes misspelled as *alot.*

a while, awhile *A while* means "a period of time." It is often used with the prepositions *after, for,* and *in:* We rested for **a while.** *Awhile* means "a short time." It is not preceded by a preposition: We rested **awhile.**

accept, except The verb *accept* means "to receive": I **accept** your apology. The verb *except* means "to exclude": The policy was to have everyone wait in line, but mothers and small children were **excepted.** The preposition *except* means "other than": All **except** Joe will attend the conference.

adapt, adopt *Adapt* means "to adjust" or "to change for a purpose": We will **adapt** to the new conditions. The author will **adapt** his short story for television. *Adopt* means "to take as one's own": They will **adopt** a new policy.

advice, advise *Advice* is a noun: They asked their attorney for **advice.** *Advise* is a verb: The attorney **advised** us to save all relevant documents.

affect, effect *Affect* is a verb that means "to influence": The lobbyist's pleas did not **affect** the politician's decision. The noun *effect* means "a result": The **effect** of his decision on the staff's morale was positive and long lasting. When used as a verb, *effect* means "to produce" or "to cause": The activists believed that they could **effect** real political change.

agree on, agree to, agree with *Agree on* means "to be in accord with others about something": We **agreed on** a date for the conference. *Agree to* means "to accept something" or "to consent to do something": The customer **agreed to** our terms. The negotiators **agreed to** conclude talks by midnight. *Agree with* means "to share an opinion with someone" or "to approve of something": I **agree with** you on this issue. No one **agreed with** his position.

all The indefinite pronoun *all* is plural when it refers to people or things that can be counted: **All** were present. It is singular when it refers to things that cannot be counted: **All** is forgiven.

all ready, already *All ready* means "completely prepared": The rooms are **all ready** for the conference. *Already* means "by or before the time specified": She has **already** taken her final exams.

* **all right** *All right* means "acceptable": The students asked whether it was **all right** to use dictionaries during the exam. *Alright* is not yet a generally accepted spelling of *all right,* although it is becoming more common in journalistic writing.

all together, altogether *All together* means "as a group": The cast reviewed the script **all together.** *Altogether* means "wholly, thoroughly": That game is **altogether** too difficult.

allude, elude *Allude* means "to refer to indirectly": The professor **alluded** to a medieval text. *Elude* means "to evade" or "to escape from": For the moment, his name **eludes** me.

allusion, illusion An *allusion* is a casual or indirect reference: The **allusion** was to Shakespeare's *Twelfth Night.* An *illusion* is a false idea or an unreal image: His idea of college is an **illusion.**

alot See **a lot of.**

already See **all ready, already.**

alright See **all right.**

altogether See **all together, altogether.**

a.m., p.m. Use these abbreviations only with figures: The show will begin at 7:00 **p.m.** [COMPARE: The show will begin at seven *in the evening.*]

* **among, between** To follow traditional usage, use *among* with three or more entities (a group): The snorklers swam **among** the fish. Use *between* when referring to only two entities: The rivalry **between** the two teams is intense. Current dictionaries also note the possibility of using *between* to refer to more than two entities, especially when these entities are considered distinct: We have strengthened the lines of communication **between** the various departments.

amoral, immoral *Amoral* means "neither moral nor immoral" or "not caring about right or wrong": Complaining that U.S. schools are **amoral,** the senator proposed the addition of prayer time. *Immoral* means "not moral": Some philosophers consider war **immoral.**

amount of, number of Use *amount of* before nouns that cannot be counted: The **amount of** rain that fell last year was insufficient. Use *number of* with nouns that can be counted: The **number of** students attending college has increased.

and/or This combination denotes three options: one, the other, or both. These options can also be presented separately with *or:* The student's application should be signed by a parent **and/or** a teacher. The student's application should be signed by a parent, a teacher, **or** both.

* **angry at, angry with** Both *at* and *with* are commonly used after *angry,* although according to traditional guidelines, *with* should be used when a person is the cause of the anger: She was **angry with** me because I was late.

another, other, the other *Another* is followed by a singular noun: **another** book. *Other* is followed by a plural noun: **other** books. *The other* is followed by either a singular or a plural noun: **the other book, the other books.**

anymore, any more *Anymore* meaning "any longer" or "now" most frequently occurs in negative sentences: Sarah doesn't work here **anymore.** Its use in positive sentences is considered conversational; *now* is generally used instead: All he ever does ~~anymore~~ **now** is watch television. As two words, *any more* appears with *not* to mean "no more": We do not have **any more** time.

anyone, any one *Anyone* means "any person at all": We did not know **anyone.** *Any one* refers to one of a group: **Any one** of the options is better than the current situation.

anyplace, everyplace, someplace According to traditional usage, each of these words should be written as two words (*any place, every place, some place).* Note, however, that *anywhere, everywhere,* and *somewhere* are each written as one word.

anyways, anywheres Unconventional; use *anyway* and *anywhere* instead: We decided to go **anyways.**

as Conversational when used after such verbs as *know, say,* and *see.* Use *that, if,* or *whether* instead: I do not know ~~as~~ **whether** my application is complete. Also considered conversational is the use of *as* instead of *who, which,* or *that:* Many of the performers ~~as~~ **who** have appeared on our program will be giving a concert this evening.

as, because The use of *as* to signal a cause may be vague; if it is, use *because* instead: ~~As~~ **Because** we were running out of gas, we turned around.

* **as, like** According to traditional usage, *as* begins either a phrase or a clause; *like* begins only a phrase: My brother drives too fast, just ~~like~~ **as** my father did. Current dictionaries note the informal use of *like* to begin clauses, especially after verbs such as *look, feel,* and *sound.*

assure, ensure, insure *Assure* means "to state with confidence, alleviating any doubt": The flight attendant **assured** us that our flight would arrive on time. *Ensure* and *insure* are usually interchangeable to mean "make certain," but only *insure* means "to protect against loss": The editor ensured [OR **insured**] that the reporter's facts were accurate. Physicians must **insure** themselves against malpractice suits.

awful, awfully Conversational when used to mean "very."

awhile See **a while, awhile.**

bad Unconventional as an adverb; use *badly* instead. The team played **badly.** However, the adjective *bad* is used after sensory verbs such as *feel, look,* and *smell:* I feel **bad** that I forgot to return your book yesterday.

because See **as, because.**

being as, being that Unconventional; use *because* instead. ~~Being as~~ Because the road was closed, traffic was diverted to another route.

* **beside, besides** According to traditional usage, these two words have different meanings. *Beside* means "next to": The president sat **beside** the prime minister. *Besides* means "in addition to" or "other than": She has written many articles **besides** those on political reform. Current dictionaries report that professional writers regularly use *beside* to convey this meaning, as long as there is no risk of ambiguity.

better, had better *Better* is conversational. Use *had better* instead: We ~~better~~ had better finish the report by five o'clock.

between See **among, between.**

breath, breathe *Breath* is a noun: Take a deep **breath.** *Breathe* is a verb: **Breathe** deeply.

* **bring, take** Both words describe the same action but from different standpoints. *Bring* indicates movement toward the writer: She **brought** me some flowers. *Take* implies movement away from the writer: He **took** my overdue books to the library. Dictionaries report that this distinction is often blurred when the writer's position is ambiguous or irrelevant: He **brought** [OR **took**] her some flowers.

bunch Conversational to refer to a group: A ~~bunch~~ group of students participated in the experiment.

busted Unconventional. Use *broken* instead: Every day he walked past a ~~busted~~ broken vending machine on his way to class.

but that, but what Conversational after expressions of doubt such as *no doubt* or *did not know.* Use *that* instead: I do not doubt ~~but what~~ that they are correct.

* **can, may** *Can* refers to ability, and *may* refers to permission: You **can** [are able to] drive seventy miles an hour, but you **may** not [are not permitted to] exceed the speed limit. Current dictionaries report that in contemporary usage *can* and *may* are used interchangeably to denote possibility or permission, although *may* is used more frequently in formal contexts.

can't hardly, can't scarcely Unconventional. Use *can hardly* or *can scarcely:* The students **can't hardly** wait for summer vacation.

capital, capitol *Capital* means either "a governing city" or "funds": The **capital** of Minnesota is St. Paul. An anonymous donor provided the **capital** for the project. As a modifier, *capital* means "chief" or "principal": This year's election is of **capital** importance. It may also refer to the death penalty: **Capital** punishment is legal in some states. A *capitol* is a statehouse; the *Capitol* is the U.S. congressional building in Washington, DC.

censor, censure, sensor As a verb, *censor* means "to remove or suppress because of immoral or otherwise objectionable ideas": Do you think a ratings board should **censor** films? As a noun, *censor* refers to a person who is authorized to remove material considered objectionable: The **censor** recommended that the book be banned. The verb *censure* means "to blame or criticize"; the noun *censure* is an expression of disapproval or blame. The Senate **censured** Joseph McCarthy. He received a **censure** from the Senate. A *sensor* is a device that responds to a stimulus: The **sensor** detects changes in light.

center around Conversational for "to center on" or "to revolve around": The discussion **centered ~~around~~ on** the public's response to tax reform initiatives.

chair, chairman, chairperson As gender-neutral terms, *chairperson* and *chair* are preferred to *chairman.* See **32d.**

cite, site, sight *Cite* means "to mention": Be sure to **cite** your sources. *Site* is a location: The president visited the **site** for the new library. As a verb, *site* also means "to situate": The builder **sited** the factory near the freeway. *Sight* means "to see": The crew **sighted** land. *Sight* also refers to a view: What an incredible **sight!**

climactic, climatic *Climactic* refers to a climax, or high point: The actors rehearsed the **climactic** scene. *Climatic* refers to the *climate:* Many environmentalists are worried about the recent **climatic** changes.

coarse, course *Coarse* refers to roughness: The jacket was made of **coarse** linen. *Course* refers to a route: Our **course** to the island was indirect. *Course* may also refer to a plan of study: I want to take a **course** in nutrition.

compare to, compare with *Compare to* means "to regard as similar," and *compare with* means "to examine for similarities and/or differences": She **compared** her mind **to** a dusty attic. The student **compared** the first draft **with** the second.

complement, complementary, compliment, complimentary *Complement* means "to complete" or "to balance": Their personalities **complement** each other. They have **complementary** personalities. *Compliment* means "to express praise": The professor **complimented** the students on their first drafts. Her remarks were **complimentary.** *Complimentary* may also mean "provided free of charge": We received **complimentary** tickets.

* **compose, comprise** *Compose* means "to make up": That collection **is composed** of medieval manuscripts. *Comprise* means "to consist of": The anthology **comprises** many famous essays. Dictionary editors have noted the increasing use of *comprise* in the passive voice to mean "to be composed of."

conscience, conscious, consciousness *Conscience* means "the sense of right and wrong": He examined his **conscience** before deciding whether to join the protest. *Conscious* means "awake": After an hour, the patient was fully **conscious.** After an hour, the patient regained **consciousness.** *Conscious* may also mean "aware": We were **conscious** of the possible consequences.

continual, continually, continuous, continuously *Continual* means "constantly recurring": **Continual** interruptions kept us from completing the project. Telephone calls **continually** interrupted us. *Continuous* means "uninterrupted": The job applicant had a record of ten years' **continuous** employment. The job applicant worked **continuously** from 1996 to 2006.

* **convince, persuade** *Convince* means "to make someone believe something": His passionate speech **convinced** us that school reform was necessary. *Persuade* means "to motivate someone to act": She **persuaded** us to stop smoking. Dictionary editors note that many speakers now use *convince* as a synonym for *persuade.*

could care less Unconventional to express complete lack of concern. *Couldn't care less* is used in informal contexts.

could of *Of* is often mistaken for the sound of the unstressed *have:* They **could of have** [OR might **have,** should **have,** would **have**] gone home.

council, counsel A *council* is an advisory or decision-making group: The student **council** supported the new safety regulations. A *counsel* is a legal adviser: The defense **counsel** conferred with the judge. As a verb, *counsel* means "to give advice": The new psychologist **counsels** people with eating disorders.

criteria, criterion *Criteria* is a plural noun meaning "a set of standards for judgment": The teachers explained the **criteria** for the assignment. The singular form is *criterion:* Their judgment was based on only one **criterion.**

* **data** *Data* is the plural form of *datum,* which means "piece of information" or "fact": When the **data are** complete, we will know the true cost. However,

current dictionaries also note that *data* is frequently used as a mass entity (like the word *furniture*), appearing with a singular verb.

desert, dessert *Desert* can mean "a barren land": Gila monsters live in the **deserts** of the Southwest. As a verb, *desert* means "to leave": I thought my friends had **deserted** me. *Dessert* refers to something sweet eaten at the end of a meal: They ordered apple pie for **dessert.**

device, devise *Device* is a noun: She invented a **device** that measures extremely small quantitites of liquid. *Devise* is a verb: We **devised** a plan for work distribution.

dialogue Many readers consider the use of *dialogue* as a verb to be an example of unnecessary jargon. Use *discuss* or *exchange views* instead: The committee members ~~dialogued about~~ discussed the issues.

differ from, differ with *Differ from* means "to be different": A bull snake **differs from** a rattlesnake in a number of ways. *Differ with* means "to disagree": Senator Brown has **differed with** Senator Owen on several issues.

different from, different than *Different from* is generally used with nouns, pronouns, noun phrases, and noun clauses: This school was **different from** most others. The school was **different from** what we had expected. *Different than* is used with adverbial clauses; *than* is the conjunction: We are no **different than** they are.

discreet, discrete *Discreet* means "showing good judgment or self-restraint": His friends complained openly, but his comments were quite **discreet.** *Discrete* means "distinct": The participants in the study came from three **discrete** groups.

disinterested, uninterested *Disinterested* means "impartial": A **disinterested** observer will give a fair opinion. *Uninterested* means "lacking interest": She was **uninterested** in the outcome of the game.

distinct, distinctive *Distinct* means "easily distinguishable or perceived": Each proposal has **distinct** advantages. *Distinctive* means "characteristic" or "serving to distinguish": We studied the **distinctive** features of hawks.

* **due to** Traditionally, *due to* was not synonymous with *because of:* ~~Due to~~ Because of holiday traffic, we arrived an hour late. However, dictionary editors now consider this usage of *due to* acceptable.

dyeing, dying *Dyeing* comes from *dye,* meaning "to color something, usually by soaking it": As a sign of solidarity, the students are **dyeing** their shirts the same color. *Dying* refers to the loss of life: Because of the drought, the plants are **dying.**

effect See **affect, effect.**

elicit, illicit *Elicit* means "to draw forth": He is **eliciting** contributions for a new playground. *Illicit* means "unlawful": The newspaper reported their **illicit** mishandling of public funds.

elude See **allude, elude.**

emigrate from, immigrate to *Emigrate* means "to leave one's own country": My ancestors **emigrated from** Ireland. *Immigrate* means "to arrive in a different country to settle": The Ulster Scots **immigrated to** the southern United States.

eminent, imminent *Eminent* means "distinguished": An **eminent** scholar in physics will be giving a public lecture tomorrow. *Imminent* means "about to happen": The merger of the two companies is **imminent.**

ensure See **assure, ensure, insure.**

especially, specially *Especially* emphasizes a characteristic or quality: Some people are **especially** sensitive to the sun. *Especially* also means "particularly": Wildflowers are abundant in this area, **especially** during May. *Specially* means "for a particular purpose": The classroom was **specially** designed for music students.

etc. Abbreviation of *et cetera,* meaning "and others of the same kind." Use only within parentheses: Be sure to bring appropriate camping gear (tent, sleeping bag, mess kit, **etc.**). Because *and* is part of the meaning of *etc.,* avoid using the combination *and etc.*

eventually, ultimately *Eventually* refers to some future time: She has made so many valuable contributions that I am sure she will **eventually** become the store supervisor. *Ultimately* refers to the final outcome after a series of events: The course was difficult but **ultimately** worthwhile.

everyday, every day *Everyday* means "routine" or "ordinary": These are **everyday** problems. *Every day* means "each day": I read the newspaper **every day.**

everyone, every one *Everyone* means "all": **Everyone** should attend. *Every one* refers to each person or item in a group: **Every one** of you should attend.

everyplace See **anyplace, everyplace, someplace.**

except See **accept, except.**

expect Conversational; use *think* or *believe* instead: I **expect** **believe** the answer is clear.

explicit, implicit *Explicit* means "expressed clearly and directly": Given his **explicit** directions, we knew how to proceed. *Implicit* means "implied or expressed indirectly": I mistakenly understood his silence to be his **implicit** approval of the project.

farther, further Generally, *farther* refers to geographic distance: We will have to drive **farther** tomorrow. *Further* means "more": If you need **further** assistance, please let me know.

* **feel** Traditionally, *feel* was not synonymous with "think" or "believe": I ~~feel~~ **think** that more should be done to protect local habitat. Dictionary editors now consider such a use of *feel* to be a standard alternative.

fewer, less *Fewer* occurs before nouns that can be counted: **fewer** technicians, **fewer** pencils. *Less* occurs before nouns that cannot be counted: **less** milk, **less** support. *Less than* may be used with measurements of time or distance: **less than** three months, **less than** twenty miles.

* **first, firstly; second, secondly** Many college instructors prefer the use of *first* and *second*. However, dictionary editors state that *firstly* and *secondly* are also well-established forms.

foreword, forward A *foreword* is an introduction: The **foreword** to the book provided useful background information. *Forward* refers to a frontward direction: To get a closer look, we moved **forward** slowly.

former, latter Used together, *former* refers to the first of two; *latter* to the second of two. John and Ian are both English. The **former** is from Manchester; the **latter** is from Birmingham.

further See **farther, further.**

get Considered conversational in many common expressions: The weather ~~got better~~ **improved** overnight. I did not know what he ~~was getting at~~ **meant.**

go, goes Unconventional for *say(s), respond(s),* and other similar words: My friends say I'm strange, and I ~~go~~ **reply,** "You're right!"

good, well *Good* is an adjective, not an adverb. Use *well* instead: He pitched ~~good~~ **well** last night. *Good* in the sense of "in good health" may be used interchangeably with *well:* I feel **good** [OR **well**] this morning.

had better See **better, had better.**

half A *half a* or *a half an* is unconventional; use *half a/an* or *a half:* You should be able to complete the questionnaire in **a half an** hour.

hanged, hung *Hanged* means "put to death by hanging": The prisoner was **hanged** at dawn. For all other meanings, use *hung:* He **hung** the picture above his desk.

hardly Unconventional when combined with a negative word such as *not.* Depending on the intended meaning, either omit *hardly* or omit the negative word: The drivers could**n't hardly** see the road.

has got, have got Conversational; omit *got*: I **have ~~got~~** a meeting tomorrow.

he/she, his/her As a solution to the problem of sexist language, these combinations are not universally accepted. Consider using *he or she* and *his or her.* See **32d**.

herself, himself, myself, yourself Unconventional as subjects in a sentence. Joe and ~~**myself**~~ **I** will lead the discussion. See **25a(4)**.

hopefully Conversational to mean "I hope": ~~**Hopefully,**~~ **I hope** the game will not be canceled.

hung See **hanged, hung.**

i.e. Abbreviation of *id est,* meaning "that is." Use only within parentheses: All participants in the study ran the same distance (**i.e.,** six kilometers). Otherwise, replace *i.e.* with the English equivalent, *that is:* Assistance was offered to those who would have difficulty boarding, ~~**i.e.**~~ **that is,** the elderly, the disabled, and parents with small children. Do not confuse *i.e.* with *e.g.,* meaning "for example."

illicit See **elicit, illicit.**

illusion See **allusion, illusion.**

immigrate See **emigrate from, immigrate to.**

imminent See **eminent, imminent.**

immoral See **amoral, immoral.**

* **impact** Though *impact* is commonly used as a verb in business writing, many college teachers still use it as a noun only: The new tax ~~**impacts**~~ **affects** everyone.

implicit See **explicit, implicit.**

imply, infer *Imply* means "suggest without actually stating": Though he never mentioned the statistics, he **implied** that they were questionable. *Infer* means "draw a conclusion based on evidence": Given the tone of his voice, I **inferred** that he found the work substandard.

in regards to Unconventional; see **regard, regarding, regards.**

inside of, outside of Drop *of* when unnecessary: Security guards stood **outside of** the front door.

insure See **assure, ensure, insure.**

irregardless Unconventional; use *regardless* instead.

its, it's *Its* is a possessive form: The committee forwarded **its** recommendation. *It's* is a contraction of *it is:* **It's** a beautiful day.

-ize Some readers object to using this ending to create new verbs: *enronize.* Some of these new verbs, however, have already entered into common usage: *computerize.*

kind of a, sort of a The word *a* is unnecessary: This **kind of a** book sells well. *Kind of* and *sort of* are not conventionally used to mean "somewhat": The report was ~~kind of~~ somewhat difficult to read.

later, latter *Later* means "after a specific time" or "a time after now": The concert ended **later** than we had expected. *Latter* refers to the second of two items: Of the two versions described, I prefer the **latter.**

lay, lie *Lay* (*laid, laying*) means "put" or "place": He **laid** the book aside. *Lie* (*lay, lain, lying*) means "rest" or "recline": I had just **lain** down when the alarm went off. *Lay* takes an object (to **lay** something), while *lie* does not. These verbs may be confused because the present tense of *lay* and the past tense of *lie* are spelled the same way.

lead, led As a noun, *lead* means "a kind of metal": The paint had **lead** in it. As a verb, *lead* means "to conduct": A guide will **lead** a tour of the ruins. *Led* is the past tense of the verb *lead:* He **led** the country from 1949 to 1960.

less, less than See **fewer, less.**

liable *Liable* generally means "likely" in an undesirable sense: If they invest money in that stock, they are **liable** to lose money. With her brains, she is ~~liable~~ likely to achieve success easily.

lie See **lay, lie.**

like See **as, like.**

literally Conversational when used to emphasize the meaning of another word: I was ~~literally~~ nearly frozen after I finished shoveling the sidewalk. *Literally* is conventionally used to indicate that an expression is not being used figuratively: My friend **literally** climbs the walls after work; his fellow rock climbers join him at the local gym.

lose, loose *Lose* is a verb: She does not **lose** her patience often. *Loose* is chiefly used as an adjective: A few of the tiles are **loose.**

lots, lots of Conversational for *many* or *much:* He has ~~lots of~~ many friends. We have ~~lots~~ much to do before the end of the quarter.

mankind Considered sexist because it excludes women: All ~~mankind~~ humanity will benefit from this new discovery.

many, much *Many* is used with nouns that can be counted: **many** stores, too **many** assignments. *Much* is used with nouns that cannot be counted: **much** courage, not **much** time.

may See **can, may.**

may of, might of See **could of.**

maybe, may be *Maybe* is an adverb: **Maybe** the negotiators will succeed this time. *May* and *be* are verbs: The rumor **may be** true.

* **media, medium** According to traditional definitions, *media* is a plural word: The **media** have sometimes created the news in addition to reporting it. The singular form is *medium:* The newspaper is one **medium** that people seem to trust. Dictionary editors note the frequent use of *media* as a collective noun taking a singular verb, but this usage is still considered conversational.

might could Conversational for "might be able to": The director ~~might could~~ **be able to** review your application next week.

most Unconventional to mean "almost": We watch the news ~~most~~ **almost** every day.

much See **many, much.**

myself See **herself, himself, myself, yourself.**

neither . . . or Conventionally, *nor,* not *or,* follows *neither:* The book is **neither** as funny ~~or~~ **nor** as original as critics have reported.

not . . . no/none/nothing The use of multiple negative words is unconventional: I did **not** want ~~nothing~~ **anything** else. Multiple negation may be used for special effect.

nothing like, nowhere near Unconventional; use *not nearly* instead: Her new book is ~~nowhere near~~ **not nearly** as mysterious as her previous novel.

number of When the expression *a number of* is used, the reference is plural: **A number of** positions **are** open. When *the number of* is used, the reference is singular: **The number of** possibilities **is** limited. See also **amount of, number of.**

off of Conversational; omit *of:* He walked **off of** the field.

on account of Conversational; use *because of:* The singer canceled her engagement ~~on account of~~ **because of** a sore throat.

on the other hand Use *however* instead, or make sure that the sentence or independent clause beginning with this transitional phrase is preceded by one starting with *on the one hand.*

other See **another, other, the other.**

owing to the fact that Considered wordy; use *because* instead: ~~Owing to the fact that~~ **Because** more people came to the concert than were expected, the stage crew set up extra chairs in the aisles.

passed, past *Passed* is the past tense of the verb *pass:* Everyone **passed** the test. *Past* means "beyond a time or location": The band marched **past** the bleachers.

per In ordinary contexts, use *a* or *an:* You should drink at least six glasses of water **per** **a** day.

percent, percentage *Percent* (also spelled *per cent*) is used with a specific number: **Sixty percent** of the students attended the ceremony. *Percentage* refers to an unspecified portion: The **percentage** of high school graduates attending college has increased in recent years.

perspective, prospective *Perspective* means "point of view": We discussed the issue from various **perspectives.** *Prospective* means "likely to become": **Prospective** elementary teachers visited nearby classrooms last Friday.

persuade See **convince, persuade.**

phenomena, phenomenon *Phenomena* is the plural form of *phenomenon:* Natural **phenomena** were given scientific explanations.

plus *Plus* joins nouns or noun phrases to make a sentence seem like an equation: Her endless curiosity **plus** her boundless energy makes her the perfect camp counselor. Note that a singular form of the verb is required (e.g., *makes*). *Plus* is not used to join clauses: I telephoned ~~plus~~ **and** I sent flowers.

p.m. See **a.m., p.m.**

precede, proceed To *precede* is to "go ahead of ": A moment of silence **preceded** the applause. To *proceed* is to "go forward": After stopping for a short rest, we **proceeded** to our destination.

prejudice, prejudiced *Prejudice* is a noun: They were unaware of their **prejudice.** *Prejudiced* is an adjective: She accused me of being **prejudiced.**

principal, principle As a noun, *principal* means "chief official": The **principal** greeted the students every day. It also means "capital": The loan's **principal** was still quite high. As an adjective, *principal* means "main": Tourism is the country's **principal** source of income. The noun *principle* refers to a rule, standard, or belief: She explained the three **principles** supporting the theory.

proceed See **precede, proceed.**

prospective See **perspective, prospective.**

quotation, quote In academic writing, *quotation,* rather than *quote,* refers to a repeated or copied sentence or passage: She began her speech with a ~~quote~~ **quotation** from *Othello. Quote* expresses an action: My friend sometimes **quotes** lines from television commercials.

raise, rise *Raise* (*raised, raising*) means "to lift or cause to move upward, to bring up or increase": Retailers **raised** prices. *Rise* (*rose, risen, rising*) means "to get up" or "to ascend": The cost of living **rose** sharply. *Raise* takes an object (to **raise** something); *rise* does not.

rarely ever Conversational; omit *ever:* He **rarely ever** goes to the library.

real, really *Really* rather than *real* is used to mean "very": He is from a ~~real~~ really small town. To ensure this word's effectiveness, use it sparingly.

* **reason why** Traditionally, this combination was considered redundant: No one explained **the reason why** the negotiations failed. [OR No one explained **~~the reason~~ why** the negotiations failed.] However, dictionary editors report its use by highly regarded writers.

regard, regarding, regards These forms are used in the following expressions: *in regard to, with regard to, as regards,* and *regarding* [NOT *in regards to, with regards to,* or *as regarding*].

* **relation, relationship** According to traditional definitions, *relation* is used to link abstractions: We studied the **relation** between language and social change. *Relationship* is used to link people: The **relationship** between the two friends grew strong. However, dictionary editors now label as standard the use of *relationship* to connect abstractions.

respectfully, respectively *Respectfully* means "showing respect": The children learned to treat one another **respectfully.** *Respectively* means "in the order designated": We discussed the issue with the chair, the dean, and the provost, **respectively.**

rise See **raise, rise.**

sensor See **censor, censure, sensor.**

sensual, sensuous *Sensual* refers to gratification of the physical senses, often those associated with sexual pleasure: Frequently found in this music are **sensual** dance rhythms. *Sensuous* refers to gratification of the senses in response to art, music, nature, and so on: **Sensuous** landscape paintings lined the walls of the gallery.

shall, will Traditionally, *shall* was used with *I* or *we* to express future tense, and *will* was used with the other personal pronouns, but *shall* has almost disappeared in contemporary American English. *Shall* is still used in legal writing to indicate an obligation.

should of See **could of.**

sight See **cite, site, sight.**

sit, set *Sit* means "to be seated": Jonathon **sat** in the front row. *Set* means "to place something": The research assistant **set** the chemicals on the counter. *Set* takes an object (to **set** something); *sit* does not.

site See **cite, site, sight.**

so *So* intensifies another word when it is used with *that:* He was **so** nervous **that** he had trouble sleeping. Instead of using *so* alone, find a precise modifier: She was **so intensely** focused on her career. See **27f.**

someplace See **anyplace, everyplace, someplace.**

sometime, sometimes, some time *Sometime* means "at an unspecified time": They will meet **sometime** next month. *Sometimes* means "at times": **Sometimes** laws are unfair. *Some time* means "a span of time": They agreed to allow **some time** to pass before voting on the measure.

sort of a See **kind of a, sort of a.**

specially See **especially, specially.**

stationary, stationery *Stationary* means "in a fixed position": Traffic was **stationary** for an hour. *Stationery* means "writing paper and envelopes": The director ordered new department **stationery.**

supposed to, used to Be sure to include the frequently unsounded *d* at the end of the verb form: We are **supposed to** leave at 9:30 a.m. We **used to** leave earlier.

take See **bring, take.**

than, then *Than* is used in comparisons: The tape recorder is smaller **than** the radio. *Then* refers to a time sequence: Go straight ahead for three blocks; **then** turn left.

* **that, which** *Which* occurs in nonessential (nonrestrictive) clauses: Myanmar, **which** borders Thailand, was formerly called Burma. Both *that* and *which* occur in essential (restrictive) clauses, although traditionally only *that* was considered acceptable: I am looking for an atlas **that** [OR **which**] includes demographic information. (For more information on essential and nonessential clauses, see **35d** and **35g**.)

* **that, which, who** In essential (restrictive) clauses, *who* and *that* refer to people. We want to hire someone **who** [OR **that**] has had experience programming. Traditionally, only *who* was used to refer to people. *That,* as well as *which,* refers to things: He proposed a design **that** [OR **which**] will take advantage of solar energy.

their, there, they're *Their* is the possessive form of *they:* They will give **their** presentation tomorrow. *There* refers to location: I lived **there** for six years. *There* is also used as an expletive (see **34a(3)**): **There** is no explanation for the phenomenon. *They're* is a contraction of *they are:* **They're** leaving in the morning.

theirself, theirselves Unconventional; use *themselves.* The students finished the project by ~~theirself~~ themselves.

then See **than, then.**

thru *Through* is preferred in academic and professional writing: We drove ~~thru~~ through the whole state of South Dakota in one day.

thusly Unconventional; use *thus, in this way,* or *as follows* instead: He accompanied his father on archeological digs and **thusly** discovered his interest in ancient cultures.

time period Readers are likely to consider this combination redundant; use one word or the other, but not both: During this **time period,** the economy was strong.

to, too, two *To* is an infinitive marker: She wanted **to** become an actress. *To* is also used as a preposition, usually indicating direction: They walked **to** the memorial. *Too* means either "also" or "excessively": I voted for her **too.** They are **too** busy this year. *Two* is a number: She studied abroad for **two** years.

toward, towards Although both are acceptable, *toward* is preferred in American English.

try and Conversational for *try to:* The staff will **try and to** finish the project by Friday.

ultimately See **eventually, ultimately.**

uninterested See **disinterested, uninterested.**

* **unique** Traditionally, *unique* meant "one of a kind" and thus was not preceded by a qualifier such as *more, most, quite,* or *very:* Her prose style is **quite unique.** However, dictionary editors note that *unique* is also widely used to mean "extraordinary."

usage, use *Use* is generally preferred to *usage* in nontechnical contexts: He designed the furniture for practical **usage use.**

use, utilize In most contexts, *use* is preferred to *utilize:* We **utilized used** a special dye in the experiment. However, *utilize* may suggest an effort to employ something for a purpose: We discussed how to **utilize** the new equipment we had been given.

used to See **supposed to, used to.**

way Conversational as an intensifier: The movie was **way utterly** depressing.

ways Conversational when referring to distance; use *way* instead: It's a long **ways way** from home.

well See **good, well.**

where Conversational for *that:* I noticed **where that** she had been elected.

where . . . at, where . . . to Conversational; omit *at* and *to:* **Where** is the library **at? Where** are you moving **to?**

which See **that, which** and **that, which, who.**

* **who, whom** *Who* is used as the subject or subject complement in a clause: We have decided to hire Marian Wright, **whom who** I believe is currently finishing her degree in business administration. [*Who* is the subject in *who is currently finishing her degree in business administration.*] See also **that, which, who.** *Whom* is used as an object: Jeff Kruger, **who whom** we hired in 2004, is now our top sales representative. [*Whom* is the object in *whom we hired.*] Dictionary editors note that in conversation *who* is commonly used as an object as long as it does not follow a preposition. See **25b(5)**.

whose, who's *Whose* is a possessive form: **Whose** book is this? The book was written by a young Mexican-American woman **whose** family still lives in Chiapas. *Who's* is the contraction of *who is:* **Who's** going to run in the election?

will See **shall, will.**

with regards to Unconventional; see **regard, regarding, regards.**

would of See **could of.**

your, you're *Your* is a possessive form: Let's meet in **your** office. *You're* is a contraction of *you are:* **You're** gaining strength.

yourself See **herself, himself, myself, yourself.**

GLOSSARY

OF

TERMS

This glossary provides brief definitions of frequently used terms. Consult the index for references to terms not listed here.

absolute phrase A sentencelike structure containing a subject and its modifiers. Unlike a sentence, an absolute phrase has no verb marked for person, number, or tense: *The ceremony finally over,* the graduates tossed their mortarboards in the air. See **21a(6)**.

acronym A word formed by combining the initial letters or syllables of a series of words and pronounced as a word rather than as a series of letters: *NATO* for North Atlantic Treaty Organization. See **43e**.

active voice See **voice.**

adjectival clause A dependent clause, sometimes called a **relative clause,** that modifies a noun or a pronoun. See **21b(2)**.

adjectival phrase A phrase that modifies a noun or a pronoun. See **20d(3)**.

adjective A word that modifies a noun or a pronoun. Adjectives typically end in suffixes such as *-al, -able, -ant, -ative, -ic, -ish, -less, -ous,* and *-y.* See **20a(4)** and **24a**. **Coordinate adjectives** are two or more adjectives modifying the same noun and separated by a comma: a *brisk, cold* walk. See **35c(2)**.

adverb A word that modifies a verb, a verbal, an adjective, or another adverb. Adverbs commonly end in *-ly.* Some adverbs modify entire sentences: *Perhaps* the meeting could be postponed. See **20a(5)** and **24a**.

adverbial clause A dependent clause that modifies a verb, an adjective, or an adverb. See **21b(2)**.

alt tags Descriptive lines of text for each visual image in an electronic document. Because these lines can be read by screen-reading software, they can assist visually impaired users. See **6e(1)**.

analysis A separation of a whole into its parts. For example, a literary work may be separated into such elements as setting, plot, and characters. See **3f(4)** and **16e**.

antecedent A word or group of words referred to by a pronoun. See **20a(3)** and **25c.**

appositive A pronoun, noun, or noun phrase that identifies, describes, or explains an adjacent pronoun, noun, or noun phrase. See **21a(5)** and **25b(4).**

article A word used to signal a noun. *The* is a definite article; *a* and *an* are indefinite articles. See **20a(4).**

asynchronous forum Online means of communication in which a period of time elapses between the sending and the receiving of a message. Internet newsgroups and electronic mailing lists are examples of asynchronous discussion groups. See **6c(1).** COMPARE: **synchronous forum.**

attributive tag Short phrase that identifies the source of a quotation: *according to Jones, Jones claims.* See **11d.**

auxiliary verb, auxiliary A verb that combines with a main verb. *Be, do,* and *have* are auxiliary verbs when they are used with main verbs. Also called **helping verbs. Modal auxiliaries** include *could, should,* and *may* and are used for such purposes as expressing doubt or obligation and making a request. See **20c** and **26a(4).**

blog Shortened form of *Web log,* a Web site that is part diary and part community forum in which users regularly post their observations or opinions on self-defined topics, maintain archives, and encourage responses from other users. See **6c(1).**

Boolean operators See **logical operators.**

bulletin board See **newsgroup.**

case The form of a pronoun that indicates the relationship of the pronoun to other words in a sentence. Pronouns can be subjects or subject complements (**subjective case**), objects (**objective case**), or markers of possession and other relations (**possessive case**). See **25b.**

claim A statement that a writer wants readers to accept; also called a **proposition.** See **8d.**

clause A sequence of related words forming an independent unit (**independent clause,** or **main clause**) or an embedded unit (**dependent clause** used as an adverb, adjective, or noun). A clause has both a subject and a predicate. See **21b.**

cliché An expression that has lost its power to interest readers because of overuse. See **33b.**

clipped form A word that is a shortened form of another word: *bike* for *bicycle.* See **43d(3).**

collective noun A noun that refers to a group: *team, faculty, committee.* See **20a(2).**

collocation Common word combination such as *add to, adept at,* or *admiration for.* See **33c.**

colloquial A label for any word or phrase that is characteristic of informal speech. *Tummy* and *belly* are colloquial words; *stomach* is used in formal contexts. See **32c(2).**

common noun A noun referring to any or all members of a class or group (*woman, city, holiday*) rather than to specific members (*Susan, Reno, New Year's Day*); also called **generic noun.** COMPARE: **proper noun.** See **20a(2).**

complement A word or words used to complete the meaning of a verb. A **subject complement** is a word or phrase that follows a linking verb and categorizes or describes the subject. An **object complement** is a word or phrase that categorizes or describes a direct object when it follows such verbs as *make, paint, elect,* and *consider.* See **20d.**

complete predicate See **predicate.**

complete subject See **subject.**

complex sentence A sentence containing one independent clause and at least one dependent clause. See **21d(3).**

compound-complex sentence A sentence containing at least two independent clauses and one or more dependent clauses. See **21d(4).**

compound predicate Predicate that has two parts joined by a connecting word such as *and, or,* or *but:* Clara Barton *nursed the injured during the Civil War* and *later founded the American Red Cross.* See **20b.**

compound sentence A sentence containing at least two independent clauses and no dependent clauses. See **21d(2).**

compound subject Subject that has two parts joined by a connecting word such as *and, or,* or *but: Students* and *faculty* are discussing the issue of grade inflation. See **20b.**

compound word Two or more words functioning as a single word: *ice cream, double-check.* See **40f(1).**

conditional clause An adverbial clause, usually beginning with *if,* that expresses a condition: *If it rains,* the outdoor concert will be postponed.

conjunction A word used to connect other words, phrases, clauses, or sentences. **Coordinating conjunctions** (*and, but, or, nor, for, so,* and *yet*) connect and relate words and word groups of equal grammatical rank. See

20a(7) and **21c(1)**. A **subordinating conjunction** such as *although, if,* or *when* begins a dependent clause and connects it to an independent clause. See **20a(7)** and **21c(3)**. COMPARE: **conjunctive adverb.**

conjunctive adverb A word such as *however* or *thus* that joins one independent clause to another. See **21c(4)** and **23d**. COMPARE: **conjunction.**

convention, conventional Refers to language or behavior that follows the customs of a community such as the academic, medical, or business community.

coordinate adjective See **adjective.**

coordinating conjunction See **conjunction.**

coordination The use of grammatically equivalent constructions to link or balance ideas. See chapter **28**.

correlative conjunctions, correlatives Two-part connecting words such as *either . . . or* and *not only . . . but also.* See **20a(7)** and **21c(2)**.

count nouns Nouns naming things that can be counted (*word, student, remark*). See **20a(2)**. COMPARE: **noncount nouns.**

dangling modifier A word or phrase that does not clearly modify another word or word group in the sentence. See **24d**. COMPARE: **misplaced modifier.**

dangling participial phrase A verbal phrase that does not clearly modify another word or word group in the sentence. See **24d**.

database An organized collection of related information, usually in electronic form. A full-text database contains the complete, or nearly complete, text of articles. An abstract database contains summaries of articles. A bibliographic database contains limited information such as the subjects, titles, and authors of articles. See **9c(1)**.

deductive reasoning A form of logical reasoning in which a conclusion is formed after relating a specific fact (minor premise) to a generalization (major premise). See **8h(2)**. COMPARE: **inductive reasoning.**

demonstratives Four words (*this, that, these,* and *those*) that distinguish one individual, thing, event, or idea from another. Demonstratives may occur with or without nouns: *This* [demonstrative determiner] *law* will go into effect in two years. *This* [demonstrative pronoun] will go into effect in two years.

dependent clause See **clause.**

determiner A word that signals the approach of a noun. A determiner may be an article, a demonstrative, a possessive, or a quantifier: *a reason, this reason, his reason, three reasons.*

direct address See **vocative.**

direct object See **object.**

direct quotation See **quotation.**

electronic mailing list See **listserv.**

ellipsis points Three spaced periods that indicate either a pause or the omission of material from a direct quotation. See **39h.**

elliptical clause A clause missing one or more words that are assumed to be understood. See **21b(2).**

essential element A word or word group that modifies another word or word group, providing information that is essential for identification. Essential elements are not set off by commas, parentheses, or dashes: The woman *who witnessed the accident* was called to testify. Also called a **restrictive element.** COMPARE: **nonessential element.**

ethos One of the three classical appeals; the use of language to demonstrate the writer's trustworthy character, good intentions, and substantial knowledge of a subject. Also called an **ethical appeal.** See **8f(1).** See also **logos** and **pathos.**

exigence The circumstance compelling one to write. See **1b.**

expletive A word signaling a structural change in a sentence, usually used so that new or important information is given at the end of the sentence: *There were over four thousand runners in the marathon.* See **20d(1).**

faulty predication A sentence error in which the predicate does not logically belong with the given subject. See **27d(2).**

figurative language The use of words in an imaginative rather than in a literal sense. See **33a(4).**

file transfer protocol See **ftp.**

first person See **person.**

flaming Heated, confrontational exchanges via e-mail. See **6d.**

ftp Abbreviation for **file transfer protocol.** The guidelines that establish the format in which files can be transmitted from computer to computer.

gender The grammatical label that distinguishes nouns or pronouns as masculine, feminine, or neuter. In English, grammatical gender usually corresponds to natural gender. Gender also describes how people see themselves, or are seen by others, as either male or female. See **25c** and **32d(1).**

generic noun See **common noun.**

genre A literary category, such as drama or poetry, identified by its own conventions. See **16a.**

gerund A verbal that ends in *-ing* and functions as a noun: *Snowboarding* is a popular winter sport. See **21a(3)**.

gerund phrase A verbal phrase that employs the *-ing* form of a verb and functions as a noun: Some students prefer *studying in the library.* See **21a(3)**.

helping verb See **auxiliary verb.**

homophones Words that have the same sound and sometimes the same spelling but differ in meaning: *their, there,* and *they're* or *capital* meaning "funds" and *capital* meaning "the top of a pillar." See **40c.**

hyperlink A Web address that is embedded in an electronic document and usually highlighted by color and underlining and that allows users to move between Web pages or sites. See **6e(3)**.

hypertext A computer-based text retrieval system that allows users, by clicking on links in a Web document, to move to other parts of that document or to other Web documents. See **6e(1)**.

idiom An expression whose meaning often cannot be derived from its elements. *Burning the midnight oil* means "staying up late studying." See **33c.**

imperative mood See **mood.**

indefinite article See **article.**

indefinite pronoun A pronoun such as *everyone* or *anything* that does not refer to a specific individual, object, event, and so on. See **25c(1).**

independent clause See **clause.**

indicative mood See **mood.**

indirect object See **object.**

indirect question A sentence that includes an embedded question, punctuated with a period instead of a question mark: My friends asked me *why I left the party early.* See **39a(1).**

indirect quotation See **quotation.**

inductive reasoning The reasoning process that begins with facts or observations and moves to general principles that account for those facts or observations. See **7h(2)**. COMPARE: **deductive reasoning.**

infinitive A verbal that consists of the base form of the verb, usually preceded by the infinitive marker *to.* An infinitive is used chiefly as a noun, less frequently as an adjective or adverb: My father likes *to golf.* See **21a(3)**.

infinitive phrase A verbal phrase that contains the infinitive form of a verb: They volunteered *to work at the local hospital.* See **21(a)3.**

inflection A change in the form of a word that indicates a grammatical feature such as number, person, tense, or degree. For example, *-ed* added to a verb indicates the past tense, and *-er* indicates the comparative degree of an adjective or adverb.

intensifier See **qualifier.**

intensive pronoun See **reflexive pronoun.**

interactive media Any type of online media that allows the user to influence and react to it.

interjection A word expressing a simple exclamation: *Hey! Oops!* When used in sentences, mild interjections are set off by commas. See **20a(8)**.

intransitive verb A verb that does not take an object: Everyone *laughed.* See **20e** and **26d(1)**. COMPARE: **transitive verb.**

invention Using strategies to generate ideas for writing. See **3a**.

inversion A change in the usual subject-verb order of a sentence: *Are you* ready? See **20e**.

keywords Specific words used with a search tool (such as Google) to find information. See **9b(1)**.

linking verb A verb that relates a subject to a subject complement. Examples of linking verbs are *be, become, seem, appear, feel, look, taste, smell,* and *sound.* See **20a(1)** and **26d(1)**.

listserv An online discussion forum consisting of a list of subscribers who share information about a specific subject by sending e-mail messages that are automatically distributed to all the other subscribers. Also referred to as an **e-mail list.** See **6c(1)**.

logical operators Words used to broaden or narrow electronic database searches. These include *or, and, not,* and *near.* Also called **Boolean operators.** See **9b(1)**.

logos One of the three classical appeals; the use of language to show clear reasoning. Also called a **logical appeal.** See **8f(1)**. See also **ethos** and **pathos.**

lurk The practice of anonymously observing how users in a given online community write and conduct themselves in order to learn the conventions before joining their discussion. See **6c(1)**.

major premise. See **premise.**

main clause Also called **independent clause.** See **clause.**

minor premise. See **premise.**

misplaced modifier A descriptive or qualifying word or phrase placed in a position that confuses the reader: I read about a wildfire that was out of control *in yesterday's paper.* [The modifier belongs before *I* or after *read.*] See **24c**.

mixed construction A confusing sentence that is the result of an unintentional shift from one grammatical pattern to another: When police appeared who were supposed to calm the crowds showed up, most people had already gone home. [The sentence should be recast with either *appeared* or *showed up,* not with both.] See **27d(1)**.

mixed metaphor A construction that includes parts of two or more unrelated metaphors: Her *fiery* personality *dampened* our hopes of a compromise. See **27c**.

modal auxiliary See **auxiliary verb.**

modifier A word or word group that describes, limits, or qualifies another. See chapter **24**.

mood A set of verb forms or inflections used to indicate how a speaker or writer regards an assertion: as a fact or opinion (**indicative mood**); as a command or instruction (**imperative mood**); or as a wish, hypothesis, request, or condition contrary to fact (**subjunctive mood**). See **26e**.

netiquette Word formed from *Internet* and *etiquette* to name a set of guidelines for writing e-mail messages and listserv postings and for online behavior in general. See **6d**.

newsgroup An online discussion group that is accessible to anyone and allows users to post messages related to a specific topic (or thread). Messages are kept on a server, organized by topic so that other users can search for, read, and respond to whatever has been discussed by the group. Also called a **bulletin board.** See **6c(1)**.

nominalization Formation of a noun by adding a suffix to a verb or an adjective: *require, requirement; sad, sadness.*

nominative case Also called **subjective case.** See **case.**

noncount nouns Nouns naming things that cannot be counted (*architecture, water*). See **20a(2)**. COMPARE: **count nouns.**

nonessential element A word or word group that modifies another word or word group but does not provide essential information for identification. Nonessential elements are set off by commas, parentheses, or dashes: Carol Murphy, *president of the university,* plans to meet with alumni representatives. Also called a **nonrestrictive element.** See **35d**. COMPARE: **essential element.**

nonrestrictive element See **nonessential element.**

nonstandard, nonstandardized Refers to speech forms that are not considered conventional in many academic and professional settings. See the **Glossary of Usage**.

noun A word that names a person, place, thing, idea, animal, quality, event, and so on: *Alanis, America, desk, justice, dog, strength, departure.* See also **common noun, proper noun, count noun, noncount noun,** and **collective noun.** See **20a(2)**.

noun clause A dependent clause used as a noun. See **21b(2)**.

noun phrase A noun and its modifiers. See **21a(1)**.

number The property of a word that indicates whether it refers to one **(singular)** or to more than one **(plural)**. Number is reflected in the word's form: *river/rivers, this/those, he sees/they see.* See **26b**.

object A noun, pronoun, noun phrase, or noun clause that follows a preposition or a transitive verb or verbal. A **direct object** names the person or thing that receives the action of the verb: I sent the *package.* An **indirect object** usually indicates to whom the action was directed or for whom the action was performed: I sent *you* the package. See **20d(2)**. The **object of a preposition** follows a preposition: I sent the package to *you.* See **21a(4)**.

object complement See **complement.**

object of a preposition See **object.**

objective case Also called **accusative case.** See **case.**

parenthetical element Any word, phrase, or clause that adds detail to a sentence or any sentence that adds detail to a paragraph but is not essential for understanding the core meaning. Commas, dashes, or parentheses separate these elements from the rest of the sentence or paragraph. See **35e**.

participial phrase A verbal phrase that includes a participle: The stagehand *carrying the trunk* fell over the threshold. See **21a(3)**. See also **participle** and **phrase.**

participle A verb form that may function as part of a verb phrase (was *thinking,* had *determined*) or as a modifier (a *determined* effort; the couple, *thinking* about their past). A **present participle** is formed by adding *-ing* to the base form of a verb. A **past participle** is usually formed by adding *-ed* to the base form of a verb (*walked, passed*); however, many verbs have irregular past-participle forms (*written, bought, gone*). See **26a(5)**.

particle A word such as *across, away, down, for, in, off, out, up, on,* or *with* that combines with a main verb to form a phrasal verb: *write down, look up.* See **26a(3)**.

parts of speech The classes into which words may be grouped according to their forms and grammatical relationships. The traditional parts of speech are verbs, nouns, pronouns, adjectives, adverbs, prepositions, conjunctions, and interjections.

passive voice See **voice.**

past participle See **participle.**

pathos One of the three classical appeals; the use of language to stir the feelings of an audience. Also called an **emotional appeal** or a **pathetic appeal.** See **8f(1).** See also **ethos** and **logos.**

person The property of nouns, pronouns, and their corresponding verbs that distinguishes the speaker or writer **(first person)**, the individuals addressed **(second person)**, and the individuals or things referred to **(third person).** See **26b(1).**

personal pronoun A pronoun that refers to a specific person, place, thing, and so on. Pronoun forms correspond to three cases: subjective, objective, and possessive. See **25a(1).**

phrasal verb A grammatical unit consisting of a verb and a particle such as *after, in, up, off,* or *out: fill in, sort out.* See **26a(3).**

phrase A sequence of grammatically related words that functions as a unit in a sentence but lacks a subject, a predicate, or both: *in front of the stage.* See **21a.**

point of view The vantage point from which a topic is viewed; also, the stance a writer takes: objective or impartial (third person), directive (second person), or personal (first person).

possessive case See **case.**

predicate The part of a sentence that expresses what a subject is, does, or experiences. The **complete predicate** consists of the main verb, its auxiliaries, and any complements and modifiers. The **simple predicate** consists of only the main verb and any accompanying auxiliaries. See **20b–c.** COMPARE: **subject.**

premise An assumption or a proposition on which an argument or explanation is based. In logic, premises are either **major** (general) or **minor** (specific); when combined correctly, they lead to a conclusion. See **8h(2).** See also **syllogism.**

preposition A word such as *at, in, by,* or *of* that relates a pronoun, noun, noun phrase, or noun clause to other words in the sentence. See **20a(6).**

prepositional phrase A preposition with its object and any modifiers: *at* the nearby airport, *by* the sea. See **21a(4).**

present participle See **participle.**

primary source A source that provides firsthand information. See **9a.** COMPARE: **secondary source.**

pronoun A word that takes the position of a noun, noun phrase, or noun clause and functions as that word or word group does: *it, that, he, them.* See **20a(3)** and chapter **25.**

proper adjective An adjective that is derived from the name of a person or place: *Marxist* theories. See **41a(9).**

proper noun The name of a specific person, place, organization, and so on: *Dr. Pimomo, Fargo, National Education Association.* Proper nouns are capitalized. See **20a(2).** COMPARE: **common noun.**

proposition See **claim.**

qualifier A word that intensifies or moderates the meaning of an adverb or adjective: *quite* pleased, *somewhat* reluctant. Words that intensify are sometimes called **intensifiers.**

quotation A **direct quotation** is the exact repetition of someone's spoken or written words. Also called **direct discourse.** An **indirect quotation** is a report of someone's written or spoken words not stated in the exact words of the writer or speaker. See **11d** and chapter **38.**

reflexive pronoun A pronoun that ends in *-self* or *-selves* (*myself* or *themselves*) and refers to a preceding noun or pronoun in the sentence: *He* added a picture of *himself* to his Web page. When used to provide emphasis, such a pronoun is called an **intensive pronoun:** The president *herself* awarded the scholarships. See **25a(4).**

refutation A strategy for addressing opposing points of view by discussing those views and explaining why they are unsatisfactory. See **8e(2)** and **8g(3).**

relative clause See **adjectival clause.**

relative pronoun A word (*who, whom, that, which,* or *whose*) used to introduce an adjectival clause, also called a **relative clause.** An antecedent for the relative pronoun can be found in the main clause. See **21b(2).**

restrictive element See **essential element.**

rhetorical appeal The means of persuasion in argumentative writing, relying on reason, authority, or emotion. See **8f.**

Rogerian argument An approach to argumentation that is based on the work of psychologist Carl R. Rogers and that emphasizes the importance of withholding judgment of others' ideas until they are fully understood. See **8f(2).**

search engine A Web-based program that enables users to search the Internet for documents containing certain words or phrases. Sometimes called a **search tool.** See **9d.**

search tool See **search engine.**

secondary source A source that analyzes or interprets firsthand information. See **9a**. COMPARE: **primary source.**

sentence modifier A modifier related to a whole sentence, not to a specific word or word group within it: *All things considered,* the committee acted appropriately when it approved the amendment to the bylaws.

simple predicate See **predicate.**

simple subject See **subject.**

split infinitive The separation of the two parts of an infinitive form by at least one word: *to completely cover.* See **21a(3).**

squinting modifier A modifier that is unclear because it can refer to words either preceding it or following it: Proofreading *quickly* results in missed spelling errors. See **24c(3).**

Standardized English The usage expected in most academic and business settings. See **Glossary of Usage.**

subject The general area addressed in a piece of writing. See **3a**. COMPARE: **topic.** Also, the pronoun, noun, or noun phrase that carries out the action or assumes the state described in the predicate of a sentence. Usually preceding the predicate, the **complete subject** includes the main noun or pronoun and all determiners and modifiers. A **simple subject** consists of only the main noun or pronoun. See **20b** and **20d(1)**. COMPARE: **predicate.**

subject complement See **complement.**

subjective case See **case.**

subjunctive mood See **mood.**

subordinating conjunction See **conjunction.**

subordination The connection of a grammatical structure to another, usually a dependent clause to an independent clause: *Even though customers were satisfied with the product,* the company wanted to improve it. See chapter **28**.

syllogism Method for deductive reasoning consisting of two premises and a conclusion. See **8h(2)**. See also **premise.**

synchronous forum Online means of communication in which messages are exchanged in real time; that is, the receiver of a message sees it on the screen right after the sender completes it. Chat rooms are synchronous discussion groups. See **6c(1)**. COMPARE: **asynchronous forum.**

synthesis Collecting and connecting information on a topic; usually involves summary, analysis, and interpretation.

tag question A question attached to the end of a related statement and set off by a comma: She came back, *didn't she?*

tense The form of a verb that indicates when and for how long an action or state occurs. See **26b–c.**

theme The main idea of a literary work. See **16b(7).**

thesis The central point or main idea of an essay. See **3c.**

tone The writer's attitude toward the subject and the audience, usually conveyed through word choice and sentence structure. See **4a(3).**

topic The specific, narrowed main idea of an essay. See **3b.** COMPARE: **subject.**

topic sentence A statement of the main idea of a paragraph. See **4c(1).**

Toulmin model A system of argumentation developed by philosopher Stephen Toulmin in which a claim and supporting reasons or evidence depend on a shared assumption. See **8h(3).**

transitions Words, phrases, sentences, or paragraphs that relate ideas by linking sentences, paragraphs, or larger segments of writing. See **4d** and **23c(5).**

transitive verb A verb that takes an object. The researchers *reported* their findings. See **20e** and **26d(1).** COMPARE: **intransitive verb.**

URL Abbreviation for **Uniform Resource Locator,** which identifies an Internet address, including the domain name and often a specific file to be accessed.

usability testing The process of soliciting reactions from potential users of a Web site or other complex electronic document in order to improve the content or design of the document. See **6e(4).**

verb A word denoting action, occurrence, or existence (state of being). See **20a(1)** and chapter **26.**

verb phrase A main verb and any auxiliaries. See **21a(2)** and **26a(4).**

verbal A verb form functioning as a noun, an adjective, or an adverb. See **21a(3).** See also **gerund, infinitive,** and **participle.**

vocative Set off by commas, the name of or the descriptive term for the person or persons being addressed. See **35b(3).**

voice A property of a verb that indicates the relationship between the verb and its subject. The **active voice** is used to show that the subject performs the action expressed by the verb; the **passive voice** is used to show that the subject receives the action. See **26d** and **30c.**

warrant According to the Toulmin model, the underlying assumption connecting a claim and data. See **8h(3).**

Web log See **blog.**

CREDITS

These pages constitute an extension of the copyright page. We have made every effort to trace the ownership of all copyrighted material and to secure permission from copyright holders. In the event of any question arising as to the use of any material, we will be pleased to make the necessary corrections in future printings. Thanks are due to the following authors, publishers, and agents for permission to use the material indicated.

Text and Art

pp. 11–12: "Jaqui's Story," Texas Department of Transportation, www.texasdwi.org/jaqui.html.

p. 19: SI Report: "Caminiti comes clean" from SI.com. Copyright © 2005 by Sports Illustrated. Reprinted with permission.

pp. 20, 22, 23, 24: From GUNS, GERMS, AND STEEL: THE FATES OF HUMAN SOCIETIES by Jared Diamond. Copyright © 1997 by Jared Diamond. Used by permission of W. W. Norton & Company, Inc.

pp. 52–53: Excerpt from "Credit Card Debt among College Students: Just What Does It Cost?" by Robyn Sylves. Reprinted by permission of the author.

p. 64: Excerpt from "ConMen" by Charles P. Pierce. Reprinted by permission of the author.

p. 65: From "Not Seeing the Forest for the Dollar Bills" by Donella Meadows as appeared in *Valley News*, June 30, 1990. Reprinted by permission of Sustainability Institute.

pp. 65–66: Excerpt from "Leg Waxing and Life Everlasting" by Anna Quindlen. Reprinted by permission of International Creative Management Inc. Copyright © 2001 by Anna Quindlen. First appeared in *Newsweek*.

p. 66: Excerpt from "Flight 93" by Randall Sullivan from *Rolling Stone* April 11, 2002. Copyright © 2002 Rolling Stone LLC. All Rights Reserved. Reprinted by Permission.

p. 67: Excerpt from "My Father's Brain." Originally published in *The New Yorker*. Reprinted by permission of Jonathan Franzen and the Susan Golomb Literary Agency.

p. 74: Excerpt from "The Better Boss" by Larissa MacFarquhar as appeared in *The New Yorker* magazine, April 22 & 29, 2002, p. 86. Reprinted by permission of the author.

pp. 83–87, 88–91, 96–99: Drafts and final version of "Working toward a Degree" by Melissa Schraeder. Reprinted by permission of the author.

p. 102: Online course: "Coding for Corporate Survival." Courtesy of Jeff Pruchnic.

p. 103: Online course: "Coding for Corporate Survival" screen: "Discussion Papers." Courtesy of Jeff Pruchnic.

p. 107: FOR BETTER OR FOR WORSE © 2000 Lynn Johnston Productions. Dist. By Universal Press Syndicate. Reprinted with permission. All rights reserved.

p. 112: Thesis statement and supporting points by Trish Parsons. Reprinted by permission of the author.

p. 122 (Fig. 6.2): Screen shot: newsgroups on programming games, Google Beta Groups. © 2005 Google Corporation. All rights reserved.

p. 123 (Fig. 6.3): CJR Daily Homepage Screen Grab. Courtesy of Columbia Journalism Review, CJRDaily.org. Photo of Protesters outside the United Nations during the U.N. 2005 Summit 9/14/05 on the CJR Daily Homepage © John Smock/AP/Wide World Photos.

p. 124 (Fig. 6.4): Instant messaging screen shot. Courtesy of Stacey Sheriff.

p. 127 (Fig. 6.5): Home page for The Green Belt Movement. Copyright © 2005 The Green Belt Movement.

p. 142 (Fig. 7.1): Cover illustration from *Diary of a Worm* by Doreen Cronin and Harry Bliss, 2003. © 2003 by Harry Bliss. Reprinted by permission of HarperCollins Publishers, Inc.

p. 147 (Fig. 7.5): Cover of 2005 *Virginia Is for Lovers Travel Guide*. Copyright © Scott K. Brown Photography, Inc.

p. 159 (Fig. 7.12): *New York Times* front page, 4/10/03. Copyright © 2003 The New York Times.

p. 165 (Fig. 7.15): Reprinted by permission of JETLOG Corporation, www.jetlog24x7.com.

p. 167 (Fig. 7.18): Line drawing of a printer from PIXMA iP4000/iP3000 Quick Start Guide, 2004. Courtesy of Canon USA, Inc. © 2004 Canon U.S.A., Inc.

pp. 181–182: "Letter from Birmingham Jail" by Martin Luther King, Jr. Reprinted by arrangement with the Estate of Martin Luther King Jr. c/o Writers House as agent for the proprietor, New York, NY. Copyright 1963 Dr. Martin Luther King Jr., copyright renewed 1991 Coretta Scott King.

p. 191: By permission of Gary Varvel and Creators Syndicate, Inc.

p. 192 (top): © The New Yorker Collection 1994 Mick Stevens from cartoonbank.com. All Rights Reserved.

p. 192 (bottom): FOR BETTER OR FOR WORSE © 2000 Lynn Johnston Productions. Dist. By Universal Press Syndicate. Reprinted with permission. All rights reserved.

p. 193: © The New Yorker Collection 1996 Warren Miller from cartoonbank.com. All Rights Reserved.

p. 195 (top): Reprinted by permission of Ed Colley.

p. 195 (bottom): © 2004 by Brian Fairrington. Reprinted by permission of Cagle Cartoons, Inc.

p. 196: Reprinted by permission of Don Landgren, Jr.

p. 213 (Fig. 9.1): Search boxes from university library's Web page. Courtesy of the James E. Brook Library.

p. 214 (Fig. 9.2): Keyword search from university library's Web page. Courtesy of the James E. Brook Library.

p. 218 (Fig. 9.3): OCLC FirstSearch. The FirstSearch Catalog screen captures are used with OCLC's permission. FirstSearch WorldCat and ArticleFirst are registered trademarks of OCLC Online Computer Library Center, Inc. WorldCat and ArticleFirst screens are copyrighted by OCLC and/or its third party database providers.

p. 221 (Fig. 9.4): InfoTrac screen shot. Result screen from InfoTrac® College Edition by Gale Group. Reprinted by permission of The Gale Group.

p. 222 (Fig. 9.5): First page of article found through InfoTrac. Result screen from InfoTrac® College Edition by Gale Group. Reprinted by permission of The Gale Group.

p. 233: Excerpt from "Bad Rapport with Patients to Blame for Most Malpractice Suits." Reprinted by permission of *The University of Chicago Chronicle.*

p. 236 (Fig. 10.1): Nobel e-Museum Web site. From http://www.nobel.se/peace/laureates/1997. Copyright © The Nobel Foundation. Reprinted by permission.

p. 240: "What Is NPR?" from www.npr.org/about/. Reprinted by permission of National Public Radio, Inc.

p. 279 (Fig. 12.1): From PROTECTING AMERICA'S HEALTH by Philip J. Hilts, copyright © 2003 by Philip J. Hilts. Used by permission of Alfred A. Knopf, a division of Random House, Inc.

p. 279 (Fig. 12.2): Reprinted by permission of Bloomsbury, USA.

p. 284 (Fig. 12.3): Page from *American Literary History* 14:3 (Fall 2002), by permission of Oxford University Press.

p. 293 (Fig. 12.4): Home page of Art Institute of Chicago. Reproduced by permission of The Art Institute of Chicago.

p. 294 (Fig. 12.5): New Yorker Web page. From NewYorker.com, November 14, 2003.

p. 298 (Fig. 12.6): Abstract page from ProQuest database. Copyright © 2005 ProQuest.

pp. 326 and 327 (Figs. 13.1 and 13.2): From "Working with People with Learning Disabilities" by David Thomas and Honor Woods. Copyright © 2003 David Thomas and Honor Woods. Reprinted by Permission of Jessica Kingsley Publishers Ltd.

p. 328 (Fig. 13.3): Adapted with permission from *Journal of Applied Social Psychology*, 2003, Vol. 33, No. 2, 423–443. © V. H. Winston & Son, Inc., 360 South Ocean Boulevard, Palm Beach, FL 33480. All rights reserved.

p. 334 (Fig. 13.4): Computer printout of abstract page from EBSCOhost. Copyright © 2005 EBSCO Industries, Inc.

p. 336 (Fig. 13.5): First page of Web article "Ethical Standards for School Counselors." © American School Counselor Association.

p. 341: Graph of sleep stages. From *Good sleep, good learning, good life*, by Piotr Wozniak, July 2000. Retrieved September 19, 2002, from http://www.supermemo.com/articles/sleep.htm. Reprinted with permission.

p. 394: "Portrait" reprinted by permission of Louisiana State University Press from *Girl at the Window* by Pinkie Gordon Lane. Copyright © 1991 by Pinkie Gordon Lane.

p. 419: Reprinted with permission from Blissitt, P. A. Sleep, memory, and learning. *Journal of Neuroscience Nursing*, 33 (4), 208. Copyright © 2001 by the American Association of Neuroscience Nurses.

p. 448: © Reprinted with permission of King Features Syndicate.

pp. 459 and 514: Boboli package directions. The Boboli trademark and directions are used with the permission of Entenmann's Products, Inc. Boboli® is a registered trademark of Entenmann's Products, Inc.

p. 660: By permission. From *Merriam-Webster's Collegiate Dictionary*, Eleventh Edition © 2004 by Merriam-Webster, Incorporated (www.Merriam-Webster.com).

Photos

p. 6: © AFP/Getty Images.

p. 11: Reprinted by permission of MADD.

p. 37: © Jeremy Woodhouse Photodisc/Getty Images.

p. 50: Courtesy of Mercedes-Benz USA.

p. 51: © Britt Erlanson/Getty Images.

p. 52: © Amy Etra/PhotoEdit—All rights reserved.

p. 54: (Kennedy) © Time-Life Pictures/Getty Images; (King) © Flip Schulke/Black Star.

p. 55: © Scott T. Smith/Corbis.

p. 60: Migrant Mother by Dorothea Lange, 1936 Library of Congress, Farm

Security Administration/Office of War Information Collection.

p. 92: © 2003 Adobe Systems Incorporated. All rights reserved. Adobe, the Adobe logo, Tools for the New Work, and Photoshop are either registered trademarks or trademarks of Adobe Systems Incorporated in the U.S. and/or other countries. Intel, Pentium, and the Pentium 4 processor logo are trademarks or registered trademarks of Intel Corporation.

p. 95: Supplied by Cheryl Glenn.

p. 144: © SpeeDee Oil Change & Tune-up.

p. 145 (top): © Bettmann/Corbis.

p. 145 (bottom): M. C. Escher's "Self Portrait" © 2005 The M. C. Escher Company-Holland. All rights reserved.

p. 148: © David Wall, New Zealand.

p. 149 (top): © Anna Palma/Corbis.

p. 149 (bottom): © Brian Gardner www.gardnerphotos.com.

p. 151: © Fotosearch.com.

p. 152: © Creative Director: David Swope; Copywriter: Neil Levy; Photographer: Curtis Meyers.

p. 168: © Bruno Joachim/Index Stock Imagery.

p. 181: © Bettmann/Corbis.

p. 198: © AP Photo/Kent Gilbert/Wide World Photos.

pp. 206 and 211: © Danny Daniels/Index Stock Imagery.

p. 225: © Charles Gupton/Corbis.

p. 252: © Michael & Patricia Fogden/ Corbis.

p. 311: Photo courtesy of Roland Schlager.

p. 364: © Bettmann/Corbis.

p. 389: © S. J. Krasenann/Peter Arnold, Inc.

p. 394: © Reuters/Landov.

p. 395 (top): © Bruce Schwartz/Worn Path Productions.

p. 395 (bottom): © Denna Bendall/Worn Path Productions.

p. 396: © Photo collection Alexander Allard, Sr./Corbis.

p. 399: © Hulton-Deutsch Collection/ Corbis.

p. 400: © Bettmann/Corbis.

p. 402: © Ali Meyer/Corbis.

p. 410: © Denna Bendall/Worn Path Productions.

p. 412: © Suzanne English/Worn Path Productions.

p. 420: © S. J. Krasenann/Peter Arnold, Inc.

p. 464: © Image Source Ltd/Index Stock Imagery/RF.

p. 504: SAKS Fifth Avenue.

p. 531: Image courtesy of the Advertising Archives.

p. 575: *Sun Rising through Vapor: Fishermen Cleaning and Selling Fish* by Joseph Mailor William Turner, c 1808 © National Gallery Collection. By kind permission of the Trustees of the National Gallery, London/Corbis.

p. 605: © Whitney and Irma Sevin/Index Stock Imagery.

p. 644: © Bruce Burkhardt/CORBIS.

pp. 647 and 653: © The Advertising Archive/The Picture Desk, NY.

p. 681: Courtesy, United States Marine Corps.

p. 706 (left): © Nigel Reed/Alamy.

p. 706 (right): © Joe Skipper/Reuters/ Landov.

pp. 731 and 745: Reprinted courtesy of the National Association of College Stores.

p. 763: © Michael Newman/PhotoEdit, Inc.

INDEX

Numbers and letters in color refer to chapters and sections in the handbook; other numbers refer to pages.

(cont.)

(cont.)

(cont.)

(cont.)

(cont.)

(cont.)

(cont.)

(cont.)